Indians in London

INDIANS IN LONDON

*From the Birth of
the East India Company
to Independent India*

Arup K. Chatterjee

BLOOMSBURY

NEW DELHI • LONDON • OXFORD • NEW YORK • SYDNEY

BLOOMSBURY INDIA
Bloomsbury Publishing India Pvt. Ltd
Second Floor, LSC Building No. 4, DDA Complex, Pocket C – 6 & 7,
Vasant Kunj, New Delhi 110070

BLOOMSBURY, BLOOMSBURY ACADEMIC INDIA and the Diana logo are trademarks of
Bloomsbury Publishing Plc

First published in India 2021
This edition published 2021

Bloomsbury Academic
An imprint of Bloomsbury Publishing Plc

ISBN: HB: 978-93-89449-17-4; eBook: 978-93-89449-19-8

2 4 6 8 10 9 7 5 3 1

Typeset in Adobe Garamond Pro by Manipal Technologies Limited
Printed and bound in India by Replika Press Pvt. Ltd.

To
Bishakha
Amrita
Asit

'We are here because you were there.'

— *Ambalavaner Sivanandan*
(Sri Lankan novelist and activist).

'As we were nearing Waterloo Station we crossed several bridges, and directing my view towards the innumerable turrets and high houses, the whole town seemed to be in a blaze, the cause being attributable to gas-lights with which the streets are lighted, as I afterwards learnt to be the case. We left our train and engaged cabs, drove through several streets, arriving at last at the Exeter Hotel, in the Strand. The brilliant lights even surpassed a bright moonlight night, and the countless people of both sexes talking up and down added fresh impulse to the spectacle, and realised, to a certain extent, the true meaning of the word *Fairyland.*'

— *Pothum Janakummah Ragaviah*
(First Indian woman traveller in Victorian London).[1]

'From Regent Street is all easy turn through Oxford Street which crosses it. This street is one of the most continuous streets of this great city. It is full of shops of all descriptions and houses suited for persons of all classes. One end of it leads to Notting Hill and the other to Holborn and the City. The Holborn side of Oxford Street leads to Cheapside at the end of which are the Royal Exchange, the Bank of England and the Mansion House. From Cheapside one can easily go into Fleet Street and the Strand, which are· not only full of shops, but also contain most of the leading publishing houses and newspaper offices. From Charing Cross to Whitehall is a very easy drive as the rush of carriages is not large enough to obstruct one's progress. Here are the various public offices of the Ministry, the Horse Guards, the Houses of Parliament, and the India Office (called by the policemen and the cabby *Indiar Office*). I shall not describe the Houses of Parliament or Westminster Abbey for the present, but cross Westminster Bridge. A more circuitous trip through Kensington brings the stranger to Hyde Park, while

---

[1] Pothum Janakummah Ragaviah, *Pictures of England: Descriptive of Her Visit to Europe* (Madras: Gantz Bros., 1876) p. 46.

a second trip leads him to Victoria Station and thence to London Bridge. Let us go towards Bayswater. I shall not enter Hyde Park now, as I wish to do so on my way back. I should like to see my Indian friends first. Most of them live in Bayswater, which has been nick-named Asia Minor, because almost all the Asiatics who visit London patronise the lodging-houses to be met with in that locality. London streets present the most varying scenes of excitement. The Metropolitan Railway or the omnibuses are pouring out their thousands, and the streets are soon full of people. They are well paved, not with sandstone or *kanker* like Indian streets, but with wood or asphalt, and they are kept very clean. In the evenings they are well lighted. I would not care to live there without an income of at least £1,000 a year.

— Lala Baijnath
(Indian traveller in Victorian London).[2]

---

[2] Lala Baijnath. *England and India: Being Impressions of Persons and Things, English and Indian, and Brief Notes of Visits to France, Switzerland, Italy and Ceylon* (Bombay: Jahangir B. Karani, 1893) pp. 27-30.

Key to Map of Indians in London (Characters and their Locations)[1]

Indians & Anglo-Indians	Borough Location	Grid Location
Ali, Choudhry Rahmat	Woolwich	F11
Ali, Master Ayub	Tower Hamlets	D9
Alley, Surat	Tower Hamlets	E9
Aly, Meer Hasan	Westminster	D5
Ambedkar, BR	Camden	C6
Anand, Mulk Raj	Camden	D7
Aurobindo, Sri	Hammersmith & Fulham	D3
Baijnath, Lala	Westminster	D5
Banerjea, Surendranath	Camden	B7
Bennett, Helene	Camden	C6
Bengal, Catherine	Westminster	E7
Bhose, Rev EB	Newham	E11
Bhownaggree, M	Tower Hamlets	D9
Bokhari, ZA	Westminster	C6
Bonnerjee, WC	Croydon	G9
Bose, Atul	Kensington & Chelsea	E4
Bose, Subhas Chandra	Westminster	E7
Cockerell, Estuarta	Westminster	D5
Dasgupta, KN	Camden	B6
Deane, Archibald	Westminster	C5
Desani, GV	Richmond	F2
Dey, Mukul	Kensington & Chelsea	E4

[1] People and locations in this map should not be considered the most exhaustive list of Indians in London between 1550 and 1947. There were many other Indians and Indian associations in London during this period. For instance, two of the exceptional architects of modern India, Sir Syed Ahmed Khan and Sardar Vallabhai Patel, who are not represented in the five acts of the book, have been mapped herein.

India Office	Westminster	E6
Indian Seamen's Welfare League	Tower Hamlets	E9
Indian YMCA	Westminster	D6
King's College	Westminster	E7
Liberal Club	Westminster	E6
London School of Economics	Westminster	D7
London School of Medicine	Westminster	D7
National Indian Association	Westminster	D4
Nayyar Bros	Tower Hamlets	D9
Northbrook Society	Kensington & Chelsea	E5
Orient Travels	Tower Hamlets	D8
Pakistan Welfare Association	Tower Hamlets	E8
Qureshi & Co	Tower Hamlets	E8
Royal Military Academy	Woolwich	F11
Shah Bros	Tower Hamlets	D9
Shah Jahan Mosque	Woking Town (Surrey)	F1
St Andrew's Waterside Mission	Newham	D11
St James' Church	Westminster	D6
St Paul's Church	Westminster	D7
Tait's School	Tower Hamlets	D9
Zoroastrian Trust Funds of Europe	Harrow	B2

Indian Restaurants, Cafés, Hotels & Lodgings	**Borough Location**	**Grid Location**
Ayah's Home	City of London	D8
Bengal India Restaurant	Westminster	D7
Coronation Restaurant	Westminster	D8
Dilkhush Delight Restaurant	Westminster	D5
Durbar Restaurant	Westminster	D6
Gator Café	Westminster	D7
Hindoostane Coffee House	Westminster	C5
Kidderpore	Croydon	G8
Kohinoor Restaurant	Westminster	D6
Mysore Restaurant	Kensington & Chelsea	E5
Number Thirteen	Tower Hamlets	D8
Oriental Restaurant	Westminster	E5
Salut-e-Hind Restaurant	Westminster	D7
Shafi's Restaurant	Westminster	D6
Shalimar Restaurant	Westminster	D6
Singh's Restaurant	Tower Hamlets	D9
Stranger's Home	Tower Hamlets	E9
Sylheti Café	Tower Hamlets	D9
Taj Mahal Restaurant	Westminster	D6
The Home	Hackney	C8
Veeraswamy's Restaurant	Westminster	E6

Contents

Illustrations

1. 'St Dionis Backchurch in the City of London.' Sketched by Frederick Mackenzie, Robert William Billings and John Le Keux for George Godwin's *The Churches of London: A History and Description of the Ecclesiastical Edifices of the Metropolis* (London: Hatchard, Seely, Weale & Williams, 1839). Courtesy: Wikimedia Commons.
   Top right: 'Site of St Dionis Backchurch,' Photograph by Simon Harriyott. Courtesy: Wikimedia Commons.
2. Top: 'Street Logo Sign of Brick Lane in English and Bengali, in London.' Photograph by James Cridland. Courtesy: Wikimedia Commons.
   Bottom: 'Children of the Bangladeshi British Community at Parfett Street in Whitechapel.' Photograph by Al Cane. Courtesy: Wikimedia Commons.
3. 'The Punjabi students "At Home" to Meet Lady Hailey, August 9, 1928 at Veeraswamy's Indian Restaurant.' Reproduced with permission from the British Library; Shelfmark: Photo 761/1(5).
4. Top: 'Ranji ... Song, Words and Music by C. T. West.' Reproduced with permission from British Library, Shelfmark: Music Collections H.1798.oo.(18).
   Bottom: 'Hon. Assistant Section Officer Noor Inayat Khan (code name Madeleine), George Cross, MiD, Croix de Guerre avec Etoile de Vermeil. Noor Inayat Khan served

as a wireless operator with F Section, Special Operations
Executive.' Photograph taken in 1943. Courtesy: Wikimedia
Commons.

5.   Top: 'George Clive and his Family with an Indian Maid.'
     Painted by Joshua Reynolds, in 1765. Gemäldegalerie,
     Berlin. Courtesy: Wikimedia Commons.
     Bottom Left: 'Charlotte Fitzroy, Daughter of Charles II, with
     an Indian Servant Girl.' Painted by Peter Lely, in 1674. York
     Art Gallery. Courtesy: Wikimedia Commons.
     Bottom Right: 'William Feilding, 1st Earl of Denbigh
     (1582-1643).' Painted by Anthony van Dyck, in 1633-34.
     National Gallery, Room 31, NG5633. Courtesy: Wikimedia
     Commons.

6.   Top: 'Robert Clive and Mir Jafar after the Battle of Plassey,
     1757.' Painted by Francis Hayman, in 1760. Courtesy:
     Primary Collection, National Portrait Gallery, NPG 5263.
     Courtesy: Wikimedia Commons.
     Bottom: 'General Lord Cornwallis Receiving Tipoo Sultan's
     Sons as Hostages.' Painted by Robert Home, in 1793.
     Courtesy: National Army Museum, Accession No. NAM
     1976-11-86. Courtesy: Wikimedia Commons.

7.   Top and Bottom Left: Portrait of Joseph Emin and the title
     page from his book, *The Life and Adventures of Joseph Emin:
     An Armenian* (London: 1792; reprinted, Calcutta: Baptist
     Mission Press, 1918).
     Bottom Right: Portrait of Mirza Abu Taleb Khan, from his
     book, *The Travels of Mirza Abu Taleb Khan in Asia, Africa,
     and Europe: During the Years 1799 to 1803*, trans. Charles
     Stewart (London: Longman, Hurst, Rees, and Orme, 1810).

8.   Top: 'Mahomed's Baths,' from *Shampooing; or, Benefits
     Resulting from the Use of the Indian ... Vapour Bath as
     Introduced*; Second edition. Reproduced with permission
     from the British Library; Shelfmark: T 12646.
     Bottom: 'Sake Deen Mahomed.' Coloured Lithograph
     created by T. M. Baynes, in 1820s. Wellcome Library no.
     6123i, Photo number: V0003787.

9. Top: 'East India House.' Painted by Thomas Malton the Younger (1748-1804). Courtesy: Paul Mellon Collection, Yale Center for British Art, Yale University. Accession No. B2001.2.1001. Courtesy: Wikimedia Commons.
    Bottom: 'The Indian National Congress Cartoons from the Hindi Punch, with a selection of the Indian Social Conference Cartoons. From 1886 to 1900. [1887-1902.] Edited by Barjorjee Nowrosjee.' Reproduced with permission from the British Library; Shelfmark: 1876.b.61.
10. 'A Portrait of an Indian Gentleman.' Painted by by A. Smith, in 1841. Courtesy: Wikimedia Commons.
11. 'Three Lascars of the "Viceroy of India," standing Behind the Wheel of one of the Ship's Tenders.' Created by Marine Photo Service, in 1930s. Courtesy: National Maritime Museum, Greenwich. Courtesy: Wikimedia Commons.
12. Top: 'Statue of Raja Rammohun Roy at College Green, Bristol.' Photograph by Not from Utrecht, in 2009.
    Bottom: 'Grave of Dwarkanath Tagore at Kensal Green Cemetery, under West London Crematorium, Harrow Road.' Photograph by Tony Mitra, in 2004. Courtesy: Wikimedia Commons.
13. Top: 'Ardaseer Cursetjee Wadia.' Postage stamp issued by Government of India in 1969.
    Bottom Left: 'Keshub Chunder Sen.' Photograph by the London Stereoscopic Company, in 1870.
    Bottom Right: 'Swami Vivekananda in London,' in 1895. Courtesy: Wikimedia Commons.
14. Top: 'London Labour and the London Poor.' Created by Henry Mayhew, in 1861. Reproduced with permission from the British Library; Shelfmark: 08275.bb.28.
    Bottom Left: Ayahs's Home in Hackney, 'from *Living London*.' Edited by G.R. Sims, 1904. Reproduced with permission from the British Library; Shelfmark: 10349.h.12.
    Bottom Right: 'Gandhi with the Vegetarian Society in the Isle of Wight, England, in 1890.' From the archives of the International Vegetarian Union. Courtesy: Wikimedia Commons.

15. Illustrations of exhibits from the Colonial and Indian Exhibition from the *Pall Mall Gazette: An Evening Newspaper and Review*, May 1886. Clockwise: 'Indian Gate'; Man at the 'Bazaar'; Man at 'Kaffir (pagan) Village'; 'Indian Pavillion'; Leopard and Elephant in an 'Indian Jungle.'

16. Top Left: 'Trailokyanath Mukharji.'
    Top Right: 'Behramji Malabari.' Photograph by G.A. Natesan & Co., in 1910s.
    Bottom Left: Syed Ameer Ali.
    Bottom Right: 'Lord Headley with Khwaja Kamal-ud-Din.' Photograph from 1913.
    Courtesy: Wikimedia Commons.

17. Top Left; 'Duplicate Passport' of an Ayah. Created on June 6, 1934, Ootacamund, India. Reproduced with permission from the British Library; Shelfmark: IOR/L/PJ/11/3/1314.
    Top Right: 'Photo of an Indian Woman and Child, from the Coronation Exhibition, London.' From 1911. Courtesy: Wikimedia Commons.
    Bottom: 'Lipton's Teas Advertisement.' From *Illustrated London News*, September 17, 1892, London. Reproduced with permission from the British Library; Shelfmark: P.P.7611.

18. Top Left: 'Frederick Henry Horatio Akbar Mahomed.' Source: J.S. Cameron & J. Hicks, 'Frederick Akbar Mahomed and His Role in the Description of Hypertension at Guy's Hospital.' *Kidney International*, Vol. 49, No. 5, May 1996: pp. 1488-506. Courtesy: Wikimedia Commons.
    Top Right: 'Rabindranath Tagore in London.' Source: Rabindranath Tagore's *Collected Works,* Edited by I.E. Bykova, A. Gnatyuk-Danilchuk and V. Novikova (Moscow: State Publishing House of Fiction, 1961). Courtesy: Wikimedia Commons.
    Bottom Left: 'The Munshi Abdul Karim.' Painted for Queen Victoria, in 1888. Courtesy: Royal Collection, Osborne House. Durbar Corridor, Accession No. RCIN 403831. Courtesy: Wikimedia Commons.

Bottom Right: 'Maharajah Duleep Bassi Dressed for a State Function.' Painted by Captain Goldingham, in 1875. Courtesy: Norfolk Museums. Courtesy: Wikimedia Commons.

19. Top: 'Photograph of Dadabhai Naoroji.' From 1892. Reproduced with permission from the British Library; Shelfmark: 14119.f.37.
Bottom Left: 'Romesh Chunder Dutt.' Photograph by Jnanendra Nath Gupta, in early 1900s. Courtesy: Wikimedia Commons.
Bottom Right: 'Mancherjee Bhownagree.' From 1890. Courtesy: Open University. Courtesy: Wikimedia Commons.

20. Top: 'Lord Sinha.' Photograph by Bassano Ltd, Royal Photographers; Bassano; Bassano Ltd., in 1920. Courtesy: Photographs Collection, National Portrait Gallery, NPG x120565. Courtesy: Wikimedia Commons.
Bottom Left: 'Portrait of Indian Philosopher Jiddu Krishnamurti.' Photograph by Albert Witzel, in 1922. Courtesy: Wikimedia Commons.
Bottom Right: 'Muhammad Ali Jinnah, as Barrister.' From 1910. Source: Matlubul Hassan Saiyid's *Muhammad Ali Jinnah: A Political Study* (Lahore: Shaikh Muhammad Ashraf, 1945). Courtesy: Wikimedia Commons.

21. Top Left: 'Bombay Emporium Advertisement: Asiatic Congress, Rome; Ceylon Students' Association and Federation of Indian Student Societies of Great Britain and Ireland.' From *Indian Student Journal*, May 1937. Reproduced with permission from the British Library; Shelfmark: L/PJ/12/475.
Bottom Left: 'Advertisement: India: If You Appreciate Indian Foods Take Your Lunch at the Indian Pavillion.' From *The Times*, May 24, 1924. Reproduced with permission from the British Library; Shelfmark: NRM MLD1.
Right: India House Collage featuring (clockwise) Madanlal Dhingra, V.V.S. Iyer, M.P.T. Acharya, P.M. Bapat, Maud Gonne, Champakaraman Pillai Vinayak Damodar Savarkar

and Anant Kanhere, with an issue of *Indian Sociologist* in the centre. Courtesy: Wikimedia Commons.

22. 'Princess Sophia Duleep Singh Selling Subscriptions for the Suffragette Newspaper Outside Hampton Court in London.' From April 1913. Reproduced with permission from the British Library; Shelfmark: L/PS/11/51.

23. 'The Indian MP Shapurji Saklatvala and his English Wife.' From 1937. Reproduced with permission from the British Library; Shelfmark: Mss Eur D1173/6.

24. Top: 'Dr. B.R. Ambedkar (first from right in second line) with Professors and Friends in the London School of Economics and Political Science.' From 1916-17. Courtesy: Wikimedia Commons.
    Bottom: 'Choudhry Rahmat Ali (seated first from left) with Muhammad Iqbal (center), Khawaja Abdul Rahim (right) and a Group of other Young Activists During Iqbal's visit to England in 1932.' Source: Iqbal Academy, Pakistan. Courtesy: Wikimedia Commons.

25. Top: 'Delegates at the Second Session of the Indian Round Table Conference, St James's Palace, London. From September 1931. Reproduced with permission from the British Library; Shelfmark: Photo 13(1).
    Bottom: 'Gandhi Meets with Charlie Chaplin at the home of Dr. Kaitial in Canning Town, London (Sarojini Naidu on the right).' From September 22, 1931. Courtesy: Wikimedia Commons.

26. Top Left: 'Subhas Chandra Bose.' From 1930s. Courtesy: Netaji Research Bureau, Calcutta. Courtesy: Wikimedia Commons.
    Top Right: 'Mulk Raj Anand.' Photograph by Howard Coster, from 1930s. Courtesy: Photographs Collection, National Portrait Gallery, NPG x126819.Courtesy: Wikimedia Commons.
    Bottom Left: 'Poster for an India League Meeting.' From November 1932. Reproduced with permission from the British Library; Shelfmark: IOR/L/PJ/12/448.

Bottom Right: 'Cover of *Britain and India* Magazine.'
Created by Josephine Ranson, in July 1920. Reproduced
with permission from the British Library; Shelfmark:
P.P.3795.c.

27. Top: 'Advertisement for the Bibliophile Bookshop.' From
1941. Reproduced with permission from the British Library;
Shelfmark: Asia, Pacific & Africa ST 1803.
Bottom: 'Advertisement for *Indian Writing* Magazine.' From
1940. Reproduced with permission from the British Library;
Shelfmark: P.P.5939.bgf.

28. Top: 'Advertisement for the Koh-I-Noor restaurant
in London.' From *Indian Student Journal*, May 1937.
Reproduced with permission from the British Library;
Shelfmark: L/PJ/12/475.
Bottom: 'Jawaharlal Nehru and V.K. Krishna Menon, United
Nations, New York.' From December 21, 1956. Courtesy:
Nehru Memorial Museum and Library. Courtesy: Wikimedia
Commons.

Acknowledgements

If my manner of thanking or expressing gratitude to someone is construed to be inappropriate by any standard, I should be immensely grateful if my apology is accepted without a great deal of suspicion. As someone who writes from a fragile cusp between history and literature, I am deeply grateful to my professors, Saugata Bhaduri, G.J.V. Prasad, Makarand Paranjape, Dhananjay Singh and Padmini Mongia in indoctrinating me in the comfortable ideology of not having one, while stirring my interest in the eccentric turns of India's colonial history. Bhaduri's pioneering work on the 'polycolonial' interactions and history of colonial Bengal have inspired me to think of colonialism as a multi-pronged tool that emphatically supersedes binaries between subjugation and liberation. To him I am also grateful for introducing the works of Jacques Derrida, that are among my literary lodestars. Prasad's avant-garde ideas on British literature galvanised my interest in Britain's interwar period, while Paranjape's trans-civilisational approaches to Indian history have helped me question many myths of India's modernity, here and elsewhere.

Although *Indians in London* is, to my knowledge, the first book length work on this precise subject, I have drawn a great deal of inspiration, besides literary and historical substance from Rozina Visram's *Asians in Britain: 400 Years of History* (2002), Antoinette Burton's *At the Heart of the Empire: Indians and the Colonial Encounter in Late-Victorian Britain* (1998), Simonti Sen's *Travels to Europe: Self* and Other in Bengali Travel Narratives, 1870–1910 (2005), Michael Herbert Fisher's Counterflows to Colonialism: Indian Travellers and Settlers in Britain, 1600–1857 (2006); Susheila Nasta (ed.), India in Britain: South Asian Networks and Connections, 1858–1950 (2013), Shompa Lahiri's Indians in Britain: Anglo-Indian Encounters, Race and Identity, 1880–1930 (2013) and the brilliant archive put up by Rozina Visram, Susheila Nasta and others in collaboration with the Open University for the digital project, Making Britain.

I am sincerely grateful to my senior colleagues at OP Jindal Global University, C. Raj Kumar, Sanjeev Sahni, Y.S.R Murthy, R. Sudarshan, Vesselin Popovski, Kathleen Modrowski, Sreeram Chaulia and S.G. Sreejith, who have indefatigably endured my verbosity and also helped fund my research at the British Library archives. That has led me into the deeply hospitable corridors of the Library, once again, and the endearing work carried out by its people, especially honourable janitors. Their zealous greeting, to the question of how they have been being 'Not too bad …', has greatly helped me to see the past and the present in a much brighter light, without judgment. Others at the British Library— including Margaret Makepeace, who has supplied rare legends from India's colonial history, and Sandra Powlette, who helped secure permission to use rare images from the collection of the Library— from coffee sellers to bakers to readers to safe-keepers to idlers to occasional gazers, a passing philosopher who had lost his sense of hearing to a budding thinker of British immigrations policy and admirer of Jomo Kenyatta, have all helped me stay wedded to this 'sneaky feeling you'll find that love actually is all around.'

(I am grateful to Hugh Grant in the role of Prime Minister David for the film Love Actually, and its director, Richard Curtis, who I hope will excuse me for quoting the above).

I am grateful to British South Asian Members of the House of Commons for their interviews (I believe they are best unnamed in the present book). I must also thank the very genial Richard Alford, former Secretary of the Charles Wallace India Trust, a mentor in the lives of several people and certainly mine with his characteristic warmth and wisdom. Will Self, his daunting literary oeuvre, knowledge of London and the patient ear he has given me have nurtured this history in some ways. Nick Papadimitriou's spirit of gallivanting into the crepuscular end of London's history has also lent to my prose, as has the sagacity of the scientist, Akram Khan. So have the writings of Peter Ackroyd, Iain Sinclair and Matthew Beaumont—the indomitable storytellers of London's past and present.

I am grateful to respected editors, Aman Khanna at *Scroll.in* and Vaishna Roy at *The Hindu*, for publishing articles concerning the history of Indians in London, which in certain altered forms have added to the masonry of this book, in a few places. Their attention to my prose has enabled me to reach a wider audience. So have the Brunel University London, the Kingston University, and the South Asia Institute at the School of Oriental and African Studies. I am grateful for the kindness of Edward Simpson, director of the South Asia Institute. I am also thankful to my friends, Anita Manoharan and Debanjali Biswas. The latter has helped me with a better practical understanding of the contemporary sociology of Indians in London. Friends in unlikely places of that city, Florian and Kristiane, in the course of the research for this book, have taught me the cherished values of hard work, courage and perseverance that perhaps migrants know best. The support of my friends, Amit Ranjan, Emon Nandi, Chandrani Dutta, Farha Noor, Nikhil Kumar and Sujay Thakur—who are very insightful scholars themselves— has been strong and steady through the months of what might have otherwise been a gloomy journey, given the famous grays of the London we know, and those that prevail in this book.

I am indebted to my friend and publisher, Paul Vinay Kumar, who has never given up on me despite adversity. Others at Bloomsbury India, including R. Chandra Sekhar, Jyoti Mehrotra, Satya Mishra and Raj Bilochan, have kept up the cheer through thick and thin. Last but not—in any manner of speaking—the least, I am grateful to my critics who are yet to incinerate my prose like Cinna's verses and the man himself were in *Julius Caesar*. It is possible that with this book I have given them a temptation too strong to resist making an attempt. If it helps anyone with a strong passion towards or against my writing, I am also grateful to be born in the country where Mohandas K. Gandhi was; for that I thank the farsightedness of my parents; as I thank my partner for guiding me in the city where Gandhi was called to the Bar, and where he launched a quiet earthquake to raise it, along with hundreds of thousands of Indians—before India.

January 16, 2020
Lalgola, Murshidabad
India

Note to the Reader

No passage, phrase or word in this book is intended to hurt sentiments with respect to anyone's race, community, religion, gender, sexuality or passionately held political beliefs. It is possible that with an intended aura and structure of Shakespearean drama, words or phrases may elicit double meaning or puns, which is entirely coincidental and unintended.

The title, *Indians in London*, refers not to migrants from India to the British capital, in general, but those Indians who visited or migrated to London from the time of Shakespeare (and a little before) until 1947 (and a little after). This is not intended to impose on anyone an arbitrary nationhood or national identity. 'India' herein refers largely to the geo-historical name given to a landmass, which even today many scholars call the great Indian subcontinent. 'Indians' should not be confounded geopolitically with the present day nation-state of India. Since this is a work of history and the prose is largely set in a time before the 1950s, older names and spellings of places and cities—Calcutta instead of Kolkata, Madras instead of Chennai, Bombay instead of Mumbai, and so on—have been used.

The history contains minimal endnotes, in order to make scholarly interruptions aesthetically unobtrusive. The complete list of references can be found in the end. Departing from the convention of mentioning scholars, historians, disciplinary experts, and so on, as part of the main text, the text from Act I through to Act V does not do so, except in endnotes in cases where someone or something has been quoted. Except very rarely, quotations in the present book preclude the use of ellipses (…) in cases where extracts from discrete portions of the quoted text have been interwoven. This has been done by way of making the text of this book a seamless whole, without aesthetic interruptions.

It is expected that if scholars wish to cite from quoted passages in this book, they should refer to this text rather than the original source. If they intend to cite or refer to the original instead, they should not make excerpts quoted in the present book a source for doing so. Those intending to read the history of *Indians in London* without the scholarly, historical and literary backdrop are encouraged to read from Act I through to Act V. The introductory chapter, 'A Chronicle Foretold', provides the backdrop to the history, as well as defines the neologism '*Typogravia*', which is crucial to the larger understanding of the history and this book. It is recommended, however, that those who wish to enjoy the introduction should have some preceding knowledge of the history of colonial India, the works of William Shakespeare and elementary understanding of modern Continental philosophy.

Shadows of London

I feel the ephemerality of my own being in the shadows of the buildings here—the shadows of other ephemeral beings
—*Will Self*

A river flows past my winter street
Warm but incomplete
Like you; or sometimes it squishes my feet
With thorns, and makes me retreat

Homewards, not too far if you think
Here, at the Strand, to the East India Dock
It will hardly take me time to sink
And drown with the spirits of my cudgelled flock

Snowflakes crackle on the dome of St Paul's
On my porous fingertips the shadows lean
By the Bankside, history bleeds new walls,
When each wall is like a shadow you've been

Slanting gray slouches to the tawny Thames,
The Globe made terracotta by a greasy day—
You are one of Tate Modern's faceless names
Where the fevered piers of Blackfriars come to pray

Where the tracks trundle in light-footed sleep,
At Harrow, by a culvert on the Station Road
A headless man with a rosary asked me, 'show me how to weep,'
I held a cigarette to his chest until his ribs narrowed

I showed his eyes to a crowd that cheered a third time
As I opened my window at thirty past two
A truant church bell has flickered a chime,
It is time for me to part as well, like a passing thing or two

My vellum is wet from your blue-eyed odes
And some purloined acts of rare kindness
As the dim mornings sigh from wooden abodes
I too am healed in London's blindness

A Chronicle Foretold

On the day he was to leave for London, Sawai Madho Singh II boarded the SS Olympia at Bombay with 132 servants, a fleet of Hindu priests, and 8,000 litres of Ganga water. In that summer of 1902 when an American Jack London chose to disappear into the East End of London, the Maharajah of Jaipur was bound for the coronation ceremony of King Edward VII. Some months ago, the British emperor's mother, Queen Victoria, had heaved her last breath. The *gangajal* on board was not for the departed queen's soul in purgatory, but to purge the person of the Rajput king off the evils of the black waters—a journey of 5,000 miles from his native land. A new dawn had certainly dawned on the British Empire as Madho Singh became a new exemplar of high-caste Hindus. Despite crossing the pernicious oceans, he retained the purity of his birth, with the help of holy waters contained in two gigantic urns manufactured in 1894 by minting 14,000 silver coins, and no less fabled a ship purchased for ₹150,000 from Thomas Cook. One of its rooms doubled up as the king's throne.

Along with Madho Singh also arrived the kings of Gwalior and Bikaner, and hundreds of others from the far reaches of the British dominions. From a grim and greasy East End, London wrote: 'in all the pomp and certitude of power, and still they come, these men of steel, these war lords and world harnessers. Pell-mell, peers and commoners, princes and maharajahs, Equerries to the King and Yeomen of the Guard. And here the conquered men of Ind,

swarthy horsemen and sword wielders, fiercely barbaric, blazing
in crimson and scarlet, Sikhs, Rajputs, Burmese, province by
province, and caste by caste.'[1] Thomas Cook & Sons—according
to the American London—could have ferried one to the obscurest
interiors of Africa, but dared not risk the descent of a Christian
soul into the precarious passages of the East End, where lane upon
lane of malodorous dampness survived rotting potatoes, flies,
fruits, beans and limbs of children thickly strewn about without
discrimination, in almost equal stages of lecherous liquidity.

Foretelling a chronicle is also chronicling acts of foretelling.
Being foretold is like being whispered to follow a ghost. Following
a ghost is like being followed by it. And to be followed thus is to
be persecuted by the chase. What appears almost doomed from its
beginning is to keep alive a séance—to speak to a ghost to speak
with it, and to liberate it to its own speech.[2] We are after a city of
ghosts. In a certain manner of recognition, is not a city of ghosts
also a ghost city?

London is a chronicle of violence. For over a millennium, it has
jealously archived its violence to gods and the violence of its gods.
'Do we hear nothing as yet of the noise of the gravediggers? How
shall we comfort ourselves, the murderers of all murderers?' asked
Friedrich Nietzsche. 'Who will wipe this blood off us? What water
is there for us to clean ourselves? What festivals of atonement, what
sacred games shall we have to invent?'[3] That archive, of museums,
libraries, abbeys, friaries, galleries, bridges, towers, fountains
and cemeteries, is a surreal brickwork of enigmas. The figure of
the Indian in London is also a living enigma of five centuries. In
his subdued voice lie embedded piercing echoes of the medieval
torture chambers of the ancient city and murky silhouettes of the
industrial ghettoes of a metropolis of modernity. The tiger skins
of Tipoo Sultan or the gouaches of Begum Sumroo, the milling
and mourning apparitions of millions of textile handicraftsmen or
the fetid footprints of barefooted tea-planters from the foothills
of the gigantic Himalayas! They have all built London, and lived
on as ghosts, spirits and spectres in all their glory and infamy
of haunting.

I am their ventriloquist. The singular language in which they died was also the language in which I have singularly loved London. 'The faithful memory of such a singularity can only be given over to the ghost,' writes the author of *The Spectres of Marx*.[4] Karl Marx was in London once. Its archives led to the *Capital* of all our lives. London fulfilled his love of tea and gave him the hungry and faceless aliens of the East End to work with. The chiaroscuro of those fixed retinas and the guttural of these departing larks evanesce into the violet twilight tottering on the edge of a melancholy bridge, quietly dissolving into a city of disappearances.[5] Beneath its towers, I disappear somewhere in the future of a past that trembles in the secret dusk of the Thames.

The Happy Few Band of Brothers

About 400 years before India became a sovereign republic, in March 1550, the last remains of an Indian named Salamon Nurr were interred at St Margaret's Church in the City of Westminster. It was then known more as a burial ground than a ground of parliamentary prorogation. Six decades later, in the City of London, at the church of St Dionis, another Indian by the name of Peter Pope was blessed in his Christian rebirth by the Archbishop of Canterbury, as he became the first Indian to be baptised in London.

In March 1949, Robert Stimson, a veteran BBC journalist who had seen Mahatma Gandhi assassinated from five yards away, wrote before returning to Britain after twelve years in the subcontinent: 'the quality of an Indian friendship, which once given is given unconditionally and for life.'[6] Almost exactly seventy years later, while reporting for the BBC radio documentary *As the World Sees Britain*, Neil MacGregor discovered that India had outgrown its Raj nostalgia, and was aggressively demanding an equitable status in United Kingdom's immigration policy. Westminster was still uncertain if it wanted a viable free-trade policy with its erstwhile colony.[7] In an unrelated episode that followed in September 2019, the

Archbishop of Canterbury, Justin Welby, offered a grovelling apology at the Jallianwala Bagh Memorial in Amritsar, for the massacre of April 13, 1919, ordered by General Reginald Dyer. The prostrated Archbishop sought forgiveness for the loss of 400 lives, not on behalf of the British government but in the name of Christ. Earlier, British Prime Ministers David Cameron and Theresa May had both verbally hung their crowns in shame, though stopping inches short of a formal apology.

By the winter of 2018, the boroughs where Nurr died and Pope was baptised could not care less about them or where they came from; nor indeed about the scars of British rule in India. Immersed in defending their own nation, nothing trampled on the fresh snow of yet another historic act of ignorance. A band of sisters and brothers was at large to save Britain from what the House of Commons had warned to be its looming vassalage to the European Union. Two people were gallantly fast-tracking Brexit proceedings on their phone-in shows on British radio. One was a former white-horse of the Eurosceptic UK Independence Party. Another was the guardian of highbrowism in Tory politics and double-breasted suits. Both had turned into inveterate adversaries of those wanting to remain in the European Union. These 'moaning' remainers had been christened as the *remoaners*. A new portmanteau word was knocking up the covers of the *Oxford English Dictionary*.

As the Labour Party—and Conservatives themselves—led one after another parliamentary coup on Prime Minister Theresa May, jargons of 'No-deal' Brexit and the great 'Irish backstop' were married to newspeak. For over three years, Britain's media had rung the daily refrain, 'in spite of Brexit,' and had it drilled into the speech of nigh on every Londoner. It was Britain's biggest crisis since the humiliation at Suez in 1956. Its public appeared generally ill-tempered as the nation's indecisiveness worsened each day without a precedent on the Richter scale of its cultural, economic and political tremors. Questions of Irish and Scottish alienation from the British Parliament haunted dailies and evening standards. Winston Churchill's majestic geometry of three circles—America,

Europe and the erstwhile British Raj—appeared to whirl into the maelstrom of a self-consuming hermeneutic void.

As Britain swung on the threshold of its memories of a world it had ruled, a new event horizon with its big-bad-world of populism was dismantling the good-old-fashioned democratic power structures, one at a time, from the press rooms of Donald Trump to the election rallies of Narendra Modi. A few years ago, Cameron had ushered Modi at the Wembley Stadium before 60,000 Indians, announcing that one day, not far, a British Indian Prime Minister would have his shack at 10 Downing Street. Modi went on to record another historic majority in the Indian Parliament after months of what gets touted as the biggest spectacle of democracy on earth. The Indian elections of the summer of 2019 totalled 900 million voters and 12 million polling staff, putting to utter shame the numbers game of Britain's referendum on the European Union. India's election machinery had travelled to far and distant and even mythical places across the Indian territory, on helicopters, trains, boats, elephants, camels and even on foot, taking as long as up to three days simply for conveyance.

Polling stations included one in Gir, Gujarat, where for just one voter in the whole constituency six polling officers were posted, and another in the Andaman Islands, closer to Indonesia than the Indian peninsula. The man who had conquered the hearts of all those scores of millions of Indians, for the second time, was well-known for cold-shouldering Britain, even after seven decades of independence. In other news, resentment was now a vital means of expression for the British. 'This is the age of British populism,' said philosopher John Gray.

> We seem to be succumbing to the forces of disruption that have for years been gathering strength throughout continental Europe. The two main parties are in steep decline, and vying for votes from an electorate that is discontented, fragmented and volatile. While the Brexit process has foundered, British politics is Europeanised. The paradoxical reality is that Britain has imported European style populism as a consequence of the failure to deliver on the result of the referendum in 2016.

If public discourse is now shaped by a language of hysteria and delusion, the principal reason is that the political classes have declined to honour the pledge they made to voters three years ago.[8]

With the albatross of Brexit round the neck, Mrs May announced her resignation and Boris Johnson became the next Prime Minister of Britain. The white-horse, who has none other than President Trump's voice announce his name for his radio-show on th   e radio network Leading Britain's Conversation, launched the Brexit Party that triumphed in the European Parliament elections of the following summer. Brexit now meant a chicken in every British pot. If that was to be chicken from United States, after withdrawal from the Union's single market, there was high risk of chlorination. Indeed, 'chlorinated chicken' was one of the things a Right Honourable Member did get called at Westminster. And beef imported from America would risk excessively high hormone-fed meat. (That epithet was yet to be taken when this was written). American ambassador to Britain Woody Johnson tried allaying fears by downplaying the European Union's 'Museum of Agriculture' standards in farming policy. The narrative of international politics around food kept going underground, never to disappear.

Priti Patel, a fervent Leave-EU campaigner, was now the new Home Secretary. She became the first Indian-origin parliamentarian to hold that position. Since the Brexit campaign, among other things, her headlines around Indian food constituted the red herring. Back in 2016, hundreds of curry house restauranteurs in London had felt betrayed by Mrs May's crackdown on immigration. Hiring chefs and staff from South Asian countries was the keystone of the £4.2 billion worth curry industry in Britain. Over that year, a thousand curry restaurants had shut store for good. Priti Patel, then the Secretary for International Development, had assured the South Asian community that Brexit would be a boon for immigrants from Asia. For South Asian restauranteurs in London, going the

Conservative way did not arouse sympathies of the government. A large population of London's curry house owners were softcore Thatcherites. They held on to their ideologies in the hope of receiving their due share of political credit after the Brexit vote. However, with new immigration policies, restauranteurs feared that small businesses would no longer be able to compete with larger restaurants due to lack of cheap immigrant labour. Labour's inroads in the electoral share of the Conservatives, in the summer of 2017, added confusion to the sensation of leaving the Union. By the end of 2018, like Honourable Mr Truth itself, Brexit had multiple versions, multiple accents and multiple ways of how not to leave the European Union. The question was—to paraphrase an old Hegelian joke from Stalinist Russia—whether one wanted to eat their curry *without the pepper or without the cream.* As English novelist Howard Jacobson remarked, Brexit kept on slipping from grasp like Hamlet's father's ghost. '*'Tis here! Horatio. 'Tis here! Marcellus. 'Tis gone! [Exit Ghost].*'[9]

Amidst the pantomimes of that Christmas, what stood out was the voice of a woman from an advertisement on Leading Britain's Conversation. It was for a restaurant in 'the heart of London,' singing the virtues of Indian food that had for hundreds of years endorsed values of bonding and sharing over which to 'make memories.' Listening to that interlude, my mind usually wandered off to the spring of 1933 when Choudhry Rahmat Ali, a young graduate from Cambridge, approached Mohammad Ali Jinnah at the Waldorf to parley over shrimps and Chablis. Over dessert, with the jolly old knife and fork at his elbow, Ali proposed the legendary course. Carve out a tender sirloin of Pakistan from the jaded shoulder of India!

Altars and Abattoirs of Authenticity

'London is now an incredibly diverse *country*', says an emphatic British South Asian Member of Parliament. 'But we had to fight for it throughout the riots of the '60s and decades of intolerance and hostility, and fight for our civil rights through

anti-discrimination legislations of the '90s.' Britain today has
over forty members in the House of Commons and the House
of Lords from its South Asian community—a staggering figure
by any standards. Their careers have been built on backbones of
many struggles and sacrifices, besides those of their forefathers
migrating to Britain from nations torn apart by conflict. Another
South Asian Member of Parliament tells me, growing up in East or
South London with Jewish or Irish communities was 'being part
of an amazing support system.' That is what the European Union
also means to these staunch remainers—proud global citizens
who are averse to distinguish between one form of diversity and
another.

> Whether they are from Asia, Africa, or EU migrants, they have
> built London's homes. Over a 100,000 people from the EU have
> worked in the construction industry or the Olympic village.
> When my father's generation came here from Bangladesh, they
> worked in the manufacturing and catering industries, building
> the nation's economy. There were people from other parts of the
> world who worked in the NHS as doctors and nurses in the '50s
> and '60s. Leaving aside Brexit, Britain is still one of the most
> inclusive countries in Europe.[10]

Modern Britain's postal service, transport service and national
insurance were cradled by the hands of South Asian and Caribbean
migrants. Here at Westminster, one of their descendants takes me
through her memory of hearing the story of Rabindranath Tagore's
loss and recovery of the manuscript of *Gitanjali* on the London
Underground. Another recounts the history of the Race Relations
Act of 1976, and what it was like to be an outsider in Britain before
that. He adds, 'Prince Charles once said, Britain's immigrants saved
the architecture of the country.' Can a politician's word be taken as
an authentic source of history?

The question of authenticity in the construction of diasporas is
also a question of authenticity of imagination. Both are invariably
entangled with the questionable authenticities in the idea of one's

homeland. Where the boundary between imagined communities and territorial homesteads are blurred, there emerges the creative inauthenticity that Bryan Cheyette has recently termed 'diasporas of the mind'. To both common sense and pejoration, Indians in London may seem semi-authentic at being either Indian or Londoners. However, South Asian communities in Britain are classic examples of globalisation from below or within. Extrovert Indian commodities like Bollywood and Bhangra have rewired the centrality of Britain's Eurocentric history.[11] This multiculturalism took a long time in making. For nearly three decades after the Second World War, race relations in Britain remained a subject of dark ages,[12] given how tense relations were between the white and 'coloured' populations even after the legislation of the Commonwealth Immigrants Act of 1962. Chinese and Jewish traders of the Edwardian years and East Europeans from the years of the Second World War were replaced by South Asians who bore the brunt of drunken vandalism and racial abuse.

Then, from the fundamentalist rows of the Parliament rose the victimology of Enoch Powell, the voice of Britain's marginalised white natives, whose old traditions and livelihoods had been allegedly robbed by aliens from the Commonwealth. In 1968, Powell's infamous speech, 'Rivers of Blood', [13] led to the foundering of the fantasy of a peaceful coexistence between Britons and multiracial immigrants.[14] Ten years later, the East End of London, still rife with tensions, witnessed the killing of the young British Bangladeshi textile worker, Altab Ali, at St Mary's Garden off Whitechapel Road. It was also the site of the burial of Richard Branson, the executioner of King Charles I. As London's history of macabre violence was repeated and South Asians drawn into its fold, Ali's murder added to the internal fragmentations of South Asia.[15] What now became the Altab Ali Park also saw the building of a Shahid Minar—a replica of the one in Dhaka—to commemorate the martyrdom of four Bangladeshi students who came under the firing of the Pakistani police, on February 21, 1952.

Ten years from Ali's death, Salman Rushdie's *Satanic Verses*, that led to a great furore in the Islamic world, became another tipping point for internal fragmentations, this time between the South Asian secular intelligentsia and orthodox Islamic ideologues. The novel was largely intended as an allegory of migration and diasporic lives in a sinister city of nocturnal witchcrafts, spelled by Rushdie as "'ell", "ow", "en", "dee", "ow", "en"'. Indian Member of Parliament Syed Shahabuddin and Iranian cleric Ayatollah Khomeini, however, were determined to launch a crusade against the *kafirs* of the Western world. 'Many Asians view their intellectuals as being as racist as the whites,' observed Bhikhu Parekh in 1989. 'This is broadly how the Hindus felt about Nirad Chaudhuri's idiosyncratic writings on India, the Bangladeshis about Faroukh Dhondy's television play *King of the Ghetto* and the Muslims about Hanif Kureishi's film *My Beautiful Laundrette* and recently about Rushdie's *The Satanic Verses*.'[16]

The event was part of the larger eventuality of integration of South Asian faiths and cultures into Britain's socio-political milieus. This was tantamount to heresy for fundamentalists back home. London's globalising influence produced conflicts but also ensured that Indian networks got intertwined with South Asian and global networks. Although the Rushdie affair consolidated Britain's sympathies with the South Asian intelligentsia, it brought under scrutiny the presumed 'uniformity of the immigrant experience', thus exposing networks of ambivalence.[17] Muslims in London, today, are made up of an overwhelming diversity. 'The reality behind the monolithic term "British Muslim" is a potpourri', writes Martin Walker. They constitute 'the wealthy London surgeon, the unemployed and barely literate textile worker in Oldham, the Malaysian accounting student intent on attending business school, the fiery newspaper columnist who dares not return to Saudi Arabia, the government clerk living with her English boyfriend and estranged from her outraged Iraqi family, the prosperous Bengali restaurant owner in East London.'[18] The city has seeped into their cultural norms and identities insomuch as the idea of home is nothing more than a 'conundrum'.[19] Take the case of Gujarati migrants who came to London in the 1960s and 1970s, and in the new millennium chose to retire to their origins around the Kutch region. It was then that they realised that if there was a 'mythical and unsullied home' anywhere, it was in Londonistan.[20]

A similar view of Londonistan is found in the world of the Punjabi diaspora seen through the eyes of Chaudhury Baldev Singh (a character played by Amrish Puri) in the film *Dilwale Dulhania Le Jayenge* (1995). In an age before Google Maps, the film created a new centre of attention for Indians in decentered pockets of London. It later became the watershed of Bombay cinema as well as middle-class Indian values. The sequence from the film in which Baldev Singh feeds the pigeons of Trafalgar Square overlaps with the scene of *shalwar-kameez*-clad women in mustard fields of Punjab, conjuring a fictitious route from Charing Cross to Bhatinda. It is likely that many Indians who subsequently visited London must have hunted for Baldev Singh's convenience store in Southall—like Americans seek out the Old Curiosity Shop on Portsmouth Street, immortalised by Charles Dickens in his eponymous novel.

In less than the first five minutes of the opening of the film, Baldev Singh walks a distance of nearly 20 kilometres—from Trafalgar Square to his shop, carrying his umbrella as a faithful subject of the Commonwealth—crossing the Big Ben, Waterloo Bridge, British Museum, the Serpentine, Hyde Park, Buckingham Palace, Tower Bridge and, finally, a drizzly St James' Park, before entering Southall. What is more extraordinary, he admits having walked the same route each day for the last twenty-two years. On each of those days the streets have asked him his name. He believes, like the pigeons he has no home. His desire to fly to India 'is a dated dream,' writes Amitava Kumar.[21] The Baldev Singhs living in Southall today would declare, rather boldly, London to be their home. Without a doubt, the mayor of London, Sadiq Khan, whose own family has Indian and Pakistani roots, wears the pride of these people like London wears curry on its crown.

No one has counted how many Taj Mahals, Rajahs, Mumtaz's, Stars of India, Curry Houses, Curry Gardens and Tandoori's exist in the UK. The decor and the lighting are identical (red flock wallpaper, ornamental hardboard Indian arches and red or orange lighting in Eastern lampshades). The serving bowls, the candle lit warmers and, for all I know, the dinner jacketed waiters are all indistinguishable. But most fascinating of all is the menu. You are as certain to get the standard menu in the standard restaurant as you are to get a postage stamp from a post office whether you are in the coves of Cornwall or the Highlands of Scotland.[22]

For a long time now, curry has been a metaphor for Indian food in Blighty. It is a culinary territory that will perhaps remain as colonial as ever, notwithstanding the decolonisation of economics and culture in Britain and the Indian subcontinent. 'Food seems to be the part of a culture that immigrants hold on to longest,' wrote Claudia Roden on London's mongrel culinary culture. Even after abandoning 'the traditional dress, the language, the music,' Indian food in London remains 'a uniquely British experience'.[23] Cooks and vendors of Balti, butter chicken or chicken tikka masala, have willingly foregone their contested Asian histories on the way to becoming British cosmopolitans, and part of a 100,000-people-workforce. This ostensible 'multiculturalism', as Elizabeth Buettner argues, 'has never indisputably been deemed "a positive force" for Britain—far more commonly, it has been imagined either as a problem or as a means of tackling a problem.'[24]

Multiculturalism in London is seen as a form of cannibalism, or of consuming other cultures in proxy. Take our own Pavlovian reflexes to a vignette depicting a Victorian high-tea. Decked up in the sheen of amaranthine and rosé chinaware, panelled and furnished by mahogany woodworks, the low murmuring coquetry that one imagines around the buffet can create in our gastric system effects similar to that of a diner in a restaurant. Reading about the history or politics of food may appear as acts of possession, or as consumption itself. Jean Paul Sartre would disagree. 'You could not make it enter your dark stomach,' he argued in his famous introduction to Intentionality, 'that knowledge could not, without dishonesty, be compared to possession.'[25] In the end, knowledge itself cannot be digested like food. Intellectually constructing the imagery of the seats where desire is gratified—far from being a possession—may well be a dispossession.

Unlike South Asian food, South Asian people were never an immediately acceptable part of British multiculturalism. Brexit controversies have only crystallised that. Chinese, Italian or Afro-Caribbean immigrants never really occupied the locus of the British population. It was always the Indians, Pakistanis and Bangladeshis who ran the most successful or the most number of non-British restaurants. They ensconced themselves 'within Britain's culinary landscape'.[26] From approximately 300 curry restaurants in 1960, Britain went on to accommodate 1,200 by the 1970s, 3,000 by 1980 and almost 7,000 by the beginning of 1990s.[27] Today, the Asian Catering Federation which represents Asian restaurants and food chains in Britain has about 35,000 restaurants under its wing, run by the South Asian, Chinese, Malayan and other Southeast Asian communities.

In February 2017, Yawar Khan, the chairman of the Federation, predicted that about 17,000 curry houses would shut down in Britain, by 2027.[28] Britain currently has about 12,000 Indian or South Asian curry-houses that outnumber its 10,000 odd fish-and-chips outlets.[29] Most of the former would be naturally wiped out by the end of the decade. The reasons cited for this, by Khan, are the inability of restauranteurs to adapt to the needs of British society, inability to service customers according to changing tastes, lifestyles and the turn towards healthy eating and the inability to source modern technology and social media. He has been backed in his claim by his co-chairman, Thomas Chan, who is also Chairman of the Chinese Takeaway Association in Britain. The Brexit clampdown on immigrants meant that curry houses would have to pay an annual tax of £2,000 instead of what was previously £1,000 per worker. Betrayal is writ large on the faces of Sanjay Shah or Oli Khan, major London-based restauranteurs.[30] In 2016 itself, the number of licensed curry restaurants had declined by 13 per cent.[31]

Given the gradual decline of the curry-industry, one is reminded of what Arjun Appadurai called a 'political economy of taste'. The real problem with curry in Britain today is that it is not exclusive enough, like the luxury commodity it was a century and a half ago.

> As the distance between consumers and producers is shrunk, so the issue of *exclusivity* gives way to the issue of *authenticity*. That is, under pre-modern conditions, the long-distance movement of precious commodities entailed costs that made the acquisition of them *in itself* a marker of exclusivity and an instrument of sumptuary distinction. Where the control of such objects was not directly subject to state regulation, it was indirectly regulated by the cost of acquisition, so that they stayed within the hands of the few. As technology changes, the reproduction of these objects on a mass basis becomes possible, the dialogue between consumers and the original source becomes more direct, and middle-class consumers become capable (legally and economically) of vying for these objects. The only way to preserve the function of these commodities in the prestige economies of the modern West is to complicate the idea of authenticity. The very complicated competition and collaboration between 'experts', dealers, producers, scholars and consumers is part of the political economy of taste in the contemporary West.[32]

To study the theatre of authenticity, one must turn to Veeraswamy. It is the oldest existing Indian restaurant in Britain. Today, it is run by Ranjit Mathrani. Built in 1926, it is as old as Queen Elizabeth II, and prides itself on being quintessentially Indian, but by no means a 'curry house'. Along with the other fine-dining restaurants in Mathrani's chain—Amaya, Chutney Mary and Masala Zone— it is as distinct from Britain's curry houses as sand from sawdust. The amber-lit walls of Veeraswamy are made of murals and sketches from the mid-Victorian noondays of George F. Atkinson's book *'Curry & Rice' on Forty Plates,* published two years after the Great Rebellion of 1857. Having had enough of their intercultural bonhomie with Indians, British families decided to monopolise the curry for their own race. With the Suez Canal thrown open to memsahibs journeying from England to India, the Company sahibs' hookahs and concubines were thrown out of the frame. What remained was an idyllic English summer home in the Indian hills, or the winter plain-tales of morally upright curry bowls. After 1858, racial discretion in food and family matters was an inalienable policy of the Victorian administration.

It is not hard to find an exciting gastronomical genealogy of curries from Charles Dickens to *Downton Abbey* or William Makepeace Thackeray to *Peep Show*. However, Eric Hobsbawm would have contended that curries, curry pastes and curry powders—that emerged on a large scale in Victorian Britain—were actually an 'invented tradition'.[33] It was a tradition designed, undoubtedly, to mask the absence of a long and organic history of a national ritual of food. 'What is an invention?' asks Jacques Derrida. 'What does it do? It finds something for the first time. And the ambiguity lies in the word "find." To find is to invent when the experience of finding takes place for the first time.'[34] An invention simulates repetition and continuity of something unprecedented. Paradoxically, only that which has a precedent in the past can be invented. Where unchanging and authentic practices of repetition and continuity come to constitute a rapidly changing world, tensions between producers' aesthetics and consumers' experiences are dramatic. London's aesthetics of Indian food is an attempt at tying it faithfully to its historical and political roots. But the ritual of consuming it is precisely the ploy to mask that history and politics.

Hobsbawm defined invented traditions as 'a set of practices, normally governed by overtly or tacitly accepted rules and a ritual of symbolic nature, which seek to inculcate certain values and norms of behaviour by repetition, which automatically implies continuity with the past.'[35] The British Indian curry was a transatlantic predecessor in invented traditions to the Italian American pizza. Christopher Columbus' waylaid medieval navigations have never been thanked enough for either. Homi Bhabha may concur: London's culinary invention was a reverse mimicry. It was an erstwhile Empire camouflaging itself against the speckled band of its erstwhile colony.

While doing so, it was caught hastily preparing a curry for its tongue that was once forked, if not a false one. The colonial tongue spoke, at once, of the mercy of Christ or Shakespeare and the dogmas of population control preached by Thomas Malthus. It was a hand that offered the benediction of Thomas Macaulay and William Bentinck—the whip of English education to foster a generation of mimic-men—if only to bulldoze millions of artisans and peasants into penury. They were then robbed of their lives before the barrels of the gun and the steam engine.

According to conservative estimates, between 1870 and 1905, about 6 million Indians died in famines in regions of the Deccan, Bengal and Malwah during a breathless expansion of railways in India. In the last three decades of the 19th century, from a trackage of a little over 5,000 miles, it had accelerated to nearly 25,000 miles of railroads—enough to chain the earth around its circumference. That was in spite of Victorian philanthropists like Florence Nightingale and Arthur Cotton campaigning 'vociferously in favour of irrigation canals, over the surplus colonial expenditure on railroads' in their last-ditch attempts to avoid the man-made famine holocausts in India.[36] The vastness of the Indian territory and the revenues and resources extracted from the large Indian population provided the British Empire a mammoth playground for administrative, economic and technological experimentation. The 400 cold-blooded murders from the Jallianwala Bagh massacre or the 3 million famine deaths in Bengal during the Second World War also added to the egotism of the likes of Colonel Reginald Edward Harry Dyer and Prime Minister Winston Leonard Spencer-Churchill. Cooking, consuming and aestheticising the multicultural colour of curry is then tantamount to whitewashing the scarlet letters of imperialism.

Curry houses in late-Victorian London started as family businesses. The fact that those mom-and-pop shops of curry came to be known as Indian restaurants is highly 'misleading' to historians, says Mathrani. According to him, 95 per cent of the pseudonymous Indian restaurants in Britain are anything but Indian. Mathrani, his wife Namita Panjabi, and his sister-in-law Camellia Panjabi, have been the vanguards of Indian food in London since the 1980s. He believes that practically every development in that segment in the 21st century has happened either in imitation of Veeraswamy and company, or in deliberate contrast to it. Chefs working for emerging Indian restauranteurs in Britain have spent months eating at his chain of restaurants to style their own version of the receipts. 'When others make curries, they sauce it up with pre-cooked meat, in a base onion and spice gravy. When the order arrives, the base-gravy is combined with a variation of about thirty dry spices, and sautéed in a skillet,' in what can be best described back in India as fast-food. 'What they do is a complete antithesis of Indian cooking. What is worse, they have given Indian names to these dishes.' Vindaloos and kormas at Bangladeshi restaurants are as different from original Indian receipts as 'Jupiter from Mars'.[37]

At Veeraswamy, Chutney Mary and Masala Zone, the connoisseur reigns supreme. Butter chickens or *do-piyazahs* are not scaled up or down on the standard of spices, cream or yoghurt to placate individual palates of the clientele, just as 'you cannot ask a French restauranteur to add more garlic or herbs to your serving.' In the same vein, Mathrani reflects on the unsung diversity of Indians in London—Gujaratis in Harrow, Punjabis in Southall, South Indians in Tooting—who are often curried into an indiscrete identity to both British and Indian perceptions. When the postcolonial wave of South Asian immigrations struck in the 1950s, West Indians in Britain worked as bus conductors, Punjabis from Pakistan and India were absorbed into construction works and the textile industry and Gujaratis of East Africa, 'fundamentally, the Patels,' came to Britain after being ousted by Idi Amin, and founded sweetmeat businesses and pickle brands. 'In fact, Britain must thank Idi Amin for chucking them out, and Edward Heath for admitting them,' Mathrani adds jocularly.

By the 1970s, Indian food in Britain had already flourished for several decades. Veeraswamy was established by the maverick Edward Palmer for fine-diners from the Indian Civil Services, the army, navy and descendants of East India Company officials. The curry houses, that mushroomed since a little before the Great War, typically catered to spike the spice levels of pub-goers. In 1932, Veeraswamy was purchased by William Steward. For three decades, he persevered in bringing chefs and staff from India, until in 1962, when the restaurant entered into a succession of unsuccessful hands. When Mathrani took over Veeraswamy, in 1996, he decided to integrate 'Indian decorative themes in all restaurants on an unprecedented scale, where they synthesised with poly-western designs. We not only represented Indian food, but also the great essence of Indian decorative idioms.'[38] Palmer's idea, says Mathrani, was aesthetically brilliant but financially ignominious. He wanted to revive the culinary tradition of the provenance. At Chutney Mary, every single receipt on the menu has its provenance in Indian family traditions from Kerala, Bengal, Punjab, Hyderabad, Central Provinces or the Deccan, besides many others. This was replicated at the modern-day Veeraswamy. To many passers-by in Piccadilly, the name of the restaurant once suggested a South Indian *dosa* establishment. Around the ninetieth anniversary of the restaurant, Namita Panjabi related the history of its deceptive nomenclature. 'Edward Palmer's grandmother was called Veera, so it was a play on "Veera Saw Me". At a later point, a printer thought it was spelt wrong as they knew of a Veeraswamy, so it was changed and remained that way.'[39] Whether this is historical or apocryphal is too trivial a question compared to the realpolitik that governs Indian restaurateuring in Britain.

Supermarkets in London have played a huge role in disseminating the desire and semantics of Indian food. Marks and Spencer, Sainsbury's, Waitrose and Tesco's, besides refrigerating Danish or German confectionaries and patisseries, Australian and American wines and noodles, pizzas, Swiss rolls, trifles and lasagnes, have seized the market of Indian food. They too have contributed to the shutdown of Indian takeaway-curry houses. Supermarket curries have a crisper sheen to the packaging, greater quantity of food at much cheaper prices, at less than even £4 for a pack of tikka masala, prawn *makhani* or lamb *korma*, along with *pilau* rice, while takeaway restaurants around Camden, Southall, Brick Lane or Wembley were not able to bring their quotations below £8 for as much quantity or less, let alone their substandard quality. In 2013, it was found that British families could not spend a fortnight without going out for the proverbial 'Indian'. While ethnic foods continued to refurbish Britain's supermarkets, the place of elite Indian catering houses such as Mathrani's was only elevated, at the cost of smaller outlets converting their stock to chocolatiers or kebabs or fish-and-chips vendors.

The supermarket cult of the invented tradition of Indian cuisine in Britain is sharply pitted against 'lack of authenticity'. The Bakkavör Group, founded by Agust and Lydur Gudmundsson back in 1986, is one of the largest food suppliers to Britain's supermarket grocery retailers today, besides leading markets in America and China. Angela McKay, the Head of Development at Bakkavör, almost ruled the present decade with her penchant for marketing the experience of the 'in-home ethnic meal'. It was all about provenance.

> There was a lack of authentic, tasty food on the UK market, and that's what I wanted to provide. We source spices from the south of India selected and picked when they're at their best. We don't spot buy. Then it comes down to using the right herbs and spices and in the right proportions. By highlighting the provenance of the product, including specific ingredients, retailers are able to engage with their customers on a more emotive level, instead of merely listing the ingredients used.[40]

Mathrani believes that this cult of upmarket authenticity has, in fact, compelled greater diversity in what was a stale variety of 'Indian food' some twenty years ago. Now, more 'authentic' types of Indian offerings coexist with groves of Bangladeshi curry houses. It is a

thesis to fetishise ghosts. What could be more spectral—what could
be a more authentic paradox—than seeking the authentic Indian
artefact in London? 'Authenticity may be sought,' writes David
Appelbaum, 'but when authentication is the play of a disguise, it's
safe to say that impasses block the itineraries to be followed, and
behind each, a ghost repression.'[41] According to Nicholas Royle,
there is an 'undecidable contamination at work in every attempt
to distinguish between the authentic and the non-authentic, pure
and impure, charlatan and non-charlatan.'[42] The quest for the
authentic is, therefore, also a sign of a historical repression of the
authentic. That which can be performed as authentic must be
induced—and in a way contaminated—with an excess of value
from its historical and social networks in order to distinguish
from the inauthentic. There is almost an academic purity to
how the experience of Indian cuisine is branded in London. It is
reminiscent of the Orientalist anthropology of Victorian times,
when tiger skins, hookahs, swords, carpets, paintings, furniture,
indeed the whole loot of 'Hindostan' was catalogued in royal
exhibitions—in Gothic boudoirs from the Victoria and Albert
Museum to Whitehall—with the clinical exactitude of trying to
graft a daffodil from William Wordsworth's Lake District on to
some forgotten Indian poet's Casuarina Tree.

Restaurateuring, unlike writing poetry or fiction, is all about
saleability, scalability and employability, says Mathrani. 'It is
entirely a function of supply and demand. And classical relics
are much less likely to survive.'[43] There will always be a Wilton's
for British cuisine, which has been in business for over 275
years, where food is as much about consuming what is on the
table as the aesthetics of the table, the furnishings and the décor.
But these heterotopias—as Michel Foucault once described
these slices of time lost in time—are not conducive to financial
scalability. Veeraswamy had become much of a relic after the war,
along with an Italian restaurant, Bertorelli, which was started in
1945. With a new wave of Italian and Bangladeshi takeaways
in London, the restaurant faced the fears of extinction, and so

did Veeraswamy. Relics of fine dining do not have the luxury of becoming museums of art, of the sort that the William Wordsworth, Rudyard Kipling, Toru Dutt or Sarojini Naidu became in postcolonial cultures. Literature may age like wine. Restaurants die out, if not modernised. The number of global professionals in London is much larger than it what it was at the dawn of the new millennium. Western banking and investment houses that employ Indians all over the world, and Indians from all over the world, now drive a new culture of food in London. More than *garam masala* or ghee roasts, it is Morgan Stanley or Goldman Sachs, for example, that now govern elite Indian restaurateuring in London, says Mathrani.

Second- or third-generation Indians and Indian immigrants in Britain no longer prize becoming chefs. Cooking is often relegated as either a domestic or a socially mediocre role in the psychology of upwardly mobile Indian middle classes in the diaspora. Gone are the days of Ranji Smile, the Indian celebrity chef whose arrival on the American culinary scene in 1899 was ushered by the *Harper's Bazaar* as 'America's King of Curry from India Who Made "Women Go Wild Over Him."'[44] A conman worth his name in gold, Smile was no stranger to the effects that his cooking had on the clientele he was targeting. 'If the women of America will but eat the food I prepare, they will be more beautiful than they as yet imagine,' he claimed. 'The eye will grow lustrous, the complexion will be yet so lovely, and the figure like unto those of our beautiful India women.'[45]

Victorian Britain prescribed a staggering volume of Anglo-Indian recipes, thanks to the likes of Sake Deen Mahomet, another celebrity chef of his time, who launched the Hindoostane Coffee House, the first Indian-owned curry restaurant in London, in 1810. Florence White's *Good Things in England* (1903) claimed that England had been savouring curries since 1390. Maria

Rundell's *Domestic Cookery* (1807), Eliza Acton's *Modern Cookery in all its Branches* (1845) and Isabella Beeton's *Book of Household Management* (1859) paid tributes to the curry.[46] 'Creatures of the inferior races eat and drink,' observed Mrs Beeton, 'man only dines.'[47] Englishwomen and domestic policies of the Victorian household were enlisted in the imperial game, as food became a centre of politics. In *Physiology of Taste, or Meditation on Transcendental Cookery* (1826), Jean Anthelme Brillat Savarin remarked that one became what one ate and, therefore, the future of nations depended on their cuisine. Steering the gastronomy of the age, Victorian wives stewed princely victuals of the Raj. Victorian cookbooks and curry receipts served as policy manuals for imperial homes and the untarnished wholesomeness of English kitchens.[48]

Indian curry recipes also started appearing in American cookbooks, such as Eliza Leslie's bestsellers, *Direction for Cookery in its Various Branches* (1840) and *New Cookery Book* (1857), Ann Allen's *The Housekeeper's Assistant* (1845) and Catherine Beecher's *Domestic Recipe Book* (1846). Before the American Revolution, colonists in the New World purchased numerous domestic items and spices such as tea, cardamom, pepper, turmeric, saffron, cinnamon, garlic and ginger from India via Britain. In 1809, America had its first dock for receiving supplies from India and China, known as the Boston India Wharf. With the Charter Act of 1813, the British East India Company lost its commercial monopoly over trade in Indian items. This opened the doors for America to receive goods directly from India, and 'chicken curry, curried veal and lobster curry were standard items on the bills of fare of Boston taverns and eating houses in the 1820s and '30s.'[49] According to Sarah Lohman, the interpretations of curry in America were largely due to British immigrants or American sailors who had visited India on mercantile missions. The recipes, therefore, were twice removed from the original delicacies.

Ranji Smile was determined to stir things up. He was first spotted by Nathaniel Newnham-Davis, a food critic, at the Savoy Hotel in London. In 1896, Smile moved to Cecil, then the largest hotel in Europe. From here, Richard Sherry, an American restauranteur, took him and his English wife over to New York, in 1899. Smile was placed in charge of the kitchen at one of the city's premium restaurants, Sherry's, located on the Forty Fourth Street and Fifth Avenue. What with his artistically sculpted beard, impeccable dressing and a lilting accent to go with, an unusual maverick was born. Items on his menu were the mysteriously titled Kalooh Sherry, Murghi Rain, Muskee Sindh, Curry of Chicken Madras, Indian Bhagi Topur, Bombay Duck and Lettuce Ceylon. Before the year ran out, Smile went missing. When rediscovered in London, the paparazzi were confused between whether he was there to recruit Indian chefs for Sherry's or on his way to India to collect his inheritance after the recent demise of his father.

Smile was originally from Karachi, and had worked in hotels in Calcutta and Bombay. Everyone knew him only as a chef. But when he checked into a London hotel this time, he registered his name after the prefix 'Prince' with twenty-six attendants waiting upon him. Smile's masquerade did not end there. He claimed to be the fourth son of the Emir of Baluchistan, a Cambridge University graduate, and a friend of King Edward VII. (The king did indeed become his patron temporarily, after believing his other astonishing claims). Later that year, when he returned to America along with his attendants, he was accosted by the press on one hand and the law on the other. The Contract Labour Law of 1885 made it illegal to offer someone an excuse for immigration to America with the promise of a job. Smile had made over two dozen of such promises. He informed the press he had never claimed to be a prince, and that the Indians accompanying him were simply tourists. He pleaded with the court that he had made no offers to them. With Sherry's staring at a damage of $26,000, Smile was estranged and left to 'giving culinary demonstrations and marrying a succession of ever-younger American women.'[50] Sometime during the First World War, he left for India with his newest American wife, with the promise of opening a new restaurant there, and was not heard of since.

Although several young Indian food entrepreneurs have strived to put the adventurous 'smile' back on Indian cuisine in London, cooking itself finds few takers. In a country of 60 million, and a powerhouse of multicultural gastronomies, there are not more than 100,000 catering colleges, a number that Mathrani considers highly insufficient. At Chutney Mary, Amaaya and Veeraswamy, Mathrani and Panjabi have tried to train many South Asians as porters and promote them to be chefs. A South Asian chef apprenticed at an Indian restaurant has to be paid the same remuneration as a French chef in a European restaurant—around £45,000 annually. This creates an additional anxiety in Indian restauranteurs for profit and scalability. The likes of Veeraswamy are then left to vacillate between whether to Europeanise their food culture in order to be financially viable, or to preserve their Indian values despite constraints on profitability. The silver lining for Mathrani's establishment is that over the last two decades, the number of Indian diners at his restaurants has gone up from almost nil to 15 per cent. Middle-class Indians in London, especially those averse to cooking at home, entertain in Mathrani's restaurants. 'While dining with their Indian friends, they may turn to an Italian restaurant. But when they want to induct a new partner at their firm or entertain a foreign client, they arrive at Chutney Mary or Veeraswamy. And Masala Zone continues to be populated by the younger Indians, a clientele that keeps returning.'[51]

Around St Valentine's day in 2018, Brick Lane geared up for its first vegan curry menu, thanks to Abdul Ahad, the new owner of City Spice, whose clientele boasts of Lord Karan Billimoria, James Nesbit, Jeff Banks, Meera Syal, Nina Wadia and Bill Nighy. Brick Lane is also one of the places in London from where Bengali road signs first emerged, going on to make Bengali the second-most popular foreign language in the city. The opening of the first branch of Zorawar Kalra's Farzi Café, in March 2019, was just another Indian milestone, *in spite of Brexit*. Along with Benares, Indian Accent, Gunpowder, Hawkyns and Kricket, it has taken Anglo-Indian food in London to incredible scales of '*farzification*' or illusionism.[52]

Trudging across Central London, I found an intoxicating range of Indo-Asian restaurants. To borrow the phraseology of one of the earliest British romantic comedies I saw, hundreds of popups appear out of nowhere, filling High Holborn right up to Tottenham Court Road. And wherever I looked, thousands of Londoners were gorging on millions of Oriental dishes, 'some genuine and some ... not quite so genuine.'[53]

Just off the intersection of Charlotte Street and Tottenham Street, in Fitzrovia, Shrimoyee Chakraborty reconstructed a piece of Calcutta in 2016. When the British journalist Michael Deacon visited her restaurant Calcutta Street, he dryly remarked, 'there was no Madras, no vindaloo, no *balti*, *bhuna* or *korma*.'[54] He was referring to the menus of Indian-styled restaurants that overpopulate the imagination of postcolonial London. The interiors of those restaurants used to be, Chakraborty recounts, heavily gadded with Bollywoodesque decors. It was a misrepresented India, where Calcutta or Bombay were misnomers. 'India speaks English now,' she contends, 'more fluently than before. It can no longer be clubbed with the *Slumdog Millionaire* trajectory. While Punjabi and Gujarati cultures are represented well enough in London, Bengali culture or Calcutta takes the fall. One recognises Hindi songs, but not Satyajit Ray, although he won the first Oscar. It is shocking to see only a few people know Tagore. Less still are those who understand that jazz was a defining leitmotif of noontimes in Calcutta.'[55] She has, therefore, built a space for food out of those very elements—Ray, Tagore, jazz, and a range of handcrafted furnishings and *haat-paakhas* (shuttered-window-styled menu cards), reminiscent of old South Calcutta. She prides herself on her prawn *malai* curry recipe, which she inherited from her mother's side. Other usual suspects—that are not so usual on a Londoner's menu—include *machher pathuri* garnished with *gondhoraaj lebu*, *laal shaag* with *kashundi*, beetroot and fish chops, and, of course, the fusion variety including *crème-roulé mishti doi* and *aam pora* with old monk. When she intends to go the full vegan way, she does not shy away from using coconut milk in *shukto*.[56]

Another Londoner from Calcutta who has amicably adapted himself to fusion is Prabir Chatterjee, with his supper club Little

Kolkata, now a brand 'not oblivious to the idea of expanding into a restaurant.'[57] Founded in December 2016, Little Kolkata has held supper events near Chatterjee's residence by the London Bridge. The culinary soirees are informal and have been a way of testing the market. In February 2018, Little Kolkata hosted a group of eighty diners at a restaurant in Canary Wharf, with Calcutta dishes such as *doi papri chaat*, Tangra Indo-Chinese chicken *pakora*, *luchi* and *chholar daal* with coconut and cashew, chicken *rezala* and *parota*, in an effort to truly represent the diaspora that Calcutta is, to the diaspora in London. With a lineage going back to the Haldar family of the Kalighat Temple in Calcutta, Chatterjee learned to cook *kosha mangsho* from the women of household, who also cooked the mutton that was offered at Kalighat. That and *mishti doi* are the heroes of his clientele, which has both White British residents and people of Indian origin, across all ages. Recreating the narrative and ambience of Bengali cuisine, he serves *luchis* in *kulos* and the main course on terracotta plates.[58] From supply chain, retail and supermarkets and designing brands for House of Fraser and John Lewis, Chatterjee has come a long way to designing his own culinary events. What truly distinguishes his brand and others like his from the 'old generation baltihouses of Brick Lane, is not simply the politics behind Brexit, but also the key themes of quality and innovation.'[59]

I met Mathrani, Chakraborty and Chatterjee during a wet winter in London. On one of its rainy evenings, I found myself behind the sleepily trundling railway tracks of Harrow. Stepping onto the high street, I was affected by a strong aroma that seemed to emanate from a Chinese restaurant. It was Steven Lee's Hakkaland. A Chinese Bengali cook, originally from Calcutta's Tangra, Lee first travelled to East Africa, and was brought to London by the founders of the well-known Chinese restaurant, Dalchini, in Wimbledon Park. From there he migrated to other restaurants in Hounslow. For the last twenty years, Lee has served his patrons for five years each, before deciding to move on in his personal quest, like Shakespeare in Southwark eyeing a plot of earth to found his Globe. Lee's theatre, the Hakkaland, came alive in mid-2016. The following year, he was awarded the 'best fusion restaurant in the UK.' 'But my greatest moment, really, was when I was asked to do the catering for the Durga Puja celebrations that year, by the Bengali community at Harrow. Although Indo-Chinese is a well-known brand in Calcutta, it was alien to a London of takeaway Indian, Chinese or pizza joints. "Indo-Chinese" not only provides a much needed versatility to the range of Indian food in London, but also evokes curiosity in a white British clientele.'[60] Kolkata chilli chicken rules the roost even in London, but Lee is also sympathetic to the needs of Marathi or Gujarati Londoners, who prefer the less spicy or vegetarian options. Unlike many others, Lee has no theories about craft or viability, except honesty to his food and budget.

I returned that night to an episode from Ben Elton's television comedy *Upstart Crow,* that fictionalises the life of William Shakespeare. One sees the bard here being as much of an esoteric artist as a shrewd entrepreneur of words. Lee did not seem very different to Shakespeare. He spoke an accent that resonated with all the languages he knew—English, Bengali, Hindi, Hakka, Taiwanese and Mandarin. Lee helped me better understand how for a merchant of language or food, the biggest asset is communication. Most other Indian restauranteurs in London emphasise authenticity. Lee's vision thrives by the sheer lack of it. He is quick to acknowledge how different Indo-Chinese is from authentic Chinese food, and even take pride in the fact that his Chinese or Japanese diners prefer his 'inauthentic' recipes more than the original. We never bother about the origins of Shakespeare's poetry. Nor does Lee bother about the provenance of his cooking. He has very little of gourmet Bengali or European or Chinese ingredients and heritage in his vocabulary, and yet his culinary language empowers the expressions of his diners all the more. Comparing him to Shakespeare is not to elevate him or his food to a national British standard. However, as newspeak, leave-hysteria and a new quest for old authenticities

rule Britain, hybridity has also emerged from this battle between
university wits and upstart crows. Perhaps for every Robert Greene
controlling the pedigrees of human expression, there will be a
William Shakespeare hailing the qualities of mercy in a work of
art. Altars cannot survive without their abattoirs.

The Shakespearean Font

The altars of hybridity in colonial history were etched out by
Bhabha in *The Location of Culture* (1994). Colonial histories are
written with the prepossession of authority. But their performance
in the years to come are in 'figures of farce'. English colonisers
wanted to create a class of Indians who could act as interpreters or
midwives of the colonial administration. It was hoped that they
would be almost English but just not quite—only marginally short
of replicas. What Macaulay and Bentinck originally intended was
reversed by the farcical mimicries that colonised Indians started
to play out. As Bhabha explained, 'the discourse of mimicry is
constructed around an ambivalence; in order to be effective,
mimicry must continually produce its slippage, its excess, its
difference. The authority of that mode of colonial discourse that
I have called mimicry is, therefore, stricken by an indeterminacy:
mimicry emerges as the representation of a difference that is itself
a process of disavowal.'[61] The character of the Anglicised Babu was
perennially capable of turning its back on the Empire—or turning
into a Frankenstein.

Colonial ambivalence succeeded on lines of psycholinguistics.
Even misinformation or misinterpretation from the colonial
language ran the risk of being considered new knowledge or being
transformed into an intelligent design through natural selection. In
Truth and Method (1960), Hans-Georg Gadamer voiced the crisis
of hermeneutics—the science of interpretation—from Friedrich
Schleiermacher to Martin Heidegger. Philosophers had always
seen the part interpreted from the whole in discrete structural
relations between the part and the whole. Interpretation, or the
act of zigzagging between the part and whole, created the aura of a

hermeneutic circle with a discrete centre.[62] As a logical metaphor of interpretation, the circle fails not so much in being a circle but in having a centre. For Gadamer and Derrida, there is no centre to the seemingly Newtonian structures of empiricism and interpretation. According to both, the relation between word and meanings lacks determinate or determining centres. In that sense, English-educated Indians belonged in an indeterminate or a decentred reality. It was hard to determine the source—a god if you will—of the intelligence of their intellectual design. They were uprooted from the language of their ancestors and never fully rooted in that of their colonisers. They considered themselves neither purely Indian nor ever purely sympathetic to imperialism.

British nobilities were infatuated with India, like Pygmalion was with his own sculpture. They believed that the untameable subcontinent had been commissioned into an enlarged statue sculpted by Britain in its own image, only twenty-times magnified. When that glorious image was inaugurated in the pomp of Bentinck's Calcutta, the serpent of imperial paranoia gradually coiled in. The language of colonial administration, art, aesthetics and culture was not an end in itself. It was subject to inappropriate mistranslations by a new class educated in the same language. Its members mimicked Europe to battle the superstitions and coquetry of the native, or behaved like Caliban when they saw the blast of imperial chicanery. The Indian Babu was neither coloured nor white. He was not shackled by the psychology of European authenticity or the neurosis of native inferiority. In his own slippages, differences, shortcomings or excesses—as opposed to the figure of the Englishman—the Babu became subconsciously feared and capable of turning dangerously inappropriate, by rebelling both against the eugenics of the European and the nativism of the native. When Macaulay wanted to protect British subjects of India under the umbrella of English education, little did he know that in twenty years the British would nearly fail to protect themselves in India, during the Great Rebellion of 1857.

With implements made of the tool of English language, both India and London came to be rewritten, reimagined and reconstructed in imperially frustrating histories, geographies and mythologies. The authors of that calumny were Raja Rammohun Roy, Dwarkanath Tagore, the Wadia brothers, Dadabhai Naoroji, W.C. Bonnerjee, Muncherji Bhownaggree, Romesh Chunder Dutt, Surendranath Banerjea, Mohandas K. Gandhi, Mohammad Ali Jinnah, Behramji Malabari, Jiddu Krishnamurti, Sophia Duleep Singh, Sarojini Naidu or Subhas Chandra Bose, to name only a few Indians who had lived in or travelled to Britain. In the age of Romanticism— with William Wordsworth, Samuel Taylor Coleridge, John Keats, Percy Shelley, Charles Lamb, Thomas Love Peacock and Thomas Macaulay himself—London was a typographical experiment in the English-educated Indian mind.

19th-century philosophers led carnivals in the minds of young Indians like Gandhi, who dared to experiment with this new typographic imagination on himself. Modernity was part of the amalgam of truths which he experimented with, and in that London became his first laboratory. For Gandhi, whatever digested or disrupted the body politic, such as the British Parliament or the Indian Railways, was unholy. Equally unholy was anything that could not be effortlessly digested by the human body, such as meat and wine. In London, Gandhi read with much greater satisfaction Henry Salt's *A Plea for Vegetarianism* (1886) than John Stuart Mill's *Utilitarianism* (1861). The city empowered him to believe that 'food reform could lead to social reform', In *A Carnival for Science* (1997), Shiv Visvanathan offered a unique explanation of Gandhi's dietary enlightenment.

> Vegetarianism in Gandhi's youth was a site for the location of alternative worldviews. It introduced him to the other West of occult philosophy, theosophy, various versions of socialism, and anti-vivisectionism as well as to Anne Kingsford's critique of diet and the Louis Kuhne's naturopathy. They combined with his readings of John Ruskin and Leo Tolstoy to provide not only an alternative view of the West but also to help him anchor his own identity in traditions. Vegetarianism linked traditional religious view of health to an alternative western philosophy of medicine.

The writings of the vegetarians, the theosophists, Ruskin and Tolstoy had in common not only a hostility to mechanistic-vivisectional science but also contained the concept of the patient as his own doctor.[63]

The ambivalence of the Gandhian mind was a stunning and sudden explosion in intelligent design. The making of a hybrid colonial subject was also an event of technology transfer, not merely from Britain to India but from the Empire to an unforeseeable posterity. With its evolutionary culturalism, this new London was a phenomenon of hybrid colonial imagination. Anglocentrism had distorted the optics of the city's evolution through migrations and networks of foreign information exchange. Paul MacReady's theory of human population explosion is rather appropriate in this regard. 10,000 years ago, human beings, their livestock and pets occupied less than 0.1 per cent of earth's vertebrate biomass. Today, as that number has risen to 98 per cent, we seem to 'have grown in population, technology, and intelligence to a position of terrible power: we now wield the paintbrush.'[64]

A similar case can be made for the transformation of London's biomass. The neural framework of the city may have been founded on the genes of Julius Caesar and the Roman Empire. But throughout the years of the industrial revolution, the two world wars and especially since the global sixties, it was sculpted with East European, South American, Chinese and South Asian experiences. Since the late 1960s, a 'multicoloured' Britain began witnessing racial riots and shrill campaigns for stricter immigration control in what was touted as a utopia or a 'Roman ideal of commonwealth.'[65] As early as 1986, Faroukh Dhondy wrote, 'On arriving at Heathrow, the first thing that catches your attention as you get off the plane is that the porters are Asians, the floor cleaners are Punjabis, the people who man the cafes are, to a man and woman, Punjabis and some of the taxi drivers are West Indians.'[66] In recent years, the Brexit campaign and Windrush scandal have exposed the limits of the British government's immigration policy based on the unsustainable nexus between its posturing of liberal cosmopolitanism and need for vote-bank politics. Today, there are over half a million British Indians living in London, which is nearly 7 per cent of the city's population. If British–Bangladeshi and British–Pakistani nationals are included in that number, a total of a million erstwhile Indian-origin people live in London, constituting 12 per cent of the population of the city.

Once the Roman bastion of imperial Britannia, London is now a dynamic phenomenon of not only its gene activities but also genetic mutations. Monica Ali's novel *Brick Lane* (2003), set around the Jamme Masjid of Tower Hamlets, reveals a kaleidoscopic view into the personal development of a third-world immigrant in the metropolis. As with capitalism, the psychology of a Bangladeshi girl undergoes a metamorphosis, so with immigration the city's traditional values of citizenship are led in to the churning of seas.[67] Several parts of London—Southall, Brick Lane, Wembley, Hillingdon or East Ham—have undergone rapid morphological transformations. Here vegetable vendors and cash & carry shops, travel agencies and fish merchants, condiment and cutlery sellers, copper and bronze sellers, incense sticks and bangle sellers, priests and restauranteurs, garland makers and car mechanics look Indian or South Asian, are to be found on Britain's maps and possess global outreach.

Echoing Appadurai, these Indian and South Asian spaces of the city have been called 'kaleido-scapes'.[68] If not in physical capacity, the city was always psychologically inhabited by Indians, who have for a long time wielded a paintbrush over its designs. Just as in human evolution, the evolution of a new hybrid colonial culture, which was both mimetic and subversive at its core, led to phenomenal transformations in how London was experienced. Before Gandhi, roughly until the time of the arrival of Keshub Chunder Sen, mimicry and subversion were like—what Charles Darwin or Alan Turing described in evolutionary contexts as— competence without comprehension.[69] Hybridity and mimicry were capable of competing against imperialism without comprehending how. Gandhi onwards, this competence was even within the reach of comprehension, and of being turned into an instrument of decolonisation.

With Gregor Mendel, the German-Austrian biologist who pioneered heredity studies, and Wilhelm Johannsen, the Danish botanist who was the first to classify organismal genetic materials and visible heredity traits, many German, Austrian, Dutch and Polish scientists made significant breakthroughs in explaining human genes. The word 'gene' itself was introduced by Johannsen, in 1905. That was when an English biologist, William Bateson, got into the act, introducing the word 'genetics' and a school dedicated to its studies in Cambridge. After the Second World War, English chemist Rosalind Franklin and New Zealand-born British molecular biologist Maurice Wilkins offered revolutionary X-ray analysis into the molecular structure of DNA. Six decades later, the *Nature* magazine published a startling discovery at the International Human Genome Sequencing Consortium organised by the National Human Genome Research Institute. The human genome, it said, comprised only about 25,000 human protein-coding genes.[70] 'We are a few human cells,' wrote quantum-healer Deepak Chopra, 'hanging on to a bacterial colony, we are the awakening of bacterial consciousness.'[71]

The absolute credibility or uncertainty of these scientific explanations notwithstanding, they can be the model to explain London's transformation from an imperial capital to a cosmopolitan consciousness. In the early 20th century, more and more of the city was crystallising into an English minority colonised by a genomic metropolis of Europeans, Russians, African–Americans, Caribbean Islanders—and, indeed, Indians. They were the bacterial colony that London wilfully imbibed to flourish in the course of its own natural evolution. It is now speculated whether the microbiome—bacterial genomes hanging on to human cells—actually listens to the thoughts of human senses. If so, the Indian community in London, throughout the years of Roy, the Tagores, Naoroji, Bonnerjee, Bhownaggree, Dutt, Naidu, Princess Sophia, Jinnah or Gandhi, was actively

eavesdropping on its daily conversations, its life on the streets and
Houses of Parliament, the kaleidoscopic cesspools of loungers
and idlers, hungry rough-sleepers and culinary fantasies, fashions
and phraseologies, cockneys and queens, its lugubrious towers
and its prodigal emporiums—by the Thames or around Hyde
Park, from Charing Cross to Spitalfields, from Bloomsbury to
Uxbridge, from Battersea to Hampstead. London seeped into
the cities, buildings, cultures and politics of India, and was itself
rendered into an Indian porringer of bewildering recipes.

The history of the reinvention of London enables us to
challenge the divisiveness of Samuel Huntington's *Clash of
Civilisations* (1996) and, indeed, the foreign policies of Britain and
India. Visvanathan argues, 'what looks marginal, what has been
sustained in little corners as a variety of imaginations has political
possibilities for receding democracies. Nationalism does not
end the conversation of cultures. We by-hearted the English, we
by-hearted the Bill of Rights, we by-hearted William Shakespeare
and Newton and Locke. And as Nirad C. Chaudhuri once said,
"The English don't write English anymore."[72] Not the kind of
English that Indians were capable of! A case can be made for the
sheer obscenity of the colonial mind that chose as its master the
English race. Even until the early 19th century, there were at least
four other formidable East India Companies—Portuguese, French,
Dutch and Danish—trading in what Saugata Bhaduri has called a
'polycolonial' Bengal.[73] Then again, it may be as easily argued that a
formidable number of Indians chose colonisation as the very pulpit
to decolonise the minds of their countrymen.

The anticolonial eccentricities of Rabindranath Tagore or
Jagdish Chandra Bose challenged the foundations of Western
empiricism and technology, making ambivalence a manual of life
and an instrument of democracy. Not contented with liberating
the oppressed, they went on to liberate the oppressor from his own
oppressiveness. The possibilities of the other Wests and the other
Londons that are quarantined from 21st-century imagination are
suddenly thrown open with the emergence of these eccentrics
who reinvented India as much as they reinvented London. Else,

it merely seems as though what is central London today once represented London for most of India. Sherlock Holmes at Baker Street, Bertram Wooster not too far at Berkeley Square, John Keats at Hampstead, G.K. Chesterton circuiting Notting Hill or Farringdon, Charles Dickens lolling about the Courts of Chancery or Holborn, Jack the Ripper scheming homicides around Tower Hamlets, was as much as the compass of the obedient Indian mind could have drawn of London. Obedience, however, does not create democracies.

Reading the 'great man' theory of Thomas Carlyle or of the 'chartered streets' of William Blake in the presidency colleges of the subcontinent, Indians were able to typographically imagine London even without visiting the city. At times, they did so even better than Londoners. For Nirad C. Chaudhuri, an unwavering confidante to the Empire, London began with Shakespeare. He was self-assured that 'no other country or people in the world has ever made one author test and symbol of literary culture as we Bengalis did with Shakespeare in the 19th century.'[74] To the Indian mind, Julius Caesar's Roman empire and its offensive citizens must have reeked of the London mob. To them, the Tiber was a metaphor for the Thames, and the Capitol for the Palace of Westminster. Cassius, who plotted the conspiracy against Caesar, may well have been Oliver Cromwell and Cinna, the poet, a prototype of John Milton.

Londoners never failed to convince themselves that the city's most famous Tower was built by Julius Caesar, whose spirit had followed Londinium into its modernity. Elizabethan London seemed to breathe the living airs of ancient Rome. Its whole purpose was to enter the past of an Italian city underneath its Italianate arches.[75] The British Empire dressed itself in insignias of the Roman Empire. Where Shakespeare's ghost travelled, Britain's Romanesque theatre followed. His plays were exploited in India for civilising through bombast.[76] His textbooks offered a colossal window of opportunity for critics to run the Empire through their commentaries. Literary criticism and essays inhabited in colonial India, what Michel Foucault called in *The Order of Things* (1966), the 'interstice occurring between the primal text and the infinity of interpretation.'[77] Before the Renaissance in Europe, commentary was an exceptionally private or scholarly activity. Printing let loose commentaries beyond the classroom lecture, or the whimsical flourish in the attic, into infinite typographical and interpretive possibilities. In the 19th century, Bengal had its own renaissance with the trinity of political reforms, public institutions and the printing revolution.

According to Gauri Vishwanathan, English literature or English studies was a British Indian invention to educate native subjects through a 'rapid institutionalisation' of Shakespeare, Milton, Wordsworth or Keats. The practice of formally teaching English migrated westwards from India.[78] A minister of Tipu Sultan once said that there was something mysterious and invisible behind the British Government—that Indians were not afraid of what could be seen, but of the unseen imperial hand.[79] Through the lure of the civil services and railways, and indeed by exporting a literary London to India, Britain tried making itself invisible. As the spectre of Shakespeare was conjured to lead the English studies movement in Bengal,[80] the Indian mind was turned into the new colonial workshop.

The semantic world of the colonised mind opened up to a melodrama of autobiographical memories and boundary extensions— neuropsychological phenomena owing to which one could recount and reconstruct much more than what was actually read or interpreted of British culture. Every name of every building or character from Britain was a lifelike persona feeding off the episodic memories of the colonial psyche. Knowledge was nothing but a 'cognitive capital', like the enormous vault where Uncle Scrooge swam in his wealth. According to Nicholas Rescher, the development of knowledge involves 'the creation of intellectual assets, in which both producers and users have a very real interest. Knowledge, in short, is a good of sorts—a commodity on which one can put a price tag and which can be bought and sold much like any other—save that the price of its acquisition often involves not just money alone but other resources, such as time, effort, and ingenuity.'[81] In that regard, London was not only an imperial capital but also a great intellectual capital, an asset, a great vault of commodities or, indeed, a super-commodity.

If London was intended to be a text, it was much mistranslated by the Indian mind. This neuropsychological eruption only served to inflate the cognitive economy of the city. 'Misunderstanding a text,' writes Pertti Hietaranta, 'in turn exemplifies the linguistic type of an incorrect choice.' In a universe where texts do not have living authors any more than living intentions of authors, mistranslation is not a flaw but, in fact, a virtue. Hietaranta adds that the cause of mistranslation is that a 'translator interprets the source text in a way which is in some respects different from the intentions of the author of the original text and thus ends up producing a translation which is considered to contain one or more mistakes due to such a misunderstanding of the original author's intentions.'[82] Macaulay did not anticipate the neurological aggression of the class of Indian translators that he wanted to unleash. Nor did he have in mind the aporia—the theatre of infinite decentred and indeterminate interpretations—that London would be subjected to. For Chaudhuri, the names of lords and royalty—Roberts, Kitchener, Buller, Methuen, Rosebery, Burke, Hastings, Queen Victoria and Gladstone—were not foreign names but an absolute language whose symphony contrived London as if by the lyre of Amphion. Another lord—Lord Alfred Tennyson—may have inadvertently traded the very idea of how Indians imagined the imperial city, when he wrote:

The city is built,
To music, therefore never built at all,
And therefore built forever.[83]

That template of an amorphous central London is still writ large on the relics of Indian history in the city. The India House of Shyamaji Krishnavarma, Madam Cama and Vinayak Damodar Savarkar was quite appropriately—however inappropriate it became for the British administration—established in Highgate, near the cemetery where Karl Marx was buried. The Indian High

Commission came up in Aldwych near the London School of
Economics, which was a hotbed of Indian Marxism in the interwar
years. The Indian YMCA guest house was rebuilt after the Second
World War in Fitzroy Square, and inaugurated by Vengalil Krishna
Menon, the first Indian High Commissioner in Britain. Visitors at
the guest house today are able to sample the displaced flavours of
Edwardian London with the City of Westminster's plaques charting
brief histories of authors, architects, scientists and statesmen, who
inhabited the various houses of its central thoroughfares. With a
Primark branch at Tottenham Court Road, which is half a mile
from Fitzrovia, scholarship moneys of students are syringed into
global capital.

The Twice-born Mimicry

History is a literary or linguistic performance of a chronology of
events in time. It is a palimpsest that mimics laboratory science.
While historical events may or may not unfold in a Newtonian
scheme of causations, history deludes one to perceive it as a stream
of sacrosanct causalities. Even at its noblest, history is nothing but
the similes of fiction mimicking the structures of fact. Those traces
of reality that are not conducive to fiction or fact are devolved by
language into a dream without language. What is never covered by
historians is the realm of the exiled or the ghostly. It belongs in
what Derrida called 'an economy of the imagination'.[84] History is
condemned to be productive. It is condemned to invent truth only
insofar as its capability of reproducing the foreseeability of future
truths. The language of history may stand or, indeed, dance in
testimony to its own imperfect origins and structures. It is contrived
to invite a predictable future. That, however, is not the future we
can content ourselves with in the history of Indians in London.

> There is a future which is predictable, programmed, scheduled,
> foreseeable. But there is a future, *l'avenir* (to come) which refers
> to someone who comes whose arrival is totally unexpected. For
> me, that is the real future. That which is totally unpredictable.

The Other who comes without my being able to anticipate their arrival. So if there is a real future, beyond the other known future, it is *l'avenir* in that it is the coming of the Other when I am completely unable to foresee their arrival.[85]

History is an act of looking at age. But in its very essence, an 'act of looking has no age.'[86] Derrida wrote in *Of Grammatology* (1976) that with the force of Western metaphysics, 'history was compelled to strive toward the reduction of the trace.'[87] The relationship between historical events and history is always one of difference, deferral and disinterment. It is always played out on an untimely and an unhomely stage—out of its time and out of its home. It is this incomplete relativism between the event and its histories that Hayden White summed up as 'metahistory'.[88] The great continental historians of the 19th century that White paid homage to—Jules Michelet, Alexis de Tocqueville, Carl Jacob Burckhardt or Leopold von Ranke—could not escape the hierarchies of dominant social perceptions of their age. The European Enlightenment's philosopher of history, Pierre Bayle, hammered the dichotomy of truth and lies into historical sciences, in his *Critical Dictionary* (1826).

I observe that truth being the soul of history, it is an essential thing for a historical composition to be free from lies; so that though it should have all other perfections, it will not be a history, but a mere fable and romance, if it want truth. Whence I conclude, that none can be well qualified to write a good history, unless he be such an enemy to lying, that his conscience does not permit him to tell lies even to the advantage of his religion, and dearest friends, nor to the disadvantage of an impious sect, and of his most implacable persecutors. I understand by lying, not only the invention of a false thing, but also the suppression or addition of circumstances, that may serve to justify others, or to lay something to their charge.[89]

It is hard to argue with Bayle's moral rationality. It is that very rationale of not 'lying'—no invention or disingenuousness, no fallacy or absent-mindedness—that informs our history of *Indians in London*. Unlike the student of physics, the agent of history is never an external observer. He is always an internal constituent of the paradigm of his own study. Following the Age of Enlightenment, and most evidently since the Romantics, history has been understood like the unearthing of the past with a pitchfork studded with realism, positivism, symbolism, liberalism, anarchism, naturalism, idealism and much else. Each of these ideologies and their piercing tips have contested with others to represent a more objectively truthful expression of social realities. Beginning with the late 18th century, Indians were an inescapable visibility in London. This may have been an ingredient for a socially realistic history of the city. It was omitted, however, as a fantastical and anarchic element, undeserving of a place in imperial imagination.

Reality can only be mimicked by history on the stage of time. The language of history is, therefore, bound to produce the slippage, excess or difference to the reality whence it emerged. London being the stage of British history—or the stage of an Indian history at the heart of Britain—does not mean that the city was entirely well-known to its historians or to those who constituted its history as it was unfolding. A character in a play knows what lines precede or follow the present, but does not fathom the spirit they emerged from. Londoners in their own hues and humdrums of history—for instance the band of Victorian authors in the Indian typographic imagination—were a coalition of several theatrical performances on several stages, synchronised and centralised as one. London's history, like the history of any metropolis, is a hypnosis where the city appears to mimic its many theatres. This performance of London was wonderfully illustrated by Raymond Williams. 'This version of a glittering and dominant metropolitan culture had enough reality to support a traditional idea of the city.' Victorian London became 'a centre of light and learning, but now on an unprecedented scale. The cultural centralisation of England was already at this time more marked, at every level, than in any comparable society. Even to oppose and reject the city, men came to the city; there was no other ready way.'[90] Indians—since even before 18th-century travellers, Ihtishamuddin, Abu Taleb Khan and Sake Deen Mahomet—accepted and rejected the city in myriad ways. Mahomet established Britain's first curry house in 1810, in London, and later became a shampooing surgeon—the first of its kind—to Kings George IV and William IV. In 2007, he was given a special place in the National Portrait Gallery's exhibition, *Between Worlds: Voyagers to Britain 1700–1850*, where 'his small red shoes, waistcoat, advertisements and portraits from his period of celebrity' were hosted.[91] Along with Ihtishamuddin and Abu Taleb, Mahomet led the early disruptions in Britain's fixations and prejudices about India and the Orient.[92] Uncannily, it is never acknowledged how much Indians themselves colonised London. They too haunted the city and made it none the holier.

While studying in England, Amitav Ghosh realised that there was something discernibly Indian about the thoroughfares of London. Not a compass or a guidebook, but a typographic imagination became the principal instrument for the narrator of *The Shadow Lines* (1988), navigating through the East End. Paradoxically, that written imagination had been passed on to him in oral form. It impersonated his personal history, and that of his uncle Tridib. It also bowdlerised the history of London. On Tridib's ninth birthday in September 1940—during the London Blitz—he was gifted an old copy of *Bartholomew's Atlas*. The narrator's oral memory of that month recreated the Middle English romance of Tristan and Isolde, where a man falls in love with a woman from another country, under the influence of a love potion. Tridib, an Indian man, had fallen in love with May, a British woman. The potion in their case was their shared memory of a tattered city, like the 'tattered' *Atlas* which the narrator rediscovered decades later. Being tattered was a testament to survival, not just of a London that survived the fury of the Luftwaffe, but also of the imagination of the city that Tridib bequeathed to his nephew.

Tridib's nephew is able to reimagine London and recognise the sites of its blitzed architecture, even before his first visit to the city. For Ila, his cousin, it is entirely incomprehensible how this bricolage of memory, history and cartography is performed. Ila is a globetrotter. For her to know a place and being able to talk about it sensibly involves physically being there and framing it in photographs. For the narrator, a place has to be 'invented in one's imagination'. He asserts that 'her practical, bustling London was no less invented' than his.[93] His and his uncle's shared love for London is consummated when the narrator is reborn as Tristan, making love to his dead uncle's girlfriend May. His journey paves the way for reimagining erstwhile imperial experiences. The *Bartholomew's Atlas* belongs to a colonised subject, not a canonical expert on London's cartography. The narrator's heretical circumambulations around central London, with his deceased uncle's memories and oral maps cultivated with the *Atlas*, are profound disruptions in that cartography. They disrupt how Indians had earlier imagined the city and how Londoners imagined themselves.

If Tridib's knowledge of London's history was a mimicry of imperial identities and spaces, his nephew's navigation through London's geography was a disruption twice-born of a twice-born mimicry. He was able to recognise the bombed out Solent Road, and House No. 44 on Lymington Road, despite the dramatic transformations those streets had undergone since the Second World War. For many, the novel appears to offer a 'feasible way of narrating what for many people is the contemporary experience of London.'[94] *The Shadow Lines*, however, is a world apart from the deifying lenses with which many Indians had seen the city for at least two centuries. Imperialism or nativism were never constant unambiguous forces. Nor was mimicry immune to its own subversions. By the sheer weight of the memory of historical dispossessions, mimicry could turn its back on itself, and undergo a cultural meiosis. Mimicry could split itself into memory and amnesia, pushing the frontiers of its own historical dualities and the frontiers of London.

The duality of memory and amnesia, or how poorly Indians have remembered their own history in London, is manifest in the accounts of Victorian Indian travellers. Not a single one of them makes a passing reference to Salamon Nurr, Samuel Munsur, Peter Pope, Catherine Bengal, or any of the few hundreds of forgotten Indian exiles in the city between the time that England first turned Protestant, in the 16th century, and colonised India, in the 18th. Whether as flesh and blood or as commodities, Indians shaped the peripheries of London since Shakespeare. Spices, textiles and artefacts had been feverishly trafficked to Britain with the inception of the East India Company in September 1600. Indian servants, Indian lascars and Indian goods constituted a sense of what was naturally fashionable and naturally English. In the worlds of William Makepeace Thackeray, Wilkie Collins or Arthur Conan Doyle, Indian merchandise and mannerisms continually pressed against older fashions of London. They were also the most visible personifications of absolute avarice in Victorian England. Yet no one stops to tell the story of the 'Hunter-Indian' or the 'lascar' population that William Wordsworth saw in London, and wrote of in *The Prelude* (1799).

> Among the crowd all specimens of man,
> Through all the colours which the sun bestows,
> And through every character of form and face.[95]

It was only in the 19th century that London actually began recognising its alien population. With reference to the Spanish exiles in the city, Thomas Carlyle wrote, 'one might mark the years and epochs by successive kinds of exiles that walk London streets, and, in grim silent manner demand pity from us and reflections from us.'[96] In his biography of *London* (2000), Peter Ackroyd too walks us between Regency's Chinese immigrants and their 'dens of inequity,' made conspicuous by London's fetish for the Asian habit of opium consumption. The Chinese were rendered unthreatening by their law abiding nature. Compared to them, Spanish immigrants or Ashkenazi Jews, as Ackroyd demonstrates, were a relatively over-accommodated presence. Immigrants from China, Spain or Ireland had been making history in London as 'examples of successful idleness' since the early 18th century.[97] They were seen as leeches on the state's charity, and were often attacked by poor-stock of the English.

> Among these riots and alarms there was another group of immigrants who, if they stirred little outrage, excited even less sympathy. They were the Indians, the forgotten ancestors of the 20th-century arrivals, who came to London as servants or slaves; some remained in employment, while others were summarily dismissed or ran away to a vagrant life. There were 'hue and cry' advertisements in the public prints—a guinea for the recapture of 'a black boy, an Indian, about thirteen years old run away the 8th ins. from Putney with a collar about his neck with this inscription, "The Lady Bromfield's black, in Lincoln's Inn Fields."' Other advertisements were placed to discover an 'East India Tawney Black' or a 'Run-away Bengal Boy.' Other Asian servants were 'discharged' or 'dumped,' having attended their employers on their passage from India, so that they were reduced to a life upon the streets.[98]

European travellers to Victorian London did mention Indians once in a while, such as when they came across a musical gig on the streets. 'There were German bands, as well as Indian drummers and blacked-up "Abyssians" who played violin, guitar, tambourine and castanets,' Ackroyd tells us. References to such stray scenes of London life are neatly ostracised from the works of civilised historians or travellers. Trailokya Nath Mukharji, a Bengali traveller who visited England in 1886, is an enduring example of London's civilising influence on the Indian mind. Mukharji was appointed a supervisor in the Colonial and Indian Exhibition. Being in the thick of artefacts and codicils of imperial knowledge, he was held captive to the idea of European progress and Britain's sovereign virtue to rule over India. Outside the Exhibition, he was also ensorcelled by the city's public institutions. The railways held a special place for Mukharji. The expanse and punctuality of the Victorian railway system had enthralled contemporary Indian travel writers such as Bholanauth Chunder or Gopináth Sadáshivji Háte, back in India. Taking a cue from their travels, Mukharji dyed his own picture of the King's Cross Railway Station. 'Engines puffing and whistling,' he gushed, 'passengers running in and out, guards shutting doors, faint hum of voices, all combined to create a grandeur of busy life which must be seen to be realised.'[99]

How Mukharji experienced the railways of London could have also been experienced in the suburbs of Calcutta. One only needed to nestle with a railway periodical of the day. What he believed to be an entirely unique experience—born out of the marvels of British engineering and industrial machismo—was only a template that could have been used to describe even a train journey in San Francisco. Turn to an issue of the *Engineering News and Contract Journal* from four years before Mukharji's visit to London. It plugs the American countryside with insignias Mukharji might have reserved for Victoria or King's Cross. 'The train suddenly emerged from a long stretch of forest,' the *Journal* went on, 'and crept slowly over a trestle-work one mile and a quarter long. *The grandeur of the surroundings must be seen to be fully realised.*'[100] Was Mukharji's English experience a facsimile of American metaphors? Was the Indian mind indeed travelling in the multitudes of London, or was its voyage sieved through the annals of the obscure American west?

———

The ceremony of travelling happened more on and off the typography of travelogues, rather than in the immediate typology of built spaces. Reading was as much an act of travelling as being physically part of the scene. Instead of the map or the atlas substituting for the territory, typefaces fulfilled the job. The printed word was a printed world. The race that had housetrained the steam engine had also naturally housetrained the modes and methods in which its colonies perceived its progress and supremacy. Caught unawares by the follies of his typographical imagination, Mukharji condemned his own race:

> The real inequality between Europeans and 'natives' rests not on the fact of the former filling a few high posts in the country. The European knows more of our mountains and rivers than we do; he knows more of the plants that grow around us, their names, their properties, even the size and shapes of their leaves: he knows more of what is interred in the bosom of our earth; he knows more about the capabilities of our land; in everything he knows more than we do of our country. Then he knows better how to use that knowledge for the benefit of men. We do not know these things; hence we are 'natives'.[101]

Partha Chatterjee called Mukharji's prose one of the sincerest 'declarations of love' for Britain and Europe, professed out of free will.[102] Mukharji belonged to the class of Indians who believed they had neither been coerced into Western education nor could they efficiently recreate their lost links with the ancient East without the British. This was the very middle-class from which stemmed the great resistance to the partition of Bengal and colonial rule—the fervour of *swadeshi* and nationalism. It was also the class that recognised how much the colonial system had debilitated British culture itself and, thus, came to love the British as its 'intimate enemy'.[103] The anti-colonial movement did not 'diminish their love for the concept of Europe that was planted in their minds— the Europe of Shakespeare and the steam engine, of the French Revolution and quantum mechanics.'[104] Anti-colonial never lapsed into anti-Europeanism.

Spawned by English prose and poetry, Indian universities 'provincialised' European aesthetics in places like Calcutta or Bombay or Madras.[105] Reading about London stimulated a bourgeois culture of homesickness for a faraway home. The city was 'hammered into banality by mass-comprehension'.[106] It was a mass-comprehension which today manifests as London being reduced to its tube-maps or its blue-eyed purlieus, such as Westminster Abbey, the Tower, London Bridge, Buckingham Palace and Madame Tussauds. In the late 20th century, Salman Rushdie proposed a new cultural contract, where he described a diaspora as an 'imaginary homeland,' into which everyone had emigrated from the country called 'the past'.[107] London, in that sense, was always an imaginary homeland for Indians. To emigrate was not so much a virtue of globalisation or class-privilege as it was the predestination of a print culture driven by Baskerville, Didot or Clarendon typefaces.

Reading English poetry in late-19th-century India could have been, at times, an experience straight out of Johannes Kepler's vision of the solar system, when the Western mind first discovered it was not the centre of the universe. Chaudhuri recounted the days of his childhood when his teacher, Bankim Babu, read English poems to him and his brothers and sisters on evenings. Once, as he was reading the Scottish ballad 'Gay Goshawk', 'the amber-coloured glare of the hurricane lantern fell on the left side of Bankim Babu's face, throwing the shadow of his nose on the right half,' as divided by an axis in the centre, like the earth. The literature of Britain shaped geographical and astronomical consciousness in the children of colonised India. Even reading Sanskrit in the Raj was like reading Latin in Renaissance Europe, for textbooks in the classical or regional Indian languages were published under the aegis of the British Government and its Orientalist reformer, the late Sir William Jones.

The algorithms that made Johannes Gutenberg's printing techniques viral during the Renaissance later fired the imagination of Indians. Macaulay's Minute and the Indian Education Act of 1835 have been subjects of unrelenting reproach. But Macaulay owed much of it to William Caxton, who imported Gutenberg's technology to England. In order to reimagine that era, we turn to Shakespeare, 'as imagination bodies forth, the poet's pen turns them to shapes, and gives to airy nothing a local habitation and a name.'[108] During the Renaissance, poets were also credited with valuable ideas for city planning, mapping and architecture. Enlightenment and the Age of Reason earmarked the language of poetic imagination and empirical science as a resolutely European language. This was then exported to the colonies. With movable printing technique, typography became the new 'natural resource or staple, like cotton or timber or radio.'[109] It was the allspice for recipes to Francis Bacon's essays, Kepler's or Newton's laws on planetary revolution, Protestant missions abroad, biblical translations in India and missionary presses in Bengal. In much of that, London was made ubiquitous. Meanwhile, Indian exiles in London since the time of Elizabeth I, were the castaways from the networks that they did not belong to in India. Like the social networks of the 21st century, Gutenberg's printing press also led to widespread public networks through the printed word.[110] Those Indians who were not a part of the oral intellectual or economic networks in India, in the first place, lost out on the immigrant networks in Britain or, more specifically, in London. The early Indian lascars, ayahs and artisans brought by the East India Company were unlettered, therefore, un-networked.

Marshall McLuhan has explored the makings of typographical man and his imagination like none else. The printing machine 'was at first mistaken for an engine of immortality by everybody'.[111] Much later, in Victorian India, the works of British authors were, to quote James Joyce, like the '*ring* man in the *rong* shop but the *rite* words by the *rote* order'.[112] One of the greatest achievements of printing presses, according to McLuhan, was that they 'made available authors of remote times. People began to imitate their styles,' and mark their pre-eminence in imagining new contexts, contours and countries in the act of writing.[113] What a city like London might have, could have, or indeed should have been, no longer commanded lecturing or storytelling. It could be read privately or aloud from penny-worth publications. The audible image of the story or the legend was transformed into a visual vault of the novel or the ode. Victorian London became a galaxy of portable metaphors shipped off to the colonies as textbooks. Its typography mimicked its geography, and was in turn mimicked by the typographic imagination of the Anglicised minds of India. There must have been hundreds of *Bartholomew's Atlases* on any given day in Edwardian India, commissioned in the name of John George Bartholomew, the 'Prince of Cartography'. Each of those was capable of building a London out of airy nothings of the local habitation of a swampy suburb in Bengal or Madras.

From Fitzrovia to Typogravia

In December 2017, the Sir John Ritblat Gallery exhibited some Shakespeare artefacts as part of the Treasures of the British Library. One of the entries mentioned a young poet, Peter Heylen, who wrote the poem 'A Dreame' in 1618. It was about a young woman who mistook him as Shakespeare and left star-struck. 'She seeing me,' wrote Heylen, 'went out and let her booke which in my trembling hands I forthwith tooke twas *Venus and Adonis*.' It has been speculated that Heylen and Shakespeare were known to each other. The entry was a window into the world of a prototypical network, hundreds of years before the internet, but certainly after the emergence of print.

In the railway colonies of India—Kharagpur, Jamalpur, Asansol or Shoranoor—where once the Kiplings and the Babus had worked the administrative mills of the Empire, Indian men wooed Anglo-Indian women to seize the opportunity of quoting Shakespeare. Given his extensive reading, the bard may have known that his British ancestors from the glorious Roman Empire had carried an illustrious trade with Arabia and India. During their heyday, a 'hundred and twenty vessels sailed annually down the Red Sea, traversed the Arabian coasts, and arriving at the Malabar shores in India, and the island of Ceylon, returned loaded with cinnamon, pepper, ginger, silk, pearls and diamonds.'[114] But was he, indeed, aware that Indians were in his city, part of 'the tag-rag people' that he was so renowned for rousing?

The first books to start talking about Indians in Britain were written by Rozina Visram and Michael H. Fisher only in the last thirty years. History had to be chutneyed and curried and pickled for it to be known that Britain was not just the nation of Churchill, the Beatles, Sean Connery, Harry Potter or David Beckham's left and right feet. It also belonged to the ayahs, lascars, apprentices and sailors from India, whom the English East India Company kept bringing on a steady fleet since the dawn of the 17th century. Culturally, if not geographically, the road to India lay through Morocco in North Africa. In *Shakespeare's Restless World* (2012), Neil MacGregor proposed that playgoers in the bard's era were 'global citizens, proud of Francis Drake's circumnavigation of the earth and willing listeners to the tall stories told by travellers.'[115] A Moroccan prince burned by the sun came as a suitor to Portia in *The Merchant of Venice*, or the 'Jewish play.' Evidently, Shakespeare knew a great deal about England. He knew the English fancy for gold which came from Marrakech, a territory much more consequential to England in Shakespeare's time than England was to it. The need for African gold to fabricate English currency was making geographical and psychological boundaries increasingly porous.

By 1600, Shakespeare's Jewish play, with the odd Moroccan prince, had run for five years. The bard must have heard of 'Muslim emissaries from Barbary to the Elizabethan court, led by the Moroccan Ambassador, Abd el-Ouahed ben Messaoud ben Mohammed Anoun,' who wanted to establish an alliance with Britain against the military regime of Catholic Spain.[116] For London, this lavish spectacle of the Moroccan ambassador and his delegation was the first glimpse of Africa and Islam, informs MacGregor.[117] The English court already accepted Moors as allies against Spain. Three years later, Shakespeare invented the character of a moor in *Othello*, to play out an English tragedy on the streets of Venice, performed at the Globe by the Thames. It was three years since the birth of the East India Company, and oriental artefacts and communities were recoloring London's demography like a chameleon or a madman's dream.

Not only were Elizabethans led to believe in their global citizenship but also their unquestionable membership in a global system of commerce. Trading with Morocco in gold, gunpowder and arms had trained the founders of the Barbary Company—a predecessor of the East India Company—to trade confidently with farther reaches of the East. India was much closer in the Elizabethan imagination than we can imagine today. Incidentally, after the alliance with Marrakech, Indians started becoming characters of Anglo-Dutch paintings, if not

Shakespeare's own writings. Some outstanding examples are Anthony van Dyck's portrait of *William Feilding, First Earl of Denbigh, Saved in a Forest by a Turbaned Indian Boy* (1633) and Peter Lely's portrait of *Lady Charlotte Fitzroy* (1674) being offered grapes by an Indian page. Two centuries later, one finds the Victorian hookah-burdar brought from Uttar Pradesh by Joseph Sedley in William Makepeace Thackeray's *Vanity Fair* (1848). Fisher called these fleets of servants, seafarers and settlers as the 'counterflows'.[118] Indians started settling in Britain almost as early as Britons began settling in India.

European British Subjects according to Census Returns.

	1931.		1921.		1911.		1901.	
	Males.	Females.	Males.	Females.	Males.	Females.	Males.	Females.
India	110,137	45,418	119,149	46,336	134,950	50,484	112,687	42,004
Ajmer-Merwara	1,172	352	1,080	320	1,369	333	644	273
Andamans and Nicobars	180	34	171	38	193	50	222	47
Assam	2,168	959	1,806	863	1,556	616	1,484	484
Baluchistan	3,795	1,219	3,967	787	3,360	809	2,961	491
Bengal	13,116	7,788	12,449	7,567	14,659	7,668	15,767	8,271
Bihar and Orissa	3,443	2,232	3,563	2,182	3,489	2,157	..	..
Bombay (*including Aden*)	16,679	7,452	23,161	7,880	21,157	7,826	19,872	7,182
Burma	7,205	3,422	5,771	2,057	8,904	2,924	6,481	2,125
Central Provinces and Berar.	3,815	1,309	4,338	1,289	5,323	1,710	3,408	1,587
Coorg	69	53	38	56	109	65	126	86
Delhi	2,879	1,330	3,401	916	622	246	Incld. in Punjab.	
Madras	6,423	4,253	5,253	4,697	8,143	4,965	7,852	4,705
N.-W. F. P.	10,116	1,427	9,397	1,056	4,898	800	4,053	587
Punjab	14,597	4,926	15,860	5,686	23,457	7,407	19,791	5,781
United Provinces	16,868	5,193	17,805	6,638	24,461	8,350	20,363	7,237
Baroda State	78	33	49	31	72	51	44	36
Central India Agency	1,788	572	2,705	614	3,414	554	3,133	580
Cochin State	38	34	19	4	Incld. in Madras		31	14
Gwalior State	54	47	489	60	Included in C. I. figures		32	29
Hyderabad State	1,760	93	2,960	543	4,251	979	2,760	387
Jammu and Kashmir State.	69	82	123	140	124	102	101	88
Mysore State	2,929	1,978	4,132	2,504	4,697	2,426	2,748	1,429
Rajputana Agency	463	393	462	342	682	445	504	381
Sikkim State	4	3	1	6	10	1	..	..
Travancore State	299	157	149	60	Incld. in Madras		310	194
W. I. S. Agency	130	79	Included against Bombay.					
			425					

Census of India, 1931, Volume 1, Part 1, Compiled by J.H. Hutton, to Which is Annexed an Actuarial Report by L.S. Vaidyanathan, p. 425

The census of 1931 of British India recorded that there were about 150,000 Europeans living in India. Going back to the end of the 19th century, this number remains largely unchanged. The number of Britons in India was anything between 130,000 and 140,000 in a total population of 330 million.[119] Visram writes that no official survey had been conducted on Indians living in United Kingdom before 1932, when the Indian National Congress recorded the population of Indians living outside India. In that survey, about 7,200 Indians were found to be living in Britain.[120] However, since ethnic minorities were not taken into account in Britain's national censuses, there is no absolute reason to deny that the number of Indians could have been much higher, especially when one comes across references to various ethnicities from India or the Indian diaspora from East Africa in colonial records. By 1939, Sikhs, for instance, were conspicuous in every large British town.[121] In the 1930s, Indian students accounted for 87 per cent of all colonial students in British universities.[122]

Back in the mid-19th century, 'tens of thousands of Indian seamen, servants, scholars, soldiers, students, envoys, royalty officials, merchants, tourists and settlers had all journeyed to Britain.' Fisher, the one to propose that score, goes on to revise the number of floating Indians in Victorian Britain to 40,000, largely constituted by sailors.[123] Around this time, the population of Britain was about 30 million.[124] If Fisher's number is anything to go by, between the 19th and the 20th-century, about 0.15 per cent of the British population was Indian, even if floatingly. Around the same time, British Europeans accounted for less than 0.4 per cent of the population in India. Arguably, the proportion of Indians living in Britain in the 19th century was over a third of the proportion of Britons living in India. After 1947, while the number of Indians in London rose dramatically, India barely had any British left. What remained was their hybrid legacy in dozens of Gothic Revivalist, Indo Saracenic or Edwardian monuments left behind in the form of the Victoria Terminus, Victoria Memorial, Parliament House, high courts, railway stations, town halls and the minor redbrick bungalows of railway towns or industrial colonies.[125] The larger public buildings of Bombay or Delhi proliferated in Hindi cinema as the muted backdrops to the rites of passage of hundreds of postcolonial heroes. Of the smaller ones, glimpses were seen in films made on the lives of Anglo-Indians. It was they who had kept running the Great Indian Railways, even at the peak of the anticolonial revolution in India, as Gandhi and the Congress were rubbing salt on the bleeding stripes of the Union Jack.

Taking after John Guare's *Six Degrees of Separation* (1990), Facebook recently published a research where it claimed that it had reduced every individual in the world, at least those on the social media platform, to 3.47 degrees of separation.[126] By that count, London's earliest Indians must have been in the bracket of one eighty degrees of separation. Thought of as few and far between until the 1960s, Indians in London 'if stirred little outrage, excited even less sympathy.'[127] Their long presence in the city can only be hinted at within the hard borders of historical facts. It is like a trace lying immediately outside the fringe of a hard bubble. No sooner than the bubble is pierced, the trace races to fill the place of what seemed like solid air. The Indian history of London is a profound interruption in the white genealogies of Europe. In this historical imagination—which is not necessarily of a new history but of a hypertext—London undergoes a boundary extension and transcends its geography. To use Derrida's expression, it emerges as 'another transcendental present, of another origin of the world appearing as such, presenting itself as irreducible absence within the presence of the trace.'[128]

Hamlet was not the only one to experience what it felt for time to be thrown out of joint. In Victorian India, time underwent a huge paradigm shift. It has been argued that the railways in India were a theatre of imperial finesse in time-administration. Standards of imperial time were introduced as the new standard of 'cosmic time'.[129] The negative capability of experiencing the passage of days was earlier achieved with the aid of almanacs and rituals. In the 19th century, the utility of time was determined beyond a shred of doubt with the *Bradshaw* which was spawned by the railway age upon a global landscape.[130] The book of railway timetables was a yet another historic British institution, founded by George Bradshaw, a contemporary and colleague of Isambard

Kingdom Brunel, that demigod of Victorian England's railway architecture.

With the blessings of Brunel's progenies, India's railway stations were built as mimicries of fortresses. Victoria Terminus, modelled largely on London's St Pancras International, is an outstanding example of railway stations built with an eye for exceptional detail and another for an exceptional historical encounter. The horror unleashed by the Great Rebellion circumscribed its Gothic architecture. The Gothicism was meant to reproduce the aesthetic of sublime awe in the native eye. Its garrisoning networks were meant to reproduce the safety of the British Empire in India. That not being enough, the *Bradshaw* was meant to reproduce routine and discipline. Kipling's *Kim* (1900) was a classic model for how the Empire fostered the duality between 'Western punctuality and eastern inexactitude'.[131] With the rationality of the railways and the routine of the *Bradshaw*, everything and everyone, including the character of the Lama, was assimilated into the British sense of punctuality. This punctuality had also impressed itself on Trailokya Nath Mukharji's memoirs. But what he mistook as the grandeurs of London were drawn from railway sequences in the American west. Immediately, *punctuality* can be seen at its workshop, inventing its others even before inventing itself.

When he rubbished the native literatures of India and Arabia, Macaulay was profoundly ill-informed about the nondual philosophies of the subcontinent. A little over a thousand years before his time, the nondual heretic Adi Sankaracharya had taken on his shoulders a reformist crusade. Derrida, who made it his gospel to demolish the foundations of Western philosophy and the logocentric letter—of Aristotle, Descartes, Levi Strauss and Rousseau—was no stranger to Eastern metaphysics. Sankaracharya's commentaries on the *Upanishads* were concerted attacks on the pedantry and ritualism of a decadent Hindu tradition. In Macaulay's India, technology appeared to have replaced theology. More precisely, the rituals of one had replaced the rituals of another. Both Sankara and Derrida would have argued that an administrative jargon like *punctuality* was everything but punctual. It punctuated reality, while the reality of *punctuality* itself was deferred to an unpunctual future. The image of the punctual Englishman could only be constructed as a binary with its other or opposite—the unpunctual native.[132] *Punctuality* and its ilk were merely symbols. Invoking a monolithic word to mean a symbol was the supreme failure of imperialism. It was here that ambivalence and hybridity triumphed.

With the English language and the railways, booksellers like A.J. Higginbotham's or A.H. Wheeler's flourished in India.[133] So did the symbolisms of London. They grew larger and larger as a cesspool of not merely idlers and loungers but also intellects of the Empire that constituted its intellectual capital. Anyone in the Empire was an inhabitant of this new *London*. The colonial tourist was indeed present in the typographical city all the more if not within its geographical territory. Typography introduced an infinite variety in the spice of its life, brought from the land once conquered for its spices. The map of a new borough was engraved and re-engraved like a reincarnation of the present. It mirrored the London of Tridib's *Bartholomew's Atlas*. One might as well invoke Gadamer's hermeneutic circle. But circles of a mind may well be the squares of a city. With that hermeneutics, a new district was born in London. From the interstices of its Georgian squares lurched a square of typographic explorations. Beyond the rich and repressed cloisters of Belgravia and Fitzrovia, a vividly throbbing Typogravia reared its crest. It was the unborn trace of the history of a foreign face in the imperial city. The colonial identity was part and parcel of living in *Typogravia*, whether one was physically or psychologically in London. For scholars, the Shakespearean stage has emerged as a new archive of smells, odours and other olfactory sensations.[134] Rose called by another name could not quell its sweetness. Could living in *Typogravia* quell the aroma of experiencing *London*?

———

It is the middle of a snowing day in the middle of January. I am in the middle of my walk to the British Library, in the middle of

London. There are traces of *Typogravia* all around. Every glimpse is like chancing upon the origin of another origin. We have stopped near St Pancras Church. This is where Thomas Carlyle began his walk, 200 years ago, looking for London's exiles. The St Pancras station and hotel were built nearly forty years after Carlyle's ramblings. Today, as Eleanor brews in the north of England and Brexit in the south, we walk towards the Regent's Canal with umbrellas tattered in the strong currents. Rain comes like shrapnel, and leaves memory in shards. The mother of Frankenstein, Mary Shelley, was born here at the brink of the 18th century. Here, in the 1820s, wandered, to borrow Matthew Beaumont's invocation, the 'noctambulant' Spanish refugees.[135] These junctures now appear like wayside chapels. What were chapels have turned into abject mausoleums in the blinding storm. The more it grows inclement, the more intimately I am drawn to some clement church. In my imagination, it is like the one Henri Lefebvre used to return to on Sunday afternoons at his French countryside hometown. And this invisible London unfolds as a devout monument.

> I hesitate on its humble, unadorned threshold, held back by a kind of apprehension. I know what I shall find: an empty, echoing space, with hidden recesses crammed with hundreds of objects, each uttering the silent cry that makes it a sign. What a strange power! I know that I cannot fail to understand their 'meanings', because they were explained to me years ago. It is impossible to close your eyes and your ears to these symbols: they occupy you, they preoccupy you immediately, insistent, insidious—and the more so for their simplicity. Already a feeling of disquiet, suppressed anger, mingled with the reluctant but tenacious memories of a childhood and adolescence. And I know that this suppressed anger is another aspect of the power, the nascent fascination of the 'sacred' object. It is impossible to free myself from it. For me this space can never be just like any other space. But precisely because I feel this obscure emotion I can begin to understand its obscure causes.[136]

As the rain holds up, I realise that the place is far from a derelict church. Just off the King's Boulevard, it is much closer to globalised territory. The Google office is barely a few hundred yards away. 'Let's Google the flamingo out of him,' someone said recently. Googling Regency's Somers Town does not guarantee one will find London's early Spanish or Indian exiles with their 'stately tragic figures, in proud threadbare cloaks.'[137] For a model, one will have to look to the imperceptible frame of some Angela Vicario, threading her twenty-year-old yarn. Google is the first global impulse to know the unknown. Our googled words and names of mistyped characters are all part of a shared hypocrisy. We question the authenticity of the act of this virtual adventure. Unlike Bayardo San Roman, we can never resist the calamitous temptation to undress the letters.[138] 'I was new here once, but now I know the moves of it,' I keep reassuring myself, like Mr Wemmick.[139] I look around on these chartered streets for Carlyle's exiles demanding my pity and my reflections. All I find are the mute shutters of hundreds of smartphone cameras. They are bluetoothing smithereens of the architecture to be teleported to an alternate planet where Mark Zuckerberg built his first satellites in 2004. Like a flaming taper, I rush to the memoirs of another Indian Londoner, in the clemency of the British Library.

———————

'Shortly after E.M. Forster published *A Passage to India*, a very young, entirely unknown Indian named Mulk Raj Anand left scandal and school behind in Amritsar to pursue a doctorate in philosophy at the University of London.' Thus begins 'Anand's Passage Through Bloomsbury,' as Kristin Blumel described it.[140] Anand's days in the Orwellian and Bloomsbury circle of authors was the foretaste of an unforeseeable future to come. In 1935, Anand's first novel *Untouchable* was published by Lawrence and Wishart, and prefaced by Forster, after being rejected by nineteen publishers. It was a book about a low-caste sweeper, which had been turned down by Gandhi in 1929. The latter dismissed it as a compendium of characters talking in Bloomsbury accents. The Mahatma's rejection would turn out to be auspicious. Now at the peak of his literary career, Anand went on to write *Two Leaves and a Bud* (1937), *The Village* (1939), *Across the Black Waters* (1940), *The Sword and the Sickle* (1941), *Letters on India* (1942), *Apology for Heroism* (1946) and *Seven Summers* (1951). Talking of his novels, Anand's friend and Labour leader Michael Foot once said that the finest novels of an age are also among its greatest political acts. Anand was as an 'overly noisy and dogmatic Marxist situated on the fringes of a Euro-American modernity, alienating the majority of his Bloomsbury friends by his anti-imperialist politics.'[141] Like Gandhi, Nehru and Menon, Anand was confident of his place in Britain and in the world as a global citizen.[142] Married to actress Kathleen Van Gelder, loved by writer Irene Rhys, befriended by Orwell, Forster and many others, and employed and then ridiculed by the Woolfs, Anand's London days remain an enigma as much as the man himself was to his contemporaries.

In 1981, Anand published his memoirs, *Conversations in Bloomsbury*, more than forty years after his trysts with the giants of English Modernism. Today, it bears uncanny resemblance to the screenplay of Woody Allen's film *Midnight in Paris* (2011). Like will-o'-the-wisps, European authors appear out of the slivers and crevices from anywhere between Little Russel Street and Great Russel Street. And then they go drinking with Anand, one after another. If 'authorise' ever had a meaning similar to 'womanise', Anand could be called a *serial authoriser*. For many, 'Bloomsbury' has the ring of an otherworldly melody. Anand's persona spruced it up with otherworldly balloons of his pomposity. In riposte after riposte, the young Indian in London affronted perfectly polite and perfectly refined European writers and intellectuals—from Bonamy Dobrée to T.S. Eliot to Aldous Huxley to D.H. Lawrence to Leonard Woolf.

Anand missed no opportunity for pretentiousness where modesty would have sufficed. There he was in the heart of the city, daggers drawn before the arrival of nigh on every artist. He subsequently adopted them as his mentors and denounced them as inadequate. All the same, he never made an effort to conceal how much of the dilettante he himself might have been when both London and he were in the thirties. The *Conversations* are at once a work of fiction—nothing less than a modernist novel. Anand recreated himself as a self-congratulatory Indian to churn out the best of the English character of his renowned friends. He was never shy of playing Eliot's J. Alfred Prufrock—that neurotic apostle of post-war London, who was disillusioned with the idea of disillusionment itself. Like Prufrock's London, Anand's Bloomsbury was a ceaseless succession of elongated dimly enlightened bookshops, taverns and cafes. Was he really as much of the *petite bourgeois* as he made of himself at the Café Italiano with Huxley?

> As we entered the long room, the warm gay little café, I wanted to recite T.S. Eliot's words: 'In the room the women come and go/ Talking of Michelangelo,' because there were intellectual looking women, mostly readers from the British Museum Reading Room, looking for places from which someone was departing or just about to leave. The fat waitress, with dark hair and a smile on her podgy face, indicated two seats to us right beneath the window overlooking Great Russel Street. Apparently she had recognised the famous writer.
>
> 'Cup of tea with shortbread biscuit for me. What about you Mr—?
>
> 'Anand,' I said. And turning to the chubby-faced waitress, I said, 'The same for me.'[143]

One's love of Anand's prose notwithstanding his persona in *Typogravia* is mortifying. It begins with his heroic calls for tea. But the sites of the café or the pub are never quite satisfactory to him. In the beginning of every conversation one finds him slouching about the British Museum. Anand ensures that he makes a princely meal out of it. Being athwart those corridors meant for him a distinguished type of passport. That is where all his *authorising* began.

No authors meet me at the British Library. I have just come down from the Asian African Reading Room. I have with me a catalogue of the cartels of calicoes and spices that other European companies were running in Britain, during and a little after Shakespeare's time. I have taken my cup of tea without nutmeg or cinnamon, indeed, without the tea. From today, it will be crushed coffee beans all the way. I can almost see Julia Roberts frowning from her *Notting Hill* days. 'Drink tea, there's lots of tea.' That is what Indians in London have always done. Tea is their jackpot of tergiversations. Tea against the backdrop of 'mullioned windows,' as goes a passage in Anita Desai's *Bye-bye Blackbird* (1971), 'the stained woodwork, the "casks" and mugs and portly British faces' of Lamb and Addison and Dryden and Jerome! Tea never falls short of the coquetry of romanticism. In his most beloved fictions, the Indian in London has been downing canisters of tea. As a work of his own art, there he stands by the undisturbed Thames, 'the spacious elegance of Wren architecture on its banks, the city coiled about with its own smoke and vapours, and he above it encompassing it all in one glance, gives him the expanding, soaring sensation of an explorer on the verge of a discovery.'[144]

Tea was never just a beverage in London. It was the fuel that drove Victorian engineering and economics. Advertising made tea deeply incestuous with other merchandised commodities. Britain's transition from trading in sugar with Mediterranean merchants to consuming its own sugar grown in the West Indies signified how tea and sugar—along with coffee or chocolate—bolstered the need for each other, as both redefined English character and its imperial metropole.[145] Horniman's 'pure tea' was advertised as the article of faith for English housewives to rule the hearts of their husbands. Tea drinking became a 'patriotic duty', adding to the national treasury for tea exports from India and Ceylon, and sugar exports from slave plantations in the Caribbean. Behind the 'domestic tranquillity' of Victorian tea artefacts lay many complex layers of the history of 'warfare and exploitation'.[146] Suppliers to France, Germany, Russia, Italy, Austria, Belgium, Switzerland, Holland, Norway, Sweden and Denmark, Horniman's was selling in excess of 6 million tea packets of black, green or mixed teas by the end of the 1880s. Thanks to Horniman's teas—sold by chemists and confectioners alike—Englishwomen were best suited to make a happy home in England, for whose pleasures every other land in the Empire had been 'ransacked'.[147]

In the summer of 1867, the year Marx was to publish the first volume of *Das Kapital*, his middle daughter, Laura, wrote him an extraordinary letter. 'I invite you to a "Hampstead tea" on your return—tea and sugar you will of course bring with you, but everything else you shall have in plenty and of the best. If this does not tempt you to come back soon—what will?'[148] Laura was on her way to being Anglicised, in an age when Englishwomen considered it their duty to master the coquettish rituals of tea. Dr James F. Johnston's in his essay 'The Chemistry of Common Life' eulogised the solitary tea-maker, who sat by the fireside in her 'humble cottage as the kettle simmers over the ruddy embers, and the blackened teapot on the hot brick prepares her evening drink.'[149] At the height of the tea-mania in the 1880s, Mrs H.W. Beecher's brief notes on English breakfast tea in *How to Make Homes Happy* (1881) trained homemakers to blend it with green or Oolong teas.[150]

For English gentlemen, tea was as much for consumption as a subject of historical exploration. Arthur Reade's treatise *Tea and Tea Drinking* (1884) brought readers up to speed with what seemed as the most momentous developments in the English tea tradition. Thomas De Quincey, it reported, drank tea from eight in the night to four in the morning, while Immanuel Kant breakfasted on tea and tobacco. The Irish nationalist and liberal historian Justin McCarthy was also a 'liberal drinker of tea,' while Samuel Johnson was an inveterate and shameless consumer in his own estimate.[151] De Quincey, whom one knows largely for his opium addiction, found his muse simply over a cup of tea. 'Near the fire paint me a tea-table,' he wrote in *Confessions of an English Opium Eater* (1821), 'on such a stormy night, place only two cups and saucers on the tea-tray, paint me an eternal teapot; paint me a lovely young woman sitting at the table.'[152] The tea-maker was for him the personification of the helpless pariah woman whom, time and again, he could not rescue from danger.[153] It was a metaphor for the Indian that he could not rescue from the jaws of British imperialism. Had it not been for the beheading of King Charles I, the establishment of Oliver Cromwell's Protectorate, the Restoration of the Monarchy by King Charles II, his wedding to Catherine of Braganza of Portugal, and the chest of tea and island of Bombay that he received in his dowry, London would never have tasted of the beverage, and India may not have known to sing 'God save the King'.

Nor would India have given to Britain those men and women who steered its destiny. Cricket, the most English game of all times, tasted its distinctly Oriental flavour with the invention of the leg glance in the early 20th century. Its inventor, the Nawab of Nawanagar Sir Ranjitsinhji Jadeja, was a forsworn opponent to English aesthetics on the cricketing field, if not off it. Born in a farmer's family that was related to the princely rulers of Nawanagar (present-day Jamnagar in Gujarat), Sir Ranji came close to becoming an heir to the state, in the late 19th century. The Viceroy, First Marquess of Ripon George Robinson, was upset on Ranji's disinheritance from the family fortune. Ranji's college principal Chester Macnaghten took him to London in 1888, the same year that Gandhi first arrived in the city. Although in theory Ranji prepared for the Bar, in practice he kept replaying in his mind the reel of a cricket match between Australia and Surrey, that Macnaghten had taken him to see upon his arrival in London. The Australian bowler Charles Turner scored a century in that match, which inspired Ranji to take up cricket three years later when he joined the Cambridgeshire County Club. One of his weaknesses in batting was to become his greatest strength. Under the mentorship of Daniel Hayward, a veteran first-class cricketer from Surrey, Ranji started practising in the nets with his right leg fastened to the ground, in order to overcome his back-foot reflexes. In the process, he improvised the then-unorthodox technique of flicking the ball behind the keeper, gradually developing the leg glance. In 1892, Ranji scored 9 centuries and 2,000 runs—an unprecedented number in English first-class cricketing history.

Over the next three years, Ranji played amateur cricket for Trinity, Cambridge and the Marylebone Cricket Club. One of his most memorable innings came in a partnership of 200 runs, with the legendary William Gilbert Grace, of which Ranji scored 94. Soon later, Ranji made his first-class debut, playing for Sussex. Crowds were enthralled by his lordship over the leg-side facilitated by the wizardry of his wrists. As Simon Wilde remarked, with 'the most disdainful flick of the wrists, he could exasperate some of England's finest bowlers.'[154] With his cricketing success followed by the death of the ruler of Nawanagar, rumours were afloat in the English press that Ranji, being the son of the ruler (*which he was not*), was the first rightful heir to the throne of the state. Ranji was both creator and beneficiary of this gossip. It helped him stay in currency, besides his glorious form in test matches with Australia, both in England and overseas. Between 1895 and 1900, Ranji scored 1,000 runs in almost every season. The white gentleman's game became incredibly colourful and exciting in his presence.

> As a writer, a text, and himself an important mediator of Empire, Ranjitsinhji did indeed suggest that the culture of colonialism could be subject to revision. Princely duties in colonial India meant that Ranjitsinhji was only a fitful presence in English cricket fields. However, when he did appear as a brilliant amateur batsman for Sussex and England his cultural impact was immense. In other parts of the Empire, too, Ranjitsinhji's studious self-fashioning as an exotic trope fed into a contemporary fascination with the Orient, and made him much in demand as an advertising tool within the burgeoning Victorian commodity culture.[155]

Even before Ranji became the ruler of Nawanagar and came to be called Maharaja Jam Saheb, his own books *The Jubilee Book of Cricket* (1897), *With Stoddart's Team in Australia* (1898) and *Cricket Guide and How to Play It* (1906)—besides P.C. Standing's *Ranjitsinhji Prince of Cricket* (1903)—and press coverage on his life, styled him as an Indian prince. Being of that elite social class legitimised him as an Englishman, despite his racial background. Not only were cricket matches remembered after his name, even railway bar sandwiches and barbers started being named after him.

It is hardly surprising that a century and two decades later, much like the commodity of tea, India has raised cricket as its very own sport.

In 1914, as Ranji left for the Western Front to fight for Britain in the First World War, as an honorary major, an infant Indian girl arrived in Bloomsbury, with her family, from Moscow. Her mother Pirani Ameena Begum was a descendant of Tipu Sultan and a poetess. Noor Inayat Khan, as the girl was called, or later as Nora Baker, studied in Sorbonne in Paris. She began her career as a writer and broadcaster. Her book *Twenty Jataka Tales* was published in London in 1939, shortly before she joined the Women's Auxiliary Air Force in the Second World War. In the early 1940s, she received training as a wireless operator in the British Special Operations Executive, with postings in Surrey and Buckinghamshire. Although Noor was brought up by her father on the nonviolence of Gandhi, she was desperate for Indians to be accepted as equal members of British society. For that she was not averse to being an accomplice to killing or being killed in Britain's war. In 1943, Noor was recruited for espionage, at a Mayfair restaurant, by Vera Atkins, a senior British intelligence officer for the Special Operations Executive. In June, she flew off to Angers as the first British woman operator in enemy occupied territory. She was given a new name—Jeanne-Marie Regnier.

Four months later, Noor was betrayed to the German secret intelligence agency, *Sicherheitsdienst*. After two unsuccessful attempts at escape, she was designated as especially dangerous by the Gestapo. In November, she was deported to Pforzheim, where she was kept in solitary confinement for ten months. Noor endured torture without revealing any information on British intelligence, even in the most intimidating hours of interrogation. From there, she was taken to the Dachau concentration camp. With three other colleagues of the Special Operations Executive, Noor Inayat Khan was killed in September 1944. As reported by a Dutch survivor of Nazi atrocities, her last word was '*Liberte*'.

Two years before she was executed, Noor had been judged by her reporting officers as 'very feminine in character, very eager to

please, very ready to adapt herself to the mood of the company.'
She lacked the intellect for intelligence operations and indeed
for anything remotely hypocritical. 'I wish some Indians would
win high military distinction in this war,' she once wrote. 'If
one or two could do something in the Allied service which was
very brave and which everybody admired it would help to make
a bridge between the English people and the Indians.'[156] More
than seventy years after the war, Noor was commemorated at the
First Aid Nursing Yeomanry memorial in St Paul's Church, with
fifty-one other Second World War heroes. In 1949, even as she
lay buried in the snows of Dachau, Noor Inayat Khan received a
French Croix de Guerre and the George Cross, Britain's second
highest military and civilian award for bravery outside the
warfront.

––––––––––

It has stopped snowing an hour ago. Tourists in London for
Christmas are headed for the galleries and museums this afternoon.
If it snows or rains again, they will sip on decaffeinated beverages
and discuss clothes and fashion from the decades following Anne
Boleyn's beheading. If umbrellas have not turned London's tourists
into time-travellers, little else has. The notion of Britain living in
a country of the past or a 'retrotopia' runs rife among detractors
of this newfound national nostalgia.[157] But travelling in time does
not only imply flying off to a pristine past. It also brings with it the
event horizon of the apocalypse that lies in an unforeseeable future
to come. Will Self can be ruthless when it comes to describing the
ruthlessness studded in our cultures like nurseries over dormant
volcanoes. London performs itself for its own eyes, back and forth
in time.

Now, you can look up to the open decks of the high-rise blocks
in my area, and see row-after-row of fake Georgian doors,
each with its mingy fanlight, implanted in the glaucous hide
of flammable cladding. Perhaps this is the best way of thinking

about it—this is the epoché demanded of us: try and bracket
the phenomena we see around us, and imagine that they're all
about to end. Most days I cycle past Selfridges, the upmarket
department store on London's Oxford Street. As the Mayor,
Sadiq Khan, brutes about his new sustainability agenda, and
egregious signs trumpet the city's Ultra Low Emissions zone, the
limos lined up outside continue to belch out a mephitic mixture
of lead particulates and greenhouse gases as they burn up the
fuel, the extraction, refining and sale of which, has afforded the
limo drivers' clients the income necessary to keep them waiting
while they spree-shop inside. I need say no more.[158]

I am back at the St Pancras railway station! Even its sighs are
gothic and sesquipedalian. One can hardly move beyond counting
and recounting its dormers, spandrels and steeples. If the gray sun
was switched off for a few hours and a face in each of its windows
was made to simultaneously whimper 'England for the English',
that would make it truly gothic. 'I am a gothic building,' St Pancras
would declare, 'but I am also an English building. To be blunt, I'm
an English building that merely happens to be a gothic building.
If, god forbid, the day should come when I would have to choose
between being gothic and being English…'[159]
Few stop to notice why this red redundant razzmatazz is here
at all. Some think this is the Houses of Parliament. Architecture is
also like food. On realising a building is not quite what one ordered
for, the visual appetite is considerably disillusioned. 'Where's the
Thames?' they wonder, standing beside St Pancras. Finding that
London is not-so-postcard-perfect, after all, they go hunting for
the nearest Pret A Manger or Café Nero. Some others are like the
pilot from J.G. Ballard's novel *The Unlimited Dream Company*
(1979), who crash-landed into the Thames. After returning from
death, he found London's suburbs invaded by apocalyptic signs
from the natural world.[160] A similar invasion by the non-human
world happens in Self's novel, *Phone* (2017). Doctor Zack Busner's
dystopic vision of a restaurant's buffet tables galvanises the mental
states of his many patients of *encephalitis lethargica*. It is the perfect

synecdoche for an overconsuming and overconsumed megalopolis. We find the doctor rapt in the bathos of culinary specimens of the buffet. These signify all that is horrifyingly cutting-edge in this culture. Busner meanders into enlightenment as Alice drifts into wonderland, or a lesser mortal into a drain.

A whole melon poised on a mound of crushed ice, its flesh elaborately tooled into tight, leafy tessellations so it resembles … *a monstrous artichoke!* Beyond this […] a steel tripod bearing a jungly mess of salad leaves and multicoloured peppers. Further away, through the misty atmosphere, Busner spots an entire Continental section: frills of ham and cooked meats, cheese slices fanned out around an entire Gouda on a wooden trencher. And there are people—*guests*—shuffling alongside the counter, tonging black bread, dill pickles, mini-muff-things and full-sized croissants on to their already high-piled plates, or spooning porridge into deep white bowls, or thrusting specialist scoops into Tupperware tubs full of organic muesli, honey-cut cornflakes and Rice Krispies […] the serving dish heaped with baked beans into … *a charnel house*: glinting, calcified slices of black pudding … oozing grease—still greasier sausages, and a great *Rattenkönig* of bacon smeared with globs of white fat, its rinds woven into a … *grisly plait.*[161]

Tourists with smartphones dash towards the thickly rusted lovelocks hung at the Westminster Bridge.[162] Once constructed from facsimiles of the world, London is obsessed with how its facsimiles are consumed or how its food is facsimiled. I am a lot like the city. London was the model for my dreaming the cities where I lived, and the cities where I went—including London. I learned to say and envisage its name before I could spell 'Thiruvananthapuram', from where the Dutch tried to supplant the Anglo-Indian nexus but failed, or 'Shrirangapattinam', where the British defeated Tipu Sultan and the French Army. I first read about London from Prince Anwar Shah Road in Calcutta, where the Sultan's sons were once exiled. Our balcony faced the entrance to a slum. It was my model for imagining 'Dickensian squalor'. There was London in much of the handiwork of my home. Arthur Conan Doyle's *The Sign of the Four* (1890) reared me in the 'questionable and forbidding neighbourhoods' of Peckham where 'long lines of dull brick houses were relieved by the coarse glare and tawdry brilliancy of public houses at the corner.'[163] I do not doubt that if I were to knock on any of those today, a turbaned Indian servant would throw open a room of Oriental figurines.

G.K. Chesterton once lashed out at Rudyard Kipling for having made the world small. The globetrotter, Chesterton argued, lived in a smaller world than the peasant. 'The telescope makes the world smaller; it is only the microscope that makes it larger.'[164] Today, Chesterton would have congratulated Kipling. Like the microscope, Brexit has made Britain larger. It has crystallised the long history of its aliens in the snowflakes of this wintry epoché. It has given London the recognition of its *Typogravia*. Seeing Mulk Raj Anand make himself scuttle in and scuttle out of the British Museum like a scullery manservant of postcolonial London, I find myself becoming more conscious each time I step into or step out of the British Library. There are millions who cannot afford to come here. Some of them are the Rohingya refugees, or those living in Malawai, Mozambique, Congo and Madagascar. The Gods of Guatemala have apparently blessed the country with giant carrots of the size of a child's foot. But its people too are not to be found in the Library. Those unable to visit also include some 8,000 rough sleepers in London alone.

Nor are Salamon Nurr or Peter Pope able to visit the Library, except as anecdotes from their lives peppering some of the records. Perhaps they nightwalk into the Library and linger about its olfactory memories, like the ghost of an odour. Santiago Nasar, the slain Saracen in Gabriel Garcia Marquez's *Chronicle of a Death Foretold* (1981), does not merely turn into a ghost. He haunts his village as the ghost of an odour. The world arrives at the British

Library or the Monument to sniff at the residues of the odour of the city's beheadings and fires. Therein also snuggles, just as in the memoirs of Samuel Pepys, the diarist of Seething Lane, the caustic scent of an Indian. Every day, just before midnight, standing by the window of an apartment in Uxbridge, I have watched the last Metropolitan Line train on its way to Aldgate, calling at Hillingdon, Wembley or Harrow. Those are also the nests of London's present-day Indians. Score after score of vacant seats inside a light-footed incandescent metallic reptile whizz past my eyes, around quarter to twelve. Then a truant chime of Westminster Quarters flickers in the dark from the nearby St Margaret's Church. My mind sketches the family portrait of James, a London beerbrewer's servant buried at St Botolph's without Aldgate, in 1618, or the plastic Indian faces in Lely's or Van Dyck's portraits. 'No man is an island, entire of itself.' The chimes seem to echo John Donne. 'Never send to know for whom the bell tolls,' they warn 'it tolls for thee.'[165]

I have brought down some notes from John Keay's history of *The Honourable Company* (1991). Besides, some rare contents of imperial history are in my hand while I stand in the queue at the coffee shop. I am behind a Bangladeshi mathematician, my semi-linguistic brethren. I know his language well and I am tempted to mimic his accent. We are being served by White Europeans at the counter. 'How the equations have changed!' he mutters to someone over the phone.

Keay explains that during the Restoration, 'imitation remained the only sincere form of competition,' for England to surpass the rest of Europe. The produce of the 'Spice Islands' was sold in Europe by the Dutch or the Portuguese at a profit of 32,000 per cent. And then the English Levant Company, that had been importing spices from Asia, started exporting them to the Middle-East at even larger profits by the mid-17th century.[166] The great ancestors of the other Bengali gentleman and my own derived great competitive strength from thoroughgoing imitations of English mannerisms. Thomas

Gray's 'Elegy Written in a Country Churchyard' marked us both for its own graveyard.

'Sandwich or shortbread?' the European at the counter asks the Bangladeshi ahead of me.

'No, but I'll come back for cha and a slice …' he continues over the phone.

'Nice walker you've got there!' says the man at the counter, attending to me. Had it been Anand in my place, the compliment would have come from no less than Virginia Woolf; perhaps King George himself! Between walking in and out of coffee houses, talking of Joyce and the Buddha, Anand informed the reader of his *Conversations* that he had taken a fancy to Dobrée for his Savile Row suits and intricate beard that made him look like the King's brother. The description of facial architecture that Anand supplied for Dobrée's could well have been for Lawrence. For the larger part of his life Dobrée only kept a moustache. Like Trailokya Nath Mukharji who took the American countryside for an English metropolis, Mulk Raj Anand may have mistaken the Englishman for the French in memories clouded by his tranquillity.

'Thanks. Espresso,' I say, steadying the crook of my umbrella upon the counter. Joyce returns in a flash, in words that an English author recently quoted to me after retrieving my walker. I had forgotten it on a conference table. 'A brother is as easily forgotten as an umbrella.' The line became the epigraph to one of his novels, and it might as well be a fitting epitaph to this chronicle. As I muster one pound ninety, a brother is about to be forgotten in a sea of snowflakes, where remoaner flamingos are twittering each to each. I take my coffee and settle down to stare into the many histories of my baptism.

———

ACT I

What Trade Art Thou

This royal throne of kings, this sceptred isle,
This earth of majesty, this seat of Mars,
This other Eden, demi-paradise ...
This land of such dear souls, this dear, dear land,
Dear for her reputation through the world,
Is now leased out—I die pronouncing it—
Like to a tenement or pelting farm ...
That England that was wont to conquer others
Hath made a shameful conquest of itself

(Richard II, Act II, Scene I)

Scene I

The Baptism

On the winter solstice of the year William Shakespeare died at Stratford upon Avon, Peter Pope became the first Indian to be baptised in Britain. They were separated by a hundred miles and eight months in death and rebirth. In Peter's story, his voice was the implacable silence of a lamb, as the faint tolling of the ancient parish church bells of St Dionis at Fenchurch Street shepherded the history of Indians in London. The curtain was lifted off the theatre of a city of spectacles, and Peter stepped on to the stage on the very first scene of the very first act of a mesmeric production, now unfolding.

For centuries Fenchurch Street has, during Christmas week, been alive with persons busily passing to and fro; but on Sunday, 22nd of December 1616, an unusual crowd surged toward the Church of St Dennis, for it had been announced that, by the rite of baptism, a lad, a native of Bengala, was to be initiated into the Church of Christ. The Privy Council, the Lord Mayor and Aldermen, the members of the East India, and the sister Company of Virginia, with difficulty, waded through the 'sea of upturned faces' overflowing the approaches to the edifice, and the congregation within the walls was densely packed. The rite was administered by Dr John Wood, and Petrus Papa, or Peter Pope, the name given in baptism, was chosen by King James, that odd compound of cant, coarseness, and sottishness, who often seemed unable to distinguish between the odour of beer and sanctity, 'the spirit of wine and the Spirit Divine,' and yet affected to be a special 'defender of the faith.'[1]

Since Roman times, London has been an avaricious carnivore. Meat was what lesser mortals, such as Orientals, would have seemed to Londoners. On one side of Fenchurch Street is Pudding Lane. It got its name—not from the commonly known dessert but—as John Stow explained in 1603 in his *Survey of London*, from puddings of meat offal. These dribbled on to the street as butchers from nearby Eastcheap waddled their carts down to Thames Street. From here they disposed of the beastly scraps into the river. Since Eastcheap was a great meat hub of the city, Pudding Lane abounded in butchers. Fenchurch Street was named from the Anglo-French word *'fein'*, meaning hay, for it was a place where hay was sold in medieval London. Then there is, of course, Mincing Lane, on another side of St Dionis Church, where one reckons meat was minced to line up London's belly. Mincing was, however, a contortion of the Middle English word *'mynchen'*, referring to the Benedictine nuns of the neighbouring St Helen's Bishopsgate. By the end of the 18th century, Mincing Lane was London's granary of Britain's global tea and spice trade. Described by English novelist Charles Dickens as 'the drug-flavoured region' in *Our Mutual Friend* (1865),[2] Mincing Lane was also the heart of the Empire's opium and drug smuggling industry. Going by the urbane alias of 'Street of Tea,' it was home to British slave traders in the early years of the Industrial Revolution. Skimming the blood-dimmed tides of that medieval history, Peter's baptism was London's Roman savagery at its subtlest. It was not the British Empire led astray into an act of compassion. It was imperialism incarnate.

The pageant was not unusual in London's vivid and uneasy century of migrations. One in every six Englishmen gravitated here, as 'the number of foreign immigrants rose at an accelerating pace, making the city truly cosmopolitan,'[3] as well as the centre of fashion. In Elizabethan London, the number of deaths bitterly rivalled the population of its newborns. To serve the demographic dividend, the workers that made up for tailors, gun-makers, dyers, weavers or needle-manufacturers had to come from France, Italy, Holland, Denmark and even North Africa. Muddled by a multitude of anonymous refugees, the history of Indians in Shakespeare's London would remain shrouded in a fog, for centuries to come.

On New Year's day, the first dawn of 1947, the fog that grovelled upon 10 Downing Street was more melancholy than ever before. The deserted and rationed streets of London—where no more than a few cars flashed and no more than a few factories had resuscitated from the bombings by the Luftwaffe—were still wriggling out of a Churchillian rhapsody. 'We shall fight on the beaches'—that speech resounded keeping Britain yet alive—'we shall fight on the landing grounds, we shall fight in the fields and in the streets, we shall fight in the hills; we shall never surrender.'[4] They had also heard the unsentimental John Maynard Keynes. The economist did not live long after the war, but his words did. 'We are a poor nation, and we must learn to live accordingly,'[5] he bluntly told Britain, after Churchill's inglorious retreat from the Parliament. Labour Prime Minister Clement Attlee was desperate to put a veneer of distraction on Britain's imminent financial catastrophe. He had chosen the great-grandson of Queen Victoria, Louis Francis Albert Victor Nicholas Mountbatten, to transact the dismemberment of the jewel in her crown and contrive the sunset once believed to be non-existent for the British Empire. Dickie, as he had been nicknamed by Victoria, his godmother, during his baptism, had an ominous contract that was to end with the independence of India. This would be the penultimate stroke in Britain's three-and-a-half centuries' long innings.

It beggared belief that the great imperial game had begun, quite simply, over peppercorns. On the afternoon of September 24, 1599, twenty-four British merchants from the City of London had huddled at Leadenhall Street, and selected as their office a dilapidated building, less than a mile from the place where Attlee and Mountbatten were tipping the hourglass on the last months of the Raj—indeed less than a mile from where Peter would be baptised. The English merchants were outraged by Dutch privateers who had escalated the price of a pound of pepper by 5s. Holland was itself dependent on the mercy of the Spanish Empire and its regulation of the market of Lisbon, from where Dutch privateers used to purchase their import goods. When Lisbon was closed to Dutch buyers, in the late 16th century, the Dutch had no choice but raise the duty on whatever spices they could manage from the East, for this was still a good decade before the United East India traders seized Batavia (present-day Indonesia). Three years before the Dutch company was founded, 125 shareholders joined the British merchants of Leadenhall, put up a capital of £72,000, and christened their little enterprise the East India Company.

In August, the following year, four months before the Royal Charter was granted to the company, William Hawkins, a self-declared ambassador to Queen Elizabeth (and later to King James), landed in Surat, in charge of *Hector*, the first Company ship to anchor in India. A pirate in his previous life, Hawkins was bred on none of the privileges as the Portuguese were at the court of Emperor Jahangir. What distinguished him, however, was that he spoke Turkish, a language for which Mughal ears had a special nostalgia. In little time, Hawkins took the rank of Jahangir's courtier at an annual salary of £3,000, and an Indian moniker, the 'English Khan'. Hawkins was also offered a fair-complexioned maiden from the emperor's harem, but he refused to marry a Moor. The emperor then presented a less fair but substantially more Christian girl—an Armenian by the name of Mariam. Her father had served in Akbar's court, and she had been raised on Mughal customs. 'Seeing she was of so honest a descent,' wrote the Khan, 'having passed my word to the King, I could not withstand my fortunes. Wherefore I took her, and for want of a minister, before Christian witnesses, I married her, the priest being my man Nicholas [Ufflet].' The ceremony took place in Agra, as Hawkins was happily wedded to the notion, 'ever after I lived content.'[6] With Mariam as Mrs Hawkins, and Mr Hawkins consumed by gambling debts, the emperor's milk of kindness began drying up. The Portuguese at the court, keen to see the back of the English merchants, promised a speedy return to London for Hawkins and his party. Mariam's relatives, who were eager to keep her in India to maintain vigilance over her increasing fortunes, would prove to be very small threats to her star-crossed future. The English Khan managed to procure two sets of passports from the Portuguese, one that allowed him and his wife to stay in Goa, and the other which was meant to take them to England. The first was used to outfox Mariam's family, who believed that the couple had left for Goa, when indeed they had set sail for London from Surat, via Bantam and the Cape of Good Hope.

Disaster struck at sea, taking the lives of many passengers, including Hawkins'. After three years of perilous seafaring, when Mrs Hawkins reached London, in 1614, she was with her husband-to-be, Gabriel Towerson, the captain of another *Hector*, that had ferried the widow and her dead husband to Albion. A week after St Valentine's Day of that year, Mariam became Mrs Towerson at St Nicholas Acons Parish Church, in the City of London—one of the churches that would be devastated by the Great Fire. The directors of the East India Company, still in the early honourable and impressionable phase of their careers, took kindly to Mariam. They agreed to settle her late husband's debts from drinking and wastrel-hood, amounting to £300, besides offering her a token of £250.

After a few years of an unhappy second marriage, Mrs Towerson returned to India and settled in Agra. She must have heard about the arrival of at least two other Indians in Britain. One of them was Coree, a servant whom Towerson had abducted in Africa and traded in London. Another was the protagonist of that historic baptism—Peter Pope—who had arrived from Surat, six months after Mariam's second marriage in London. As Mariam braced for a life unremembered in India, Towerson sailed for Britain, from where he was deputed as the Company's chief merchant to Amboyna, the Dutch stronghold in the Indonesian islands. In February 1623, detectives at the Dutch enclave suspected him of betraying their confidence and organising a rebellion against them. In what was recorded in English history as the abominable Amboyna Massacre, Towerson was one of the ten English Company officials—besides a Portuguese merchant and nine Japanese conspirators—who were tortured for treason, before being beheaded in March. His head was put up on a post to be displayed to the natives. Thirty years later, Oliver Cromwell, Lord Protector of the Commonwealth of England, Ireland and Scotland, ended a Civil War by gratifying the mob of London with the truncated torso of King Charles I. The end of the English Civil War coincided with the liberation of the Dutch Republic from the clutches of the Spanish and the Holy Roman Empire. With the Peace of Westphalia—that brought a thirty years' war of European religions to an end in the summer of 1648—the golden age of Dutch industry had commenced. Cromwell and his Parliamentarians felt their bloodlust once again. When he needed a fertile stratagem for going to war with Holland, he resorted to reminding his citizens of the lurid image of Towerson's amputated head. Of that barbarous British mob, drunk with its own theatre, none could be bothered about the vagaries of the Arabian Sea, which Mariam, Peter and hundreds of thousands of Indians would cross to reach London. The western coastline of the Indian peninsula was now becoming a cliff-hanger on the map of the imminent Anglo-Dutch wars.

Scene II

Brewing a Colony in a Tea Cup

About half a mile from Fenchurch Street where Peter was baptised, lies the Monument. From here, on the street called Pudding Lane, broke out the Great Fire of September 1666. It started from the bakery of Thomas Farriner, who was the supplier of bread to the English Royal Navy during the first war with Holland. The 'pudding' of the Lane was what the city's most daunting edifices were reduced to in the five days of the seething conflagration. On September 3, English diarist John Evelyn saw what were the first signs of the fire's Hitlerian fury, threatening to engulf the whole of London.

The fire having continued all this night when conspiring with a fierce eastern wind, in a very dry season; I went on foot to the same place, and saw the whole south part of the city burning from Cheapside to the Thames, and all along Cornhill, Tower Street, Fenchurch Street, Gracious Street, and so along Bainard's Castle, and was now taking hold of St Paul's church, to which the scaffolds contributed exceedingly. There was nothing heard or seen but crying out and lamentation, running about like distracted creatures, without at all attempting to save even their goods, such a strange consternation there was upon them, so as it burned both in breadth and length, the churches, public halls, exchange, hospitals, monuments, and ornaments, leaping after a prodigious manner from house to house, and street to street, at great distances one from the other; for the heat, with a long set of fair and warm weather, had even ignited the air, and prepared the materials to conceive the fire, which devoured, after an incredible manner, houses, furniture, and everything. Here we saw the Thames covered with goods floating, all the barges and boats laden with what some had time and courage to save—as, on the other, the carts, & c., carrying out to the fields, which for many miles were strewed with moveables of all sorts, and tents erected to shelter both people and what goods they could get away. The clouds also of smoke were dismal, and reached upon computation near fifty miles in length. Thus I left it this afternoon burning, a resemblance of Sodom, or the last day. It forcibly called to my mind that passage—*We have here no abiding city;* the ruins resembling the picture of Troy. London was, but is no more![1]

For poet John Dryden, the year was England's *annus mirabilis.* It altered India's history for completely different but not entirely unconnected elements. First, it marked the death of Shah Jahan, the last known humane ruler of the Mughal dynasty in India, followed by the reign of Aurangzeb, who had seized the throne after imprisoning his father. It also cleared the way for European colonial powers in India, once and for all. The Portuguese and Dutch companies had already ensconced themselves in Malabar and Coromandel. The French were still trickling into Surat and Masulipatnam. The Danish (Denmark and Norway) were dispatching steady fleets to South India. They too had established enclaves of great commercial value in Masulipatnam and Tranquebar. Within a 100 years, the Swedish East India Company would also be feverishly smuggling tea and spices from China to Europe.

Beginning with these multinational corporations that harvested the seeds of their intercontinental fracases in India, the eastern and the western hemispheres conspired to gear history in the direction of the conquest and ruination of the colony. In early 2018, Boris Johnson, the then British Foreign Secretary, perplexed Belgium and Britain by calling the European Union a 'teleological construct'.[2]

The implication was that the Union had single-mindedly pursued the sinking of United Kingdom into a larger economic power-zone, which patriotic Britons ought to have shunned. Around the burning Brexit controversies, political gaffes seemed to be headed for farce. The Raj, however, was indeed shaped by a crafty catalogue of freakish incidents, as non-teleological as Johnson would have approved. Where there was fire, there was bound to be the smoke of tea. Britain's imperial destiny came to be written as books of accounts against a few of the simplest necessities of daily life. Arguably, large provinces of India were first annexed to the East India Company's estates purely to sustain the business of brewing—what was to become—a very British beverage.

———

Four years before the Great Fire, King Charles II was betrothed to the Portuguese princess, Catherine of Braganza. The ceremony redefined the English figure of speech known as zeugma. A classic example of this came in the King's zeugmatic dowry—a chest of tea with the island of Bombay, among other dictions and addictions from the court of John IV of Portugal. However, any form of pleasantry was a very distant cousin-in-law during the handover of Bombay by Portugal to Britain. The Portuguese rallied up a disheartening resistance to the liveried English troops sent on King Charles' fleet to the island. Local Hindus, who had seen the worst of the Portuguese, now assigned some Brahmins of the community to persuade the English to steer the helm of Bombay. Even while Goan natives retained their loyalty to Portugal and the idols of Christ (which they worshipped as yet another Hindu deity), Bombay's Brahmin delegates were deployed to Surat to supply the English with intelligence to conquer the island. Only in 1666, however, Humphrey Cooke, Bombay's first English Governor, was able to take possession of six of the seven islands—Salsette, Mazagaon, Parel, Worli, Sion, Dharavi and Wadala—away from Portuguese control. Samuel Pepys, a friend of King Charles and London's most popular gossiper and intelligencer at the time, had closely followed the crisis in India. Before the island was passed over to the British at an annual lease of £10, Pepys desponded that 'Bombaim' was a 'poor little island', far from what King Charles had been given to understand. It was bound to bring misery.[3] Pepys should have known better.

Portugal was not the sole contender in the East. The *Vereenigde Oostindische Compagnie* (or the Dutch East India Company) had been on a marathon shopping spree for thirty years. It had decimated Portuguese control over factories and settlements in South India. Heads of the four other East India families had also been stoned at sea by Holland's naval prowess. By mid-17th century, Cragnore and Cannaonore in Kerala passed into Dutch hands. So did Ceylon and its entire pepper operations. Back in Bombay, the Golconda rulers now refused to curry favour with the Portuguese. No longer did they apply for their travelling passes from Portugal, which had been hitherto customary. In the previous century, even Akbar the Great had allied with the Portuguese to acquire passes for his ships carrying pilgrims to Mecca on the Hajj. Now, as a substitute to Portuguese tyranny, the princes and natives of Malabar and Coromandel were defecting to the manners of the Hollanders.

Portuguese strongholds in the colony suffered heavy losses at the time of the Iberian Union between Spain and Portugal. In mid-16th century, Portuguese India was ruled by Kings Philip II and III of Spain. Marred by inefficient negotiators and culturally backward administrators, India had become more of a liability than an asset to Spain. Even when Madrid attempted to sell off its territories and businesses in the colony, disasters wrecked its fleet on the Indian Ocean. While Antonio, the titular lead from Shakespeare's *The Merchant of Venice*, awaited the return of his ships from the English Channel, several fleets of Spanish merchants and messengers had drowned in the storm-tossed seas on their way to India, as though even the heavens had withdrawn their alliance from Portugal.

As England prepared for Restoration, the Portuguese in India were staring at two unholy choices. One was to have their last bastions in the Indies robbed by the Dutch Company. The other was to put down the signature of their King on a peace accord with Holland, thus arming up against the English. In 1662, Cochin fell to Dutch assault, days after the Portuguese called for a ceasefire. Holland had enjoyed stupendous military success in the last three decades. About twenty years ago, during the English Civil War, it had also sent enormous subsidies, through the House of Orange, to Charles I, for purchasing firepower from Holland and France. Not unreasonably then, the Dutch were past chagrin by the handover of Bombay to Charles II. Although they had never held the city itself, it had been controlled for 130 years by an inferior European power that the Dutch fleets had just unequivocally muzzled. And yet, now, the island of Bombay had been handed over to a profligate British monarch without even the whiff of gunpowder. Both the English and the Portuguese now feared that Holland's vengeance was frothing at the mouth of the Indian Peninsula.

Humphrey Cooke was still wading through the Bombay negotiations when the fire raged across the banks of the Thames. The 'East India House in Leadenhall Street stood about 400 metres from the seat of the fire. Books, papers, goods, and treasure were hurriedly removed for safety to outlying Stepney.'⁴ Owing to the conflicts overseas between England and Holland, London's suspicions immediately fell on the Dutch for having started the fire. A Dutch baker, Cornelius Rietveldt, was nearly beaten to death and his house was looted in front of him. One Lady Hobart wrote to Sir Ralph Verney, ''Tis the Dutch who fire, there was one taken in Westminster setting his outhouse on fire and they have attempted to fire many places and there is an abundance taken with grenades and power.' As many as 13,000 houses and 89 churches perished in London. The Dutch did indeed rejoice over that incendiary week, although as far as in Cochin, where they celebrated the Fire of London by burning effigies of Charles II.

Holland's naval ascendancy was approaching its twilight. By introducing tea in Europe in the early 17th century, the Dutch had inadvertently invented a rod for their back. Abetted by the firm J.J. Voute & Sons, Holland had ruthlessly exploited the incapacity of the British East India Company to supply tea to its thriving domestic elites and coffee houses. Even when the Industrial Revolution took off in Britain, Holland was smuggling about 8 million pounds of tea annually, which occupied almost half of the entire British import. However, by this time, Dutch teas had become a 'name for all teas that are bad in quality and unfit for use.'[5] What England needed was a royal campaign to dress the foreign herb as authentic at home and monopolise the authenticity to manufacture it. Even hell had no such fury like a nation of merchants that wanted to brew its tea but could not acquire it. With its entry into the court during King Charles' wedding, tea was turned into a poster-child of the English Restoration. The herb had been available in Europe for forty years now, and in England, for at least ten. Yet, it was only in 1661 that the first known evidence of tea appeared from the pen of an Englishman. Pepys wrote about his first drink of the exhilarating potion in late September. Although not an immediate fancier himself, his entry seems almost like an advertisement for what he described as 'that excellent and by all Physicians, approved, China drink, called by the Chineans Tcha, by other nations Tay alias Tee.' It was being vended 'at the Sultaness Head, a Cophee-house, in Sweeting's Rents by the Royal Exchange, London.'[6] Around the time of the Great Fire, England was drinking tea for prices as high as between £3 and £6 per pound of the herb, equivalent to the annual rent of that rocky Indian island in the Western Ghats.

Bombay was to serve as the incubator of British India's opium and tea trade with China to outmanoeuvre all European— especially Portuguese and Dutch—operations. With a slice of India in his hamper, Charles II was happy to sign off the Island of Run in Indonesia. The Treaty of Breda, signed between England and Holland in 1667, brought the Second Anglo-Dutch War to an end.

Burning the King's effigy in India was all that the Dutch Company had done to exact retribution for the irreversible commercial and military damage they now began to suffer. Towards the end of the 17th century, with the beginning of the Fourth Anglo-Dutch War, Holland's fortunes in the East nearly collapsed. Had it not been for tea, and the machinations of the English Company to police the borders of Britain for smuggled European varieties of the herb, England may not even have launched an offensive on the Dutch navy, in and around India, on such an unprecedented scale.

What the English later spent in their opium wars with China, they took in compound interest from the Brahmaputra Valley, rendering India—a nation of teetotallers—into a tea-guzzling gizmo. By the time of Queen Victoria, nearly two centuries later, the virtues of Indian tea were aggrandised in London to advertise the backwardness of China. Neither India nor Indians necessarily, but nostalgic varieties of Indian tea were strutted as the glow-signboards of Anglo-Indian solidarity on the streets of London, such as in this advertisement from A Pure Indian Tea Supply Agency:

INDIAN TEAS ARE PURER. INDIAN TEAS ARE MORE AROMATIC. INDIAN TEAS ARE STRONGER. INDIAN TEAS ARE CHEAPER. INDIAN TEAS ARE MORE WHOLESOME AND ARE BETTER IN EVERY RESPECT THAN CHINESE TEAS.[7]

China was condemned for its insanitary methods of growing tea in the treatise, *Indian Versus Chinese Teas. Which are Adulterated, Which are Better?*, written by Edward Money in 1884. Indian tea, as it endorsed, was grown by educated Englishmen, aided by sophisticated machinery, on large Indian estates. Chinese tea, on the other hand, was hand-rolled and spiked with microbes of nude Chinese bodies and sweat. With the advent of Sir Samuel C. Davidson's Sirocco Tea, Indian pedigrees of tea colonised London—as well as Ireland, Scotland, Europe and the United States. The Indian Tea Store came up on Oxford Street, in 1881, not long before many of its replicas were placarded in the city. It was impossible not to be seduced by the beverage in London, as if it was a demystified Cleopatra—cloned into hundreds of thousands of Darjeeling or Assam boxes, snaffled out of the timber forests of Deyrah Doon or Simla.

————

The reverberations of maritime battles and the grinding mills of imperial merchandise throw us precipitously away from the history of Indians in London. The Monument on Fenchurch Street is a living testimony to the mysterious relationship between the construction of this building, the cost of reconstructing London after the Fire and the British East India Company's box office collections in the subcontinent. It also dates back to the time after the Renaissance in Europe, when empires and their etiquettes, cities and townships, and people and commodities were flung into a highly networked world, more than ever before. Even in the Shakespearean age, social networks tilted in favour of scandal, or the propensity for spinning 'details of new scandal to fictional stories that were sure to find a substantial audience.'[8]

It was no scandal either in London or India, that Indians had been purloined to London, indeed, where they lived in states of servitude. However, it was deeply scandalous that three Brahmin priests crossed the Arabian and the Mediterranean seas in the 19th century to retrieve a fictional diamond, the Moonstone—a pseudonym for the Kohinoor. *The Moonstone* (1868), by Wilkie Collins, toyed with the binary of a printed will and an oral myth. In the novel, Colonel Herncastle had bequeathed in his will the stolen diamond to his niece, Rachel Verinder, while the pious Hindu vanguards of the Moonstone were out to enforce their myths as the gospel, in a quest to restore the pious artefact to the temple of Somnath. What shone supremely in the hands of the women of the Verinder household as the Moonstone was merely an isotope of coal. Coal was to London that pristine commodity whose marine alchemy had brought tens of thousands of Indians to the city even before they learned to read or write. It was the mastery over coal that led the English Company's headquarters in London to swell up with proceeds from spices, silver, gold, textiles and gunpowder, in quick succession, in their new-found empire in India. It was coal that brought Indians as commodities to the imperial capital. Under King Charles II, coal became a metaphor for Indians. As *The Moonstone's* scoundrel, Godfrey Ablewhite, remarked cynically to the family butler, 'Carbon, Betteredge! mere carbon...'[9] The face of carbon, in its crudest form, defined not only the complexion of Indian labourers and lascars in London, but also the treatment meted out to them.

The Coal Tax instituted in 1667, meant to recoup the damages caused by the fire, was supposed to last for ten years; and then an additional thirteen years. However, it continued for 160 years. Between 1613 and 1669, the Company's exports to India—as well as the other new and darker parts of the world—were estimated at £2.5 million. By 1700, they had raced to £6.5 million. Either directly or indirectly, India contributed enormously to rebuilding London after the fire. By 1800, the East India Company's exports rocketed to £43.2 million. In 2016, the damages caused by the Fire of London were estimated at £37 billion in today's currency—£10 million, back then. Notionally, the Company's spice and textile trade could itself have contributed to rebuilding the city four times over, without any economic inflation—or thrice over, with it. The Company exploited the Coal Tax, as merchants from Liverpool or Cork were left to starve of the profits that went exclusively into the cases of London merchants, while wholesale deposits lined the city's warehouses. Victorian London's demand for coal to work the mills and the foundries, as well as due to the emergence of steam locomotion, was considered 'steady, natural and inevitable'.[10] The railways led to faster locomotion of textiles, dyes and steel. This meant that the East India Company was not merely fetching London tens of millions from all around the Empire, but that the Coal Tax was making the City of London clear its large debts by cannibalising England's own foreign and domestic trade. England, like Bill Clinton, went about campaigning to its colonies, it was all about the economy, 'stupid'.[11] London, like George W. Bush, was hardening the military capacity of the Company, for the miniature Iraqs of its age—namely, Bengal and Mysore.

With one eye on his foreign tea and another on his domestic coal, King Charles II spawned a third eye for the consolidation of the British textile industry.

> The Dutch kept declining spice trade in Indonesia. The textiles trade quickly surpassed the spice trade. By the 1680s, the Dutch imports from Bengal was already exceeding its imports from spices from the Indies. Now England had exclusive rights to this trade. As a result of this agreement the sales of the British East India Company overtook that of the Dutch by 1720s. The profits of the British East India Company also exceeded that of the Dutch. English imports of cotton and calicoes were surpassing imports of nutmegs, cloves, peppers and other spices.[12]

If the Dutch or the Danish were smuggling tea—refused by the rest of the continent—into Britain, England was determined to smuggle into East Europe and the colonised regions of East Africa textiles or undyed cotton that America refused to consume in the 19th century. Following the Restoration, the East India Company began deploying its artisans to teach the Indians in Western and Oriental fashions.[13] Indian cotton was the gasoline for the British Industrial Revolution as well as the accelerator for railway projects in the colony.

Since the 16th century, India had exported cotton and fabrics to Europe, paving the way for its own slavery, and that of Africa. What most 'European trading companies had in common was that they purchased cotton textiles in India, whence they might be consumed domestically or shipped to Africa to pay for slaves to work the plantations just beginning to take root in the New World. Slaves, after all, could only be gotten by exchanging them for the cottons from India.'[14] Before the Lancashire mills came up, Dhaka muslin was a lavish article in Britain. 17th-century French travellers in India, Francois Bernier and Jean-Baptiste Tavernier, throbbed with delight at the delicateness of Indian cotton. 'White gold', what it was hailed as, was ubiquitous in Mughal harems and on royal personages. Due to their sublime textures, Indian muslins were known as *aab-e-rawan* (running water), *shabnam* (evening dew) or *beft hawa* (woven air). Between 1681 and 1685, when the English first arrived on the Indian cotton scene, the East India Company paid India 240 tonnes of silver and 7 tonnes of gold for its imports of cotton textiles. After the Battle of Plassey in 1757, the Company assumed control over 70 per cent of the world's saltpetre in Bengal. Even then, cotton continued to be its principal export to Europe, occupying in the 1760s, three-quarters of the Company's total trade.

The use of cotton in pre-Victorian England appeared as unwholesome to some as drug abuse. English author and creator of Robinson Crusoe, Daniel Defoe, lamented in his *Weekly Review*, that the English had taken to dressing in Indian carpets, which until a few years ago even their chambermaids would have frowned upon. Chintz from India 'crept into our houses, our closets, and bed-chambers; curtains, cushions, chairs, and, at last, beds themselves were nothing but calicos or Indian stuffs. Almost everything that used to be made of wool or silk, relating either to the dress of women or furniture of our houses, was supplied by the Indian trade.'[15] With the success of King Charles' cotton campaign, importing cotton became a national evil in England. The Dutch had been relegated to the East Indies, the Portuguese to the Malabar, the French to the Carnatic and the Arab and Bania merchants practically ousted from the eastern part of the subcontinent. By the early 18th century, Britain acquired a monopoly of trade in Bengal and Gujarat. Militarised and bureaucratised by late-18th-century naval and industrial expansion, the Indian cotton trade became a three-continent-spanning enterprise. As Surat and Dhaka became fortified by the English Company, 'cotton from India, slaves from Africa, and sugar from the Caribbean moved across the planet in a complex commercial dance.'[16]

Britain's textile Hollywoods—Lancashire and Manchester—profited tremendously from the market that Indian cotton had created in pre-industrial Europe. As the British mined out white gold from India, the mourning spectres of the weavers of Bengal, Mysore and Gujarat and their handloom industry haunted the Raj

in—what a philosophical descendant of Karl Marx later called—
'a ghostly silhouette'.[17] At least a hundred years before the Victorian
nabobs retired from the colony to London, with their Indian cash and
concubines disguised as maidservants, Indian textiles, muslins, print
designs, upholstery and furniture had invaded the city's fashions. At
the time King James' Bible was released, London 'was a surfeit of
silk shops, selling everything from gold thread to silk stockings.'[18] In
1618, a 'Benguella Quilt' was auctioned at a large price in London.
Shakespeare himself would have seen artisans exchanged between
Britain and India to facilitate the growth of the imperial textile
industry. As early as 1609, one found in the city, Easterners like
'John, the Indian' who worked as a weaver. John lost his thumb in an
accident, whereupon he took up work at the Company's docks as a
lascar. Tens of thousands like him could be found languishing upon
the docklands of Southwark, Newham, Tower Hamlets or Greenwich,
over the next hundred years, laying the foundations for the fabled
factories and marketplaces of London. Rebuilding the city after the
fire also included the cost of rebuilding fifty-two of the city's burned
churches, spearheaded by Christopher Wren. The churches that were
eviscerated in 1666 included St Dionis Backchurch, where Peter Pope
was baptised. Much of that restoration was courtesy of England's
textile trade. St Dionis Backchurch was demolished in 1878 and a
new church of the parish was built at Parsons Green in 1886. Today,
a Marks & Spencer and a Nando's guard the entry to the Leadenhall
Market, where the city had witnessed for the first time how an Indian
became a Christian in a foreign land. India kept furnishing the fabrics
to clothe the souls of England while the English would reciprocate by
exporting a new idea of soul altogether to dwell in Oriental wealth—
one that was to putrefy the pristine subcontinent from within.

By the time London's coal duties were annulled in 1831, Indians
had enjoyed—or rather been writhing from—two centuries of
existence in the city. Indian labourers and settlers were turned into
industrial cocaine—an unseemly dependency issue. Unlike the
cigar or the pipe, these Indian chattels were not lit up openly. They
were consigned to a few hidden wallets or domestic quarters, to be
sneakily sniffed and put out of sight.

Scene III

An Indian Fish, Dead or Alive

Peter Pope's memory became a casualty amidst the manic expansions of king and country. Reverend Patrick Copland, East India Company's Chaplain to Masulipatnam, had escorted him to the heart of Britannia as a prospective *cavea porcellus* to test the effects of the fruits of its civilisation. According to another version, Peter was brought to England by Captain Best, and handed over to Copland, who was supposed to have him 'taught and instructed in religion, that hereafter he might upon occasion be sent unto his country, where God may be pleased to make him an instrument in converting some of his nation.'[1] Copland trained the Indian youth 'to speake, to read and write the English tongue and hand, both Romane and Secretary, within less than the space of a yeare.' Copland petitioned for his baptism, and the insemination of the faith of England into the 'first-fruits of India'.[2]

'What have we here? A man or a fish?' asked Trinculo, the Shakespearean fool in *The Tempest*. When Victorian readers recovered Copland's journals, they were quick to see Peter's resemblance in his baptismal scene to the misshapen character of Caliban in that play.

Dead or alive? A fish. He smells like a fish, a very ancient and fish-like smell, a kind of not-of-the-newest poor-john. A strange fish! Were I in England now, as once I was, and had but this fish painted, not a holiday fool there but would give a piece of silver. There would this monster make a man. Any strange beast there

makes a man. When they will not give a doit to relieve a lame
beggar, they will lay out ten to see a dead Indian.[3]

Shakespeare finished writing *The Tempest* not before 1610. The
age for the arrival of 'strange beasts' of the East had just set in.
For a decade now, the East India Company and the two Virginia
Companies had been plying to the Indies and America. At
Fenchurch Street, where the Indian Caliban was Anglicised, the
entire body politic of England flocked to celebrate. The Archbishop
of Canterbury blessed Peter's baptism. King James' hand in the
pageant warranted the presence of directors of the two trading
Companies and members of the Privy Council. Peter's entry into
London was a manifestation of the Shakespearean dream of an
intensely networked experience as though the various parts of the
undiscovered world were but the human protrusions of a child in
birth—a renaissance dream that London was besotted by. It was
the dream of a 'boy stolen from an Indian King,' that Shakespeare
dreamed about in *A Midsummer Night's Dream* (1605), a dream
wafted across the Thames by the 'the spiced Indian air by night.'

Peter Pope was in London for only a year. Copland took him
back to India in 1617, on the ship *Royal James*. Four years later,
Copland returned alone to England. Soon after, he was asked to
preach before the Virginia Council. In his sermon *Virginia's God
Be Thanked*, he reproduced Peter's letters in Latin and English,
written to Sir Thomas Smith, a Company Governor, and Martin
Pring, commander of the *Royal James*. After much ado over little,
the boy from the 'Bay of Bengala' almost disappeared from history.
When he left London, he was intended to be the rock on which
the Church of England would build its temples in India—and
eventually reap the moolah for rebuilding London when the leaden
roofs of St Paul's came down haemorrhaging by the Thames during
the Great Fire. But the eagerness with which Peter had agreed to
be baptised did not come so naturally to the rest of his tribe, often
particularly due to the subhuman treatment meted out to them.
Even in Victorian London, one found examples such as the Countess
of Londesborough, of Mayfair, who purchased an Indian domestic

by the name of Bimbi, who was made to dress in motley robes and a pink turban, and dance on her marble stairwell.

In 1720, an Indian youth of sixteen was purloined from his family in Madras and trafficked to London by one Captain Dawes. He was gifted to Elizabeth Turner, who christened him 'Julian'. Despite her best efforts or coercions, the Indian lad was intractable when it came to learning English or adopting Christianity. While Julian stuck to his Pagan conflict with the benefits of the new civilisation, Mrs Turner went Trinculo on him, forcing him to dance and croon before her guests. On August 8, 1724, Julian fled with 20 guineas stolen from the household, leaving the sheets and the house on fire. The police captured him immediately. Julian confessed before the lady's husband and Sir Francis Forbes, pleading all the while that he had been forced into clownery and animalesque acts to entertain humans. Mrs Turner refuted the charge of knowing about Julian's dissatisfaction. As customary, her claim was given more credence over his. Julian was executed publicly at the Tyburn tree, but not before he had acquiesced to being baptised and rechristened as 'John', likely as a last-ditch attempt at the commutation of his sentence. On the day of his execution, he asked for a penknife from one of the prisoners, to take his own life. However, his Lord—whoever it was at the time—saved him to live a few more hours until the London mob could fulfil its appetite watching him die at the gallows.

The historical crisscrossings between Peter's baptism under King James, King Charles' absorption of tea and the execution of John are indeed not as convoluted as they appear. There is something tremendously macabre beneath the decorous flurry of English faces, whether one sees them at a retail store in London or imagines their congregation for the public hangings at the Tyburn. London's theatricality was played out at its best at the Tyburn or Newgate prison, where executions were 'essentially a form of street theatre'.[4] One often turns to Pepys while recounting the legends of London between the time of Shakespeare and the Great Fire. One of his lesser-known contemporaries, William Schellink, a Dutch visitor to London in 1663, also left several diaries. In one of them, he audited a row at the Tyburn, annotating what was probably the first public hanging of a black or coloured woman in early modern England. She was classified as a 'negress or coloured woman', which made it impossible to ascertain if she was African or Indian.[5]

Beyond doubt, Indians lived and died in London even before the birth of Shakespeare. On March 22, 1550, one Salamon Nurr was buried at St Margaret's in Westminster. Conjecturally, his name was the Anglicised form of Suleman Noor. In that, he is likelier to be Indian than the 'coloured woman' hanged at the time of Charles II. Another Indian, Samuel Munsur, described as a 'blackamour,' was married to one Jane Johnson on December 28, 1613, at St Nicholas Church in Deptford, about five miles from Shakespeare's Globe Theatre in Southwark. More Indian betrothals, baptisms and burials followed. From the period between Peter's baptism and John's hanging, as many as fifteen burials and baptisms have surfaced from the various parish churches in London. Of the many records from this period that mention blackamours or negroes or negresses, or just people of colour and do not specify their places of origin, it is not improbable that one, or more, is also of Indians. According to the Company's official records, many labourers or servants who wished to return to India were eventually brought to London as blacks. Not all Indian converts to the Church of England were necessarily baptised, thus, leaving the glaring possibility that there were more Christian Indians in London than officially recorded. That number was obviously much smaller than those Indians who did not convert at all. Of those who did, the present list of baptised Indians has survived from old parishes of 17th and 18th-century London.

> St Botolph Aldgate: 8 Sept 1618, burial of 'James (an Indian), servant to Mr James Duppa, beerebrewer' (GL Ms 9222/1)
> St Katherine by the Tower: 20 August 1623, baptism of 'Phillip, an Indian blackmore, borne in the East Indies at Zarat' (GL Ms 9659/2)

St Andrew Holborn: 17 April 1633, burial of 'Thomas a[n] Indian, out of the Lord Brooke's house, was layed in the Church as Catumelant' (GL Ms 6673/2)

> *'Catumelant' in the entry above appears to signify that the individual was a catechumen, a Christian convert under instruction prior to baptism.*

St Olave Hart Street: 29 April 1675, baptism of 'George an India[n] servant of Mr Robert Andrews, chirurgeon, aged 16 yeares or thereabouts, christened in the publique congregacon' (GL Ms 28868)

All Hallows Barking: 24 February 1681/2, burial of 'Trumbelo, an Indian black, Catechumus' (GL Ms 3713/2A)

St Olave Hart Street: 14 June 1681, burial of 'Loreta, an India woaman, buryed in the near [new?] churchyard in Seething Lane' (GL Ms 28869)

St Olave Hart Street: 14 February 1682/3, burial of 'An Indian[n] slave boy of Mr Charles Gray was buryed in church yard' (GL Ms 28869)

St Mary Woolchurch Haw: 7 March 1683/4, baptism of 'Marck Anthony an Indian, by Frank Sclater. Witnesses—Mr Thomas Rannd, Mr James Watkins, Ms Elizabeth Howard' (GL Ms 7644)

All Hallows Barking: 25 January 1688/9, baptism of 'Mary Alphabet, an Indian black aged about 16, servant to Mrs Richardson of this parish' (GL Ms 3713/2A)

St Edmund Lombard Street: 9 November 1690, baptism of 'Joan Hill, a black of about 30 years, servant to Lt. General Hill, of the Cariby Islands' (GL Ms 20204)

St Katherine Cree: 6 December 1691, baptism of 'Daniel Mingoe, an Indian boy, servant to the Lady Ann Godwin, baptised at the font' (GL Ms 7889/1)

St Ethelburga Bishopsgate: 19 May 1695, baptism of 'Francis Brewer, laite servant to Mr Thomas Rutter, a black or Indian' (GL Ms 4236/1)

St Augustine Watling Street: 20 May 1697, baptism of 'Sarah Bamoo, a black Indian about 20 years of age' (GL Ms 8872/2)

St Dunstan in the West: 27 January 1714/5, baptism of 'Titus
Vespatian, aged 15, born in the East Indies, a servant to Mr
Thomas Robinson baptised this day at the font' (GL Ms 10349)
All Hallows Lombard Street: 12 February 1721/2, baptism of
'Thomas James Campbell, an Indian youth' (GL Ms 17614).[6]

For one reason or another, London's servants were almost always
fleeing the homes of their employers. It became such a common
feature during the reign of Queen Anne that advertisements on
real estate, fashion goods and absconding servants throve side
by side in the newspapers of the day. A *Morning Chronicle* issue
from the spring of 1795 reported missing the fourteen-year-old
Bengali servant, Hyder, in the employ of one Mrs Ramus of
58 Baker Street, Portman Square. Hyder had stolen several items
from his lady's wardrobe, which outlawed his future employment
in the city. Britain was used to waking up to such notices since
long before John was hanged.

> In 1685, a Bristol man offered a reward of 20s. for his 14-year-
> old runaway 'Indian Boy'; in 1702, another was searching for an
> 'Indian Black' servant 'with long hair' called Morat, aged 15 years,
> who had absconded from Westminster. There had been sightings
> of the runaway in Hampstead, Highgate and Tottenham. Another
> advertisement, for an 'East India Tawny Black' was issued in
> 1737, and yet another tried to find a 'Run-away Bengal Boy' in
> 1743. In 1772, Thomas Hornsey, 'a Black, a Native of the Coast
> of Malabar' ran away from his master's house in Epsom. He was
> reported as having offered himself as a servant to several gentlemen
> in areas as far apart as Highgate, Deptford and London. In 1767,
> the *Dublin Journal* advertised for 'a mulatto East India Boy,'
> eloped from Eyre Evans Crow at Aughrim near Ballinasloe, and
> in the same year the *Belfast Newsletter* was looking for a 'black
> boy,' native of Bengal.[7]

Indian servants were usually found in the prosperous nabob
households of Stepney, Tooting, Marylebone, Whitechapel,

Lewisham, Greenwich or Essex. While most advertisements described the absconders as the generic 'negro', some specified the Indian origins of the servants. One such announced a reward of 10s. for anyone who could return 'a Slender middle-sized India Black, in a dark gray Livery with Brass Buttons,'[8] escaped from the house of Mrs Thwaits in Stepney. Another bore the following:

> Went away from his Master's House in Drury Lane, upon Monday the 6th Instant, and has since been seen at Hampstead, Highgate and Tottenham Court, an Indian Black boy, with long Hair, about 15 Years of Age, speaks very good English; he went away in a brown Fustian Frock, a blew Wastecoate, and scarlet Shag Breeches, and is called by the name of Morat; Whoever brings him to, or gives Notice of him, so as he may be brought to Mr Pain's House in Prince's Court, Westminster, shall have a Guinea Reward, and the Boy shall be kindly received.[9]

During and after the Restoration, most Indians in London remained in undocumented servitude. After 1657, it was easier for them to find themselves on the shores of England than the coasts of Coromandel or Malabar. The Company's board of directors passed a resolution that those intending to go to India needed to have an official license, which cost £12 (about £1,500 in today's currency). Penury left Indian labourers stranded in the metropolis. On the road to insolvency, many started to beg or offer themselves up for dockyard or domestic labour. Many were purchased as servants by Company officials. Instances of the Company's benevolence were not entirely rare. In 1667, Captain Lord, of the ship *St George,* brought to London a group of ten lascars from Surat. Their *sarang*, the contractor who had travelled with them, complained to the Company's directors that Lord had not paid his men their wages and instead had sold some of the seamen to be trafficked to America. It was later discovered that a publican from Shadwell had sold two of the seamen to one Captain Tilman of the vessel—ironically named—*Constant Friendship*. It had already set sail for Virginia. The Company's directors immediately summoned a committee to preside over complaints of forced servitude and unwarranted traffic of Indians. The committee contacted the customs collector at Downs, on the coast of Kent, to refuse the *Constant Friendship* its final permission to sail abroad. Tilman was apprehended. However, he declined to give up the custody of the Indian men without compensation. This too was provided by the Company, the sum of which and the costs of the lascars' maintenance, £42 3s. 8d. (about £6000 in today's currency), were extracted from Lord's pay. The Indians were given food and lodging and employed on the ship, *Return*, which sailed for Surat later that spring.

English lawyer and diarist William Hickey was among the most esteemed chroniclers of amusements of the Raj in late-18th-century Bengal. In Warren Hastings' Calcutta, going out of favour with the hookah implied going out of fashion. The hookah was an emblem of British integration into Indian culture as well as of their supremacy. With the employment of the *hookahburdar* (hookah-bearer), smoking became a ritual of Indian vassalage and Company Bahadur's prestige. British diplomat Philip Dormer Stanhope wrote in his *Genuine Memoirs* (1784) that even writers, whose annual salaries did not exceed £200, employed *hookahburdars*. Addiction to the hookah was not merely olfactory but also highly visual. Without the sight of *hookahburdars* carrying the nabobs' serpentine tobacco instruments, or *khansamas* currying up mutton or pillauing rice, London's elite households would have been little better than wildernesses. The cost of employing a servant in India was one-eighth that of having one in London. Hickey's own household staff included 360 people, with butlers, bearers, valets, grooms, coachmen, gardeners, cooks, bakers, tailors, barbers and washermen. His contemporaries in Calcutta followed suit. Reverend William Tennant lived in a household served by 500 domestics, while that of Philip Francis was served by 110.

Although African slaves could also be purchased in Calcutta or other metropolitan centres in India, the cost of buying them, along with commissions, was ten times that of employing Indian domestic staff. When Hastings retired to England, he and his wife took four maidservants and two teenaged boys. When he visited London in 1780, Hickey brought his favourite servant-boy, Nabob. When he finally retired to England in 1808, he was accompanied by Munno. Hickey had purchased him from his affectionate mother for ₹500. The diarist's final years at Beaconsfield saw his Indian companion in the Anglicised avatar of William Munnew. In 1750, an East Indian, versed in Portuguese, German and six other languages and baptised under the Church of England, sought for a footman's position. In 1775, another Indian, nearly of age, who had been in Britain for over a decade, offered himself up to any noble household. The following year, an East Indian with a footman's skills, and recently returned from America, offered himself up to service. And the year after, a twenty-two-year-old from Bengal, who had been in Britain for a decade-and-a-half, was also in the market for domestics.

> Indian servants were as familiar in East London as in St James' and the Mall or Marylebone. Gravestones in churchyards bear witness to the fact that many Company agents retired in the East End, forming a visible presence. Places like Stepney may be poor today, but in the 18th century these areas were gentrified and desirable residences, and it was this that attracted the India-returned nabobs. A random search of parish registers illustrates the point: the presence of Indian servants in places as far apart as Tooting, Marylebone, Whitechapel, Greenwich, Lewisham and Essex.[10]

All Indian servants in London were expected to be baptised, conversion being the only pathway to their emancipation. At times, even that was not enough to save them from perdition, as in the case of 'Catherine Bengall'. Catherine arrived in London about 130 years after Shakespeare's death. Her life perfectly rounds off the saga of Indians from the time that moulded the bard's chronicles or those that his histories later occluded. In *A Room of One's Own* (1929), Virginia Woolf created the character of Shakespeare's fictional sister, Judith. Nudging citations from Professor Trevelyan's most recent *History of England* (1926), Woolf recapitulated several incidents in Englishwomen's lives that had been otherwise conscribed to domestic hells. In Woolf's archaeology, Shakespeare's 'extraordinarily talented and gifted sister remained at home. She was as adventurous, as imaginative, as agog to see the world as he was.'[11] Like her brother, Judith Shakespeare too left Stratford upon Avon for London. While she was still in her teens, she was impregnated by the actor-manager Nick Greene, and found herself with his illegitimate child, sans a character and a living. Judith was compelled by the indifference of the sordid world around her to take her own life, and was brusquely 'buried at some cross-roads where the omnibuses now stop outside the Elephant and Castle.'[12]

Just as theatre could not promise the blossoming of Judith's genius, the Anglican Church could not fulfil the pledge of Catherine's liberation. She had been purchased in Bengal at the age of ten and trafficked to London by one Suthern Davies, who gifted her to his relative, Ann Suthern. On November 26, 1745, Catherine was baptised at the St James Church in Westminster. Kinder than expected, the Sutherns set her free in a few months. Catherine followed Judith's footsteps, momentarily climbing the social ladder as the concubine of one William Lloyd. By the summer of the following year, she was thrust into a pitiable pregnancy and pennilessness. Found in that state on the streets of the city, she was lodged at the local parish workhouse of St Martin in the Fields, by the order of the local magistrate. Here, Catherine found food and shelter—and social humiliation. Her son, born in September 1746, was christened William after his father and—coincidentally indeed—Judith Shakespeare's renowned brother. Within a few years, either due to death or destitution, the names of Catherine and William faded from the annals of the East India Company, just as Shakespeare's sister had vanished from London 150 years ago.

ACT II

Lays of Little Bengal

… in the spicèd Indian air by night
Full often hath she gossiped by my side,
And sat with me on Neptune's yellow sands,
Marking th' embarkèd traders on the flood,
When we have laughed to see the sails conceive
And grow big-bellied with the wanton wind
　　　　　(A Midsummer Night's Dream, Act II, Scene I).

Scene I

An Armenian in the City

Every day, hundreds of London's tourists file in for the city's ghost tours, to experience the eerie nighttime of St James' Park. In the middle of it lies the Blue Bridge, upon a lake, both haunted by the phantasm of a headless woman, and many others of her ghoulish ethnicity. The lake divvies the murky landscape into the Duck Island and the West Island. If you keep Buckingham Palace towards the left, the London Eye and the Shard loom in the east as reassuring but remote rays of civilisation upon this haunted moorland.

Our scene began here, one summer evening, the year before the Battle of Plassey, when with a chance meeting between an Armenian and a Briton, the long history of Indians in the city turned a new leaf. Soon enough, the day was forgotten with the rustling of the poplars opposite the Buckingham House, like a waylaid cog from the engines of Brittania on the faraway seas. Less than fifty-years from that day—less than three miles from the place where they met—the hallowed squares around Baker Street would be popularly known as 'Little Bengal'. That was how an 1837 issue of the *Quarterly Review* designated 'that European Elysium of Asiatics—the streets north of Cavendish and Portman Squares.'[1] Even a century before the world's first and only consulting detective, Sherlock Holmes, shot to fame and his Baker Street Irregulars came to public notice from the vintage neighbourhood, the districts of Mayfair and Marylebone had been breeding grounds for chronicles of the Little Bengal Irregulars. From here, Indians, now exiled in

London, began adventitiously shaping the Empire in ways that usually went unacknowledged, but not undetected.

———————

In the winter of 1749, the young son of an Irish solicitor relocated from Dublin to London. At twenty, he aspired to become a lawyer. His esteemed tutors at school had been admirers of his extraordinary intellect, while his peers were enthralled by the 'truest affection from his warm-hearted disposition.' He characterised an inborn aversion to hatred and oppression of all kinds, and an indiscriminate love for liberty. Wandering around the Houses of Parliament and St James' Park, he often dreamed of a seat in the House of Commons. Listening to the hours toll by in the churchbells of Westminster Abbey, he wondered if someday he too should have his 'resting place in this grand cathedral, side by side, with the great men who are now calmly sleeping after their lives of usefulness.' Many of the speeches that he had delivered in London's private debating clubs made his contemporaries realise that the young scholar was made of sterner stuff than the inertia of the statutes and decrees of the Age of Reason.

As the Irish prodigy was still making his mark on the English intelligentsia, a fierce military campaign led by Nadir Shah had reduced to his obedience capital after capital in the middle-eastern and southern parts of Asia. His empire comprised vast territories of what are today Iran, Armenia, Azerbaijan, Georgia, Iraq, Turkey, Turkmenistan, Afghanistan, Uzbekistan, Bahrain, Oman, Pakistan and India. Dubbed as the 'Persian Napoleon', Nadir Shah proclaimed to have conquered India in 1739, with his entry into Lahore and Delhi. When his scribe challenged the proclamation, interposing that all of India had not been invaded yet, the Shah declared, 'where the chiefs of the people choose to live in this effeminate manner, it will cost me little trouble to conquer them.' The Shah's life and campaigns had a deep impact on Napoleon Bonaparte's military strategies sixty years later. With a horse-blanket for a couch and a saddle for a pillow, the Shah pillaged Asia for nearly two decades, making his Great Persian Empire the blight of local dynasties and the pestilence of refugees. Two such fugitives were the Armenians—Hovsep Émïn (Joseph Emin) and his father—who fled from Hamadan to Baghdad in the 1730s, and thence to India in 1744.

In the early 17th century, the Safavid emperor, Shah Abbas, sacked the Armenian town of Julfa, thus, leading to a mass exodus of Armenians eastwards, into Persia, central Asia and India. The Persian township of Isfahan was given the sobriquet New Julfa by Armenian settlers. The primary objective of Abbas driving away the Armenians was to usurp their monopoly over silk trade. A century marked by religious persecution of Armenians and conflicts resulting from converting them to Catholicism or Islam in Safavid Persia, following the invasion of Aghanistan in 1720s and Nadir Shah's tyranny after 1745, saw hundreds of Armenian families flocking into India. European port settlements in India showed considerable strategic efforts to usher Armenians into the commercial life of the emerging colony, with nearly every East India Company recruiting Armenian intelligencers in its wing to scout trading opportunities in Asia.

Some Armenians had also been operating from London as negotiators of trade and diplomatic relations between the directors of the British East India Company and the Indo-Armenian community. One of them was Khwaja Panos Kalandar. The British administration was initially hostile to the free settlement of Armenians in their Indian enclaves. In 1688, Khwaja Kalandar forged an agreement with the Company to allow equal rights to Armenians as to Britons to settle in the Company's Asian protectorates. They were permitted to buy land and profess their branch of Christianity. In return, the Armenians promised to use British vessels in promoting their own trade between South Asia, the Middle East and Europe. They were also agreeable to promoting British commercial interests in Asia by exploiting their influence with local princes and nawabs. Eight years later, Khwaja Kalandar died in London. However, the political pact he had settled with the British for the Armenian community continued well after the Battle of Plassey. Following that trail of the spillikins of imperial history, shaped by the bizarre expanse of traffic between Westminster and Howrah in the 18th century, Emin arrived in London. Here, at St James' Park, on that afternoon in 1756, he walked into the young Irishman, who was now a solicitor. After diffidently inquiring who he was, Emin was told: 'Sir, my name is Edmund Burke, at your service. I am a runaway son from my father, as you are.'[2]

Emin and Britain were yet to recognise the radical reputation that Burke's name was capable of. After their meeting, Emin and Burke entered a lifelong correspondence and everlasting friendship. Their bond reinforced Burke's growing inquisitiveness over Indian matters, and Emin's desire for English education. The latter, in his early life, had often been cautioned by his friends and 'admonished not to open his mouth in praise of the English; but he could not help it.' When he was eighteen, Emin's father gave him the option of learning French, Portuguese or English, of which he chose the last. He studied at Mr Parrent's English School in Calcutta, where he was enchanted by English manners and the English language, its democratic ideals of freedom from oppression and slavery as he saw them, and the English celebrations he would later witness during the American War of Independence. In the exploration of this utopic English spirit, the Armenian spent thirty-five years of his life, essayed in his book *The Life and Adventures of Joseph Émin* (1792). It was published when he was sixty-six. He had managed to acquire many powerful friends in that journey. Drafts of his work were sent to Mrs Montagu, Warren Hastings and Sir William Jones—who made copious corrections and suggestions on Emin's style of panegyric, grammar and orthography. Through his literary work, Emin hoped to be accepted as a naturalised English speaker, although he was well-versed in Armenian, Persian, Turkish, Portuguese, French and Bengali literary conventions. He paid £50 for the publication of his book in London, to which there were seventy-three subscribers. Four-fifths of them were European, including five women.

Back in the 1740s, when Emin migrated with his family from the Middle East to Calcutta, it was a great deliverance from the Mahomedans and Christian evangelists of Persia and Afghanistan. Emin's tale began in 1722, with the siege of Hamadan by Ahmad Pasha, the governor of Baghdad, during which 60,000 Persian Muslims were butchered. The blood of 800 Armenians also stained the apses of the city's churches. Over the next thirty years, the provinces of Hamadan and Baghdad were continually besieged by Turks and Persians. In the midst of battle and terror, Emin lost his mother and brother to ordinary diseases, while he lived a charmed life, barely escaping being killed by Turks. He finally fled with some members of his family to India, where they joined about 4,000 Armenians there, precariously surviving between numerous European and Indian power-zones. Emin first reached Cannanoor, thence to Cochin, Surat and finally Calcutta, where he found his father selling small merchandise goods. Emin's father and uncles had been visiting Bengal since the 1720s. His family had suffered losses of over ₹110,000 at Basra followed by three subsequent trade losses for his father in Bengal. His ships were seized by Commodore Griffin of the Royal Navy, due to suspicions of his allying with French interests. When Emin visited London to represent his father's case at the King's Bench, he found many other Armenians being abused for allegedly siding with the enemy.

Even before Emin landed in Calcutta, Armenians had had a long presence in the city. During Akbar's reign, they were exempted from taxes on the merchandise they traded with the Persian Gulf. In the 16th century, they settled in Surat (Gujarat), and in Chinsurah (West Bengal) in the late 17th century. In 1665, they were allowed to form a settlement in Saidabad, in the Murshidabad district of Bengal, after a royal *farmaan* issued by Aurangzeb which adjusted the duties on two Armenian trade items—piece goods and raw silk—at 3.5 per cent. Both Surat and Murshidabad assumed robust identities as towns of silk-crafts due to these early modern Armenian settlements. Armenians in Calcutta, as well as in other port cities such as Dhaka, distinguished themselves from other migrant trading communities in their singular talents 'to create networks of trust, shared information and mutual support based upon the fact that they were a distinctive ethnic and religious minority.'[3]

A thoroughfare—Armenian Street; a neighbourhood—Armanitola; and a riverside junction—Armani Ghat, came up in Calcutta, due to rituals of loading and offloading goods from the Armenian vessels connecting to Persia, Turkey and China. The Armenian Ghat was a key to Calcutta's urbanisation. The first ticket reservation room of the East Indian Railway Company was situated here between 1854 and 1857. The Calcutta Tramway Company, opened in 1873, ran a metre-gauge horse-drawn tram service between Sealdah and Armenian Ghat until 1902. The *ghat* was built in 1734 by an Armenian, Manvel Hazaar Maliyaan, also known as Huzoorimal. He had also helped build a tank at the city's *baitakkhana*, the Armenian Church, and a bathing site near Kalighat. From then till the end of the 19th century, Armenians in India numbered from anything between 5,000 and 25,000 according to various English or French records. At the turn of the century, there were about 1,000 Armenians in Calcutta alone—greater than one-fourth of the population of British settlers in the city who numbered about 3,200. An elderly member of the Calcutta Armenian Community observed during his visit to the city, in 1934, that there were not less than 3,600 Armenians living there at the time, largely engaged in coal mining, jute industry and construction works. After 1947, most of them left for America, Britain and Australia.

Armenians felt no pangs while changing their names and converting their faiths as a commercial strategy. A noted Armenian, Khoja Wajid, also referred to as the 'merchant prince' of Bengal, was the son of Mhamet Faziel, who had espoused Islam in India. He negotiated with Indian nawabs both for the Dutch and the British. For the former, he was a Moor or Muslim; to the latter, an Armenian. Both Faziel and Wajid held business transactions with the French and the Dutch, with ships trading with Mocha and Basra. As a century of Armenian immigrants were *uberised* in India, many of them acquired great stations in the history of the various East India Companies in Bengal. Some prominent names were Agha Nazar, who established the Armenian Church in Calcutta, in 1724, while working as an agent for other Armenian merchants in Bengal; Avak di Aratoon, who worked in Calcutta as an agent for merchants in the city as well as in Basra; Khachik di Khojamal, who operated between Calcutta and Isfahan; and Khoja Petrus Aratoon, a leading merchant in 18th-century Bengal, who maintained close links with Saidabad and the Mughal durbar in Murshidabad. Aratoon's two brothers were Khoja Barseek Aratoon and Khoja Gregory Aratoon. Barseek operated from Saidabad, as a salt merchant. Gregory rose as a textile merchant in Hugli to a commander-in-chief in the army of Mir Qasim, the second Nawab of Bengal installed by the British after the Battle of Plassey.

The pivotal role of the Armenians, Petrus Aratoon in particular, in Robert Clive's victory at Plassey cannot be overemphasised. In 1756, anticipating French and Dutch movements in Bengal, the British began reinforcing their troops at Fort William. This enraged Siraj ud-Daulah, the last independent Nawab of Bengal. He attacked the Fort and the neighbouring church and, on June 26, 1756, the British forces surrendered to Siraj ud-Daulah. Before attacking the British troops in Calcutta, Siraj had taken over the British settlement in Cossimbazar, near Murshidabad, and captured several British officers, including William Watts and a young Warren Hastings. Besides the Dutch—who were now friendlier with the British than in the previous century and who garrisoned the Fort's evacuees for the next six months—Petrus Aratoon provisioned the English Company after the fall of the Fort and the Black Hole of Calcutta. Aratoon was later placed in the direct employ of Clive and Company, as a confidential agent during the negotiations with Mir Jaffar for the overthrow of Siraj ud-Daulah and the Conspiracy of Plassey. A year ago, for Clive, Hastings and the rest of the Company, Plassey had been a mirage. But for Petrus Aratoon secretly supplying 'them for about six months— during the interval between the tragedy of the Black Hole and the arrival of the Army of Retribution from Madras—with boat-loads of provisions from Calcutta,'[4] the histories of Bengal, India and

Britain would have been dramatically different. Had it not been for the humane Armenians, wrote an eminent Armenian historian, 'British fugitives at Fulta might have been starved to surrender.'[5] The Fort William rebuilt into a mosque by Siraj would have remained so, and Calcutta would have been his Alinagar for times to come. Petrus Aratoon was later made a member of the East India Company's Council in Madras. With that he turned into a putative ambassador for the Armenian community in Bengal, henceforth characterised by their philanthropy, piety and steadfast loyalty to British imperial interests.

Plassey was a watershed for modern London, consummating mixed interests of Indian courtiers, domestic merchants, banking agencies and foreign fleets that amalgamated to conspire the new triumphs of the City of London and the Bank of England with the total decimation of Mughal and Muslim dynasties in India. In this new cesspit of imperial and military concentrations, Armenian settlers milked the tide of warring monopolies. They were able to operate alongside modern joint-stock European companies. The 17th and 18th-century imperial interactions were the ages of partnership and regulated conflict. Within that fold, Armenians trained themselves to be willing mercantile subjects affiliated to the goodwill of more than one East India entity at a time. Plodding on with their own stock, the Armenians were clearing the way for new corporate structures of European trade and settlement in 18th and 19th-century India. Besides an imperial Calcutta, that was shaped by them, the lustful lungs of Britain were also breathing their blood's toil.

When Emin first met Burke, Siraj ud-Daulah was a young man of twenty-three, yet to be spoiled by the recklessness of youth. He sat on the throne of Bengal after the demise of his grandfather Ali Vardi Khan. The encounter between Emin and Burke, on one hand, and the siege of Calcutta or Plassey, on the other, were much more than mere coincidences. The friendship between Burke and Emin terminated only with their lives. Burke's intense interest in matters of English rule over the Indian empire 'was first excited by his acquaintance with the brave and high-minded Armenian.'[6] Burke's growing penchant for imperial politics, along with the contemporaneity of the plunder at Plassey, made the history of British Bengal all the more imperative to the annals of Little Bengal in London. With the connivance of Siraj's uncle, Mir Jaffar, and the Armenian merchant, Khoja Wajid, Clive's victory would have appropriately compensated for England's loss of America, which came twenty years later. Overnight, and by no virtue of a judicious or tactical attack, England came to reign over a population to whose geography, cultures or religions even Europe was oblivious at the time.

> It was Plassey which made England the greatest Muhammadan power in the world; Plassey which forced her to become one of the main factors in the settlement of the burning Eastern question; Plassey which necessitated the conquest and colonisation of the Cape of Good Hope, of the Mauritius, the protectorship over Egypt; Plassey which gave to the sons of her middle classes the finest field for the development of their talent and industry the world has ever known; to her aristocracy unrivalled opportunities for the display of administrative power; to her merchants and manufacturers customers whose enormous demands almost compensate for the hostile tariffs of her rivals, and, alas! even of her colonies; to the skilled artisan remunerative employment; to her people generally a noble feeling of pride in the greatness and glory of the Empire of which a little island in the Atlantic is the parent stem, Hindustan the noblest branch; it was Plassey which, in its consequences, brought consolation to that little island for the loss of America, to her children the sense of responsibility, of the necessity of maintaining a great position, the conviction of which underlies the thought of every true Englishman.[7]

Mir Jaffar's traitorous plan was to humidify Siraj ud-Daulah's artillery and infantry. The Bengal army, of about 60,000 soldiers,

300 cannons and 300 elephants, outnumbered twenty times Clive's 3,000 men. The former simply ended up deserting or surrendering. The English army suffered a negligible casualty of seven European and sixteen native soldiers—fewer than any battle of such titanic stakes had ever seen, or is ever likely to. It was a victory to be least proud of, lost by soldiers who did not fight, and won by generals or *subedars* not exactly heroic. The English navy and army were each paid a tribute of £275,000 (about £32 million in today's value). Between 1757 and 1760, the Company received from Mir Jaffar a sum of £3 million (about £308 million in today's currency). Clive's own *jagir* proceeding from the Plassey plunder was estimated at £34,567 (£3.5 million in today's currency).

Clive had grown up as a mafioso of teenage ruffians in Shropshire, extorting pennies and fruits from merchants for the service of not damaging their property. When he joined the East India Company as a writer in Madras, his annual salary was £5. When he returned to England in 1767, he had written upon his name the epithet 'Clive of India', and for the British Empire an annual trade revenue of £4 million, more massive than any other European kingdom. Following a peerage in Ireland, he purchased seats for himself and his father in the House of Lords, where he filibustered with the heat of his Bengali loot. His County Clare estate was renamed 'Plassey' for the new Baron Clive of Plassey in the Kingdom of Ireland, who never visited. Clive's return to England compelled the Whig politician and author Horace Walpole to lament how machinations of the Company had 'starved millions in India by monopolies and plunder, and almost raised a famine at home by the luxury occasioned by their opulence, till the poor could not purchase bread.'[8]

Joseph Emin was loyally wedded to British imperialism, and believed that Plassey was a righteous acquisition. As the Eastern exile turned his gaze towards English forts flanked by cannon throwers and marvelously attired soldiers, English ships fanning the far seas and English technology in every dimension of science, commerce and the arts, he realised instinctively that the English were a race born to rule. Britain was for Emin a resurgence of the glories of the older Safavid dynasty, his oneiric childhood in Hamadan, and the opulence of Isfahan. He was convinced all along that the British would soon conquer India, and with the benefits of their civilisation he would become a crusader of his beloved Armenia. Emin's father refused to pay for his permit to sail to England. After several remonstrations, Emin acquired permission from an English captain to be employed on a ship, for 15s., during his passage to England, loading cargoes of rice, redwood, turmeric and saltpetre, or cleaning the ship and occasionally tying ropes. He arrived at Wapping, in August 1751, with 'four shirts and four coarse drawers to wear in all weather.'[9] Emin spent his wages on tuition at Mr Middleton's Academy for Boys in Bishopsgate, while he also worked as a servant in the neighbourhood. Unable to manage the fees for very long, he took up bricklaying work in Drury Lane and as an unskilled labourer for a grocer in the City of London. He even signed up for indentured labour in Jamaica, but withdrew his papers soon after. When his master went bankrupt, Emin tried his hand as a porter and a copying-clerk for an attorney. Failing at both, he was stranded on the streets of London. When his father came to know of his destitution, he offered him a loan of £60 to secure his passage back to Calcutta. Emin refused.

During his early days in London, Emin stayed at a lodge in Wapping, run by a Swedish family, at a weekly rent of 1 shilling. He had fallen in love with the maidservant of the lodging, a woman called Sally, whom he considered to be an angel. Since she was married to a sailor, he circumscribed his affections to mere siblinghood. Emin's wanderings led him to the Armenian jewel merchant Stephenus Cogigian at the Royal Exchange, as well as other Armenians; but he consciously distanced himself from them as well as from Catholics Frenchmen, Jews and Muslims. Since Cogigian was also a Catholic convert, Emin saw little of him, being all too alert to the inferior place of Catholics and French in English society. He even thought Cogigian resembled Shylock, 'the avaricious Jew in *The Merchant of*

Venice.' Ironically, Emin was taken for a Frenchmen by one of his employers. When told he was an Armenian, the employer mistook him again, this time for a German: 'Germans and Armenians are all alike,' he said, 'as long as you are not a Frenchman.'[10]

One Sunday afternoon, at St James' Park, Emin saw an American lawyer, by the name of Bodley, whom he had met in Calcutta. Accompanying him was Edmund Burke. Emin could not muster the courage to speak with the lawyer. He came up to Burke, instead, who patiently heard the tale of the fugitive and took him to his lodgings in Fleet Street above Pope's Head. He offered Emin half a guinea, to which the wretched Armenian returned him his entire savings of three-and-half guineas. He told Burke even if he was offered a thousand pounds, he would gladly exchange it 'if you will continue your kind notice of me, that is all I want; and I shall value it more than a Prince's treasure.'[11] Propping an issue of the *Tatler* into Emin's hands, Burke agreed to be his friend. He brought more books to Emin, and introduced him to William Burke, for whom the Armenian began copying manuscripts. Emin also copied Burke's own writings, including the *Vindications of Natural Society* and *On the Sublime and the Beautiful* (1756–57). Although Burke was three years younger to Emin, he became an avuncular figure in the Armenian's life, giving him literary and philosophical guidance, as well as joining him over political gossip, drinks and chess.

Emin also formed acquaintances with the Dukes of Northumberland and Cumberland. His candour was hard to resist for the English elites. In a letter to her husband in July 1757, Mrs Montagu wrote, 'I had a letter from Mr Emin that the Duke of Cumberland had received him in the most gracious manner, and he is so pleased, I believe he thinks one more step will put him on the Persian throne. It is happy to be born of a hoping constitution.'[12] The description walked a tightrope between sarcasm and endearment. Emin was of course not unaware. He pigheadedly chased that segment of London society which would have had an abiding interest in his exotic legends and Oriental inflexions, just enough to keep alive the occasional invocation of his name. The Duke of Northumberland even invited him to write an autobiographical essay on his life and the political climate of Persia and Armenia, which he then circulated among 300 British elites. With the bearings of Northumberland and Cumberland, Emin went on to receive training at the Royal Military Academy at Woolwich, and joined the English Army. The British painter Arthur Pond was commissioned by Lord George Lyttleton to paint a portrait of Emin. It was preserved at Hagley Hall, the home of the Lyttleton family in Worcestershire, until 1925, when it was destroyed by a fire. Emin was also a part of an expedition to the port of St Malo at Brittany, where he fought against the French. As an international diplomat at Georgia, he presented Prince Heraclius with a proposal to emancipate the condition of his fellow Armenians. In 1772, Clive recommended a military promotion for the Armenian at Burke's solicitation. Hastings, the first Governor General of Bengal, had ably filled in the shoes of his predecessor, by robbing the state, waging wars with the Marathas and Hyder Ali, and stage-managing the shocking execution of Maharajah Nandakumar of Birbhum. In 1788, Hastings was brought to trial by the Whigs. His impeachment was led by Edmund Burke and Richard Sheridan, in nothing less than a grand social spectacle, at Westminster Hall. In a letter to Emin, Burke confessed that his views on India were not popular in the Parliament. 'Who could have thought,' he wrote, 'the day I met you in St James' Park, that this kingdom would rule the greater part of India? But kingdoms rise and pass away—emperors are captive and blinded—pedlars become emperors.'[13]

Burke's letter reached Emin in 1789. That was four years after Emin returned to Calcutta and had written to Burke for the first time in over a decade. Enervated and dejected after the Regency Crisis and the acquittal of Warren Hastings, Burke was now turning to a higher wisdom—the virtue of that friendship that had occasioned an Asiatic from Calcutta to fight for Armenian freedom, inspired by the ideals of the English race. With an inglorious retirement in prospect, Burke consoled his friend and himself in the hope of making 'the burden of the English Government over the people of India a little more tolerable,'[14] even as the English Company went about annexing Buxar, Seringapatam, Mysore and the Malabar.

Scene II

The Orient Arrives

After Plassey, the almost exclusive traffic of Indian servants, delegates, scholars or retiring British nabobs from Bengal brought to London a distinctly Oriental flair. In the 18th century, thousands of servants were shipped to the city from India. While in the first half of the century, many of them came from the Coromandel Coast, in the latter half, most of them were from Bengal. Almost all were Muslims, with the exception of a few Catholics, and almost no Hindus.

It was also the time when the first travelogue was written by an Indian upon visiting England. Its author, Mirza Sheikh Ihtishamuddin, arrived in London in 1766. Ihtishamuddin was born in a family of *muftis*, who hailed from the town of Chakdah, a neighbourhood now known as Kazipara, in the Nadia district of Bengal. His elder brother, Ghulam Mohiuddin, worked as a *mufti* in the court of Ali Vardi Khan. Ihtishamuddin began his career as a scribe, in the court of Mir Jaffar, moving on to the court of Mir Qasim. In 1762, he joined the East India Company as a Persian scribe. He was a member of the camp of John Carnac during the Battle of Buxar in 1764, when, under the command of Hector Munro, the East India Company defeated the combined forces of Mir Qasim, Nawab of Awadh and Shah Alam II. The British Army, with a strength of 7,000–10,000, outflanked a combined military strength of over 40,000 Indian soldiers. Unlike Plassey, this was achieved without the aid of traitorous generals and *subedars* in the Indian camp.

After the battle, Ihtishamuddin joined the court of Shah Alam, as a scribe for the Persian drafts of the Treaty of Allahabad. It was this document with which the Mughal Emperor was to hand out the *diwani* of Bengal to the British. Having written off his empire to the Company, Shah intended to return to Delhi. However, the British were loath to provide him the necessary military entourage. Clive asserted that only the King of England could permit the Company to oblige the Shah's remonstrations. The Shah sent as his delegates to London, Captain Archibald Swinton, a former Company official, and Ihtishamuddin, as his transcriber. The Mirza was paid an honorarium of ₹4,000 for his foreign mission, which would soon prove to be 'much more onerous than he had expected.'[1] Shah Alam sent a dossier for King George III, with an offering of ₹100,000, numerous gifts and souvenirs and a letter written in Persian pleading the King to restore him to the throne of Hindustan at Delhi, with an army of 5,000 men trained for war. Clive did not want the letter to reach the King, although he could not officially prevent the emperor from sending his delegates to London. Through the directors of the Company in London, and officials at the Calcutta Government, he tried to delay the imperial mission. After a year's adjournment, in January 1766, Swinton, Ihtishamuddin and his attendant, Muhammad Muqim, set sail for England aboard a French vessel, from Hijli in East Midnapur. In London, Ihtishamuddin realised that Clive had intercepted the letter from the Shah, back in India itself. The imperial mission was a catastrophe, *ab initio*, without any possibility of meeting the King. Swinton too had been an accomplice in Clive's conspiracy. Even the *nazr* of a lakh of rupees, that King George was to receive, mysteriously disappeared in the Company's transactions in Bengal.

Left to his own ministrations in *vilayet*, Mirza Ihtishamuddin plunged himself into what he did best. While on his journey to London, he began recording his observations on European expertise in navigation, and the paraphernalia of compasses, maps and charts. He also witnessed a scene of smuggling of silver, gold and textiles from the Company's cargo at Nantes in France, where his ship had halted. Swinton was a party to this crime as well, and French customs officials too were amply rewarded for their connivance. Ihtishamuddin did not know English, which made him dependent on Swinton for his communication. Throughout the journey and his stay in London, the Mirza stuck to a halal diet and was averse to give up his turban and shawl. That made him all too conspicuous on the streets of London. The English knew well about the kingdom of Bengal, but only through legends and memoirs. They, therefore, expected a traveller to behave and appear with a touch of the dramatic. He chose to parade accordingly, through the streets of London and indeed through his own narration of how the character of a *munshi* was perceived by Georgians. It was an aesthetic pact of mutual curiosity between himself and the '*franghees*', with which to glorify his own status.

The English had never seen an Indian *munshi* before, but only lascars from Chittagong and Jahangirnagar, and were consequently unacquainted with the clothes and manners of an Indian gentleman. They took me for a great man of Bengal, perhaps the brother of a *nawab*, and came from far and near to see me. Whenever I went abroad crowds accompanied me, and people craned their heads out of windows and gazed at me in wonder. Children and adolescents took me for a curious specimen and ran into their houses crying, 'Look! Look! A black man is walking down the street!'—at which the elders would rush to the door and stare at me in amazement. Many children and small boys took me for a black devil and kept away in fear. Within a couple of months, everyone in the neighbourhood became friendly. The fear which some had felt vanished completely, and they would now jest with me familiarly. The ladies of the bazaar approached me and, smiling, said, 'Come, my dear, and kiss me!'[2]

Ihtishamuddin triumphed as a colonial historian in smuggling a chameleonesque image of himself. More than the unfolding of history, he was interested in unfolding as history himself. From one moment being taken for a 'black devil' by Londoners around, to the very next he turned himself into someone whose Oriental kiss charmed their days and nights. In his own drama, he was himself the spectacle before the spectacles of *vilayet*. Women tittered with comic relief at his appearance during dances, as Ihtishamuddin ravished them visually from a distance. 'How ironic,' he mused, 'that I, who had gone there to enjoy a spectacle, became a spectacle myself.'[3] The Mirza's candid confessions added more credibility to his attitude. London's street lamps, rituals of garbage disposal, supply systems of clean drinking water, windmills, spinning mills, public theatres, the progressive rhythms of metropolitan life that tolled away in the unison of hundreds of public clocks and the unanimity of watches, stupefied him. From scene to scene, he carried the torch for the lofty pillars of European enlightenment just as he had for the 'emporium of beauty' of Englishwomen at the balls.[4]

In British eyes, Ihtishamuddin seemed to rise in comparison with lascars. He came to be respected as a man of noble birth. Women on the streets begged him for flying kisses. His hosts even suggested to him to settle down in London as a Persian Professor, and take up an English wife. The appreciation that came by his way inspired his perambulations around London. At Vauxhall Gardens in Kennington, Ihtishamuddin was smitten by Francis Hayman's painting *Lord Clive Meeting Mir Jaffar* (1760). The widely available inexpensive books, periodicals and journals of the Age of Reason also had a deep impact on him. The Mirza was affected by the printed words of modern London in ways similar to his contemporary, Joseph Emin. Ihtishamuddin found the English to be much more democratic and systematic in their expenditure on luxurious lifestyles, while also being more advanced in science and in religion, than the nations of the East. He was convinced that England's riches were distributed as public wealth and welfare. 'Worldly riches ought not to be,' he concluded after seeing what he believed to be London at large, 'appropriated for eating and drinking alone, or for leading a luxurious life, or for collecting together a great number of women, or for sitting and viewing dances night and day,' as the elites of 'Hindoostan' were accustomed to.[5] Ihtishamuddin's admiration of British institutions and culture was not merely for its perceived superiority to Indian races, but also to the French. When the Mirza visited Calais in France, he wrote 'that the whole conversation of the French was an attempt to display their own superiority, and without any good reason they abused other castes.'[6]

Ihtishamuddin was impressed to see how Europeans immersed themselves in education, commerce and travel, until the age of forty, before enjoying luxurious retirements. By contrast, the men of Hindustan, he lamented, married young and went about in pursuit of employment, leaving their wives behind to compose poems of grief and despair in separation. The Mirza 'imbibed something of the new bourgeois morality that was becoming dominant among the growing middle classes of Britain in the second half of the 18th century.'[7] Although he was immediately persuaded that Britain's sciences and religion had contributed greatly to its emerging supremacy over the other nations of the world, he wrote almost nothing in his book of the conquest of Bengal or the presence of the English Company. Even as far back as then, the Mirza was seeking what constituted—or would go on to constitute—the identity of an Indian diaspora in England. The great madrassa at Oxford enchanted him, and upon seeing the model universe in the University's physics laboratory, he shuddered at the thought of the proximity that Europe had achieved with the higher truths of the universe. Although never shy of conceding the backwardness of India, he ensured that he was not perceived as inferior in any way. He brazenly challenged professors at Oxford that even Sir William Jones was no match his talent for Persian, nor could Christian clerics override him in a debate on Islam and the vindication of polygamy.

Ihtishamuddin's *Travels* were completed around the same time as the impeachment of Sir Elijah Impey and Warren Hastings.

Charges against the latter included the judicial killing of Maharajah Nuncomar (Bengal's collector of taxes), supporting the Rohilla War, and misappropriation of the state treasury while sucking dry the once-infinite wealth of Bengal. Hastings was seen as a supreme model of unscrupulousness and lack of accountability in public wealth. Drunk with the ambition of political fame, he may well have been a tyrant of tyrants, but to be a swindler was way beneath his salt. He once admitted to the Supreme Council of Calcutta that the 'desire for applause in public life'[8] was his guiding principle. And, he pursued it feverishly. On his way to London, in 1785, he would be finishing writing his defence on *The State of Bengal*. Burke had chosen to make an example out of Hastings to prove to Britain that he had not entered politics to mint blood-money, unlike the nabobs of the Raj. Intent on creating a new model for British statesmen in India, 'Burke cast Hastings as his antitype.'[9]

If Burke wanted Hastings to speedily withdraw from India, a namesake of Hastings went on to prophesy the withdrawal of the British Empire itself. Three decades from the time of the impeachment, this Hastings, the Second Earl of Moira, chipped in with his two cents. 'A time, not very remote, will arrive when England will, on sound principles of policy, wish to relinquish the domination which she has gradually and unintentionally assumed over this country.'[10] Blissfully ignorant of such a possibility, Ihtishamuddin was tipping the final dots on his travel account, which would be later translated from Persian as *Shigurf Namah-e-Vilayet* (1827) in Urdu, *Bilayetnama* (1981) in Bengali, and *Wonders of Vilayet* (2001) in English. Although the Mirza had returned to India in 1769, his oral tales and the manuscript tided along for the next sixty years. That is when he was first translated by James Edward Alexander and Munshi Shumsher Khan into Urdu. His experiences were now the leitmotifs to understanding England and its customs—a private handbook to many an Indian envoy visiting the imperial city until the reign of Victoria.

In the Deccan, at the court of Peshwa Raghunathrao, a small band of courtiers still bowed before their powerless hero. Having been betrayed by his own family and ousted from the Maratha Confederacy, the Peshwa was now a dethroned ruler. In March 1775, during the outbreak of the First Anglo-Maratha War, he had signed the Treaty of Surat with the Bombay Government, which was to reinstate his position as Peshwa, protected by 2,500 troops. This came at the cost of conceding the territories of Bassein and Salsette, a pledge of ₹600,000, and an annual tribute of ₹1,875,000 to the Company, as part of revenues from Surat and Bharuch. Ironically, both the Marathas and Warren Hastings were opposed to this treaty. Instead, the Marathas recognised as their king Sawai Madhavrao, the infant son of Peshwa Narayanrao who was assassinated in 1773. Even from the Company's ranks, the only visible support for Raghunathrao came from the Governor of Bombay, Henry Oxendon. Hastings derecognised the Treaty of Surat, and sent Colonel Upton from the Supreme Council of Bengal to Pune, to sign the Treaty of Purandhar with Maratha ministers. It retracted the position of Raghunathrao as the Peshwa, although the Company itself retained the territories and tributes he had signed off in its name. As soon as he scented the sabotage, Raghunathrao initiated dialogues with the Portuguese and the French, while simultaneously contemplating seeking the help of King George III, to challenge the hegemony of the corrupt Bengal administration over the regional politics of Bombay. Like Shah Alam, the dethroned Peshwa decided to send a delegation to London. Hanumantrao, a Brahmin scholar from Rajapur, was chosen as his ambassador, and Maniar Ratanji, a Parsi gentleman, and his son Cursetji Maniar, as the ambassador's assistants.

Like Ihtishamuddin, Hanumantrao knew no English. And just like the Mirza, the Brahmin ambassador continued observing strict dietary and sartorial practices. The delegation left India in 1780 and reached London in 1781. Raghunathrao's letter addressed to King George was handed over by Hanumantrao to the directors of the Company in London. It solicited an enquiry into the Bengal administration under Hastings. The Peshwa's delegation

commanded the immediate attention of Edmund Burke. Sir
Charles William Rouse Boughton, a former administrator of the
Company in India, also jumped into the controversy. Having
returned to England in 1778, he was elected a member of the
House of Commons just the year before Hanumantrao arrived
in London. The delegation was also abetted by Harry Verelst,
a former soldier in the Battle of Plassey and later a governor
of Bengal under Clive. During Hanumantrao's sojourn, Verelst
was serving as a director of the East India Company. The
need for the enquiry was also exacerbated by recent reports of
rampant corruption. These included the much-publicised case
of Sir Thomas Rumbold, Governor of Madras, who had deserted
his post in 1780 and packed off to London with a fortune of
£700,000, leaving the Carnatic vulnerable to famines and
invasions. Another was Hastings' own subordinate at the Calcutta
Supreme Council, Richard Barwell, who too had amassed a
wealth of £400,000 under the watch of the Governor General.
Besides that, the bevy of powerful supporters that Hanumantrao
galvanised compelled the Secretary of State Earl of Hillsborough
and Company directors in London to study Raghunathrao's
petition even more seriously than they would have otherwise.
Burke, well-known by now for his Indian sympathies, hosted
Hanumantrao at his Beaconsfield greenhouse. Here the Brahmin
was given the peace and comfort to prepare himself to defend the
overthrown Peshwa and the Maratha confederacy, in the British
Parliament, where he would be turned into a key agent in the
prosecution of Hastings.

An account of Hanumantrao's stay at Burke's greenhouse in
Beaconsfield was given by Burke himself to Mary Shackleton, the
daughter of his old friend Abraham Shackleton. Miss Shackleton
reproduced it and it was later included in the book of Burke's
Correspondences. Notwithstanding the help of the Maniars, and
also that of a servant, Hanumantrao cooked his own dinner. It
was closely guarded from even the sight of meat or wine. He was
used to eating on the floor, wearing almost nothing waist up. If
someone came within visible distance during his dinner, he would

instantly discard the food in keeping with his rigid Brahminical rituals, which prohibited the presence of a non-Brahmin during meals. 'Burke was unusual in treating with respect Hindu practices,'[11] which were otherwise regarded in England as obnoxious superstitions. All the same, Hanumantrao formed very affectionate bonds with Sir Joshua Reynolds and Burke. He would often compliment their visage, asking his interpreter to tell them that their looks had sustained him, despite their alien tongue, like a rhinocerous feeds her young ones by gazing upon them. Touted as a humble servant of the English race and the oppressed millions of India, Hanumantrao's testimony in the Parliament was used to prepare the case for the impeachment of Hastings, four years later. His account was taken for 'the most authentic Source of Information concerning the Usages and Religion of the Hindoos.'[12] Rouse himself acted as an interpreter to Hanumantrao during the impeachment of Hastings. *Reports from the House of Commons* described him as following:

> ... his Name is *Honwontrow*—That he comes from Poonah, a Gentoo Government, of which Sittarab is the Capital—That it is governed by the Peshwah, who is a Brahmin—That he is come to England with Letters to the King, and the East India Company—That he is a Brahmin—That his Caste, as well as all others, is obliged to observe particular Rules and Modes of Life—That the Object of Worship is alike to all Casts; but that there are many Sects and Distinctions, each of which has its peculiar Rules—That there are Four principal Castes; and within there, there are a great many others; and that it is criminal for any Gentoo, to transgress the Rules of his particular Caste—That he may lose his Caste entirely, or, according to the Nature of the Offence, it may admit of Expiation.[13]

The account went on for several pages, including the battles of Bengal, northern India, the Maratha wars and treaties, besides traditions and rituals of the Hindus and Brahmins and the casualty to Hindu lives during the 18th-century European conquests of India. The trial of Hastings provided great publicity both for Hanumantrao as well as his country in England. The Parliament investigated particularly into Hanumantrao's testimony against Hastings in the execution of Maharajah Nuncomar. The imminent impeachment of the Governor General was meanwhile a matter of great disconsolation in Calcutta. It was later documented by Phoebe Gibbes in her novel, *Hartly House, Calcutta* (1789). One of its characters, Sophia Goldburne, writes to her friend Arabella about the departure of Hastings from Calcutta.

> The Company it is affirmed by those who appear well informed, will, by this event, be deprived of a faithful and able servant; the poor, of a compassionate and generous friend; the genteel circles, of their best ornament; and Hartly House, of a revered guest. A more uniform good man, or so competent a judge of advantages of the people, he will not leave behind him; nor possibly can a successor be transmitted, of equal information or abilities.[14]

The mood in London, however, was far from sympathetic towards Hastings. The proceedings featuring Hanumantrao contributed greatly to William Pitt's India Act of 1784, which ended the East India Company's administrative monopoly over the subcontinent. The Act came as a personal injury to Hastings, who while presiding over the last meeting of the Supreme Council in Calcutta, in February 1785, knew that his days in government were numbered. The Company's political sovereignty in India would now remain subservient to the British Government, until entirely subsumed into the auspices of the Crown in 1858. In the Parliament's last session of 1785, Burke pledged to prosecute Hastings, who had arrived in London earlier that year. Before Hanumantrao's departure, the Company's directors hastily prepared an official response to Raghunathrao, with some ambiguous assurances. Hanumantrao sent his Parsi assistants to collect the letter. Finding the letter sealed, the father and son demanded to see the contents therein, but were refused. What was meant to be a peaceful rendezvous turned confrontational, as the envoys were thrown out of the Court.

Burke, that time-honored comrade-in-arms, once again leaped to the rescue. He urged the Secretary of State and the directors to offer their 'National Hospitality' to the delegation from India 'and to send them away in good humour.'[15] Burke also managed to elicit from King George himself, a most favourable response to the three Indian men in England—presents amounting to about £270, and the acknowledgement that 'nothing can be more shameful than the conduct of the East India directors towards the Agents.'[16] In addition, the delegation was offered £1200 for the return journey to India, which they set sail for on August 15, 1781. The letter from the East India Company to Raghunathrao was, however, delayed by a year, along with the presents sent by the King. Raghunathrao would go on to thank Burke profusely for the magnanimity he had shown to the delegation. Statesmanly as ever, the Irish solicitor, who had by now turned into a philosopher, wrote back with utmost tact and diplomacy.

Hummond Row has done me the honour of being my guest for a very short time; and I endeavoured to make my place as convenient as any of us are able to do, for a person so strictly observant as he was of all the rules and ceremonies of the religion to which he was born, and to which he strictly conformed, often at the manifest hazard of his life. We have, however, sir, derived one benefit from the instructions he has given us relative to your ways of living; that whenever it shall be thought necessary to send Gentoos of high caste to transact any business in this kingdom, on giving proper notice, and on obtaining proper license from authority, for their coming, we shall be enabled to provide for them in such a manner, as greatly to lessen the difficulties in our intercourse, and to render as tolerable as possible to them a country where there are scarcely six good months in a year. The suffering this Gentleman underwent at first was owing to the ignorance not to the unkindness, of this Nation. I am sorry, sir, to inform you that I can give you no sort of hope of your ever obtaining the assistance of the troops you require. It is best at once to speak plainly, when it is not in our power to act. Hummond

Row is a faithful and able servant of yours. And Mamear Parsi
and his son used every exertion to second his. If your affairs have
not succeeded to your wishes, it is no fault of theirs.[17]

Although Hanumantrao had succeeded in causing a minor
upheaval in the British Parliament, Raghunathrao's dream of the
Peshwai would remain unfulfilled. The Treaty of Salbai, signed in
May 1782, consigned him to the life of a pensioner at ₹300,000
annually. Madhavrao II was made the new Peshwa of the Maratha
Confederacy, and under him, the Marathas joined the British in
Mysore—against Hyder Ali, the father of Tipu Sultan—reinforcing
the Company's forces to pillage southern India in yet another gory
decade to follow.

———————

After the impeachment of Hastings, the East India Company
adopted an unofficial policy of turning a blind eye to petitions
by descendants of deposed rulers or nawabs of conquered Indian
territories, for pensions, titles and exemptions. The petitioners in
such cases had to travel to London to present their case before the
Company's directors, who in turn were disinclined to add to the
bulk of piling paperwork. One such petitioner, Mirza Odu-din
Khan, was the son of Maazad Khan, the former Nawab of
Bharuch. English forces had stormed the province in November
1772, under the command of General Wedderburn. In May
1794, the Bombay Government was apprised in a letter from the
Court of Directors in London, of the recent arrival of Odu-din
Khan. The letter went on:

He has delivered a representation to us in his own behalf, and
in the behalf of five other descendants of the said nawab, a copy
of which is enclosed, and we direct that you cause inquiry to be
made into their claim to a house at Surat, and to a duty, said to
have been vested in their family, on all goods imported there,
and that you use your endeavours to procure them such redress

as the nature of the case may require. If you should be perfectly satisfied of the identity of Mirza Odu-din Khan, we have agreed that you shall make him an allowance of ₹200 per month so long as he shall conduct himself to your satisfaction. Should either of the other descendants of the *nawab* of Broach make a similar application to you, we authorise you to grant them a like allowance, provided you shall be satisfied that they are really the descendants of the said nawab. Mirza Odu-din Khan and his two attendants have, during their continuance in England, been subsisted at the company's expense, and we have furnished them with a passage to Bombay in the ship Sir Edward Hughes.[18]

Mirza Odu-din had managed to secure just enough money to travel to London along with his secretary Mustafa Khan and servant Adun Mahomet. He demanded from the Company arrears worth ₹180 million and nearly a million in annual pension. Impressed by the victory milestones of the previous diplomatic missions to London, Odu-din Khan even paid for legal advice from Henry Frederick Thompson. Between March and April 1794, the directors agreed to offer the Mirza foodstuffs for the month of Ramzan, later an accommodation, as well as a daily stipend of 3 guineas plus carriage fare. However, when they realised that Odu-din Khan had every intention of overstaying his welcome, they promptly arranged for his passage back to India, in addition to a grant of £100, on the condition that he take the offer immediately or else all his further grants and petitions would be rejected. The Mirza's existing grants were contingently halved and his carriage allowance invalidated at once. He did not take the insult lying down, and threatened to humiliate the Court of Directors by making public the litany of abominable depredations they had caused to his dynasty.

Fairly alarmed by the Mirza's threats, the directors took to consulting the Board of Control. By summer, the negotiations with the Mirza had shaped into a full-fledged dispute. Just as he was beginning to make his presence turn into a veritable nuisance, Odu-din Khan changed his mind and decided to accept the court's offer. He returned to India with an English servant,

Henry Monmouoth, and even tendered a letter of thanks to the
same directors whom he had earlier sworn to shame and avenge
in London. Odu-din Khan forged an agreement that he and his
brother would each receive an annual pension of ₹2,400 from the
Company, and that he would be compensated with a share of the
percentage of the pensions of his brothers to make up for his own
travel expenses, during his visit to London.

After returning to India in the winter of 1794, Mirza Odu-din
Khan set sail for Europe, along with one of his brothers. In April
1795, from Greece, he intimated to the Company's directors his
intention of visiting London again. The directors warned him
to never contact them again, vouching 400 guineas as the price
for his withdrawal. The Mirza took the offer, and indeed much
else besides. Perturbed by his visit to Europe, the anxiety of his
imminent return, and a procession of other descendant nawabs,
the Company was eventually led to enhance the pensions for the
family. Henceforward, its directors became especially cautious of
Indian delegates or travellers in England, arriving without prior
notice. The traveller and scholar, Mirza Abu Taleb Khan, who was
in London in the early 1800s, was initially mistaken by the directors
as an Indian ambassador come forth to submit a royal petition
before the King. In 1799, Abu Taleb had received an unlikely
offer from a Scotsman, Captain David Thomas Richardson, that
of travelling to Europe. Richardson was a former officer of the
East India Company's Bengal army. Being fluent in Persian and
Hindustani, he had helped establish the Company's staff college
in Barasat, on the outskirts of Calcutta. 'As you are without
employment,' the Captain told Abu Taleb, 'let me request you to
accompany me. The change of scene, and the curiosities you will
meet with in Europe, will disperse the gloom that now hangs over
you. I will undertake to teach you English during the voyage, and
provide for all your wants.'[19] In a world of impoverished lascars and
insufferable diplomats, he was perhaps the first Indian to travel to
England primarily for pleasure. Knowing that full well, Abu Taleb
donned the Oriental minstrel's hat.

Scene III

From an Indian Harem to a London Tavern

In February 1799, Richardson and Abu Taleb left for Cape Town on the Danish ship *Christiana*. From Cape Town, Lady Anne Barnard, a leading socialite, wrote a letter introducing them as her friends to Lord Henry Dundas, the First Viscount of Melville, who was then the Secretary of War in the government of William Pitt, the Younger. She recommended Abu Taleb as 'a Persian chief, a clever agreeable and good man, a man of letters also and far superior to most of the grandees of Indostan—he has the Honour to be a particular friend of Lord Cornwallis and travels chiefly to see the world.'[1] In September, they boarded the *Britannia*, and reached Cork three months later. In his later life, Richardson would be the casualty of a fatal hurricane while returning from England to India, in 1808, aboard *Lord Nelson*. The ship disappeared at sea, leading to the presumed deaths of all its passengers, including Richardson and his family. Before that, the former army man did, however, enjoy twice the pleasures of life, being married to one Violet Oliver while fathering a son with one Sarah Lester. Understandably, Abu Taleb was not a man to remain unaffected by his English benefactor.

———

The East India Company may have planned Abu Taleb's journey to England to use him as a foil in Awadh. Abu Taleb hailed from Lucknow, where his father Haji Mohammad Beg Khan had settled after escaping Persia during the siege by Nadir Shah's army in the late 1740s. Employed in the court of Lucknow, Mohammad Beg Khan rose to become a deputy to Mohammad Kuli, who was a nephew of Awadh's ruler, Safdurjung, and a deputy-governor of the province. After Safdurjung's death, his son and successor to the throne, Shuja-ud-Daulah, ordered the execution of Mohammad Kuli Khan. After losing his chief patron, Haji Mohammad Beg fled to Murshidabad in 1754. Abu Taleb, who was born two years before that, stayed with his mother in Lucknow, until 1766, when they too moved to Murshidabad. After the death of his father, he took up several employments with the East India Company, coming close to Hastings, as well as brushing shoulders with Sir Charles Cornwallis, the commander of the English forces that defeated Tipu Sultan at Seringapatam. At the peak of the Hastings' administration, Abu Taleb became an important emissary in Lucknow, and a noted intelligencer for the Company.

Unlike his predecssors, Abu Taleb was familiar with English customs and even willing to experiment with them, if not wholly adopt. His travelogue on Europe would rival Sake Deen Mahomet's book of *Travels*, which was otherwise the first known book by an Indian author to be written in English. One of the reasons for the popularity of Abu Taleb's *Travels*—although largely modelled on the observations of Joseph Emin and Ihtishamuddin—was that it was translated into English in 1810 by Charles Stewart, a preeminent Professor of Persian at Haileybury College. Despite lacking in powerful endorsers or subscribers, the book created a niche of its own over the long 19th century.

A profligate in his use of language, Abu Taleb included in his book the 'Ode to London,' which was written in imitation of the 14th-century Persian poet, Hafiz. Inevitably, much of its original insobriety may have been watered down in Stewart's prosaic translation.

Henceforward we will devote our lives to London, and its heart-alluring Damsels:

Our hearts are satiated with viewing fields, gardens, rivers, and palaces.

If the Shaikh of Mecca is displeased at our conversion, who cares? May the Temple which has conferred such blessings on us, and its Priests, flourish!

Fill the goblet with wine! If by this, I am prevented from returning
To my old religion, I care not; nay, I am the better pleased.

If the prime of my life has been spent in the service of an Indian Cupid,
It matters not: I am now rewarded by the smiles of the British Fair.

Adorable creatures whose flowing tresses, whether of flaxen or of jetty hue,
Or auburn gay, delight my soul, and ravish all my senses!

Whose ruby lips would animate the torpid clay, or marble statue! Had I a renewal of life, I would, with rapture, devote it to your service!

These wounds of Cupid, on your heart, Taleba, are not accidental: They were engendered by Nature, like the streaks on the leaf of a tulip.[2]

Abu Taleb Khan's holiday in London was ostentatious, to say the least. His accounts of meeting with King George III or Queen Charlotte (the second black queen of England, who hailed from the African branch of the Portuguese royalty) were not very remarkably different from his rendezvous with Englishwomen. If the author could be believed, they often turned up at his residence in Rathbone Place which, although a den of prostitutes, was rendered decorous by his stay. Invariably, he happened to take English hospitality as a bounty exclusively reserved for him. 'Princes, and the Nobility vied with each other in their attention'³ to Abu Taleb Khan, while Englishwomen frequently sent him invitations to the opera, which he was happy to sacrificially distribute among young Englishmen. Meeting the 'handsomest women'⁴ of England made up the Mirza's average days, almost to the point where he was obsessed by them, besides his meetings with distinguished thespians, music connoisseurs, writers, portrait artists, scholars, members of the Royal Society, and so on.

Once, Abu Taleb was overwhelmingly affected by the 'angelic perfections'⁵ of one Miss B. He dedicated three of his odes to her in his poetical volume, *The Mesnevy*. Abu Taleb claimed that during a banquet thrown by the Lord Mayor of London, the Mayoress apparently rose from her seat to welcome him, by way of making a great exception for an Indian. Elsewhere, he found himself luxuriously smitten by the 'angelic charms' of yet another Englishwoman, in his own words, 'one of the greatest beauties in London.'⁶ When the lady tried to converse with him in a private corner, his flattery of her broke all shackles. The fact that he had been overheard and turned into the subject of London gossip, the following day, only made him gloat. How seriously Londoners actually took him did not quite merit investigation. However, Thomas Williamson, a retired captain of the Bengal army, would often remark that Abu Taleb's much flaunted association with the female of the English species was a figment of his regrettably fraudulent imagination.

From how the Mirza looked at Englishwomen, evidently he saw himself as an ambassador in London, in whose honour the city and its women were stockpiled into a social masquerade. Being extremely literal-minded about interpreting body language, to Abu Taleb every female nod was literally as good as a feminine wink. At a public parade in Windsor, he was awestruck by the 'immense multitude of spectators' that had gathered, along with 'five-thousand carriages, filled, both in the inside and on the tops, with handsome women, dressed in their best attire.'⁷ Unable to contain his excitement upon seeing so many of them at once—in a rather indelicate imagery likening them to cattle or poultry—the Mirza declared: 'During the whole of my residence in Europe, I never saw so much beauty assembled as on that day.'[8] The panoply of women in his chronicles, or the liberal canvas he took to frame how they socialised with him, were bewilderingly at odds with the laws that governed daily lives of Englishwomen at the time. Even until the early 19th century, married women in Britain were liable to be beaten by their husbands as a legally permissible *immoderation*. Women were prohibited from travelling without their husbands or chaperones, therefore, from mingling with other men. Without doubt, London was perplexed as to how the Mirza managed to seek out the single ladies with that extraordinary frequency and clinical precision.

From Hampstead to Highgate or from Westminster to Portman Square, Abu Taleb proceeded with his social liaisons, meeting on the way ambassadors, generals and officials (some who had returned from India), and their wives and daughters, of course. In almost one and the same breath, he met the Prince of Wales, London's chimney sweepers and Hindustani women living in the city—either as widows remarried to Englishmen or divorcees, on an alimony—in that order. There was hardly a nobleman, rarely a building and never a social occasion upon which the Mirza failed to leave his impression, even if a very ephemeral one, but not without its immediately gratifying results. Just before he was to attend a charity event at Vauxhall Gardens, the newspapers hailed him as 'Prince Abu Taleb' and 'The Persian Prince'. He mostly travelled free of cost to near and distant parishes in the carriages of the Englishmen he befriended. In the process, he even went up to Windsor, the country residence of the King; the township of Oxford; Blenheim, the seat of the Duke of Marlborough (the future residence of Sir Winston Churchill); thence to Chipping Norton; and eventually to Sezincote, the Indian styled palace of the Cockerell family. For each of these places, he journalled ethnographic accounts, with miscellanies of characters and their chores of sporting and husbandry from rural England. All along, he never failed to make himself the 'hero of his own tale.'[9] King George—on whom he left quite a mark as well—apparently urged his ministers to procure letters of recommendation for the Mirza, addressed to the King's envoys and ambassadors at the courts where he was likely to stay during his return to India.

The naked sinews and arteries of London—as it must have appeared to Abu Taleb in the city's vast refurbishments—came alive before his eyes. In between paying homage to the Bank of England and the London Stock Exchange, and without being discernibly bothered about the larger imperial significance of these structures, the Mirza smugly found himself in the thick of some of the world's biggest engineering innovations. He witnessed the beginnings of the construction of an underwater tunnel between Gravesend and Tilbury—which would be later taken up by Ralph Dodd, in the late 18th century. The project was the inspiration behind the world's first underwater passageway, the Thames Tunnel, built in 1843 between Rotherhithe and Wapping, by Marc and Isambard Kingdom Brunel. Like megalosauruses being reared for the future, the city's dockyards, iron foundries, factories, mills and the stereotypical cheap inns acted as the subterranean world of Abu Taleb's London, exhaling soot, steam and quarantined to the periphery. Far from the satanic din, he enjoyed dwelling in the London of taverns, coffee houses, musical societies, the Royal Society and, indeed, clubs—the Indian Club, to be precise, comprising members from a class of gentlemen who had 'resided for some years in the East.'[10]

For all his soft-headedness, the Mirza was not ignorant of the monopoly of Indian cotton in England around this time. The sight of a spinning engine in London became his unique feast of physics: 'By the turning of one large wheel, a hundred others were put in motion, which spun, at the same time, some thousand threads, of sufficient fineness to make very good muslin.'[11] Amidst the glittering balls and banquets, dissonant noises of the jangling and juggernauting of industrial hardware marked in the mental diaries of travellers Britain's transition from being the cultural and architectural Acropolis to a flourishing Ephesus of engineers and businessmen. What Abu Taleb saw in the effects of automation, the English 'passion for mechanics'[12] as he called it, was still unfolding as the bedrock of imperial commerce in the Indian subcontinent. Ambassadors to Albion would henceforth shower eloquence upon those spinning or grinding manufactories of England which produced cement, lime, needles and oils, while from their picturesque lenses the impoverished English working classes would be ruled out, along with the fatally impoverishing conditions that would effect in India in the next fifty years. The Mirza was no Marx ahead of his time; he merely wanted to be assimilated into the English aristocracy. From the subjects of town planning, transportation, administration, politics, government or education, he was able to effortlessly enter the domain of visually consuming the ironworks, glassware, cutlery, furniture and, indeed, ammunition—the tell-tale signs of the second Roman Empire.

How genuinely strong his associations with the nobility were, after all, was tested in his plans of establishing an academy in England for the teaching of Hindustani, Persian and Arabic. The learning of Oriental languages was gaining steady purchase in 18th-century London. Abu Taleb must have been inspired by the industrial and entrepreneurial genius of the Age of Reason. He dreamed of setting up an academic enterprise suited to the intellectual and linguistic needs of 'the English as were destined to fill important situations in the East.'[13] After lobbying with Company directors and ministers of His Majesty's Government, Abu Taleb was met with general apathy towards his idea. Although he was offered an annual salary of £750—a remarkably handsome package—to teach at an institution of his choice in London or Oxford, the Mirza had already resolved to leave England, 'politely' excusing himself from the affair.[14] Here too his account may have been disingenuous. Both British and Indian instructors at the future Oriental colleges for military officials and civil servants were paid much less salaries than what Abu Taleb was promised.

It could also as easily imply that the Mirza was not prepared to accept the cultural vassalage of Britain. Even two decades after the battles of Plassey and Buxar, the psychology of the Indian middle classes was not entirely colonised. Rather, their own manners and customs were colonising London.

One of the Mirza's friends was an Englishman returned from India, where he had 'acquired a large fortune in the most honourable way.'[15] As a result, he was the host of lavish banquets, comprising several hundred people of high rank. At one of these, where the Mirza was also invited, he saw the diners feasting off fruits produced by artificial heat, replicating the climate of the tropical regions. By the 1780s, Indian artefacts, culinary items such as spices and condiments, the English chatterati conversing on fragments of Indian history and occasional Indian words started crowding London's Little Bengal. Fleets of returning Britons had Indianised themselves as nabobs—the demi-princes who had minted their retirement pensions on the Company's muslin, silk and saltpetre trade. Thousands of cadets and civil servants in Britain were setting store by the warring kings and dying industries of India. Anticipating the needs of these young British aspirants, it was fashionable for Persian scholars to accompany sahibs from India, in the hope of advancing their teaching careers at schools meant for training British officers for the tropics. In 1772, Munshi Ismail travelled to London with Claude Russel, a senior officer in the Bengal civil services, and in 1785, Munshi Mohammad Sami followed Sir John D'Oyly, the British Member of Parliament for Ipswich. Both sought vocations of training young Britons in the finesses and subtleties of Persian culture, as close as possible to what had prevailed in India during the reign of Akbar the Great.

Scene IV

Nurseries for Nabobs

British rule in the East stressed the rational importance of a strong executive armed with various legal and penal codes, a system of doctrines on such matters as frontiers and land rents, and everywhere an irreducible supervisory imperial authority. The cornerstone of the whole system was a constantly refined knowledge of the Orient, so that as traditional societies hastened forward and became modern commercial societies, there would be no loss of paternal British control, and no loss of revenue either. From the days of Sir William Jones, the Orient had been both what Britain ruled and what Britain knew about it: the coincidence between geography, knowledge, and power. To have said, as Curzon once did, that 'the East is a University in which the scholar never takes his degree' was another way of saying that the East required one's presence there more or less forever.[1]

To be able to know about the Orient, in order to command its administration, required the British to be in the Orient, in flesh and blood, or to reproduce the Orient in miniature systems and replicas of various Orients scattered in and around London. At the beginning of the 19th century, the East India Company was increasingly pressed with the need for Company officials visiting India to possess at least a working knowledge of Hindustani, Persian, Arabic, Bengali or Sanskrit, rather than having to pick up their dregs in India, adulterated by its harems, hookahs, concubines and nautch ceremonies. Pitt's India Act had been in force for over twenty years. The powers of the Company's governing council were greatly reduced, with many of the Board of Directors' administrative rights now ceded to the British Government and the Crown. Cadets recruited to the Indian service by Her Majesty's Government needed to be much more efficient in the lay of the land than the lackeys of Clives and Cornwallises. To this end, two new colleges were established in England, meant for educating India-bound officials in basic Indology, the idiomatic nuances of Indian languages, along with Indian manners and customs. One was opened at Haileybury in 1806, for training civil servants, and another at Addiscombe in 1809, for training military cadets.

The first Indian teacher to join Haileybury was Sheth Ghulam Hyder, who came from Darbhanga in Bihar. During his application, he submitted a few pages of Persian verses which he had copied in calligraphy. His scarce knowledge of English acted as a qualification in his case, for that could only keep any possible subversive designs at bay. Hyder was employed as a writing master—an assistant to the Professor of Persian, Charles Stewart, the man who was at the time engrossed in translating Abu Taleb's *Travels*. While Stewart's annual salary was £500, Hyder received £200, which was equivalent to the salaries of Indian language instructors at Fort William College, in Calcutta, but less than one-tenth of that of British professors who taught Arabic, Sanskrit or Persian. Hyder's primary job was to teach basic Persian vocabulary to British pupils, with a pronunciation as accurate as possible. This was to be followed by lessons in copying the Persian script from inscriptions engraved on copper plates, teaching them elementary skills of writing the language.

In the year that Hyder joined Haileybury, the Company's directors sent an invitation to Abu Taleb, who they knew was staying in India since returning from Europe in 1802. The directors recalled his offer of establishing an institution in England for the study of Indian languages, inquired if he was still in Bengal, and if he would like to accept the post of a munshi at Haileybury. The Mirza had passed away a few days before the letter reached his family in December 1806. However, since his memoirs had created a deep impression about European life in the Persian-speaking society of India, Company officials were able to track two other men with the desired qualifications to take up teaching positions at Haileybury. By 1808, Moolvey Meer Abdul Ali from Benares and Moolvey Mirza Khalil from Lucknow were recruited at an annual salary of £600, which was even higher than the highest paid British professors at Haileybury. The Moolveys, who enjoyed the rank of assistant professor, were rather dissatisfied with their salaries, and wrote to the Board of Directors, asking for an additional house rent allowance of £25, a furniture allowance of £15 and an annual rebate of £5 on income tax. Rather than lose the first of their hard-earned recruits, the directors agreed to the bargain.

In the winter of 1808, Abdul Ali married an Englishwoman, now known as Elizabeth Moolvey. He bought a horse and a landau, subsequently relocating to a lavish residence near the college, rationalising his new lifestyle as his willingness to stay in the vicinity of his employers and students, who could then call upon him at any hour. Ali spent about £200 in refurbishing his house and buying additional furniture. He splurged himself dry in the process before the spring showers turned the house into a waterlogged mess. Ali was in debt already, and had to apply for a pecuniary aid of £200 from the college administration, promising to never bother them again with his financial problems. Abdul Ali had failed miserably in adapting to English snobbery as well as the English climate and, in 1811, he was stricken by paralysis. He died the following year. Elizabeth was given £120 in salary and gratuity, to mourn the passing of her husband, with an annual pension of £25. Moolvey Mirza Khalil, the son of a Shiite trader in Awadh, stuck to his religious puritanism, eating separately and keeping mostly to himself. After a largely unsocial decade at Haileybury, he resigned in 1819, after being assaulted by a Briton. Khalil was asked to return to India with an annual pension of £360 for life. He remained in London, however, until 1826, and when he returned to Lucknow he was richer by £2500—seven years' pension saved up, untouched.

Ghulam Hyder, who earned considerably less than the other two, still managed to spend a fruitful life initially. He too managed to persuade the directors to pay him £40 annually as house rent allowance. Although he had two wives in India—one of them deceased—he married a third, an Englishwoman named Rose Slocomb. She was the daughter of William Grant Slocomb, the headmaster of the Green Coat School in Hertford. The wedding took place in 1810 at St Botolph's Church in Bishopsgate. Hyder's polygamy was often a subject of amusement for his students, who even took to writing a doggerel on him.

> How oft alas! poor Hyder's looks express'd,
> He wished his wife at Mecca or Modena,
> And often too, his trembling lips confess'd
> His great regret, that he had ever seen her,
> For though she was exceedingly well drest,
> And always very modest in demeanour
> Her drinking wine, and eating of pork sausages,
> Appeared to him as very great monstrousities!
>
> Lucky that Hyder's prophet did allow,
> His faithful followers to be well supplied
> With wives for Hyder, ere he left Lucknow,
> Had married three, tho' one of them had died,
> But if from grief or want, I do not know,
> That is a question, which I can't decide,
> His English wife was the hardest to control,
> Because she had the advantage of a soul!
> …
>
> Lovewell would say, 'Come Hyder tell us how,
> 'That charming wife of your's, your English rib is,
> 'When did you last get tidings from Lucknow,
> 'About your children and your Indian *bebees*?

'What are they like to, are they black or no?
'And are they handsome, Hyder, as your *jib* is?'
Hyder scarce knowing if to speak or not
Would answer him, *hah! Sahib, khoob surut got!*[2]

In 1811, Hyder ran into arrears with his doctors after falling
miserably ill. The Company increased his annual salary to £250.
His relentless share of domestic disturbances and conflicts was a
constant source of trouble for his landlord. The following year,
when his landlord asked him to vacate the house, he made a
petition to the Company to increase his house rent allowance to
£50. At the Company's mercy, his salary was increased to £350,
in addition to the accommodation allowance requested by him.
Hyder continued teaching at Haileybury over the following decade,
without much luck with a promotion or much improvement in his
family situation. He passed away in 1823, leaving four children
and his wife, Rose Hyder, three months' pregnant and suffering
from cancer in her leg. Rose lived for the rest of her life on an
annual pension of £40, while Hyder's children each received £15
annually. Of these, John Master Hyder and Emma Hyder died at
ages sixteen and ten respectively. The family received about £20
for their funerals, put together. Ghulam Hyder's surviving son,
Sullivan Law Hyder, became an apprentice to Richard Watts, a
publisher of Oriental books. Later, the Company saw it best to
transfer him to Bengal, the presidency where his father was born.
In India, Sullivan Hyder married Amelia Botellho, an illiterate
woman of Indo-European ancestry, preserving his hybrid lineage.

In 1809, Meer Hasan Aly arrived in London, looking for
employment as a teacher of Arabic, Persian, Hindustani or
Bengali. He was formerly employed at the court of the King of
Awadh and was also associated with the Company in Lucknow.
Hasan Aly came from a family of highly dignified scholars. He
was the grandson of Nawab Birem Khan, whose knowledge and

proficiency in Arabic, Persian and Hindustani was considered second to none. In his first month in London, Meer Hasan Aly applied to Haileybury, without any hope of getting through, since the college was known to employ very few Indians. He also applied to Addiscombe that year, and joined the faculty of Indian languages in the summer of the following year. Hasan Aly began at an annual salary of £250, which in a year was raised to £400. Like Hyder, his job was to teach Persian vocabulary, pronunciation and writing, besides Persian and Devnagri orthography, to military cadets. He was to also assist John Shakespear, Professor of Oriental Literature at Addiscombe.

English cadets at Addiscombe were extremely apathetic towards learning Indian languages, often frustrating Shakespear and Ali, even as the latter was expected to give two or three extra tutorials every week. When Abdul Ali died, Hasan Aly applied for his position at Haileybury. Once again, he was unsuccessful, despite recommendations from his friends and colleagues, including Mirza Khalil and Ghulam Hyder, and despite threatening the authorities that he would resign from his position at Addiscombe. The same year, he had also compiled the *Grammar of Hindoostanee Language* in three parts. The first was Hindustani as it was taught in India in the native fashion; second, a set of grammatical rules 'reduced to the English scale, and accompanied as far as possible to the Rules of Grammar received in' Britain; and finally, a 'selection of Vocables, Dialogues, and Exercises very useful to Hindoustanie scholars'[3] in the early stages of learning to read or write. The research committee at Addiscombe rewarded Meer Hasan Aly with a grant of £100 towards the costs of publishing his work as a book. At its completion, the directors of the committee sent the book for evaluation to Charles Stewart and Alexander Hamilton, Orientalists in the academic circles of Georgian London. Their response was not as congratulatory as Hasan Aly had expected:

> It must be premised that Hasan Aly has attempted one of the most difficult undertakings in Literary acquirements, viz. that of translating from his own into a Foreign language, and therefore it

could not but be expected that a person who has resided but a few years in this country should in some measure fail in explaining in English the intricacies of Oriental Grammar, in the attempt he has however manifested a very considerable acquaintance with the English language and an extensive knowledge of the Hindoostany, but as Doctor Gilchrist had many years ago completely sifted that dialect, and left scarcely anything new to be explained, all that was required was an abridgement of that Gentleman's quarto grammar, in the Oriental and English characters. In this particular Hasan Aly has been anticipated by a recent publication, we are therefore of the opinion that the utility of Printing this book would not be adequate to the trouble and expense but take the liberty of suggesting that the author should be distinguished by the Hon'ble Company with some mark of their favour and the Book be deposited in their Library as a Literary curiosity.[4]

The cold and condescending reception to Aly's magnum opus fractured its spine. More than a review of Aly's scholarly achievement, Stewart and Hamilton chose to highlight the achievements of British Orientalists like John Borthwick Gilchrist and John Shakespear, with the implication that theirs were *a priori* more advanced than a native's fluency in Persian and Hindustani. According to them, Aly's *Grammar* was a queer example of Indian literacy, but not a tall enough study in linguistics worthy of renown. Nonetheless, Hasan Aly continued working as a writing master at Addiscombe and went on to translate the *Gospel of St Matthew* into Hindustani in collaboration with an Englishwoman, Biddy Timms, who had been a domestic employee to Princess Augusta, the second daughter of King George III. In 1816, Hasan Aly quit his job due to failing health. He was now set to return to India on a pension of £120 and a travel allowance of £205 for his passage back home, to be borne by the Company. But before that, in March 1817, he married Miss Timms at the St James Parish Church in Piccadilly.

The couple left for Lucknow, and within a few years, Hasan Aly, now weary of his crossbred wedlock, would remarry Indian women of his own religion. The former Mrs Hasan Aly, distraught though enriched from the Indian nightmare of a life in the *zenana*, returned to Britain in 1829, to write an autobiographical and epistolary account, the *Observations on the Mussulmauns of India*. It was published in 1832 in London for private circulation. Sympathising with Indian women in the *zenana*, she observed that they were, in fact, 'happy in their confinement, and never having felt the sweets of liberty, would not know how to use the boon if it were to be granted to them.'[5] Their lives, she added, were about striving to be exemplary wives, sisters, daughters, mothers, mistresses, friends and benefactresses, in the service of the prince and the pauper. The book was dedicated to Princess Augusta. Muslim men, as Mrs Aly had observed, ventured out into promised Meccas of culture and education, leaving their women back home, even those from elite or erstwhile royal households, who were largely uncultured or uneducated—as they appeared in eyes of British travellers. Maria Graham, who was married to a Scottish naval officer in India, began writing her *Journal of Residence in India* at the time when Hasan Aly was putting the final touches to his *Grammar*. Published in 1813, Graham's experiences spoke to the patrician ears of England, of the backwardness of Muslim women, especially those from the courtier families of Awadh or the Carnatic that had been driven from glory to decadence. Her journal spared no words of cynicism.

> Prepared as I was to expect very little from Mussulman ladies, I could not help being shocked to find them so totally void of culture as I found them. They mutter their prayers, and some of them read the Koran, but none in a thousand understands it. Still fewer can read their own language, or write at all, and the only work they do is a little embroidery.[6]

By 1820, the two new English academies had grown into nurseries for breeding xenophobia towards Indian instructors. To allay the fears of Indian recruits, the chairman of the board of Haileybury

College took to addressing the graduating batch of 1817, in the presence of Indian faculty members. He issued a cautionary note to the students against any form of racial, colour or linguistic discrimination for the times when they were to arrive in India. Indians, he believed, were 'a mild, inoffensive, well-disposed, benevolent race of Men, and earnestly recommended that they should on all occasions be treated with humanity and kindness.'[7] Be that as it may, after 1823, the Company adopted a new policy of no longer employing Indian scholars as language instructors. Since the beginning of the language courses, English students considered Englishmen more suited to the job—one that had been originally intended for the pursuance of Indian customs and was meant to be taught by Indians. Indian scholars at Haileybury and Addiscombe came to be seen as progressively deviant in their clothing and social customs, morally unsound, financially irresponsible and unable to master the English language—all of which was no less than a pestilence for students and authorities. The Company's directors were especially perturbed by Indian scholars taking up jobs around London, followed by British wives, whom they frequently left behind as penniless or widowed, or both. In either case, their upkeep depended upon the expenses of the Company.

One Mirza Abdullah arrived in Britain in the 1820s to further his prospects, after having served the Company for two decades in the Customs Service in Bengal. Eager to please the administration, he even converted to Christianity, adopting the name Daniel Abdullah. Following what had by now become quite a convention, he married a British woman, Mary Callesteur, and with her he had a daughter, named Mariam Julia Clementine Abdullah. Despite several attempts at integrating into British society, Abdullah's application to Addiscombe was rejected. He finally became a destitute, with no option but to accept the Company's free passage back to India. In 1826, Company officials did, however, employ an Iranian scholar, Mirza Muhammad Ibrahim, simply because he was Persian and not Indian. Ibrahim made great progress in Anglicising himself, learning the English language and socialising—even cohabiting—with his English colleagues. He worked for eighteen years as an assistant to the Professor of Arabic and Persian, Henry George Keene. In 1844, he returned to Iran. After Ibrahim's departure, Asians in general were avoided at the Company's academic institutions. In the 1850s, the applications of two independent scholars, Hafiz Ludroo Islam Khan and P. Joyaloo, for teaching Persian, and Telegu and Tamil, were rejected at Haileybury and Addiscombe, respectively. The Board of Control was of the opinion that too much of time and resources had been devoted to Oriental studies without the project yielding any of its desired results.

The seeds of Indian flavours had already been sown in the streets of London. Disgruntled Indian princes, soldiers and zamindars were gearing up for the Great Rebellion of 1857. By then London was already in the grip of a mutiny of sorts, fought not with arms but with vapours and spices.

Scene V

For the Sake of Mahomet

Although early-19th-century England was marked by the aftermath of 'the worst excesses of the French Revolution,' to quote Lady Bracknell from *The Importance of Being Earnest*,[1] and the Napoleonic Wars, in large parts London was characterised by a singular nostalgia for the Raj, a phenomenon still very much in its infancy. Retirees in the city, who had once fought in the fabled battles of Hindostan would, as one satirist wrote, idle away their forties doing nothing but 'eat Mulligatawny soup, smoke the Hookah, talk about Tippoo Saib, Seringapatam, and tiger hunting.' The kind of Orientalism which constructed a Little Bengal within the imperial metropolis was far more alarming than their nabobery overseas. The curry had conquered Victorian tastes, and was well on its way to becoming more English than it was ever Indian. Although Britons in India were discouraged to consume it, in London's England it became a packaged commodity of great celebrity status. Eastern spices and cuisines acquired great cosmopolitan appeal in London. It was no surprise to see Maria Eliza Rundell's *Domestic Economy, and Cookery, for Rich and Poor* (1806) taking readers through an Oriental culinary education: 'The *mulakatanies* and curries of India; the sweet *pillaus*, *yahourt*, and cold soups of Persia; the *cubbubs*, sweet *yaughs* and sherbets of Egypt have been inserted with a view of introducing a less expensive and more wholesome and a more delicate mode of cookery.'[2]

In the 21st century, the British curry industry would go on employ over 100,000 people, adding nearly £4 billion to the British economy annually. In March 2017, an antique chicken curry recipe was discovered in the tucked away records of a Benedictine monastery at Downside Abbey at Stratton-on-the-Fosse in Somerset. Apparently, the recipe dated back to 1793. Instead of cooking chicken, monks had been using it to cook 'calves head turtle fashion' and 'fricassee of pigs' feet and ears.'[3] It was speculated that this might be the oldest existing singular curry recipe in the world. Hannah Glasse's recipe for curry from her book *Art of Cookery* (1747) is perhaps the oldest known published recipe of the Indian gastronomical delight. By way of comparison, the first restaurant in London to serve curries came up fifty years before even the first London fish-and-chips shop. And, nearly 150 years before migrants from the Indian subcontinent made chicken tikka masala popular as Britain's national takeaway food, curry-mania wafted across the streets of central London.

The Norris Street Coffee House came up in London's Haymarket in 1773, being the first English restaurant to serve curries. A similar establishment, the Jerusalem Coffee House, had already been opened in Cornhill, to serve East India Company officers and merchants. About 5,000 miles away, in Warren Hastings' Calcutta, hookah-smoking had turned into the dominant custom for imperial evening soirees. These fashioned the city's dramatic transformation into a major urban centre and the capital of British India, from what had been a meagre cluster of villages, a hundred years ago. If Lord Macaulay wanted to turn Indians 'English in taste, in opinions, in morals and in intellect,'[4] it was only half a century after the British had themselves gone native in Calcutta, in each of those attributes. William Hickey wrote that in British Calcutta, going out of favour with the hookah implied going out of fashion. The hookah was an emblem of British integration into Indian culture as well as of their own racial supremacy. With the employment of the *hookahburdar* (hookah-bearer), smoking came to signify a ritual of native subjugation. The unforced fecundity of the colony cast its colonials into imperial boredom. The hookah was both its aggravator and therapy—an apology for ruling by pleasure and lassitude. In European history, the hookah appears as a sinful creature in the manors of India, accompanied by a sweet fragrance affected by the punkah of toddy leaves. Colonials in 18th-century Bengal were slaves to breakfasts of cold ham, fish, rice and fruits that gave way to the hookah, chaperoned by brandy-pawnie (brandy and water), while the sahibs emitted smoke in 'odoriferous spicy gales; crowds of Bengallee servants in attendance.'[5]

An advertisement from 1792 for the sale of a hookah by a European firm in Calcutta read: 'Elegant Hookah bottoms—urn shaped, richly cut, with plates and mouthpieces.'[6] Earlier, Charles Bendysh's inventory of 1675 mentions 'Chamolet Hoake (sic) with a green baise.'[7] The retired British army official Thomas Williamson's copious accounts in *The European in India* (1813) reported many Europeans as being slaves to their hookahs. Williamson's accounts were illustrated with engravings by Sir Charles D'Oyly, a British painter and government official, born in Dhaka in 1781. His Tom Raw series of paintings feature several scenes of hookah smoking in private or public milieus of colonial life in India, besides his paintings of hookah-smokers in Williamson's travelogue, and hookah instruments as showcased in his own drawing room in Patna. Paintings by Francesca Renaldi took to featuring Indian women in Bengal, smoking the hookah. The hookah was most widely adopted by the Europeans in the 18th century, given the increasing contact with Indian society which the French wars inaugurated. In his *Voyages* (1798), the Dutch traveller John Splinter Stavorinus gave an account of a dinner at the residence of the governor of Calcutta, hosted for the benefit of a Dutch Director in 1769. The dinner was followed by a hookah session which went well past 12:30 in the night. Smoking habits determined the quality and degree of pleasures that imperialism afforded its European denizens in the colony—and later in London. With dreams of making it to the British Parliament, each army man, bureaucrat, polygamist and gossiper walked

into his palanquin with his hookah in one hand—without his
retarded conscience in the other—to come out into a dazzling
Chowringhee, not unlike the debauchery of tuberose-wearing
latter-day Bengali *zamindars*.

Exploiting the Oriental course that imperial commodities were
taking, a Bengali immigrant in London, Sake Deen Mahomet,
opened the Hindoostane Coffee House, in 1810, at George
Street. Here, for the next three years, aficionados of Oriental
cuisine and addictions could savour their honest English curries
and puffs of the hookah. The coffee house was envisaged as a
heterotopia—a slice of India replicated in London. Its clientele
was intended to be those 'Europeans who had worked and spent
several years in India, and who wanted that same experience "back
home."'[8] The joy of curry was supplemented by exotic Asiatic
paintings, bamboo-cane sofas and the activity of smoking, where
'underlying the noise of clinking dishes and conversation would
be the hiss and bubble of the hookahs.'[9] The India-returned nabob
was defined as a 'hookah-smoking, curry munching inhabitant
of a palanquin.'[10] Even Englishwomen were so smitten by the
Orient that India-returned memsahibs were referred to as Lady
Kedgeree or Lady Hookah Smith. Other satires testified that
the '"fleshpots of Egypt" were not more holily longed for by
the murmuring sons of Israel, than were the hookah and hot
curries of India, both *sadha* and *dho'-peeaza*, daily sighed for and
regretted'[11] by the expatriate servants of the East India Company.
This kind of Oriental fantasy was a palimpsest or phantom—of
arbitrary signs and fabulous suggestions of the East—but not the
East itself.

Mahomet well understood the architectural trappings of that
fictional Orient. That was what he precisely set out to recreate
for the likes of William Makepeace Thackeray, who had made
a fortune during his tenure as a collector in the Sylhet district
in Bengal. Thackeray traded elephants from Sylhet, transporting
them from Calcutta's Chowringhee to Westminster in London.
Sylhet's virgin mineral resources offered him the perfect
opportunity to quietly plunder the wildlife of the area, eventually

earning him the sobriquet 'the elephant-hunter of Sylhet'.[12] In a passage from the *Correspondences of William Ritchie* (1920), Thackeray is described as 'a collector of revenue, a maker of roads and builder of bridges, a *shikari* or hunter, a magistrate, judge, policeman and doctor in one.'[13] Trading of elephants was added to his resume sometime in the 1760s, when only sixteen elephants out of sixty-six survived among those that were supposed to be marched out of India by the East India Company. Thackeray pursued the matter at the judicial tribunal. He went on to sue the Company in the Supreme Court of Bengal—a case that he won and claimed damages of £3,700, approximately £7 million in today's value. In 1776, he married Amelia Webb, the daughter of Lieutenant-Colonel Richmond Webb. For the nine-and-half years that he was posted at Sylhet, Thackeray lost no opportunity to mint ivory into sterling. He left with so much wealth that there was no need for employment for three generations to come. Following the example of Lord Clive, nabobs like Thackeray were buying not only estates, but also seats in the Parliament, boosting their social and professional ranks.

Naturally, the British aristocracy felt outraged by what they considered to be the influx of corrupting social upstarts and Oriental opulence into upper-class society. These later became subjects of mockery and satire in the novels of the more famous William Makepeace Thackeray (grandson of Thackeray, the elephant-hunter). On November 28, 1846, an anonymous poem was published in *Punch Magazine*, titled 'Kitchen Melodies—Curry'. It was revealed in a collected edition of the author's ballads and humorous writings that the work belonged to William Makepeace Thackeray, the collector's very own progeny.

> Three pounds of veal my darling girl prepares
> And chops it nicely into little squares
> Five onions next prepares the little minx
> The biggest are the best her Samiwel thinks
> And Epping butter, nearly half a pound
> And stews them in a pan until they're brown'd

What's next my dexterous little girl will do?
She pops the meat into the savory stew
With curry powder, tablespoonsfulls three
And milk a pint (the richest that may be)
And when the dish has stewed for half an hour
A lemon's ready juice she'll o'er it pour
Then, bless her, then she gives the luscious pot
A very gentle boil—and serves quite hot
PS beef, mutton rabbit, if you wish
Lobsters, or prawns, or any kind of fish
Are fit to make A CURRY. 'Tis when done
A dish for emperors to feed upon.[14]

In Thackeray's satirical novel *Vanity Fair* (1847), one of the major characters, Jos Sedley, was an imitation of the novelist's grandfather. Sedley, a civil servant, had returned from Uttar Pradesh with a *hookahburdar*. In order to seduce Sedley, Becky Sharp pretended to be fascinated by all things Indian, and even dared a hot curry cooked by his mother. Even in Mahomet's time, the average Englishwoman was not comfortable or acquainted with the over-seasoned flavours of the Raj. Naturally, Becky Sharp had a hard time reconciling to Sedley's palate. To be able to replicate the flavours of the East was an imperial triumph for British cooks in London. Victorian Britain marked itself as distinct by taming the alien cultural forces of what was erstwhile deemed as uncivilised or racially impure.

By mid-19th-century, Britain saw a flurry of Victorian cookbooks that tried to assimilate the curry into familiar realms of British culture, in the process leading to an inflation in the price of packaged curry powder. Alexis Soyer, Victorian London's celebrity and philanthropic French chef, lamented in his book *The Modern Housewife: Or, Ménagère* (1849), over the steep rates of curry powder 'as it is one of those stimulating condiments which would be invaluable to the poor.'[15] Eliza Acton's *Modern Cookery for Private Families* (1845) dedicated a whole chapter to the Indian curry. Even the inanest curry recipes appeared to embody a miscellany of racial and cultural politics over India. Acton's emphasis on the freshness of the curry powder and detailed insights into Indian recipes turned cooking into a political act. Acton wrote: 'The natives of the East compound and vary this class of dishes, we are told, with infinite ingenuity.'[16] Why this was at all significant and appealed to Victorian readers was due to the phenomenon unleashed by Mahomet, as early as 1810. Notwithstanding the contempt for the nabobs in the English society, Mahomet designated them as the desired regulars of his Coffee House.

> Sake Deen Mahomet, manufacturer of the real currie powder, takes the earliest opportunity to inform the nobility and gentry, that he has, under the patronage of the first men of quality who have resided in India, established at his house, 34 George Street, Portman-Square, the Hindoostane Dinner and Hooka Smoking Club. Apartments are fitted up for their entertainment in the Eastern style, where dinners, composed of genuine Hindoostane dishes, are served up at the shortest notice.[17]

That was one of the first advertisements of Mahomet's coffee house that London read. In his later life, he was known for a variety of other talents and enterprises. In 1838, his book *Shampooing; Or, Benefits Resulting From the Use of the Indian Medicated Vapour Bath* went into its third edition. Being a discourse on medicated Indian baths, vapors and shampooing, it was dedicated to King George IV of Great Britain and Ireland. The patrons of Mahomet's bath included the King as well as the crème de la crème of English society. Situated in Brighton, the Indian Vapor Bath was a concept that, as Mahomet claimed, had been pioneered by him, and was capable of curing the worst afflictions plaguing modern Britain. These included dyspepsia, flatulence, rheumatism, metastatic diseases, vertebral pains, asthma, nervous or muscular contractions, early-stage paralysis and even hoarseness or loss of voice. Indeed, Brighton 'was the theatre where his name became patent for the alleviation of suffering mankind.'[18]

Even without his shampooing micro-industry, Mahomet was a famous man. His book *Travels of Deen Mahomet, Through Several*

Parts of the Eastern Territory, published in 1794, was the first English book ever by an Indian author. In October 1822, in *The Brighton Gazette*, *The New Times* and several other publications, there appeared an ode to Deen Mahomet. This was only one of many that helped keep his name in currency: 'Would it avail to give thee joy,/ If sickness were the sad alloy?/ Ah no, alas!—then turn thee here,/ See *Mahomet's high dome* is near!/ *There, there,* behold the power of steam/ Of *Milton's* pen a worthy theme'[19] For Mahomet to reach that stage, it took much more than shampooing or learning courteous phraseology of the English language. Not only did he have to first convert to Anglicanism, but he also needed to convert the culinary sensibilities of the gentlemen of Marylebone. In the process, he also became the first known entrepreneur of the hookah in Great Britain. He made the right to addiction a matter of etiquette and social delicacy. For all intents and purposes, the Hindoostane Coffee House was a hookah parlor, better known to India-returned veterans as the 'Hooka Club.' It did not sell any coffee, whatsoever. Today, the 'Life in the UK' test—which needs to be passed as a qualification for British citizenship—requires its aspirants to know 'the year Emperor Claudius invaded Britain, the year that Sake Deen Mahomet launched the first curry house in the country and the age of Big Ben,'[20] in the same breath. Mahomet's *Travels* might still be the rightful claimant to the plot of a bestselling picaresque novel. In 2002, *The Guardian* made a generous opening to its article 'And Mr Mohamed Too', asserting that 'when the complete history of Britain is written a paragraph or two should be reserved for Sake Deen Mahomet.'[21]

Large parts of central London bear witness to the popularity of Mahomet's tool of addiction. A few minutes' walk from Baker Street—where the Hindoostane Coffee House was situated—takes one to Marble Arch, whose main thoroughfare is populated by a line of very popular and crowded shisha (hookah) bars. Mahomet shared a special bond with the hookah. Its traditional make was the indelible sign of power and luxury, which Mahomet probably first encountered, in all its grandeur, as a child of fourteen, in service of the East India Company. That was when he visited the palace of Nawab Mubarak-al-Daulah in Murshidabad in 1773. Around twenty years later, an account of that hookah, reproduced from his memory, became part of his *Travels*.

> His pipe was of a serpentine form, nine cubits in length, and termed hookah: it reached from his lips, though elevated his situation above the gay throng, to the hands of a person who only walked as an attendant in the train, for the purpose of filling the silver bowl with a nice compound of musk, sugar, rose-water, and a little tobacco finely chopped, and worked up together into a kind of dough, which was dissolved into an odoriferous liquid by the heat of a little fire made of burnt rice, and kept in a silver vessel with a cover of the same, called *Chilm*, from which was conveyed a fragrant cool smoke, through a small tube connecting with another that ascended to his mouth.[22]

The curious instrument had enticed Mahomet to linger on in the Nawab's court. In his adolescent imagination, the hookah dressed with fruits of the Orient, or decked in satin, silk, muslin, gold, silver and diamonds, steered the unwritten chronicles of colonial India. The character of the *hookahburdar* was a highly sought-after domestic exhibit in an age when the British supposed they could employ the unlettered, unemployable and the uncivil in fulfilling the imperial fantasy of civilising natives. For them, smoking the hookah became intertwined with other evangelical and administrative obligations. And the Sake had struck gold in his discovery of that artefact

Mahomet joined the East India Company as a surgeon's assistant, at the age of ten, rising to the rank of a captain. After an early teenage spent in Calcutta, he set sail on the Danish ship *Christianborg*, and in 1784, he landed in Cork as a Company lascar. Two years later, he eloped with Jane Daly, an Irishwoman, and married her at the local church. In Ireland, he found a patron for his book in Colonel William Annesley Bailie, to whom he dedicated the *Travels*. The book was intended as a guide for Englishmen travelling to India, unravelling its secret Oriental charms. Meanwhile, Mahomet was

employed on the estate of one Godfrey Baker, who was one of his
fellow passengers on the *Christianborg*. Baker died in the year that
Mahomet was married, but not before he had made provisions for
sponsoring his stay in Ireland. Godfrey Baker's brother, Captain
William Massey Baker, returned from India the following year,
and Mahomet was promoted as a manager in the estate. Over the
next two decades, he managed to raise sufficient capital for his own
venture, finally deciding to move to London in 1807. He worked
for a while at a shampoo store run by Sir Basil Cochrane, another
wealthy nabob recently returned from India. Here, Mahomet
began conceiving plans for the Hindoostane Coffee House. Coffee
houses in London, at the time, 'resembled the latter-day *addas*
of Kolkata, informal versions of gentlemen's clubs or New York
nightclubs. Which coffee house you patronised said a great deal
about your politics, your interests and your social standing.'²³ The
Hindoostane Coffee House had separate smoking rooms where
the diners were treated to gilded hookahs, dressed with tobacco
blended with Indian herbs and spices. His customers were assured
that 'the spices, oils, and herbs, both for the curries and for the
hookah tobacco, were all specially procured in India,'²⁴ thus being
virtually transported back to the colony. The menu contained an
elementary spread of meat and vegetable receipts. Spiced in the
Indian style, the curries, made of meat, cumin and coriander seeds,
salt, peppercorns and lemon juice, were served with rice.

Even in its short career, the Hindoostane Coffee House
penetrated into the world fiction. Edward Nares' novel, *I'll
consider of It! A Tale, in Which 'Thinks I to Myself'* (1812), featured
a character, Thomas Jenkins, who confesses to have frequented
the Hindoostane Coffee House, and even been a subscriber
to its 'Hookha Club'. East India sahibs and Indian gentlemen
belonging to that club, he added, were exceedingly wealthy and
conceited. *The Epicure's Almanack* (1815), the most sought after
guidebook to the eating and drinking tastes of London during the
Regency, also gave Mahomet's coffee house a promising review.
However, in 1812, the Hindoostane Coffee House went out of
business. Despite its popularity, Mahomet found it hard to draw

customers, since a large number of ex-India officials had their own domestic chefs trained to prepare authentic Indian cuisine. The coffee house continued under the ownership of Mahomet's partner John Spencer until 1833. Soon after Mahomet left the scene, its clientele shifted to the likes of the Oriental Club, the Calcutta Club or the Madras Club, which were established one after another immediately after the Napoleonic Wars. Although forced to declare bankruptcy, Mahomet had 'created a concept that was to become something of a phenomenon, a hundred years later.'[25]

If Sake Deen Mahomet had given Britain two of the most delicious ingredients to die sooner of blood pressure, his grandson, Frederick Akbar Mahomed, went about discovering how by reducing blood pressure human life could be prolonged. The Victorian doctor from Brighton was the first to undertake some of the most historic researches into nephritis and hypertension, that would later help introduce the system of British Medical Association's Collective Investigation Record. Akbar Mahomed was in the audience, when William Gull and Henry Sutton—after whom the Gull-Sutton Syndrome was named—first demonstrated their new studies in Bright's disease, at Guy's Hospital, in 1872. Akbar Mahomed had joined the hospital three years ago after briefly attending the Sussex County Hospital. He distinguished himself at Guy's Hospital by winning the Pupil's Physical Society Prize in 1871 for his work on modifying and improving the use of the sphygmograph, the instrument for measuring pulse and blood pressure. Mahomed's new sphygmograph better calibrated these measurements, and helped diagnose various cardiac or renal diseases. Even as a doctor, he had retained the poetic verbosity of his grandfather. 'The pulse ranks first amongst our guides,' he wrote, 'no surgeon can despise its counsel, no physician shut his ears to its appeal. We should study the pulse in its marvelous changes of character and form.'[26] Much before the use of the sphygmomanometer, Mahomet was able to outline 'characteristic features of the pressure pulse in patients with high blood pressure and in persons with arteriosclerosis consequent on aging.'[27]

In 1871, Akbar Mahomed joined the Central London Sick Asylum, where he studied sphygmographic tracings of many of his patients with symptoms of Bright's Disease. He was also a resident medical officer at the London Fever Hospital. Mahomed deduced hypertension to be a primary and separate event causing functional kidney damage, preceding the discharge of albumin in urine. While demonstrating that high blood pressure could exist even in apparently healthy individuals, he also clarified how high arterial tension could affect heart, kidney and brain without the onset of renal diseases, until an advanced age. In 1881, he qualified for the degree of Bachelor of Medicine at Cambridge, following his thesis on Chronic Bright's Disease without Albuminuria. He had already been awarded a Doctor of Medicine at University of Brussels, and the Fellowship of the Royal College of Physicians. In a few years, he would be leading pioneering studies into surgical cures for appendicitis. When Mahomed wrote to the *British Medical Journal* to introduce the idea of Collective Investigation, he was endorsed by the president of the British Medical Association, Sir George Murray Humphry. He also collaborated with Francis Galton to collate photographs of over 400 tuberculosis patients, arriving at the conclusion that facial appearance had no relation with the disease, as was hitherto believed. The Collective Investigation Committee was established in 1881, with Akbar Mahomed as its secretary. Within two years, the Committee published a seventy-six-page record of over 2,000 patients. By 1888, the collective investigation saw over 300 families coming forward to submit the details of their family history.

Like the Hindoostane Coffee House, Akbar Mahomed's glory was short-lived. Nor did he live long enough to witness finale of his breakthroughs. In November 1884, at the age of thirty-five, Akbar Mahomed passed away after suffering for three weeks from a typhoid fever which he contracted from a patient. Ada Chalk, who was the nominee and the trustee in his will, ensured, while purchasing a plot for his burial at the Highgate Cemetery, that Akbar Mahomed's gravestone remembered both him and his legal wife, Ellen Mahomed. The Medical Press and the *British Medical*

Journal mourned the premature demise of Akbar Mahomed as a national and international loss.

Although Mahomed was a beneficiary of modern British medicine at Guy's and Cambridge, racial prejudice often raised its ugly hood during his lifetime and afterwards. Some of his students at Guy's considered his methods 'as foreign as his name to the atmosphere of the place.'[28] His obituaries highlighted his Irish-Indian complexion, and *The Biographical History of Guy's Hospital* (1892), written by Samuel Wilks and G.T. Bettany, drew undue focus upon his 'Oriental strain'.[29] Akbar Mahomed's son, Archibald Deane, also grew up to be a doctor, obtaining a Doctor of Medicine from Aberdeen University in 1910. He practised at the Children's Hospital at Paddington, the East Suffolk Hospital, the Brompton Hospital and Princess Alice Memorial Hospital, finally becoming a medical officer at Morris Motors. Archibald Deane was the first of the Mahomeds to use the new surname—an Anglicised version of his great grandfather's first name—Deen. As recounted forty years later by Jane Deane—Akbar Mahomed's youngest daughter—the family changed its name around the time of the Great War, since mixed marriages were out of favour and xenophobic attitudes were fast thickening. Over time, practically nothing remained in public memory of the Deanes or even the revolutionary doctor, save a green plaque in Mayfair. Today, hundreds of curry houses in Southall or Brick Lane, spawned by several waves of Asian, or more particularly Bengali immigration, have been converted into chocolatiering joints. By and by, Nutella has eclipsed peppers and cardamoms—and the Deanes.

The Deanes' misfortunes were nearly mirrored in another Muslim family in London, whose origins went back to the years of the Hindoostane Coffee House. Born in 1811, in Bombay, Mahomed Palowkar came to London at the age of twenty-three, with his father, to move the board of directors of the East India Company over the usurpation of their estate. The young Palowkar was smitten by an Irishwoman, Eleanor Deegan, whom he married in February 1835, at St Leonard's Church in Shoreditch. In a couple of years, he had secured a listing as a tobacconist in the city's gazettes, operating from San Street in Bishopsgate. He carried on in that capacity until his death in 1855. One of Palowkar's sons, William, joined a general merchant as an apprentice; another, Ricky, became an engineer; while the third, Frederick Mahomed, left for Australia, abandoning his wife Elizabeth and their children in England. When the Great War broke out, Elizabeth and her children were flung to the rage of the English mob that terrorised them, under the impression that Palowkar was a German surname; even as four of her sons were bleeding on the battlefront in France, fighting Britain's war. The chain of events, that Elizabeth found herself trapped in, preluded the horror of the Italians and Austrians stranded in London during the Second World War. The Palowkar family became the Wilsons, and it is under that name one can find their descendants across Britain today, joined in their star-tossed destiny with many posterities of the Dean for whose sake London used to disguise itself as Little Bengal.

ACT III

Begums, Baboos, Seamen and Spirits

There is a tide in the affairs of men,
Which, taken at the flood, leads on to fortune;
Omitted, all the voyage of their life
Is bound in shallows and in miseries.
On such a full sea are we now afloat,
And we must take the current when it serves
Or lose our ventures
(Julius Caesar, Act IV, Scene III)

Scene I

Married to Empire

In 1795, Colonel John Cockerell of the Bengal Army retired from the services of the East India Company. He and his Indo-Portuguese wife, Estuarta Cockerell, returned to England. Cockerell purchased the Sezincote House in Gloucestershire, where he lived for the next three years, until his death. Mrs Cockerell and her children, however, were left in London, in the care of Samuel Pepys Cockerell, a brother of Colonel Cockerell and a great-grand-nephew of the 17th-century diarist Samuel Pepys. After the death of the Colonel, Samuel Cockerell designed the neo-Mughal palace at Sezincote for the benefit of another elder brother, Sir Charles Cockerell. Even then, the widow of the Colonel was consigned to exile in the metropolis. When Mirza Abu Taleb Khan was staying in London, he came across several such Indian women, whom he wrote about in his *Travels*. One of them was the wife of Gerard Gustavus Ducarel, who had rescued her from the funeral pyres of her first husband during her Sati. The Ducarels believed her to be a daughter of the King of Purnea in Bengal. Before marrying Ducarel in India, she converted to Protestantism. Unlike Estuarta Cockerell, she was proficient in English manners. Besides, given her fair complexion, she was easily mistaken for an Englishwoman. Her children grew up to be perfectly Anglophonic—English in all manners of appearance and custom.

Borne of biracial parentage must have had its peculiar advantages when compared to those of Indian lineages. Another Indian woman who was in London around Ducarel's time was Helene Bennett (or Benoit), the wife of a Frenchman, General Benoit de Boigne. Helene Bennett, or Halima Begum as she was known before her marriage, was the sister of Faiz Bakhsh, a Begum from Awadh. The latter was married to General William Palmer, who became famous as the founder of the banking firm Palmer & Co. of Hyderabad. De Boigne, on the other hand, belonged to a modest mercantile family from Savoy in France. His aspirations threatened to exceed his grasp. After arriving in Madras in 1778, he joined the British army as a pallbearer. Later, he became an independent mercenary soldier and an associate of Warren Hastings who introduced him to Palmer. In the late winter of 1782, de Boigne travelled to Lucknow, in order to consolidate his military connections. While his days were immersed in the study of Persian, Urdu and the local culture, on one of the evenings he came across Halima Begum 'on the frontiers of the Company's dominions in a city that brought together many high-profile interracial couples.'[1] The following year, de Boigne joined the Maratha forces, and in 1788, he led the army of Mahadji Scindia to a decisive victory over the Mughals in Agra. He was now an eminent mercenary commander, who could afford to retire for a few years to start a family with Halima. In 1789, the couple gave birth to a daughter, and three years later, to a son. After a second stint with the Maratha army, de Boigne secured an annual pension of over ₹1.5 million, and enduring fame as a military strategist who altered the course of Maratha and Mughal history.

Before he left India, de Boigne's property was estimated to be worth £400,000. He made generous allowances for his mistresses, granting them permission to marry, while he and Helene Bennett set sail for London, in 1796, with their two children, Banu Jain and Ally Bux. They lived in a small mansion in Portland Place, where their children were baptised as Ann and Charles Alexander. Within a couple of years, the London air had worn down Halima's Lucknawi charms, as General de Boigne found his affections swayed by Charlotte Louise Eleonore Adele d'Osmond, the young daughter of Marquis d'Osmond, an exiled French ambassador of King Loiuse XV, then living in London. By 1803, having left Halima for Adele, de Boigne was well settled into his second marriage and was now living in Savoy. Adele too, however, could not hold on to her prize long enough. The following year, the general separated from her. The former Mrs Bennet stayed on in London on an annual allowance of £300 from her husband. After the accidental death of Ann, during a visit to France, Mrs Bennet retired to Sussex in an old cottage known as Great Ground House. Before she left for the country, she wrote to her former husband, mourning the death of their daughter and urging him to secure the future of their son, Charles.

> I don't know what to write upon my misfortune. I think you ought to give thanks to God for having many relations, friends and acquaintances, where poor I had very few of next to none. I see by your letter that you have provided for Charles and also for me. As to myself, I don't much care, but only for Charles. How easy one may wrong him out of his rights by destroying the papers. I sincerely hope you will act like a father towards your son. You may have many more but you are not sure that they are yours.[2]

The Begum had been introduced by her former husband to a network of influential members of British society, including Edmund Burke and his wife. After the death of Ann, several noble-hearted Englishmen came forward to help the Begum secure a larger share in her husband's property, in accordance with the provisions of British law. Given to a melancholy strain of modesty, she refused all pecuniary aid. As she hailed from the Mughal court, she carried on with a few vestiges of her bygone Begumhood, one of them being the habit of smoking hookahs and pipes. Yet, she was generally regarded as a pious Catholic woman—having converted to her husband's religion before marriage—and was also known for being exceptionally charitable to the poor, notwithstanding her own meagre possessions. It has been speculated that the romantic poet, Percy Bysshe Shelley, saw her roaming about St Leonard's Forest as a 'Black Princess'[3] during his own wanderings with his younger sisters. If that is to be believed, she possibly inspired Shelley's *Fragments of an Unfinished Drama* (1839), as well as an essay published in *Indicator* in July 1822, which has been variously attributed to Shelley, Charles Lamb and Benjamin Disraeli. The author of that piece, titled 'A True Story' ('A Tale of Wonder' in later versions), wrote that he 'was suddenly startled by the sight of a tall slender female looking sorrowfully and steadily in my face. She was dressed in white, from head to foot, in a fashion I had never seen before; her garments made of the richest silk.' Nowhere did the writer mention if she was Indian, but the passage was certainly replete with the origins of the feminine Victorian Gothic, with all the undercurrents of an Oriental mystery. The author went on, 'altogether she looked like a lovely picture, but not like a living woman. I closed my eyes forcibly with my hands, and when I looked again, she had vanished.'[4]

Mrs Bennett died in December 1853, at the age of eighty-one, and was buried in Horsham. Her lasting solace was the reconciliation of her son Charles with de Boigne, that occurred over a poignant reunion in 1814. In the remainder of his life, de Boigne worked as a philanthropist and was ennobled as a Count by the Italian King, Victor Emmanuel. He honoured the solicitation of his first wife, and duly arranged for his title and property to pass over to his son. After his father's death in 1830, Charles assumed his title and came to be known as Count de Boigne. That was a rare instance of Anglo-Indian inheritance, for children of Anglo-Indian marriages or intercourses were not considered worthy of being proper family members in European households. In order for children of interracial intercourses to travel to London, and assume their fathers' social stations, they had to be passably fair-complexioned. In a letter to Hastings, John Palmer, son of General William Palmer, and a Company agent at Calcutta, wrote that one of his orphaned step-grandsons had failed to reach 'a complexion that could possibly escape detection.

It was decided in the end that the "dark" child should stay in India and try to make his way as a clerk.' The other two orphans, 'almost as fair as European children,' were shipped to England, *en route* to gentrification. Hastings, and his council, was of the opinion that a Scottish accent was as damaging to the prospects of candidacy for English society, as a murky complexion.[5]

Some Anglo-Indian children did happen to reach Britain for higher education. Not surprisingly, a majority of them went to Scotland. One such young girl, Jane Cumming Gordon, was the first known Anglo-Indian pupil in a Scottish school. She was the daughter of George Cumming Gordon and his Indian mistress from Calcutta. After Gordon's death, his mother, Lady Helen Cumming Gordon, brought Jane to a school in Edinburgh. Jane's quick-spirited mother had, meanwhile, lost no time in contracting a romantic alliance with an English military official in Bombay. Although Lady Cumming and her son had fallen out over his racial transgression of taking an Indian partner, she came to believe that the way to the peace of her deceased son's soul lay in the path of caring for young Jane. In 1810, the Anglo–Indian girl came to be involved in a historic lawsuit. That is one of the reasons her name still stands out. The case of Miss Marianne Woods and Miss Jane Pirrie against Lady Helen Cumming Gordchief would shock Britain out of its vanity of moral decorum. It involved a sexual scandal in a girl's boarding school in Edinburgh where Jane was also a student and boarder. One night, in 1809, the fourteen-year-old Jane found the owners of the boarding, Marianne Woods and Jane Pirrie, engaged in a sexual act. Based on the evidence of young Jane, Lady Helen Cumming withdrew her granddaughter from the school, influencing other guardians to do the same. She filed a case of 'improper and criminal conduct,' against Pirrie and Woods, two female lovers who were seen as profane offsprings of the French Revolution and Mary Wollstonecraft's feminist campaigns. In 1811, the lovers retaliated by suing Lady Cumming for libel. Later that year, they lost the suit in the Scottish Court of Session. The following year, they challenged the original verdict and, on this occasion, it was ruled in their favour. For all the love of Jane, Lady

Cumming had to pay damages to the boarding school owners. A vital fact, hitherto ignored, that created public doubt was that Jane was herself a biracial child. A verdict of sexual misconduct based on her evidence could only have further jeopardised the sexual morality of the British Empire.

Jane was not alone in her history of Indo-Scottish ancestry. Born of a Scottish father and Indian (Bengali) mother, John Campbell became a noted Victorian missionary and author. Campbell was educated at Tain, and later at the University of Aberdeen. He returned to Calcutta, to preach at the Bhowanipore Institution, under the London Missionary Society. One of the prominent Anglican evangelists of Victorian India, Thomas Aveling, mentions Campbell in his recollections: 'I was born of idolatrous parents, but through the great mercy of our Lord Jesus Christ, and the kindness of the Missionaries of London Missionary Society, I was admitted as a pupil in the Christian Institution, under the care of Rev John Campbell, where I was taught to read and write in Bengalee, and also learnt a little English.'[6] Then there was the Anglo-Indian son of Panna Begum, who sprang to notice with her long letters to Warren Hastings written in Persian. She was the wife of Colonel Pearse. Their son, Mr Tommy, went by the alias of Muhammad. He was possibly admitted at Harrow—being among the first Asians to enter the school—thanks to his mother doggedly persuading the Bengal Council. Tait's school at Bromley-by-Bow in East London was another sought-after school for the education of Anglo-Indian children.

Although the run-of-the-mill Anglo-Indian stock did not always acquire easy access to imperial culture, there were phenomenal exceptions. Robert Banks Jenkinson, Second Earl of Liverpool and a liberal Tory, rose to become the Prime Minister of Britain, and steered the nation through the final years of the Napoleonic Wars. He was the son of Charles Jenkinson—an adviser to King George III—and Amelia Watts, who was the daughter of Begum

Johnson, who had herself led a life of famously ravishing twists.
As speculated, Begum Johnson's mother, Isabella Beizor, believed
to be of Portuguese descent, was actually of Anglo-Indian origin.
Born as Frances Croke in Madras, the Begum saw her first two
husbands die before she was twenty-four. William Watts, her third
husband, was a senior official in the East India Company and a
key imperial agent in Bengal. A year before the Battle of Plassey,
when Siraj ud-Daulah attacked British factories and settlements
in Calcutta and Cossimbazar, Begum Johnson and her children
were severed from her husband. They were rescued by the widow
of Alivardi Khan (the grandfather of Siraj), and cleared off to
safety in the French enclave at Chandernagore. After the battle,
William Watts was united with his wife and children. He was
rewarded by the Company and made the governor of Fort
William. Watts and his family retired to England, purchasing
estates in Berkshire and Buckinghamshire, just before his death
in 1764.

A decade later, the Begum, now back in India, having 'previously
buried three husbands,'[7] married Rev William Johnson, a chaplain
to the British forces at Fort William. He would later help establish
Calcutta's first Anglican cathedral, St Johns Church, built in
1784, where the Begum was herself interred upon her death. Four
years after the cathedral was built, the Begum separated from the
Reverend—the man from whom she had taken her fifth surname.—
That was, in fact, the one that she would be known by for over two
centuries to follow. It was never confirmed, however, whether it
was owing to the honorific Indian epithet of *Begum*, or the alleged
biracial identity of her mother, that Robert Jenkinson came to be
known in closed circles as Britain's first Prime Minister of Anglo-
Indian descent.

Begum 'Sumroo', a contemporary of Begum Johnson, was
the second wife of the 18th-century soldier mercenary Walter
Reinhardt Sombre. She is credited with giving the British
Parliament its first Anglo-Indian member in David Ochterlony
Dyce Sombre. That is, if one were to overlook Robert Jenkinson's
alleged Asiatic lineage. Accounts of Begum Sumroo, the Queen

of Sirdhana in Meerut, populated many Victorian journals and travelogues. Like Begum Johnson, she led an adventurous life, if not more dangerous and extremely vindictive. She was a close aide of David Ochterlony, the British Resident of Delhi and a fellow hookah-smoker. Ochterlony was a deeply eccentric character himself. He was also known as 'Loony Akhtar' (a contortion of 'Ochter-looney', which in Urdu meant 'a lunatic star'). Of his many wives and mistresses, the most well-known was Generallee Mubarak Begum. Through Ochterlony, she controlled the administration of Delhi while her husband devoted himself to imbibing the Persian airs of the medieval capital.

Begum Sumroo, who shuffled her lovers like cards, tolerated no man's intervention in her reign. In the 1770s, as as a young nautch girl in Delhi, going by the name Farzana, she met Walter Reinhardt Sombre. She was married to him at the age of fourteen. Sombre was notorious for changing his employers before and after the Battle of Plassey, allying both with the British and the French, in Bengal and around the Carnatic. He died in 1778, leaving the estate of Sirdhana and inestimable wealth in the hands of the young Begum, much of which was to later flow into London through a series of muddled coincidences, not untypical of the Raj.

Sumroo was of Kashmiri descent, and relatively fair-complexioned. She was easily distinguished by her masculine features, notwithstanding her short stature. As early as 1828, Mary Martha Sherwood's novel *The Lady of the Manor* featured a character called Begum, the mother of an Anglo-Indian girl, Gertrude. Although the 'Begum' remained nameless in the book, the fact that she was a *'Cashmerienne,'* 'a little corpulent old woman' dressed in Banarasi silk *'paunjaummahs'*, a silk-trimmed muslin jacket, and a Cashmere shawl around her shoulders, made her a striking likeness of the Indian tyrant.[8] Louisa Stuart Costello, an Irish-born French travel writer, also gave a lavish description of a portrait of Begum Sumroo, which she chanced upon at the Château d'Eu in France. This was one of the several sights of the Begum that Europe had seen, as the eyes of the continent gorged on what seemed to taste like voluptuous malevolence.

Although the Begum never visited England herself, her name was a resident devil, and tales of her cruelty made up the chatter of London. Subjects who ran out of her favour had their ears or noses chopped off, as Sumroo watched 'the mutilation with gusto, whilst she placidly smoked her hookah.'⁹ Godfrey Charles Mundy, a lieutenant in the British army, once saw the Begum in the '*Jagire* of Sirdhana', in all her palpable majesty, smoking her instrument during a European styled repast.¹⁰ While counting the corpses of revolters with her stone-cold retinas, she appeared as a living imitation of art that reminded one of Sir Walter Scott's character, Madame Montreville, from his Waverley novels. Daughter of a Scottish immigrant, Montreville was generally regarded as a despotic Oriental with a devious sexual drift, bordering on an unhinged masculinity. Scott's own epithets for Montreville were 'the tyrannical Begum', 'female tyrant' and an 'unsexed woman who can no longer be termed a European.'¹¹ Victorian novels did cast characters on Sumroo, while her gouaches from India travelled to England, where they overlooked the balustrades of many an English manor house.

Sumroo's malevolence extended even to her own family. Her second husband, the Frenchman L'Oiseaux (or La Vassu), was the commander-in-chief of her army. In 1795, the Begum's sepoys mutinied against her. Sumroo was captured by Zafaryab Khan, known to the Europeans as Aloysius Reinhardt, the son of Walter Reinhardt. Leading the mutiny, Khan ordered for the Begum to be stripped of her *jagire*. A more fabulous version of the legend went that the mutiny was a bluff hatched by the Begum to eliminate her own husband, besides disaffected rebels in her army. She had elicited a promise from La Vassu that they would both commit suicide rather than be taken alive by the rebels, in the likelihood of an uprising. This he duly carried out, shooting himself clean through his temple when he heard the news of the Begum's captivity and imminent execution. Barely hours before Sumroo was to be tied to a cannon by her stepson and blown into smithereens, she appealed to her newfound Irish lover, Thomas, who immediately came to her rescue. By now, the mutineers had grown tired from

Zafaryab Khan's constant intoxication and indecisiveness. They returned their allegiance to the Begum, and Zafaryab Khan was taken a prisoner. Before his death in custody, Khan left a daughter, Juliana. She later married an Anglo-Indian by the name of George Alexander Dyce. Their son David Ochterlony Dyce Sombre— named after Sumroo's old English beau at the court of Delhi—was adopted by the Begum and made her heir. After the term of Sir David Ochterlony, the Begum and her heir maintained close links with the new Resident at Delhi, Sir Charles Metcalf. Once when Metcalfe was bound for London, aboard the ship *St George*, Dyce Sombre, who was also visiting England at the time, changed his tickets at the very last moment only to travel with him.

In 1836, when the Begum died, she left her estates and wealth to Dyce Sombre. The Company seized most of her territory as Sombre stood fleeced by English law and a host of relations and friends who hounded him for shares and loans. These included his own father, who sued him in the Calcutta Supreme Court for a slice of the Begum's wealth. Even after agreeing to pay him ₹10,000 and a monthly allowance of ₹1,500, and whatever that was annexed by the Company, Sombre was left with a hefty fortune. That he took to London in 1838, where he became the evening toast for each matrimonial prospect in town. Before long, Sombre was married to Mary Anne Jervis, a highly musical and vivacious woman, and daughter of the Second Viscount St Vincent. Given Sombre's opulence, the family was not particularly inclined to ascertain his racial pedigree. In 1841, Sombre became a Member of Parliament for Sudbury, but only to quit politics the following year, after a dispute over the constituency seat. As his social relevance began waning, his marriage hit the rocks. Sombre suspected his wife of adultery with several men, including her own father. In complicity with Sombre's half-English sisters, English doctors and English law, Mrs Dyce Sombre pressed charges of lunacy on her husband, claiming that her alleged infidelity was courtesy of her husband's delusions, and that she was 'as virtuous and chaste a woman as ever lived.' Not only the wraith of the Begum's property, but also the spirit of the looney-star, Ochterlony, was haunting London now.[12]

Sombre's entire wealth was ordered to be transferred to a trust to which his wife was decreed as the sole heir. None of his high-ranking friends came forward to support him for fear of losing their reputation. Sombre went into hiding in Paris. Here he survived hand-to-mouth while making a violent dash for his six-hundred-page dossier titled *Mr Dyce Sombre's Refutations of the Charge of Lunacy Brought Against Him in the Court of Chancery*, even as he was being finished off by millimetres and inches from a dishonorable disease called syphilis. He returned to London, and took up temporary residence at Fenton's Hotel, on St James' Street. On July 1, 1851, at the age of forty-three, he met with a death as sombre as three generations of his ancestors. Although he left a will placing most of his property in the trust of the Deputy Chairman and the Court of Directors of the East India Company, 'the will was negatived in every Court as that of a lunatic; and the whole property devolved upon the widow, as sole heir at law.'[13]

After Reinhardt's death, the Begum had inherited an annual revenue of ₹2.5 million (the equivalent of today's £20 million). That, and her three palaces at Sirdhana and Delhi, were plattered before Mary Anne Dyce Sombre, which probably made her the richest woman in England for a brief span. Mrs Sombre spared all her qualms in selling the Delhi palace to a bank— whose manager and his family were butchered ten years later during the Great Mutiny. A part of her bound to a jot of charity disbursed a small portion of her inheritance to refurbish the walls of the palaces at Sirdhana, and some towards the building of a local hospital and school, as was intended in the will of her late lunatic husband. With her old linen and upholstery now crispened, Mary Anne Dyce Sombre came out of mourning and married George Weld-Forester, a Conservative Member of Parliament, and the future Third Baron of Forester. With the turning of myriad imperial screws, the stumbling estates of Sumroo imploded like a supernova into a black hole, as its shrapnel became the property of English peerage. When Mary Anne Forester died in 1893, the palaces at Sirdhana were bought by the Catholic Mission of Agra. One of them was turned into St John's Seminary and another into the St Charles Inter College.

Scene II

Ragtag of the Raj

For over six centuries, at least, the dominant colour of London has been red. When a victorious Henry VI returned to London in 1432, after his two-year-long exile in France, a commemorative poem written to mark his entry into the kingdom described him as garbed in 'Reede velvette.'[1] Red makes up the underbelly of the London bridge where little children were sacrificed. In Roman Londinium there was a preponderance of ruddy buildings, and archaeology has unearthed swathes of red ash beneath the city's streets, believed to date back to the first century when the British Celtic Queen, Boudica, led a heroic but failed revolt against the Romans. 'Red', the colour of royalty, is also the cockney word for gold. Red were London's telephone booths and red are its buses. London has often sided with madness upon seeing the colour of its own people painted unto themselves, as during an exhibition in 1838 displaying a portrait of the Paddington Railway Station, painted by the Victorian panoramist William Powell Frith, which had to be protected from an erupting crowd that roared to catch of glimpse of it.

That was already half a century since the city's Gothic canvas had been spattered with a brush of Indianness by the architect George Dance, who redesigned the grand entrance of Guildhall in a Hindustani Gothic style. Two years before Dance perfected that Oriental façade, *The Public Advertiser* commented on the Indian vagrants in town, that 'those poor wretches who are daily begging for a passage back, proves that the generality of those who bring them over leave them to shift for themselves the moment they have no further occasion for their services.'² Even an Indian visitor to London took to complaining in *The Times* that Indian beggars in the city were a menacing presence, not just for Londoners, but also for Indian gentlemen. India was much visible now, not just in forms, functions and folklore, but as a fact itself in London. The city's regalia and public works doggedly tried to hide from public memory the images of an Indian past that had been, in one way or another, born from the scarlet womb of London.

———

Portraits of Indians who themselves did not visit England were nonetheless trafficked as artworks, in many of which Indian ayahs occupied a prominent place. Francesco Renaldi's unfinished painting of *The Palmer Family*, from 1786, featured William Palmer with his two Muslim wives, three children and an ayah for every child in the frame. While this scene was captured in India and later shipped to London, Sir Joshua Reynolds had the distinction of painting ayahs in England itself. Painted in 1759, Reynolds' *The Children of Edward Holden Cruttendon with an Indian Aayah* was a testament to the indispensability of Indian ayahs in the lives of Anglo-Indian children, especially after the Battle of Plassey. Cruttendon's wife died during the siege of Fort William led by Siraj ud-Daulah. The presence of the ayah in the portrait added both visual richness and melancholia, and her dark complexion enabled Reynolds to portray her as a benevolent alien who was also the singular maternal presence in the Cruttendon household. Reynolds' painting of George Clive with his wife, their two-year-old daughter and an Indian ayah (1763), acted as a visual record of a woman from a colonised territory, who had chosen to dedicate her life towards nourishing the future generations of her magnanimous coloniser. The colonisation of Bengal was, indeed, the immediate context. George Clive, a close associate of Robert Clive, travelled to India in 1755. During the Battle of Plassey, he was an army agent for the

East India Company. George Clive returned to London in 1760 to join the banking firm Sir Francis Gosling and Co., where he served as a partner until his death. He was also an attorney to Robert Clive, handling his transactions at the East India House. Reynolds was himself a shareholder in the East India Company, and was abreast of its recent military and economic accretions. Naturally, Clive and his child's ayah in the painting would have been Reynold's first-hand metaphors for the captor and his docile subject.

Another 18th-century painting that emphasised the growing importance of ayahs in British families was Johan Zoffany's *Portrait of Sir Elijah and Lady Impey* (1783). The couple were painted as enjoying Indian festivities, while witnessing how three of their daughters learned to appreciate Indian culture. The oldest daughter, Mariam, in the centre, formed the axis of the painting, with two ayahs to her left and her parents on the right. Besides telling the story of British integration into Indian culture, it was an illustration of the emergence of the new English mother—intellectual, independent and intrepid, which Mary Impey herself was—and the emergence of the new child, dressed in Indian muslins, who had the freedom to experience an unadulterated environment, true indeed of the Impey daughters in India. Both feminine identities were held together by the background activities of the ayahs, whose judicious attention to the upkeep of Anglo-Indian family values was most essential to the cosmopolitan experiments of the Company nabobs. Arthur William Devis' portrait of Emily and George Mason (1794–95) took the racial narrative ahead into an aesthetic ideology. The ayah and the servant of the family were cast into the distant background, too far to adulterate the utterly benign foreground, where the two children of the Mason family played in loose Indian muslins, woven for no other purpose than to clothe their delicately fair skins. From these visual depictions the image of the Indian ayah started to haunt English society at large.

By 1825, London could no longer pretend to overlook the reality of racially different characters in domestic English households. Thomas Strange, a Calcutta-born judge at the Madras High Court, travelled to England in 1861 with his wife Emily and her two sisters. They were accompanied by a footman and a nurse, both from Madras and named 'Mair Mooto', according to the census of that year.[3] The following decade, Brinoo, a widow from Calcutta, joined another English family at Ealing Southall. After the Government of India Act of 1858, and the transfer of the Indian administration from the East India Company to the Crown, a much larger number of Britons travelled to India to take up alluring career paths in the military, bureaucracy or industry. The opening of the Suez Canal in 1869 is widely held as a watershed moment in the history of Memsahibs arriving in India—either to hunt for husbands or the heads of their husbands' concubines. As more and more British children were conceived and schooled in the colony, family life and domestic morals became progressively important features of Victorian British administration. Indian ayahs and servants, vital as they were to childcare and household management, were readily employed in Anglo-Indian families. Rebecca Solomon's novel *A Young Teacher* (1861) honoured and idolised the position of Indian ayahs in British society. In *The European in India* (1878), Edmund Hull censured the overused services of ayahs that led to English children becoming alienated from the core morals of Englishness. While others actively advocated for the employment of English nannies, Flora Annie Steel and Grace Gardiner, authors of the bestselling etiquette book *The Complete Indian Housekeeper and Cook* (1889), and Anglo-Indian wives themselves, refused to blame Indian ayahs for the moral deficiencies of Anglo-Indian children. Writing against that motion, Doctor Kate Platt raised concerns in her book, *Home and Heath in India and the Tropical Colonies* (1923), of ayahs drugging Anglo-Indian children with opium to keep them from whining, or children missing an environment to properly master the English language.

Notwithstanding the usual disapproval with which ayahs were met in English society, they were quintessential to staging imperial identities, and were often asked to accompany the families in the course of their annual visits 'back home', or upon the families' retirement to England. For most of their childhoods, many Anglo-Indian children spoke Urdu or Hindustani much better than English under the influence of their ayahs. An almost prohibited

relationship in some cases, the love of an ayah for her employer's
children was a standard occupational hazard of colonial rule. In *Tales
from Sholapur* (1994), George Roche, who was born in India in the
early 20th century, recounted his childhood picnics and afternoon
naps 'in the shade of trees and, when we woke, clambered on to our
ayah's hips to be given forbidden sweetmeats.'[4] The predilection
of Anglo-Indian children to parrot the ayahs' languages or idioms
was a much-feared source of the breakdown of imperial and racial
distinctions. Oftentimes, the ayahs 'bore the brunt of complaints'
about the child's behaviour, thus establishing a deeper bond with
the adolescents.[5]

Rudyard Kipling confessed to have been very close to his ayah,
whose memory he preserved in the short story, 'Ba Ba Blacksheep'
(1888). For him she represented an idyllic nation—a pseudo-pastoral
reality in which most Anglo-Indian children grew up. Not only did
these children see India through the eyes and physiognomies of their
ayahs, but in their care also understood the social expectations from
the future life of a childhood spent in the colony. Colonial children
who were exceedingly badly behaved in the presence of English
or Eurasian nannies, felt instantly tamed with the arrival of their
Indian ayahs. By the late 19th century, ayahs came to be seen as the
feminine counterparts to the noble savages that the British had been
civilising for two centuries in India—an amalgamation of evangelical
benevolence and Indian womanhood. Cast in this new aura, they
turned from being a liability to an imperial responsibility. Many
paintings of the Victorian artist Helen Allingham featured an ayah,
whom she had seen in the company of an Englishwoman and her
children at a beach around Dover. Owing to dark complexions, the
eclectic colours of their native costumes, bangles, nose-rings, shawls
and other paraphernalia—that were visually appealing to British
society—ayahs often made fascinating subjects for photography.

Many ayahs were abandoned in London as an increasing
number of English families disregarded the old policy of providing
their servants with a return ticket or equivalent fare. As early as
1855, the East End was home to about sixty ayahs. By 1870, over
a hundred of them were travelling each year to England with their

employers, and by 1875, over a hundred unemployed ayahs had boarded in lowbrow lodging-houses of the city. Living between rowdy men and rank poverty, with weekly rents going up as high as 16s., the ayahs may very well have been driven to livelihoods of loose morals. If not the deplorable conditions in which ayahs lived, the fact that they lived so far from Christian graces and sermons was, indeed a deep concern for Victorian Londoners. Around 1863, Mr and Mrs Rogers opened an Ayah's Home at Jewry Street in Aldgate. Administrative failures led to the temporary shutting down of the Home in 1891. The establishment was taken over by the London City Mission after protests by a committee of white British women. It was rebuilt ten years later. Joseph Salter, a missionary and human rights activist, who had absorbed several Indian dialects while working with lascars in London, dedicated his energies to the re-establishment of the Home in the final years of his life. Salter wanted to defend the vulnerable minds of the heathens from the sins of their native lands as well as those of Europe.

The Home, in its new avatar, relocated to King Edward Road in 1900. In 1921, it shifted to a larger building in the same locality where it was inaugurated by the wife of Lord Chelmsford. In 1908, Mrs Dunn, the Matron of the Home, recorded in her testimony an instance where an ayah had been abandoned. She had accompanied a British woman to England. Upon her arrival, Thomas Cook and Sons—noted travel agents of the time who doubled up as agents for hiring Indian servants—directed her to a family in Scotland. It was understood that the ayah would leave for India with the family when they sailed from London. Instead, the family abandoned her at King's Cross Station with a hapless pound in her hand, with which she was expected to find her way to the Thomas Cook office. The agents transferred the case of the ayah to the Home. Mrs Dunn, unable to accommodate the destitute and ticketless boarder, went knocking on the door of the India Office, that then arranged for the woman's passage back to India. Owing to the increasing number of abandoned servants in England, the Committee on Distressed Colonial and Indian

Subjects was instituted in 1910 to look into the welfare of these trafficked denizens. It worked closely with the Ayah's Home.

The Home had thirty rooms that provided yearly housing for over a hundred ayahs from India, China or the Malayan Peninsula. The governing spirit of the Home was to Christianise the ayahs in the guise of philanthropic work. Religious practices, such as the learning of hymns and church visits, though optional for the residents, were highly valued. Superintendents of the Home were expected to be conversant in Indian languages to add a touch of Oriental familiarity to the evangelical mission. It was a prototype of modern employment agencies for domestic help services. Shipping offices in London listed the Ayah's Home as an important address. Every ayah that came to stay here was given a return ticket to India (or another Asian country) by the English family she had accompanied to London. The return ticket stayed with the matron of the Home, and was sold to any new family that wanted to employ the ayah's services. The weekly rent for the Home was 14s., but the ayahs did not pay it themselves. It was taken care of by the sale of their return tickets. Whatever more was required to run the Home came from charitable donations, including from the Viscountess of Chelmsford. Albeit reluctantly, the India Office also stepped in to clear its moral deficits. Lives in the Home were briefly documented in an article by Alec Roberts, 'Missionary London', which he wrote for *Living London* (1901), picturing a dozen ayahs as reading, sewing and fraternising in a Christian way, to portray the establishment as a vehicle to guide those it believed to be unenlightened alien women on to the path of sacred domestic ideals.[6] Roberts' article, which was widely read and popularised, attempted to inoculate this small community of female outsiders for contemporary readers, lest the sanctimony of London's homes was disrupted by fears of racial contamination.

A similar class of Indians, whose population became significantly thicker in the 19th century, and even came to be termed or seen as marginally 'British', was that of the lascars. In 1849, the British Parliament repealed its 200-year-old Navigation Acts to encourage free-market capitalism, which had earlier been considered particularly detrimental to the formal growth of the British Empire due to European or American smuggling of tea, sugar, molasses, textiles and the like. As more free-trading enterprises came to be legislated for, modern industrial Britain and its shipping industry was more frequently employed with Indian lascars than ever before. In 1823, the Merchant Shipping Act or the 'Lascar Act' laid down political and economic restrictions on the employment of lascars. Accordingly, lascars were not to be considered as British citizens and, hence, they could not be paid or discharged in British territory. Lascars left behind in Britain had to be repatriated to India, with damages borne by the East India Company. Captains failing to report the arrival of a lascar into Britain were to be penalised with £10. Although the Lascar Act was not repealed until 1963, the repeal of the Navigation Acts did have a partially ameliorative effect on the regulations and legislations for the employment of lascars in Britain.

With the expansion of steam navigation, British ships needed sturdy seamen to work in the furnaces of engine rooms. In 1823, the East India House resounded with debates on the East India Trade bill, introduced in the House of Commons by William Wynn, chiefly to 'admit East-India-built ships to all privileges of British registry.'[7] The debates investigated the effects new lascars would have on the environment of London dockyards. Lascars, as one viewer stated, 'were a very acute and cunning set of people,' and that 'when once they entered this land flowing with milk and honey, the devil himself would not be able to get them back.'[8] Shipbuilders and ship owners who could have hired an Indian lascar for the monthly rate of a dollar would have had to pay £2 for a British seaman, roughly ten times the Indian rate. Naturally, it was profitable for industrialists to have more lascars stranded in England, instead of being officially reported or deported to India. However, there was always the possibility that it would inflate the number of poor Englishmen at the dockyards and London streets, if lascars were to be considered of the same rank as them.

The beginning of the 19th century saw systematic efforts at regulating the working conditions of lascars. In 1814, the Government of India brought in specifications for clothing, food and spice rations, bedding and sleeping and healthcare provisions for Indian seamen. The regulations were, however, not strictly followed, leading to up to 40 per cent risk of lascar deaths on England-bound ships. The risk rose to 50 per cent on ships bound for India, especially in cases where lascars returned home unemployed. The next year, the British Parliament set up the Committee on Lascars and Other Asiatic Seamen in order to look into the system of recruiting and regulating the working conditions of seamen. Stricter regulations were placed on lascar recruitments that now required attestations by Governors of Presidencies in India, stating that the captains or shipowners were, indeed, unable to hire British seamen in the given town or district, which is why Indian lascars had to be recruited. Until 1834, the Company provided very modest lodgings for lascars in England. Indian seamen who usually met with fellow lascars on ships to Britain, huddled up later in groups of anything between seven and twenty-five, all living and cooking in the same quarter. However, a few weeks of staying in a foreign land awakened their inhibitions over ethnic and religious barriers, and very soon Muslim or Hindu lascars would not permit the shadow of the other to fall upon their food.

There was also the imminent danger of riots between lascars and British workers on the streets of London. In 1803, three lascars armed with cutlasses broke into the City of Carlisle public house in Whitechapel, seeking to recover a sum of £150, which they claimed local sex-workers had stolen from them. The incident alarmed the Directors of the Company, not necessarily for the security of the British public, but for the safety of the lascars who had apparently been poor preys at the hands of the 'women of the town'.[9] Two years later, in October, lascars hijacked the streets of Shadwell. The incident was followed by a deadly riot. Nineteen people were taken into custody; fifteen hospitalised. In November, lascars thronged around the Tower of London, protesting the abduction of a colleague by a local sex-worker. At times, Englishwomen became the bone of contention between seamen of different ethnicities. In 1806, 300 Chinese and a few Arab seamen rioted with about 150 Indian lascars to settle old sexual rivalries concerning a few Englishwomen. A couple of years later, a Muslim Indian lascar called Imambacchus was killed by three Malay Muslim lascars. Imambachhus had been living with one Sarah Williams on Cable Street in East London. On the night of the episode, Williams left with one of the Malay seamen, agreeing to offer him sexual favours in exchange for drinks at the Blue Gate public house on the Ratcliffe Highway. Imambachhus returned to find his partner with another of the Malay lascars. The Indian was attacked by the Malay seamen along with two other men. They were later convicted of manslaughter. Other minor scuffles often featured Indian and British sailors. In 1808, a duel broke out between a lascar and an armed and inebriated British seaman. 400 lascars gathered in support of their fellow seafarer. The crowd had to be quelled with bayonets by a squad of British military men who were in the vicinity.

In 1834, when the East India Company lost its trading rights in Asia, its obligation to operate lodging houses in London's docklands for lascars and traders also ended. In came a new generation of entrepreneurs who set up their own lodging houses, at times in partnership with British women, to temporarily accommodate inbound seamen. These lodges came to be known as 'Oriental Quarters'. In Liverpool and Salford, Meer Jan and Jan Abdoolah ran lodging houses. At Bluegate Fields, one of the typical Victorian slum areas, Abdul Rhemon ran two lodging houses in partnership with his English wife. Having arrived in London from Surat in the 1830s, he worked his way up from being a crossing-sweeper around St Paul's Cathedral to a translator in the suite of the Nepalese ambassador, Jung Bahadur, who visited London in the 1850s. Rhemon's lodging houses were allegedly dens of opium and prostitution. A similar whorehouse, or 'quarters', was run by a Bengali Indo-Portuguese woman and her English partners, who boarded Indian and Chinese lascars.

Victorian London abounded in Indian drum players, musicians, curry-powder sellers, snake-charmers, jewellery hawkers, some of them who had arrived as lascars and converted to Christianity. Calcutta's Jhulee Khan jumped ship in 1841, and took to making a living by performing in musical events in Scotland and England. In 1857, he surfaced in Tottenham, and probably under the influence of his future English wife, he was baptised John Carr, who now sang hymns and preached the Gospel on the city's streets. He returned to Calcutta as a missionary in 1866 with his wife and five children. Then there was Joaleeka, in his fifties, who had travelled extensively in India as a baggage servant to a European army man. He came to London with an Indian prince, and while staying in Oxford Street, contracted an alliance with an English maidservant. Joaleeka converted to Christianity and took up several wives who bore him three children.

Seeing lascar deserters shack up comfortably in London, even in their seedy skins and quarters, might have been mortifying for Victorians. However, more than the fear of their contaminating London, evangelical missions were regularly concerned about London contaminating these naïve 'heathens'. Evangelical journals of the day decried the 'deplorable' state of lascars in the city. 'O yes, it is in London,' read an 1843 issue of *The Mariner's Church Gospel Magazine*, 'that the poor ignorant Lascar is to be seen drunk from morning to night, rolling in the vilest debauchery, so that very little ship's duty can be done by them until they are forced to sea again, from Shadwell, or Limehouse, or Stepney.'[10] Officers of the East India Company confirmed that it was impossible to keep lascars 'out of the brothels and public-houses, the moment they reached London.' Indeed, London seemed to have indulged them with a certain depravity which their 'own heathen temples never exceeded.'[11] The British press was also critical of new capitalist policies of the government that were leading to London's dockyards being crowded by lascars, forced to live in fatal poverty. On November 20, 1843, a gloomy report on the death of a lascar appeared.

Lascar Seamen—On Saturday, an inquest was held on board the Thames East Indiaman, now lying in the East India Docks, on the body of a Lascar seaman, named Mamarie, aged twenty-six, alleged to have died from want of medical assistance. The stench emitted from the cabin in which the body lay, and in which the Lascar slept daring the voyage, was so great, that the jury were unable to remain in it more than a few seconds. The Thames was the property of Mr Greek, of Bristol. On leaving Calcutta, there were ninety-five Lascars on board, but twenty-three had died from scurvy and dysentery on the voyage homewards. The surgeon on board left the ship along with the captain on her reaching Margate, without providing medical treatment for any of the crew who might be sick. 'The Lascars lived on fish, rice, and split peas, but had no meat. The deceased had been ill about four days, and on Friday was found dead in bed. Several of the jury severely animadverted on the treatment the Lascar seamen received, and the coroner said it was the duty of the owners to provide medical assistance; and should death ensue in consequence of not having it, they were guilty of manslaughter. The chief-mate in reply to the question, said there were twenty Lascars now ill on board without medical assistance, and it was not unusual for a great many Lascars to die during the voyage. They have no hammocks to lie upon, but only rugs, which they find themselves. Mr H. Hornfield, surgeon, said he had been on board the vessel, and had seen the body. He was of opinion that consumption was the cause of death. He had examined all the crew, but there was no evidence of dysentery being prevalent on board. With the exception of about four, nearly the whole were suffering from scurvy; four or five of them so bad, that he could remove their teeth with the greatest ease. This he should say was caused by diet. The coroner said they must adjourn for the attendance of the owners, and also for a post mortem examination, as it was necessary that the most searching investigation should be pursued, for if death was proved to have resulted either from the neglect of the captain or the owner, it amounted to manslaughter.'[12]

The inquest was lengthy. Although the jury did not positively chastise the captain or the shipowner, it held that the welfare of the lascars were the duties of both. The captain, in this case, promised that if any lascar under his command was taken ill, in future, he would pay for the surgeon's fee if the shipowner refused or delayed doing so. It was hard to keep off the apparition of the Indian lascar from the eyes of English public, or keep off the English public from sympathising with them, given how integral they were to the Industrial Revolution and British overseas commerce. The susceptibility of Indian lascars to drunken acts, indiscipline and insubordination was still seen as less threatening than that of their European or British counterparts. Lascars were also less likely to be unionised than British seamen. Without the muscle power of lascars, 'the British merchant fleet in the Indian Ocean would have ground to a complete standstill.'[13] Since the 1840s, the Peninsular and Oriental Steamline, the Bibby Line, Harrison Line and Clan Line annually recruited an increasing number of Indians as their firemen. Traditionally, they came from the port cities of Surat, Goa, Bombay, Cochin, Calcutta, Sylhet or Chittagong. Later, lascars from the landlocked cities of Punjab, Peshawar, Bengal, Assam and the North-West Frontier Province also came to be employed due to increasing labour requirements on the seas. Beginning with a majority of Muslims, Hindus and Christians also later added to the lascar population in England or the Indian Ocean. Besides London, Glasgow, Cardiff and Liverpool were the new cradles of Anglo-Indian lascar communities.

An audit from 1855, conducted by Lieutenant Colonel R.M. Hughes of the East India Company, suggested that there were about 12,000 Indians, Chinese and Australian seamen in the employ of British merchant services, and about half that number was being transported to Britain annually. In the 1850s, there came a change in the recruitment policy of British shipowners, owing to new legislations that discouraged lascar settlements in England. Following the Merchant Shipping Act of 1854, shipowners were to be fined £30 for lascars left behind in Britain. In 1871, Lascar Transfer Officers began to be deputed by the Board of Trade at all important ports for the task of transporting lascars to London, and thence to India. In order to prevent the destitution of lascars in English docklands, the new Merchant Shipping Act of 1894 brought in the binding clause that any unemployed lascar in Britain, by dint of a prior agreement signed with his shipowner, was to head to a British port and sign a fresh agreement to sail as part of the crew upon a ship bound for any Indian port. The legislation was often manipulated to interpret any failure to meet the guidelines as a criminal offence by the lascars. Written in 1873, Joseph Salter's *The Asiatic in England: Sketches of Sixteen Years' Work Among Orientals* records several instances of maltreatment of lascars in England, as well as on the high seas, particularly in one macabre incident when Muslim seamen were hung by their feet with weights tied, before being flogged with a rope. They were also force-fed pork and the intestines of a pig were hung about their necks. One terrified lascar who tried to escape the torture flung himself into the sea and drowned. Many lascars were also imprisoned on false or unsubstantiated charges, especially because they were unable to plead for themselves in a language intelligible to the authorities. One of them was Sadiq, who was arrested on charge of assaulting a woman. The fact that she had robbed him of his money prior to the assault went unheeded by the police. Sadiq was, however, miraculously rescued from prison by a missionary, after securing his release papers from the Home Secretary, barely hours before his ship was to sail for India.

With support from the Seamen's Hospital Society, the National Appeal for East India and China Sailors drew up an impressive campaign for delivering homeless lascars in London from moral, spiritual and physical degeneration, and from the harsh open streets into a Christian and economical shelter. Salter was himself instrumental in agitating for the establishment of a sailor's home in London along with Colonel Hughes. Together, they amassed donations worth £15,000, with £5,000 coming from Indian donors. Their efforts culminated in the founding of the Strangers' Home for Asiatics, Africans and South Sea Islanders on the West Indian Dock Road in Limehouse. The foundation stone of the Strangers' Home was laid by Prince Albert in May 1856, and it officially opened its doors in 1857. A generous donation of £500 was offered by Maharajah Duleep Singh, the last King of the Sikh Empire. Other regular contributions came from directors of the East India Company and the Peninsula & Oriental Steam Navigation Company. Later, the India Office also contributed £200 for the repatriation of destitute lascars. 'It was a happy day,' wrote Salter, marking the occasion when 'flags of all nations and gay streamers of every colour floated in the air over the site of the future Home.' Maharajahs and lords, princesses and nabobs, Mohammedans and Hindus, Parsis and Persians and Africans and Burmese were among those who attended the ceremony, threatening to steal the thunder of those homeless seafarers whose own history was being finally written.

> The longing eyes of the starving hundreds of Asiatics in London were hopefully turned to the new building, and daily crowded round its door for help, and to have their name registered for service. Each one had his tale of woe and suffering to tell. Fraud, robbery, begging, imprisonment, starvation, formed the common history of each. Shoeless, shirtless, in rags and dirt. The Asiatic Home in London is the centre of attraction to the stranger coming from the East; often in starting from his home he has that destination in view. Ruined nobility, and even scions of the royal root seeking to re-establish their lost fortunes by coming to London, have had 'the Home' in London in view, and have never been disappointed in their application. Asiatic seamen who have landed at Liverpool, and even Glasgow, have arrived by rail, if they could afford it, and many have tramped up all the way, if destitute.[14]

In the course of its eighty-year-old journey, the Strangers' Home went on to have 220 beds, luggage-room, reading and smoking rooms and kitchens and dining rooms, where boarders had the independence to cook their own meals. In the first twenty years of its existence, the Home had only a little over 5,700 lascar boarders. Hughes, who became the secretary of the Home, acquired the specialty of tracing and repatriating London lascars. The Home was a nucleus of all wandering lascars in the city, as well as a missionary centre, where Salter cautiously played the role of a benign evangelist, whispering in their ears the 'unsearchable riches of Christ.' Salter also helped set up the Asiatic Rest at the East India Dock Road. At Tilbury Dock Road came up the London City Mission's Lascar Institute. Both were meant to be social and recreational centres for lascars, aimed at their moral edification. Besides in English, both places had signboards in Bengali and Persian.

Just before the outbreak of the Great War, nearly 17.5 per cent of British seamen, numbering about 51,000, were constituted by Indian lascars. In the same year that the London Home was established, the Glasgow Sailors' Home came up in Broomielaw. In the early 20th century, it received over 5,000 lascar boarders annually. By the end of the war, another home was started in Queen's Dock at Glasgow. In 1908, a group of Indian students, supported by Rose Majumdar, organised a cultural event at the Royal Albert Dock for the benefit of the London lascar community. In 1909, K. Chowdry, a former secretary of the Manchester Indian Association and assistant secretary to the British Indian Seamen's Institute, steered the foundation of the Lascars' Club at Victoria Dock Road. The club drew an illustrious list of subscribers, including Princess Sophia Duleep Singh, the Maharajahs of Scindia and Burdwan, Sir Ratan Tata and Lord Curzon. Within a year, the club had opened its gates to about 5,000 lascars.

In 1880, St Luke's Lascar Mission founded the St Andrew's Waterside Mission at the Victoria Dock Road. A Bengali Christian missionary, Reverend E.B. Bhose, was placed in charge of it. Like Salter, Bhose was fluent in many Indian languages by virtue of having worked with Asiatics, although in the West Indies. In 1887, he became chaplain of St Luke's Mission, and helped convert several lascars. Until his death, in 1905, Bhose ran a Sunday school and a mission club room from his rented apartment. Four years after his death, a Muslim convert by the name Luqa, originally Yusuf Sayah, became an assistant at the Mission. Sayah hailed from Bombay, where he was a priest at a mosque, and was also trained in medicine and Islamic law. A contemporary of

Bhose and Luqa in Glasgow, Aziz Ahmad, was highly critical of Christian missionaries. Being a Muslim convert to Christianity, Aziz was sent for missionary training by the Indian Missionary Society, from Lucknow to Scotland, in the 1880s. From Glasgow, he contributed to periodicals in Amritsar and Lahore, which were allegedly seditious, even leading to his investigation by Scotland Yard. He was later reported as clean and unworthy of being executed. Despite his privations, Ahmad did not stray from the path of Christ. Rather, he plunged himself into the works of his Lascar Mission, which he used as an evangelical as well as a literacy campaign among the seamen. The mission is said to have survived until well after the war.

Immigrants were the scourge of London, behind whom more immigrants took shelter. The 100,000 Jews of Spitalfields and Whitechapel were an ideal front for Asian immigrants to hide behind until they were inseparable from the phizog of the East End.

> Because it did indeed lie towards the east, it became associated with that larger 'east' which lay beyond Christendom and which threatened the borders of Europe. The name given to the dispossessed children of the streets, 'street-Arabs,' offers some confirmation of this diagnosis. The East End was in that sense the ultimate threat and the ultimate mystery. It represented the heart of darkness.[15]

English wives of Indian lascars were to be found a dime a dozen in the East End. They muttered a strange mixture of Cockney English and Hindustani, spiked with opium and alcohol. Their children grew up to be the crudest anomalies of the great imperial racial miscegenation. These Englishwomen, better known by their pejoratives, 'Calcutta Louise,' 'Lascar Sally,' 'Mrs Janoo,' or 'Mrs Peeroo,'[16] made for the sleazy surpluses of Britain's global commerce that were now dotting the docklands of the imperial city. They were seen as victims of impregnation by those who were seen as the lowest-born of the Orient. The life of one such

woman, Audrey Ann Mahomet, came to be recorded in the book
From Street Arab to Pastor, written in 1894 by her son Albert
John Mahomet. Born in 1858, Mahomet was perhaps the first
known British-Indian photographer. His father John was born in
Calcutta, and had probably landed in Britain as a lascar. He began
selling watches, knives, scissors and jewellery in Norfolk before
marrying Audrey Ann Jenkinson. Along with their six children,
the Mahomets came to live at Bow in East London before John
decided to abandon his family and set sail for Calcutta, never to
return. The Mahomet family lived in clichéd squalor, where Albert
was exposed to gangs of criminal youths, drunken brawls, racial
abuses and, at times, unexpected acts of kindness by neighbouring
slum dwellers. Still a young boy, Mahomet was chosen as the
leader of a gang of slum children. When he was eight years old,
his elder brother Eli was caught stealing, and was transferred to
a reformatory at Feltham. Audrey Ann was arrested for public
indecency and her children were put up at a Limehouse factory.
In 1868, Albert lost his brother Sake Husson to consumption.
His eldest sister, Rosa, stricken by the responsibility of managing
the entire family at a tender age, died when she was eighteen.
Albert and his two sisters were sent to Thursford, a town near
Wells-Next-the-Sea. After several years of odd jobs at inns and
hotels, apprenticed to a doctor and a lawyer, a blacksmith and a
school superintendent, Albert became a Sunday School teacher.
Having converted to Christianity in Norfolk, he became a
preacher at a United Methodist Free Church school in Lincoln,
later going on to preach in Lincolnshire, Nottinghamshire,
Lancashire and Yorkshire. With his wife, Paulina Gill, who was
a fellow missionary, Albert returned to London for a few years,
and settled in Littleborough. In 1893, they returned to Wells-
Next-the-Sea, where Albert continued with his evangelical work
and also began a career as a photographer, spawning generations
of Mahomets, who probably still live in Norfolk and other parts
of Britain.

In 1877, an English civil servant, Thomas Henry Thornton, undertook the organisation of the 'Delhi Durbar' to mark the official transfer of administration from the East India Company to the Crown, proclaiming Queen Victoria as the Empress of India. Although the Queen did not herself grace the ceremony in India, it was attended by maharajahs, nawabs, politicians and leaders of great affluence, led by the Viceroy of India, Lord Lytton. To mark the ceremony in England, a Durbar Room was ordered to be built in Osborne House, Queen Victoria's royal residence at East Cowes on the Isle of Wight. The Durbar was designed by Rudyard Kipling's father, John Lockwood Kipling, and built by Ram Singh of Lahore. In 1887, three days after the Golden Jubilee ceremony of the Queen, an Indian delegation of servants arrived at Balmoral Castle, in Scotland, to participate in the royal carnival staged in honour of their empress. The Indian who was given the task of serving the Queen at her table was Abdul Karim, a twenty-four-year-old clerk from Agra, accompanied by his friend Mohammed Bux. A reticent, handsome and remarkably tall man, Karim left an immediate impression on the Queen. Over the following months, she decided to learn Hindustani from him—lessons that were peppered with snippets of the cultural and religious myths of India. He also had the privilege of cooking the Queen her first curry.

Within a couple of years, Karim was the Queen's own munshi. The progress she made in the language served only to exasperate her own coterie, for it paved the way for her to greet Indian visitors in Hindustani. Victoria intended for Karim to go down in history in a hazardous way. Through Lord Lansdowne, the Viceroy of India, she arranged for a large plot of land for Karim just outside Agra. She also gifted her own houses—Frogmore Cottage and Arthur Cottage at Balmoral—to her 'dear good Munshi'. What seemed to have begun as one of her many eccentric seasons was now tottering on the threshold of a historic scandal. Victoria went on to stay with Karim at Glassalt Shiel, an isolated cottage in her Scottish estate. She had often visited the place with her Scottish attendant and close friend, John Brown. It was speculated even during the Queen's own lifetime, that she was engaged in an affair with the Scotsman after the death of King Albert. Recent evidence of a letter from Victoria to Brown does little to suggest the contrary. Since Brown's death in 1883, the forlorn Queen had passed many a twelvemonth as a twice-widowed ruin. Whether or not Victoria exactly took Karim for a substitute to Brown, her royal household certainly did.

The Queen continued to wear a cataract in the face of the rebellious gossip all around. She travelled with Karim to her annual holidays in the French Riviera, gave him a special place during Christmas celebrations and presented him to King Umberto I of Italy. On her eightieth birthday, Victoria appointed him as a Commander of the Royal Victorian Order. When the munshi was indisposed, she looked after him personally like a mistress or mother. She also commissioned Heinrich von Angeli to paint his portrait, and wrote several letters to him signed with affectionate endearments and kisses. In 1892, when Karim's father Waziruddin visited Britain, the Queen arranged for him to stay at her own castles in Balmoral and Windsor. Two years later, she promoted Karim to the rank of Hafiz (royal guardian scholar). The munshi was not satisfied. What he truly wanted was a peerage, possibly a knighthood. Lord Elgin, the new Viceroy of India, was furious at the hint of having a vernacular clerk promoted to the order of a knight. He prevailed upon the Queen to override the prospect at once. As the looming racialism of a new age was brewing its venom, Victoria adamantly handed over a Hindustani phrase book to each of her servants and staff, for them to fraternise with Karim in his own language. 'For a dark-skinned Indian to be put very nearly on a level with the Queen's white servants was all but intolerable, for him to eat at the same table with them, to share in their daily lives was viewed as an outrage.'[17]

On one occasion, the Queen's Assistant Secretary, Sir Fleetwood Edwards, refused to sit at tea with the munshi. Victoria was rather contented to alienate her staff and members of the royal household, including her son and the next King, Edward VII (Albert Edward), over the contretemps surrounding Karim's alleged kleptomania, promiscuity and lowly family background.

The gravest of all accusations was his disestablishmentarianist associations with the Muslim law student Rafiuddin Ahmed. 'Bertie', as the future king was known to her, is said to have fought bitterly with his mother over her orders for Karim to be allocated a seat among the royalty during an entertainment hosted at Edward's residence at Sandringham House in Norfolk. After almost a decade of tensions in the royal household, coupled with the munshi's mounting ambitions, the Queen and Karim seemed to have fallen out. Sir James Reid, the royal physician who was used as a foil by Edward, managed to unearth startling details about Karim's past life, including his alleged gonorrhoea, to expose him before her. Simultaneously, he would use her shocking proximity to the munshi as cold data to his theory that Victoria was gradually lapsing into the tight grip of insanity. Reid had deputed the Queen's Equerry, Frederick Ponsonby, to chase the last piece of scurrilous detail on Karim. Ponsonby even had him shadowed in India by the Thuggee and Dacoity Department when the munshi was on a holiday in 1896. Much of Ponsonby's investigation was inconclusive. Even Ahmed—the political brain behind the seditious movement that Karim was allegedly involved in—was found to be an honourable and unimpeachable scholar.

Back in the royal household, Reid revolted from the thought that the Queen had made Karim more important than him in the royal household. He cautioned her that unless she distanced herself from the munshi, her mind would be clinically termed as 'foundered',[18] declared mad, and King Edward announced as the regent. In early 1900, he publicly confirmed that the Queen had entered the initial stages of dementia—but not before she duly testified before the Court and Prime Minister Lord Salisbury that the munshi had no access to state papers. Besides, he was not even conversant with the English language, and would not have been able to read anything of consequence in government matters. Lady Curzon—wife of Elgin's successor and the architect of the Partition of Bengal—took more kindly to Karim. 'The Munshi bogie,' she wrote 'which had frightened all the household at Windsor for many years had proved a ridiculous farce, as the poor man had not only given up all his letters but even the photos signed by Queen and had returned to India like a whipped hound. All the Indian servants have gone back so now there is no Oriental picture and queerness at Court.'[19]

When Victoria died in 1901, all papers and letters in possession of Karim were confiscated from his residence at Frogmore cottage and burned under orders from the King. The munshi was the last to see Victoria's corpse before the coffin was taken away. Forthwith, he was relieved from his duties. Along with his relatives employed at the royal household, he was packed off to India. Karim died eight years later, quietly in his cottage in Agra. King Edward had the remaining papers and correspondences between the Queen and the munshi seized from Karim Lodge and sent to him by the Commissioner of Agra, W.H. Cobb. When Viceroy Lord Minto along with the civil servants of the India Office, made known to the King his disapproval, he relented by returning four letters subject to be sent back to him after the death of Karim's first wife. The munshi's exploits that roused the royal household against the Queen were probably worth finding him a statue at Madame Tussauds. Since that was not to be, Abdul Karim became a Black British hero in 1988 in Salman Rushdie's *Satanic Verses*. Besides the many things Rushdie became notorious for there was also Karim's waxwork statue that could be seen at the fictitious Hot Wax Nightclub in that fateful novel.

Scene III

Scent of Steam

In April 1831, the socio-religious reformer, linguist, journalist, and founder of the Brahmo Samaj, Raja Rammohun Roy, arrived in Liverpool, along with his adopted son Rajaram, two servants and several cows for his daily milk consumption. Roy was the first known Hindu of an established social standing, often claimed as the first Brahmin, to visit England. He was sent as an envoy of the Mughal Emperor Shah Akbar II to petition before the Company's directors to increase his annual pension. By the end of his stay in England, Roy was successful in swelling up the Emperor's coffers by £30,000 annually. His name had of course already reached the English press, owing to his aggressive campaign against Sati, his continued advocacy of renewal of the abolition bill passed by the William Bentinck Government in 1829 and the memorandum he had submitted to the Parliamentary Committee on Indian Affairs in 1830. For most British people, 'he was India incarnate'.[1]

Upon his arrival in London, Roy was consensually lionised across the Whig and Tory ranks, women's rights campaigners and London society in general. Besides his several other accomplishments, the Raja's acquaintances in England often alluded to his consummate command over the English language. That went down as one of the first attributes that London would celebrate for the coming century, whenever it recognised an Indian worth his salt—or an Indian with guts worth hating.

────────

'The fame of Rammohun Roy had preceded him,' wrote a reviewer, 'but the official character in which he came, together with the state of public affairs, necessarily brought him forward to public notice even more than might otherwise have been expected.'[2] Roy was well known in London's Unitarian circles, by 1818, when several of his essays on Vedanta appeared in issues of the *Monthly Magazine*, alongside works by Jeremy Bentham, P.B. Shelley, William Godwin and Thomas More. One of these was even passed on to Samuel Taylor Coleridge, and although the two never met in person, Roy's writings continued to opiate the English poet. With the gradual proliferation of his works during the Bentinck administration, England and Europe were beginning to come to terms with Roy's 'Hindoo Reformation' of Bengal. He was considered to be a fierce Vedantin, critical of the concept of the Trinity. In popular English imagination, he was seen as a convert to Protestantism. When he finally arrived in London, *The Satirist* broke its principle of avoiding religious matters by publishing a review of his essays that had previously appeared in England in 1824. London's theological enthusiasm around Roy soon became a transatlantic phenomenon, as his Unitarian stardom trickled into the American press, whetting popular spiritual appetites in Boston and New York. The American Unitarian Joseph Tuckerman, who met Roy in London, was also a key broadcaster of his views in the United States. In addition, Roy had now put on the garb of a free-trade advocate. That too was in no way scandalous to Londoners. *The Times* described him as 'decidedly in favour of the present system of government as administered through the East India Company, and is not backward in acknowledging the benefits which India has derived under it.'[3] Whether or not he was against British policies, he never gave an impression of being against British rule in India.

To keep up appearances, he even 'seemed unwilling to avow the radical principles he had espoused in Bengal.'[4]

On the day of his arrival, the Liverpool East India Association deputed John Crawfurd to book a hotel for Roy in London. Crawfurd, who was a well-known peasant rights and free-trade campaigner, was responsible for spreading Roy's views on Indian economy in England, and introduced him to the editors of several radical periodicals. Crawfurd had booked rooms for Roy at Long's Hotel in Bond Street, but the Raja turned up at the Adelphi Hotel in Charing Cross. Meanwhile, David Hare, a friend of Roy in Calcutta, had recommended him to his brothers in London. They helped put him up at 48 Bedford Square— an address marked today by a blue plaque, characteristic of postcolonial London. At the hotel where he stayed, visitors left behind their cards. A public figure of the stature of Bentham personally called upon him. Roy was introduced to Bentham by one of the English philosopher's close associates, Colonel J. Young, rather glowingly: 'Not only has he no equal here among his countrymen, but he has none that at all approach to equality, even among the little "sacred Squadron" of all disciples whom he is slowly and gradually gathering around him.'[5] Bentham waited late into the night, finally leaving a note for the Bengali visitor. The father of Utilitarianism would later recommend to the Parliamentary Candidate Society to have in the House of Commons, 'Rammohun Roy as a representative of British India, a half caste, and a negro, in order to subdue the prejudices of colour, and to hold out encouragement and hope to the rest of these races.'[6] Politicians of the day did not really take Bentham's suggestion very seriously, largely owing to his unconventional anti-imperial beliefs. However, under his influence, Joseph Hume, a member of the Parliamentary Candidate Society, did much to persuade the Raja to join Parliament. The campaign never quite matured owing to Roy's ambivalent religious and political ideology.

Roy came to London furnished with letters of introduction from Bentinck, who was, although untrusting of people in general, remarkably well-disposed towards the Raja, despite his disestablishmentarianism. In London, Unitarians, Anglicans, Quakers, singers, members of the Royal Asiatic Society, actresses, reverends and aristocrats compelled Roy to their company, even forcing him to dine on nine consecutive nights. Roy had a formidable grasp over the *Upanishads*, besides Arabic and Persian. He charmed London's audiences with his expositions on how Sanskrit was, in fact, the mother of Greek, and the roots of the New Testament were contained in the Vedanta philosophy of ancient India. Roy's earliest biographer, Sophia Dobson Collet, was only ten years old during his stay in London. She was to grow a keen interest in the workings of the Brahmo Samaj and 19th-century Hindu reform, while compiling *The Life and Letters of Raja Rammohun Roy*, which was published posthumously in 1900. In studying Roy's life, Collet went on to write significant tracts on Brahmo philosophy and Brahmo reformers, thus, keeping the memory of the Bengal Renaissance well in currency in late-Victorian Britain.

Roy enjoyed special attention from Lord Henry Peter Brougham, the Lord Chancellor of Great Britain. Brougham was a furious legislator and activist for popular education, legal reform and gender and religious equality. Roy also established close links with the third Marquess of Lansdowne, Henry Petty-Fitzmaurice, who was the Home Secretary and Lord President of the Privy Council. He invited Roy to the Council during sessions covering debates on the overturning of the Bill that had abolished Sati in 1829. An important member of the royal family, responsible for bringing Roy unequalled access to the English political class as well as the Unitarians, was the first Earl of Munster, George FitzClarence, an illegitimate son of King William. Coveting the governor-generalship of India, FitzClarence had turned into a devout Orientalist, following Bentinck's example. He was one of the founders of the Royal Asiatic Society in London, where he invited Roy as a keynote speaker at a session presided over by the Duke of Sussex, Augustus Frederick, brother of King William and Unitarian supporter. Armed thus with royal, political, religious and social endorsements, Roy went on to republish for English readers his most prominent essays on Sati, *Brief Remarks*, *Translation of Several Principal Books*, and *Passages and Texts of the Veds, and of Some Controversial Works on Brahmunical Theology* in 1832. He received many more invitations than he had time to accept. In one of the gatherings where he was an invitee, Thomas Babington Macaulay is said to have waited for him until midnight, only to be disappointed. Roy was himself a witness to the widespread circulation of extracts from his lectures and sermons in contemporary epistolary exchanges within the English intelligentsia. In the letters of the writer and historian, Lucy Aikin, Roy was said to have been a great triumph in women's circles, owing to his admiration for the cerebral qualities and natural intelligences of Englishwomen. Aikin and Roy came very close, far too visibly. She was rumoured to have been his mistress. It was surmised after his death that he had secretly married Aikin.

At a literary gathering conducted by Aikin, Roy was introduced to the Scottish author, Joanna Baillie. She had been central to the literary lives of William Wordsworth, Sir Walter Scott and Lord Byron, among others. Baillie was seemingly won over by Roy during a discussion over Arianism, the heretical principle which defied Christ's divinity. Inspiring a whole new generation of Bengali and Brahmo reformers and transcultural theologians, Roy championed the notion that Christ had Asiatic origins. The following—from a letter written by Aikin to Rev Doctor William Ellery Channing, in June 1831—is how Roy was described on almost any given day while he was in London. Although he was a lifelong Hindu, she introduced him as a Christian, either going by his reputation of collaborating with the Baptist missionary William Carey, or the theological proximity of Christianity with Brahmoism, the religious movement that Roy spearheaded in Bengal. Unitarian missionaries and activists in India, as well as Britain, were convinced that Roy was a Christian convert, a fabrication that possibly sprang from the Unitarian missionary ranks in Serampore. Since the Serampore press had been a bedrock for Roy's popularity in England in the first place, he probably did little to quell the rumours of his conversion. Even as Christian missionaries were eager to adopt him as their exemplar, Roy actively talked against Christian dogmas, such as original sin, across London, Manchester and Bristol.

> In the intervals of politics we talk of the Christian Brahmin, Rammohun Roy. All accounts agree in representing him as a person of extraordinary merit. With very great intelligence and ability, he unites a modesty and simplicity which win all hearts. He has a very great command of the language, and seems perfectly well versed in the political state of Europe, and an ardent well-wisher to the cause of freedom and improvement everywhere. To his faith he has been more than a martyr. On his conversion to Christianity his mother cursed him, and his wife (or wives) and children all forsook him. He had grievous oppressions to endure from the Church party on turning Unitarian. This was at Calcutta; here it is determined to court him. Two bishops have noticed him, and the East India Company show him all civilities. But his heart is with his brethren in opinion, with whom chiefly he spends his time. I hear of him this remarkable saying—that the three countries in Europe which appear even less prepared than Asia for a liberal system of religion, are Spain, Portugal and England.[7]

Roy's popularity among women included his brief but poignant spell of interactions with the author and actress, Fanny Kemble. At their first meeting, he gifted her a translation of Kalidasa's *Abhijnan Shakuntalam* by Sir William Jones. Kemble lovingly offered him a copy of *The Merchant of Venice*. A 'darling of the stage,' Kemble had apparently sent Roy into 'fits of crying' during her performance in the Irish dramatist Thomas Southerne's 17th-century play, *The Fatal Marriage*.[8] He was equally touched by her conscientiousness. Doctor Channing, who happened to be a mutual friend, had inspired Kemble into Unitarianism which, in fact, facilitated a common intellectual ground between her and Roy. At a party hosted by Basil Montagu—Roy's literary neighbour at Bedford Square—Kemble found Roy's attire especially picturesque. She thought it made him 'a remarkable object in a London ballroom'. Kemble was an instant admirer of his sweetness and benign demeanour, not to mention his 'moral force' which deeply attracted her.[9]

In less than the three months that he spent in London, the Raja's name became a phenomenon. One Rev D. Davison—in whose guardianship Roy had placed his son in London—even decided to christen an infant boy as 'Rammohun'. Roy patiently sat through several hours of the baptism. In August, Roy was invited by King William IV to the inauguration of the new London Bridge. The following month, he was formally introduced to the King. The Duke of Cumberland introduced Roy to the House of Lords, where he sided with the Tories to prevail upon them for the passage of the 1832 Reform Bill, while the renewal of the Charter of the East India Company was being discussed in Parliament. At Bristol, Roy had found another influential friend in Dr Lant Carpenter. His daughter, Mary Carpenter, was deeply affected by Roy's life and work and would come to visit India on four occasions. She was also instrumental in the making of the Bristol Indian Association, which was established thirty-seven years after Roy died at Stapleton in Bristol in 1833. That year, his son Rajaram was offered a temporary employment as a clerk at the East India House, less than a decade after Charles Lamb began writing his retirement essay, 'The Superannuated Man', from the same place. It was this building from where India was governed by clerks, scholars and bureaucrats who had never set foot in the colony. Although the sun never set on the British Empire, an exception had been cast upon the mildewed corridors of the East India House, where, as Lamb wrote, 'candles for one-half the year supplied the place of the sun's light.'[10]

———

In the 1830s, Britain had done a lot to invite the jealousy of Russian emperor Nicholas I. The First Reform Bill of 1832 was Britain's window to whitewashing the bars of electoral democracy.

More people could now vote in Britain as the patronage of peers operating as pseudo-electoral godfathers in rotten boroughs was eliminated. Democratic Britain's chief adversary, Imperial Russia, was meanwhile feared to be stoking the fires of civil unrest in Central Asia and Afghanistan, in alliance with local leaders of Kabul and the growing clout of the Sikh Empire in northwestern India. Lord Henry Palmerston and Lord George Auckland were among the first to raise the alarm that Afghan leaders like Dost Mohammad Khan, whom the British had been humouring for a decade, might well have shuffled their loyalties to Russia in a bid to retrieve Peshawar, which had been invaded by the Sikhs. The French too had trained a ferocious army of Sikh fedayeens and soldiers, known as the Dal Khalsa, to fight the British in and around Central Asia.

Britain's own diplomacy with the Ranjit-Singh-led Sikh Empire was treading a shifty ground in which the East India Company found itself playing the second fiddle until Singh's death in June 1839. Two months later, the first Anglo–Afghan War broke out, even as the British went into the first Opium War with China. When Britain invaded Kabul, Dost Mohammded fled to India, and Shah Shuja Abdali Durrani was placed on the throne of Afghanistan. The Great Game between Britain and Russia had now been formally ushered with land conquests merely being the face of the sixty-year-long Cold War that ensued. Most of it was concentrated around expanding the public infrastructure of either nation. For over fifty years now, Britain had been incubating the golden egg of Boulton & Watt's steam engines, that had handloomed the Industrial Revolution beginning with the proverbial mills of Lancashire, Newcastle and Manchester. Capturing seas and navigational expansion had found a new language in Henry Bessemer's innovation in making steel from pig iron, leading to an unprecedented technology of land mobility in the railways that would create the sense of infinite power in infinitesimal time.

Irrefutably, the railways in Asia were a surrogate child of the Great Game. They were meant to accelerate British militarisation of the subcontinent. India's first passenger railroad, managed by the Great Indian Peninsular Railway Company, was opened in April

1853. Not only did it change the way Indians travelled forever, but it also changed the way battles were fought. At the peak of the Rebellion of 1857, the dethroned Mughal emperor Bahadur Shah Zafar promised in his Azamgarh Declaration that if the Badshahi regime was restored in Delhi, he would build Indian-owned railways for native merchants. A few visionary Indians saw in the Great Game an enormous wealth of opportunities for Indian industry and, what was to later become, a modern swadeshi fervour. The road to swadeshi, however, crossed through a passage made up of steam. In November 1839, Ardaseer Cursetji Wadia, the scion of the Wadia family of Bombay, travelled to London, to study marine engineering and waterworks. Building on this experience, Wadia would later go on to be the first Indian official of the East India Company to supervise Europeans in India. London's dockyards and canals had exposed his horizons to rapid inventions in steel and steam, in a rapidly changing Britain. The next year in spring, he witnessed the wedding ceremony of Queen Victoria and Prince Albert, perhaps being the only notable Indian visitor to have left an account of the day.

Ardaseer Wadia had been introduced to the Queen in February. The leverage he took from that meeting, along with his work and connections with the engineers in the city, earned him the post of an Associate of the Institute of Civil Engineers. In 1841, he became the first Indian to be elected a Fellow of the Royal Society. He was also invited to the House of Commons, where he presented clinching evidence on the opium trade between British India and China. Just before Ardaseer Wadia's departure from India, 20,000 opium bales from British and Indian merchants had been seized in Canton by Chinese officials. Wadia's intelligence was crucial from the point of view of the war as well as to help the British circumvent Chinese restrictions on free trade. While in the previous century, the British wanted Indian businessmen and zamindars on their side on Indian soil, under Queen Victoria, Indians would become a visible part of the Empire's goings-on in London and beyond. Ardaseer Wadia was not the first of his family to visit England. His brothers Jehangeer Nowrojee and Hirjeebhoy Meerwanjee had preceded him to

London in 1838. The city overwhelmed them with its bewildering traffic, omnibuses and swelling crowds, astounding architecture, and at times also amused them with its sleeping parliamentarians at the House of Commons. However, coming from an industrial background, their real hypnosis lay on the couch of steam. Between furnishing industrial and military strength, steam appeared to have penetrated into English currency, libraries, drawing rooms, dining rooms and the most basic elements of daily life. 'What is there in England that cannot be done by steam,' wondered the Wadia brothers. In their account, *Journal of Residence of Two Years and a Half in Great Britain* (1841), they wrote:

> Carriages fly upon iron railroads heated by coal, wood is sawn by steam, iron is hammered into anchors, and rolled into plates, bars and wires by steam. The very fires to get up all these powerful machines are blown up by steam, water is pumped by steam, butter is churned by steam, books are printed by steam, money is coined by steam, ships heedless of wind and tide, navigate the seas by steam, guns are fired by steam, and every article of clothing from head to foot is made by steam.[11]

The three Wadia brothers were enthralled by the pageantry of the royalty, clothing fashions and steam technology. Ardaseer Wadia was perhaps one of the very few Indian travellers around this time to find anything remotely dissatisfactory in London. Published in 1841, his *Diary of an Overland Journey from Bombay to England* described London's roads in the pea-soup fog—that ubiquitous megalosaurus of the Dickensian era—to be absolute nuisances. He found London's cab drivers unbearable and the competition between tradesmen and shopkeepers to be stifling. All of that made him long to return to India, and when he chanced on an advertisement in *The Times* for the job of Chief Engineer and Inspector of Machinery at a foundry in Bombay, he wasted no time to bid adieu to Blighty.

Scene IV

The Baboos' Last Sigh

Nine years after Rammohun Roy's death, his close compatriot, Dwarkanath Tagore, arrived in England. Tagore was originally an 'implacable foe' of the Raja.[1] Around 1818, having just come of age, Tagore began attending the Upanishad study sessions organised by Roy in Calcutta. Tagore was far from interested in spiritual learning but was curiously drawn to the enigma around the 'strange maverick' at the helm of these meetings.[2] Two and half decades later, Tagore was himself on a mission to complete the unfinished work of Roy, who over the years had transformed into his 'friend, guide and philosopher.'[3] It was Tagore who transferred Roy's last remains in Bristol to the Arnos Vale cemetery, and commissioned the building of a mausoleum around his grave. About 180 years later, Tagore's own gravestone—at London's Kensal Green Cemetery—lies overshadowed by the memory of Roy's mausoleum in Bristol.

On January 9, 1842, Prince Dwarkanath Tagore boarded the ship *India*, accompanied by his brother, Ramanath Tagore, his nephew Chunder Mohan Chatterjee, his friend Purmananda Moitra, and the oldest son of Rammohun Roy, Radha Pershaud Roy. Also on board were Dr MacGowan (Tagore's physician), Sir Edward Ryan, Messrs Parker and Walker, and a few Italians and Frenchmen. The list of passengers also included three Hindu servants and a Mussalman *khansama* in Tagore's employ. The *khansama* became much sought after in London, where his curries and pilaus were highly prized items. In the city's epicurean circles, they came to be known as 'Dwarkanath dishes'. Tagore's *khansama* was a legend in his own right, and was often consulted to teach 'the *Chef-de-cuisine* in several English households the art of making curries.'⁴

After halting at Egypt, Alexandria, Malta, Italy, Germany, Belgium and France, Dwarkanath Tagore reached London in early June. He and his touring party were hosted at St George's Hotel in Mayfair. Within a couple of weeks, the Hyde Park household of William Prinsep—renowned British painter, merchant and banker—was to be Tagore's residence in London. The city's parks and gardens held a special place in Tagore's travel diary. Known for taking evening walks around Hyde Park, Regent's Park and Kensington Gardens, Tagore was overjoyed to visit the Chiswick Garden Horticultural Festival. He was also introduced to Robert Peel, the then prime minister; Lord Palmerston, the future prime minister; Lord Fitzgerald, president of the Board of Control; and the Marquis of Lansdowne, the home secretary. Lord Brougham, a champion of educational reforms who had been on intimate terms with Roy in the last decade was also quick to make Tagore's acquaintance. Like Roy, Tagore's fame had also preceded him in London—not for spirituality but for his business empire. After founding the Union Bank in 1829, the Bengal Coal Company in 1832, and Carr Tagore and Company, the first Indo–European partnership firm in 1834, Tagore turned his gaze on the prospects of steam locomotion and railways in India. By 1840, he was 'a major thespian on the stage of the colony's private investments and banks, as well as the Bengal Renaissance,' covering a vast portfolio of managing agencies and businesses such as silk, indigo, tea, coal and sugar.⁵ His visit to London was meant to garner the goodwill of the Company and the administration in order to consolidate his plan of connecting his coalfields in Ranigunj with Calcutta and Delhi.

Tagore's itinerary was rather frantic. All of the above meetings took place within the first two days of his arrival in the city. In the first week, the Marquis and Marchioness of Lansdowne organised a lavish dinner for him. In the following, he was entertained by the Court of Directors of the East India Company at the London Tavern. This was just a few days after he was hosted at a banquet given by Queen Victoria and Prince Albert. The Duchess of Kent followed suit. In one of the royal dinners at Buckingham Palace, the duchess proffered to play a game of whist with Tagore, whilst Prince Albert discussed Indian politics with him. The Queen herself was noticeably affected by Tagore, especially after his ornate greeting to her: 'I have overcome the prejudices of myself and all my friends and relations. I have travelled some thousands of miles under trial and privation to see your Majesty—Queen of this great nation. Now if I went back tomorrow, I am amply repaid.'[6] All aquiver with his accolades, she gifted him three gold coins that had been freshly minted earlier that day. She would note in her diary how intelligent he was, and how 'remarkably well' he spoke English.[7]

Victoria was eager to see more of him. Along with the Dukes of Cambridge and Wellington, she soon received Tagore at her annual review of the royal troops. In his third meeting with Victoria, he was shown around the royal nursery. Accompanying him here were also Lady Lyttleton, wife of Tory leader George William Lyttleton, and the Prince and Princess of Wales. For the benefit of his letters back home, he also frequently toured London's zoos, horticultural and artistic exhibitions and galleries, schools, hospitals, factories and docks, as passionately as though he were 'the eyes and ears of India.'[8] In a letter written to his son Debendranath, Tagore seemed to suggest that he had struck new roots in London. The capital and its people surpassed everything that had hitherto charmed him on his grand tour.

After seeing everything on the Continent, I did not expect that I should be so much taken by this little island; but really London is the *wonderful city*; the bustling of the city, the carriages, the shops, and the people, quite bewildered me. From 8 AM till 12 at night, I am engaged either in receiving or returning visits and invitations. Two days after my arrival, I had a very gracious reception by Her Majesty. All the royal family and the principal nobility have made my acquaintance, and the present as well as the late ministers have shown me every attention. If a man has wealth, this is the country to enjoy it in. I was at Westminster Abbey this afternoon. The solemnity of the sermon and prayers, with the singing and organ, was much imposing. I have seen some noblemen's gardens; you may write anything you like about my garden now; I have completely given it up.[9]

In his own estimate, Tagore's princely house in Calcutta, known as Belgatchia Villa, which he had purchased in 1823 from Lord Auckland, was a humble underdog in comparison with the Duchess of Sutherland's Stafford House (known as the Lancaster House today) or the Duke of Devonshire's Chatsworth House. The prince had spent ₹200,000 in renovating his Calcutta mansion. In the course of a month's sojourn in London, he was to obtain over ten times that amount in sheer goodwill. Tagore followed the footsteps of Roy in a rather business-like fashion, only keener to glorify British engineering, commerce and military, than matters of Vedanta and spiritual brotherhood. Dwarkanath's perceptions of the city were sieved through his own notions of European civilisation, or those of his contemporaries alloyed by their own agendas. Karl Marx's partner-in-crime, a thirty-three-year-old Friedrich Engels, who was also in London around this time saw a very different city altogether. In the 1840s, the heart of Albion swarmed with cesspits of ashes and stinking sepulchres.

The corpses have no better fate than the carcases of animals. The pauper burial ground at St Bride's is a piece of open marshland which has been used since Charles II's day and there are heaps of bones all over the place. Every Wednesday the remains of dead paupers are thrown into a hole which is 14 feet deep. A clergyman gabbles through the burial service and then the grave is filled with loose soil. On the following Wednesday the ground is opened again and this goes on until it is completely full. The whole neighbourhood is infected by the dreadful stench from this burial ground.[10]

Tagore shied away from that city. Instead, he was wonderstruck at the Printing House Square upon seeing 20,000 copies of *The Times* packed off in a couple of hours, or the hundreds of thousands of newspapers and letters that were dispatched at the post offices, and he must have inevitably drawn his comparisons with printing businesses back in India, a few of which he too controlled. With Tagore's expedient flattery of their ways, 'English noblemen and gentlemen, men distinguished in the walks of literature and science, men holding the most conspicuous position in the political and legal world, sought his acquaintance, and delighted to honour him.'[11]

Dwarkanath was no stranger to highbrow society or populist means of grabbing public attention. Back in Calcutta, he was a prominent patron of European theatre. In 1835, he purchased the Chowringhee Theatre, which he ran until it was damaged by fire in 1839. While in London, Tagore hired a steamer from Richmond upon Thames to conduct a ride for a literary gathering. He even commissioned a portrait of himself from the painter F.R. Say, around the same time as he was making the acquaintance of Charles Babbage, the inventor of the calculator and father of the modern computer. At the annual dinner of the Lord Mayor of London at Mansion House, Tagore's sympathy towards the Englishmen of India was a point of commendation. The mayor described him as an ornament to English society. Seizing the first opportunity for headlines, Dwarkanath burst into a speech that lasted half an hour. India, he said, 'had been saved from utter destruction by the national friendship and humanity of England.'[12] It was unlikely that Tagore's praise was meant for the British Parliament for impeaching Warren Hastings, or the compassionate hospitality provided to Indian travellers by the likes of Edmund Burke in the previous century. Instead, he showered plaudits on the Clives and the Cornwallises of the Empire, for

their political acumen and military intelligence. English rule, he
believed, had rescued India from the 'tyranny and villainy of the
Mahometans, and no less frightful oppression of the Russians,'
just in the nick of time.[13]

The speech bewildered both Indians and British subjects in
India. Radical factions in London held that Dwarkanath had
compromised humanity itself in exalting Britain's military and
economic prowess. The doughty prince was unmoved. In response
to one of his fierce critics, Joseph Pease, the first Quaker Member
of Parliament in Britain, Tagore reiterated his stance on the Muslim
question, even more unambiguously, or rather emphatically. It was
due to the benevolence of British rule, he said, 'all things considered,
my nation has been benefited by its deliverance from the yoke of
the Mahometans.'[14] Although known for a deeply cosmopolitan
and egalitarian outlook, Tagore's open contempt of the Sultanate
and Mughal periods may well have been more for political
milestones than personal grievances. He intended a lot of it to be
savoured by the British ruling class which was beginning to harvest
its first fruits of the communal divide-and-rule policy in India.
The Tagores believed they had been uprooted from their erstwhile
socio-economic glass palace due to events partly influenced by an
elite Muslim family from Bengal. The Tagore family was of high-
caste Brahmins, until one of the Tagores, Purushottam, 'brought
lasting disgrace upon his family.'[15] He had either inhaled the aroma
of forbidden meat, or had inadvertently married the daughter of
a family of Muslim converts—depending upon which legend one
chose to believe. Later, one of Dwarkanath's great-grandfathers,
Joyram Tagore, who was a secretary in the Bengal administration in
24 Parganas, suffered a blow to his otherwise uninterrupted career
due to the attack on Calcutta by Siraj ud-Daulah's army, in 1756.
After the Battle of Plassey, however, Joyram was given the contract
of reconstructing Fort William. For several generations, the Tagores
nursed the grudge of having been beaten in their fortunes by the
Muslim aristocracy in Bengal, and had finally taken to uniting
the ideals of a Hindu renaissance with the ambitions of Company
directors in London.

As for Tagore's gratitude to Westminster for having kept out the Russians, his timing could not have been more impeccable. Although Russia had no plans of invading India even at the peak of its imperial expansion in Central Asia, fears of losing the 'jewel in the crown' ran rife among the administrators of the East India Company. After the Anglo-Afghan War, Britain's growing power of steam, iron and textile operations in the colony was used as the diplomatic excuse for British industrial settlements and Europeanisation schemes in Central Asia. Empowering the native tribes of Afghanistan, Uzbekistan and beyond was the British front for observing the military movements of Nicholas I. That, as well as the ongoing Russian invasion of Kazakhstan, must have been well known to Tagore. The Great Game had grown even more complex with the decline of the Ottoman Empire, emerging British strongholds in the power vacuum around the Arabian Gulf, and the imminence of the Crimean War with Russia. These were not far from Tagore's motivations behind conceding the suzerainty of the British Empire, and stimulating the ego of its directors in the imperial capital.

In return for his eulogies, London threw open its bounty to Tagore. While his afternoons were hued with cherries, strawberries, currants, gooseberries and the horticultural pageants of Covent Garden, his dinners were decorated with eels, flounders, trout, whitebaits, fowls, lobsters, curried vegetables, tarts and tartlets and puddings and blancmanges. Alongside his brush with royalty, Dwarkanath also had his own share of radical supporters. Perhaps the most influential one of them was Lord Brougham, one of the founders of the Whig-leaning British India Society established in 1839, to address the growing needs of the Indian peasantry, women and the future of educated British subjects. Tagore was Brougham's 'particular and old friend, at the head of everything liberal in India; a man of the world, of excellent natural parts, and master of English to a wonderful degree.'[16] Greatly helped by the press coverage that Brougham had arranged for him, Tagore filled in the shoes of Roy with his own commercial and political intelligence. Leopold von Orlich, a German traveller, counted

Tagore among the most distinguished people in India, 'next to Rammohun Roy.'[17] Like Roy, Tagore's Hindu cultural identity had taken a leap towards Christianity, for that is how Europeans came to identify him.

When he took leave of Queen Victoria and Prince Albert, in October 1842, this is what London remembered him as—a man with features not exactly 'masculine,' nonetheless a dominant and steadfast 'partner in Empire.'

His limbs are beautifully moulded, his hand being the most slender and delicate we have ever seen belonging to one of the male sex; his countenance, in a state of repose, bears an aspect of peculiar thoughtfulness, but, when lighted up, is one of great expression and striking beauty. We have had the opportunity of seeing much of him during his visit to England. We have seen him surrounded by a dozen persons, each directing his attention to a different subject, and have admired the facility with which he can pass from topic to topic, conveying his thoughts on all with singular fluency and equally singular terseness and emphasis. We have seen him at one and the same time dictate letters of business and letters of compliment; make engagements, answer inquiries, receive new-comers, recognise old friends, exchange jokes, strike bargains, and smoke his hookah. By those who have known him longest we have been assured that he is firm in his friendships—proof against the whispers of slander—ever ready to help the honourable struggler in his exertions to secure success in trade—and of incorruptible integrity in all his engagements as a man of business.

The eminent position to which Dwarkanath has placed in his hands the means of being of incalculable service to his country. We believe he feels his responsibility, and fervently desires to exert his vast influence for the good of his brethren. We look forward to his return to this country with high expectations. Informed as he now is of the nature of our institutions, the genius of the British people, the constitution and character of the government, and the true state of things at the India House; and freed as he will be in a great degree from those claims upon his time, which during his present visit have rendered it impossible to devote himself to the great objects to which he stands so deeply pledged, we trust he will come back with a determination to mingle and co-operate with the growing party in this country who are anxious to labour in the cause of India—that justice may, though late, be done to the countless millions of his brethren who have been brought into the situation of subjects to the British Crown, and are entitled to enjoy the blessings of the British Constitution.[18]

Around the time of Tagore's departure, the gossip of a possible knighthood commenced from Lord Brougham's quarters, who was pressed by some of his colleagues to have at least a baronetcy conferred upon the prince. Tagore too had sniffed a royal title. When he returned to Calcutta, he sought the help of his friend, Laurent Dent, to register for a coat of arms. It was awarded to him by the College of Arms, with the shield comprising a ship in the sea, an open book, and an elephant carrying a lotus. On the coat, Tagore adopted as his motto, 'Works Will Win'.

———

Of the most fabled aspects of Tagore's life was his perturbing popularity with Englishwomen. It neatly exceeded the female following of Rammohun Roy; that in itself was an extraordinary benchmark. On his return journey to Calcutta, Tagore was joined in Bombay by one Elisa Reade, who deemed him to be her 'great acquisition'. She seemed especially disturbed by the bigotry of Indian gawkers who expected to see him 'transformed into some beast or other.' Sympathising most affectionately with 'Dwarky,' her nickname for the prince, she wrote that he 'had been more stared at since his return to Calcutta than he was in London.' Tagore's romantic life was the subject of much speculation in London and Bengal.[19] Rammohun Roy's adopted son, Rajaram, wrote to Hare's daughter about Tagore's liaisons with the young wife and mother-in-law of an English ship-captain. The mother in question was English actress Esther Leach. Despite the staggering range of female associations that he contracted, Tagore 'made no attempt to conceal his liaisons. Perhaps, unconsciously, he meant to convey to the British that "partnership" must embrace all aspects of British–Indian relationships.'[20] He was also rumoured to have had affairs with Charlotte E. Harvey, a singer at the Italian Opera Company, and Caroline Norton, a divorced Victorian poet. His allegedly immoral personal life degenerated all the more due to his complicated relationship with his pious wife, Digambari Devi, who in her final years had exiled her husband from her life. Before Tagore left for London, she had passed on, leaving him a free man to India's cause. However, upon his return, the Tagore family at Jorasanko decided to excommunicate him for his refusal to purge himself of the sins of having crossed the oceans, dined in European company and much else that was beneath contempt.

Tagore's commercial success did deflect the public attention, willy-nilly, from his personal strife. While he was in Britain, he kept a distant but alert eye on his coalfields in Ranigunj, and closely studied the progress in the steam industry. After returning to India, he dived straight into lobbying for the merger of the Calcutta Steam Tug Association—a client of Carr Tagore and Company—with the newly formed India General Steam Navigation Company. He also prepared to take advantage of the railway project in Bengal and the rest of India. Rowland MacDonald Stephenson, British banker-turned-engineer and founder of the East Indian Railway Company, turned to Tagore for intelligence, finance and support. Tagore had shares in the newspaper *Englishman*, a predecessor of *The Statesman*. In 1844, he sold it to Stephenson, who started using its columns for his railway promotions. Tagore had promised him of raising a third of the capital for India's first passenger railway service if his coalfields were united to Central India.

'Having flirted with officials of the East Indian Railway Company for a few months, over an idea of building a railway network from Calcutta to collieries in Ranigunj and Burdwan, Tagore decided to plunge into the act himself,' by floating the Great

Western of Bengal Railway Company in 1845.[21] He was desperate
to improve Bengal's education. When Tagore returned to London
that year, he took with him four Bengali students. With the help
of other philanthropists in Calcutta, he sponsored their education
at the University of London for degrees in medicine. They were
Suruji Kumar Chuckerbutty (or Suruji Goodeve Chuckerbutty),
Bholanath Bose, Gopal Chandra Seal and Dwarkanath Bose, each
of whom went on to have a highly accomplished medical career in
India. On this visit to England, Tagore was also accompanied by
his youngest son Nagendranath, and his nephew Nabin Chandra
Mukherji, besides Major Henderson, William Prinsep and other
Englishmen and Europeans. Nagendranath was supposed to have
an education in Latin and the liberal arts, while Nabin Chandra
was employed at Roberts Mitchell and Company. To them, London
seemed like a paradise, where they could lounge in theatres, read
the hallowed literary periodicals of the day, listen to the lectures
of Michael Faraday at the Royal Institution and challenge English
fledglings to debate on the great political events of the day, such
as the Anglo-Sikh Wars, the fall of Peel's cabinet and America's
conflict with the Northwest territories.

The weary old Tagore resumed 'the racket of London life,'
rubbing shoulders with the future Prime Minister William Ewart
Gladstone or authors Charles Dickens and William Makepeace
Thackeray or twittering on religious, political or literary subjects,
until the year waned into a dreary London winter that would
plague him incurably. He left for a short stint in France to regain
his health. When he returned to London, it was clear he would
not survive the summer.[22] On August 1, 1846, Tagore breathed
his last at St George's Hotel. 'A terrific thunderstorm passed over
the great city at the hour of his death,' wrote J.H. Stocqueler, an
English author and journalist, and a friend of the prince. It was, as
Stocqueler remarked,

> … only natural that so truly great a man should pass away in a
> moment of striking solemnity. I had never heard such peals of
> thunder, or saw such vivid flashes of lightning, even during a

mountain storm in Armenia, or the commencement of a rainy monsoon in India, as that which accompanied the divorce of the soul from all that was earthly of the noble Dwarkanath.[23]

Dwarkanath's death left the teenaged Nagendranath immoderately high—but not quite dry—as an alcoholic who would waste himself junketing around England. A disconsolate Nabin Chandra returned to Calcutta to find Tagore's elder sons—Debendranath and Girindranath—excommunicated from the Bengali Hindu society for performing their father's last rites according to Brahmo rituals. In December that year, a campaign was started by a group of European and Bengali intellectuals to raise a trust in the memory of Tagore for supporting the education of Indian students at University College London. With the collapse of the railway bubble and the banking crisis in England, the plan was thwarted. Stephenson, whose only ambition now, at any rate, was to run the first passenger railway in India, had much to rejoice for. In April 1847, with a strong backing from its London committee, his East Indian Railway Company purchased the Great Western of Bengal, burying with Tagore the last sighs of his dream of a swadeshi railway in India.

———

Tagore led the departure of India's destiny from England in ways that were less perceptible in his lifetime than later. But for his amorous ways of doing business with London, he and his sons would not have been outcastes in their own family. Like a Shakespearean spectre, the dead Tagore would come back to alter the religious and economic currents of Bengal and London. After being anathematised over his father's last rituals, Debendranath did not stay quiet for very long. Over the following decade, he fortified the Brahmo Samaj into a religious citadel from where to attack both Hindu and Christian dogmas in Bengal. As he assumed almost presidential control over the Samaj, the reverence that had been earlier accorded to Unitarianism and Universalism by Roy, now came to be reserved for Vedantism.

With Debendranath's support, young Keshub Chunder Sen rose on the theological horizon of the Bengal Renaissance. Keshub was the son of Ram Comul Sen, treasurer of the Bank of Bengal and an old loyalist of the Empire. The bank itself had been founded to sponsor General Richard Colley Wellesley's wars against Tipu Sultan and the Marathas. It later became the Imperial Bank and, later still, the State Bank of India. Keshub Chunder Sen lost his father very early in his life. Orphaned, but not impoverished by any means, he became a self-taught iconoclast with extensive knowledge in the Vedas, the *Bible* and the histories of India and England. In 1859, he opened a Sunday School as part of the Samaj, and began writing and lecturing widely on the necessity of religion as the remedy to the spiritual degeneration brought about by British rule.

In 1870 came the turning point in his career, when his sermons were published in London as *The Brahmo Somaj Lectures*, edited by Collet. It was time for Keshub now to have a snifter of the Thames and, in April that year, he became the third Bengali to be 'lionised' by London in half a century. One of Keshub Chunder Sen's early Indian biographers summed up the zeitgeist of the city rather cynically. 'English cities sometimes take strange fancies to idolise certain individuals for a season,' he inked with ingratitude, 'and London specially suffers from such fits of sporadic hero-worship.'[24] A scholar no less than Max Müller believed that Sen had become a household apostle in Britain. There was hardly an English newspaper that did not cover the news of his arrival in London. As his official reception in the city, the British and Foreign Unitarian Association organised a tea-soiree in his honour at Hanover Square Rooms. The *Punch* magazine carried an invitation in characteristically cheeky limericks for Londoners to come and discover more about the Brahmo Baboo from Bengal.

Who on earth, of living men,
Is Baboo Keshub Chunder Sen?

I doubt if even one in ten
Knows Baboo Keshub Chunder Sen ...

The name surpasses human ken—
Baboo Keshub Chunder Sen!

From fair Cashmere's white-peopled glen
Comes Baboo Keshub Chunder Sen?

Or like 'my ugly brother Ben,'
Swarth Baboo Keshub Chunder Sen?

Big as ox, or small as wren,
Is Baboo Keshub Chunder Sen?

Let's beard this 'lion' in his den—
This Baboo Keshub Chunder Sen.

So come to tea and muffins, then,
With Baboo Keshub Chunder Sen.[25]

Over English tea and muffins, Keshub Baboo inaugurated his mission to systematically shame Western theology—not unlike Roy from forty years ago. At a lecture in St James' Hall, he put forth the question: 'Does not London life tell me every moment that there is an attempt in every Christian sect to follow both God and mammon?'[26]

Stout with the legumes of the Industrial Revolution, London was a ghastly forest of posters, advertisements and handbills as though the faces on the streets had been posted with placards—a city of the dreadful night awaiting the spectre of Hamlet's father, where women pleaded for the elbows of gentlemen before entering a banquet hall lest a wine glass broke at their feet, where lavish English beef, fowls and fish bedecked tables of mahogany and rosewood— where the western hemisphere of London gallantly battled dead sautéed beasts, armed with knives and forks, and the East End lay shrouded in the darkness of narcotics and the pandemonium of poverty. There was no better place for Sen to confront 'sectarian antipathy and unbrotherliness,' the lack of female education and political rights, the vast standing army of Britain, its immoral liquor industry and its long betrayed obligation towards India.[27] In early May, he delivered an address at Mr Spurgeon's Tabernacle in Newington. It came to be famously titled 'England's Duties to India'. As a consequence, Sen was brought to a vicious media trial by the Anglo-Indian press. A Briton living in Bombay even issued a putative fatwa on him, offering a reward of ₹500 to anyone who was willing to read Sen's lecture in the presence of this exasperated man who would stand with a 'horsewhip in his hand.'[28] London, however, was deeply entertained at how Sen turned biblical passages into clouds and brought down tropical showers of Vedantic wisdom. Owing to his linguistic exploits, *The Saturday Review* renamed him as 'Conundrum Baboo'.[29] *The Spectator* also reported a very favourable response from the large audiences in London who heard him lecture on the 'sublime egotism of Christ'.[30]

Sen's audiences included clergymen, members of the Houses of Parliament and preeminent literary and scientific men of England. *The London Quarterly and Holborn Review* gave a very compassionate reading to his books—*The Brahmo Somaj Lectures* and *Keshub Chunder Sen's English Visit* published between 1870 and '71—more compassionate, however, to Christianity than Sen himself. The review cast Sen as a representative of one of the greatest achievements of the Christian Church. It was a fashionable opinion in England that Christian missions had played an unacknowledged role in the establishment of the Brahmo Samaj. Sen's philosophy was considered eccentric and somewhat less than true spiritualism, while Sen himself appeared to be a semi-Christian Hindu. A lot of the credit for how he was portrayed in such reviews was owing to Sen himself.

Sen knew that his chances of staying alive in the memory of the literary and spiritual world of England depended on how well he embraced the garb of a Christianist reformer. He frequently spoke of universal brotherhood, temperance and the temptations of sin. Although his language promised to be fiery, his ideas gradually seemed like old wine bottled anew. His pulpits were largely chosen with the blessings of Unitarians or Congregationalists.

Conscientious Londoners, nursing the guilt of the colonisation of India and the massacres during the Great Rebellion, regularly came forth to his lectures by way of expiation. Sen gave lectures to the Peace Society, the Ragged School Society, the Swedenborg Society, to slum-dwellers at London's East End and various temperance societies. Expectedly, he also drew several friends from the Female Suffragette Society. Sen also came to be in the company of Professor Max Müller, William Ewart Gladstone, Queen Victoria and several other eminent members of the English political class, with all of them featuring in his accounts as passing mentions. Sen was also invited to the Lord Mayor's annual dinner. All throughout these meetings he consciously avoided becoming a glitterati spiritualist. Uniquely enough, his fancy was reserved for the natural phenomena of London—a draught of snow in March for instance. 'For the first time in my life,' he wrote, 'I see snow falling in flakes. Within a short time, everything becomes white—streets, housetops, trees, and even the umbrella and the dress of those who are going about. I cannot resist the temptation of going out into the veranda, and receiving a good sprinkling of flakes on my overcoat.'[31]

At the opening ceremony of some of the new buildings of the University of London, Sen saw the Queen for the first time. He found her to be 'plain-looking in plain dress,' distinguished only by her dignified speechlessness. In the regard that he owed to the ruling class of English society, Sen was far from the etiquettes observed by Roy or Tagore. When John Stuart Mill came to visit him after his address at Hanover Square, Sen was writing a letter back home. Much to the chagrin of his Indian companions, he made Mill wait and ponder over a newspaper, while he lazily finished writing the letter. Mill, the champion of Utilitarianism, and Sen, the apostle of nondual Vedanta, were supposed to have met as chalk and cheese. In a later lecture delivered in India, Sen described the Christian spirit to be made of utilitarianism and devoid of morality. It was stuffed with John Stuart Mill not Jesus Christ, he often lamented. But Mill was much closer to Sen than it would have been understood back then. In his book, *England and*

Ireland (1868), Mill had expressed a similar discontentment with the English administration of India. In Mill's opinion, since the English had 'insular prejudices' to begin with, their governance in India was deeply obsessed with the pursuit of 'common English habits and notions,'[32] instead of the welfare of Indian cultures and spiritual beliefs. At the end of their meeting, Mill must have made a deep, if only fleeting, impression on Sen. The latter, in his diary, termed the philosopher as 'the leader of English thought, the greatest thinker of the age.'[33]

For the next four months, London was Sen's nucleus to navigate through the cities of Liverpool, Southampton, Glasgow and Birmingham, among others. While he was in Bristol, Roy's old friend, Mary Carpenter, took advantage of his visit to establish the National Indian Association. Later, when he was at Leeds, the Unitarian missionaries there opened a branch of the association in the city to honour his visit. In late August, Sen was formally invited to meet Queen Victoria, at the Osborne House, where he wore none of the pomp of Roy or Tagore. Over a vegetarian luncheon, they discussed female education and the challenges for British rule in India. He also showed her pictures of his wife which impressed the queen so much that, following their meeting, she and her daughter, Princess Louise, expressed their desire to 'possess' photographs of him.[34] He blushed, but did not refuse. Before he left for India, the Queen gifted him a life-sized engraving of herself and the two books she had authored—*The Early Years of His Royal Highness The Prince Consort* (1867) and *Leaves from the Journal of Our Life in the Highlands* (1868). They were both inscribed with her own hand, 'To Keshub Chunder Sen, from Victoria, Re. Sept., 1870.' On his departure, the satirical magazine *Judy* (a late rival to *Punch*) published a reasonably unsatirical farewell poem for Sen. It was titled 'A Valediction'.

What think you of England's glories—
West-End fashions, dinners, soirées?
Friendly censure do not taboo:
Tell us how things struck you, Baboo!

What say you on public questions?
People oft accept suggestions
Plainly stated by a fresh ob-
Server, like you, Baboo Keshub!

At the shops, with gaslights blazing,
In the streets, whose noise is crazing,
Did you stare in silent wonder?—
Tell us, Baboo Keshub Chunder!

Well, your thoughts of us, we'll risk 'em;
Bon voyage, sir—*Pax vobiscum*!
Farewell, till we meet again,
Baboo Keshub Chunder Sen![35]

Sen returned home to a celebration by deafening crowds.
However, he was to soon witness an acrimonious theological split
within the Brahmo Samaj. His views had now undergone a sea
change from those of Debendranath and his followers. To him,
the Samaj was nothing better than 'a ridiculous caricature of the
Church of God.'[36] Choosing faith over frustration, Sen broke away
from the Samaj and converted to Christianity. London had brought
about his own renaissance. Ironically, it was only as a Christian that
he discovered the greatest bliss of his spiritual life, that too in the
company and the gospel of the mystic Hindu saint Ramakrishna
Parmahansa, who knew no more than ten words of English.

Sen passed away in 1884. Hearing the news, people from all
corners of Britain and beyond, including Victoria, mourned
his death. The Queen sent condolences to his family through
the office of Lord Ripon, the Governor General of India. In
London, Müller wrote a brief but endearing life sketch of his
dear departed friend, as part of his *Biographical Essays* published
that year. According to Müller, he had helped the Brahmo Samaj
unyoke itself from the scriptures of the Veda, wooed Christianity
and embedded both in a comparative science of theology.[37] But,
Sen's most unsung contribution to the Indian history of London

was perhaps condensed in a striking imagery. It endured in the imagination of a new generation of Indian travellers to the city. Evidently, Keshub Sen had read the Romantics. By the time of Wordsworth, London's culture of fairs had started assuming a whole new theatricality. As an audiovisual stage, Victorian London was a world hollowed of its soul with advertisements and salesmen's cries. Latter-day Indian travellers to the city were aghast at seeing advertisements such as the one for Pears soap that promised to wash *black* boys into *clean* white or dyers that pledged to *dye* in order to live. With more vintners and liquor shops in the city than bakers and Bibles put together, London had succumbed to an 'inordinate desire to make the largest fortune within the shortest space of time.'[38]

In his 'Residence in London,' from the *The Prelude* (1799), Wordsworth compared the city to the cacophony of Babel, where every shop and every house was like a title page to an empty novel. Lamb was more ambiguous. To him, London was a splendid pantomime of the 19th century. 'The wonder of these sights, impels me into night-walks about her crowded streets,' he confessed, 'and I often shed tears in the motley Strand from fullness of joy at so much life.'[39] Macaulay, who was fresh from having fathered the tradition of English studies in India—much of which sprang from London's Romantic circles—was dazzled by the age of its science and spectacles. The imminence of the city's high-velocity transport would come to substitute life itself.

Then in characteristic London fashion the single placard-carriers were put together in order to create a kind of pageant or pantomime; a group of them were placed inside paste models of blacking pots, for example, and paraded in line to advertise the efficacy of 'Warrens Blacking, 30 Strand,' the very place where Dickens himself began his tortuous London childhood. Then arrived the advertisement as the horse-drawn gig, surmounted by an enormous hat or an Egyptian obelisk. The search for novelty was always intense and the passion for posters blossomed into the 'electric advertisements' of the 1890s when 'Vinolia

Soap' was hailed in illuminated letters above Trafalgar Square. Advertisements in lights soon began to move; at Piccadilly Circus could be seen a red crystal bottle pouring port into a waiting glass, and a car with turning silver wheels. Soon they were everywhere—above the ground, under the ground, and in the sky.[40]

Not for all were the genteel sights of London. Dickens, for one, saw the squalid state of sandwiched men as 'a piece of human flesh between two slices of pasteboard.'[41] In a century where a world was busy selling the rest of the world in London, including London itself, Sen took to disentangling its maya. 'The first thing that struck me,' he told the audience during his welcome address at Hanover Square, 'and dazzled my eyes in London was the brilliancy and splendour of your shops; but their number bewildered me. I thought, "Surely the English must be a nation of shopkeepers; but if everybody sells, where are the buyers?"'[42]

ACT IV

A Nation Known by Stage

But from thine eyes my knowledge I derive,
And, constant stars, in them I read such art
As truth and beauty shall together thrive
If from thyself to store thou wouldst convert:
Or else of thee this I prognosticate,
Thy end is truth's and beauty's doom and date

(Sonnet 14)

Scene I

City of Counsellors and Clients

By the last decades of the 19th century, London had become the city of Empire; the public spaces, the railway termini, the hotels, the great docks, the new thoroughfares, the rebuilt markets, all were the visible expression of a city of unrivalled strength and immensity. It had become the centre of international finance and the engine of imperial power; it teemed with life and expectancy. Some of its gracefulness and variety had now gone; its Georgian compactness and familiarity had also disappeared, replaced by the larger scale of neo-classical or neo-Gothic architecture which somehow matched the aspirations of this larger and more anonymous city. Nelson's Column in Trafalgar Square, erected in 1843, was conceived upon the model of a column in the temple of Mars the Avenger, in imperial Rome, while a revised classicism was employed for the new buildings along Whitehall. If it was a more public and more powerful city, it had also become a less human one.

Victorian London was fostered in great architectural pomp and unassailable individual ambitions. With a phenomenal density of labourers from all parts of the world, in the City of London around the Bank of England, other banks, financial buildings and smaller enterprises mushroomed. Faster technologies in concrete and steel meant buildings grew taller and elevators more numerous. Thomas Edison's helium spirits were imported from New York. The Gothic

English capital, whose mysteries consisted of the uncanny play of chiaroscuro elements on melancholy or forbidding architecture, was now preparing for an alien century. In the early 19th century, tallow candles and oil lamps were replaced with the proverbial gaslights, and the London fog acquired its customary creepiness. The French impressionist painter Claude Monet lived in the city only to serenade the fogs. From Southwark to Waterloo, from Oxford Street to Knightsbridge, from Kensington High Street to Notting Hill, from Piccadilly Circus to Leicester Square, their yellow shadows flickered sombrely. With the electrification of London in the 1890s, office indoors no longer required the sun, as, indeed, the age of England's enlightenment had been far surpassed by the age of imperialism. From a working population of less than 200,000 in 1870, London grew into a workforce of over a third of a million in 1910. A great bulk of them was constituted by clerks clobbering down the cobbled streets from Fitzrovia to Kentish Town. Others were doctors, engineers, bankers, architects or salesmen. For a few, like the poet, Thomas Stearns Eliot, it was an 'unreal city' simmering beneath the brown fogs of winter twilights and careless crowds over the London Bridge.[1] At Charing Cross or Bloomsbury, the trotting of horse-drawn carriages reverberated with the hootings of steam or motor-driven transport on major thoroughfares. The rich grew richer and looked the part evermore; the poor went from looking hoggish to increasingly hideous. Every night, nearly 500 rough sleepers choked the fountains of Trafalgar Square. Besides old kettles, crockery, dead pets, castaway shoes, chinaware, rotten fruits and sandwiches, London was also littered by epidemics, savagery and crimes. The Whitechapel murders of 1888 shed a dark crimson light on the awkward conurbations of Tower Hamlets in the East End, and the grisly poverty appertaining thereto. If the blurry motions of this new London were marked elsewhere by the sinister decadence of Oscar Wilde, the journey of Indians in the city was guided by the incandescent hand of the law.

In 1864, Womesh Chunder Bonnerjee, another young Bengali who would alter the future of Britain and India, enrolled at Lincoln's Inn. Three years later, he was called to the Bar at the Middle Temple. Three Indians before him who had had the distinction of being called to the Bar were Gyanendra Mohan Tagore at the Inner Temple in 1862, and Michael Madhusudhan Dutt and Monomohan Ghose at Gray's Inn and Lincoln's Inn, in 1866. Gyanendra Mohan, the son of Dwarkanath Tagore's brother Gopi Mohan Tagore, did not return to India. Ghosh did, and became the first Indian barrister to practise at the Calcutta High Court. Pherozeshah Mehta, also called the 'uncrowned king of Bombay,'[2] was the first Parsi to be called to the Bar. In 1868, he took his barristership from Lincoln's Inn. Towards the beginning of that decade, the first Indian medical graduate, Muncherji B. Kolah, had received his Fellowship of Royal College of Surgeons from London. A little away from the city, Bombay's Cursetji Maneckji Shroff enrolled at the University of Oxford in 1864 as the first Indian undergraduate student there. His brother, Jahangir Maneckji Cursetji, was still finishing matriculation at Trinity College in Cambridge. Another Bombaywalla, Badruddin Tyabji, had been living in London since 1860. He was a student at Newbury High Park College, and later the University of London. In 1867, he too was called to the Bar at the Middle Temple.

In 1869, Syed Ameer Ali came to London to prepare for the civil services but instead enrolled as a law student. The following year, he was called to the Bar at the Inner Temple and returned to India to take up practise at the Calcutta High Court. His affair with London had only just begun. Although Ali's family hailed from Awadh, his father was settled in Orissa, where Ameer Ali was born. Later, the family migrated to Chinsurah, near Calcutta. Ameer Ali was to rival Bonnerjee, neither as a barrister nor as a Bengali, but in rattling the history of the subcontinent. He was in London during the visit of Keshub Chunder Sen, and also became friends with the social reformers and women suffragettes of the day. Besides law, his preoccupation was the gospel of Mohammad. Ali described the prophet as another face of Jesus, who 'preached gentleness, charity and love.'³ After biding his time for over thirty years, Ali's old beliefs in universal spiritual brotherhood took a more political hand. As a young barrister, Ali had warned against the sort of jingoism that plagued Jews during the time of Christ, and their 'nation animated by a fierce love of their country, creed and individuality.'⁴ As an older politician, he was lobbying to establish a fund for the Shah Jahan Mosque at Woking, the first to be built in London. Ironically enough, its founder was a Jew named Gottlieb Leitner, also a former Registrar of the Punjab University. The mosque was merely the dome of the iceberg that had just started baring its hood, dividing Hindus and Muslims in India, as well as in London.

———————

By the late 1870s, the elite Indian stronghold in and around London was exacting heavy concessions from the British Government in India. Bonnerjee, the fourth Indian to become a barrister, would go on to be a founding member and the first President of the Indian National Congress. In 1892, Bonnerjee was the Liberal Party's candidate for Barrow-in-Furness, a constituency where he was unsuccessful. In the same election, his contemporary, Dadabhai Naoroji, won from Finsbury Central, becoming the first Indian Member of the British Parliament. Naoroji, who was also an old resident of the city, belonged to the Parsi community of Bombay that became a dominant force in London although they were the tiniest minority in their nation. Bonnerjee's arrival in London in the 1860s was funded by a scholarship from Sir Jamsetjee Jejeebhoy, another Parsi Bombaywalla and businessman, who had made his fortune trading in opium and cotton with China. Bonnerjee rose to become the most prominent barrister in his time at the Calcutta High Court and the first Indian Standing Counsel. Despite his Anglicised name, he remained a Hindu, but his wife Hemangini converted to Christianity. More than his family or professional name, however, what was of much greater significance was how he redefined London and Calcutta with his grandiloquent Victorian mansions in the hearts of the two cities.

When his eldest was ready for Oxford, he had purchased a three-storey, ten-bedroom mansion just outside London, adding a new wing to accommodate a billiard room and smoking den. Named Kidderpore after the family ancestral estate on the Hooghly River, the spread included tennis courts, an orchard, gardens and a stable. After settling his wife and eight children under its roof, W.C. returned to Calcutta to amass his wealth and reside in an equally grand residence on Park Street. Its grounds also included a tennis court and stable, as well as an aviary, two fern houses, and a veranda wide enough for a coach and four.[5]

The eastern and western wings of Bonnerjee's barristocracy were his two houses, at 6 Park Street in Calcutta and 8 Bedford Park at Croydon. They were built as aesthetic twins. The interiors of both households—from the lavatories to the dining halls, the smoking room to the billiards room, the carpets to the balusters—were designed to articulate the ornamental sensibility of the age as well as the cultural legacy of the Bonnerjees. The linen, crockery, cutlery, furniture and the domestic staff of the Park Street home were as Victorian as 21st-century film adaptations of Edwardian novels. The downstairs staff and domestic administration at Kidderpore in Croydon would have easily equalled Carson's army of servants in some *Downton Abbey*. Janaki Agnes Penelope Majumdar, daughter of W.C. and Hemangini Bonnerjee, was educated at Cambridge and became the first Indian woman to have a degree in the natural sciences. In her *Memoir* (1935), she described their Sundays at the Croydon residence and the flurry of its visitors as quaint artefacts of Anglo-Indian life from the spliced history of the two imperial cities. The Bonnerjees began their days of the lord,

> … with breakfast in bed, as when the elder sisters began their medical work in London they had a very early start and late return all the week and liked to get up late on Sundays to make up, and we younger ones thought it a marvellous idea, so my mother would send up as many as 6 trays sometimes! Attendance at the Iron Room was compulsory for the younger ones, and on our

return we usually found two or three young Indian students and other friends awaiting us who had arrived for lunch—Mr K.N. and Mr P. Chaudhuri were frequent visitors, also Basanta Mullick and his brothers, Sir B.C. Mitter, Sir B.L. Mitter, Mr C.C. Ghose, and a great many others. After lunch there was a 'spread tea' in the dining room and after that 'Hymn' in the drawing-room. Each of us in turn chose our favourite hymn, and Nellie played the piano while the rest of the family sang. Sometimes we used the 'Ancient and Modern' Hymnbook and sometimes 'Sankey and Moodie's.' Immediately after this ceremony my mother used to go down to the kitchen to cook a real Indian dinner, and as soon as I was old enough I always used to help her. The servants were all given the evening off, and we used to dish up and carry up the things ourselves—My Aunts always sent the spices to us ready ground in tins and we and our visitors all greatly enjoyed this meal. Sometimes my father would come and help, and I remember him and Mr R.C. Dutt once spending a whole evening cooking a wonderful duck curry that no one could eat because it was too highly spiced ('*jhal*')! At first the servants were rather 'superior' about Indian food and my mother always left plenty of cold meat and pudding out for their supper. But she gradually noticed that however many curries might be left over on Sunday nights, there was never anything on Monday morning, and at last a deputation came to her from the servants asking her to cook just a little more of everything if she didn't mind, as they all so much enjoyed it.[6]

Furnished by the London firm Fox & Co., the three-storeyed Kidderpore was a meat of Victorian London leisurely curried with slivers of India. Many Indian students were Sunday diners at the Bonnerjee household. Not dozens or scores, but hundreds of those Indian characters—into whom the age of steam was breathing new life with the maddening cadence of an incantation—were no longer merely visitors in the city. They were the new citizens of London.

By the beginning of the 20th century, ghettos of colonial students in the city were a much less cordial sight than in days of Victoria's youth. Gone were the times of exotic Asiatics, Rajas and their ambassadors, when residents of the city flocked to welcome them or cachinnated at their charming accents at social gatherings. Doctor Thorndike, a forensic scientist and real-life contemporary of Sherlock Holmes, during one of his walks around Bedford Place—not far from the house where Rammohun Roy had once stayed—twitted irately, 'the Asiatic and African faces that one sees at the windows of these Bloomsbury boarding-houses almost suggest an overflow from the ethnological galleries of the adjacent British Museum.'⁷ The growing population of Asian and African students in London was largely owing to a wave ushered in by Dwarkanath Tagore, and later by a fraternity of Indian luminaries who began their careers as students in the city. Surendranath Banerjea, who came to London in the 1860s and kept returning in the following decades, saw what he called a growing 'Indian colony' of students.⁸

One of the first in that line was Romesh Chunder Dutt. In 1868, while he was still a student at Presidency College in Calcutta, he left for London after winning a scholarship to the University College. Although his family was against his crossing the Arabian Sea, Dutt set sail for Albion, accompanied by Behari Lal Gupta and Surendranath Banerjea. Dutt wanted to qualify for the Indian Civil Service. That feat had so far been achieved by only one Indian—Satyendranath Tagore, grandson of Dwarkanath Tagore and brother of Rabindranath Tagore. Dutt's political views would be profoundly shaped by life in London, where he saw, for the first time, democracy in action among a race of people who were considered to be self-reliant, liberated and keenly 'determined with an eye towards utility and not towards sentimental idealism.'⁹ The young student was also deeply impressed by the town planning of Victorian London, the palatial buildings and the spacious parks. However, the fourteen-hour-study days at the university kept students away from enjoying the pleasures of the city. Gloomily, from Bloomsbury, Dutt wrote to his brother:

> I need scarcely tell you that never before did we study so hard and so unremittingly as during the past year. We attended classes of the University College, London and also took some private lessons from some of the Professors of the College. We passed our days in the University College, either in the classrooms or in the library. In the evening, we returned to our lodging houses, took our dinner, went out for a stroll, returned and took a cup of tea and then resumed our studies, which we kept up as long as we could. And in the morning, after a hasty bath and breakfast, we went to the college again.[10]

In 1869, both Dutt and Gupta qualified for the civil services; both were called to the Bar at the Middle Temple two years later. Dutt chose to become a civil servant. Their quiet companion, Banerjea, also passed the civil service examinations, not once but twice. After passing the first time in 1869, he was disqualified due to an age discrepancy. Later, while working in the Indian Civil Service, he was dismissed from his posting in Sylhet in 1872. He would return to the city to argue his case, although unsuccessfully. Banerjea began teaching at what came to be known as the Ripon College, named after Viceroy Lord Ripon. After independence, it would be renamed as Surendranath Banerjea Law College. Even as a lecturer in Calcutta, Banerjea visited London, where Indian scholars were now a common sight. Dutt rose to the post of divisional commissioner in Orissa, being the first Indian to achieve that designation. In 1897, he came back to live in London, where he taught for a few years as an honorary lecturer at his alma mater.

During his first furlough which he spent in London, Dutt saw the earliest signs of the Indian diaspora in the city. With the political reforms initiated by Lord Ripon between 1880 and 1884, India was at the threshold of provincial legislatures. Following a resolution brought in by the Ripon administration in May 1882, local state bodies and non-governmental bodies in India were handed over the charge of public works, education, finance, taxation and local administration. The impact of the legislation was palpably felt on Indian attitudes in London. Indian nationalists resolved to 'flood Great Britain with pamphlets, leaflets, newspapers and magazine articles.'[11] In 1888, 10,000 copies of the report of the annual meeting of the Indian National Congress were disseminated across Britain. The next year, the journal called *India* was founded in London, which continued to be published until 1921.

Not only for Indian students or politicians-in-the-making, a journey to London was the watershed moment for many Indian travellers who brought closer to India the sights and scenes of the imperial city in progressively irreverent accounts. They also dramatically changed the perception of Indians in England. Even loyalist Indian subjects began writing back to the imperialists from the very heart of the Empire. Trailokya Nath Mukharji, appointed as a supervisor by the Government of India to the Colonial and Indian Exhibition of 1886, was astonished to see that Indians themselves were objects of sheer wonder on display. They were the ready exhibits in the city, as 'parents explained to their children, and young men to their sweethearts, the various points of interest found in the innumerable products and manufactures which India sent to the Exhibition.'[12] Being both a spectator and the spectacle, Mukharji wrote in *A Visit to Europe* (1889) how he and others 'were pierced through and through by stares from eyes of all colours.'[13] The majority of those eyes belonged to women.

The number of wives we left behind at home was also a constant theme of speculation among them, and shrewd guesses were sometimes made on this point, 250 being a favourite number. You could tell any amount of stories on this subject without exciting the slightest suspicion. Once, one of our number told a pretty waitress—'I'm awfully pleased with you, and I want to marry you. Will you accept the fortieth wifeship in my household which became vacant just before I left my country?' She asked— 'How many wives have you all together?' 'Two hundred and fifty, the usual number,' was the ready answer. 'What became of your wife, number 40?' 'I killed her, because one morning she could not cook my porridge well.' The poor girl was horrified, and exclaimed—'O you monster, O you wretch!'[14]

Unlike Mohandas K. Gandhi—who concealed his marital status for fear of derision or being deprived of female company— Mukharji was urbane, assertive and unfazed by racialism. Once, in a London restaurant, he noticed a man and his daughter staring at him. When the young lady finally spoke to him, she was delighted by his 'knowledge of English.' All she wanted was to be able to 'brag about seeing and talking to a genuine Blackie.'[15] Mukharji was quick to differentiate himself from Africans and Caribbeans in the city—owing to the relatively privileged status of Indian subjects. At the same time, he felt the bitter irony of Africans, Caribbeans, Australian-aborigines, 'the Negroes, the Kaffirs, the Hottentots, the Egyptians,'[16] along with Indians of course, referred to as *natives;* whereas, the French, the German or the Italian was a distinguished *foreigner. The Spectator* found Mukharji to be 'a very favourable specimen of the educated Hindoo,' who had no radical delusions about his nationhood.[17] That also had partly to do with the fact that he was, after all, an imperial loyalist. Even while safeguarding the 'the benefits of civilisation,'[18] he was firmly opposed to the Irish Home Rule movement.

Scene II

Trains of Fact and Folklore

Macaulay's Minute and colonial textbooks in India threatened to turn the English language and the English imperial capital into a run-of-the-mill experience. Indian travellers to London often had an intellectual template of what to expect and what was expected of them. The city's Romanesque and Gothic structures featured liberally in Indian travel accounts, which were also meant to 'take their stay-at-home audiences through the British Museum, the Parliament House, Westminster Abbey, the Crystal Palace, the Royal Academy, Madame Tussaud's and so on. Descriptions of palaces and towers invariably meant going down memory lane,' for Indian travellers, 'and confident as they were in their knowledge of history, the visitors gave themselves every liberty to do so.'[1] London did not disappoint them in offering either Hellenic grandeur or Dickensian squalor.

'On arriving in London from India,' Krishnabhabini Das wrote in 1885, 'one feels sort of dazed and stands pulverised for everything looks so different—dress, way of speaking, houses, traffic—all seem to be entirely new. If you look above you will see a number of fuming chimneys, you will not find a soul on the roofs which are sloping on both sides and covered with black slate.'[2] Das, the wife of a Cambridge lecturer, was one of the very few Bengali women who wrote an account of her stay in the imperial capital. Although Toru Dutt had studied in Cambridge in the 1870s, and Sarojini Naidu at King's College London in the 1890s, their travels and memoirs are largely unknown or unpublished. Das's experiences of London as a 'city of shops', a 'city of theatres' and a 'city of riches'³ did stand out in that era.

In the effort to appear as naturalised as European travellers, some Indian observers conjured London as the hand with a 'magic touch in every trivia and every greatness, from Hyde Park to the Houses of Parliament.' Amritlal Roy, a student in the University of Edinburgh, wrote: 'London means the centre of the world-wide empire, a repository of wealth and a reservoir of energy, a whirlpool of activity and a deep sea of thought, a point where the ends of the world may be said to meet.'⁴ Mukharji was captivated by the railway system of the city, which he believed to be 'one of the wonders of the world.' 'Engines puffing and whistling,' as he marvelled, 'passengers running in and out, guards shutting doors, faint hum of voices, all combined to create a grandeur of busy life which must be seen to be realised.'⁵ Another Indian student, Syed Shah, after spending an afternoon in 1893 at the Tower of London, expressed profound gratitude for being 'born in the glorious reign of our noble Queen-Empress Victoria. Through her government we are protected from all sorts of dangers, and also our property and our sacred religions: this is the real blessing which we, the British subjects, enjoy under our good Queen-Empress, upon whose rule the sun never sets.'⁶

A surge of disenchantments was also catching up fast. In 1874, one Naoroji Ferdoonji, in a lecture to the city's East India Association, attacked England's dangerous ignorance of poverty, racial violence and gross human rights violations in India. The imperial superstores, the Harrods and Selfridges of the future, swaggering with the *objets de curiosité* of the world, were also a blatant reminder of Indian servitude. 'This feeling,' of gloominess in the city, wrote A.K. Roy, 'is, perhaps, more acute in the Indian than any other observer; for inured as he is from infancy, to associate splendour and magnificence, with dazzling brilliancy, the dull dismal and foggy, muggy look of London adds a touch of sadness to his disappointment.'[7] Debaprasad Sarbadhikari, first private Vice-Chancellor of the University of Calcutta, found the city to be a cluster of 'chimney stacks and advertisement hoardings,' while Krishnabhabini Das wrote that the English were 'advertisement maniacs.' Rabindranath Tagore, who first visited London in 1878 to attend lectures at the University College, was also disappointed. True to his innate spirit resistant to formal education, he returned to India without a degree. Admittedly, he had come to England to experience the resonance of Tennyson's verses, the eloquence of Gladstone's speeches, of 'Max Muller's Vedantic exposition, Tyndall's scientific theories, Carlyle's profound thoughts and Bain's philosophy.'[8] Instead, London only offered him women discussing fashion and men toiling in factories. To several other conscientious Indians of the latter-day, like Shibnath Shastri, the easy virtues of the city were to appear endangering to the moral fabric of India.

> At ten-thirty in the night I came to King's Cross from Waterloo Station by bus. As the night grew everyone around appeared drunk. Even the booking clerk at the station was in a particularly jocular mood. He asked me with a smile, 'Are you alone?' A woman came up enquiring, 'Are you coming my way, dear?' Getting no reply, she realised that this was not the right place to look for business. Another lady had drunk so much that she had lost her ability to move. The workers on the station were similarly out of their senses. When the tram came at twelve in the night I found that almost no passenger could stand up properly. One needs to see to believe how dangerous London night-life is.[9]

Moored in the melancholy aura, London's railway stations came to occupy a special place in the Indian imagination. That was not merely because they were ancestors of the designs of the grand metropolitan railway stations of the subcontinent. On one occasion, the London Tube became the protagonist of an unforgettable chapter in India's cultural heritage.

Rabindranath Tagore was to return to London in 1912. He was eager to show the English translation of *Gitanjali* to the English painter and art critic, William Rothenstein. Tagore wanted to request him to urge the Irish poet, William Butler Yeats, to write an introduction to the book. Tagore's son, daughter-in-law and Soumendra Deb Burman (of the royal family of Tripura) are also known to have accompanied him on this journey. In mid-June, Tagore and his party travelled from Dover to London, thence on the underground service to meet Rothenstein at his Hampstead residence. However, the attaché case in which Tagore was carrying his manuscript was nowhere to be found. After some panic-stricken hours, the poet asked his son Rathindranath to inquire with the London Underground authorities. Astonishingly for the Tagores, the case was found and returned safely by the office of 'lost property' at the Baker Street station. Sherlock Holmes, the most famous tenant of the neighbourhood, had just solved 'The Adventure of the Devil's Foot', and was in all likelihood involved in 'The Adventure of the Dying Detective'. But he, almost certainly, had no hand in the retrieval of Tagore's case. The railway incident catapulted Tagore into instant celebrity. Meet Rothenstein he did, the following day. Needless to say, he was carrying the manuscript, which was later read and reviewed by Yeats, who also wrote the famed introduction to *Gitanjali*.

Through the summer of 1912, Tagore continued to revise the translations of his Bengali verses. He had a temporary residence in Hampstead Heath. Rothenstein also passed on copies of the book to the writer Stopford Brooke and critic Andrew Cecil Bradley. In July, at Rothenstein's house, the writers Evelyn Underhill, Ernest Rhys, Alice Meynell and Arthur Fox Strangways gathered to listen to a reading by Tagore. He was embarrassed with joy at the 'excessive enthusiasm' of the influential English literati.[10] 'Nothing could exceed,' Rhys remarked, 'the simplicity and unpretentiousness of this visitor from an older world. He was content to take things as he found them, and did not expect one to discourse all day on philosophy.' What India had been taught of Wordsworth or Keats, London rediscovered in Tagore. Rhys added, 'if the English sun was only good enough to shine, it was pleasure enough for him to sit on the grass in a Hampstead garden and listen to the noises of the town carried over the roofs and treetops. His understanding of life, his acceptance of its cares, his delight in its common occurrences, were not those we had hitherto associated with the notion of an Indian ascetic.'[11] Soon after, another gathering was organised at the Trocadero Restaurant. This time, it was Yeats who read out the translations. In November, a limited edition of an anthology of 103 poems by Tagore was published by the London Indian Society. It was sponsored by Rothenstein. *Gitanjali* was published in March the following year, by Macmillan. By the time Tagore was awarded the Nobel Prize for literature, in November 1913, 'he was a global phenomenon.'[12] The greatest conceit of western technology and civilisation—the railways—had cast a strange inscription on a book of Eastern spiritual wisdom. Tagore's poems would become the comfort of an entire generation of Europeans over that decade of ceaseless bloodletting and terror.

In 1961, a blue plaque and an Indian tricolour went up at 3 Villas, Hampstead Heath—Tagore's old residence in London. In 2011, at the Tagore Centre in Golden Square, Prince Charles inaugurated a bust statue of the poet. Seventy years before that, Tagore had written to Rothenstein that it was not at all important to his 'own reputation that I should find my place in the history of your literature. It was an accident for which you were also responsible and possibly most of all was Yeats.'[13] An accident indeed, which led to the railways redeeming many souls, instead of the loss of lives!

The British exuberance around Tagore was the outcome of six decades of fetishising Indians in London. Yet, it was also an expression of how successfully India had adopted the conventions European print culture, beginning with the rise of print journalism in the colony since the 1850s. James Augustus Hicky had founded the first Indian newspaper in the form of *Hicky's Bengal Gazette*, as early as 1780. However, British censorship came in the way of the emergence of a journalistic tradition in India. It was not until 1838 that *The Times of India* started printing, then known as *The Bombay Times and Journal of Commerce*.

Upendrakishore Ray Chowdhury, a 19th-century Brahmo intellectual, also pioneered print technology in South Asia, beginning with bicolour and coloured block making. To perfect the technology, he imported equipment and publications from Britain. In the process, he also contributed several articles to the London-based journal of printing arts *The Penrose Annual*, between 1895 and 1912. Extolling his wisdom in printing technology, the editor of the journal, William Gamble, wrote, 'Mr Ray is obviously possessed of a mathematical quality of mind and he has researched out for himself the problems of half-tone work in a remarkably successful manner.'[14] Upendrakishore's accomplishments included the invention of the sixty-degree screen, his pathbreaking studies into diffraction and his patented gadget, 'the automatic screen adjustor,' which was sold to the process camera of the Penrose Company.

Just before the outbreak of the Great War, Upendrakishore set up U. Ray & Sons, soon to become one of the finest printing houses in South Asia, almost at par with global technology of colour printing. The *Sandesh* magazine, founded by Upendrakishore and managed by the Ray household since 1913, was a prized chauffeur to Bengal's arts and literature. Many of his early illustrated collections of Indian folklore inspired the artistic awakening of the graphic artist and filmmaker—Satyajit Ray. He was Upendrakishore Ray's grandson and India's first Oscar-winning filmmaker. In 1911, his father Sukumar Ray was sent to England by Upendrakishore for a degree in printing arts. Both Upendrakishore and Sukumar Ray collaborated with the Tagore family. The latter even met Rabindranath Tagore in London, in 1912. Sukumar Ray wrote back several letters to his family, describing soirees at Rothenstein's house, where besides Tagore, Prasanta Chandra Mahalonobis, the renowned statistician, and Ramananda Chatterjee, founder of the influential magazine *Modern Review*, were also present. During Tagore's visit, Sukumar Ray read a paper at the London Indian Society, titled 'The Spirit of Rabindranath,' which was published in the magazine *Quest*.

Given the support of Gamble and his fellow-editor of *The Penrose Annual*, R.B. Fishenden, young Sukumar was well-ensconced in the London art scene. Here, his old admiration for Lewis Carroll and his masterpiece, *Alice in Wonderland*, grew manifold. Ray was to be one of the greatest proponents of Bengali nonsense literature in his later life, and considered as the Lewis Carroll of Bengal. In London, he also attended the first post-Impressionist arts exhibition, organised by the art critic Roger Fry. Experiencing the emerging artistic styles of Futurism, Cubism and Expressionism led him to write the essay 'Exaggeration in Art.' Meanwhile, he attended a course at the London County Council School of Photo Engraving and Lithography at Bolt Street, while residing at the Northbrook Society situated on Cromwell Road. From here, Sukumar often visited his family friends, Dr and Mrs Ray. They introduced him to Kali Narayan Gupta, whose granddaughter, Suprabha Das, would later become his wife. E.B. Havell—Principal of the Calcutta School of Art where Sukumar Ray had studied—also came to his aid in London. Then there was Rothenstein who wheedled Ray to take up subjects such as Ajanta and Ellora caves, and reproduce them in colour. From London, Ray contributed to *The Penrose Annual* as well as *Sandesh*. In 1912, just before leaving for the Manchester School of Technology, he became a member of the Royal Photographic Society. Ten years later, when he was back in India, he was made its Fellow.

Anglo-Indian camaraderie played a prominent role in the progress of Indian arts. William Winstanley Pearson, a science scholar from Cambridge who met Tagore in London, went to

teach English at Santiniketan. After the war, he supported Mukul
Dey, then a young painter from Santiniketan, as the latter was
about to join the Slade School of Art. Dey was also helped by
artists, writers and architects such as Thomas Sturge Moore,
Laurence Binyon and Edwin Lutyens. In 1922, he became the
first Indian to be awarded a Diploma in Mural Painting from the
Royal College of Art. The next year, the Royal Academy exhibited
his paintings, and, in the year after, he was invited to decorate a
segment of the Indian Pavilion at the British Empire Exhibition.

Atul Bose, another artist from Bengal in London at the time,
was also a member of the Royal Academy. He refused the invitation
to join Dey in working on the Indian Pavilion. Bose was already
famous on account of his sketch, *The Bengal Tiger*, depicting Sir
Asutosh Mukherjee—the second Indian Vice-Chancellor of the
University of Calcutta, a Member of the London Mathematical
Society and Fellow of the Royal Society of Edinburgh. Besides
being a barrister, a towering educationist, polyglot and social
reformer, Mukherjee was a devout nationalist. In 1924, *The Times
Literary Supplement* published Bose's sketch alongside its obituary
of Sir Asutosh. Five years later, when the Government of India
announced a competition for painters to reproduce the royal
paintings from Windsor Castle, for the Viceregal Lodge in New
Delhi, Edwin Lutyens selected Bose. Later, he even commissioned
Bose for his portrait. Then there were William Archer and John
Conran Irwin, keepers of the Indian Section of the Victoria
and Albert Museum. For several years after the Second World
War, they curated the paintings of Jamini Roy with leading
commentaries. Without their backing and gratifying reviews in
The Statesman newspaper of Calcutta—most notably by its editor
Sir Alfred Watson—Jamini Roy could not have possibly sustained
his name in India, especially since he had broken away from the
Tagores and their famed Bengal School.

The unexpected warmth of Londoners notwithstanding,
Behramji Malabari believed that the English often overdid 'their
part of friendliness.'[15] The patronising behaviour of Englishmen
was partway due to the nostalgia for the early days of the Raj.

But there was also the uncomfortable realisation of the increasing visibility of Indians in Britain. Malabari, an eminent poet, journalist and reformer from Bombay, came to England in 1890 to campaign against child marriage and oppression of widows. His book, *The Indian Eye on English Life* (1895), differed considerably from the usual travelogues on London. Malabari's experience in the city of handbills and advertisers was aggravated by the smoky tunnels of the underground railways, silhouettes of naked women on billboards, uncouth cab drivers, the poverty of London's East Enders and multitudes of disempowered women. While most other Indians wrote home of the architectural genius of the Westminster Abbey, Malabari found it void of the very woman's spirit that gave birth to its makers.

> There was not a single bust in the Abbey or the Cathedral, that I could see, devoted to the memory of women. This omission cannot be accidental. If it is designed, it may be taken as another instance of the disfavour with which Mother Church has viewed the liberation of her daughters from religious thraldom. Is it now too late to deny that there have been women in England worthy of a place side by side with some of their illustrious countrymen whom they have aided materially in winning a niche in the Temple of Fame?[16]

Malabari's lodgings were around South Kensington and Bayswater. The area came to be known as 'Asia Minor', due to its mounting Oriental population, in the 19th century. His landlady was one Mrs M, a twice-married Englishwoman, whom Malabari held in high esteem. Together with her Scottish maid, Maggie, she was the perfect example for him to study Victorian London's domesticities. G.P. Pillai, another Indian traveller and barrister, saw English landladies as snobbish fakes who while accommodating Indian students pretended to host nabobs, 'because on them rested the foundation of their fame.'[17] *The Times, The Illustrated London News* and the *Saturday Review* often featured stories about Indians in Britain. The journal of the National Indian Association, *Indian*

Magazine and Review, was also a regular source of information for Indians in the city to plan their boarding, itineraries, sightseeing and occasional gourmandising retreats.

SITE OF
ST DIONIS
BACKCHURCH
DEMOLISHED
1878

CITY OF LONDON

The Manipuri Students "At Home" to meet Lady Hailey, 9th August 1928 at Veeraswamy's Indian Restaurant.

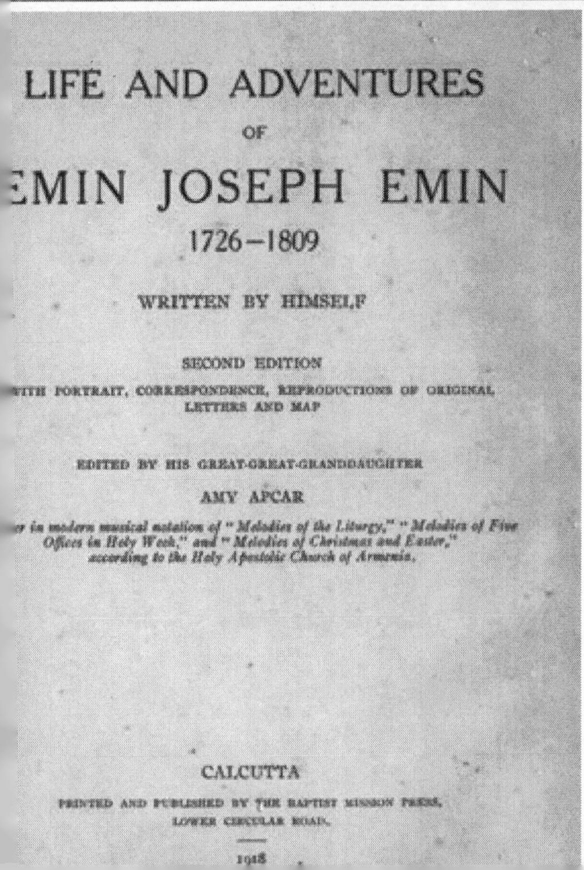

LIFE AND ADVENTURES

OF

EMIN JOSEPH EMIN

1726–1809

WRITTEN BY HIMSELF

SECOND EDITION

WITH PORTRAIT, CORRESPONDENCE, REPRODUCTIONS OF ORIGINAL
LETTERS AND MAP

EDITED BY HIS GREAT-GREAT-GRANDDAUGHTER

AMY APCAR

*er in modern musical notation of "Melodies of the Liturgy," "Melodies of Five
Offices in Holy Week," and "Melodies of Christmas and Easter,"
according to the Holy Apostolic Church of Armenia.*

Mirza Aboul-Faleh Khan

CALCUTTA

PRINTED AND PUBLISHED BY THE BAPTIST MISSION PRESS,
LOWER CIRCULAR ROAD.

1918

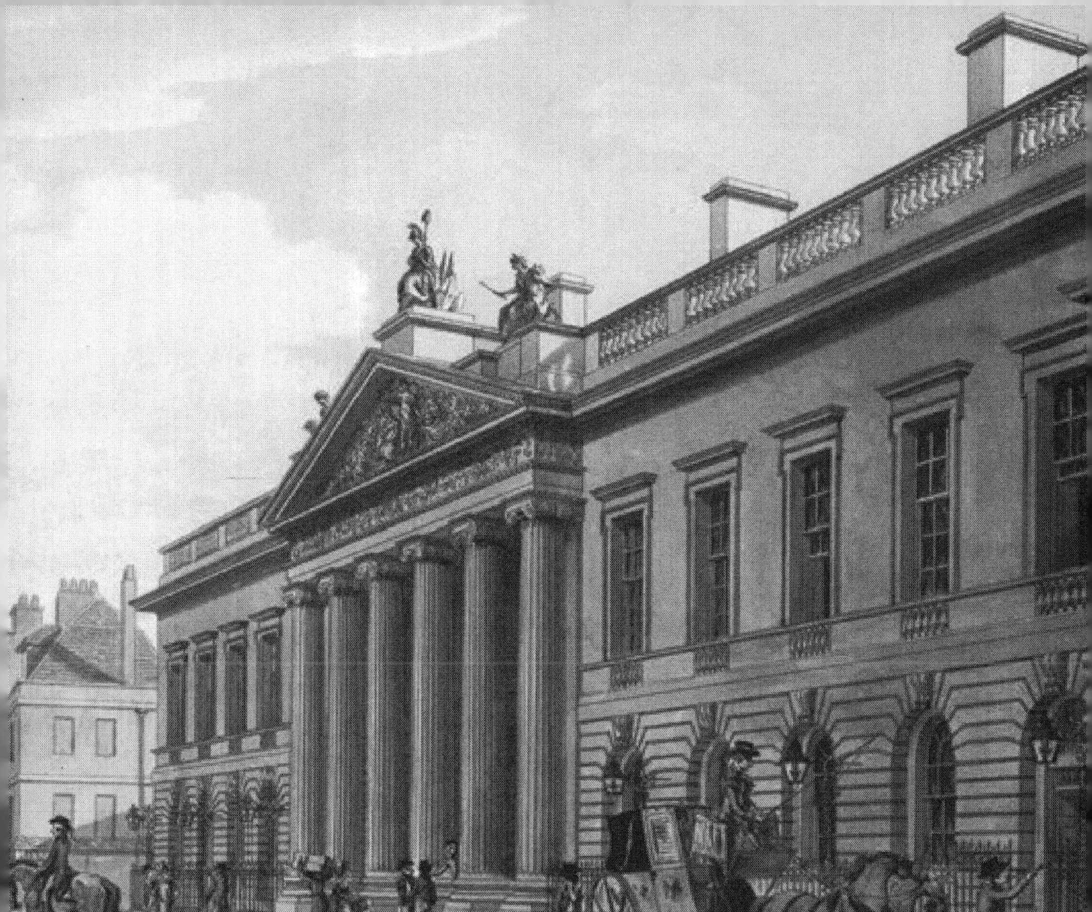

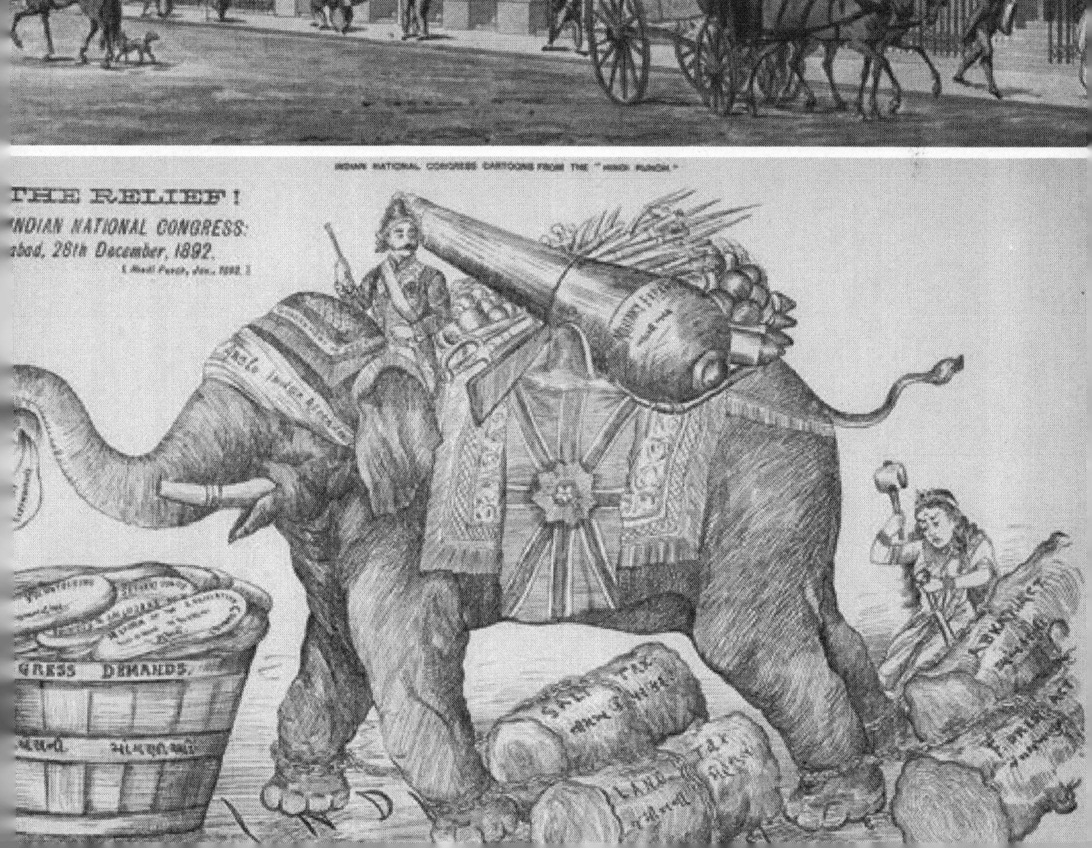

INDIAN NATIONAL CONGRESS CARTOONS FROM THE "HINDI PUNCH"
THE RELIEF!
INDIAN NATIONAL CONGRESS:
abad, 28th December, 1892.
(Hindi Punch, Jan., 1893.)
GRESS DEMANDS
SALT TAX
TAX
LAND
ARMS ACT

अरदेसर खररसेदजी वा[ह]

RDASEER CURSETJEE WADIA 1808

HINDOO TRACT-SELLER.

[From a Daguerreotype by BEARD.]

Indian Woman & Child.
Coronation Exhibition, London, 1911.

Р. Тагор в Лондоне
(1879—1880)

[From a photograph by   Franz Baum, New Bond Street.]

Mr. D. Naoroji.

مسٽر ڏي نوروزجي *

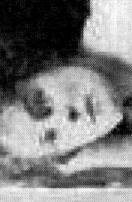

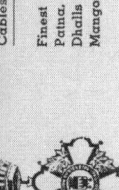

Princess Sophia Dhuleep Singh selling "The Suffragette" outside Hampton Court Palace, where she has a suite of apartments.

Mr. Shapurji Saklatvala, the Indian M.P., photographed with his English wife at their home in
London yesterday. He is Labour member for North Battersea—and "member for India," he says.
wife is a loyal supporter of his political views.

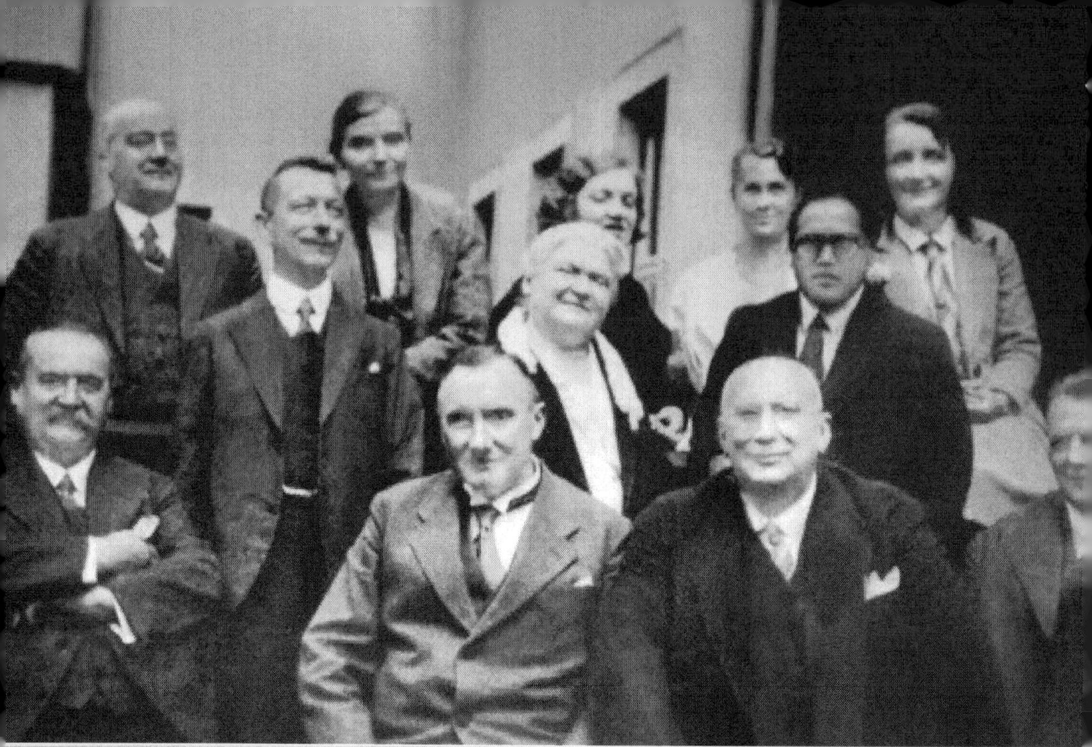

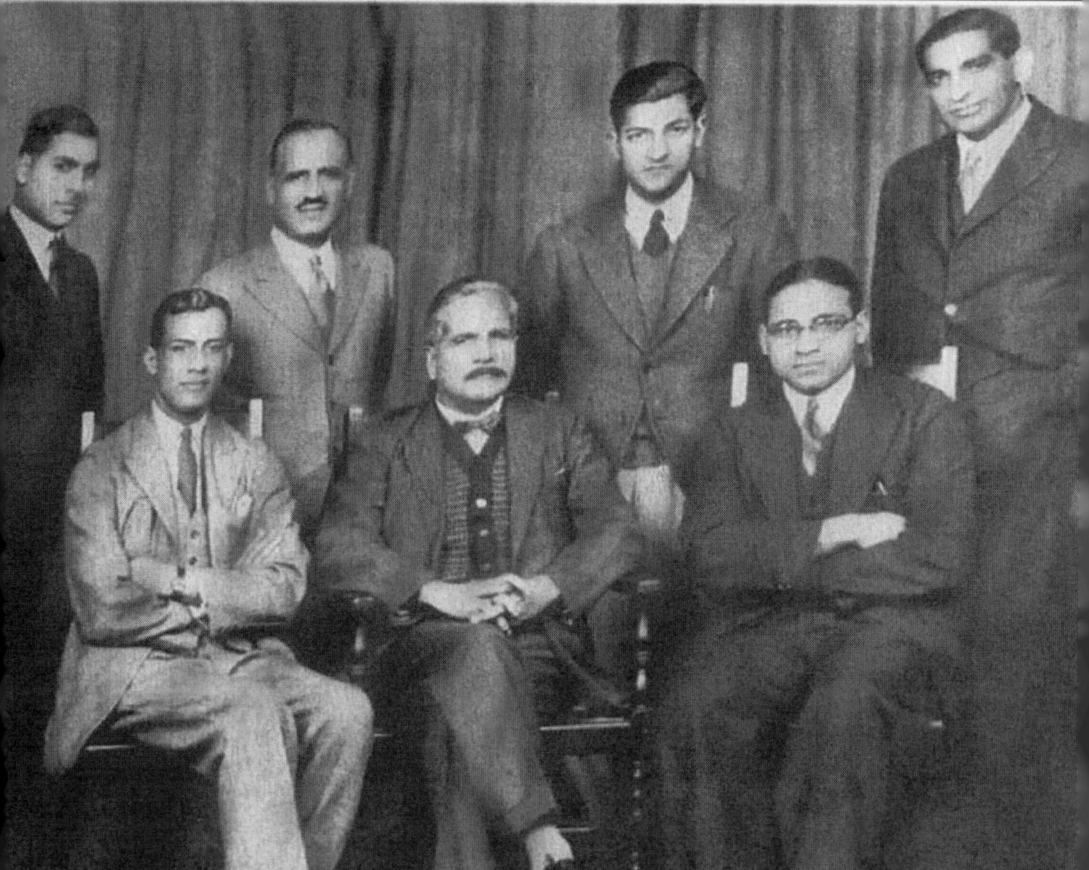

INDIA

SATURDAY, NOVEMBER 28, AT

KINGSWAY HALL

CONFERENCE 3 P.M.

CHAIRMAN: BERTRAND RUSSELL

SPEAKERS:

DELEGATION TO INDIA

ELLEN WILKINSON

MONICA WHATELY

LEONARD MATTERS

V.K. KRISHNA MENON

ADMISSION 1:-

PUBLIC MEETING 7 P.M.

SPEAKERS AS ABOVE
ADMISSION FREE

THE INDIA LEAGUE, 146, STRAND, LONDON, W.C. 1.

Vol. 1 No. 7   July 1920

BRITAIN
and
INDIA

A
Monthly
Magazine. 1/-

Edited by Josephine Ransom

Special Articles:—

India and Internationalism
Interview: Rabindranath Tagore
Hindu *versus* European Dancing
Women's Congress at Geneva

Offices: 7 Southampton Street, High Holborn, W.C.1

Scene III

Raising the Bar

By the onset of the 20th century, the number of newspaper advertisements calling for Asian boarders multiplied. So did the number of restaurants around Holborn, Bloomsbury and Mayfair, serving rice, curries, chutneys and pickles. In 1910, the number of students in British universities had already crossed 700. Among the places most frequented by young Indian students was the National Indian Association. It operated from the residence of Elizabeth Adelaide Manning, at Maida Vale in north Paddington. The association was founded in Bristol, in 1870, by Mary Carpenter, the old *protégé* of Raja Rammohun Roy. The next year, the London branch of the association took off from Manning's house in Victoria Street. In 1877, following Carpenter's demise, Manning became the association's new honorary secretary, moving its official work to London. Here, it also doubled up as a clearing house for students from the subcontinent until the years of the Great War. In a letter written to his parents, in 1911, Sukumar Ray noted that in the parlance of young Indians, the house went by the sobriquet, 'Miss Manning's Association.'

The Indian Magazine and Review, published by the association and edited by Manning in her lifetime, ran features and opinions on Indian women's education and the colonial administration of India. Inter alia, it was also the first publisher of several rare tracts by Indians, one of them being *Extracts from the Diary of the Nawab Mehdi Hasan Khan Fathah Nawaj Jung* (1890). A civil servant from Hyderabad, Mehdi Hasan Khan was in London in the late 1880s, to represent the Nizam's Deccan Mining Company before the British Government. In 1888, he was presented before the Queen at Buckingham Palace. But for *The Indian Magazine*, many such colourful accounts of British social life would have been lost to the public eye.

———

Among notable visitors to Manning's house was the young Gandhi. It was here that he first met his lifelong friend, the Bengali writer and fellow-vegetarian, Narayan Hemchandra. The first Indian female barrister, also the first female graduate from the Bombay University and the first female law student at Oxford, Cornelia Sorabji, also stayed with Manning in 1889. Along with Mary Hobhouse, Manning helped Cornelia acquire a scholarship to Oxford with recommendations and financial support from Sir William Wedderburn, Florence Nightingale and others. A letter written to *The Times* by Hobhouse, in April 1888, on the 'progress of female education in India,' aroused great public sympathy for Cornelia. 'Difficulties, chiefly of a pecuniary character,' wrote Hobhouse, had prevented her from coming to Oxford despite her successful tenure as a senior Fellow at the Gujarat Arts College.[1]

London opened its arms to Cornelia—especially the arms of elderly Christian missionary ladies very keen to convert her. She was often at a loss to explain that she was already as Christian as could be, her father being a long-serving agent for the Christian Missionary Society. Yet, owing to the 'so very heathen'[2] appearance that Cornelia wore about her, she was expected to look more Christian, if only through conversion. As an Indian Christian, Cornelia was a walking advertisement. Although she strongly opposed the activities of Christian evangelicals, she worked towards raising funds for the Society, from all across Britain. Her later accomplishment in the field of law overshadowed her literary talent. In 1902, she wrote a play called *The Clay Cart*, which was an English adaptation of a Sanskrit play by Sudraka. A brusque 'suggestion for improvement'[3] from George Bernard Shaw led her to abandon the work. Six years later, she wrote *Between the Twilights* (1908), and over the next decade, *The Purdahnashin* (1917). Both were based on her experiences in social reform and women's activism. When she returned to London, in 1924, after a long career in India, she wrote at least one more drama, namely, *Gold Mohur Time: 'To Remember'*, which was published in 1930. As a journalist, Cornelia's journey was staggering. In that decade, she also published two autobiographies, *India Calling* (1934) and *Indian Recalled* (1936). Later, she also contributed to the *Queen Mary's Book for India* (1943), which was meant to collect donations for the India Comforts Fund during the Second World War.

Back in the day, at Manning's house, Cornelia stayed with Rukhmabai, who had come to appeal to the Queen for the dissolution of her oppressive marriage with Dadaji Bhikaji. The Bombay High Court had earlier ruled that if Rukhmabai did not return to her husband, she could face a prison sentence of six months. On hearing her tale of misery, Victoria overruled the verdict. Amidst high controversy both in India and Britain, Rukhmabai's marriage was dissolved. The case led to the Government of India legislating the Age of Consent Act of 1891, which raised the age of consensual sexual relations for Indian women from ten to twelve. While in London, Rukhmabai studied at the Royal Free Hospital, and in 1894, she was awarded a physician's degree at the London School of Medicine for Women. She was only the second Indian woman to practise Western medicine, after Kadambini Ganguly.

London was the land of alchemy for most middle-class Indians. More than a decade before the city gave the subcontinent its first Nobel laureate, it shaped the early career of the 'Nightingale of India', Sarojini Naidu. During her undergraduate years at King's College, Naidu was surrounded by literary geniuses. Edmond Gausse and Arthur Symons took her under their wing. When Gausse recognised her strains were borrowed from Shelley and Keats, he issued her a strict injunction. He expected to see nothing less—or perhaps nothing more—than the soul of India in her poems. After all, Naidu was in London for her poetry, funded on a scholarship from the Nizam. On the brighter side, some of her early poems were published in *The Savoy*, which was founded in 1896 by the controversial author and publisher Leonard Smithers, and the illustrator and author Aubrey Vincent Beardsley. Symons too was a co-founder.

Born as the face of the Decadent Arts movement, and named after the hotel where Oscar Wilde was known to have burned the midnight oil with his partners, *The Savoy* shut down by the end of the year as the controversy around Wilde's alleged depravities further intensified. Although the magazine boasted of publishing many popular and distinguished writers, including W.B. Yeats and Joseph Conrad, by the end of its career, booksellers refused to stock it on their shelves. Naidu's early eminence was, therefore, quite transitory. After returning to India, she resumed her poetic career and began publishing in the *Indian Magazine*. London had already given her her first major publication—*The Golden Threshold*—which was published as a limited edition in 1896. It was largely owing to Gausse, to whom she dedicated the book. Naidu was successful in teasing the exotic sensibilities of the city with characters such as palanquin bearers, snake charmers, corn grinders and Coromandel fishermen. The book was republished by William Heinemann, in London, with an introduction by Symons.

While at King's College, Naidu met her future husband, Dr Govindarajalu Naidu, who was a student of medicine at the University of Edinburgh. It was also in London that she first met her political guru, Mahatma Gandhi. In 1914, upon returning from South Africa, Gandhi stayed for a few months in London before leaving for India. He was to be joined by Gopal Krishna Gokhale, the stalwart Congressman, who had been campaigning in England for Indian Home Rule since the 1870s. As the war broke out, Gokhale was detained in Paris. Naidu was asked to meet Gandhi— alone. Her second book of poems, *The Bird of Time* (1912), had just been published from London, and she had started working as a volunteer at the Lyceum, a women's club which contributed to the war effort by sewing uniforms. Gandhi was himself involved in organising an ambulance unit for the war. In August 1914, Naidu came to meet Gandhi at the old Kensington apartment where he was staying. She found him in the company of 'a battered tin of parched groundnut and tasteless biscuits of dried plantain flour.'[4] She would later recall that rainy afternoon in a letter to Hansraj Jivraj Mehta, another Indian student activist in London in those years: 'The Great South African leader who, to quote Mr Gokhale's apt phrase, had moulded heroes out of clay, was reclining, a little ill and weary, on the floor eating his frugal meal of nuts and fruit.'[5] Although Gandhi had not seen her before, he recognised her instantly from her mischievous laughter: 'Ah, you must be Mrs Naidu!' he exclaimed. 'Who else dare be so irreverent.'[6] Later that day, she taught Gandhi to sew, and a few days later, he entrusted her with the mission of mobilising supporters for the war from the Indian quarters in the city. That tryst in London matured into a long attachment over a series of correspondences. From calling him 'Bapu', she went on to name him 'Apostle of Peace', 'Mystic Spinner', 'Little Man' and, finally, 'Mickey Mouse'. Unsurprisingly, Western cinema audiences often spoke about the resemblance of Gandhi with Mickey Mouse or with 'the socialist Charlie Chaplin whom he met in East London in 1931.'[7]

London had grown into a realm of uncanny first-meetings and a minefield of transcultural exchanges—a rapidly evolving citadel of Indian solidarities. 'When you meet an Egyptian, an Algerian, an Indian and a Turk in London,' Naidu remarked two years later, 'what matters that Egypt was the motherland of one and India the motherland of another?' The gift of Indian brotherhood that Mughal rule had bestowed on the subcontinent, 'this great sense of human justice,'[8] as she called it, was increasingly manifesting in the city. It was here that one saw 'thousands and thousands of young hearts' beating as one independent nation, here that one discovered 'such a thing as the Indian renaissance.'[9] Congressmen like Gopal Krishna Gokhale and Mohammad Ali Jinnah had turned to London to westernise themselves, on the road to India's freedom. Giving up on his turban, Gokhale took to an English top hat, while Jinnah even seriously contemplated on a career on the London stage. His artistic aspirations were forestalled when he was called to Lincoln's Inn in 1895. At nineteen, Jinnah was the youngest Asian at the Bar. From there he would go on to become Bombay's first Muslim barrister in the late 1890s and, by the 1920s, a decadent and dangerous intellectual in London. His opus consisted of a house in Hampstead, with a black Doberman and a white West Highland terrier. There was an English chauffeur who tended to his Bentley, and Indian and Irish chefs to his curries. During the day the barrister attended the Privy Council, and read Shakespeare aloud to himself by night, still nursing his old dream of playing at the Theatre Royal, Drury Lane.

Jinnahbhai—as was his original family name—was still far from coming of age, when his father 'deposited money enough to his account in a British bank to allow Jinnah to live in London for three years. There is no record of precisely how many hotel rooms or "bed and breakfast" stops he rented before moving into the modest three-story house at 35 Russell Road in Kensington.'[10] He replaced his Indian wardrobe with bespoke English suits from Savile Row, impeccably starched shirts, two-tone leather shoes, and silk ties which he was known not to wear twice. The Victorian Jinnah wore the Edwardian expression much before P.G. Wodehouse, who actually coined it: 'there is no time, sir, at which ties do not matter.' Jinnah even had his own Wodehouse-moment 'during a visit to Oxford, when he was arrested. He, along with two of his friends, "caught up with a crowd of undergraduates," came across a cart and "pushed each other up and down the roadway." They were arrested and taken to the police station, where they were let off with a caution.'[11] Jinnah's mimesis of the life and manners of English aristocracy in India left even Londoners ill at ease. Among Indians, his fashion was equalled perhaps only by Motilal Nehru, a barrister and Jinnah's colleague in the Congress and the Privy Council.

When he was not flaunting his signature monocle or devouring politics and biographies at the British Library, Jinnah closely followed the movements of William Ewart Gladstone. Gladstone was elected the prime minister of Britain for a fourth term in 1892. The young Jinnah was in the visitor's gallery on the July afternoon that year, when Naoroji made his maiden speech in the House of Commons. Many years later, a British general's wife recounted meeting Jinnah at a Viceregal dinner in Simla: 'He talks the most beautiful English.

He models his manners and clothes on Gerald du Maurier, the actor, and his English on Edmund Burke's speeches.'[12] His long residence in London after the war and his purported attempts to enter the British Parliament made many wonder if he was not the future Viceroy of India. Naidu herself was infected by his 'virile patriotism.'[13] Jinnah was undoubtedly the man, she believed, who 'symbolised everything attractive about modern India.' She thought he aspired to be the 'Muslim Gokhale.' Young Naidu was smitten, even if platonically, and was not shy to mark it in her prose.

> Tall and stately, but thin to the point of emaciation, languid and luxurious of habit, Mohammad Ali Jinnah's attenuated form is a deceptive sheath of a spirit of exceptional vitality and endurance. Somewhat formal and fastidious, and a little aloof and imperious of manner, the calm hauteur of his accustomed reserve but masks, for those who know him, a naive and eager humanity, an intuition quick and tender as a woman's, a humour gay and winning as a child's. Pre-eminently rational and practical, discreet and dispassionate in his estimate and acceptance of life, the obvious sanity and serenity of his worldly wisdom effectually disguise a shy and splendid idealism which is of the very essence of the man.[14]

Motilal Nehru, a Cambridge graduate and a towering barrister in Victorian India, had chosen to break away from almost all of Eastern wisdom, including its languages. Without English, he reckoned, his clan would be bound for a speedy decline. He did forget, in the process, that several women of the Nehru household were not schooled in English or, indeed, schooled at all. In 1905, his son Jawaharlal Nehru was admitted to Harrow. It was the same school Winston Churchill had been to, fifteen years ago, before proceeding to the Royal Military Academy at Sandhurst. The school that had also produced Sir William Jones, the founder of the Asiatic Society of Bengal, taught Churchill to take India for nothing more than a 'geographical expression'. Spending his time between football, cricket, the writings of George Bernard Shaw and clippings from Indian newspapers sent by his father, Nehru took both to Jones' fancy for institutions and Churchill's fantasy for reinventing nations. It was Harrow after all that would turn Nehru into 'a queer mixture of the East and West, out of place everywhere, at home nowhere.'[15]

The Irish Home Rule Movement and the life of Giuseppe Garibaldi—whose biography Nehru had won as a prize at Harrow—brought him closer to the Indian freedom struggle. In 1907, he enrolled at Trinity College, Cambridge. Although he was a member of the debating societies of the time and also came in contact with the Congress extremist Bipin Chandra Pal, the raw chords of nationalism were yet to be struck in Nehru's organs. Pal's theatricality seemed to fall upon deaf ears during a speech delivered in Cambridge.. 'The volume of noise was so terrific,' Nehru later disparaged, 'that I could hardly follow what he was saying.' Nehru's outlook on life was of an ambivalent 'Cyrenaicism,' summed up as a 'desire for a soft life and pleasant experiences.'[16] He too had taken the contagion from the age of dilettantism popularised by Oscar Wilde and Water Pater before the *fin de siècle*. When he joined the Inner Temple, the discordant songs of Fabian Socialism were about to be heard in the neighbourhood. At the London School of Economics, where Nehru attended some lectures, his political views had their inception. Among his many Indian friends in London, around this time, was Khan Abdul Jabbar Khan, a medical student at St Thomas' Hospital. He was the younger brother of Khan Abdul Ghaffar Khan, better known as Frontier Gandhi— an inveterate antagonist to the partition of India and diehard campaigner for an independent Pashtunistan. Nehru would later be counted among those who betrayed Abdul Ghaffar Khan, as the Congress gave its consent to the Partition. Writing to Gandhi in 1946, Khan bemoaned the foreseeable disaster of his nation and tribe: 'We Pakhtuns stood by you and had undergone great sacrifices for attaining freedom, but you have now deserted us and thrown us to the wolves.'[17]

In 1912, Sidney and Beatrice Webb, Fabian Socialists and founders of the London School of Economics travelled to India. They persuaded Sir Ratanji Tata, the second son of Jamsetji Tata, to award an annual grant of £1,400 to their lately-founded university. It was meant to fund research in legislative and administrative processes for alleviating poverty and economic inequality. At first approved for three years, the grant was renewed in 1916, and again in 1921 and 1926. Even later, it continued as part of the Ratan Tata Fellowships. Back in India, the Tatas would aid the war effort with iron and steel for railway tracks, war-wagons and finished textiles for soldiers. They had been pioneers of swadeshi textile mills, as well as iron and steel manufacturing, with over half a century of entrepreneurial legacy in India. From London, the Tatas began authoring their chapter of international philanthropy.

The family business had already forayed into Europe by establishing the headquarters of the Tata Limited in London in 1907. Ratanji's brother, Sir Dorabji Tata, appointed his cousin, Shapurji Saklatwala, as the manager of the Manchester branch of the company. In 1909, Saklatwala joined the Independent Labour Party, beginning his twenty-year-long political career. Another cousin of the Tata brothers, the teenager Rattanbai Petit, or Ruttie as she was better known, was about to be the second Mrs Jinnah. Jinnah and a pregnant Ruttie were in London in 1919. Before the midnight of August 14—the day Pakistan later became an independent nation—the couple were visiting a theatre, when Ruttie went into labour. Jinnah, on the other hand, was gradually going out of favour with Secretary of State Edwin Samuel Montagu and the British Government. With the Jallianwala Bagh massacre of April that year, and the heat of the Khilafat and Non-Cooperation movements, Jinnah plunged into the work of revolution, sparing little time for his family. In October, Sarojini Naidu wrote to her daughter Padmaja, from London, that the young and lonesome Ruttie was now adrift like a jaded moth, whose black and gold spots were recklessly growing gray as the weather.

Even before the war, nearly all shades of Indian politics and passion had been cradled in London. During his second visit to the city in 1913, Jinnah found himself in the company of several Congressmen. Naidu and Gandhi were there as well, and Gokhale too, for the last time before his death. Gokhale was a neighbour and guest to Ratanji Tata and his wife at York House in Twickenham. Even in his final years, Gokhale delivered stirring lectures on patriotism and self-sacrifice to Indian and British students in London. On certain evenings, he was seen with Sarojini Naidu at Kensington Gardens, lending an avuncular shoulder to the wild imaginings of the poetess. He continued to be a regular invitee to elegant luncheons, an avid theatre-goer and a ladies' favourite for many a card game at the National Liberal Club. Established in 1882 at Whitehall Place, the Club was Gladstone's brainchild to give members and campaigners of the Liberal Party a respectable clubhouse. Three years later, Naoroji became the first Indian member of the club. He was followed by Gokhale and Jinnah. Before Jinnah began rubbing shoulders with the bureaucrats of Whitehall, he founded the London Indian Association—named as though in portmanteaux between the London Indian Society and the East India Association. Its promise exceeded its prospects; its ambitions undermined its affluence. The objective of the association was 'to provide a permanent centre to focus the scattered student life in London and to build up such staunch tradition of co-operation and fellowship that this young association might eventually grow into a perfect miniature and model of the federated Indian of the future, the India of their dreams.'[18]

That was already thirty years after the great Congress barristocracy first rose to the stage of British electoral politics. In the late 1890s, Romesh Chunder Dutt's popularity as a scholar, journalist and political campaigner was on the ascent. He was approached by the Yarmouth constituency to stand for election. Naoroji offered to loan him the money for the campaign, but Dutt refused to contest. However, he canvassed for the Liberal Party, and in his speeches he attacked the British foreign and war policy in Afghanistan and Central Asia, the plight of Indian taxpayers and the Indian state policy on sedition. Dutt never passed on an opportunity to promote Indian nationalism, contributing prolifically to newspapers such as the *Daily News*, *The Times* and the *Manchester Guardian*. While at the University College, where he started lecturing in 1898, Dutt worked on revisions of his book, *England and India* (1897), and on his abridged English translations of the *Mahabharata* (1898) and *Ramayana* (1899). He lectured on the civilisation and religion of the Hindus, Indian history, Indian epics and ancient Indian poetry. Even while he was associated with a colonial academic institution, Dutt protested against a bill introduced in the Bengal Legislative Assembly which intended to reduce the number of elected representatives in the Calcutta Municipality from fifty to twenty-five. With tempers running high in Calcutta, Dutt was designated as the representative of the constitutional agitation in Britain in 1899. Although the bill became an Act of Parliament, Dutt enlisted strong supporters from the House of Commons and the press. That year, he was elected as a Fellow of the Royal Society of Literature, and President of the Indian National Congress session in Lucknow. He was also the London correspondent for the *Indian Mirror*, a journal based in Calcutta. Over the twenty columns that he wrote, his subjects ranged between current affairs, book reviews, excerpts from his speeches and questions on Indian economy, politics and literature. In one of his columns, he remarked:

> It is an age of Imperialism we live in; all over Europe there is the unending struggle for material interest, for conquests, annexations, extension of markets, increase of profits. Never since the Crimean War has Imperialism been so rampant in England; never have the purely animal instincts of self-love or self-aggrandisement been stronger or more violent. The close of the 19th century, like the close of the 18th century, is marked in England by the coarsest form of Imperialism.[19]

In his final years in London, Dutt's magnum opus, *The Economic History of India* (1902), was published in two volumes. As Britain came to learn of the mass exploitation and millions of famine deaths in India, its workers, labourers, women and oppressed classes came forward to sympathise and toe the campaigns of the Indian nationalists. Dutt understood this when he saw Lalmohan

Ghose rouse rabbles in the city with his fiery speeches in 1880. Ghose had been called to the Bar along with Dutt. He practised at the Calcutta High Court for six years before coming to London, in 1879, to protest against two highly repressive acts enacted by the Government of India. These were the Arms Act (which prohibited Indians from possessing, manufacturing or selling arms) and the Press Act (which prevented Indians from critiquing British policies). Under public pressure, the latter was repealed in 1882. Ghose also agitated for relaxing the age limit for candidates appearing for civil services examinations. In London, he made the acquaintance of William Gladstone, the then leader of the opposition party, and John Bright, a Liberal statesman and free-trade campaigner. While addressing a meeting at St James', chaired by Bright, Ghose tapped into the city's growing appetite for internationalism: 'the various races are being gradually welded together into the common nationality, they are beginning to cooperate with each other in the discussion and agitation of political questions and the national pulse is beginning to beat with unison.'[20] The stream of passion around which political activists in Calcutta, Bombay, Delhi or Madras held their rallies and protest meetings, was beginning to overflow in London.

After the rescindment of the Press Act, Surendranath Banerjea published some inflammatory pieces in his newspaper, *The Bengalee*, which were held in contempt of court. Calcutta, Agra, Amritsar, Lahore and Pune erupted, as Banerjea was taken into custody. Ghose, who was in London, took to defending Banerjea in his and the many rebellions seething in India. In 1885, the Liberal Party offered candidacy to Ghose to contest from the Deptford Constituency, which had a large working-class Irish population. Ghose, who was also an ardent supporter of the Irish Home Rule Movement, sensed an immediate opportunity to foment the nascent ideas for Home Rule in India. But the Tory-leaning British press launched a concerted effort to malign the moral and social reputation of Ghose, while elevating that of his opponent, the Tory candidate W.J. Evelyn. After losing the contest, Ghose stood again the following year. On this occasion, Naoroji also stood as a Liberal candidate. Although both of them lost, Naoroji had a lot to look forward to after his election as President of the Indian National Congress. Six years later, he was to return to London for the British general elections of 1892. Once again, he stood for the Liberals, this time from Finsbury Central. Naoroji won the seat by a historic majority—three votes. 'We have heard of Indian "nabobs,"' wrote *The Guardian*, 'buying up a rotten borough here and there and seated themselves in Parliament; but that a native Indian should find a place in that Imperial assembly and take part in the legislation and administration of the Empire would have been considered too wild an idea to be ever realised.'[21] As Naoroji became the toast of the Indians and Irish in London, Ghose's exploits were far from forgotten. In Deptford, his farewell meeting witnessed huge crowds of Britons and Asians. When Banerjea visited London in 1890, hundreds of Deptford constituents came forward to recount Ghose's 'power and eloquence that excited the admiration of all.'[22] In 1903, eight years after Naoroji completed his term as Member of Parliament, Ghose also became President of the Indian National Congress.

In 1888, when Mohandas K. Gandhi set sail for London, he was given four letters of introduction addressed to Indians in London. One of them was for Naoroji. Gandhi was one of 200 Indian students in the heart of Albion. He reached Tilbury on the ship *Clyde*, and then London by train. Gandhi's 'badly cut Bombay clothes flopped over his undersized body like loose sails on a becalmed ship,' as he waded his way through the city like a crow in a foreign country. Chosen by nature to be unimpressively small, his colleagues in the Inns of Court would sometimes mistake him 'for an errand boy.'[23] Foreseeing the challenging times ahead, Gandhi boarded at the Victoria Hotel, one of the most ostentatious hotels in London at the time. Pranjivan Mehta, a law student from Kathiawar, came to see him the next day. It would be quite a while before Gandhi met with Naoroji. In the interim, he began his quest for a new identity in London with lessons on elocution, violin and dancing, fraught with constant anxieties of English etiquette and sartorial tastes. What ailed Gandhi must have been a historical reality for most Indian students in London and the rest of Britain. Beset by the memories of his mother and his motherland, a lonely and homesick Gandhi wrote on his nineteenth birthday from his secluded quarters in Richmond:

> I was very uneasy even in the new rooms. I knew of nothing that would soothe me. Everything was strange—the people, their ways, and even their dwellings. I was a complete novice in the matter of English etiquette and continually had to be on my guard. There was an additional inconvenience of the vegetarian now. Even the dishes I could eat were tasteless and insipid. England I could not bear, but to return to India was not to be thought of.[24]

Gandhi's lethal essay, *Hind Swaraj* (or *Indian Home Rule*, published in 1909), described how British newspapers had poisoned the minds of the electorate, and turned the British Parliament into a rationed pleasure seeker.[25] Gandhi's early days in Richmond were spent in reading at least three English dailies— the right-leaning *Daily Telegraph*, the liberal *Daily News* and the somewhat eclectic if not eccentric *Pall Mall Gazette*. Besides staying abreast of developments in Britain's workers' unions, financial policies and the Irish Home Rule movement, Gandhi was also able to greatly improve his English. He closely followed reports of criminal cases, and it is not unlikely that he came across reports of the Whitechapel murders committed by Jack the Ripper in the very year of his arrival in London. He kept those newspaper cuttings in his treasury, which would travel with him to India, twenty-five years later. Not only in Victorian proverbs, but Gandhi also preceded Jinnah in Victorian sartorial experiments. A starched collar, he believed, was his first passport to imperial acceptance. It was his English dressing that, later on in South Africa, made him immune to many forms of racism reserved for Asians and 'coolies'. Gandhi picked up a gadabout lifestyle, and within his first two years in the city he could be seen promenading about the Piccadilly Circus, 'wearing a high silk top hat burnished bright, a Gladstone collar, stiff and starched; a rather flashy tie displaying almost all the colours of the rainbow under which there was a fine striped silk shirt.' His hair was plastered to his skull, and he had a silver-topped walking stick to pay suit to his white gloves and patent leather shoes.[26]

The one thing, however, that Gandhi would have protected with his life was his food. Boiled potatoes and cabbages, raw lettuces and tomatoes, blanched carrots and half-seared scarlet mutton slices sickened him aesthetically, before choking him gastronomically. Gandhi was rather comfortable with caste hierarchies, in general, minus the evils of the caste system, of course. Not surprisingly, in his *Guide to London* (1893), he wrote how, by making a few compromises, food could have been easily obtained in the city without imperilling one's caste. 'For an ordinary Indian who is not overscrupulous in his religious views,' he instructed, 'and who is not much of a believer in caste-restrictions, it would be advisable to cook partly himself and get a part of his food ready-made.'[27] Gandhi lived on breakfasts of oatmeal porridge, luncheons and suppers of spinach and bread, and the intellects of Jeremy Bentham, John Ruskin, Ralph Waldo Emerson and Oscar Wilde while being enrolled at the Inner Temple. Later that year, he moved to West Kensington, living as a paying guest with a widow and her two daughters. It was a four-storeyed house in a row of houses behind which trundled the District Line trains that had started plying twenty years ago.

A month after his moving in, Gandhi made the extraordinary discovery of the vegetarian Central Restaurant, off Farringdon Street, while looking for the Porridge Bowl Restaurant around High Holborn. Armed with a copy of Henry Salt's *Plea for Vegetarianism* (1886), Gandhi memorialised first hearty meal since his arrival in London. Following his epicurean adventure, he purchased all the works on vegetarianism he could lay hands on, including those by the authors William Howard, Anna Kingsford and Thomas Allinson. Gandhi's sleuthing stints for vegetarian food around Marylebone and Holborn were a constant source of vexation for his friend and fellow student, Dalpatram Shukla. From Bond Street to Piccadilly Circus, Gandhi ambled about fulfilling the necessary conditions of his 'dramatic experiment,'[28] trying to conform to British dressing and sociability, as well as learning how to subvert it. In 1889, when he moved to Store Street in Bloomsbury, he continued his practise of walking eight to ten miles every day.

During a trip to Brighton, Gandhi encountered an English widow, who became his friend back in London. Occasionally, she invited him to Sunday luncheons at her house, where she introduced him to young ladies to help him overcome his shyness. Mild flirtation was encouraged and even cultivated by Victorian English families for sculpting the romantic sensibilities of young men and women. Gandhi was not unfamiliar with that convention. He passed himself off as a bachelor, although he was already married to Kasturba and was the father of a young son back in India. In this faraway sanctuary, he commenced on a close friendship with an English lady who lived as the widow's tenant. Gandhi possibly overestimated his own charms for he was mortally afraid that the landlady dreamed of making a match for her ward with a shy and coy young Indian law student. Racked by guilt, he finally unburdened his secret in a confessional letter of apology to the old woman. A cheeky response followed: 'I have your frank letter. We were both very glad and had a hearty laugh over it. We shall certainly expect you next Sunday and look forward to hearing about your child-marriage and laughing at your expense.'[29]

Two of Gandhi's most prominent female acquaintances in London were Annie Besant and Helena Blavatsky. Well known, even back then as the co-founders of the theosophical movement, they left a deep impression on Gandhi's early life and influenced his turning to Hindu theology, which he had hitherto stayed away from lest he was seen as un-English. The English theosophists, Bertram and Archibald Keightley, who introduced Gandhi to Besant and Blavatsky, would later seek his help in translating the *Bhagavad Gita*, which led him to a lifelong study of the holy book. In 1890, he moved to Tavistock Street at Covent Garden, to further economise his lodging costs. By now, he had started collecting material for the *Guide to London* and writing articles for *The Vegetarian*, on diet and travel. He was also serving as a board member of the London Vegetarian Society. As his culinary explorations continued around Holborn, he discovered as many as ten vegetarian restaurants in the neighbourhood. At Waverley, a restaurant in Borough Street, Gandhi lectured to diners on the diversity of Indian food. Impressed by his scholarship, Josiah Oldfield, a doctor and barrister, and the editor of *The Vegetarian*, invited him to the International Vegetarian Congress. In spring the following year, he moved in with Oldfield at an apartment in Bayswater.

Most of the places that Gandhi visited in his time for his getaway meals were later demolished to make way for Sainsbury's supermarket stores. Nonetheless, his tutelage in the vegetarian counter-culture of modern London went a long way in a career shaped by the politics of the streets—one that his colleague Jinnah could never endorse even to save himself. The vegetarian restaurants and journals to which Oldfield introduced him, provided him with object lessons in organisation and campaigning. The Vegetarian Society, on whose executive committee he served from 1890, was a haven for a variety of renegades of the 'late Victorian revolt'.[30] A broad church embracing dissenters from various ideologies, its members included Fabian socialists like Shaw, along with spiritual seekers and Irish nationalists such as Besant and Yeats. Gandhi's revolution was one of self-inquiry—dietary, political and spiritual, and all very likely in the same orbit. It was an experiment to rise to the biblical solemnity of the virtues of honest agricultural toil over the cannibalistic intellects of civilisation, that John Ruskin had inspired in him.

In his first week in London, Gandhi was told he would not survive without meat. As it turned out, 'the British faith in its mythical power was quite equal to the Indian faith in the purifying and polluting potential of food.'[31] Ten days after he was called to the Bar in June 1891, Gandhi gave an interview to *The Vegetarian*, where he proudly asserted that he would now be returning to India 'without having taken meat or wine.'[32] Being associated with the magazine, Gandhi came to be in touch with footballers and even saw the coming up of the West Ham United Football Club in

Stratford. Arnold Frank Hills, the founder of the club—as well as the founder of *The Vegetarian*—was the one who introduced Gandhi to the London Vegetarian Society. In 1888, Hills became the first president of the society, later serving with Gandhi on its executive committee. When Gandhi returned to London in 1931, to attend the Second Round Table Conference, he stayed for three months at the Kingsley Hall community centre in East London. Just off the Green Street—that became one of the many 'Little India' crossroads in millennial London—lies the Boleyn Tavern, once frequented by West Ham United fans. Gandhi, who enjoyed immense popularity with the East Enders, is said to have enjoyed cream soda at the tavern over discussions on football and politics with local Londoners. Owing to his love of football, he even helped establish three football clubs in South Africa—at Durban, Pretoria and Johannesburg. Just like he later did with railway platforms in India, he might have hoped to transform football grounds in South Africa into theatres and battlegrounds of *Satyagraha*.

———

It was at the London Indian Society where Gandhi finally met Naoroji. The society was established by the Grand Old Man of India in 1865, to bridge the gap between Englishmen and Indian scholars. Its active members included co-founder Bonnerjee, Mehta, Tyabji, Ghose, Tagore and Dutt. Besides, they were also members of the East Indian Association, founded in 1866, for studying and advocating the public interests of India. It was the breeding ground for debates on holding simultaneous civil service examinations in England and India, the 'Drain of wealth' theory (popularly credited to Naoroji and Dutt), and studies into the dire need for irrigation canals and humane agricultural policies in the heydey of railway expansions in India. Almost every member was to be later elected president of the Indian National Congress. The nub of the Congress brain could be traced to these men largely from Bombay and Calcutta who had been operating from London, off and on, since the 1860s. Their long presence in the social circles of the city had deeply familiarised them with British politics. To impress British voters, Naoroji had to choreograph a lot of his identity. He exchanged his Parsi turban for an English hat to supplement his Caucasian-English appearance and steadfast loyalty to the Queen. It made a remarkable change to the damaging impact of the racist overtures of the British press, which had strategically shortened the career of Ghose. No less than Prime Minister Lord Salisbury referred to Naoroji as a 'black man'.[33] Much of it turned to political advantage, as Naoroji was staunchly defended by the leading liberal dailies of the age, *Glasgow Mail* and *Newcastle Leader*, and affirmed by influential liberal voices such as William Digby and even an ailing Florence Nightingale.

After Naoroji's victory, however, *The Guardian* was perhaps the only mainstream voice to consider it 'an honour to England.'[34] *The Times* played down Naoroji's entry into the House of Commons as an 'almost romantic event, if romance can enter into politics.'[35] The English public was pitted against having an Indian member in the House. Naoroji went about his term, undaunted by the hostile environment. He was a passionate supporter of temperance activism, trade unionism and working men's societies. He also supported women suffragettes and played an active role in promoting the Women's Franchise League and the Women's Liberal Federation, established in the late 19th century, to campaign for the rights and liberties of women, the latter being a part of the Liberal Party. Naoroji's attendance in Parliament was impeccable and he voted on over 90 per cent of the issues debated in the House. He also helped the formation of the Royal Commission on Indian Finance and the Welby Commission, in both of which he was an appointed member. Naoroji steered the Indian Parliamentary Committee which, in 1893, put forth before the House about 400 questions on Indian finances, civil services, public works and socio-political reforms. He also introduced the East India Bill, originally moved by fellow-Liberal, Herbert Paul, for simultaneous civil services examinations in India and Britain. Although the resolution was passed by a majority in the Parliament, the bill was turned down by the Secretary of State for India, fearing that it would only strengthen the Indian Home Rule agitation. Much of Naoroji's term was shadowed by the cloud of the Irish Home Rule Bill. The preoccupation with Irish Home Rule in the House paved the way for Irish parliamentarians to footnote and rake up matters of imperial misrule in the Indian administration. Frank Hugh O'Donnell, an Irish Member of Parliament, fed the intelligence offered by the Indian Parliamentary Committee to his propaganda for an independent Ireland, in the process filibustering and frustrating the House and the India Office. Naoroji himself ran an inquiry campaign on the high frequency of suicides among indentured Indian labourers in the Caribbean islands.

The expansion of the railways in India, that both Naoroji and Dutt strongly criticised, had been shaping a new national and geographical imagination, which marked the origins of a nationalist self-consciousness in India. Naoroji's electoral campaigns did much to transplant that consciousness into London. Six years after the end of his term, his imposing thesis, *Poverty and Un-British Rule in India*, was published in London, in 1902. His political career did not quite end with that, while that of Indians in Britain had only just begun. As Naoroji made his way out of the House, another Indian, Sir Mancherjee Merwanjee Bhownaggree, walked in as a Conservative Member of Parliament from Bethnal Green Northeast. Throughout his career, he would maintain cordial relations with Naoroji. However, when the Liberal Party organised a banquet to celebrate Naoroji's victory, in 1892, Bhownaggree launched a campaign to challenge the Liberal monopoly over Indians. He offered himself stridently as a candidate for the Conservative Party for 'declaring the opinions of conservative India,'[36] and to create a lasting dent in what he believed to be the great radical conspiracy of poaching Indians. He was a robust defender of the British Empire, which explained his unpopularity in India. He was also an advocate of global capitalism, being one of the strong voices in Parliament to promote the rights of Indian enterprises in Transvaal, even while Britain was reinforcing its military operations during the Second Boer War to control its imperial influence in South Africa. Bhownaggree believed that Turkey, China and Egypt were living testimonies of the failure of anti-European states. He could be no less concerned about balancing his political beliefs with 'mob moods'.[37] Against the mounting rhetoric of Irish and Indian Home Rule in late-Victorian London, Bhownaggree was decorated as a 'conservative voice of India,'[38] both by the British press as well as the India Office.

Bhownaggree was a latecomer to London's political scene. He was educated in Bombay and was called to the Bar at Lincoln's Inn, in 1885 when he was thirty-four. That year, he was also awarded a silver medal by the Royal Society of Arts for his research on women's education. He was appointed as a Judicial Counsellor by the Maharajah of Bhavnagar in Gujarat. Subsequently, he was made Companion of the Order of the Indian Empire. The following year, he returned to London as an executive commissioner for the Colonial and Indian Exhibition, where he was accompanied by his beloved sister, Ave. Her premature death in 1888 left him shattered. Her memory inspired many charitable and benevolent Anglo–Parsi institutions of women's education and empowerment, both in Bombay and London. In 1893, the Imperial Institute (later the Commonwealth Institute) at Kensington inaugurated the Bhownaggree Corridor on the fifth death anniversary of Ave, with support from the Prince of Wales and Queen Victoria herself. After the 1895 elections, combined with unflinching Tory support and his own wit and wealth, Bhownaggree sat in the House for eleven years. Two years into his term, he was knighted. In a controversial move, the India Office deputed him to draft a pamphlet meant to 'project the Indian confidence in British rule,' in 1916.[39] It was commissioned by the War Publications Department and was aimed to be a response to the German War propaganda against British violations of human rights in the Indian subcontinent. Bhownaggree's fifty-one-page response reaffirmed the indispensability of the British Empire to the cultural and economic aspirations of Indians, solidifying the defence of the 'ancient glory of their motherland.'[40] The India Office was so impressed by the brochure that it planned to translate it into Urdu and Gurumukhi, largely to motivate Punjabi soldiers fighting in the First World War.

Along with Naoroji, Bhownaggree also spearheaded the progress of the British Zoroastrian community. It has been speculated that he played a key role behind the acquittal of George Edalji, who was sentenced to be imprisoned for seven years in 1903, after being accused of mutilating animals in Great Wyrley. Edalji was an English solicitor, and the son of Reverend Shapurji Edalji (a Parsi from Bombay who converted to Christianity) and Charlotte Stoneham, the daughter of a vicar from Shropshire. The vicarage of Great Wyrley was a wedding present to the Reverend. In 1888, the Edalji family began receiving a series of poison-pen letters which threatened them with damage to their home, property and lives. That was followed by a slur campaign against the Edaljis and their neighbours, where it was also alleged that Shapurji was a sodomite and an occultist. In 1903, in the infamous case of the Great Wyrley Outrages, where horses and other livestock were found maimed or mutilated, George Edalji was falsely charged and convicted based on poison-pen letters and other circumstantial evidence. When Bhownaggree heard of the case, he immediately moved the Home Office and members of the judiciary. After three years of re-investigations, George Edalji was released, although kept under surveillance. Alongside Bhownaggree's crusade, a privately led investigation by a sleuth, no less than Sir Arthur Conan Doyle, led to the official pardon of George Edalji by the Home Office enquiry committee.

Bhownaggree also served as chairman or distinguished member in various organisations, one of them being the Northbrook Society, through which he came to lobby with Indian students in England as a Conservative influencer. In 1927, he was elected as chairman of the Parsi Association of Europe (earlier the Zoroastrian Association and later the Zoroastrian Trust Funds of Europe). It was originally founded by Muncherji Hormusji Cama and Dadabhai Naoroji, in 1861, at Kensington and was the first Asian religious association in Britain. Naoroji was its first chairman. The early flow of Parsis to the city would make London the 'home to the oldest Zoroastrian community in the Western world.'[41] Along with Muncherji Cama and Dadabhai's cousin Kharshedji Rustomji Cama, Naoroji started the first fully-Indian firm in Britain, with offices in London and Liverpool. Both Dadabhai and Kharshedji later resigned due to their misgivings over the business of alcohol and opium, but the former had already made large profits to fund his political career in London. After the unseating of Bhownaggree, Naoroji returned to recontest in the elections of 1906 from Lambeth North. He was accompanied by another Indian barrister from the Middle Temple, Manmath Mallik, who stood as a Liberal candidate from St George's at Hanover Square. Both lost on this occasion. This was Naoroji's final stab at electoral politics. Mallik, who stood again from Uxbridge, in 1910, was yet again unsuccessful. His political ambition came full circle when his grandson, Lord Pratap Chidamber Chitnis, became a political organiser for the Liberal Party in 1966.

Scene IV

A House of Uncommons

From the apogees of their political careers, both Naoroji and Bhownaggree had backed the formation of India House at Highgate. They were both unaware of the incendiary designs of its residents. The founder of India House, Shyamaji Krishnavarma, came to England in 1879 as an assistant to a Sanskrit professor in Oxford. He returned to India in 1884, only to come back to London thirteen years later and settling at Highgate. The next year, he was joined by his future political disciple, Sardarsinhji Raoji Rana. After becoming a barrister in 1899, Rana travelled with Krishnavarma to Paris. When Bengal's partition was announced, a spate of subversive events broke out in the province, the rest of India, and even Paris and London. The Anushilan Samiti, a recently founded revolutionary organisation in Bengal, had started radicalising Indian youths through an ideology born curiously and effortlessly from the teachings of Swami Vivekananda and the history of the Carbonari revolutionary societies in 19th-century Italy. In London, Naoroji, Rana and Krishnavarma established the Indian Home Rule Society. Only Indians were to be allowed to be its members, as it openly challenged what it saw as the pseudo-imperial obsequiousness of the Indian National Congress.

In its early months, India House was widely considered to be a thrifty residential home and Hindustani restaurant catering to Indian students in the city. Secretly, however, it operated as a hub of Indian revolutionaries, and often as a stopover for rebel recruits from India for their journeys to or from Paris or America. The House published an anti-colonial magazine under the deceptively scholastic title, *The Indian Sociologist*. Its agenda was to subtly broadcast to English readers that they could 'never succeed in being a nation of freemen and lovers of freedom so long as they continue to send members of the dominant classes to exercise despotism in Britain's name upon the conquered races.'[1] Even after the Government of India proscribed the import of *The Indian Sociologist* in 1907, copies of the magazine continued to be smuggled in. Bhikaji Rustomji Cama—better known as Madam Cama—who lived as an Indian expatriate in Paris, was also closely associated with the House and its magazine. She first came to London to convalesce from the bubonic plague that hit the Bombay Presidency in 1897, that she too had contracted while nursing for plague relief. Hearing Krishnavarma's speech at the Speaker's Corner in Hyde Park, she found herself in the grip of a new fever that they called *swaraj*. In 1905, she established the Paris Indian Society along with Sardarsinhji Rana and Munchershah Burjorji Godrej. Earlier that year, she had been warned by officials in the British Government to refrain from political activism, or else she would not be permitted to return to India. Far from being stubbed, she went on to be a leading face of the Hindu-German conspiracy of the following decade, which threatened Britain's power in India through a series of minor mutinies and political uprisings.

Cama kept the émigré Indian revolution in Paris up to speed with news from its headquarters in London. By 1906, India House had about fifty residents, including Vinayak Damodar Savarkar, V.V.S. Ayer, Barendranath Chattopadhyaya, Madanlal Dhingra, M.P.T. Acharya, Lala Hardayal, H.H. Koregaonkar, Govind Amin and G.M. Bapat. Many of them were in London on fellowships of ₹5,000 or ₹10,000 organised by Krishnavarma and *The Indian Sociologist*. Unknown to the other inmates, Savarkar had forged links with revolutionary organisations in India and the United States, such as Mitra Mela and Abhinav Bharat. His idols were Mazzini, Chhatrapati Shivaji and the Indian kings, queens and warriors who were either killed or exiled during the Great Indian Rebellion of 1857. Along with Krishnavarma, he was at the forefront of mobilising students from Oxford, Cambridge and Edinburgh to join the activities of the House, especially during the commemoration ceremony of the fifty-first anniversary of the Great Rebellion. It was here that Savarkar's book, *The War of Independence, 1857*, became the first public expression of the 'Sepoy Mutiny' as an Indian war. On Guru Gobind Singh's birthday that year, a pamphlet titled *Bande Mataram Khalsa* was circulated to an audience largely comprising Sikhs. It served to provoke them against the British government, the strength of whose armies, in India, Afghanistan, Europe and Africa, lay on the shoulders of its Sikh battalions.

Behind the scene, Russian bomb manuals and a stock of Parisian pistols made their way into India House, as the young renegades turned to a rifle range in Tottenham Court for shooting lessons. Vinayak Savarkar's brother, Ganesh Savarkar, helped in smuggling seditious material from India to Europe and back. He and a few of his associates were arrested on conspiracy charges in India, following the assassination of the district magistrate of Nasik, Arthur Mason Jackson. By 1909, the Scotland Yard, Lord Minto's secret agents, and King Edward VII himself, were closely watching movements in and around India House. Savarkar's dream of becoming a barrister was quashed when the Scotland Yard relayed its suspicions to members of the Bar—a grievance that he was to nurse for the rest of his life.

India House was not the only grain of sand in Lord Minto's eye. There was also the Hind Nationalist Agency, founded by Bipin Chandra Pal, G.S. Khaparde and Barendranath Chattopadhyaya. The organisation published a journal called *Swaraj* which, despite its brief career, acted as an important source of covering fire for the propaganda of *The Indian Sociologist*. In 1908, Krishnavarma went into exile in Paris, which indirectly handed over the reins of the House to Savarkar. Events at the India reached their culmination in July 1909, when Dhingra, an engineering student, killed Sir William Curzon Wyllie. Wyllie was a political *aide-de-camp* to Lord George Hamilton, the Secretary of State for India, and had been a decorated veteran who served in the Second Anglo-Afghan War. Kharshedji Lalcaca, a Parsi doctor from Shanghai, who tried to save Wyllie, was also killed. The assassination occurred at the Imperial Institute in South Kensington, where Wyllie and his wife Amelia, were at an event of the National Indian Association.

In October 1907, *The Indian Sociologist* had framed Wyllie as one of the 'old unrepentant foes of India who have fattened on the misery of the Indian peasant every day since they began their career.'[2] Under orders by Minto, Wyllie and his men had been tailing students and associates of India House for a few years, and reporting back to the India Office that students in the city were 'neither afraid nor ashamed to openly manifest their disloyalty.'[3] It was also known that Wyllie had been deputed to Paris to gather actionable intelligence on Savarkar and the others. Apparently, Dhingra's family in India was vexed by his continuing association with the India House rebels. They had even written to Wyllie, urging him to oil Dhingra off the treasonable syndicate. After the assassination, Gandhi had quietly inferred that Dhingra 'was egged on to do this act by ill-digested readings of worthless writings,' and that those guilty of inciting the crime should be the first to be punished.[4] Once, during a Dussehra dinner at India House, Gandhi was mocked by Savarkar over his vegetarianism, in the middle of an argument about Ram Rajya. With almost no love lost between the two, there was little doubt as to who the instigator of the assassination was in Gandhi's insinuation.

The Indian Sociologist, on the other hand, applauded Dhingra's courage. 'Political assassination was not murder,' it declared.[5] Others, like H.M. Hyndman, the editor of the magazine *Justice*, saw Dhingra as the unfortunate outcome of Britain's sustained strategy of 'an unceasing and ever-increasing bleeding' of India.[6]

Surendranath Banerjea, who was in England at the time, distanced himself from all possible association with India House. Malik Umar Hyat Khan, once an associate of Savarkar at India House, went so far as to call the conspirators 'low-caste men'. Bipin Chandra Pal and the Hind Nationalist Agency, that had by now visibly reduced its anti-imperial literature, condemned the killing. So did Aga Khan, Bhownaggree and Ameer Ali, who dubbed it a 'national disaster'.[7] And the British Parliament geared up to use Dhingra's transgression as the red herring to forestall Indian reforms.

Scotland Yard shared Gandhi's theory. It believed that Dhingra had been hoodwinked intellectually. The trail of the crime dotted back to Krishnavarma and Savarkar, who had personal reasons for plotting the murder. Dhingra had learned to rifle at a hideout in Tottenham Court Road, but besides that, there was precariously little evidence to link him with the revolutionary brainwaves of India House. A raid at his lodgings could merely elicit two postcards, one illustrating a scene of mutineers blown from the mouth of a cannon, and another featuring Lord Curzon with the moniker 'heathen dog' pencilled on it.[8] Dhingra's family denied any history of his seditious views; nor was Scotland Yard able to trace any of his political ties in London. Although the government believed he was merely an instrument in the hands of others, the trial had to take his word that none but his 'conscience' had spurred him to act. It was his chosen way of discharging retribution for the murder of his countrymen, and the loot of £100 million that the British annually extracted from India. 'In case,' Dhingra argued, 'this country is occupied by the Germans, and an Englishman not bearing to see the Germans walking with the insolence of conquerors in the streets of London, goes and kills one or two of Germans, then that Englishman is to be upheld as a patriot of the people of his country.' He added, 'then certainly I am a patriot too.'[9]

On August 17, 1909, Dhingra was hanged at the Pentonville Prison in Highbury and Islington. Krishnavarma sold India House and recommended the publication of *The Indian Sociologist* from Paris. The following March, Savarkar was arrested at the

Victoria Station while returning from Paris. Savarkar was in a police van headed to the Bow Street Magistrate Court when an attempted rescue operation was foiled. The plan had been directed by Barendranath Chattopadhyaya, Madhav Rao, David Garnett and Maud Gonne. The last of the conspirators, besides being an Irish revolutionary, actress and female suffragist, was also the renowned muse to the poetry of W.B. Yeats. She had refused Yeats' proposal for marriage on at least four occasions, leaving him with the consolation, 'you make beautiful poetry out of what you call your unhappiness and are happy in that. Poets should never marry. The world should thank me for not marrying you.'[10]

Savarkar, however, had no time to thank Maud Gonne. Extradited by a London court to India, he was immediately sent for his homeland, where he would be sentenced, in all likelihood, for at least one life. In July 1910, he attempted another escape, this time from a lavatory of the ship where he was a captive. In that he was successful, but only to be rearrested by the French Police and returned to the British. In Paris, Cama used her links to have the struggles of Savarkar and the other India House residents covered in leading Socialist journals like *L'Humanité* and *Action*. Even as Savarkar's book on the Indian War of Independence was banned by the British government, his case reached the corridors of The Hague Tribunal. In India, he was tried on charges of sedition and plotting the murders of Jackson and Wyllie. In December, he was sentenced to two life terms, and deported to the Cellular Jail in Andaman, where he was united with his brother, Ganesh. After a slew of mercy petitions to the British government, he was released from prison, fourteen years later, although his future movements were confined by severe restrictions that barred him from any form of political association. For over a decade, Savarkar was kept under police watch at Ratnagiri, being granted no other form of employment besides an annual stipend of ₹720.

In 1937, India attained provincial autonomy and the Indian Muslim League began coining its first slogans for Pakistan. That year, Savarkar, the man who was among the first to see the

Rebellion of 1857—jointly fought by the two major religious communities of India against the British—as the dawn of an independent nation, was elected as president of the Hindu Mahasabha.

Wyllie's assassination and the flare-up at India House had ruffled the feathers of Whitehall. Lord Minto and company now unleashed an awkward but systematic crackdown on Indian students. The Simla Department of Criminal Intelligence deputed John Wallinger to London to form a secret branch at the India Office. This later became the Indian Political Intelligence department. Under Philip Vickery, who headed a division of undercover agents salaried by Indian taxpayers, the department filed surveillance reports on Indian students and visitors. Its documents remained classified until fifty years into the Indian independence.

The Secretary of State, John Morley, had set up the Lee-Warner Committee in 1907, to report on a course of action on the question of youth campaigns, proposed to be led by the administration. Following its recommendations, three public offices were established. First was a Youth Advisory Committee, comprising local Indians and British advisors. This was followed by a Bureau of Information headed by the office of the Education Advisor to tender information on courses, boarding houses, sources of funding and recommendations for students in London. The committee further recommended bolstering ties between the National Indian Association, the East India Association and the Northbrook Society.

Rather than visibly and violently suppress the resistance that was emanating from the ranks of Indian students, the British administration hoped to gradually beguile them into the fold of the Empire. In 1910, the proposed Bureau was inaugurated, along with boarding facilities for Indian students, at Cromwell Road. Ten years later, the Young Men's Christian Association Hostel came up in Keppel Street. In 1923 it moved to Gower Street. The man behind the conception of a new lodgement to imperialise

young Indian minds was K.T. Paul, the general secretary of the
National Council of the Association in India. The president of the
Association, Sir Arthur Yapp, tried shortening old sherry in a new
bottle with a campaign that advertised the hostel as 'little bit of
India, not a little bit of England, with Indians as hosts,'[11] although
a lot of Britain had already turned notoriously Indian over a
century ago. Morley, and later administrations, were successful in
quelling extremist elements in the process of exploiting the hostel
as 'the sounding board of public opinion of Indian affairs.'[12] For
seventeen years, the Gower Street building continued to house
Indian students and noted diplomats, writers and nationalists
until the Blitz ravaged its thunder.

Scene V

A Theatre of Theatres

Late Victorian London was an unsung stage for training the *dramatis personae* to the theatres of nationalism in India, and latter-day Pakistan and Bangladesh. Since the 1880s, the city grew into a historic confluence for Indian dramatic performances. Britain's fixation with the Orient, even until much after the War of Independence, could be regularly seen in Victorian drama or fiction titles such as *The Nautch Girl or The Rajah of Chutneypore, The Prince of India, The Great Mogul, The Nabob's Fortune, The Saucy Nabob, Carylon Sahib* or *Carnac Sahib*. Most of these plays were written and staged between the time of the Colonial and Indian Exhibition, in 1886, and the outbreak of the Boer War, in 1899. By then, London's audiences had grown accustomed to—and even somewhat weary of—white actors playing Indian roles.

In 1885, the Parsee Victoria Dramatic Company was invited from Bombay to stage an adaptation from *Abhijnan Shakuntalam*. The audience responded derisively to Indian actors—otherwise trained to perform in Hindi—acting to an English screenplay. The performance was a disaster. Undaunted by the edgy precedent, William Poel, the founder of the Elizabethan Stage Society, directed another production of *Shakuntala*. It was performed at the Royal Botanical Gardens in 1899. For this, the cast was constituted entirely of Indian players based in London, including the veteran economist and dissenter, Romesh Chunder Dutt. Over the following decade, Poel was actively engaging the Indian student population on the London stage, while organising talks by South Asian playwrights and drama critics like Thyagaraja Paramasiva Kailasam and Ananda K. Coomaraswamy. He also staged adaptations of Indian and Middle Eastern classics for raising funds for the Indian Women's Education Association based in London. On one of his productions, adapted from Kalidasa's *Kumarasambhava* (circa 500 AD) and Omar Khayyam's *Rubaiyat* (circa 1100 AD), *The Indian Magazine and Review* remarked: 'The London public had a rare opportunity of seeing a true representation of the East, not a substitute provided by people dressing up and pretending to be somebody else.'[1]

In 1912, Poel's production of *Buddha* was staged at the Royal Court. It was adapted from Edwin Arnold's poem *The Light of Asia*, by Sarat Chandra Bose, a young barrister who later joined the Indian freedom struggle. He was also the elder brother of Netaji Subhas Chandra Bose. Not surprisingly, nearly all the flammable spirits of India House had either evanesced from London or transmigrated into an Indian theatrical movement. For some months after Savarkar's deportation, Bipin Chandra Pal continued to frustrate the government, although his methodology was now much more moderate than before. In November 1909, along with his son Niranjan Pal and some other Indians including Kedarnath Das Gupta, J.M. Parikh, Asaf Ali and D.P. Mukherjee, Bipin Chandra Pal founded a new organisation called the Hind Biradree. It was later renamed as the Hindustan Society. That too had its own journal, *The Indian Student*, which was started with financial assistance from the Gaekwad of Baroda. The society and its journal led ephemeral lives. By the summer of 1911, both were disbanded. In September, the retiring shadow of Bipin Chandra Pal quietly made its exit from London. Reports of the Indian unrest in the city were now submerged by telegraphic interceptions foreboding war.

Kedarnath Das Gupta took on himself to amend the reputation of Indian students in the city. After a sketchy career in publishing and political campaigning in Bengal, Das Gupta was sent to London, in

1907. Contrary to his family's wishes of seeing him as a barrister, Das Gupta did not proceed beyond graduating in the arts. With continued involvement in stage activity, he became a business manager in Poel's theatre group. He was also very likely the unacknowledged co-director of the 1912 production of *Buddha*. In his stage career, Das Gupta inspired the confidence of noted scientists, politicians, suffragettes, authors, art critics and politicians like Sir Oliver Joseph Lodge, James Bryce, Sir Francis Younghusband, Keir Hardie, Charlotte Despard, H.G. Wells and Surendranath Banerjea.

Das Gupta organised several prized events on Indian art, literature and the political and cultural links between Britain and India. His motto was, 'a nation is known by its stage.'[2] Before the war, he founded the Indian Art and Dramatic Society to bring before Western audiences the dramatic arts of India and foster stronger cultural ties between Britain and its colony. Many prestigious names from the British stage, such as Henry Ainley, H.K. Ayliff, Arthur Bourchier, Ben Greet, John Martin Harvey, Miles Malleson, Herbert Beerbohm Tree, Sybil Thorndike and William Poel himself, were part of this society. Situated in Cromwell Road, it also housed the head office of the National Indian Association and the Bureau of Information. During Tagore's visit to London in 1912, Das Gupta organised a seminar on his writings at the Royal Albert Hall. It featured readings from Tagore's poems, performances from his dramas and a keynote by William Rothenstein. The musical score for the evening was composed by Inayat Ali Khan, an acclaimed Hindustani classical musician in the city. By leaps and bounds, Das Gupta had quarantined himself and much of India from extremist politics. He now simply adhered to pacifist—at times even obscure—principles of art. 'My society,' as he would later write during his retirement in America, 'was like a green bamboo. It could be made into a flute of praise, but not a stick of censure.'[3]

In London, Das Gupta's repertory worked tirelessly to organise plays for raising funds for wounded Indian soldiers, a million and half of whom were fighting Britain's 'war to end all wars.' He joined Gandhi and Gokhale as a volunteer to the Indian Field Ambulance Corps for the war effort. Das Gupta's plays offered free admission to soldiers convalescing in British hospitals. The performances were usually adaptations of *The Mahabharat* (800 to 900 BCE), *The Arabian Nights* (Middle Ages), extracts from the plays of Kalidasa and, indeed, Tagore, who was by now 'a figure of ever-growing international significance.'[4] In 1920, Das Gupta would accompany him to the United States, where the writings and ideas of the Nobel Laureate were turned into a vehicle of international peace and humanism. In New York, Das Gupta established the American wing of the Union of the East and West, a repertory he had founded in pre-war London. Throughout the pessimistic years of the war, from The Hill to the Prince of Wales's Theatre to Drury Lane, Das Gupta and his players entertained London with one Indian masterpiece after another. His plays were the garden-fresh silos of cultural fodder not only for theatre lovers of the West End but also British aristocrats and political men, besides eyeing the approval of esteemed Indians like Aga Khan and the Maharajah of Baroda.

The aftermath of the war saw the emergence of a new theatre group called the Indian Players. In 1922, with Niranjan Pal at its forefront, the Players began the marathon run of its new production, *The Goddess*. It was adapted by Pal from Tagore's drama, *Bisarjan* (*Immersion*). Beginning with the Duke of York's Theatre, the Ambassadors Theatre and the Aldwych Theatre, the play ran for sixty-six performances at a stretch, across playhouses in Britain. Due to the play's incredible success, plans of establishing an Indian Repertory Theatre were announced during its fiftieth performance. Pal had been involved with London's theatres since 1912, with Poel's production of *Buddha*, where he had assisted Bose and Das Gupta. He would visit Poel's house daily to school himself in the company of the celebrity stage artists who frequently gathered there. From his lodgings, he 'walked the whole six miles from Russell Square to Putney every evening and back and would sit enraptured listening to Poel till past midnight.'[5] For Pal, the London stage was also an education in cinema. In the 1920s, he authored several Indian-themed plays, including *The Magic Crystal, Singh Sahib* and *Shiraz,* in collaboration with Himansu Nath Rai, who too had come to London to study law. Rai was Tagore's student at Santiniketan and was introduced to the stage at the age of eleven. London came to know him better with his role as the lead protagonist in *The*

Goddess. Later on, Pal and Rai worked together on cinematic productions, their first venture being *The Light of Asia*, which released in Britain in 1925. The film was co-directed by Franz Osten, a German filmmaker, who also collaborated with Pal and Rai in the making of the silent films *Shiraz* (1928), *A Throw of Dice* (1929) and *Untouchable Girl* (1936). Each of these became a masterpiece of its time. When *A Throw of Dice* was restored and rereleased in 2007, it was described as 'a surge of visual pleasure,'[6] and 'a rare and fascinating gem.'[7] That was nearly eight decades after Pal and Rai returned home to enjoy a glorious run in the Indian film industry as screenwriters, directors and founding members of Bombay Talkies, the Mecca of early Indian cinema.

Syed Ameer Ali could have gone down as another charismatic actor from that legacy; that is to say, if his theatre had not dramatically digressed from the stage of Indian nationalism and the stage of Indian arts. Since the 1870s, he had quietly counted the tolling of years on a flagging rosary. As the first Indian to sit on the Judicial Committee of the Privy Council in 1909, Ameer Ali was the first Asian to be addressed as 'The Right Honourable…' More legendarily, a year ago, he had laid the foundation of the London Muslim League in collaboration with S.H. Bilgrami. Mohammad Iqbal, still a young barrister and not yet the hardline exponent of Pakistan that he would become, was also a member of that League. It was instituted as a political body for voicing the rights of Muslims in England and elsewhere, independent of its recently founded parent organisation, the All India Muslim League. By the time of the war, sensing that the London Muslim League's ideology had turned too shrill for his ageing lungs, the Right Honourable Indian gentleman resigned from it.

Ameer Ali's twilight in London coincided with the university years of Sir Malik Firoz Khan Noon, who would later become the seventh prime minister of what was still to be Pakistan. A few years before that eventuality, Noon sent a letter to Jinnah to urge him to establish a Muslim press in London.

India Office
Whitehall
12 July 1944

My dear Jinnah,

Please find enclosed a letter from Ikbal Ali Shah—he has written it at my request. I am sending it to you for your information. I shall personally discuss the matter with you when I am in India. I hope to be there early in August ...

Yours Sincerely,
Firoz

[PS.] Some people are about to start a Muslim paper here now. I am in touch with them and shall help them too.

Enclosure

Ikbal Ali Shah to Firoz Khan Noon

4 Turl Street,
Oxford
7 July 1944

Dear Sir Firoz,

The background of the necessity, the great necessity of Muslim representation in London, is well-known to you; and in this connection, I wish to make the following suggestions so that, if possible, the whole thing could be got going before you actually leave these shores for India.

If there might be difficulty, or delay in having an Indian Muslim League office here, let us start a Muslim News Agency with which we could couple a Muslim Information Centre, the object of such an agency being to send all kind of Muslim news and reactions from London to Muslim India; and notably to the Muslim papers in India; and the Information Section of it to give news and interpretation of the kind that Muslim League wants to the British press and institutions in this country.

Naturally, a Muslim League office is desirable, but I am suggesting the News Agency and the Information Section, in case Mr Jinnah may not feel disposed to give full authority to anyone in London. If that be the case then the News Agency and the Information Centre will do all, or nearly all, that work which the League may wish to be done in London.

This organisation (Muslim News and Information Centre) in London should be housed in an office of at least two room in some central part of London, maybe in Fleet Street or the Strand.

The work of this London organisation should be to receive and give Muslim India news to the British and American press in London and to other offices, to publish small pamphlets on Indian Muslim point of views, to meet Members of Parliament in order to give them facts about the Muslims of India.

In policy, it may not necessarily 'go for the Congress,' but only give its version of the Indian political situation to the British people. But if the Congress confuses the issues, and deliberately gives the wrong impression to the British men and women, then most certainly challenge the Congress views and facts, and correct the impressions …

If the Muslim League cannot set down its seal upon an organisation under its own name, then, one can start or rather re-start the old movements entitled the London Muslim League, with which I was intimately connected in London during the lifetime of the late Syed Ameer Ali. At that time, of course, we had a weekly English journal, too, called the *Muslim Standard*. If the Muslim League cannot muster £1500 a year at the moment, then let us have half of this sum, or one thousand from other Muslim sources, or other sources in Britain, so that we could start the work at once ...

I am willing to take on its Directorship, and represent the best interests of the Muslim League ...

I am waiting to release the enclosed booklet, but you see that I have not yet given my name to it, because I have nothing permanent going here, and unless I know that I can keep this sort of publications going, I will not feel that I should be doing real good to the Muslim cause in India: for what after all is one pamphlet in the face of a hundred already published by the Congress workers in London? Also, its publication will cost me fifty pounds; how can I afford to spend this fifty pounds on a venture of my own: for I do not seek personal publicity through this kind of thing; my forty-eight books are big enough publicity for me ...

... May I have your early reply, which I shall treat confidentially.

Yours Sincerely,
Ikbal Ali Shah[8]

Jinnah would come to be revered as Quaid-e-Azam for almost as long as Hitler was hailed as Führer. After 1940, the Muslim League announced Jinnah as its rival contender to Bapu for the sobriquet of 'Father of the Nation.' Noon was not ignorant of the possibility that Jinnah would be 'Pakistan's King Emperor, Archbishop of Canterbury, Speaker and Prime Minister,' test-tubed and precipitated as one mythical identity.[9] Jinnah, meanwhile, knew that the British would have never objected to the Partition. They did not in Ireland; nor would they in Palestine. An Empire impoverished by the war, he reckoned, would have gladly taken back to London the map of not one but two nations, with the egregious prospect of a third.

Noon's appeal from London had not yet arrived in India when Jinnah's associate, Begum Firdaus Rizvi, wrote a terse letter to C. Rajagopalachari, the man who would become the last Governor General of India. 'You know it fully well,' she told a placid Rajaji, 'that he is leader of a nation which has democracy in its blood.'[10] Jinnah was to take the Muslim fear of Hindus and turn it into a virtuous bloodletting. Once a figure of speech for the Muslim League, 'Partition' would now be groomed as his birthright. On August 16, 1946, the eighteenth day of Ramzan, Jinnah and the League declared Direct Action Day in Calcutta. They took Whitehall into confidence about the inalienable rights of Muslim India. The dreadful silence back at the India Office, and the failure of British law and order in India, was a vindication of the Great Calcutta Killings of that year. 'Today Muslims of India,' roared Quaid-e-Azam, 'dedicate their lives and all they possess to the cause of freedom.'[11] On that road to freedom were soon littered the entrails of 4,000 corpses and the debris of 10,000 broken homes. For the next ten days, anybody in Calcutta could have slaughtered anyone with anything—almost nothing capable of battering a human skull was left unused that month.

> Like water-soaked logs, scores of bloated cadavers bobbed down the Hooghly river toward the sea. Other corpses, savagely mutilated, littered the city's streets. Everywhere, the weak and helpless suffered most. By the time the slaughter was over, Calcutta belonged to the vultures. In filthy gray packs they scudded across the sky, tumbling down to gorge themselves on the bodies of the city's six thousand dead.[12]

The Black Hole of Calcutta finally found something of an equal to go down with it in history. Any vestigial dream of an undivided India had vaporised by now. British eyewitnesses, struggling to describe what had unfolded, thought it was 'a cross between the worst of London air raids and the Great Plague.'[13] With an inglorious retreat written on the wall, Whitehall was now loath to part with even a penny to be spent on saving the subcontinent.

Exactly two years before the Great Calcutta Killings, the London Library at Drury Lane was reeling from the destruction of 16,000 books and London from that of 6,000 lives at the hands of the Luftwaffe. Ikbal Ali Shah was convinced that Jinnah was eyeing a base for the Muslim League in the battered city. His letter to Firoz Noon betrayed his ambition. He would no longer hesitate to offer himself into a power vacuum that Muslim London was grappling with, after Ameer Ali. Three other things were also clear from Shah's letter. As the Second World War entered its climactic years, the idea of a Muslim India had been catapulted into reality. Pakistan was now a force, not just against a Hindu India, but over and above the Congress party itself—the erstwhile fortress of most leaders of the All India Muslim League. It was profoundly clear that any new Muslim stronghold in London would be used to detonate all possible channels of information and goodwill that the Congress had assembled in Britain.

Shah, who had fled to Oxford in the year of the London Blitz, was one of the most unlikely actors to throw his hat in the theatre of Muslim nationalism. Occasionally, he was known to work on Middle Eastern assignments of the British Foreign Office. He had worked with Ameer Ali during the Khilafat Movement, been a member of the Royal Geographical and the Royal Asiatic Societies, and had once enjoyed the company of Kemal Ataturk, Nadir Shah of Afghanistan and Aga Khan. He was now at the dusk of his life as he wrote to Noon. Shah had recently turned to compiling the biographies of some of his influential allies, besides the life of Prophet Mohammed, selections from *The Quran*, Sufi doctrines and tales from *The Arabian Nights*. With a short-lived fame that was now extinguishing, Shah hoped to spark his dying flame with a great controversy. His book, *Pakistan: A Plan for India* (1944), was purported to provoke Muslim India's discontents on English soil. But his success as an ideologue would be overshadowed by a middle-aged barrister and Cambridge scholar. Eleven years ago, Choudhry Rahmat Ali had stupefied India and Britain by inventing the name for a new Muslim nation. More famously known as the 'Pakistan Declaration,' his pamphlet 'Now or Never; Are We to Live or Perish Forever?', published from England, was the doctrinal gauntlet for Pakistan. Come fury of hell or high water, Rahmat Ali would not allow his Muslim brethren to be crucified on what he saw as the the gibbet of Hindu nationalism.

When he came to England as a student, Rahmat Ali was hosted by Sir Umar Hayat Khan Tiwana, a former Rajput soldier in the British army. Tiwana had served as aide-de-camp to George V, George VI and Edward VIII in between. During Rahmat Ali's stay in London, Tiwana was spending his retirement years as an elite member of the Carlton Club, an erstwhile haven of the Conservative Party, and the president of the Falconer's Club. Unlike his benefactor, Ali's career was modest. He began with a poor record in academics. As a barrister, he 'barely eked livelihood from his law practice.'[14] But like Tiwana, he was excellent at churning his acquaintances into his exploits. At the First Round Table Conference of 1930 in London, Rahmat Ali was introduced to Sir Muhammad Iqbal, who had also been a student in Cambridge and London before the Great War. Iqbal was the first to demand an independent province for Muslims within the larger dominion of India, in his presidential speech at the Muslim League session of 1930 in Allahabad. His two-nation theory was, quite simply, the proposed formation of a Muslim India within the territorial and constitutional boundaries of the future independent Hindustan. Earlier that year, he had inadvertently coxswained Rahmat Ali to coin the acronym for a new Muslim nation. 'I told him,' Iqbal would later recollect, 'that if you take the first word of each province in the northwest of India and the "tan" of Baluchistan, you get a meaningful and nice word, Pakistan. That will be the name of the government.'[15] A few months later, while travelling on a route 11 London bus, Rahmat Ali found the brainwave for christening his utopia.

'I am enclosing herewith an appeal on behalf of the thirty
million Muslims of PAKISTAN, who live in the five Northern
Units of India—Punjab, North-West Frontier (Afghan) Province,
Kashmir, Sind, and Baluchistan,' a forty-year-old Rahmat Ali
wrote from an unremembered cottage in Cambridge in the early
winter of 1933. 'It embodies their demand for the recognition
of their national status, as distinct from the other inhabitants of
India, by the grant to Pakistan of a separate Federal Constitution
on religious, social and historical grounds.'[16] Ali was aware of its
potential to be misunderstood and—more menacingly—to be
canonised. By the time of the Second Round Table Conference, he
had finished scripting his battle cry. Iqbal, who was in London for
the conference, remained his long-distance counsellor all along.
Ali was now campaigning in the city for young Muslim signatories
to his pamphlet. 'This proved to be a long and laborious search,'
he reflected, 'for so firm was the grip of "Indianism" on our young
intellectuals at English Universities that it took me more than a
month to find three young men in London, who, after reading
and discussing the Declaration, offered to support and sign it.'[17]
These were Mohammad Aslam Khan Khattak, Sheikh Mohammad
Sadiq and Inayat Ullah Khan. Khattak was the president of the
Pakistan National Movement based in London. The other two
were students of law and engineering when Rahmat Ali met them.

Jinnah and the Muslim League found the declaration too radical
at the time. A decade later, when Rahmat Ali was squarely excluded
from mainstream Muslim politics and left to wither in Cambridge,
Jinnah took to zealously fostering his brainchild. That did not settle
the matter of a Muslim leadership in London. Mohammad Abbas
Ali, who came in 1945 to study law, quickly assumed the leadership
of the Bengali Muslim community in the city. Backed by others
like Master Ayub Ali, Shah Abdul Majid Qureshi, Sheikh Abdul
Ghafur, Dewan Monfor Ali, Abdul Mannan Chhanu Mia and
Saidur Rehman, Abbas Ali vowed to revive Ameer Ali's legacy. His
residence at 33 Tavistock Square was turned into Pakistan House,
the headquarters of the All India Muslim League in London. He
considered no one but himself as the perfect man to head the new
London Muslim League.

I had the cooperation of my great friend Samjed Ali, who runs a restaurant at 36 Percy Street, London, W1. He enabled me to hold a meeting at his restaurant which remained closed for the day, incidentally at a heavy loss to the proprietor. At this meeting with the assistance of Mr Samjed Ali, I recruited a number of members for our movement. On 5 August 1945, we called a General Meeting for the purpose of electing the officers of the League. Frankly, I considered myself to be the most suitable choice as President. I was, therefore, not surprised when my name was proposed for this post, and I was elected without opposition. I proposed Mr Saidur Rahman as Secretary, and he too was elected.[18]

In March next year, the London League celebrated Pakistan Day, under the Nelson Column in Trafalgar Square. On March 24, the *Reuters* reported:

The green Muslim flag was flying, and a red banner on a white background proclaimed 'Pakistan or Muslim Revolt,' while 5,000 people gathered in the Square to hear the League leaders under the brilliant sun. This was one of the biggest demonstrations in London. The members of the All India Muslim League branch in London, headed by their President Mr Abbas, addressed the crowd on the aims of Pakistan. Muslim students, including girls in beautiful saris, clustered around the microphone, singing national songs by Iqbal.[19]

The idea that Ikbal Shah had proposed to Noon was now a reality, with Abbas Ali assuming the editorship of *Our Home* and *Voice of Pakistan*—two popular newspapers voicing Muslim opinions in London. December onwards, the All India Muslim League leaders, including Jinnah, began visiting the London branch. On December 14, Jinnah delivered a lecture at the Kingsway Hall in Holborn, with the melancholy thesis that nothing but the creation of Pakistan could save Muslims from being historically wronged in India. Later in the day, the leaders of the London League held a meeting with Jinnah at Mayfair's Dorchester Hotel.

Quaid-e-Azam assured his coterie that Pakistan was now merely a gunshot away.

Forty years ago, Jinnah had styled his monocle after the Liberal Member of Parliament, Joseph Chamberlain. His son, Neville Chamberlain, became the prime minister of Britain in Jinnah's time. In September 1938, as Hitler's whimsical meetings with European leaders were knocking up Britain, the second Chamberlain, after his return from Munich, was contented to declare 'peace for our time.' A year after the end of the world war that the prime minister could not withhold, Jinnah was fresh from his exploits of the Direct Action Day and in no mood to copy the Chamberlains a second time. He was more in tune now with the spirit of Chamberlain's successor—Winston Churchill—prepared to 'persevere in making war until the other side had had enough of it.'[20] When Jinnah's meeting began at Dorchester, less than four miles away at the East London Mosque, in Tower Hamlets, the evening's azan was just about to commence. He was embarrassingly untutored in Islamic prayer ritual, but his predecessor in the League, Sir Syed Ameer Ali, was not.

Ameer Ali had quietly settled into English life a year before the partition of Bengal. Soon after the assassination of Wyllie and the fall of India House, he was quick to remind the India Office about the urgency of enlisting Muslim loyalties in the face of mounting Hindu sedition against the Empire. He had been a part of the Muslim delegation that met Lord Morley in 1906, just before the formation of the All India Muslim League. Ali considered himself to be a 'bridge builder'[21] between the British and the Muslims on foreign shores. He recognised the importance of a mosque in London, and how that could act as a centre for cultural and political negotiations while eradicating Britain's misconceptions about Islam. Since the 1830s, northern towns like Manchester and Cardiff had seen temporary Muslim settlements of sailors from Morocco, Arabia, Somalia, India and elsewhere. They used their boarding houses as makeshift mosques. One of the first rudimentary mosques in Britain was set up by Abdullah Quilliam in Liverpool. In 1887, Quilliam turned his house on Mount Vernon Street into a mosque. After being expelled from there, he took the mosque to his new residence at West Derby Road two years later. That was also when Gottlieb Leitner established the Shah Jahan mosque in his private estate. Although Leitner was not ready to allow religious conversions inside his premises, he hoped to use the mosque as evidence of British toleration. When he died in 1899, he took the mosque into his grave. For thirteen years, private premises lodging Muslim tenants acted as provisional mosques for *ad hoc* religious gatherings, celebrations and festivals in London.

By 1910, Ameer Ali had galvanised a group of Muslims and Islamic enthusiasts from well-known walks of London's public life, some of them highly influential and affluent. It comprised Sir Hassan Suhrawardy, a surgeon in the British Indian Army (later the first Muslim Vice Chancellor of the University of Calcutta), Aga Khan III, Nathan Rothschild, Lord Lamington, T.W. Arnold, Sir John Woodhead and the Earl of Winterton. They met in November at the Ritz Hotel to discuss the formation of a London Mosque Fund and organise a plan for hiring temporary premises for Friday prayers for Muslims in London. In 1911, Ali also set up the Red Crescent Society for providing medical aid to Ottoman soldiers wounded in the Tripolitan and Balkan Wars. When Turkey entered the Great War on the German side, many British politicians, including Prime Minister Lloyd George, mouthed expletives against Turks that were coloured on racial lines. Ameer Ali argued 'that Islamic feeling towards England, especially among Indian Muslims, was changing for the worse, and that this would prove harmful to British interests.'[22] Later, when tens of thousands of Indian Muslim soldiers battled in the British ranks against Germany, British opinions did change.

The London Mosque Fund acquired rented housing, first at Russel Square and later at Notting Hill Gate, for Muslim congregations, prayers and meetings with the Imam of the Woking Mosque. In 1913, the Shah Jahan Mosque was revived under its new imam, Khwaja Kamaluddin. The imam had come to London only a year ago to pursue a court case for a client of his father, the respected Indian judge, Khwaja Abdur Rasheed. Kamaluddin rose to the scene from a public lecture at Speaker's Corner in Hyde Park. Backed by Ameer Ali and the London Mosque Fund, he founded the Woking Muslim Mission and Literary Trust and its journal— *The Islamic Review*—which continued publishing for the next fifty-three years. In November 1913, Rowland George Allanson-Winn, the Fifth Baron of Headley, outraged London by converting to Islam and becoming an ardent follower of Kamaluddin. Within a year, he engineered the British Muslim Society and authored his controversial treatise, *A Western Awakening to Islam* (1914). In their initial years, both ran successfully. However, after campaigning for over twelve years for donations from Muslim rulers and patrons around the world, the Fund appeared to have dried up. In 1926, Headley returned from India with a bounty of £60,000 from the Nizam of Hyderabad and, two years later, the Nizamiah Mosque Trust was established with premises procured in West Kensington for another new mosque.

Ameer Ali had only meant to empower Britain's Muslims— to raise the bars of their basic welfare, religious respectability and an environment free from racial abuse. For most of the Muslims living around Tower Hamlets, this was still a distant dream. However, in some cases, they asserted their presence quite disturbingly to the English. One such case occurred in the 1920s, when the Jamiat-ul-Muslimin, a local Muslim organisation, called for an apology from the author H.G. Wells, whose book *A Short History of the World* (1922) had allegedly insulted Prophet Mohammed. Members of the Jamiat led several East Enders to burn copies of Wells' book in protest. Having fought a war in Europe, Britain was fighting another on the streets and docklands of London, this time against African, Caribbean, Chinese and Indian immigrants. In May 1919, 'large crowds assembled outside the Strangers' Home for Asiatic Seamen in West India Dock Road and any coloured man who appeared was greeted with abuse and had to be escorted by the police.'[23] Little colonies of Punjabi Muslims had become a nuisance in London, besides in several cities of Scotland and Wales. Here, not only lascars, but also Indian workers in collieries, steelworks and iron factories and the manufacturing industry found themselves unemployed. They were marked as aliens to be dispensed with, now that the Allied resistance on the theatres of the Western Front was done and dusted with.

In 1921, the India Office was neck-deep in documents of repatriation or incarceration of idling Indians or deserters around Britain's docks. It was also the year when the travel diary of a little-known Indian woman was published. Titled *Zamana-e-Tahsil* (*A Time of Education*), it was written by Atiya Fyzee during her teacher's training course at Maria Grey College in the years immediately following the establishment of India House. Fyzee was born in Istanbul to an elite Bombay merchant family from the Tyabji clan, and was one of the first English-educated Muslim women from India. Being the princess of Jinjira (a minor suburb of Bombay), she was rather well off and at liberty to offend the sensibilities of her time with her literary contributions to leftist publications such as *Tahzib un-niswan* (*Women's Culture*) and *Khatun* (*Woman*), published from Lahore and Aligarh, respectively. What brought her greater infamy was her association with the public intellectuals—Maulana Shibli Nomani and Mohammad Iqbal among others—with whom her friendship was speculated to have gone beyond the frontiers of acceptable or discreet proximity. Her correspondences with them, published between 1930 and the Partition, further stoked the fires of scandal.

Fyzee took encouragement from her friend Cornelia Sorabji, first to apply for a scholarship to London and, later, to spread herself quite thin among the *nouveau riche* of London. The English journalist, Mary Billington, in her articles for the *Daily Graphic* and her late-19th-century book, *Women in India*, described Fyzee as an 'exotic creature'.[24] On finally arriving in London, Fyzee let herself be admired at the Henley Royal Regatta, the city's pre-eminent social season. *Lady's Pictorial*, a well-known women's magazine, approached her for a picture and an interview. Atiya's brother, cousin, cousin-in-law and nephew were in Britain around this time—the last of them being Camruddin Abdul Latif, a scholar of languages from Cambridge, and later a barrister, as well as a member of the London Mosque Fund. Atiya's brother, Ali Azhar Beg, had come to Britain to pursue a higher degree in medicine but took up tennis as a career, which lasted nearly thirty years and stellar performances in Wimbledon and Davis Cup. In her first few months in London, Atiya was absorbed into the fold of the National Indian Association. Among other Indian women there, she met Krishnabhabini Das and the Brahmo reformer and writer, K.G. Gupta, and was well-exposed to the ever-sprouting who-to-meet-and-greet societies of the metropolis. One of her bosom friends, Flora Sassoon, came from the wealthy Jewish family of merchants who once ran Bombay's David Sassoon & Sons. She would send her car for Atiya to be picked up from college and chauffeured over to her home in central London. Atiya was also spotted in the company of Ameer Ali and, even more startlingly, beside the Maharaja and Maharani of Baroda. She was as liberal at befriending Englishwomen (Catherine Firth, Malvina H. Green and M.H. Goldsmith) as she was perceived to be in her taste in men. And that most squarely distinguished her—besides her religion—from the other Indian women studying in London, or her own college, at the time.

Imaginably, both Edwardian and Muslim eyes had been measuring Atiya Fyzee's movements. By the time she got married in 1912, to Samuel Rahamin, her clammy reputation in the conservative circles in India was clutching on to a tenterhook. Such a scandal was the princess driven into that her literary genius was brushed under the carpet of her premarital indiscretions. Those, in the case of her contemporary Sarojini Naidu, may have simply been perceived as the passionate twittering of the 'Nightingale of India'. Fyzee rivalled her in being the 'Nightingale of Hind,' but the love she received from a future Pakistan was a dismal fraction of what Naidu was showered with in India. 'Nightingale' was the epithet that Iqbal had given Fyzee when he fell in love with her

in Europe. In Cambridge and London, the two had found each
other in arms, when Iqbal confessed to her: 'I am pragmatic and
utilitarian outside but a mystic inside.'[25] When Fyzee returned to
India, Iqbal wrote her a poem titled 'Union'.

Hark ye Nightingale!
    the flower I was restlessly in search of
    I fortunately got
When I heard your melody I invariably blushed.
Like mercury my heart was in constant flush.
Perhaps the sin of love made it so impatient[26]

Fyzee had waited for Iqbal to marry her, but fearing barriers
of class—Atiya was of a substantially higher social station—he
did not even propose. On the other hand, Samuel Rahamin, the
'Jew of Pune,' embraced Islam to marry her. Being a poet, painter
and playwright, he was far from being a disappointment to Atiya.
His paintings found a gallery in the British Empire Exhibition of
1924 at Wembley, as well as the Arthur Tooth & Sons Gallery,
in a sequence named 'Water-Colours, India, Vedic, Mythological
and Contemporary,' which inspired *The Burlington Magazine* to
review his work. Rahamin went on to be an art advisor under
the State of Baroda, and a painter of the imperial frescoes at the
Imperial Secretariat in New Delhi. He also devoted his energies
to reorganising the section of Asian paintings at the Victoria and
Albert Museum. When his plays, *Daughter of Hind* and *Invented
Gods,* were staged in London, in the 1930s, Atiya played the music
composer and choreographer for her husband. Her own book on
classical Indian music went into three titles, *Indian Music* (1914),
The Music of India (1925) and the *Sangt of India* (1942).

After the Partition, Atiya and Samuel relocated to Karachi at the
request of Jinnah, who had been a neighbour of Samuel at Malabar
Hills in Bombay. Quaid-e-Azam gifted the couple a section of
the city's Burnes Garden, where they rebuilt their Bombay home,
Aiwan-e-Riffat, that soon became a salon for artistes. However, after
1950, they were unceremoniously ousted from their residence by

the new administration. Having been forced to live in local hotels and makeshift lodges paid for by friends overseas, and conned into a protracted legal battle, when Atiya was finally given proprietary rights over Aiwan-e-Riffat, her husband had already passed away, and she had only a few years left in her.

Among the Indian women mentioned in the Princess of Jinjira's travel diary was another princess, who was born a year before Atiya herself, and who died in 1948, the year Fyzee and her husband moved to Karachi. Evidently, Atiya had lived a floral life, one that was ever so often peccable. What if she had been feistier—like this other princess whom she had met in London along with members of the National Indian Association? Perhaps she may have been remembered for a few more wrong reasons. But would that not be so much more apposite than Atiya being almost not remembered at all? Karachi, the very city that had once beckoned her with all the love of a benefactress, would disown her, in independent Pakistan, like some Havisham disowning her Estella.

ACT V

Defending the Island

Then shall our names,
Familiar in his mouth as household words ...
From this day to the ending of the world,
But we in it shall be remembered—
We few, we happy few, we band of brothers;
For he today that sheds his blood with me
Shall be my brother; be he ne'er so vile,
This day shall gentle his condition;
And gentlemen in England now abed
Shall think themselves accursed they were not here ...
(Henry V, Act IV, Scene III)

Scene I

Jewel in the Crown

Seven years after Gandhi's birth in Porbandar, Sophia Duleep Singh was born in Belgravia, not far from Buckingham Palace, the residence of her godmother and the recently crowned Empress of India—Queen Victoria. At the evensong of that moralist century, Sophia was one of the most dreaded women in Britain, guided by her dangerous pursuit of creating and courting strife on the streets of the imperial capital. That was how most Edwardians would have imagined the suffragette movement.

Princess Sophia was the daughter of the last Sikh Emperor of India, Maharajah Duleep Singh. Known as the Black Prince of Perthshire in his later life, he had ascended to the throne of Punjab at the age of five, and was one of the first to be conferred the Order of the Star of India. It was perhaps the richest order ever received by a subject, for it came in exchange of the most coveted diamond. The setting was the British conquest of Punjab in 1849. By the tenets of the Last Treaty of Lahore, Lord Dalhousie oversaw the surrender of the ancient Kohinoor to Sophia's godmother. As a suppliant was the eleven-year-old emperor. 'His Highness Duleep Singh shall receive from the Honourable East India Company,' the treaty went on, 'a pension of not less than four, and not exceeding five lakhs of Company's rupees per annum.'[1] Two years later, at the Great Exhibition in London, the diamond failed to dazzle European visitors. A crestfallen Prince Albert ordered Royal Coster Diamonds in Amsterdam, to recut the diamond. Back in London, suspicions regarding the arrival of the blood-stained diamond were running rife, 'with Prime Minister Peel dying on the very day it landed in England, in July 1850, and also with Queen Victoria getting injured the same day.'[2] British author Wilkie Collins cut a new literary edge to the diamond in his book *The Moonstone* (1868). The fictional gem found itself in the hands of Rachel Verinder and her opiated sleepwalking lover, Franklin Blake, after a series of transcontinental adventures. It had been once stolen by chieftains in Tipu Sultan's army, from a Hindu temple in Somnath. The destiny of the moonstone was to tail the manifest plight of the Kohinoor. Rumours about the fateful stone would keep resurfacing for the rest of the century.

———

In the autumn of 1895, Swami Vivekananda was returning to India from the United States after his oratorical feat in the World Parliament of Religions and a marathon of lectures on Vedanta, when he halted midway in London for three months. London's sympathies with India were on an upsurge, with Dadabhai Naoroji and Muncherji Bhownaggree in the thick of its political affairs. Although not lionised in quite the same capacity as Raja Rammohun Roy, Dwarkanath Tagore or Keshub Chunder Sen, Vivekananda was still a beneficiary of the ascending interests in Indian culture and aesthetics. In the reminiscences of a Londoner:

> Clubs, societies, drawing-rooms opened their doors to him. Sets of students grouped themselves together in this quarter and that, and heard him at appointed intervals. His hearers, hearing him, longed to hear further. The Indian students resident in London naturally looked to him for guidance. The Swami endeared himself to them all by making them feel quite at home with him and helping them in various ways. And so when on July 18, a social conference of Indian residents in Great Britain and Ireland was held under the auspices of the London Hindu Association, it was he who was asked to preside.[3]

Vivekananda lived with one of his old friends, E.T. Sturdy, at 63 St George's Road. By and by, his plans of hibernation melted away with the snows. By summer next year, he had taken considerable stock of the glitterati in the city. In May, he wrote to an associate that the 'City of London is a sea of human heads—ten or fifteen Calcuttas put together. One is apt to be lost in the mazes unless he arranges for somebody to meet him on arrival.'[4] That very month, however, he inaugurated a series of Sunday lectures on Yoga at the Royal Institute of Painters in Watercolours at Piccadilly. In the following month, he wrote, 'we have already got funds to start a London Centre. What will be the good of my going home?—This London is the hub of the world. The heart of India is here.' The city had brought so many unforeseen godly possibilities to the swami, that he was now in England for the second time, within a year.

In Vivekananda's lifetime, numerous influential Western intellectuals and activists were spurred to Indian spirituality. One of them was the Irish schoolteacher from Wimbledon, Margaret Noble, who in later life would be his favourite disciple—the revered Sister Nivedita—and one of the chief strategists behind the Ramakrishna Mission, founded in 1897. Noble was introduced to Vivekananda in November 1895. 'Suppose he had not come to London that time!' she remarked. 'Life would have been a headless dream.' Nivedita believed she had waited throughout the prime of her life for a spiritual saviour. Over next autumn, she was among the chief organisers for Vivekananda's seminars in London. He well understood that for thousands of Indians in the city, the path to spirituality lay in the struggle for freedom. 'Not all of us come as trailing clouds of glory,' rang the swami's caution, courting William Wordsworth's paean in a dark century. 'Some of us come as trailing black fogs.'[5] Albeit confined to its drawing rooms, private clubs or select galleries, where the swami spoke, London had started to recoil from the berries of its own maya. 'The work in London has been a roaring success,' Vivekananda later wrote. 'The English are not so bright as the Americans, but once you touch their heart, it is yours forever.'[6]

In an interview to the *Sunday Times* that winter, he stated unflinchingly, 'England will be conquered in her turn. Today she has the sword, but it is worse than useless in the world of ideas.'[7] The *Indian Mirror* ran several reports covering the successes of the swami's lectures in London, and his much talked about camaraderie with Max Müller, who regularly hosted him in Oxford. By Vivekananda's own admission, the professor overshadowed Indians in his consummate love for Vedanta, Sri Ramakrishna and India. Friedrich Nietzsche, the guardian angel of nihilism, had argued that god was dead. Yet, the frequency with which audiences sprang to attend the speeches of the swami was clinching evidence of the compatibility of Indian spirituality in the epicentres of European modernity. His voice had struck roots in the hearts of Londoners, insomuch as there was even an air of Christian sombreness when Vivekananda bid his last farewell to the city in December 1896.

It was Sunday in London, when shops were shut, business at a standstill, and the city streets silenced for a while from some at least of the rattle and the rumble of their heavier traffic. Londoners wore their Sunday clothing, their Sunday bearing and manner, and gray, subdued, and semi-silent folk wended their way to church and chapel. This afternoon the friends of Swamiji were to say 'Good-bye' to him whose coming had meant so much to them. In the hall of meeting, dedicated to the use of the artists, paintings hung upon the walls: palms, flowers and ferns decorated the platform from which Swamiji would utter his final speech in England's great metropolis to the British people. All sorts and conditions of men were there, but all alike were filled by one desire: to see him, to hear him, even if it may be, to touch his garment once again.[8]

No sooner than the swami had recrossed the Mediterranean, the dark underbelly of London was once again exposed. Within a few years, Sir Arthur Conan Doyle would have begun serialising *The Hound of the Baskervilles* in *The Strand Magazine*. It was published in 1902, the year that also marked the end of the Boer War in South

Africa. Doyle's titular beast was a metaphor for the patent fear of
the loss of empire. It had hounded many a Baskerville Hall in the
memory of many a reluctant English custodian of the white man's
burden in the colonies. What with the sinister fogs of Dartmoor
and the sordid obscurities of the Great Grimpen Mire, London was
a prisoner of the spoils of its Oriental plunder. Its 'so-called trailing
beauty was but a prison-house,' the swami had warned before his
departure.[9] This palpable paranoia could not have been crystallised
any better than in the life of the Kohinoor. After Victoria's death, the
diamond was studded in the crowns of Queen Alexandra, Queen
Mary and Queen Elizabeth, and enshrined at the House of Jewels
in the Tower of London. Despite being jealously guarded by the
British royalty and the Parliament—even in the 21st century—the
controversy around the diamond would remain quite luminescent
in the consciousness of Victorian and Edwardian England. So
would Sir Duleep Singh.

A year before the transfer of the Kohinoor to the Queen, Duleep
Singh became a Christian—a decision he later regretted deeply. In
1886, after thirty-two years in England, he espoused Sikhism once
again. However, when the young usurped emperor had first arrived
in London, he was far from any guilt or want of glory. The East India
Company had him lodged at the Claridge's Hotel, from where he was
shifted to Wimbledon, and thence to Roehampton. Hailed as the
darling of the Queen, the teenaged Duleep Singh was as distinguished
a guest as Osborne House had ever seen. 'Those eyes and those teeth
are too beautiful,' Victoria exclaimed while sketching him, as if in a
prolonged juvenilia.[10] She also commissioned portraits of the young
Maharajah by the German lithographer and artist, Franz Xaver
Winterhalter, renowned for his magical brushstrokes to the faces of
European royalty. Courted by aristocrats and adored by noblewomen,
Duleep Singh passed his days as the cynosure of London's elite society.
There was no dearth of women who 'defied convention to flirt, accept
his gifts and agree to secret liaisons with him.'[11]

Along with his steadfast companion, the Prince of Wales (later, King Edward VII), the young Maharajah rollicked and whored around Victorian London, daring both the composure of the Queen and the scorn of the English society for his inferior race. Both she and her son, however, were responsible in varying degrees for making a profligate out of the deposed king. As early as 1855, Duleep Singh was made a member of the Royal Photographic Society, just after a year of his arrival. He was then sardined off on a grand tour of Europe. On his return, the Queen and the Company · thought it best to appoint Sir John Spencer Login as his de facto pater in London. Originally a physician from Edinburgh, Login had served in the British army in Bengal and under the Nizam. He would go down in history as the man to escort Duleep Singh and the Kohinoor to London. Under Login, the Maharajah 'developed into a Christian gentleman, an English courtier, and a Scottish laird.'[12] In a childlike portmanteau of the Hindustani equivalents for 'mother' and 'father,' Duleep Singh called Login by the noun, '*Ma-Baap*.' It naturally fell on the physician and his wife to take charge of him during his later teens in Perthshire, where they took lease of the Castle Menzies to lullaby the Prince of Punjab.

The story of the Kohinoor's journey provided an uncanny subplot to the novel *Kim* (1901), written by Rudyard Kipling. Its character, Lurgan Sahib, who ran a curiosity jewellery shop in Simla, is said to have been based on the life of the jewel merchant, Alexander Malcolm Jacob, whose name lent itself to the Jacob Diamond. The diamond was also known as the Imperial or, not uncannily, the Victoria Diamond. In the 1890s, it was advertised for sale by Alexander Jacob, and nominally sold to Mahbub Ali Khan, the sixth Nizam of Hyderabad. His son, Mir Osman Ali Khan, the seventh and last Nizam, briefly became the richest man in the world. Inter alia, he had inherited from his father an enormous wealth of jewellery, which today survives as a 173-piece collection, that 'displayed at various museums across India includes the legendary 187.75 carat Jacob diamond, the world's fifth-largest diamond which is valued at over £100 million.'[13] Both the Nizams and the Jacob had little to do with London or Victoria, especially in comparison with Duleep Singh and the Kohinoor. But the history of the diamond, its journeys and those of its possessors, is inseparable from the history of queen and country. The Jacob emerged from a mine in South Africa. 'This gem of blue-white colour,' read an advertisement in *The Times* of August 20, 1884, 'similar to the finest stones from the Jagersfontein Mine, which is said to be (and most probably is) the true locality of this gem. There is somewhat of a mystery attached to the true origin of the stone, and from the secrecy displayed at its first discovery, it is not improbable that it has been procured through an "illicit" at the mine from which it is reported to come.'[14] It had arrived in London in July. From there it was traded off first to the King of Portugal, and thence to the Queen of Holland. Before reaching the Nizam, the diamond had been cut several times, on the last occasion by the Dutchman, M.B. Barends, who cut it with 58 facets. With the diamond arriving in India, Alexander Jacob had just plotted the 'most audacious diamond sale in history.'[15]

The Jacob was arguably the most expensive diamond to be advertised on the market. Even in the late 19th century, the value of the diamond was estimated to be as much as £800,000. The Nizam managed to cajole its sellers to pass it on for half that sum. When the Jacob finally reached Hyderabad, Mahbub Ali, disillusioned by the cut of the crystal, reluctantly parted with just a little more than £200,000. So indifferent was the Nizam towards the acquisition that when he died, his son, Osman Ali, found 'the duck-egg-sized diamond hidden in his father's slippers and used it as a paperweight.'[16] Until 1948, the Jacob lived a thoroughly unremarkable life, until it came to be ineradicably associated with the blood and trauma of the Partition. Before the state of Hyderabad became a part of the Republic of India, Osman Ali transferred £1 million to Habib Ibrahim Rahimtoola, the Pakistani High Commissioner in London. Over the next seven decades, the deposit had multiplied three times, before Pakistan and India decided to settle the dispute out of court. The story of the Jacob still nestles behind what was to become infamous as the 'Hyderabad Funds Case', although the diamond was never itself a part of the disputed inheritance. Thanks to the seemingly more adventurous and bleeding history of the Kohinoor, Duleep Singh and John Spencer Login lived fuller lives in public memory. In Kipling's novel, Lurgan Sahib assigned to himself the role of recruiting Kim to the cause of the Empire's Great Game in countering Russian espionage. In his old curiosity shop, Lurgan Sahib had trained Kim in a jewel game. Login's burden in real life was the cataloguing and taxonomy of the bulk of jewellery looted from Punjab. If the Kohinoor was the jewel in the crown of Victoria—a crystallised edict of Indian destiny—Login was, indeed, the most trusted envoi in the whole of the Empire. Duleep Singh was destined to a regally curated life in a casement of the imperial capital. He was to Login as Kim was to Lurgan Sahib. Except, the last Maharaja of Punjab was both the jewel as well as the game.

Victorian England attended to superstitions around the Kohinoor with the due diligence of midwifery. One of the most controversial statements came from Wilkie Collins himself, partly to popularise his novel. He is said to have incensed Charles Dickens for nursing the 'prediction, which prophesied certain misfortune to the persons who should divert it from its ancient uses.'[17] Collins was well aware of the genealogy of incidents that surrounded the lives of the diamond and Duleep. Two days after the Kohinoor came to London, and about a week before it was offered to Victoria, she was assaulted by the mentally unstable Robert Pate, a retired army lieutenant. Suspicions for this and other similar incidents fell on some supernatural agency acting on behalf of the stone, as though it were 'an invisible germ mysteriously carried in the air and over the seas.'[18] In June 1871, *The Spectator* reported that superstitions had led the English to 'firmly believe that the Queen in accepting the Kohinoor accepted the destiny which accompanies that jewel, and will either have to endure severe misfortunes or be left without successor to her throne.'[19] Such premonitions did not fail to remind the English public of the Doctrine of Lapse, devised by Lord Dalhousie, decreeing that kings and rulers in alliance with the British East India Company would have their kingdoms and estates annexed to the Empire if they were incompetent or were to decease without a male heir.

As Dalhousie shooed away such shilly-shallying attitudes, his gratifying doctrines of governance and the railways roused the colony to the War of Independence. That was only more grist to the mill for the English who attributed the massacre of 15,000 British and Indian subjects to the curse of the ancient diamond. As late as January 1880, an 'unknown correspondent' of *Vanity Fair* wrote in a satirical piece that the Kohinoor could even be used by the former prime minister, the Earl of Beaconsfield, as a cursed present to be sent to the new Liberal Prime Minister, William Ewart Gladstone, to replenish Conservative politics by means of the occult. That was only one of the many nifty deployments that the fatal diamond could be put to, as suggested by the writer.

The fatality which attaches to the Kohinoor is only too well known, and a recent publication has brought it very prominently before the anxious mind of this thoughtful nation. The owner of it, or his near descendants, have always lost their dominion over the country, where it has been considered for ages as a treasure unparalleled in magnificence, and, at the same time, ruinous to its possessor—not to go so far back as the Malwah Rajahs, whose dynasty disappeared when the fatal jewel passed from their hands into those of the Moguls; it ruined the Moguls, who lost it to Nadir Shah; and then it ruined Nadir's family, who lost it to the Durani's; and then it ruined the Duranis, who lost it to Ranjeet Singh; and then it ruined the Sikhs, who lost it to John Company; and then it ruined John Company himself; and then it became the property of somebody else—and has been shown at some great exhibitions as an inestimable treasure. If a great lump of pure crystal could have been manufactured out of condensed carbonic acid gas, it would have been quite as pretty to look at without carrying inveterate ill-luck with it. The only question to be considered then would have been—what should be done with the original Kohinoor? I should have suggested that it should be sent back to the Durani chiefs of Afghanistan as a simple and efficacious way of subjugating that rebellious people, whom all the bishops and clergy ought to be instructed weekly to curse (as some few, I believe, are doing) for being so dull as not to understand that our only wish is for their welfare, though official reserve and political complications prevent us fully explaining to them how and why that is. Or it might be offered as a tribute of respect and admiration on our part to the great Prince who conquered Tartary, and so pass on to him our own bad luck and the loss of empire which unavoidably awaits the possessor of the Kohinoor ...

Or, to come nearer home, why should it not be made a present of to Mr Parnell as part of the regalia of the future King of Ireland, and as a certain means of making his Majesty's first Parliament in College Green an utter failure? But perhaps, what between Catholic Connaught and Munster and Presbyterian Ulster, that disruption is a foregone conclusion already which requires no Kohinoor mysteriously to bring it about. If it were privately offered him however in his capacity as a Member of Parliament, it ought to do something towards disorganising the Home Rule Party, always supposing that the said Party is organised at all-this is only thrown out as a suggestion. But as it is the brightest jewel in the British Crown, and as Lord Beaconsfield has the temporary charge of the Crown and its jewels, why should not he send it to Mr Gladstone in a registered letter, with a post-card in pretty terms requesting his acceptance of it. So would fatal ill-luck attend the Opposition ever after, and the hand of destined destruction be averted from the Empire which his Lordship may be said to have created when he gave it an Empress, and so would the stone be turned against the man and the Party who dislike the title of Empress, but have never expressed aversion to the possession of the Kohinoor.[20]

Whether or not at the behest of the Kohinoor, misfortune had indeed befallen Victoria in the winter of 1861. Neither the diamond nor Duleep—nor indeed a sliver of hope from her Eastern jewels—could rouse the Queen from bitterly mourning the loss of her husband. He had been the chief architect in transforming and sculpting the Kohinoor. One might as well have said of the Queen's summer retreat, the Osborne House, as Gabriel Betteridge wrote of the Verinder household in *The Moonstone*: 'here was our quiet English house suddenly invaded by a devilish Indian diamond.'[21]

A year after the War of Independence, the guardianship of Duleep Singh was transferred from Login to Sir Charles Phipps, the Queen's Treasurer. As the lease of Castle Menzies gave over, Duleep Singh was shifted to the house of the Earl of Breadalbane in the hamlet of Auchlyne, about forty miles from the Maharajah's previous residence. Prince Albert's death was followed by repeated remonstrations by Duleep Singh's mother, Jindan Kaur, to see her son. In 1856, Duleep first wrote to his mother, who was exiled in Kathmandu, to come to London. That and several other couriers sent by him were seized by the British. When the Maharajah finally managed to send an inquiry to the British Resident in Kathmandu, he was told his mother's health was failing miserably. Duleep Singh was too precious a subject to be lost to 'any native influence.'[22] Jindan Kaur alone had been a dozen thorns in the side of the Company, having single-handedly organised a Sikh uprising against its forces in 1849. After her capture, she had hoodwinked prison guards and tramped 500 miles off to Nepal. However, since Jindan's erstwhile connections with the rebels of Punjab had paled away, the civil servants at Whitehall considered it prudent enough to unite the mother and son in Calcutta.

In 1861, Jindan arrived in London, as discussions of Duleep Singh's marriage were underway between Phipps and Login. The bride that the two loyal queensmen had chosen for Duleep Singh was the Queen's own god-daughter, Victoria Gouramma. She was the daughter of Chikka Virarajendra, the ruler of Coorg, who had surrendered to the forces of James Stuart Fraser in 1834. Exiled to Benares, Virarajendra travelled to London, in 1852, along with his daughter, to petition before the Queen for the restoration of his wealth purloined by the Company. Victoria royally welcomed the father and daughter, agreeing to godmother the latter the same year, with the benediction of the Archbishop of Canterbury. What could be a better compensation for Virarajendra that his child was rechristened in the Queen's name, and she and her father were consigned to their new home in London, where he counted his last months as the young Victoria came of age?

Gouramma was given to the care of Edith Dalhousie Login, the wife of John Spencer Login. Having had a similar upbringing to Duleep Singh, albeit much less adventurous, she was considered the ideal partner for the Maharajah, in what was to be an Indian match made in the imperial heaven. In 1863, Duleep Singh's putative father, Login, passed away. Later that year, Duleep's mother, 'the frail and partially-blind queen who had spent much of her life raging against the British Empire, died in her bed on the top floor of a Kensington townhouse.'²³ She looked decades more wrinkled than her forty-six-year-old mortal frame. Although the living Jindan was not as much of a nuisance as apprehended, in her death she left the British with ample inconvenience. A burial was planned for her in London, but her servants who came to know of the impending desecration of their Maharani's body, noised up *The Times* to demand her cremation. Fearing the disaffection of Sikhs in India, and to avoid any local turbulence in London, the India Office had it arranged for the remains of Jindan Kaur to be preserved at the Kensal Green Dissenters' Chapel. Here she lay for over a year, while attempts were made to quietly pass over her remains to India.

The India Office also purchased an estate in Elveden in Suffolk, whose 17,000 acres of territory was transformed by Duleep Singh into a sanctuary for hunting game. Cossetted in the Oriental architecture of his renovated mansion at Elveden, he prided himself as one of the best shots of England. His marriage plans had been upset with the passing away of Login and, even before that, Victoria Gouramma choosing to marry Lt Col John Campbell instead. She named her daughter Edith Victoria Gouramma after the Queen and Lady Login. In 1864, Gouramma also died, and was buried at the Brompton cemetery. That year, while Duleep

Singh was in Alexandria, he married Bamba Müller, the daughter of Ludwig Müller. Twelve years later, their fifth child and third daughter, Sophia Alexandra Duleep Singh, was born to be caressed, baptised, reared and to be feared royally.

———

Princess Sophia was a broadside face of the British women's suffragette movement. She was an active campaigner in the Women's Social and Political Union founded by Emmeline Pankhurst and her daughters, Christabel and Sylvia Pankhurst, in Manchester, as a breakaway faction of women from the Independent Labour Party. She was also a passionate activist in the Women's Tax Resistance League born out of the Women's Freedom League, which campaigned for women's political and gender equality. In June 1911, during the coronation of King George V and his wife, Queen Mary, 60,000 women in London marched from Westminster to Albert Hall. The Indian representation in the procession, and their Oriental dressing and diversity, gave it a 'particularly striking and picturesque' character. The faces of the movement appeared to be 'without race, or creed, or boundary,'[24] unlike other contemporary movements in England and beyond. These included the Maharani of Baroda and, of course, Sophia Duleep Singh.

The princess grew up at Faraday House in Hampton Court Palace at Richmond upon Thames. As a young Englishwoman, Sophia learned music, visibly taking after her mother's taste in Western classics and the opera. What was the use of being in Europe, Bamba used to say, 'if one hears no music?'[25] Besides that, Sophia was fond of pedigreed dogs and riding the bicycle. Like many upper-middle-class women of her time, she attended ballroom parties and charities. Unlike most of them, she was a photographer who also played hockey. Even before her teens, she had to stomach rumours about her father's many mistresses. As if that aggravation was not enough for her mother and sisters, the Maharajah abandoned his family in the 1870s by dint of a public notice in *The Times*. As the debts of the Maharajah shadowed the family, Bamba took to alcohol, while Whitehall grudgingly arranged for a pension of £6,000 for the downtrodden Maharani. It also helped send their two eldest sons to the Sandhurst Military Academy and Cambridge. Duleep, on the other hand, was plotting a game far more insidious than what Login had taught him in Perthshire or Lurgan Sahib had taught Kim in Simla.

In 1884, Duleep Singh's cousin, Thakar Singh Sandhawalia, travelled to England along with his sons and a Sikh priest. The Maharajah had been eyeing a ceremony in India to mark his reconversion to Sikhism. He had also established communication with Moscow and St Petersburg to persuade Tsar Alexander III to foment a rebellion in Punjab, if not commit to a full-fledged invasion of India. The Russian government was not moved, but the Russian press certainly was. Mikhail Katkov, the editor of *Moscow News*, stirred up his columns with news about the Maharajah's rebellion, while lobbying extensively to grab the attention of the Russian administration. In 1886, following a severance of all his political ties with the British Empire, Duleep Singh set sail for India. During a halt at Yemen, he underwent the conversion ceremony organised by his cousin and the Sikh priest he had brought over from India. His next stop was Aden, where he was arrested and brought back to London. This humiliation acted as the last straw in the Maharajah's soured ties with the Crown.

It was almost a fresh lease of life for Duleep Singh that, in 1887, Bamba quietly passed away, paving the way for his mistress and future wife, Ada Wetherill, to enter the semi-royal household. His daughters were yet to come out of mourning when, with the aid of Wetherill's contacts in Russia, Duleep Singh planted his bait before the Tsar. He was in Russia the next year, ardently reasoning with Alexander III: 'I guarantee an easy conquest of India.'[26] Assuring him the unswerving allegiance of Sikh soldiers in the British army, Duleep Singh promised to blow up the bridges, railways and all telegraphic communication in British India. Just as his name began pulling some weight with the Soviets, Katkov, who had by now helped publish several of his interviews, died unexpectedly. The Maharajah's letters to the Tsar went unanswered, as well as his prayers of a sovereign Punjab, forcing him to an exile in Paris. The Tory Member of

Parliament, Lord Randolph Churchill (father of Sir Winston), was the one to hammer the last nail in the coffin of Duleep Singh's battle-plan. On a delegation to meet the Russian administration, Churchill wrote from Moscow that there was no basis, whatsoever, to the complete 'absurdity of the alarmist theory of the English jingoists according to which Russia is a constant threat for the English Empire in India.'[27] The morally crushed Victorian Maharajah died in Paris, in 1893. Before his death, the Queen granted him a royal pardon for his conspiracy against the Empire, and also ensured that Sophia and each of her sisters inherited a pension of £23,000.

Where the Great Game ended, Sophia's dangerous career began. She would be remembered from her iconic image circulated in the English press—a non-White Edwardian, standing outside Hampton Court, dressed in lavish furs, armed with a satchel and copies of *Votes for Women*, the official journal of the Women's Social and Political Union. A voracious smoker and an insufferable radical in the eyes of the law and the crown, Sophia's links with Indian nationalists like Gopal Krishna Gokhale and Lala Lajpat Rai were just one more reason in her resume to qualify her as an abnormal transgressor. However, she was exceedingly disillusioned with any form of publicity, including notoriety, after her first two visits to India, where British condescension had been regularly impressed upon her. Sophia was unmoved when William Carrington, treasurer to King George V, couriered to the Secretary of State for India and the India Office, pictures of her engaged in hazardous business. She had been peddling women's rights magazines, including *The Suffragette*. The King wanted her gone from Hampton Court, without possessing the nerve to act on it personally. Buckingham Palace wanted Lord Crewe to work it out covertly. And Crewe, under the advice of the King himself, had to avoid making headlines out of Sophia.

Faraday House had been given to Sophia by the King's own grandmother, the late Queen. Tailed by British intelligence, the King's assistants, the paparazzi and her own affectionate supporters, Sophia's life was turned into the royalty's nightmare, much of what was its own making. In 1911, she was fined £3 by the Spelthorne Petty Sessions Court for keeping an unlicensed coach, five dogs and a roll of arms. When she refused to pay the fine, she had her diamond ring, gold bangle and pearl necklace confiscated and auctioned at Twickenham Hall. They were bought back by Jopling Rowe, a colleague of Sophia from the Women's Tax Resistance League, and returned to her. A couple of years later, she was tried again. The *Daily Mail*, in its article 'Princess's Unpaid Taxes. Fines Upon Four Summonses', gave a report of Sophia's appearance in the Feltham Police Court. The charge was that she owned a horse, a carriage and two dogs, without the necessary licences, therefore, without paying taxes. She appeared in court wearing the badge of the Women's Tax Resistance League, in the company of Kineton Parkes, the secretary of the body, and six of its other members. Her response was summed up by the *Mail* as a refusal to pay either tax or fine until the 'women of England were enfranchised.'[28] *The Times* published a much longer excerpt of her insolent persuasions.

I am unable conscientiously to pay money to the state, as I am not allowed to exercise any control over its expenditure, neither am I allowed any voice in the choosing of members of Parliament, whose salaries I have to help to pay. This is very unjustified. When the women of England are enfranchised and the State acknowledges me as a citizen, I shall, of course, pay my share willingly towards its upkeep, if I am not a fit person for the purposes of representation, why should I be a fit person for taxation?[29]

The judge was indifferent to Sophia's politics. He fined her with £12.10, which she had no intention of paying. Back at Crewe's office, along with pictures of Sophia and cuttings from the *Daily Mail*, records from the trial went into the safe harbour of a file that the Secretary of State had been asked to keep on her activities. The princess was determined to make much more mayhem. Between protesting for rights of lascars and supporting bomb-makers and arsonists in Britain, she once threw herself before the car of Prime Minister Herbert Asquith, outside 10 Downing Street. It was in February 1911, a day when the King was to address the Parliament. Sophia was waving a placard that read: 'Give Women the Vote.' She was not even dressed for revolution but what seemed like dinner, in 'a wide brimmed hat tipped low over her face and an expensive fur muff.'[30] That itself must have miffed Downing Street even more, while in a gilded hallway of Buckingham Palace, King George V cried exasperatedly, 'Have we no hold on her?'[31]

Sophia's epithet 'Princess' was frequently flagged by her Union's colleagues to shock the aristocracy. Back in November 1910, as 300 female protestors marched from Caxton Hall to Westminster on the Black Friday protests demanding the vote for women, many of them were assaulted or tossed about like playthings. The Home Secretary, Winston Churchill, issued strict orders not to arrest the suffragettes. Nicknamed at school as the 'bull dog,' he allowed a freehand to his own dogs to brutalise the fasting marchers on the streets. The London mob disagreed, treating the princess to the pomp reserved for royalty. 'Jostling crowds parted to let Sophia pass. She was the darling of ladies' magazines and newspaper society columns.'[32] She came out unscathed, preceded and protected by her fame. In the words of her sister Bamba, Sophia was 'very very lovely, rather like our grandmother Jindan.'[33] When the Great War broke out, Sophia and her colleagues from the Women's Social and Political Union, headed by Emmeline Pankhurst, stopped their suffragist campaigning for the war effort. They led an army of 10,000 women for the Women's War Work. That too had to fight to make its place and presence strongly felt by the War Office, that was otherwise rather opaque to the notion of women joining the war. The militant feminist turned into a nurse looking after Sikh and English soldiers wounded on the Western Front, scandalising Whitehall, which believed feminism and nursing were antithetical roles.

Although the services of Indians in the war would never be seen on an equal footing with those of the British or French, the India Office tried to deploy fair measures for the recreation of Indian soldiers in England. As many reckoned, it would be to Britain's own advantage if Indians were exposed to the metropolitan air, not to say its grandiose architecture, which would have perhaps drugged them into worshipping the wealth and power of the Empire.

Starting in December 1914, the India Office arranged for
small parties of 24 at a time, either all Muslims or all Hindus,
to be taken to London to see the sights: St Paul's Cathedral,
the Tower of London, the Houses of Parliament, Buckingham
Palace, Queen Victoria's Statue, the Natural History Museum,
Hyde Park, the Albert Museum and the Zoo. An hour's
shopping at Selfridges and a ride on London's underground
train were also included. Such an itinerary could be on any
tourist list. It might be argued that there was a genuine desire
on the part of the India Office, expenses notwithstanding, to
give some of the wounded a day out, away from Brighton. The
India Office might also have considered that the soldiers were
missing out on an experience if, having been in England, they
had then not seen the metropolitan capital, especially as some
had shown a desire to do so. Commenting on the 'excellent
effect' these 'joy rides' were having on the minds of Indian
soldiers, R.C.F. Volkers wrote how, in 'sympathetic hands,'
these men 'expand wonderfully,' so that while giving them
a pleasant day out, it was possible to 'direct their attention
and with it their minds' in such a way that 'they obtain an
impression of England's greatness, wealth and power,' which
would not only remain with them, but 'through them react on
other Indians of their class.'[34]

The India Office had convinced itself that the ostensibly
invincible edifices of London—one of the most fragile cities in
Europe during the Second World War—were the closest that
Indians could have come to the pomp of Roman antiquity. That
was close enough to inspire them to fight Britain's war. Besides
120,000 men in the Imperial Service Troops comprising forces
from the Indian princely states and men in the Indian Labour
Corps, the colony sent a million soldiers to fight in the Great War.
They fought in France, Belgium, Africa, Gallipoli, the Persian Gulf
and Aden. It was the single largest contribution in terms of number
of soldiers from any other nation of the British Dominions.

Besides contributing £100 million to the war effort, India sent about a quarter of that sum for each year of the war. Gandhi and other Congressmen urged Indians in London to dedicate their lives to imperial service, in the hope that once the war was over, Indians would be given the same status as British citizens. Indian medical students, R.N. Cooper, G.C. Chatterjee and Cawas Homi, were among those who devoted their early years as house-surgeons during the war. Dadabhai Naoroji's grandson, Kershap, was one of the rare Indians who got a commission in the armed forces. He fought as a private in France, and as a lieutenant in the Hazara Pioneers in Iraq. Two of Sake Deen Mahomet's great grandsons, one of them being Lieutenant Claude Atkinson Etty Mahomet of the Scots Guards, died in the war. Second Lieutenant H.S. Malik was one of four Indian students in British universities, and the only one to survive, who were given short-term commissions in the Royal Flying Corps. Another Indian pilot in the Royal Flying Corps, Second Lieutenant Indra Lal Roy won ten decisive victories for Britain in 1918, before he was killed in action at the age of nineteen. He was awarded a Distinguished Flying Cross, posthumously.

Sophia's elder brother, Frederick Duleep Singh, a Cambridge graduate, also fought in the war at the Western Front as part of the Norfolk Yeomanry. After the war, Sophia became a lifelong member of the Suffragette Fellowship. On one hand she remained a princess, surrounded by her family's relics dating back to the Stuart period—the last years of Shakespeare when the first generations of Indians came to be visible in London. On the other, when asked to contribute to *Women's Who's Who* in 1934, she noted her only abiding passion had been women's empowerment across the globe. Frederick returned to collect relics and writing his *Portraits in Norfolk Houses,* co-authored by Reverend Edmund Farrer, and published three years after his death in 1926.

Scene II

The Spirit and the Spectre

The heroism of Princess Sophia invited other Indians into the struggle for women's electoral rights. One of them was Sarojini Naidu herself, also a prominent face in London's feminist circles during and after the years of the First World War. Another was Herabai Tata, whom Sophia had first met in Kashmir. After her initiation into spirituality through the route of the Theosophical Society, Herabai was radicalised by Sophia Duleep Singh, during the latter's visit to India in 1911. Herabai's daughter, Mithan, later recounted their meeting in Srinagar with Sophia, who had donned her characteristic white and yellow 'Vote for women' badge. It was the turning point in Herabai's life. 'Her talks with Princess Sophie,' wrote her daughter, 'and the literature she sent immediately roused my mother's interest.'[1] Around the same time, Herabai also met Annie Besant. The headquarters of the Theosophical Society in Adyar developed close links with the Women's Indian Association, which too was first set up in that town. Herabai became a member of the Women's Association and later its honorary secretary in Bombay.

In 1918, Whitehall deployed the Southborough Franchise Committee to India to collect intelligence on communal and territorial electorates, and commercial and other interests of political representation. When it came to the issue of female electoral rights, the Committee interviewed respondents only from Bengal and Punjab. With supreme haste and brevity, it concluded that Indian women were not ready for the vote. Sir C.

Sankaran Nair, the sole Indian member of the Viceroy's Executive Council, was one of two members of the committee who tirelessly lobbied for Indian women's voting rights to be recommended to the Joint Select Committee in the House of Commons. Towards this end, he needed a women's delegation from India to voice their concerns in London. In August 1919, supported by funds from the Theosophical Society and the Indian Women's Association, Herabai and her daughter accompanied Nair to represent the Indian women's movement at Westminster.

As Mithan enrolled for postgraduate studies at the London School of Economics, what was to be a sojourn of four months for Herabai became a four-year-long crusade. Not only women's organisations, but a wide range of associations came ahead to support her to transform the perceptions of Indian women in English minds, and pursue their enfranchisement. These included the National Union of Women of Great Britain and Ireland, the Quakers' Friends' Mission, Congregational Church Institute, Social and Political Union of Bedford College, the Women's International League Council, Westfield Ladies' College, Wood Green Unity Hall, Wesleyan Mission Adult School, the Croydon Women's International League, the Women's Cooperative Guild at Holloway and the British Dominion Women Citizens' Union. Mithan Tata was called to deliver a lecture to members of the Women's Freedom League, at the Minerva Café in London, which was publicised in the popular radical magazine, *The Vote*. Mother and daughter toured across Glasgow, Harrowgate, Bolton, Liverpool, Manchester, Birkenhead and Newcastle, managing to win an influential aide in Harriet Newcomb, the Secretary of the British Dominion Women Citizens' Union, who wrote a persuasive letter to the Joint Select Committee soliciting for imperial support to the cause of gender equality in India, on the principles of the League of Nations. In 1920, the women's rights campaign took Herabai to Geneva as part of an Indian delegation to the International Women's Suffrage Alliance, along with Mrinalini Sen and Sarojini Naidu.

In Edwardian London, theosophists and feminists had forged a formidable solidarity on nationalist lines. On June 3, 1920, the British

Committee of the Indian National Congress organised a meeting at Kingsway Hall to protest against the Jallianwalla Bagh massacre. Naidu's speech, 'The Agony and Shame of Punjab,' was a riot of 'images of female assault to describe the betrayal of the bonds of Empire and thereby to launch her most vitriolic attack on the British.'[2] *Britain and India*, a magazine founded by Australian theosophist Josephine Ransom, covered Naidu's tirade with all sincerity.

> Not only were the men mown down as if they were grass that is born to wither; but they tore asunder the cherished Purdah, that innermost privacy of the chaste womanhood in India. Therefore, Englishmen and Englishwomen, my sisters were stripped naked, they were flogged, they were outraged. Should they hold their Empire by dishonouring the women of another nation or lose it out of chivalry for their honour and chastity? You deserve no Empire. You today have lost your soul; you today have the stain of blood-guiltiness upon you.[3]

The House of Commons was stunned and split. In theory, the Secretary of State for India, Edwin Montagu, was a Liberal Party leader. In practise, he must have seemed to Naidu as illiberal as an act of god. He demanded that Naidu hand over the proof of her scandalous claims or act on a speedy withdrawal of her inflammatory metaphors. She answered the former demand, detailing to the Secretary of State how she herself was hit and spat on, and how women were unveiled one after another before being spewed on with burning profanities. Naidu challenged the House of Commons as a fearless critic of the purblind intellectual slavery to the West that India had undergone for over three generations. What Indians demanded, she told Westminster during the debate on Punjab, was not revenge but reparation in order to 'transmute bitterness into something that might mean redemption both for ourselves and the British race.'[4] Montagu remained as thick and impassive to Sarojini's magniloquence as Churchill had been in the last decade to Sophia's magnanimity.

In May 1970, a mystic—endeared by the East and the West though very little understood—delivered a lecture in London on the subject of 'The Religious Mind'. Cast in his singularly unorthodox style, it was simply a eulogy on conscious life led against violence. He held that the secret to overcoming the violence of the self was in transcending greed and grief, egotism and economics, religion and gender, ambition and politics, nation and nationality and sundry other seemingly narcissistic or noble identities. A world where meditation had become a masquerade, where the wholesomeness of daily life had been dissected into manifold pigeonholes, where spirituality itself was conditioned luxury and the self, but a proxy concert of other identities, the mystic merely asked to renounce knowledge and adopt silence. He had spent his teens and young adult life in the city, and had failed the examination to the University of London in each of his three attempts. Jiddu Krishnamurti was as much of a discovery as an invention. In 1910, along with his brother Nityananda Krishnamurti (or Jiddu Nityananda), he was recruited for the Indian Theosophical Society by Charles Webster Leadbeater, a controversial occultist and clairvoyant. The brothers were placed in the care of Annie Besant. Jiddu was an emaciated Brahmin child, almost without a brain, almost unintelligent, almost unread—the perfect clay to be moulded into a theosophical cross between Christ and the Buddha.

Leadbeater had seen in Jiddu all the makings of the messianic world teacher or *Maitreya*, as the theosophists called their revenant. The arrival of the messiah had been prophesied in the conception of the Masters of the Ancient Wisdom, which was a theosophical illuminati of sorts. Helena Blavatsky, the Russian philosopher who founded the Theosophical Society in 1875, also referred to the messianic notion in her influential book, *The Secret Doctrine* (1888). Being fluent in French, English, Hebrew, Tibetan, Sanksrit and Hindi, Blavatsky had access to a large corpus of religious literature. Her efforts at popularising theosophy in Europe and America had been attacked on charges of plagiarism and posturing. Theosophy, in her vision, was the salvaging of esoteric and ancient wisdom, scientism, cosmic union and the enigmatic processes of doubling the self in astral projections to manifest the immaculate immortality of the soul. She claimed that Pythagoras, the ancient Greek mathematician, had learned about reincarnation in India. Blavatsky and her lifelong associate, the American lawyer Henry Olcott, came to meet many spiritual leaders in the colony. One of them was Dayanand Saraswati, founder of the Arya Samaj, with whom they had corresponded from America. In the 1880s, Saraswati and the theosophists fell out over conflicting spiritual ideologies. Blavatsky decided to temper the spiritual zest of theosophy, especially in India, where she attempted to harmonise it with the Swadeshi Movement.

By 1882, Blavatsky and Olcott set up the headquarters of the Indian Theosophical Society in Adyar. Hardly a year had passed since the publication of *The Theosophist as Fragments of Occult Truth* by Allan Octavian Hume, an early Indian theosophist and official in the Government of India, better known as one of the founding fathers of the Indian National Congress. As that glorious age of eccentrics would have it, Hume was also a devout scientist of sorts—an ornithologist to be precise. While he was posted as a Company civil servant at Etawah, in the Central Provinces, his large collection of specimens of birds was destroyed at the hands of the mutineers, during the Great Rebellion. Undaunted by that loss, and despite the lack of interest in ornithology at the time, he launched the quarterly *Stray Feathers*, in 1872, and continued to build an archive of avian and horticultural specimens at Simla. In Hume's oeuvre, theosophy was also a science. His gleanings from the lectures and works of Blavatsky emboldened the links between the theosophists and the Congress. Several Congressmen themselves were closeted theosophists. Although he never openly admitted to it, even Gandhi was much too theosophical ever since his meeting with Blavatsky and Besant in London. Understandably, theosophy must have been a welcome change of seasoning for Indian nationalists, after over half a century of Vedantism in Victorian Britain.

Jiddu Krishnamurti would grow up to spare no sympathy for either. In May 1909, he was a lad of fourteen when Leadbeater met

him for the first time. His father had been an old theosophist and
an employee of the Adyar branch of the society. Jiddu was given
the *nom de plume* Alcyone, a cosmic and mythological character
whose reincarnation he was believed to be. Alcyone's first book, *At
the Feet of the Master,* was published in 1911. In January, George
Arundale founded the Order of the Rising Sun in Benares. Three
months later, it was replaced by the Order of the Star in the East,
instituted by Annie Besant. Jiddu 'Krishna' was proclaimed as
its supreme head. He was meant to be an amalgam of Jesus and
Krishna, a pinnacle of cosmological wisdom and the ecstasy of a
new century.

Jiddu's father was deeply annoyed by the deification of his
son as a surrogate Christ, while devotees queued up to prostrate
themselves before the teen. After a bitterly fought court battle,
Besant won the case of Jiddu's legal guardianship against his father.
However, the alarum had rung piercingly in the Theosophical
Society with Jiddu's elevation as a godman. A.E. Wodehouse, the
Secretary General of the Order, was thoroughly offended. With
bare minimum heed to Wodehouse's dissent, Jiddu was safely
ensconced in the house of English theosophist Esther Bright
at Drayton Gardens in South Kensington. When theosophists
of London saw him at his first public appearance overseas at
Charing Cross, they instantly hailed him as their messiah. While
Princess Sophia and other female suffragettes were steering past
the potholes of Palmer Street during the Coronation march,
Krishnamurti was being groomed in the heart of the Empire to
possess 'a cosmopolitan outlook and an otherworldly, almost
beatific detachment in his demeanour.'[5]

Arundale had offered to tutor the *Maitreya*. Besides with him,
Jiddu also developed an affectionate bond with Emily Lutyens, the
daughter of the former Viceroy of India, Edward Bulwer-Lytton.
She was somewhat better known as the wife of Sir Edwin Landseer
Lutyens, who was known a great deal better as the architect of
New Delhi. A year after Jiddu moved to London, the British
administration decided to move the Indian capital from Calcutta
to New Delhi. In between keeping an eye on Sophia and Indian

student revolutionaries, Crewe had handed over the charge of designing the new imperial capital to Sir Lutyens, who in his later life would also go on to design several war graves and memorials in England and France. Before Sir Lutyens left for India to survey New Delhi, he designed a building for the Theosophical Society at Tavistock Square. In Delhi, he sculpted the Rajpath on the model of Whitehall and designed both the India Gate and the Cenotaph. As a consequence of his imposing architectural imagination, 'London was less emphatically an imperial city than New Delhi.'[6]

The money that had bled for nearly two centuries from Howrah to Westminster had bolstered London's Italianate facades, but in several recesses of the city, Indian faces lay scattered. One such in central London quietly pointed to the memory of a Parsi, the second of his clan to be given the Order of the Star of India by Victoria. By the year Lutyens took to Londonising New Delhi, Readymoney's memorial had stood for a good forty years.

Regent's Park in London is home to a drinking fountain, a structure that might draw little attention to itself except that it was paid for by a well-known 19th-century philanthropist from Bombay. The Gothic fountain's sculptural features reveal the connection between Britain and its empire. Each side of the basin has a triangular pediment. The sculpted visage of Sir Cowasjee Jehangir Readymoney, the fountain's donour, is flanked on one side by the face of a European lady and on the other by a European gentleman. Beneath each of the four pediments is an arcuated frame. These contain a dedication stone, a coat of arms, a lion with a palm tree, and a horned Indian buffalo with a palm tree. Even without portrait and dedication of Jehangir, the animals and vegetation suggest a tropical empire beyond Britain. The plaque announces that the fountain was raised by the Metropolitan Drinking Fountain and Cattle Trough Association and was gifted by Sir Cowasji Jehangir.[7]

Sir Readymoney's worth far exceeded the weight of his name in gold. He had invested and donated large sums of ready money towards the building of modern Bombay in the 1870s. The fountain at Regent's Park was built and inaugurated by Princess Mary, the Duchess of Teck, in 1869, three years before Readymoney was knighted. Sir Lutyens wanted to uphold that cosmopolitan tradition in his architectural ideas, rowing in shades of London back to Delhi. Chiefly responsible for that Indianisation was his wife. A passionate vegetarian, Mrs Lutyens was the representative for the Star of the Order of the East in England, and was in charge of the publication of the *Herald of the Star*, the Theosophical Society's journal. It was originally founded in Adyar in 1912, but was shifted to London two years later. Until 1927, when it finally folded, Jiddu Krishnamurti was its general editor.

From being a second mother to the two young boys from Madras, Lady Lutyens became a special devotee of Jiddu. Her youngest daughter, Mary Lutyens, was to be the most well-known biographer of Krishnamurti. In one of his biographies, she recollected her mother's reaction on seeing him for the first time, as Besant presented Alcyone before a hysterical crowd at Charing Cross.

> I had eyes for none but Krishna, an odd figure with long black hair falling almost to his shoulders and enormous dark eyes which had a vacant look in them. He was dressed in a Norfolk jacket. Mrs Besant piloted him along the platform anxious to keep the crowd from pressing on him.[8]

From Ashdown Forest, to Robert Street, to Wimbledon, to the West Side Common, the brothers lived in several parts of London, mostly in the residences of English theosophists. Since Jiddu was unable to fulfil his dream of entering Oxford or acquiring formal education in London, he was sent to Paris to study languages. Nityananda prepared for the Bar while managing to infatuate a young Mary Lutyens.

Nitya was chosen to replace Wodehouse as the Secretary General of the Order. In his twenty-sixth year, Jiddu also plunged himself into the work of the Society and the Order. The arrival of the messiah was announced in 1927, but the messiah himself was all too reluctant. A rapid disillusionment had overtaken him, and by now he was flying in the face of Besant, slamming the very pedestals that deified him. His pessimism first set in around 1925, when Nityananda died of tuberculosis. He was further distanced from his manufactured identity after falling out with Helen Knothe, a young American theosophist whom he had met in London, and with whom he had fallen in love after returning from Paris. They parted around the time of Nitya's death, for the *Maitreya* was prohibited from worldly relations. Embittered by his losses, Jiddu dismissed the Order in 1929. The next year, he resigned from the Theosophical Society, followed by Emily Lutyens' resignation.

Krishnamurti headed to Ojai in California. It was here that, in 1922, he had had his first mystical experience or spiritual awakening. Not Knothe or Besant or Lutyens, but his own otherness—his spiritual glimpses into an otherworldly freedom—was to be his lifelong companion now. During and after the Second World War, Krishnamurti was secretly watched by the Federal Bureau of Investigation in America because of his deep pacifist leanings. However, 'K', as he was referred to by his colleagues in London, loathed all forms of organised spirituality or hero-worshipping orders. He lectured all over America, Europe, India and the East. Jawaharlal Nehru is said to have learned from Krishnamurti the mysterious language in which the perpetually observing self could converse with a troubled mind. And, it is supposed that, his daughter, Indira Gandhi, was softened to relax some of her policies during the fatal years of the Emergency under Krishnamurti's influence.

Fifty-five years after Jiddu resigned from the Theosophical Society, he was back in London—barely a few years before his death. The Conservative Party was fuming from the ignominy of Prime Minister Margaret Thatcher being denied an honorary degree by the University of Oxford. She was the first British prime minister since the Second World War to own that unfortunate distinction. Krishnamurti had owned it for over six decades. Unfazed by the stifling atmosphere of Thatcherite policies, he quietly made for his tailors at Savile Row. Much like M.K. Gandhi, M.A. Jinnah or even Sophia Duleep Singh, K too was bound to the sagas of fashion that London had parented since the time King Charles II held his court wearing the first waistcoat in history.

> K always went to Huntsman in Savile Row when he came to London if only to take in a pair of trousers to be altered. The evening before coming to London he would carefully choose the suit he was to wear and lay out the shirt and tie to go with it and polish his shoes, even the insteps. His suit would always look pristine, yet he took pride in showing one how old they were by looking inside the inside pocket of the jacket where a good tailor always inscribed the date. London-tailored gentlemen vied with each other over the longevity of their suits. But on this occasion K ordered a new suit and a pair of new trousers, very heartening to us because it showed a confidence that he did not expect to die soon. So little pleasure did he have in his life that it was a joy to see him at Huntsman. Strangely enough he looked more at home in this masculine English shrine than when speaking on a platform.[9]

Contrary to the expectations of his colleagues of an overly long life from him, Krishnamurti passed away in 1986 in Ojai. In London, he had received premonitions of his death, and although he was asked severally how long he thought he would live, K pretended he still had a few good years in him—never betraying the slightest notion that it would be the very next year.

———

Back in 1921, when Jiddu returned to London from Paris, a spectre was haunting Europe. It had been conjured by Karl Marx in the previous century. In the aftermath of the First World War and the Bolshevik Revolution, the Communist International or the Comintern was founded by Vladimir Lenin, with the dream of Communism as the new world order. Shapurji Saklatvala, a member of the Independent Labour Party for over a decade now, fell for that dream.

Saklatvala had been on the files of the Criminal Intelligence Office since as early as 1910 when he hosted Bipin Chandra Pal at his residence in Manchester. Pal's lecture on 'Socialism and Empire' was attended by 700 mill workers and other employees of the firm Messrs Howard and Bullough, which had undertaken large investments in India. Saklatvala too came into the notice of the public and Scotland Yard. His interest in the student movement in London and correspondence with Bhikaji Cama soon earned him a file at the India Office. Besides, there was also the rumour that he had been sent to England by the Tatas after he had embarrassed the family business by foul-mouthing the British administration. An early instance of Saklatvala's extremist reaction to British imperialism was recorded in a letter of condolence written to his son, after his death, by his friend Spitam Cama.

Sometime during the outbreak of the Great War, Spitam was at a meeting with Shapurji Saklatvala and Mancherjee Bhownaggree at a London restaurant. Their discussions commenced with what should have been India's reaction to Britain over the course of the war. The Indians should have 'to kill as many Englishmen as possible,' Saklatvala propounded in cold blood.[10] He added that the Bombay water supply could be poisoned, killing British troops at once. Furious beyond words, Bhownaggree left instantly. Saklatvala's real intention was, however, to poison British imperialism from within the British Parliament.

Shapurji Saklatvala was a feminist perhaps even before Princess Sophia, and certainly before the reddening of his own politics. In 1908, he had marched with female suffragettes headed by Sylvia Pankhurst and Minnie Bowles. 'Sak,' Bowles later wrote, had calmly restored peace at a house near Battersea Park Road, where domestic violence had broken. 'Now why do you beat your wife?' he asked the husband. 'She is not your enemy. You have real enemies. Think of the landlord who charges you rent for this slum; or your boss who pays your wages, hardly enough to keep you alive.'[11] Saklatvala also enjoyed the lifelong support of the Anglo–Irish suffragette, Socialist leader and novelist, Charlotte Despard. She was an important bridge between the Women's Social and

Political Union, other women's rights organisations and the Labour Party. Saklatvala's wife, Sarah Marsh, whom he met in Derbyshire, was also from a working-class background. Around the time of his marriage, while travelling in England, he first confronted the brutal reality of 'the slums and unemployment, the ruthless exploitation of the industrial and agricultural workers.'[12]

Saklatvala's Communist ideals had their origins in England. In the Independent Labour Party, his chief comrade-in-arms was Rajani Palme Dutt, an Indian-origin journalist, with whom Saklatvala formed the Left Wing Group of the party. Rajani Palme Dutt was the son of Upendra Dutt, a Bengali surgeon settled in Cambridge, and his Swedish wife, Anna Palme. Later, as a member of the Communist Party of Great Britain, Rajani founded the party's journal, *Labour Monthly*, which he conducted throughout his life. He was also one of the editors of the party's newspaper, *Worker's Weekly*. In 1921, Dutt and Saklatvala both resigned from the Independent Labour Party to join the Communist Party of Great Britain, established the previous year with the merger of the Communist Unity Group of the Socialist Labour Party, the British Socialist Party, the South Wales Socialist Society and other smaller Marxist circles in Britain. As for Krishnamurti, 1922 was the year of reckoning for Saklatvala. In October, he stood for the Parliament from Battersea North as a Communist candidate. It was one of the six constituencies in which the party fielded its candidates in its first elections. His former colleague from the Independent Labour Party, now a member of the Communist Party, J. Walton Newbold, stood from Motherwell. Unlike him, Saklatvala was also supported by the Labour's United Front. To the utter astonishment of Westminster, both Communists were victorious.

Saklatvala and Newbold achieved phenomenal success in campaigning for cheaper housing and house rents. In 1923, some radical members of the Lascar's Welfare League, in whose formation Saklatvala had dedicated yeoman's service, established the Indian Seamen's Association in London. He had also been a member of the General and Municipal Workers' Union, the National Union of Clerks, the Cooperative movement and the London chapter of the Indian Home Rule League, founded by Annie Besant during the war. Saklatvala was also an eminent member of the Workers' Welfare League of India founded by C.F. Ryder and Arthur Field. From these platforms, he raised a powerful campaign for equal labour and protection rights for Indian workers in Britain. After an unsuccessful strike by Bombay cotton workers in 1923, Saklatvala had hoped to establish a shared consciousness between the mill workers of Britain and India, by shedding light on the shared struggles of the jute mill workers of Dundee and Bengal. He believed that 'unless there was a uniform standard of wages in the Jute Industries of Bengal and Dundee, the black worker terrorised in Bengal would deprive the Scottish worker and his children of the necessities of life.'[13] Owlishly, the campaign was muffled by E.D. Morel, the Labour Member for Dundee.

Saklatvala refused to be browbeaten. He launched another campaign, this time with Trades Union Congress workers in London, supplementing their agitation with the plight of the lascars in Britain. When the All India Trades Union Congress was founded in 1920, Saklatvala was chosen as its representative in England. Known in his party as 'Comrade Sak,' he was considered to be one of the finest and fieriest orators, whose knowledge on Indian industry and economics was second to none. At many a roadside meeting upon cold winter nights, he had breathed comfort with the fire of indignation, inflaming the spirits of his party workers. His speeches, that usually began with dry wit and moved on to black humour, ended with every fibre of his writhing like a feather on fire, in a disdain for the imperial state that 'irresistibly seemed to transmit itself to his audience.'[14] While the Communist Party saw him as its trump card, he was indispensable to the Labour whip in Parliament. His constituents swore by his rhetoric and the bravery of Indian soldiers in the Great War. From taxi drivers to charwomen, ex-army men to factory workers and Irish rebels to West African students, Saklatvala was championed by all. In 1924, he was elected to the House of Commons for the second time—the only Communist candidate in the Parliament for that term.

Labour had suddenly turned wary of Saklatvala's meteoric rise. The party's first Prime Minister, Ramsay MacDonald, arranged for weekly intelligence on Saklatvala to be wired to his office. He openly declared on the floor of the House that his Honourable Friend, the Member for Battersea North, had been ordered by Moscow to cause a split in Labour votes and the party. By the time of MacDonald's second term in office, Britain would be hit by its worst decade of unemployment. There were nearly 3 million redundant Britons in North England, Wales and Scotland, by the 1930s, which was half as lethal as the unemployment rate in Hitler's Germany. MacDonald wore hats for all seasons of the London weather. To deflect attention from the nation's plummeting economy, he reached for the hat of a conspiracy theory. It would have been to his sheer credit if a Communist plot to shatter British democracy—even a fictitious one—could somehow have been apprehended. The *London Evening Standard* was an instant ally. It published an article to sensationalise Saklatvala's Bolshevik connections, alleging that armed Communist gangs had been hiding in Battersea to assassinate a Liberal candidate. When the *Portrait of the Labour Party* was written in 1929, MacDonald was painted gloriously. 'In the slums of the manufacturing towns and in the hovels of the countryside,' Ramsay MacDonald had 'become a legendary being—the personification of all that thousands of downtrodden men and women hope and dream and desire.'[15] The Honourable Member for Battersea North, warranting an equally large portrait in that history, was heavily cornered by Labour's chicanery.

Saklatvala's grit was only hardened by MacDonald's whispering campaign. After being voted to the House, he had published a collection of his speeches titled *The Class Struggle in Parliament*, and seen it become a runaway bestseller. His eleven-point dossier on the Labour Party's policy for the colony, 'The British Labour Government and India,' was submitted to the Parliament in July 1924. Cold-shouldered by Sydney Olivier, the then Secretary of State for India (and uncle of the English actor Sir Laurence Olivier), the blueprint rotted in Whitehall. True to Labour policy in the interwar years, Lord Olivier maintained a dispassionately conservative line over matters pertaining to the administration of India. This marked the beginning of Saklatvala's split from Labour's affections, even as his girth within the Communist Party was increasing. The following year, he helped establish the Communist journal, *Sunday Worker*. He had, by now, also resigned from the post of manager of the Cotton Mills Department of the Tatas, lest his political reputation affected the investments and goodwill of the firm. Saklatvala would stir up the Parliament again by tabling an amendment to the Irish Bill, the irony being that both the Conservative and the opposition parties supported it. Farce turned into fury when Saklatvala himself voted against the amendment. Marx had once argued—and Rajani Palme Dutt often reaffirmed— that the antipathy between the English intelligentsia and the Irish working classes was 'the secret of the impotence of the English working class.'[16] Saklatvala would not have settled, at any cost, for tokenistic resolutions to the Irish question—or, indeed, the interlinked Indian question for which he had fought bitterly.

Obsessed with India in his parliamentary speeches, he was described in 1925 by the *Daily Graphic* as the 'Member for India,' instead of Battersea North.[17] Saklatvala was known for filibustering without digressing into objectionable remarks on his adversaries. Around the same time that he was re-elected to the House, Edward Turnour, the Sixth Earl of Winterton, became the Under-Secretary of State for India. Being a Tory, he found an old-world charm in Saklatvala's oratory, which he reckoned had 'a flow of what is commonly known as Babu English which greatly amuses the House.'[18] Saklatvala put it to good use while raking up issues of British militarism in Egypt, Persia, Iraq and Afghanistan and the 'constant unseen war'[19] that its imperial expansions were waging on the masses of America and Europe. Richard Chaloner, the First Baron of Gisborough, a lifelong Conservative and a Member of the House of Lords, could not but have thrown his hat into the controversy around Saklatvala's speeches. Lord Gisborough believed it was an outrage that an Indian should be allowed to hoodwink and infect the very British hand that fed him. 'Either he ought to be deported,' said the Lord, 'or if that were illegal, shut up in some room where he would be safe ... that would be a lethal chamber.'[20]

One of Gisborough's Fellow-Lords in the House was Baron Satyendra Prasanna Sinha. He had travelled to London from the small district of Birbhum in Bengal on an annual scholarship of £50. Sinha attended Lincoln's Inn much before Gandhi or Jinnah, where another annual scholarship of £100 sustained him until he became a barrister. His brother, Narendra Sinha, also accompanied him to England, where he studied medicine. In Calcutta, Barrister Sinha was appointed a Standing Counsel to the Government of India in 1903, two years before he created history by becoming the first Indian Advocate General of Bengal. Sinha was unsure whether to take up the position. His own practise was yielding in excess of £10,000 annually. Serving the government would have meant pocketing a much reduced remuneration. Jinnah stepped in as the devil's advocate, coaxing Sinha to fill in the rank. It was a decision he would not regret. By the end of the decade, in the event of the imperial legislatures for India proposed by the Morley-Minto reforms, and under the recommendation of Viceroy Lord Minto, Sinha was chosen to be the first Indian member of the Viceroy's Executive Council. His appointment came through despite the disapproval of King Edward, who was deeply pessimistic about exposing the officialdom of the Viceregal office to Indians. Minto, however, stayed true to his word and Sinha, equal to the task of loyalty, ended up resigning from the Council when Minto's tenure concluded in 1910.

The Sinha family was built upon old links with the Brahmo Samaj. Lord Sinha was arguably the most famous Brahmo in late-19th-century Calcutta, thriving on a strong network with the Tagore family. He also promoted the Church in the city and was a zealous philanthropist. No other lawyer in his age, 'was so courted by the British bureaucracy, and no other lawyer achieved so much.'[21] While keeping his long association with the British government, he also remained an active member of the Indian National Congress. He was elected as president for its Bombay session of 1915, the same year that he was knighted. Riding on the back of a brief stint in the Imperial War Cabinet, Sinha travelled to England as an assistant to Edwin Montagu in 1917. After the end of the war, he was designated to be the Under-Secretary of State for India. As legend would have it, he was offered ten minutes to withdraw his plans of returning to Bengal, and instead agree to succeed John Dickson-Poynder, the First Baron of Islington, as the Parliamentary Under-Secretary. Sinha, 'with the caution of the lawyer, was always slow to accept responsibility when it could be avoided,'[22] but he did accept it on this occasion.

Another historic first knocked on Sinha's door when the King presented him with the baronetcy of Raipur in Bengal, as he became the first Indian to sit in the House of Lords, and the third Indian then at Westminster, also joining Ameer Ali in the Privy Council. As a member of the Upper House, he had impressed upon the Viceroy, Lord Chelmsford, ample cause for increasing the electoral and political rights of Indians. The Government of India Act, which met with royal approval in December 1919, was a tremendous milestone for Sinha. In the aftermath of the Jallianwala Bagh massacre, the British government realised that its despotism had to be replaced by a gentler hand of governance in the colony. They deemed that it should fall on an Indian— expediently in the form of Sinha—to ensure that the Act survived the filibustering of other Lords in the House. While legislating for India and enjoying his status of the Freedom of the City of London, which was awarded to him after the war, Sinha gradually turned more cautious about daring the civil servants of Whitehall. He made an exit from the Congress over the hardening of its extremist elements. Saklatvala, on the other hand, was not contented with administrative rewards for himself. Not an acre short of the global elimination of imperialism would have satisfied him.

As the 'lone voice in the halls of Westminster, Saklatvala saw no contradiction between the interests of British workers and those elsewhere.'²³ When the Prince of Wales was to visit Africa and South America on a grant of £2,000 of public money, Sak shocked the Parliament once again by calling him a 'Royal nob'.²⁴ He was also the first and mostly likely the only Member of Parliament to address the Speaker as his 'comrade'. Even while he was a Member of Parliament, Saklatvala's house was raided more than once. He was also imprisoned on charge of sedition in 1926, during a General Strike at Hyde Park, while speaking to protestors who included soldiers of the British Army. After sentencing him for two months at the Wormwood Prison, Whitehall thought it best to make amends. He was offered to be made Under-Secretary of State for India, if he softened his Communist line. Sak refused to be quieted 'except by force majeure.'²⁵ For his wife Sarah, his prison sentence was a matter of pride. She celebrated it by buying a pup for their daughter Sehri.

Sak had a dangerous reputation even across the English Channel. In 1925, Frank Kellogg, the American Secretary of State, passed orders for banning him in the United States. The *New York Times* called the move an overreaction. As the American Workers' Party and the Civil Liberties Union protested, William Borah, Chairman of the American Senate's Foreign Relations Committee, spared no words of condemnation for Kellogg. *Daily Herald*, published from Chicago, contended that the real reason behind banning his entry was that his native country was 'under the domination of Britain, a domination of which the mass of the American people strongly disapprove.'²⁶ In his own estimate, Saklatvala was Indian as much as his conscience throbbed for the milling multitudes of all disenfranchised democracies, one of which was Ireland. In a letter to Gandhi, Saklatvala wrote:

> I was just walking down the main street of Dublin last night. I saw around me a new Ireland with a new Irish soul arising out of the ashes of their 1916 rebellion for independence. I can send you no better message from the Irish heart than the one that I saw in this street, carved on the Parnell monument, and once uttered by Parnell himself: 'No man has a right to fix the

boundary to the march of a nation. No man has a right to say to his country, 'Thus far thou shalt go and no further' We have never attempted to fix the ne plus ultra to the process of Ireland's nationhood, and we never shall.'[27]

Sak's persistent shaming of British foreign policy was duly reciprocated by the Foreign Office, which banned his entry into Belgium and Egypt as well. When he visited India in 1927, the alarm bells of the India Office and the Foreign Office struck again. The *Bombay Chronicle* compared the triumph of his arrival in the city to that of Gandhi's return to India in 1915. Saklatvala addressed rallies in Bombay, Delhi, Calcutta and Madras and met many Congress leaders, including Nehru and Gandhi. The Londoner was highly sceptical of Gandhi's romance with the charkha and khadi. He believed that Gandhian pastoralism had distanced the freedom struggle from the history of industrial exploitation and the birth of class struggle. Equally strong was his distaste for the honorific 'Mahatma' with which the folded hands and devoted eyes of millions greeted their Bapu. 'Be a good old Gandhi,' Sak pressed on the spinner to return to his good old London days. 'Put on an ordinary pair of *khaddar* trousers and coat and come out and work with us in the ordinary way.'[28] The spinner was not impressed. Nor was Sak, when Gandhi marched from Sabarmati to Dandi with hundreds of thousands of khadi-clad satyagrahis. He felt that Gandhi had cautiously left the Salt Police and his wealthy salt manufacturing friends out of the picture of the public sentiments that he had marched for.

Saklatvala too had wagered a great deal for the Indian freedom struggle. His house in Highgate was an unofficial London branch of the Indian national movement. Following his return from India, the Foreign Office banned his entry even into the subcontinent. In May 1928, Britain, France, United States and sixty-two other nations agreed to renounce war under the Kellogg-Briand pact. Saklatvala lambasted the sitting members of the House—many of whom were in the army or businesses that governed colonies—for the sheer hypocrisy of their being 'at war even as they signed the pact.'[29] That was to be his last major intervention in Westminster. The following year, he lost his seat to Labour candidate William Sanders. Although Despard came back to march for him, and Nehru sent a £100 donation for his election rallies, the Labour Party's slur campaign against him—including the rumour that he had abandoned his old constituency for North St Pancras—got the better of Comrade Sak. From over 50 per cent of the vote share in the previous election, his tally had dropped to below nineteen. From its daydream of Westminster being a stone's throw once again, the Communist Party was shunted out of the House of Commons. It would take six decades for the next Asian Member of Parliament to surface in Britain, as Keith Vaz—whose origins were from Goa and Aden—went in for Labour in 1987.

Saklatvala's bitter loss was aggravated by a heart attack. He retired with his family from London to Surrey, although not quite from politics. In 1930, he pulled out another stunt by contesting a by-election from Glasgow. Against the common enemy of Labour, he even resumed his old friendship with Bhownaggree. Comrade Sak came fourth, after the Labour, Conservative and Scottish Nationalist Party candidates. Four years later, with two more unsuccessful attempts for the London County Council for North Battersea and the St Pancras Borough Council, his political career had folded. He stood a dismal fourteenth at St Pancras, where he was defeated by Krishna Menon, the rising Indian star of Labour. Yet refusing to bite the dust, Saklatvala continued campaigning around Britain, and went on a lecture tour to Russia. By the time he returned to Britain, his heart had run its course.

In January 1936, a massive stroke finished the old comrade. Even on the day prior to his death, he delivered a lecture on Socialism at the Marx Memorial Library. In his obituary, Harry Pollitt, the founder of the Communist Party of Great Britain, called him the 'greatest and most sincere champion' of India.[30] Clement Attlee lavished about his 'very vivid sense of humour,'[31] while Nehru described him as the greatest Indian nationalist outside India. Comrade Saklatvala was cremated at the Golders Green Crematorium, and his remains passed on to the Brookwood

Cemetery. His elder son became a doctor and his younger went on to serve in the British Air Transport Auxiliary during the Second World War. His older daughter trained as a barrister and later as a psychologist. His youngest, Sehri, planted 120 trees in lieu of a memorial stone for her father at her birthplace in Derbyshire. She worked for the India House before joining the Greater London Council. Sehri passed away in 2017, forty years after her mother. Back in India, Baron Sinha was made the first Governor of Bihar and Orissa, and accepted the editorship of the *Bengalee*. Even as he continued to be a bencher in Lincoln's Inn and the Judicial Committee of the Privy Council, compared to the euphoria of his pre-war years, Sinha's future life was reasonably uneventful—if one ignored the frequent bouts of hypochondria in his final years. He passed away in 1928. The baronetcy continues.

Scene III

The League of a Nation

'I lived in England for twenty-eight years—the greatest part of my adult life,' wrote Vengalil Krishnan Krishna Menon in an article for *The Sunday Times* in 1963. 'London like Madras,' he added, 'is an overgrown village and homely. Though a large city, one does not get lost in London.'[1] That is exactly what happened to Menon, however. He was lost in the city, until he found a new calling. While being a law student in Madras in the 1920s, he came to be acquainted with Besant, as a radical pursuant to the Home Rule League. Besant was keen to recruit another theosophist to the cause of nationalism, and Menon was taken in as a member of her nationalist society, 'Brothers of Service,' as she began arranging for a fellowship for him to study a course in theosophy in England.

———

When Menon joined the Labour movement in Britain, he naturally came under the influence of Saklatvala's campaigns. After arriving in England in 1924, he took up a teaching assignment at St Christopher's School in Letchworth, Hertfordshire, that would fetch him an academic diploma. The following year, he joined the London School of Economics, where his early career was moulded in the Socialist ideals of Harold Laski.

Laski's long academic career would culminate in his becoming the chairman of the British Labour Party after the Second World

War. He had joined the London School of Economics in the early 1920s, as a lecturer of Political Science, while continuing as an active member of the Fabian Society. Fabian Socialism, which was, in fact, the foundational philosophy of the London School of Economics, would be the lodestar in Menon's politics as well. After a bachelor's degree in political science, Menon received an M.A. from the University College London in 1930, and an M.Sc. from the London School of Economics four years later, when he also became a barrister. Although he had left the theosophical society far behind, his association with Besant had, by no means, dwindled. As a student in Madras, he had joined Besant's Home Rule for India League, which was founded in 1916 to agitate for Indian independence on lines of the Irish Home Rule movement. After the war, it was renamed as the Commonwealth of India League.

Unable to find any extremist connections, Whitehall had no choice but to give the clean chit to the League. When Menon became its joint secretary in 1928, however, the League toughened its stand on the total independence of India versus the third-rate dominion status that the Simon Commission report would recommend. In 1929, Jiddu Krishnamurti's disbanding of the Order of the Star of the East had taken a great toll on Besant. She resigned from the League, leaving it entirely in Menon's hands. The word 'Commonwealth' was speedily dropped from the name of the organisation. What now became the India League, at 146 The Strand, garnered hundreds of new members from its thirteen branches in London, and others at Hull, Manchester, Bournemouth, Cardiff, Birmingham, Wolverhampton, Bradford, Leeds, Bristol, Liverpool and Southampton. Over that decade, the India League would set up offices in Edinburgh, Glasgow, Coventry and Wales, as well as a branch office in America, membered by Indian students, trade unionists, members of cooperative societies and many university and political elites.

Whitehall had been instructed to keep the imperial propaganda alive in defence of the report of the Simon Commission. The refrain was to be that India was not yet ready for legislative governance. Sir Michael O' Dwyer, former Lieutenant Governor of Punjab, and an avowed sympathiser of the British atrocities in Jallianwala Bagh, was called upon to consolidate the most hard line imperialists from India and Britain. In July 1930, he called for the first meeting of the India Empire Society at Caxton Hall. The Society had been rustled up as a competitor to the India League, and Winston Churchill made one of its strategic spokespersons. Well past his mid-life, Churchill was out to pulverise the Congress and its 'half-naked fakir'. That phrase would later augment Gandhi's celebrity just as Robert Greene's phrase, 'the upstart crow,' had augmented Shakespeare's. The Congress bowdlerised it heavily and made Gandhi wear it on his absent sleeves, as Churchill's original words were nearly forgotten. While delivering that speech at the West Essex Conservative Association, Churchill believed he was acting not merely in the nationalist cause, but also the cause of national decency and moral hygiene—as much as the man he was denunciating.

> It is alarming and also nauseating to see Mr Gandhi, a seditious Middle Temple lawyer, now posing as a *fakir* of a type well known in the East, striding *half-naked* up the steps of the Viceregal Palace, while he is still organising and conducting a defiant campaign of civil disobedience, to parley on equal terms, with the representative of the King-Emperor. Such a spectacle can only increase the unrest in India and the danger to which the white people there are exposed.[2]

If anyone truly wanted to set a hound upon Gandhi, it was Churchill. Condemning the Mahatma was his *cri de coeur* to safeguard the Empire and its mills of erstwhile glory. When Ramsay MacDonald tried persuading Viceroy Lord Irwin to propose an armistice to the Congress—and bring over Gandhi to London for the Second Round Table Conference—Churchill was left cornered and fuming. Quoting Irwin's failure to protect the grandeur of Great Britain, he resigned from the Tory Shadow Cabinet.

When Gandhi arrived in Britain, everyone worth making a headline wanted to meet him, except for Churchill—the man whom Adolf Hitler would refuse to meet the year after in Munich. Churchill was on the brink of becoming a nobody then, as Gandhi threatened to scorch the magnum from his future opus, *A History of the English-Speaking Peoples* (1956). From Jan Smuts to George Bernard Shaw, to the Archbishop of Canterbury and Maria Montessori—from miners to their children, and even the textile-mill workers who were now unemployed because of Gandhi's boycott of English clothes—all flocked by the fakir's side. He was still sallow from his imprisonment. After the Dandi March, the Mahatma's overlong curriculum vitae included the craft of manufacturing salt at his own sweet will. Rubbing exactly that now on Churchill's wounds were Gandhi's goat and pots and pans, which had followed him to London that winter.

Outside Buckingham Palace, after his meeting with a disgruntled King George, some journalists asked Gandhi if he believed he was suitably dressed for the weather and the occasion. He answered with cheek that the King was wearing enough for both of them. The wisecrack must have whacked the face of Churchill. Ten years ago, as a member of the Liberal Party, Churchill had written to Montagu that Gandhi deserved to be 'laid, bound hand and foot, at the gates of Delhi and then trampled on by an enormous elephant.'[3] To many commentators, the name of Gandhi, the city where he wanted the man trampled, and the animal to be deployed in the act, seemed to exhaust Churchill's knowledge of the Indian subcontinent. During Churchill's days as the prime minister, his own Secretary of State, Leo Amery, remarked that he understood India only as much as George III had understood America. What his colleagues failed to understand was that,

> Churchill loved India with a violent and unreal affection. He had gone out to India as a young subaltern with his regiment, the 4th Queen's Own Hussars, and done all the Kiplingesque things. He

had played polo on the dusty *maidans*, gone pigsticking and tiger hunting. He had climbed the Khyber Pass and fought the Pathans on the Northwest Frontier. He was, forty-one years after his departure, still sending two pounds every month of the year to the Indian who had been his bearer for two years when he was a young subaltern. His gesture revealed much of his sentiments about India. He loved it, first of all, as a reflection of his own experience there, and he loved the idea of the doughty, upright Englishman running the subcontinent with a firm, paternalistic hand.[4]

His resignation from the Shadow Cabinet, notwithstanding, Churchill was a towering smokescreen for the India Empire Society, which drew most of its other members from former governors of Indian presidencies, and most of its mandates and resolutions from the India Office. For the following years, the meetings, conferences and debates organised by the India League were a direct response to the Society's white supremacist attitude. The League rallied for issues around India's independence, civil liberties, gender equality, education and health, besides its annual celebrations of Amritsar Day and Independence Day in its drive to enlist more funding and members. Saklatvala's absence from London chalked the way for Menon to become the face of the Indian rebellion in the city, which both the British Press and Scotland Yard had accepted as the harsh realities of English life by now.

Prime Minister MacDonald had been going from bad to worse at being out of touch with the reality of Britain's poverty. To take the edge off, Labour leadership threw up Oswald Ernald Mosley as its new pantomime hero. 'We live in a period,' he told Britain with a poker face, 'in which politicians are not very popular. And believe me, you have my sympathy.'[5] He himself inspired the sympathies of none but his mistresses who shared his anachronistic fantasy for the aristocracy. 'Vote Labour, sleep Tory,' was his undying motto. Originally a Conservative member, Mosley joined the Labour Party in 1922. By the end of the decade, he was seriously planning to import Benito Mussolini's public works policies to England. With chaos in the Labour leadership, massive government cuts on wages, and many avatars of Socialist sloganeering on London's bridleways, Krishna Menon seized the hour by firming up his place in the Indian minds of the city.

Menon took to addressing gatherings of students, mill-workers and miners, church and women's groups, youth organisations and trade unions, local Labour Party groups and the Fabian Society, peace groups and the Communist Party, indeed anyone who was prepared to listen to him. Whitehall's surveillance reports on Menon in the interwar years suggested that although India was at the centre of his activities, his audiences flocked from all spheres of London. Reginald Sorensen, a Labour Member of Parliament, came to learn about the India League from an old woman distributing its leaflets, and invited Menon to address a Unitarian group that he ran. Menon cast such a spell on the small audience that it felt as if he was addressing an entire nation of people. Sorensen was instantly won over as a staunch supporter of India.

In 1931, the Gandhi–Irwin Pact, and the resolution by the British government to lift the tax on salt and release all political prisoners, was not enough to pacify the raging subcontinent. Gandhi was arrested in India within a few days of his return from England. The new Governor General, Freeman Freeman-Thomas, First Marquess of Willingdon, reinforced the suppression of the Congress movement and the freedom of press. As 80,000 people were imprisoned in India, the League unleashed its militias of protestors in London. At a meeting in its Leytonstone branch, in East London, the brutal ordinances of the British government were squarely condemned by the India League. As its chief campaigner, Menon came to be very well known electorally, as he rose to be Labour' prized candidate for the ward elections. In 1934, Menon was elected as a Labour councillor for Ward 4 of St Pancras. Even in its despair, Whitehall sighed with the relief that Menon had no acumen for Communism.

Opinions would remain divided on whether Menon was indeed not a Communist. During the years of the war, 'British intelligence was already tapping Menon's phone and reading his letters,' fearing that 'he was both a prescription drug addict and a closet Communist.'[6] The India Office credited Menon neither with the cerebral touch necessary to engage in Marxist dialectics, nor the modesty to be bribed with any intellect by those who had it. With his intimate links with the Congress high command, to many observers, Menon appeared to be a Nehru-in-the-making. Except that he had fallen short by a silver spoon and a continent! Yet, no other second-in-command could have been more faithful to the original. Nehru, who had inherited the guardianship of Indian morality from Gandhi, needed the shield of Menon's anti-Western bombast, his teetotal vegetarianism and overall austerity. The *Time* magazine, on whose cover Menon appeared in 1962, called him a 'Mephistopheles'[7] camouflaged in Savile Row suits—perhaps the only luxury that he allowed himself.

Barring an affair with author Marie Seton, officially speaking, Menon lived a bachelor's life 'that married emotional instability to political petulance.'[8] In the words of Sir Alec Clutterbuck, the British High Commissioner in an independent New Delhi, Menon was 'Nehru's evil genius,'[9] reputed with a penchant to damage India's foreign policies. As India's High Commissioner in London, Menon would also be accused of laundering funds from India's defence budget to subsidise Meridian Books. This was the publishing wing he had founded as part of the India League, which in turn had subsidised a portion of the royalties for Nehru, for his book *The Discovery of India* (1946). Being Nehru's publisher, Menon wanted him to believe that his book had sold more than it indeed had.

Both Menon and Nehru were irascible; both enjoyed dictatorial ranks in their own outfits. In 1937, Nehru parodied himself in a piece of satire written in the *Modern Review* of Calcutta, under the pseudonym Chanakya: 'Jawaharlal is certainly not a Fascist, not only by conviction but by temperament. He is far too much of an aristocrat for the crudity and vulgarity of Fascism. His very face and voice tell us that.'[10] Menon too was only some half-blood kin to the crude forms of Communism that the British adored bashing. Being rooted in constitutional methods, he was a safe adversary for the India Office. In fact, Menon was rather useful to Whitehall as a noisy repellent to budding Fascist ideologues. At the Brussels World Peace Congress, in 1936, Menon emerged as a powerful champion of colonised and oppressed peoples—not just in India, but also the Caribbean, Abyssinia and Spain—where he confronted imperialism and its hidden Fascist fineprint. Two years later, at the National Independence Demonstration, the India League aligned its struggle for freedom with the aspirations of the Chinese, Africans and the Spanish. Portraits of their leaders, alongside those of Nehru, Gandhi and Tagore, were paraded past Trafalgar Square before 3,000 spectators. Many notable black intellectuals and activists joined the League as advocates for Indian independence, including Wallace-Johnson, Jomo Kenyatta, Rudolph Dunbar and C.L.R. James. Along with the League, they denounced Fascism as the 'blood-brother' of imperialism.[11] In June that year, Menon introduced Nehru to Paul Robeson, the African American artist and activist, at a meeting of the League in Kingsway Hall, where they all condemned in unison the Fascist and Nazi risings in Italy and Germany.

———

Fascism, Nazism and Communism were born as sisters in England, if not in its European neighbourhood. At Swinbrook House in Oxfordshire, two legendary sisters, Unity and Jessica Mitford, fought through their teens against each other—one on the side of Hitler, the other, Lenin. Unity was conceived in the town of Swastika in Ontario. She was destined to deck Hitler's arms, being rumoured as well to have given birth to their lovechild in wartime Britain. In 2007, speculations ran rife about Hitler's progeny still living there.[12] Jessica, too, would remain honest to her adolescent fantasy, eloping with her second cousin, a Socialist journalist, who died fighting the Nazis in the Second World War.

By 1930, Mosley realised that the farce was slipping out of his grasp. In 1932, after several rejections by MacDonald's Cabinet to his proposals for economic reforms, he took matters into his own hand. As Mussolini was about to call for the invasion of Abyssinia,

Mosley launched the British Union of Fascists. In earnest, he wanted to give his nation a fighting chance to have a slice of German and Italian progress. Mosley approached no less than Baron Israel Sief, the Jewish industrialist—and later chairman of Marks & Spencer—to raise funds for his anti-Jewish propaganda in Britain. Despite his million detractors, the *Daily Mail* openly rose in support of Mosley and his British band of black shirts. When Sir Mosley married a second time, his wife was none other than Diana Mitford, sister of Unity and Jessica. The ceremony was conducted in October 1936 at the house of Joseph Goebbels, the Reich Propaganda Minister of Nazi Germany. Hitler was a guest of honour. The newly married couple returned to London with an autographed photograph of the Führer. In that very month, Mosley led a march of 5,000 Fascists across the East End of London, in what came to be known as the Battle of Cable Street. Expectedly, it ended in his hilarious defeat.

The India League was a shining crusader among the many groups and organisations that came ahead to restore Britain's political sanity against Fascism. It held dozens of rallies in London, from the west to the east, agitating against the rise of European ethno-nationalism. As a councillor, Menon also put a check on the movements of the British Union of Fascists, as well as putting pressure on the administration to forestall the activities of the German Nazi Party in London. Before the outbreak of the Second World War, a strong faction had broken away from the Indian National Congress. It believed in organised armed struggle and guerrilla warfare as the only means of driving the British away from India. The leader of that movement was Subhas Chandra Bose, one of the most dangerous enemies the Home Office would be forced to wrestle during the Second World War. Netaji, as he was better known, went on to lead the Indian National Army, or the Azad Hind Fauj. The army had been raised in 1942 by the exiled Indian nationalist Rash Behari Bose. Britain had for two centuries used militaries of colonised men to fight against its colonies. Now the Boses were daring to replay the gigantic scheme—battling against Britain with its own prisoners of war.

Since the dramatic rise of his popularity in the party, Netaji knew that the Congress orthodoxy was in no mood to cast off its

Anglophonic slumber. At the Haripura session of the Congress, in 1939, Subhas fell out with Gandhi and resigned from the party. Those aligned with Netaji could not possibly stomach the idea that the Congress stood in opposition to Hitler and Mussolini, who were challenging the colonisers of India. It fell on the shoulders of Menon and the League's members in London to convince the India Office, Clement Attlee, George Lansbury and Stafford Cripps, that India was predominantly united in its condemnation of Nazism and Fascism. However, the task was much steeper than Menon had expected.

In January 1938, as Bose reached London, he was welcomed by Attlee, Cripps, Lansbury and other Labour leaders. Political and constitutional experts, including Harold Laski, J.B.S. Haldane and Ivor Jennings, also came forward to brush shoulders with him. Bose's pleasant demeanour was infectious to people at large. It astonished many who had been taught to believe that he was a misled radical. Several receptions were held in his honour, while the *Manchester Guardian* praised him for his decisive attitude towards the future of India. Two months later, Hitler led the Wehrmacht into the heart of the erstwhile Austro–Hungarian Empire which had been balkanised by the Treaty of Versailles. Two years ago, when the Nazis had marched into Rhineland, the British High Command was seduced by Hitler's coquetry. Neville Chamberlain was duped into thinking that the German comrade was simply recovering his own backyard that had been confiscated from him by that ignominious treaty. Hitler believed that history would prove him right, as he was the one righting it himself. A helpless Chamberlain was left parroting the promises of the Anglo-German naval agreement as Hitler conquered Poland. Chamberlain did not survive the taste of disaster, but Churchill certainly did. As the First Lord of the Admiralty, Churchill was the face behind the phenomenally disastrous Gallipoli Campaign, by which Britain had hoped to reduce the Ottoman Empire in the First World War. When Britain's obsolete navy nosedived in the Dardanelles, the bull dog lost as much of his reputation as Hitler would soon, when Friedrich Ebert, the first German president, put his signature on the Treaty of Versailles. A fellow painter and oratorical genius, Churchill understood and even admired Hitler, being well aware of what monstrosities he was capable of.

Churchill too had an admirer in Bose, who understood what monstrosities he too was capable of. Bose had been educated in England in the years following the Treaty of Versailles. He took his matriculation degree from Fitzwilliam College in Cambridge in 1921. He moved to London to stand for the Indian Civil Services. As if it was not impressive enough that he came fourth in that examination, Bose turned himself into the stuff of legends by testing his own interviewers. London had schooled Gandhi in the dangerous heroism of humility, and Jinnah in making a virtue out of vanity. Thirty years later, it taught Bose the weight of his nation's blood. He preferred war over being undressed in shame. If any Londoner truly influenced him, inadvertently, it was Sir Winston. Like Churchill, Bose was a conservative among radicals and a radical among conservatives. When the Luftwaffe aircrafts roared across twenty miles of the London skyscape during the Blitz, Churchill pleaded with his countrymen that he could not offer them much beyond blood, toil, tears and sweat. At the climax of the War of Liberation that Bose masterminded, two years later, he would resurrect Churchill's metaphor before the Indian National Army in Rangoon. While Netaji's troops went into war against Churchill's army, he reminded his countrymen that blood alone could offer 'the price of freedom. Give me blood and I shall give you freedom!'[13] Like Churchill, he was prepared to die with a sabre in hand, than live in coerced peace.

In London, young Subhas had turned down the employment of an alien nation. The best way to terminate a government, he argued, was to withdraw from it. As an explanation to his family and friends, he cited the precedent of Aurobindo Ghose, the nationalist-turned-mystic who was educated at Cambridge in the 1880s. Ghose was an English idealist in his soul, as much as Rudyard Kipling was an Indian loyalist in his mind. In the spring of his Anglophilia, Ghose was a regular at the Liberal Club in South Kensington, not far from his residence at Stephen's Avenue in Shepherd's Bush. The secretary of the Club, Sir Henry John Cotton, was a friend of Aurobindo's father, Krishna Dhun Ghose, an attaché in the Bengal Civil Services. After ranking eleventh in the Civil Services examination, a strange conversion came over Aurobindo. He was bent upon disqualifying himself from the post. He executed that feat by deliberately failing his horse-riding test. In India, Ghose was charged over a conspiracy to kill the Calcutta Magistrate in the months of the political turmoil that followed the Partition of Bengal in 1905. During his term at the Alipore Jail, Aurobindo claimed to have been visited by the spirit of Swami Vivekananda, and here his spiritual journey began.

Bose, who was a keen admirer of Sri Aurobindo, also underwent a conversion in England. He attended lectures at the London School of Economics, where he came in contact with Fabian Socialists. They inspired him, just as they had many an Indian before and after him. It was staggering how much the imperial city contributed to the political upbringing of British Empire's enemy number one. Bose's interpretations of Socialism were rather at odds with the statutory visions of Nehru or Menon. In 1935, the London-based publisher Lawrence and Wishart brought out the first of his two-part history of the freedom movement, *The Indian Struggle*. Under orders from Whitehall, the book was banned in India. It was with this book that Bose's Socialism seemed to take a distinctly rightward turn. While Bose was exiled in Europe, his book spoke for his person in secret circles in India. His high regard for Nazism and Fascism 'weighed little against him, and the onset of his ideas encountered a Congress for a time too unsure of itself to answer.'[14] Towards Gandhi, to whom 'the entire intellect of the Congress' had been mortgaged,[15] Bose became increasingly irreverent. During the war, with the German offensive at its climax, Bose was tearing down the glory of the good old metropolis.

> During the last few months, the British Empire has been passing through its darkest hours. Gone are the days when London was the metropolis of the world. Gone are the days when kings and statesmen had to wend their way to London in order to have their

problem solved. Gone are the days when the American President had to come to Europe to meet the British Prime Minister ... the British Prime Minister has now to run to New York and Washington, and Americans in Britain are declared to be outside the jurisdiction of British laws. Thus, Britain and her Empire are fast becoming a colony of Roosevelt's 'New Empire.'[16]

Netaji's meetings with Mussolini and Hitler had convinced him that India's salvation stood near the address of an Axis victory. Hitler, however, stuck to being an old guard to the Munich Agreement of 1938, which he had signed with Chamberlain. He was determined to stay clear of any intervention in matters of the British Empire. In doing so, Hitler made the Allies labour under the impression that he desired to conquer all of Europe and much of Russia, but not the blessed shores of Britain. The primordial Nazi distrust of Indians did not prevent Bose from seeking the Führer's munitions to wage India's war against the British. If not anything else, it gave him a remarkable publicity coup with which to ruffle the India Office. As a Faustian accord, Bose chose the enemy's enemy over a long-drawn winter of the passive resistance that Gandhi's nonviolence had been being reduced to. Worse still, he feared that the Communists of India were turning against their own nation. Many of his ideas were crystallised in an interview he gave to Rajani Palme Dutt during his visit to London, which was later published in *Daily Workers*. Reflecting on Karl Marx, the *Communist Manifesto*, Vladimir Lenin and the Communist International, Bose believed that all of these single-mindedly pointed towards India's struggle for national self-determination.

In short, Bose wanted a union between Communism and National Socialism. He idolised the Gestapo (the German Secret Police) and German civil obedience. It was a futurism too complex for the Congress to sympathise with; too inevitable for Bose to overlook. He had the blueprints ready for the new institutions of independent India—the police force, the postal system and communications, industrial policy and factories—enough to capture the imagination of the German public if not the government itself. In 1942, it was widely reckoned that after invading Russia, the Nazi army would head straight for India. Bose's Indian National Army had become a substantial threat to the Allies. Before the yuletide of 1941, Japan had sent its blood-curdling missive to America at Pearl Harbour—an attack that catapulted both nations into the war. Two years later, with the aid of the Japanese army, Bose began planning a long march to India through the Eastern frontier, via Burma and Kohima. He was confident that the approach of the Azad Hind Fauj near the borders of Bengal would trigger an armed civilian uprising in Calcutta.

About two decades ago, when Bose was still at Cambridge, a letter dated September 23, 1920 arrived at Professor Herbert Foxwell's office at the London School of Economics. It was written by Edwin R. Seligman, an economist from Columbia University, introducing an exceedingly talented scholar—Mr Bhimrao Ramji Ambedkar. Two months later, Foxwell wrote to the secretary of the School that there was no more intellect that the Columbia graduate could conquer in London. The first Dalit to study at Bombay's Elphinstone College, Ambedkar, was awarded a Baroda State Scholarship that took him to Columbia University in 1913. Three years later, he found his way to London, desirous of becoming a barrister as well as finishing a doctoral dissertation on the history of the rupee. Ambedkar enrolled at Gray's Inn, and attended courses on geography, political ideas, social evolution and social theory at London School of Economics, at a course fee of £10.10s.

In 1917, Ambedkar was invited to join as Military Secretary in Baroda, earning at the same time a leave of absence of up to four years from the London School of Economics. Back in India, he taught for a while as a professor in Sydenham College in Bombay, while also being one of the key intelligencers on the condition of 'untouchables' in India for the government, during the drafting of the Government of India Act of 1919. In late 1920, Ambedkar was to return to London, determined more than ever before, not to spare a farthing beyond his breathing means on the city's allurements. Each day, the aspiring barrister woke up at the stroke of six. After a morning's morsel, he moseyed into the crowd of London to find his way into the British Museum. At dusk, he would leave his seat reluctantly—after being scurried out by the librarian and the guards—his pockets slogging under the notes that would finally become his thesis, *The Problem of the Rupee*, some of whose guineas would eventually find their home in the Constitution of India that he was going to author about three decades later. Back at his lodging at King Henry's Road in Primrose Hill, mostly on foot, Ambedkar would live on sparsely whitened tea and poppadum late into the night.

It was here that the daughter of Ambedkar's landlady, Fanny Fitzgerald, a war widow, found her affections strangely swayed by the Indian scholar. Fitzgerald was a typist at the House of Commons. She lent him money in difficult circumstances and volunteered to introduce him to people in governance, with whom he could discuss the Dalit question that was raging in India. An apocryphal story goes that Miss Fitzgerald once gave Ambedkar a copy of the Bible. On receiving it, the future Father of the Indian Constitution promised to dedicate a bible to her of his own authoring. True to his commitment, he would fondly dedicate his book *What Congress and Gandhi Have Done to the Untouchables* (1945) to 'F'. The incident, when that promise was exchanged, occurred after Ambedkar was called to the Bar in 1923. In March that year, his doctoral thesis ran into trouble possibly because of its radical approach to the history of Indian economy under the British administration. He might have taken the subtle hint that passages in his work needed tempering—a notion that a man of his vision was likely to have quietly pocketed more as a compliment than an insult. Ambedkar would have been happy to chisel the nose from his David for the show, like Michelangelo had four centuries ago in order to appease the connoisseur-like pretense of Piero Soderini, who had quipped, 'Isn't the nose a little too thick?' That done, Ambedkar resubmitted his thesis in August. It was approved two months later and published almost immediately thereafter. He expressed gratitude to his professor, Edwin Cannan, who, in turn, wrote the preface to his thesis, before Ambedkar travelled to Bonn for further studies.

Babasaheb, as he was now beginning to be called, was to return to London for each of the three Round Table Conferences held between 1930 and 1932. Two months before the Third Round Table Conference—in which both Labour and the Congress were absentees—Ambedkar and Gandhi reached a historic settlement in the Poona Pact. In September 1932, from the Yerwada prison near Bombay, Gandhi began a fast unto death protesting against the Ramsay MacDonald administration that was determined to divide India into provincial electorates on the basis of caste and social stratification. In the pact signed with Madan Mohan Malviya, Ambedkar settled for 147 seats for the depressed classes. But the pact to which he was forsworn—tacitly made in London with Fanny Fitzgerald—that of writing the bible of modern India, was brewing like a storm that would take the form of an open battle between him and Gandhi, in the years of the Second World War.

Despite the strong network of Indians at the London School of Economics, Ambedkar chose not to hobnob with India League members. What might have been a sort of marriage-made-in-heaven between him and Menon was forestalled. If Menon was Nehru's alter ego, he would also be instrumental in shaping the early career of the man to become an alter ego—principal secretary—to Indira Gandhi. In the winter of 1935, a twenty-something Parmeshwar Narain Haksar arrived in London, enrolled as a student at the University College. The following year, he made an unsuccessful attempt for the civil services. In 1937, Haksar became a Fellow of the Royal Anthropological Institute, a distinction conferred on him with support from noted anthropologist Bronislaw Malinowski. Although Haksar also studied at the London School of Economics, it probably never became public knowledge if he had acquired formal degrees from either university. Whether or not he did, as a scholar he commanded great attention from British intellectuals, especially in his arguments on the crisis of education in India, which he reckoned had been tailored to perpetuate British imperial interests and low levels of literacy in the colony.

Haksar was to be called to Bar at the Lincoln's Inn, but, at the beckoning of Nehru, he would join Indian Foreign Service in 1948. His red days in London were to yield him lifelong companions. In the 1930s, the Comintern came up with the policy of hatching popular fronts all across Europe with which to counter the growing threat of Nazism and Fascism. It was a phase in European ideologies that strongly affected British politics, and popular movements led by Labour leaders and student communists in London—a cosmopolitan and unswervingly left-leaning outlook that shaped much of the administration and policies of independent India until the years of the Emergency. A socialist himself, Haksar held an influential position in the Federation of Indian Societies in UK and Ireland besides becoming the editor of its magazine, *The Indian Student*. His links with the Communist Party of Great Britain, Rajani Palme Dutt and the Soviet undercover agent at Cambridge, James Klugman— indeed with almost anyone of some consequence who supported the cause of Indian liberation—was more than enough for Scotland Yard to keep him closely watched in London.

In September 1941, when the India League organised a commemoration at the Conway Hall in Red Lion Square for the late Rabindranath Tagore, a few months after his demise, Scotland Yard obliged by adding a leaf to their surveillance files. Inaugurated by M. Maisky, a Russian ambassador, it was just one in a sea of events concerning India that the Yard and other intelligencers of His Majesty's Government would tolerate during the interwar years. Almost all such gatherings featured subversive pamphlets and books published by the League and similar organisations that were openly lauded by Soviets and Soviet sympathisers. It was just as well that Nehru also had to tolerate that under the shield of Haksar's own watch a new romantic plot thickened around Primrose Hill, that of his daughter Indira and future son-in-law, Feroze. Feroze had his flat at Abbey Road and Haksar lived half a mile away, at Abercorn Place. Haksar was befriended by the Gandhis—Indira and Feroze—who introduced him to Sasadhar Sinha of the Bibliophile Bookshop. That, besides the India League and Allahabad connection, not to mention Haksar's enviable culinary skills, ensured that he was soldered to the future of the Gandhis.

The future of the man who had leant the family his coveted surname would also take a blow on the burning issue of caste. Gandhi was not to be remembered as the sole nemesis of the British Empire. In an interview given to the BBC in 1955, Babasaheb indicated that one of the biggest reasons behind Clement Attlee handing over the reins of the Indian administration so suddenly was the persistent fear of a massive armed uprising in the colony. He implied that the road to independence had already been paved by the Azad Hind Fauj brigadiered by Netaji. Bose had departed from London during Ambedkar's days in the London School of Economics. But, he would return in Haksar's time.

In the early winter of 1938, Menon was hardly surprised when Bose made no attempt to meet him. Betrayed by the Congress, Bose was convinced that the party would in turn be betrayed by the British government. Menon believed otherwise. Not only was the latter a fierce opponent of armed resistance, but also devoutly constitutional. He was also, by now, a bona fide citizen of Britain. As a councillor for fourteen years, Menon had worked tirelessly for slum dwellers at King's Cross, serving in all major committees of his ward, including Baths and Cemeteries, Sewers and Public Works and Highways. He had served as chairman of the Education and Public Library Committee, in which capacity he campaigned to make libraries as numerous in the borough as there were pubs. He took to organising exhibitions, concerts, conferences, gramophone records, a travelling library and much else to popularise reading and literature. The St Pancras Arts and Civic Council founded in 1944, with Menon at its helm, introduced the St Pancras Arts Festival—the precursor to the Camden Arts Festival.

Menon was also the political mentor to Nehru's daughter, Indira Gandhi, while she was a student in Somerville College at Oxford. Putting together his political clout and university ties, he persuaded some of the finest minds and influencers of the era to join the India League. Bertrand Russel was its chairman and J.F. Horrabin, one of its vice-chairmen. In 1934, as part of the report prepared by an official delegation sent to India, Russell famously quipped: 'so long as the British insist upon governing India, they have no right to ignore what is done in their name by the Government which they have elected.'[17]

Other leading Londoners associated with the League included Fred Longden, Saeed Mohamedi, H.N. Brailsford, A.A. Purcell, Dorothy Woodman, Harold and Frieda Laski, Reginald Bridgeman, Rajani Palme Dutt, Sir Stafford Cripps, Sybil Thorndike and J.B.S. Haldane. As many as forty Labour Members of Parliament were suspected of maintaining strong links with the League. Among them, Reginald Sorensen, William Dobbie and Alex Sloan were cronies to the cause of Indian independence. Rajani Palme Dutt, now a veteran member of the Communist Party, had been mentoring Indian communists in interwar Britain. His disciples included Jyoti Basu, who went on to become the Chief Minister of West Bengal, staying in power for a record of five terms in the state assembly. Inspired by the legacy of Menon, Basu attended lectures of Harold Laski at the London School of Economics, and played an active role in student politics, until he was called to the Bar at the Middle Temple in 1939.

Throughout the 1930s, from The Strand, Menon had stoked the bonfire of the ledgers of India's slavery under British rule. The League's publications, *Indian News* and *Information Bulletin*, became vehicles of countering fake news, while his columns in *Manchester Guardian* and the *New Statesman* grew shriller by the day. The latter was founded in 1913 by Sidney and Beatrice Webb, with the backing of George Bernard Shaw and his Fabian circle. As Menon milked that Socialist legacy, he also kept the Intelligence Branch hot in his pursuit, by squeezing out every last drop of horror tales from his secret Indian sources. He reported that while there was one nurse for less than 450 people in Britain, in India the ratio was 1:86,000. If Britain had a doctor for every 800 people, India had one for every

9,000. And after 150 years of colonial rule, the mortality rate in India had fallen to a ghastly 23 years and 6 months.

All this and much more is what Menon unearthed and charted up as part of the economic research of the League. Except the Leader of the Opposition, George Lansbury, almost every other Labour member had their correspondences intercepted by the Bureau, only to ensure that Menon was not a beneficiary of any news from them. He had grown into a sultan of statistics, 'in such a way as to make them stand up and raise their arms in social protest.'[18] He also drew support from *The Daily Worker*—the Communist Party's newspaper with a circulation of over 40,000—that worked as a propagandist for the League. Although Menon and the Communist Party parted ways following the Nazi invasion of Russia, the newspaper continued to publish news of human rights violations in India, if not directly on the League's activities. At the same time, Menon was also reporting from London for quite a few Indian newspapers, including the *National Herald*, published from Lucknow.

In 1934, Allen Lane, while returning from a visit to Agatha Christie, stopped at a railway platform in Exeter. Lane was a publisher at Bodley Head, and unable to find anything worth reading at the station, he conceived the plan for the Penguin Company, formerly meant as an incubator of affordable paperbacks of literary classics. Three years later, along with Menon, he co-founded the Pelican book series for Penguin, meant for the more academic and intellectual titles of the time, beginning with George Bernard Shaw's *The Intelligent Woman's Guide to Socialism, Capitalism, Sovietism and Fascism*. Menon conscientiously ploughed back his earnings from publishing and writing into the work of the League. By the 1940s, it ran into severe scarcity of funds, affecting its publications. Jai Kishore Handoo, a League member, put up a subscription plan for the League's journals, targeting well-to-do Indian doctors and businessmen in Britain and India. Fallen on hard times, the League had to compete even with Indian organisations in London.

First was Saklatvala's New Indian Political Group, which folded after a brief run in the 1930s. Since the 1890s, the Cambridge

Majlis and the Oxford Majlis had been the greenhouses for preparing university graduates for political debates on issues of electoral equality, democracy and fighting British imperialism. In its initial days, the Cambridge Majlis held its sessions at the house of Rajani Palme Dutt's father, Upendra Kishore Dutt, an Indian doctor who had come to study at the University of London on a Gilchrist Scholarship back in 1875. Among those who became involved in the Oxbridge Majlis circles, either as student members or visiting lecturers, were Jawaharlal Nehru, Aurobindo Ghose, Gopal Krishna Gokhale, C.F. Andrews, E.M. Forster, M.K. Gandhi, Mohammed Ali Jinnah, Subhas Chandra Bose, Shapurji Saklatvala, Govinda Krishna Chettur, Indira Gandhi, Mohammad Habib, Humayun Kabir, Basanta Kumar Mallik, K.P.S. Menon, Frank Moraes, Huseyn Shaheed Suhrawardy, Laurence Binyon, Ernest B. Havell, Sarojini Naidu, Rabindranath Tagore, Lala Lajpat Rai, K. L. Gauba, Fazl-i-Husain, Mohan Kumaramangalam, Mirza Abol Hassan Ispahani, Rajni Patel and Shankar Dayal Sharma. Around 1935, the legacy of the Majlis led to the formation of the London Majlis, largely engineered by the Communist Party. Jyoti Basu, who became a member in 1936, was elected as its general secretary the following year. Along with Rajani Palme Dutt and other Communists, he helped create the Federation of Indian Students' Organisations, and set up its journal, *Indian Students and Socialism*.

The Majlis and the Federation went hand in glove, running missions for lascar communities in London and around, and fomenting the fires of labour unrest. With the clarion call of 'Quit India', in 1942, several other Indian organisations sprang up in London, beginning with the Committee of Indian Congressmen, founded by Amiya Bose, a nephew of Subhas Chandra Bose. The Friends of India Society was started by A.S. Kamlani. Suresh Vaidya, a member of the Committee of Indian Congressmen and a London-based correspondent for the American magazine, *Time and Life*, broke away to launch Swaraj House. Unlike the League, it enlisted only Indian members. Swaraj House was merged into the more powerful Indian Workers' Association, or the Hindustani

Mazdur Sabha, to form the Federation of Indian Associations in Great Britain. The Workers' Association had become very prominent during the Second World War, with its bimonthly bulletin, the *Indian Worker*, a mouthpiece for seamen, factory workers and students. The Association was founded in Coventry in 1937, predominantly with members from Sikh labourers. Some of them had been sympathisers or old hands of the Ghadar Party that had been aggressively training rebels in America and Canada for the Indian freedom struggle. The first members of the Association were Charan Singh Chima, Thakur Singh Basra, Ujjagar Singh and Kartar Singh Nagra. Their objectives were to disseminate the message of the Ghadar Party and drive subscriptions for *Desh Bhagat Parwarik Sahaik Committee*, a magazine published from Amritsar to aid Punjabi nationalists and their families. Beginning with Bradford and Birmingham, where the Sikh and Muslim populations were strong, the Association's membership spread across Manchester, Wolverhampton, Newcastle, Liverpool and finally to London during the war.

In the autumn of 1941, even as France fell to German occupation, British atrocities in India continued unabated. The India League launched a massive campaign in London to protest against the imprisonment of Nehru and other Congressmen. During Nehru's visit to London, in 1938, he was accompanied by Bhicoo Batlivala, his personal assistant, who later became an important member of the League. At her suggestion, H.G. Wells was also roped into the League. His exchanges with the Secretary of State, Leo Amery, on the Indian question, intensified the London chapter of the Congress. By 1942, the India Office was torn between supporting Lord Linlithgow's claims of India being a lawless state and appealing to the Congress to join the Allies in the war. Britain needed India desperately, as Singapore and Burma fell to the Japanese in February, and British prisoners of war captured by the Axis powers were handed over to the Azad Hind Fauj.

As the threat of an Eastern invasion of India grimly approached reality, Stafford Cripps, the then Leader of the House, was sent to India to convince the Congress to stand by Britain. Amery was prepared to show his fairer hand while secretly abiding by what Churchill had told him; that 'he would sooner give up political life at once, or rather go out into the wilderness and fight, than to admit a revolution which meant the end of the Imperial Crown in India.'[19] Unbeknownst to the Congress, Cripps had been instructed to keep alive Hindu-Muslim conflict, which had acted as the bulwark of the Empire for over a century. For all Nehru knew, the delegation might have done better to discuss dying animals in circuses. The Congress was in no mood to sign on Cripps' 'post-dated cheque drawn on a failing bank,' as Gandhi described that mission.[20] The Muslim League, however, found it deeply enriching; so did the Hindu Mahasabha. Strangely united by the attempted treachery, Jinnah and Savarkar had scented the flesh and blood to their demand for independent theocracies. To champions of the Partition it must have brought an odd sense of relief, as amidst reports of his death and an avalanche of speculations about his resurgence, Subhas Chandra Bose vanished like a broken meteor somewhere in Japan or Russia or Europe or beyond—or somewhere very much in India, as some continued to hope.

In March 1906, a platoon of German uniformed soldiers had goose-stepped past Oxford Street, drilling terror in the heart of Londoners. It was not the real invasion that had haunted London throughout that decade but, in fact, a publicity campaign by the *Daily Mail* for a war novel it was about to serialise. Ten years from the Treaty of Versailles, a similar sight—this time far from being a media stunt—would be enacted near the Victoria Terminus in Bombay. The Nazis had carved in India a discreet headlock by the Arabian Sea. Their creed of Aryan supremacy was in elegant harmony with Savarkar's own two-nation-theory. From his exile in Andaman, and later in his solitary confinement near Bombay, Savarkar had paid intense scrutiny to the communally polarised political landscape. The Germans, who had heard of the legends from his London days, now wanted to exploit his old resentment that had been exacerbated by British prisons.

In the 1930s, motor cars with Nazi flags smarted across south Bombay, as secret meetings of German spies unfolded on private ships in the Bombay harbour. Where it came to ethnic Socialism, the Germans knew that Savarkar was cast in the Führer's own mould. Even during the outbreak of the Second World War, the Berlin Radio was broadcasting lectures on India and musicals on the Taj Mahal. The Nazi influence on India was more of an intellectual distraction than political derangement. Three years into the war, as the strength of the Gestapo and the Luftwaffe was approaching a decline, Gandhi struck a fatal blow to Whitehall with his call for the Quit India Movement. Having been winded in the Blitz, the India Office dreaded parting with the last days of the Raj. Nearby, at the Strand, Menon went on cluttering breaking news from the subcontinent. Reports of the Bengal Famine of 1943, that killed 3 million, as Churchill rerouted their staple to feed English soldiers in Australia, were followed by those of Royal Air Force aircrafts machine-gunning crowds of protestors in India. One frustrated civil servant at the India Office exclaimed: 'It's time Menon was machine-gunned!'[21]

Someone had indeed been gunned down. While Hitler's panzers were crossing the Maginot Line into France, Udham Singh—an old Ghadar activist—shot dead Michael O'Dwyer at an East India Association meeting in Caxton Hall, on March 13, 1940. O'Dwyer had been the governor of Amritsar during the Jallianwalla Bagh massacre. Singh had successfully pulled off a reprise of Madanlal Dhingra's assassination of Curzon Wyllie back in 1909. Udham Singh was sent to the gallows three months later. That did little to quell the tensions that were mounting for Whitehall across the Atlantic. That year, Batlivala, Menon's associate at the League, left for America on a six-month academic tour. Menon had planted her as a secret envoi to induce President Franklin D. Roosevelt to recognise India as a free nation. Just as Archibald Wavell, the new Viceroy of India, was about to be sworn in, Menon's ploy foreshadowed a new predicament for Churchill and the India Office. Although it could not officially ban the activities of the India League, or its publication, *News India*, it compelled the Paper Control authority to restrict its paper supply so as to reduce its circulation. Whitehall also deputed Sir Alfred Watson, the editor of the journal, *Great Britain and the East*, to write a scurrilous report against the fanaticism and seditiousness of the League, which was then circulated to about 850 publications across Britain. Inside the British Parliament, Labour was whipped to take charge over Sorensen and Menon.

Whitehall foregrounded to its national frontiers Lord Amery's book, *India and Freedom* (1942), and other concocted versions of the success of the Cripps' Mission, as prescribed literature on the political situation in India. It also subsidised several unofficial bodies to counter the League's propaganda, one of them being the India-Burma Association. Ironically, it was reinforced by none other than Cornelia Sorabji, who had been spotted by Amery's men as a forthright opponent to Menon. All that Whitehall wanted to broadcast to the London proletariat was how divided India was between its communities, castes, languages and even genders— indeed how hopelessly undeserving of freedom. As part of public lectures and panels underhandedly organised by the India Office, Menon was brought on the same platform against the likes of the Imam of the Woking Mosque or Barrister Yusuf Ali. The latter were manipulated to paint a picture of the oppressed Muslim minorities of India in the face of the trenchant rhetoric of unity being voiced by the Congress. Sir Hassan Suhrawardy, former Chairman of the East London Mosque, was also called upon to nominate Muslim intellectuals to spark divisions on communal lines. As Churchill's men oversaw the conspiracies to disunite India, little did he know of the disunity of the British electorate that was itself conspiring to strike him down with a feather.

In the late winter of 1944, the Labour Party passed a resolution stating that the freedom of India was absolutely central to the war against Fascism. Tabled by Labour leader, C.W. Bridges, the resolution was seconded by Sukhsagar Datta, an Indian Labour member from Bristol. Datta's days in London dated back to the time of the student revolution and the assassination of Curzon Wyllie. He had been a resident of India House and a close associate of Savarkar. After India House came down, the two moved to a flat in Red Lion Passage. Following a brief stint in Morocco, fighting a battle of resistance against the Spanish army, Datta returned to London in 1911. His association with Savarkar ended after the latter was deported to Andaman. Datta went on to take a degree in medicine, from the Bristol University Medical School, in 1920. Six years later, he joined the Labour Party, rising to become its chairman in the Bristol North division just after the war. In his later life, he would administer the revival of the Bristol Indian Association that had been founded in the memory of Raja Rammohun Roy.

Hitler's defeat in the war was followed by the unforeseen collapse of the Tory citadel in the House of Commons. Led by Attlee, who was Britain's second-in-command through the war as the nation's first ever deputy prime minister, Labour members were themselves taken aback by the rout they had effected. Churchill had once described Attlee to President Harry Truman as a modest man with much to be modest about. Now reduced to being an overridden monarch in his antiquated empire, Sir Winston had little to fall back on but the echoes of his own speech, 'if necessary alone ... we shall fight on the beaches.' In the minds of the British voters, two toxic decades of unemployment, homelessness, poverty and starvation appeared to have battered London more than the Blitz. The man who had led Britain through the war with his speeches and his impassioned letters to President Roosevelt—like a lover beseeching his mistress—was now woefully short of words and friends. In the summer of 1942, before the echoes of the Quit India Movement began buzzing outside 10 Downing Street, Roosevelt had written a cautionary note to Churchill.

> The feeling is almost universally held that the deadlock has been caused by the unwillingness of the British Government to concede to the Indians the right of self-government, notwithstanding the willingness of the Indians to entrust technical, military and naval defence control to the competent British authorities. American public opinion cannot understand why, if the British Government is willing to permit the component parts of India

to secede from the British Empire after the war, it is not willing to permit them to enjoy what is tantamount to self-government during the war.[22]

Menon's dossier had crawled to the President of America. During the war, Churchill may have threatened to resign over the crisis of the Indian Empire. There was no need for it after the war. Joseph Stalin, 'the great Russian bear,' as he was known to Churchill,[23] had predicted an 80 per cent majority for the Tories in the general election of 1945. Instead, after returning from the Potsdam Conference held outside a devastated Berlin, Churchill was treated to booing at his rallies, with vigorous chants of 'Attlee', and a sharp swing of the constituencies towards the left, beginning from London. Not just India, even Churchill now seemed better out of the British Empire than within. His biggest arch nemesis after Hitler—Gandhi—had fasted himself to abysmal health and reputation. Both their parties secretly hoped for them to saddle up. After defending its little island, it was time for Britain to liberate its colossal South Asian peninsula. As Churchill left the scene of the Empire's nightfall with forebodings of the Cold War, Gandhi resignedly moved into the sunsets of Noakhali in the deep interiors of Bengal, where the ceaseless blood of the crown's lost jewel begged for a moment's rest to clot. After the inevitable sunset, the Partition's genocide blotted the stars.

Scene IV

Between the Ink and the Deep Sea

Mulk Raj Anand, an Indian writer in interwar London, had quietly observed the developments of the India League since the late 1920s. He had also broken bread with the theosophists after being introduced to the society by Mary Lutyens. The India League's future chairman and the face of modern British philosophy, Betrand Russell, was the subject of his dissertation for which he received a doctorate in philosophy in 1929. Having been in the city as long as Menon, initially as a scholar in the University College London, Anand had struck an affinity with the Bloomsbury circle of writers led by Virginia and Leonard Woolf, and the poet whose fame for the post-war saga of *The Waste Land* preceded his name— Thomas Stearns Eliot. The latter ran the *Criterion* magazine, while the Woolfs managed Hogarth Press. Both had ushered the high-tide of modernism in Britain. Both patronised Anand at one point or another.

———

Anand's rendezvous with London's literary pundits often revolved around gastronomic digressions from literature. In fact, these digressions themselves became Anand's preliminary career. Besides writing on the arts, he was also a food writer for a while. Anand first met T.S. Eliot in the company of the author, Bonamy Dobrée, who, being French, had much more distinction in the eyes of

Anand, whether on account of his Savile Row suits, or his beard that imitated King George V, or simply that he was not English. The two had met courtesy of Anand's friend and fellow poet, Nikhil Sen, at Harold Monro's bookshop on Great Russel Street. Dobrée had, as Anand later recounted, 'demolished my sense of inferiority by suggesting, "Why don't you both come and have a drink with me in the Museum Tavern."' The Bloomsbury intellectuals used to dine together frequently. Dobrée was their culinary connoisseur. On his first meeting with Eliot, Anand was far from being overwhelmed in his presence. He would recall Dobrée's words that he had read somewhere: 'how unpleasant to meet Mr Eliot.'[1] In fact, he was more impressed by the restaurant itself, which was not an unlikely infatuation for an Asian in post-war London.

> I had often gone past this select place which had a few tables outside on the pavement, and menu cards written and framed in silver. On occasions, while on my way to cheap Italian restaurants on the same street, I would get a glimpse of the inner sanctum, with its elegant interiors and rich diners, through the half-opened door. It had never occurred to me that one day I would partake of the luxury of French cuisine in this exalted place.[2]

Anand's luncheon outshone Eliot's pearl pin and check necktie, not to mention the otiose conversations about the London weather, which had almost made the young Indian 'ask why Londoners continually talked about the weather.'[3] The lunch had dragged on over soup, fish, goulash, wine and conversations upon Gandhi, Rainer Maria Rilke, Kipling, the Buddha, *kaliyuga* and doomsday. Past dessert, Eliot asked Anand to telephone his secretary at the office of the *Criterion*. Notwithstanding his enviable rapport with some of the greatest authors of that age, Anand himself was not much of a success as yet. The turning point in his literary career came in 1934 when, one night while walking around Mayfair, he entered a bookshop and chanced on a copy of *World's Great Short Stories*, published by the Odhams Press. The first story in the collection was his own, 'The Lost Child,' which had been first published in another collection five years ago. Soon, London's critics started taking note of Anand. Over the next decade, he published his first nine novels, including his masterpieces, *Untouchable* and *Coolie*. By the time he would return to the colony, in 1946, he was the most well-known contemporary Indian author. That would not have been possible without an extraordinary contribution that he made to Indian literature—and, indeed, to the Indian legacy in the city—one that also began in a restaurant in central London.

In 1931, Sajjad Zaheer, then a young student at Oxford, returned to India for six months. He joined a band of insubordinate subjects of the Empire, that included Rasheed Jahan and Ahmad Ali. In 1932, he published *Angaray* (*Embers*), a belligerent anthology of short stories. It was a scathing account of orthodox Muslims within the framework of British colonial rule. Infuriated Islamic clerics issued fatwas on the authors. The book was banned in the United Provinces, Zaheer's own birthplace. Two years into the controversy, Zaheer and his blood-brethren set up the League of Progressive Authors. In a few years, as Fascism began combing the streets of London night and day, Zaheer, now a much mellowed version of his youth, would pen down one of the most endearing odes to the metropolis to be ever written in Urdu. Published in 1938, *London ki ek Raat* (*A Night in London*) was a doughty experiment in modernist writing, in many ways moulded by one of the lodestars of the movement—Virginia Woolf's *Mrs Dalloway* (1925). Woolf's mantra was alluring. Walking in London— those everlastingly lit up streets that no darkness could ever have assailed—was remarkably better than walking in the country. A compliant semi-Londoner, Zaheer's protagonist moseyed past Tottenham Court Road, seeing its vivacious supermarkets, theatres and ballrooms intervalled by a pesky form—copies of the *Socialist Worker* peeping out of the rows of newspapers at wayside stalls. On careful inspection, one spotted the headline, 'A Glorious Procession of Hungry Workers.'[4]

Anand too had struggled to reconcile social quandaries with modernist prose. Like his idol Gandhi, he was a man of action, if not

as abstemious in his diet. One foggy Autumn night in the London of
1935 would later be recounted by Anand as the hour of emergence
of the exiled writers of India. The All India Progressive Writer's
Association was carved out 'from the slough of despondency of the
cafés and garrets of Bloomsbury.'⁵ A surreptitious ceremony was
lined up in the backroom of the Nanking Restaurant on Denmark
Street, where Mulk Raj Anand, Sajjad Zaheer and Jyotirmaya
drafted the manifesto of the Association. They wanted to find in
their writings a concrete home for those antique predicaments of
India—poverty, hunger, illiteracy, communalism, gender inequality
and caste—that in the name civilisation and imperialism had
chafed the nation to bits.

A year after being founded, the Association held its first
conference in Lucknow, where the pearl of Urdu literature, Munshi
Premchand, was chosen to preside. Within a few years, far away
from the intelligence of the *Kapellmeister* of those 600 Luftwaffe
bombers from the diabolical orchestra of September 1940, another
stellar work was born out of the Association. It was Ahmad Ali's
Twilight in Delhi, published that year by Hogarth Press. Woolf's
press miraculously survived the air raids. However, Paternoster
Row—the heart of the city's publishing industry—had been wrung
like a chicken's neck. Thirty printing houses and their 5 million
books were barbequed to ashes. In October, Woolf walked past
the bombed out granite of Bloomsbury, Warren Street, Chancery
Lane—and Tavistock Square where her old house and its furniture
had been gutted. London was the face of a tormented prisoner,
smoking from its ears, its teeth scattered about, and its puddings
degorged from its bones in this Second Great Fire of London, 274
years after the one in Pudding Lane. Six months later, Leonard
Woolf found the suicide note of his beloved wife. She lay drowned
in River Ouse by her old country home in Yorkshire. Virginia had
stuffed her overcoat with stones. Like her London, she too had
gone underground.

Sixteen of Christopher Wren's churches—built after the Great
Fire of 1666—were also reduced to pepper on the rubble. While
rebuilding St Paul's Cathedral, Wren had asked one of his workmen

to fetch a slab of stone from the wreckage of London. With that he anointed the reconstruction of London. The stone brought to him had written upon itself in bold letters the unmistakable inscription—'Resurgam'. It meant 'I will rise.' Wren buried it in the centre of the cathedral. During the Second Fire of London in December 1940, even after 114 nocturnal bombings, St Paul's survived like some leviathan from a legend. Another thing that survived with the promise of London's resurgence was the London stone, around which Victorians fashioned the myth that it had been brought over as a relic by Brutus of Troy, the first king of Britain, and it was around this stone that London had been built. When Wren rebuilt the St Swithin's Church, the stone was set in a casement at the centre of its front wall. Although the church was destroyed in the Blitz, its front walls and the stone survived. The Victorian myth had gone on to proclaim: 'So long as the Stone of Brutus is safe, so long shall London flourish.'[6]

By the last of his days in London, Anand was recognised as a stalwart in Indian culture and politics. Along with Rewal Singh, M.F. Boomla, Jai Kishore Handoo and others, he started the Central Indian Committee which worked in tandem with the India League and extended the work of bringing Indians in Britain under one umbrella. As an informal spokesperson of the Indian National Congress, he published a short volume called *Letters on India* (1942), to convey the nationalist side of the story of the freedom struggle to the diaspora. He also presented and wrote scripts for the BBC's Indian Programme, along with other leading Asian authors of his generation. They included Cedric Dover and J.M. Tambimuttu, the Sri Lankan poet and scholar, who had founded *Poetry London* in 1939, going on to publish for the next thirteen years the poetry of William Empson, W.H. Auden, Stephen Spender and many others. Not without the relentless backing of his London ilk, Mulk Raj Anand became one of the first English novelists of modern India. He shared that distinction with R.K. Narayan, Raja Rao and Anand's colleague from the BBC, Govindas Vishnoodas Desani.

Born in Nairobi, Desani belonged to a merchant family from Karachi. Landing in London a year after Anand, he gradually started working as a correspondent with several leading Indian presses, beginning with the Associated Press, Reuters and *The Times of India*. Having left for India in the late 1920s, he returned to London barely a month before the siege of Warsaw. He took up employment as a broadcaster and writer for the BBC Eastern Service and also served as a lecturer with the Ministry of Information and the Imperial Institute, which took him to several English schools, universities and war battalions. In 1943, the journals on his experiences of lecturing across England during the war were broadcast on the BBC, both in English and Hindi. Just as the years of Modernism were on their way out, the experimentalist spirits of Virginia Woolf and James Joyce dawned upon Desai's residence in Kew Bridge Court. Out came from his typewriter the highly eccentric though widely acclaimed novel, *All About H. Hatterr* (1948). The name he made for himself in London could have earned him the position of Jawaharlal Nehru's cultural ambassador. He refused that and chose to continue with his journalism, before going on to teach philosophy at the University of Texas in the 1970s.

By the 1980s, the BBC's Indian services had been warming the ears of millions of South Asians. Founded in 1922, the BBC's affair with India began almost as soon as it was born. Its founder, Sir John Reith, was an Indophile. Like many Indophiles of his age, he regretted not being able to visit the subcontinent in his lifetime. Fortunately for him, however, the first radio operation in India— the Indian Broadcasting Company—went into bankruptcy in 1930. With the Government of India Act of 1935, the dire need for a more centralised radio network was felt in the colony. Reith came to the rescue, cajoling Viceroy Lord Willingdon to steer his vision. The result was the All India Radio, with Lionel Fielden as its programmes head. Fielden was a BBC producer with a volatile artistic temperament, and plans of amalgamating British and Indian radio networks. In the bandwidth of young and energetic

Indians that rallied around Fielden were the Bokhari brothers of the All India Radio, who were so vital to the network that it came to be rechristened as the 'Bokhari Brothers' Corporation', or the 'Indian BBC'.[7] The older between them, A.S. Bokhari, became the first Director General of the All India Radio. The war sirens were on air when Desani was introduced to the younger Bokhari from the Bombay Station of the All India Radio. Syed Zulfiqar Ali Shah Bokhari, who left as a director of the station, went to London after being invited by Sir Malcolm Lyall Darling to join as a Programme Organiser. He was given charge of setting up the Indian network of the BBC Eastern Service, one that could possibly override Berlin's wooing of Indians on shortwave with its Axis propaganda.

Darling was a well-known British author, civil servant and peasant rights campaigner. He headed the BBC India Service during the war, where his larger plan had been to recruit Orwell for the Eastern Service. Orwell had a long history with India and Burma, being born in the former and having been once posted in the latter as an Assistant District Superintendent of the Indian Imperial Police. Orwell and Anand had both fought in the Spanish Civil War, on the side of the Republican alliance. Anand too had been on Darling's list of wanted men for the BBC. Through Bokhari, Darling managed to persuade Orwell to broadcast for the network, and Anand to ally as a freelancer. Bokhari assisted Orwell in many of his radio scripts and himself broadcast to millions of Indians in Urdu, from the BBC office at 200 Oxford Street. By late 1940, Bokhari was a household name in India, reporting from the warfront in France on the state of Indian soldiers in the British Army. He was a teacher, poet, writer, actor, broadcaster and also an administrator with an iron fist. Bokhari was also instrumental in establishing the BBC Hindustani service in May that year—a team largely consisting of Indians with Hindi or Urdu as their first language—strategically aimed at building an Indian audience otherwise beyond the reach of elitist English language broadcasts.

Among Bokhari's finest recruits was Princess Indira Devi of Kapurthala, who had arrived in Britain in the previous decade with the dream of becoming an actress. After studying briefly at the Royal Academy of Dramatic Art and working with Alexander Korda—who had promised to make her Britain's next leading actress after Merle Oberon—Indira Devi decided to appear for the St John Ambulance examination. After driving motor ambulances during the early months of the war and a brief stint as a postal censor, Indira Devi joined the BBC in 1942, where she anchored the iconic programme, 'The Debate Continues', based on Indian proceedings in the British Parliament. She was, at the time, the only woman to enter the press gallery of the House of Commons.

As a broadcaster for the BBC Home Service, Indira Devi was dubbed as the 'Radio Princess', and was offered a tenure with the Overseas Service Division within a year of her joining the BBC. Another Indian at the station was the future film actor, Balraj Sahni, who had broadcast for the Eastern service along with his wife Damjanthi Sahni. Balraj Sahni, who had been a Hindi lecturer in Tagore's Visva Bharati University and fought alongside Gandhi in the freedom struggle, also made a deep impact on Indian listeners. Despite the success of the Eastern Service, Bokhari believed that it was virtually impossible for the English to beat the Germans through propaganda alone, and if at all they wanted to win the loyalty of the Indian mind, they would have to leave their intellectual footprints on it. To a large extent the BBC implemented his views, and through the years of the war, the Indian broadcast of the network was geared towards enmeshing the cultures of the two nations, with Orwell being accompanied by E.M. Forster, J.B. Priestly, Louis MacNeice and T.S. Eliot.

In 1941, another young Indian, Narayana Menon, joined the BBC Indian Service in London. An accomplished *veena* player, he first came to light with his musical recital at the East End at a charity event in 1938. Three years later, the Carnegie Scholar was awarded a doctorate at the University of Edinburgh for a thesis on the poetry of W.B. Yeats, that was published subsequently. After a glowing review of his book by E.M. Forster on BBC, an enduring friendship ensued between them. Bokhari and Orwell commissioned Narayana Menon to write and broadcast talks in Hindustani and English. He also collaborated with Anand on the BBC poetry series 'Voice', conducted by Orwell, besides writing scripts for the network's series on 'Friends of Bengal' and adapting Tagore's play, *The King of the Dark Chamber* (1916) and Premchand's short story, 'The Shroud' (1936). Even while producing the Music Programme of the Eastern Service, Narayana Menon continued to be a regular performer at the events of the India League, where his admirers included Rajani Palme Dutt and Krishna Menon. The League's own offering to the BBC was the radical Communist, Krishnarao Shelvankar, who was also recruited by Orwell for the Eastern Service. He was a co-editor of the Progressive Writer's Association's journal, *Indian Writing*, and a compelling author himself. Shelvankar's book, *The Problem of India* (1940), was censored by the India Office. His first book, *Ends are Means* (1938), was a controversial rejoinder to Aldous Huxley's *Ends or Means* (1938). Shelvankar had been schooled at the Theosophical Society in Adyar before coming to the London School of Economics under Harold Laski's wing. He was, therefore, a curious amalgamation of Eastern mysticism, Fabian socialism, Marxist dialectic and Congress-led nationalism.

In founding *Indian Writing*, Shelvankar was companioned by Iqbal Singh and Sasadhar Sinha, as well as the Sri Lankan author, Alagu Subramaniam. Iqbal Singh was also a member of the India League, which he discovered after being sent to England by his family to shield him from being radicalised by the Congress in India. His contributions to English literature included the life of *Gautama Buddha* (1937) and one of the earliest biographies of Allama Iqbal. Sasadhar Sinha, who was a contemporary of Krishna Menon and Mulk Raj Anand, began his career as a scholar at the London School of Economics, where he was awarded a doctorate in the 1920s. After several unsuccessful attempts at securing a job as a journalist in India, largely owing to his disestablishmentarianism, Sinha returned to London to create the Bibliophile Bookshop at 16 Little Russell Street, with Subramaniam as his assistant. Besides being one of the places that stocked copies of *Indian Writing*, the Bibliophile Bookshop grew into a secret nest for radicals of the India League, and Indians in general. Sinha's wife, Marthe Goldwyn, was a teacher at Prendergast Girls' School in Lewisham. Sinha was often found researching at the British Museum, where, under the vigilance of Scotland Yard and the India Office, all his reading requests were monitored. That was partly triggered by his opting to be a conscientious objector during the war, while he went about lecturing on the history, economics and culture of India at various literary institutes at Dulwich, Lewisham and Eltham in south and south-east London. In 1942, when the Bibliophile Bookshop ran into debts, it was sold to Krishna Menon, although Sinha continued to be the manager. Three years later, Sinha left for Calcutta for the finale of India's freedom struggle and the civil unrest.

Another endearing Indian presence in London was that of Attia Hosain. Like her namesake from the previous generation, she came from the Muslim landed aristocracy. Her father was a Cambridge graduate and her mother, a women's rights activist in India. Attia graduated from the University of Lucknow in 1933, one of the first women of her clan to achieve that distinction. It was also the year when she attended the All India Women's Conference in Calcutta, covering it for publications in Lucknow and Calcutta—an event that underscored the beginning of her journalistic career. Besides the classical influence of Urdu and Persian, her early adulthood was also shaped by the political fervour of Zaheer and Anand. Gradually, Attia seasoned into a torchbearer for the Progressive Writers' Association. So profound was her love of India that when the country was partitioned, rather than leave for Pakistan, she and her husband, Ali Bahadur Habibullah, travelled to Britain. In 1949, she took up broadcasting at the Indian section of the BBC's Eastern Service, sampling themes in faith, art, culture and cinema from the subcontinent, besides working as a correspondent for the *Weekend Review*. In that, Attia was able to lean on the stern backbone of Indian journalism from the heart of an Empire that had ended barely a few years ago.

Several figures from the Progressive Writers' legacy and the India League were correspondents for Indian publications, and broadcasters, either in London or in India (and later Pakistan). From London, Shelvankar reported for *The Hindu* newspaper in Madras, and in 1944 he was chosen as an advisor to the Federation of Indian Student Societies in Great Britain and Ireland. In independent India, he would become Jawaharlal Nehru's Press Advisor. Narayana Menon took up the directorship of broadcasting in the princely state of Baroda before joining the All India Radio, rising to be its director general in 1963. Bokhari, who left for India immediately after the war, joined the Calcutta All India Radio as its director and, later still, found his final destination in Karachi as the broadcasting controller for Radio Pakistan. By then, his legacy of the Hindustani service was so soldered to the spirit of the BBC, that with India's partition, the service was also bifurcated into Hindi and Urdu services for the two new nations. This was followed by a system of secondments forged with the All India Radio and Radio Pakistan, and a stream of informal opportunities for Indian and Pakistani students to earn a few pounds as a perquisite to walking the hallowed corridors of the public broadcasting network at 200 Oxford Street and, later, at Bush House in Aldwych.

With Sophia Duleep Singh's sequestration from activism and the demise of Shapurji Saklatvala, lascar politics might have come to a standstill in London, but for Surat Alley and his confrères. One of them, Aftab Ali, had lobbied indefatigably for over a decade to unite the various seamen's welfare unions formed in India after the First World War. In 1937, the five principal bodies for lascar representation in India, the Indian Seamen's Union, Indian Quartermasters' Union, Bengal Mariners' Union, the Seamen's Welfare League of India, the National Seamen's Union of India and the Karachi Seamen's Union merged into the All-India Seamen's Federation. Aftab Ali, a former lascar himself, was elected as its president. He travelled to London the following year to agitate for the rights of Indian seamen working in British territory. The government had earlier thwarted all their demands for higher wages, safer working conditions, vindication of the rights of lascars and protection from dire punitive action in cases of desertion. Many lascars who jumped ships in Britain changed their names and took to the streets selling curios, spices or incenses.

The All-India Seamen's Federation now had a strong membership of at least 50,000 seamen in Britain and India. Less than a week after the Nazi invasion of Poland began, hundreds of lascars went on strike in Britain. Thrown into sudden panic, the Board of Trade approached Firoz Khan Noon, the India High Commissioner in London, to control the pandemonium at sea. Lascars had started demanding for their wages to be doubled, for new uniforms, an extra bar of soap and bonuses. Stranded by the eventide of the Empire, Noon went from being frantic to ineffectual. He could not dare to openly affront the India Office, nor could he reason with the seamen of his own country. Meanwhile, shipping companies reckoned that yielding to the demands of lascars would be none the wiser than surrendering to Hitler. In October 1939, the British crew of *SS Oxfordshire* went on a nine-day strike. The death of a crew-member made matters worse for the ship owner. Their demands were finally met with 100 per cent raise in their wages, along with a £10 wartime bonus. For the next two months, on one ship after another, scores of Indian seamen went on strike. By the end of winter, nearly 400 of them were convicted, with sentences of up to three months' imprisonment and fine of a week's wages. Liberal Indian newspapers, such as the *The Statesman* and *Jugantar*, rose in solidarity with the seafarers.

Surat Alley, who hailed from a poor Muslim family of Cuttack in Orissa, was an old hand at lascar politics in Britain. He had come a long way, becoming the head of the Colonial Seamen's Association, the Hindustani Social Club and the London representative of the All-India Seamen's Association. Besides being a well-recognised face to seamen of various nationalities in London, Alley was also marked by Scotland Yard. He had peeved the administration many a time, running May Day rallies where his speeches fuelled the discontent of the 'coloured' proletariat in London. A few months before the outbreak of the war, he organised the Indian Workers' Conference in Whitechapel, where R.S. Nimbkar, general secretary of the Bombay Textile Workers' Union, delivered the keynote. With the help of

Aftab Ali and two other old lascar activists, Tahsil Miah and M.A. Jalil, Alley frustrated London with pamphlets and striking seamen. At a rally in Whitechapel, held in November, Alley informed the lascars that 150 of them had been killed in action and another 500 were serving sentences in British prisons—naturally provoking uncontrolled fury. The protest campaign brought Krishna Menon to compel Reginald Sorensen to raise the matter in the Parliament.

Alley went about knocking the doors of the Ministry of Shipping and the India High Commissioner, trying to reach the Ministry of War Transport, without any significant gains. Instead of working towards improving the conditions of lascars, the India Office acted on garrotting the disturbances in London's dockyards. By the end of that year, Tahsil Miah was deported to India. Aftab Ali, who returned to the colony soon after, was barricaded in by the mediational strategy of H.S. Suhrawardy, the Bengal Minister of Commerce and Labour. Left alone, Alley was gradually pushed into redundancy over the issue of lascar welfare, as the Government of India began appointing Lascar Welfare Officers both at home and in London. Whitehall ensured that all the credit for that development went to Noon, the Shipping Federation and the shipping companies, instead of Alley. Reports of acts of lascar-bravery in the war were frequently announced to the public, and the seamen were now held in great virtual esteem. In December 1941, the Information Department published its tactical memorandum on the lascar situation, *Indian Seamen in the British Merchant Navy*. A month later, Viceroy Lord Linlithgow inaugurated Calcutta's first Indian Seamen's Home.

Alley had been defeated back in London, even before his battle was over. He continued unionising lascars in Liverpool, where he founded the All-Indian Seamen's Centre in 1943. Two years prior to that, he had independently released his own memorandum, *Indian Seamen in the Merchant Navy*, which he kept updating with comparative statistics of lascars' wages and working conditions over the next three years. One of the major issues that Alley raised in his campaigns was the plight of seamen who had been attacked on British ships. They had to recuperate in Britain or await their turn for repatriation for up to five months without any pay, before the bureaucracy cared to pass their papers, while their families starved in India. Another crisis was that lascars were subjected to incredible quantities of inedible stale mutton until they were one with their food. By the end of the war, the India Office realised that the only way to keep lascar unions at bay was to be a part of them. In 1946, the All-India Seamen's Federation was established with governmental support. Over the course of the year, the protracted struggles of Surat Alley and Aftab Ali finally led to some piecemeal reforms for the lascars. Compared with the situation in the beginning of the war, their wages had increased four times, in several instalments, but were still much behind those of white seamen.

Alley's London days did not entirely revolve around lascar unions. He was simultaneously unionising Indian cinema artistes. In 1939, Hungarian filmmaker Zoltan Korda adapted A.E.W. Mason's war novel, *The Four Feathers* (1902), for the celluloid. The memory of Niranjan Pal and Kedarnath Das Gupta, who were now transforming cinema in India, was still very much alive in London. Korda's film paved the way for casual Asian labour in English productions. Said Amir Shah, a silk merchant from Whitechurch Lane, and a frequenter of the India League, also opened shop as a contractor and agent for films. He used to help South Asian artistes find small roles and employment in the British film industry. Sensing an opportunity of extending labour rights campaigns to cinema, along with Akbar Ali Khan, Surat Alley established the Oriental Film Artistes' Union. Alley knew the power of performance to unite communities and foster political consciousness. In December 1939, even at the peak of the lascar agitation, he organised a special matinee performance by the Indian dancer Ram Gopal and his company, at the Vaudeville Theatre, as part of the Hindustani Social Club's cultural calendar. The event was sponsored by D.N. Dutt, a doctor from north-west London. Through such initiatives, the Club was able to maintain the façade of being a cultural organisation meant for the intermingling and entertainment of Indian and British aficionados. Behind all of that, Alley ran a clandestine membership drive for the Indian National Congress.

Thanks to Alley and his associates, many lascars who had deserted their ships, and ran the danger of arrests and imprisonment, survived in the city, working their way through odd jobs. Unskilled labourers joined in factories as firemen or as porters in shops and tailoring houses in the East End. Jobs that English workers refused on account of very low wages were, however, enough to see the lascars through the years of the war. Others with appetites for risk took to the clothing industry. Imitating the methods of Jewish immigrants, many 'Indians sold ready-made garments. With a suitcase containing items of light clothing, shirts, socks, ties, scarves, lingerie and aprons, working six days a week, in all weathers, they travelled miles to establish their own patch and build up a regular clientele.'[8] Given the backing of their communities, as well as the English nostalgia for Indian silks, lascar traders in London, especially in the East End, grew into familiar entities.

At Church Lane in Aldgate, Ahmad Din Qureshi ran Qureshi and Company, with merchants C.L. Nayyar Brothers in close vicinity. Said Amir Shah and Fazal Shah started Shah Brothers in Whitechurch Lane, while Fazal Ali looked after his tie business at Clifton Street in Shoreditch. At Poplar High Street in the East End, Hashmatrai Rewachand ran his business of hosiery and artificial silks. His agents collected orders from Indians all over Britain, as Rewachand's merchandise was purveyed to Glasgow, Inverness, Torquay and Norwich. Allegedly, he reinforced his human resources by billeting deserting lascars in London, and later even sponsored the travel fares of his staff sourced from India, with each passage costing him nearly £20.

The docksides of Poplar and Stepney and Spitalfields in Tower Hamlets became infamous for housing lascar communities. Lascars were also to be found in the far east of London—Canning Town, Tidal Basin, Plaistow and Customs House. Kartar Singh, a cloth-vendor from Punjab and his English wife lodged many Sikh workers in their house in Spitalfields. In west London, the Bhupindra Dharamshala provided another safe haven for Sikhs in the city. The East London Mosque and the Woking Mosque acted as makeshift homes for wayside Muslims. According to the conservative estimate of B.R. Hunter's *Report on Seamen's Welfare* in 1939, the lascar population of London was 3,000. Many others migrated to Glasgow, Lancashire, Manchester, Birmingham, Liverpool, Coventry or Leicester, where they peddled smuggled clothes or French imports as India cotton. Scotland Yard even suspected these Indian hawkers to be undercover anarchists. When it was discovered that they were peddling cottons available for cheaper rates on the streets of London, the administration supplicated British housewives not to purchase what they called a 'positive peril' to their domestic budget and health.[9] On reading these impassioned reports written by *patriotic* journalists, British housewives came to believe that the counterfeit silks and cottons were major causes of skin disease. They also learned that contrary to the lascars being on a day's break from their seafaring contracts, they had but deserted their ships and were pilfering the tawdry goods of the metropolis into the unsullied homes of the counties. In their own unofficial ways, the lascars too were Congressmen, waging small battles with the English every day, drawing closer with each to the tide of freedom.

Scene V

If Empire Be the Love of Food

The Congress bandwagon in London seemed much more united than in India where the nation's communal harmony was the chief casualty of the war. Krishna Menon, who had resigned from the Labour Party at the time of the Cripps' Mission, now returned to its fold to witness the overthrow of Britain's domination over the colony. In 1946, he was at the peak of his form at the United Nations General Assembly Meeting held at Lake Success in New York. However, the legacy of the India League was much more than political. It triumphed, quietly but maturely, in spawning a new architecture in the minds of a new generation of Indians. London now seemed to have expanded beyond its Edwardian thoroughfares or its alabastered cathedrals. To the new Indian, the strangulating squares of Mayfair and Marylebone were now stretched into the working-class neighbourhoods of Tower Hamlets, Wembley, Harrow, Slough, Tooting and Southall.

The many Indians that the League brought together in London—directly as members or indirectly as part of its extended circle—included Tarapada Basu, P.C. Bhandari, B.B. Ray Chaudhuri, P.T. Dalal, R.J. Deshpande, Joseph Devli, Feroze Gandhi, Sunder Kabadia, Surat Alley, C.L. Katial, Dr Kumaria, M. Majumdar, S. Menon-Marath, S.P. Mitra, Rajni Patel, Renuka Ray, Krishnarao and Mary Shelvankar, Harbhajan Singh, Reval Singh, Marthe Sinha, Sasadhar Sinha, Parmeshwar Narayan Haksar, Narayana Menon, Shah Abdul Majid Qureshi, Ayub Ali,

Said Amir Shah, Venu Chitale, Savitri Devi Chowdhary, Narayana Menon, Ahmed Ali and Mulk Raj Anand. Either during their short or prolonged stays in London, they reinscribed the cultural contours of the city. The India League's hungry revolution ran parallel to London's hunger for Indian cuisine. Restaurateuring in the city was conceived as a close cousin of the incendiary spirits of nationalism. Most of these restaurants were run by lascars from the Sylhet district of Bengal, who after 1971 would be known as Bangladeshis.

Master Ayub Ali's café, Shah Jolal Restaurant, at 76 Commercial Street in the East End, was one of the India League's best kept secrets. Started in 1920, the café came to be a meeting place of the League's members. Originally a lascar from Sylhet, Ali escaped from a ship in America after the First World War, and sneaked into London through Tilbury Docks. His house on 13 Sandy's Row at the East End—popularly known as 'Number Thirteen'—doubled up as a temporary refuge for lascars and Sylheti workers, who were often directed to the India League to run its small errands. Owing to his gift for words, Master Ali was trusted to become the treasurer of the League's East End branch, as well as a key strategist in Muslim politics in London during the Second World War. He later found himself at the helm of the London Muslim League. Another activist in seamen's politics in London, Shah Abdul Majid Qureshi, had been in the city since 1936. He had fled from a New York-bound ship at Tilbury, and gone underground in East London with other Bengali labourers. Qureshi began working as a chocolatier in pubs around the East End before entering the Bengal Restaurant in Percy Street. He was taken in as a partner in Nogendro Ghosh's café, the Dilkush Delight, on Windmill Street at Soho. From there he climbed the professional ladder of restaurateuring, owning cafés around Tower Hamlets.

Asif Khan ran the Punjabi restaurant, the Shalimar, on Wardour Street. Back at Percy Street, one also came across Asok Mukherjee's

Durbar and Jobbul Haque's Bengal India, while the Oriental Café de Colombo beamed as a prominent highlight at West India Dock Road. A well-known Indian restaurant and affordable lodging house for Indians was The Hindustan Community House, managed by Kundan Lal Jalie since 1937. Inter alia, it also provided free medical services by Indian doctors, and functioned as a cultural centre stocked with English and Indian newspapers, besides the services of a radio and a gramophone. The community house was wrecked in the London Blitz. So was the Dilkush Delight. Grounded underneath the devastation all around him, Qureshi was, however, able to revive his fortunes in 1944 when he built his second restaurant, the India Centre, on Charlotte Street. This, too, became a den of the India League's meetings in wartime London. Along with Master Ali, he was the co-founder of the Hindustani Social Club, where they entertained the lascar community of London, largely comprising Sylhetis. In 1943, the duo was also instrumental in setting up the Indian Seamen's Welfare League at 66 Christian Street in East London, in the process shoring up their café clienteles. Qureshi became its *de facto* president and Master Ali, its general secretary.

One of the most undervalued reasons for the resurgence of Sylheti cuisine in Britain during the Second World War was this: the war itself. Bangladeshi food in London today, and the British Indian catering industry in general, owes a lot to Mussolini. In June 1940, Italy declared war on France and England. The Allies had sustained a humiliating defeat in the Battle of France, that compelled Britain to undertake the epical evacuation of a third of a million soldiers from Dunkirk. The brunt of the battle was also borne by European immigrants in London. The *Daily Mail* had committed itself to haranguing Italians in the city. They were seen as an indigestible population. London's paranoia came disguised as fury. Italian coffee-shop owners in the city became its first targets. Many of their sons had been serving in the war, but that was no mitigating factor. Nearly 5,000 Italians were rounded up and taken into safe custody under Churchill's orders—not before several of them had their properties plundered and their persons slain. By July, they were followed by Germans and Austrians. The Europeans were then packed off to the Isle of Man until the end of the war. Resigned to their fate, they set up makeshift bohemian libraries, philosophy cafes, patisseries and clubhouses. It was not those 10,000 Europeans that London lost that year, but European culture indeed. George Orwell lamented that one could not get a proper lunch in London anymore for the Italian chefs at the Savoy, Café Royal, the Piccadilly and all around Soho and Little Italy had been subtracted from the terrain, as violently as speedily.

> Disgusting though these attacks on harmless Italian shopkeepers are, they are an interesting phenomenon, because English people, i.e. people of a kind who would be likely to loot shops, don't as a rule take a spontaneous interest in foreign politics. I don't think there was anything of this kind during the Abyssinian war, and the Spanish war simply did not touch the mass of the people. Nor was there any popular move against the Germans resident in England until the last month or two. The low-down, coldblooded meanness of Mussolini's declaration of war at that moment must have made an impression even on people who as a rule barely read the newspapers.[1]

The European establishments left behind in Soho or Spitalfields or Piccadilly or Bloomsbury were purchased or rented by Indian restaurateurs. As the Luftwaffe unloaded on London the biggest engines of fire Europe had ever seen, the curry's destiny grew thicker in that fire.

———

David Beckham reportedly celebrated his football feats with chicken korma at Manchester's Shimla Pinks Indian Restaurant. Meanwhile, mock-political slogans from T-shirts and cartoons such as 'Keep Curry British' and 'Curry is Your Birthright'[2] had started pushing against the limits of late-20th-century British culture. In

August 1998, *The Guardian* asked its readers what share of Britain was defined by chicken tikka masala. For many, it was a colourful creolisation for British tongues, for others an overspiced babel. One end of the spectrum seemed to suggest there was a great contradiction between Britain's multicultural consumerism and its inherent racism. Another held that culinary multiculturalism was, in fact, another form of racism, which involved consuming another race in proxy.[3] Some went on to add that chicken tikka masala 'was not a shining example of British multiculturalism but a demonstration of the British facility for reducing all foreign foods to their most unappetising and inedible form.'[4] The tragic flaw of the dish was not that it was insipid, for Britons had been weekly consuming about eighteen tonnes of it. It was perceived to lie instead in its blatant inauthenticity—very often cooked by Bangladeshi immigrants from a district not necessarily celebrated for its cuisine, and served for naïve and very often very tipsy British palates.

That did not stop Robin Cook, the Labour Foreign Secretary, from enshrining chicken tikka masala as the great symbol of Britishness and a living testament to pluralist British ancestry. Cook's proclamation came on April 19, 2001, about five months before the twin towers fell in Lower Manhattan. Geared by its Secretary of Defense, Donald Rumsen, and the aggression of President George W. Bush, America went to war with Iraq, to capture not only Osama Bin Laden but also Saddam Hussein. Led by Tony Blair, United Kingdom followed suit. Cook had not foreseen that. His intention was simply to take the edge off the bombast against liberal immigration policies; the onslaught on the political sovereignties of Scotland, Wales and Northern Ireland; English displeasure caused by Britain's perceived humiliation in the European Union; and the alleged contamination of white British identity. Britain has often contemplated on issues of authenticity. Any authentic history of British cuisine—if one such could be written—would be hollow without chippy questions such as 'why did the Brits, a nation famed for a love of bland food, end up with chicken tikka masala being hailed as their favourite dish?' or 'how you got hold of cardamom in Glasgow in the 1880s.' There would also be contemporary ones such as 'how did Indian cuisine as vast and varied as the country of its origin end up in restaurant after restaurant as regimented and branded as McDonalds without a master plan or billion-dollar marketing deal?'[5]

It is widely believed that the curry first crossed the Mediterranean on the Commonwealth's immigration splash on postcolonial Britain's shores. Under the premierships of Alec Douglas-Home and Harold Wilson, United Kingdom would embrace immigrants and refugees, especially from the economically underdeveloped corners of the world which were once part of its Empire. A legend dating back to the early 1970s points to the invention of chicken tikka masala by Pakistani chef, Ali Ahmed Aslam, in the Shish Mahal Restaurant in Glasgow. Descendants of Sultan Ahmed Ansari, who ran the city's Taj Mahal Restaurant, later claimed that the dish was Ansari's invention from the 1950s. Since in those years Glasgow did not even have a tandoor oven—the most essential equipment for chicken tikka masala—such and many other claims took a backseat. In 2009, Mohammad Sarwar, the Labour Member of Parliament from Glasgow Central, wanted to have the fabled recipe honoured as part of Britain's founding 'fashion for "fusion" cuisine.'[6] The seeds of that phenomenon, that were supposedly hatched in the global sixties, were, in fact, sown in London towards the end of the First World War, or even before.

In 1891, the food magazine *Caterer* wrote that 'the civil service of our great Eastern dependencies is ever expanding, and it must ever be that a perpetually growing population of persons having Indian tastes in matters gastronomic must be located in London.'[7] In that decade itself, Behramji Malabari had seen rice and curries and condiments 'struggling into favour.'[8] New refrigeration technology, by the turn of the century, led to an explosion in restaurant businesses—an avenue where enterprising immigrant restauranteurs from Italy, France, Austria, Germany, Turkey, China or, indeed, India, reaped the largest profits. Meats imported into the British dominions from the southern hemisphere could be purchased at Smithfield, fish at Billingsgate and fruits and vegetables at the good old Covent Garden Market. Since 1885, the Falcon Restaurant, near the Strand, had catered Indian and Malaysian varieties of curries so blisteringly spicy as to easily revive the dead. The Crown Hotel in Leicester Square and Purssell's at Cornhill in the City of London had employed curry-chefs since the 1880s. St James' Hall Restaurant had its sous-chef in M. Futymed—from Calcutta—who managed the Indian segment of the kitchen. For twopence, the District Line would take Indian students from central London to Hammersmith, where Mrs Turner's Indian restaurant was a much-savoured retreat for curries.

By 1905, London was witnessing a full-fledged renaissance of the curry. Back then, there was at least one Indian café each, in Shaftesbury Avenue and Holborn. There was also the Indian Catering Company on Ledbury Road and the Eastern Café on Chancery Lane. Bengali restauranteur K.N. Dasgupta ran the Coronation Hotel and Restaurant on Gray's Inn Road. In 1911, Nitisen Dwarkadas set up his spice trading company chiefly to import for the Salut-e-Hind restaurant in Holborn. When Subhas Bose and Krishna Menon first came to London, Bengali galley chefs had already been ruling the gastronomical roost, albeit covertly. Most of them had escaped from their ships docked in London's harbours and set store by the legacy of Sake Deen Mahomet, transforming East London into a cultural laboratory of—what would be after the Partition—East Pakistan. Scotland Yard too, played its part by keeping files on these culinary mutinies and counting them in its brochures and advertisements. According to official records, there were at least sixteen curry-and-rice restaurants in 1937 in London itself. By the end of the war, the number had leaped to over twenty. Israel Miah and Mosharaf Ali were forerunners in a British Indian catering industry largely led by lascars. Their restaurant, Anglo-Asia, at Brompton Road near Knightsbridge, was one of their many joint ventures. Ward Lock & Co. travel guides had been advertising The Indian Restaurant Ltd. since 1920. In his memoirs, A.S.P Ayyar wrote about dining there in 1919, while he was a student at Oxford.

Shafi's restaurant on Gerrard Street was a great culinary hospital for Raj nostalgics in the interwar years. It was started by

Mohammed Wayseem and Mohammed Rahim, who arrived as students when the demand for Indian food in London was just about to peak. During her time in the city, Attia Hosain used to frequent Shafi's, which she included in one of her vignettes: 'it was a rendezvous for Indians—visitors, expatriates and students alike. For all who came from a country where food and companionship went naturally together, Shafi's was like being back home. The owner was host, friend and confidant to all who came, whether to eat, or just to relax and talk.'⁹ Even in the 1930s, Shafi's was mentioned on the list of restaurants published by the Post Office London Directory. The West End too fell to the curry invasion, with the coming up of the Taj Mahal Restaurant at Cambridge Circus and the Kohinoor on Rupert Street. Both were regularly advertised in the *Indian Student*. Another Taj Mahal restaurant, although not run by the owners of the one in West End, was opened in Glasgow. The Scotland Yard recommended the Café Indien located at Leicester Square, which was later renamed as the India and Burma Restaurant.

As vindaloos, kormas, kebabs and dopiazas became the rage, these restaurants also ventured into private catering. Kohinoor's owners, the Bahadur brothers—Bir, Sordar and Shomsar—came from Delhi to Britain as students before schooling a whole new pedigree of cooks and culinary entrepreneurs. From their first establishment in London in 1934, the Bahadurs spread to Brighton, Oxford and Northampton by the name Taj Mahal. In Manchester and Cambridge, they operated as Kohinoor. Soon after, Liverpool and Cardiff were also won over. In Manchester alone, the Bahadurs established three more branches. Almost all latter-day restauranteurs in London 'learnt their trade from the Bahadur brothers. They learnt the skill of cooking and serving, also management, step by step.'¹⁰ Regardless of how lavish a restaurant one had previously worked in, the Kohinoor was their finishing school. Not just as the imperial diamond, but also as a cuisine, Kohinoor had invaded the essence of being British for generations to come.

Defying—and redefining—the Sylheti tradition of catering in London, Veeraswamy stands at Regent Street in Piccadilly Circus as the oldest existing Indian restaurant in the city. It was created not by Indian immigrants but a retired English army officer, Edward Palmer, in 1926. He was the grandson of William Palmer, the banking tycoon of the Raj. An 18th-century painting of the Palmer family by Johann Zoffany later found a place on a wall of the Oriental and India Office of the British Library. After the year-long British Empire Exhibition organised in Wembley in 1924, Edward Palmer evidently succeeded his grandfather's fame. The exhibition was a grand success, attracting over 27 million visitors, who were treated to a miniature Empire spread across its various geographies. In the aftermath of the Great War, the exhibition offered a much-needed vindication to a reeling Raj that 'was missing and mourning a generation of young men and enduring dire financial crises.'[11] The segment on India, represented 'in a pavillion modelled on the Taj Mahal, had the usual mock jungle, jugglers, and snake charmers, a display of *shikar* trophies, a model of the Khyber Pass, and a jumble of Indian goods, including carpets, silks, indigo, and tea.'[12] Its café, the Mughal Palace Restaurant, served tea in a make-believe Indian tropical forest, and was conducted by E.P. Veeraswamy's & Co., Indian Food Specialists. It had already made a name selling chutneys, spices, curry powders and pastes imported from Hyderabad, under the brand 'Nizams'.

Edward Palmer had founded the company in 1896. It is very likely that he named it after his grandmother Veera, one of the many mistresses of William Palmer. Having grown up on artefacts and legends of the Raj, Edward Palmer well understood the importance of Indian settings as the entrée to the main course. Veeraswamy was contrived as the conjuration of 'a fantasmatic vision of imperial opulence, where there were tiger skins on the wall, where *punkah wallahs* worked the fans and where Indian doormen held umbrellas as customers returned to the rain-soaked streets of London.'[13] The interiors were decorated with lamps from the Mysore Palace; its palms and cane chairs imitated the tropics. Palmer's original flooring plan adhered to ancient Vedic architecture. The kitchen equipment and the staff were manifestly procured from India. The paintings on the walls, the uniforms of the stewards and waiters, the drapery and the cutlery were all classically designed to deceive diners into an imperial perihelion—as though Plassey had been conquered just the day before.

Veeraswamy opened to a satiating review in E. Hooton Smith's *The Restaurants of London* (1928). Besides Mughlai chicken pilau, Madras chicken curry, mutton curry, daal curry and prawn curry, the menu also flattered Londoners with English rump steaks, prawn cutlets and sundry other indulgences. Distinguished by its old-money clientele, the restaurant was soon hailed as the 'ex-Indian higher serviceman's curry club.'[14] Even after its first decade, Veeraswamy had not lost the zing of its Oriental condiments. Johnny and Fanny Craddock's *Where to Dine in London* (1937) lauded the restaurant's sharp vision for culinary and cultural detailing, just as middle-class Britons were beginning to come to terms with the subtle, startling and, at times, surreptitiously spiced nuances of Indian cooking.

> Veeraswamy's India Restaurant, 99 Regent Street (the entrance is in Swallow Street) gives the lie to those who fondly imagine that curry is the only Indian dish. There is curry, of course, and curry powder plays no part in its composition: it is made entirely with spices. Madras Chicken Curry is the speciality, and it consists of the whole wing of a chicken appropriately treated. Also there are vegetable curries. But this is by no means all. There is Indian Omelette, which is delicately flavoured with spices; Chicken Biriani, steamed in butter with special rice; Grilled Kabab; and some succulent fruit sweets, Mangusteeni, Lichi and Mangoes. There are no less than six different kinds of Indian bread.[15]

Palmer's branding of Indian food attracted competitors such as Mr Friday, whose shop at Brompton Road in Knightsbridge sold canned curry pastes and spices, or Mr Edmund's at Stonefield Terrace in Islington selling gold medal 'Empress' curry powder. These new luxury items on the city's market were aggressively advertised as necessary education in Indian cooking for amateurs or as a crash-course in the history of 'old East Indians at table, and of millionaire nabobs regaling on delicacies of which the West only knows little or nothing.'[16] The interwar extravaganza of Indian food in London was just one of the symptoms of how anxiously Britain needed India on its side of the table. In the wake of Veeraswamy, at least two other upper-crust restaurants opened in the city. One was Mysore at Glendower Place, in South Kensington. As a result, aubergine and lemon chutneys, poppadum and Bombay duck and lassi and filter coffee took off as catchphrases on the English tongue. 'Going for an Indian' turned into a glamorous activity as King Edward VIII, King Gustav of Sweden, Charlie Chaplin and the King of Denmark joined the clientele of Veeraswamy. How realistically all of them took to the curry-mania can be witnessed in a legend that was floated by the restaurant's advertising agent in the 1990s, and subsequently the fiction was taken for fact. Accordingly, the King of Denmark dined at Veeraswamy's whenever he was in the city. However, he was past chagrin, when unable to combine 'a glass of his beloved Carlsberg beer to have with his meal. So, being king, he ordered a minion to arrange a delivery of Denmark's finest to 99 Regent Street, thus, beginning the great British tradition of washing down a curry with a glug of beer!'[17]

Veeraswamy reinvented not just the craze for curry, but Indian commodities in general. It was not objectionable anymore to British middle-class propriety that even the less fashionable areas of London started getting decked up with shops peddling Indian spices. The Oriental Restaurant came up in Broadway and Singh's Restaurant at Whitechapel in Aldgate. Nearby, at 36 Percy Street, was the Basement Café or Gator Café, run by Abdul Mannan Chhanu Mia. His house at St Mary Abbots Terrace in Kensington and his other restaurant, Green Mask, were hubs of political meetings of East Bengalis in Britain. Mannan was a key architect of the East Pakistan House set up in the late 1950s, which later became the Bangladeshi Bhaban, an unofficial wing of the Bangladeshi High Commission in London. London's reconstruction after the war owed a lot to its East Bengali settlers who were employed in the railways, public works, constructions and the London underground, besides their very own thriving catering micro-industry. Razaur Rahman Jagirdar, who fled from his ship during the London Blitz in 1940, stayed up all night on the day of his escape, barely surviving the bombing all around him. The morning after, he discovered the Sylheti Café on Commercial Road, from where he was guided to the Gator Café. Like many other lascars, Razaur found a home in 'a terraced four-bedroom house that he shared with between 35 and 40 other Sylhetis.'[18]

Many lascars employed themselves in menial—and often what seemed like exotic—professions. Some became perfumers selling homespun penny-bottled Oriental scents; many others took to vending herbal medicines or smuggled Japanese trinkets and haberdashery; others, meanwhile, roamed around as Indian masseurs and shampooers. Another popular and cheap merchandise sold by former seamen was 'real Indian toffee' made by spinning sugar.[19] These pedlars were mostly Sikhs or Muslims. A large population of them had taken to hawking in a Britain hit by the Great Depression in the late 1920s, while many also worked on odd jobs at Greek and Egyptian cafes, Wimpy bars and Lyon's Corner Houses during breaks from seafaring labour. One seaman, Nawab Ali, slogged at an Egyptian café on Cannon Street Road, dishwashing, sanitising and peeling vegetables, before he managed to enter the staff of the Savoy Hotel, whence he came in as a bearer at Veeraswamy's. Assigned the task of serving rice, Ali observed that diners usually never ate the entire serving, and at the end of each day, the restaurant would have dustbins full of rice. In order to economise on the wastage, he began reducing the quantity of each serving by neatly spreading rice around the plates. When the proprietor saw Ali at his new technique, he was impressed and raised his salary. However, Ali had unwittingly piqued the jealousy of the kitchen staff, and had to resign from his job.

Ali's previous jobs afforded him ample savings to start the Calcutta restaurant in Cardiff which, when gambled away by a friend of Ali's, was revived by him as the Bengal Restaurant in Plymouth. Another lascar, Haji Kona Miah, who worked in the kitchen of a Greek restaurant around Tottenham Court Road earning £2 weekly, also entered the catering industry. Dockside cafés turned into extremely lucrative outlets, in the process bringing in an unhurried but persistent transformation in the commercial aesthetics of London. Besides shares in the profits, some cooks and workers were able to earn up to £9 every week in the restaurant business. As the Bengali Muslim community started turning into the largest ethnic minority in London, the catering industry came to be almost synonymous to their history.

The menus were copied from Veeraswamy's, Shafi's, and the Bahadur brothers' chain of restaurants, where the first Syhleti restaurant owners had learned their trade. Veeraswamy's served the curries beloved by Anglo–Indians: coloured *pilau* rice; sour vindaloos, hot with chillies; creamy chicken kormas, thickened with almonds; hot Madras curries, spiked with lemon juice; *dopiazas*, thick with fried onions and sweet yellow Parsee *dhansaks*. The various owners of Shafi's, and the Bahadur brothers, from northern India, followed the lead of the few restaurants that existed there, serving a version of Anglo–Indian, Punjabi, and Mughlai cuisine, which included chicken biryanis, *rogan* joshes, mushroom curries, and spinach and potato side dishes. This ensured that while in India Mughlai cookery never became a national cuisine, outside India Mughlai dishes were regarded as the national food of all Indians.[20]

Reflecting on the success of Sylhetis in London, Nawab Ali recounted many years later that the reason why there were so many of them, in the first place, was because they were a tight-knit community who never set out with well-chalked out economic plans. Their primary purpose was to help men from their communities; their secondary, to have relatively better means of survival when they were to return to India (or East Pakistan). Ali himself brought twenty men before, and about 200 during the war. Each of them were prepared to help at least twenty others. It was hard to find a chink in that chain of scores of Sylhetis becoming Londonis by the month. Even as lascars, they would have managed to save enough to return to Bengal. Just a year's work on an English ship, although humiliating and jeopardising in many ways, would have fetched a seaman the capital to buy a liveable property in Purbo Bangla (East Bengal). Those who did return to Sylhet—if only to come back to Britain eventually—did enlarge their houses with indoor bathrooms and painted verandas. For those who did not return, forlorn women hummed the folk-songs of separation that began being composed since the years of the Second World War with new trends in Bengali emigration to Britain.

> How can I accept that my husband has gone to London?
> I will fill up a suitcase with dried fish
> All the mullahs—everyone—have gone to London
> The land will be empty—what will I do?
> When my brother goes to London he'll give orders at the tailor's
> He'll make a blouse for me
> How can I accept that my husband has gone to London?[21]

Even after the Partition, East Bengalis felt no serious dismay at being pigeonholed as 'Indian'. They realised, it was good for the business, for it evoked a sensory recuperation for the Raj-sick middle-aged Britons. In the hours that the Sylheti children were supposed to finish homework or prepare for examinations, they were made to cook or help with the arrangements for the next day's menu. Consequently, even second- and third-generation Bangladeshis in London, as elsewhere in Britain, were sucked into the food business. Far from the culinary sophistication of something like Veeraswamy's or Shafi's, the food in these curry houses 'was awful, the greasy-spoon side of Indian cooking,'[22] and yet it was probably the resonance of Indian utensils with the twang of the East Bengali dialects that created the onomatopoeia of the East for intoxicated ears of the Brits.

The *dum-pukht* or slow-steaming processes of Indian cooking, freshly ground spices, marinades, the browning of the base gravies, and so on, had been left behind in the decadent mohallas of Old Delhi or the untouched backwaters of Bangladesh. Firing the palates of beer-guzzlers in London were the reincarnations of kormas, rogan-joshes, vindaloos or Madras curries, which tasted only a little different from each other, by virtue of being cooked in the same sauce. Boiled onion purées replaced browned onions, and packaged spices and curry pastes were used instead of blended garam masalas and gravied tomatoes. To compensate for the want of flavour, the food was then daubed with instant appetisers like asafoetida, fenugreek, tomato ketchup or monosodium glutamate. The latter two ingredients were then mostly unheard of in the Indian subcontinent. What further enhanced this new species of British 'Indian food' was the liberal use of tartrazine or ponceau as colouring agents. And the clientele would binge over Britain's redness manifested in this creolised culinary conspiracy.

In the decade following the Partition, new British immigration policies welcomed the entry of East and West Pakistanis. With the former firmly entrenched in the food business, the latter went up to Birmingham or Manchester to work nocturnal hours in car-manufacturing and textile factories. Jobs that had hitherto been abegging in food-processing, plastic and rubber industries in west London around Southall, or rag trade in east London around Tower Hamlets, readily assimilated South Asians. By 1970, with the third wave of Indian immigrants from Africa—the twice-born refugees of Uganda and Kenya—Drummond Street near the Euston Station developed into another 'Little India'.

Around Tolmer's Square near Drummond Street—a neighbourhood that was ravaged by property speculation and real estate battles in the 1970s—Mohammed Salique ran his restaurant, the Diwana. It was claimed to be the first vegetarian South Indian restaurant in Britain. Ambala, that would later become a large chain of Indian sweetmeat sellers, opened shop in 1965, selling their produce largely to the East Pakistanis. By the time their clients had a new nationality—that of Bangladeshis, after 1971—Ambala began servicing the upmarket boroughs of central London. Over and above the lethal fluorescence of spurious Mughlai food, *barfis* of condensed milk, *laddus* of gram-flour, *gulab jamuns* of cottage cheese, *samosas* of potatoes and flour, Gujarati-styled pickles and Bombay-*bhelpuris* mellowed the air and incensed many a native British, with the synesthaesia of Indian aromas. The first tandoor had already arrived in London, the chicken tikka masala had been invented, and over 2,000 Indian restaurants had been opened in Britain, close to a quarter of that number in London alone. Dining in these, a new postcolonial England sat down to learn about a subcontinent over sixteen times the volume of Albion.

As Britain began recovering from the economic downfall of the Cold War years, the mythologies around the Indian independence started to change both at home and abroad. Britain wanted to reclaim and relive the Raj, and simultaneously honour the heroic and homoerotic strains of the colonial years that had produced many a British and Indian stalwart in London's cosmopolitan imagination. In Mrs Thatcher's Britain, Raj nostalgics found a sensational hobby horse when, in 1984, Granada Television adapted Paul Scott's *Raj Quartet* novels for the television series, *The Jewel in the Crown*. Two years ago, in Richard Attenborough's *Gandhi*, Lord Irwin had asseverated: 'Mr Gandhi will find it needs a great deal more than a pinch of salt to bring down the British Empire.' The Salt March of 1930 had made Gandhi the *The Time* magazine's 'Man of the Year.'[23] However, the last prime minister of the Empire—Clement Attlee—later judged that it was Subhas Chandra Bose's Indian National Army that uprooted Britain's blind trust in Indian loyalties. When asked about what impact Mr Gandhi had had on Britain's withdrawal, Attlee had replied with a sheepish grin, 'minimal.'[24]

It had taken not a great deal more, however, than a spring dinner at a gilt-edged London restaurant, to unsplice the Indian subcontinent into three nations. Rather, four nations—if one also cheekily counted London that had for so long operated, and would continue to operate, as a country of Indians in exile! As far back as 1891, the *Chamber's Journal* ran a survey on London's immigrant populations essayed as 'Our city of nations', where Indians too had found a modest occupancy.²⁵ Willy-nilly, London's true escalation into a cosmopolitan universe began with its restaurants and bakeries and cafés—that remorseless romanticism around gastronomy turned into a *gastromanticism*!

Half a century before the *The Jewel in the Crown* premiered in Britain—three years after the historic march that was fictionalised in Attenborough's film—a penguin-suit banquet was hosted at the Waldorf Astoria by Aga Khan. Muhammad Ali Jinnah was one of the guests of honour. At the pre-dinner reception, Jinnah was accosted by Choudhry Rahmat Ali. The latter sat him down to have a famous word—man to man, barrister to barrister, Muslim to Muslim—over French oysters and Chablis. Rahmat Ali handed over the pamphlet *Now or Never*, baring the plan for Pakistan to its future Quaid-e-Azam. Through with the salt-fish and having downed the glass of Chablis, Jinnah responded placidly: 'Don't be in a hurry; let the waters flow and they will find their own level.'²⁶ In the spring of 1943, at the Muslim League session in Delhi, Jinnah gave the clarion call for 'Pakistan.' It was a proper noun he had refused to baptise ten years ago at a restaurant in Aldwych. Millions of myrmidons would baptise it now with their own blood and marrow.

After their meeting with Quaid-e-Azam at the Dorchester Hotel in the winter of 1946, Qureshi, Master Ali, Chhanu Mia and others were convinced that India was not theirs. Only Pakistan was! But it was not the Pakistan they had been promised; so they realised after the Partition. The newly set up Pakistan High Commission in London refused to issue passports to Bengali lascars without a hefty security deposit. Failing miserably to match up to their Punjabi leaders in the postcolonial standards of skin colour or linguistic flair, the Bengalis of Pakistan were its new second-rate citizens. On February 21, 1952, four Bengali students of Dhaka University— Salam, Barkat, Zabbar and Rafiq—were shot dead in broad daylight in the capital of East Pakistan. It happened during a march led by university students protesting against the imposition of Urdu as the official state language of the western and the eastern wings of Pakistan. Hundreds of protestors were wounded in the firing. Forty-seven years later, UNESCO declared the day of the martyrdom of the four young Bengali students as the International Mother Language Day.

About a year after the shooting in Dhaka, Chhanu Mia led a gang of East Pakistanis into Mukhter Mia's café at 9 Hessel Street. A few hours later, the Pakistan Welfare Association was formed, with Chhanu Mia as its president and Dewan Monfor Ali, its vice president. On February 21, 1954, the Association published the first issue of its magazine, *Desher Daak* (*Call of the Nation*). With their camaraderie of over twenty years, Chhanu Mia, Master Ali and Qureshi would go on to create the Pakistan Caterers' Association to unionise Bengali cooks in Britain. Master Ali's travel agency, Orient Travels, turned Sandy's Row into a covert station for parachuting in more Sylhetis. Suitably enough, it was moved to Brick Lane, the future curry capital of London. Channu Mia's Green Mask restaurant, Mukhter Mia's café and Abdul Matlib Chowdhury's residence at 144 Bethnal Green were used for crepuscular meetings of East Pakistani delinquents. By daybreak, the men went into stewing and sizzling their way through the mutilated skeletons of the Raj, in a city that was once 'the great cesspool into which all the loungers and idlers of the Empire were irresistibly drained.'[27]

The Bard of Avon may even have been tempted to paraphrase the song of Ariel for the imperial city. Of its bones were corals made, and those were pearls now that used to be its eyes. Nothing of it had faded, however, but had merely suffered a 'sea-change, into something rich and strange.'[28] Pakistan—the tormented territory of the pure and pristine—that lay 4,000 miles away, was not a nation that the men of a future Bangladesh had chosen for themselves. However, this London, they were making their own, with a dozen Karachis, Bombays, Calcuttas and Delhis scorching and dazzling diners from every possible curve of the globe with the curries of Madras and Sylhet, made to scurry indistinguishably into each other. Neither was this the beginning nor the end—neither the end of the beginning nor the beginning of the end. This was the timeless past, present and future of India, called by whatever name its citizens were—the city where Peter Pope was baptised and the plunder of Plassey cargoed to embroider the prodigious palaces of Westminster.

At 143 Strand, Krishna Menon's India League was rehabilitated into something it had always been predestined for—a new Anglo–Indian haven of old-world curries. Menon was now India's first High Commissioner to United Kingdom. In 1951, he founded the India Club, warranting that its rites of passage were led by no less than Jawaharlal Nehru and Louis Mountbatten. The two men had shared much more than the cachinnations of Cambridge and the catacombs of Calcutta. They had also shared the broken dream—of giving birth to an undivided India—turned into a prolonged nightmare. Lady Edwina Mountbatten too was on the list of the founding members. The India Club was first built on Craven Street at Charing Cross. It was later moved to the old address of the League. This was where Indian journalists, writers and ministers stayed during their visits to London, as the League reincarnated into a unit of the Congress party to enact postcolonial India before the eyes of postwar Britain. For most visitors, however, it was quite undisguisedly a time-travelling chamber of linoleum floors and green-leather-topped mahoganies, where one could raise a toast to the confected heritage of Mughlai bird-recipes or prawns wriggling out of a mephitic onion sauce.

Where one could ponder over the pound of pepper that had now come full circle after its worldwide excursions—a journey of over 350 years! A gallant crusader of the British Empire once wrote that 'the beginning of everything was in a railway train upon the road to Mhow from Ajmir.'[29] The two railway stations in the then Central Provinces of India would be barely remembered. Far less remembered is that even the beginning of that beginning had begun merely a couple of miles from here, at the Strand, with twenty-four English merchants conspiring at Leadenhall Street on how to defeat a handful of Dutch entrepreneurs in the spice trade with the Indies. Thus was born an Indian London; a city and a nation; the resurrection and the life. Thus were reborn India and London. In the words of Charles Dickens, their lips kissed as they blessed each other solemnly. Behind the murmuring voices and the upturning faces waylaid by pageants dividing the swelling crowd, the invisible knitting-women of many forgotten revolutions had sewn the two destinies; where little did it matter what was Indian and what Londoni; where *gangajal* and the Thames were one great splash of cosmic water; and where *moluga*, spelled as pepper, still tasted of the untold chronicle of our ancient footprints.[30]

Notes

A Chronicle Foretold

1. London, *The People of the Abyss*, pp. 144–45.
2. Derrida, *Specters of Marx*, p. 10.
3. Nietzsche, *The Gay Science*, p. 181.
4. Derrida, *Archive Fever*, p. 62.
5. Iain Sinclair, *London: City of Disappearances*.
6. Stimson, 'Goodbye to India', p. 4.
7. MacGregor, 'India and How It Sees Britain,' *As the World Sees Britain*, *BBC*, March 20, 2019.
8. Gray, 'British Populism and Brexit', *A Point of View*, *BBC*, July 19, 2019.
9. Jacobson, 'The Language of Leaving', *A Point of View*, *BBC*, July 14, 2019.
10. British South Asian Member of Parliament, January 2018.
11. Henry, McEwan and Pollard, 'Birmingham: Postcolonial Workshop of the World?', pp. 124–26.
12. Panayi, 'A British Race Riot of the 1960s?', pp. 139–41.
13. Powell, '"Rivers of Blood" Speech', *The Telegraph*, November 6, 2007.
14. Lewis, 'An Introductory Note to the Study of Race Relations in Great Britain', p. 12.
15. Keith, *After the Cosmopolitan?*, pp. 144–45.
16. Qtd. in Fisher and Abedi, 'Salman Rushdie's *Satanic Verses*', p. 111.
17. Sharma, 'The Ambivalence of Migrancy', pp. 617–18.
18. Walker, 'Europe's Mosque Hysteria', pp. 17–18.

19. Karmakar, 'The Conundrum of "Home"', pp. 80–84.

20. Ramji, 'British Indians "Returning Home"', p. 659.

21. Kumar, *Bombay-London-New York,* p. 215.

22. Qtd. in Buettner, 'Going for an Indian', p. 882.

23. Roden, 'London's Mongrel English Cuisine', p. 69.

24. Buettner, 'Going for an Indian', p. 866.

25. Sartre, 'Intentionality', p. 4.

26. Buettner, 'Going for an Indian', p. 881.

27. 'Curry Statistics', p. 18.

28. 'Britain's Curry Houses Disappearing', *The Telegraph,* February 23, 2017.

29. Grose, 'Indian Food Curries Less Favor in the UK', *US News,* December 14, 2016.

30. Kesvani, 'Curry in Crisis', *New Statesman,* November 18, 2016; Rodionova, 'Brexit-backing Curry Industry Says It Feels "Betrayed"', *The Independent,* November 4, 2016.

31. *Ibid.*

32. Appadurai, 'Commodities and the Politics of Value', pp. 44–45.

33. Hobsbawm, 'Inventing Traditions', pp. 1–14.

34. Derrida, *Psyche,* p. 23.

35. Hobsbawm, 'Inventing Traditions', p. 1.

36. Chatterjee, *The Great Indian Railways,* p. 130.

37. Mathrani, January 2018.

38. *Ibid.*

39. Kebble, 'Veeraswamy: Adding Spice to London for 90 Years', *The Resident,* June 27, 2016.

40. Qtd. in Gander, 'Ethnic Foods Shaping UK Market', *Food Manufacture,* August 12, 2013

41. Appelbaum, *Jacques Derrida's Ghost,* p. 89.

42. Royle, *After Derrida,* p. 11.

43. Mathrani, January 2018.

44. Cited Sen, *Curry,* p. 56.

45. 'A Chef from India: New York Women go Wild over Him', *Park County Bulletin,* November 17, 1899.

46. Zlotnick, 'Curry and Cookbooks in Victorian England', pp. 58–60.

47. Cited in Beetham, 'Dining with Mrs Beeton', p. 391.

48. Zlotnick, 'Curry and Cookbooks in Victorian England', pp. 64–68; Sen, 'The Saracen's Head', p. 419.

49. Sen, *Curry*, p. 47.
50. *Ibid.*, p. 56.
51. Mathrani, January 2018.
52. Morrissy-Swan, 'Deconstructed Cottage Pie and Indian Scotch Eggs: Meet the Man Taking Anglo–Indian Cuisine to the Next Level', *The Telegraph*, January 28, 2019.
53. Michell, Roger (dir.), *Notting Hill*.
54. Deacon, 'Next Time, I'm Bringing Goggles and a Black & Decker', *The Telegraph*, October 13, 2016.
55. Chakraborty, January 2018.
56. *Haat-paakha*: hand-fan; *machher pathuri*: steamed fish in banana leaves; *gondhoraaj lebu*: kaffir lime; *laal shag*: red spinach; *kashundi*: mustard sauce; *mishti doi*: sweet curd; *aam pora*: mango pulp; *shukto*: a bittersweet vegetarian recipe from Bengal.
57. Chatterjee, January 2018.
58. *Doi paapri chaat*: a snack made of curd, crisps and tangy sauces; *luchi chholar daal*: deep fried flatbread with stewed lentils; *rezala*: Mughlai meat recipe; *parota*: fried flatbread; *kosha mangsho*: thick gravy of mutton; *kulo*: jute basket.
59. Chatterjee, January 2018.
60. Lee, January 2018.
61. Bhabha, *The Location of Culture*, p. 122.
62. Gadamer, *Truth and Method*, pp. 291–93.
63. Visvanathan, *A Carnival for Science*, pp. 133–34.
64. MacCready, 'An Ambivalent Luddite at a Technological Feast', *Designfax*, August 1999.
65. Buchan, 'Multicoloured Britain', p. 530.
66. Dhondy, 'An Emergent Ethnic Culture in Britain', p. 209.
67. Ziegler, '"Brick Lane", Capitalism, and the Global Metropolis,' pp. 165–67.
68. Nasser, 'Southall's Kaleido-scape', pp. 76–103.
69. Dennet, *Intuition Pumps*, p. 232.
70. 'Finishing the Euchromatic Sequence of the Human Genome', *International Human Genome Sequencing Consortium,* pp. 931–45.
71. Qtd. in Senapathy, 'Bacteria Listen to Our Thoughts', *Forbes*, January 27, 2016.
72. Visvanathan, 'Ethics, Memory and Innovation', May 2015.

73. Bhaduri, *Polycoloniality: European Transactions with Bengal.*

74. Chaudhuri, *The Autobiography of an Unknown Indian*, p. 190.

75. MacGregor, 'London Becomes Rome', *Shakespeare's Restless World*, *BBC*, May 9, 2012.

76. Miscellaneous Notices, *The Calcutta Review*, 1855, Vol. 24, p. 3.

77. Foucault, *The Order of Things: An Archaeology of Human Sciences* (New York & London: Routledge, 2002) p. 45.

78. Vishwanathan, *Masks of Conquest*, pp. 7–8; 45–46; 160–61.

79. 'Minutes of Evidence Taken Before the Select Committee on Indian Territories', *Reports from Committees, East India*, p. 155.

80. Bengal functioned as the first laboratory for experiments with Shakespeare in India. The first attempts to stage Shakespeare in India were as early as 1753. See Dahiya, *Shakespeare Studies in Colonial Bengal*, pp. 4–6

81. Rescher, *Epistemology*, 54.

82. Hietaranta, *Cognitive Economy and Mental Worlds*, pp. 442–43.

83. Tennyson, *Poetical Works*, p. 279.

84. Derrida, *Psyche*, p. 41.

85. Derrida qtd. in Dick & Kofman (dirs.), *Derrida.*

86. *Ibid.*

87. Derrida, *Of Grammatology*, p. 71.

88. White, *Metahistory.*

89. Bayle, *An Historical and Critical Dictionary*, p. 173.

90. Williams, *The Country and the City*, p. 229.

91. Bartlett, 'Dean Mahomet', p. 8.

92. Narain, 'Dean Mahomet's "Travels"', pp. 610–12; Fisher, *Dean Mahomed.*

93. Ghosh, *The Shadow Lines*, p. 23.

94. Huttunen, 'Representation of London in *The Shadow Lines* by Amitav Ghosh', March 2004.

95. Wordsworth, 'Residence in London', p. 180.

96. Carlyle, *The Life of John Sterling*, p. 57.

97. Ackroyd, *London*, p. 693.

98. *Ibid.*

99. Qtd. in Sen, *Travels to Europe*, p. 77.

100. *Engineering News and American Contract Journal*, p. 284.

101. Qtd. in Chatterjee, *Lineages of Political Society*, p. 47.

102. Chatterjee, *Lineages of Political Society*, p. 47.

103. Nandy, *The Intimate Enemy.*

104. Chatterjee, *Lineages of Political Society*, p. 48.

105. Chakrabarty, *Provincializing Europe*.

106. Self, 'Tough Tough Toys for Tough Tough Boys', p. 120.

107. Rushdie, 'Imaginary Homelands', p. 12.

108. Shakespeare, *A Midsummer Night's Dream*, p. 135.

109. McLuhan, *The Gutenberg Galaxy*, p. 164.

110. For claims that draw parallels between the print revolution and social media revolution of the 15th and 21st centuries, respectively, see Ferguson, *Networks and Power, from the Freemasons to Facebook*.

111. McLuhan, *The Gutenberg Galaxy*, p. 202.

112. Joyce, *Finnegan's Wake*, p. 176.

113. McLuhan, *The Gutenberg Galaxy*, p. 192.

114. Dr Black, 'History of the Smallpox', pp. 187–88.

115. MacGregor, 'From London to Marrakech', *Shakespeare's Restless World*, in BBC, May 2, 2012.

116. Johanyak, 'Early Modern English Orientalism, and Shakespeare's *Othello*', p. 80.

117. MacGregor, 'From London to Marrakech', *Shakespeare's Restless World*, in BBC, May 2, 2012.

118. Fisher, *Counterflows*, pp. 1–3.

119. Hutton and Vaidyanathan, *Census of India, 1931*, pp. 425–429.

120. Visram, *Asians in Britain*, p. 254.

121. Ballard, 'Family Organisation Among the Sikhs in Britain', p. 12.

122. Schaefer, 'Indians in Great Britain', p. 308.

123. Fisher, 'Early-Nineteenth-Century British-Indian Race Relations in Britain', pp. 304–05.

124. Wrigley and Schofield, *The Population History of England*, pp. 208–209.

125. Chatterjee, *The Great Indian Railways*, p. 132.

126. Bhagat, Burke, et al, 'Three and a Half Degrees of Separation', *Facebook Research*, February 4, 2016.

127. Ackroyd, *London*, p. 693.

128. Derrida, *Of Grammatology*, p. 47.

129. Adam. *The Cosmic Time of Empire*.

130. *Ibid*, p. 6. Also, for the importance of the Bradshaw to London life, see the discussion on Sherlock Holmes' intricate knowledge of the Bradshaw, in Chatterjee, *The Great Indian Railways*, pp. 36; 300.

131. Adam. *The Cosmic Time of Empire*, p. 90.

132. Sahibs in aristocratic clothing, carrying accoutrements and symbols of imperial civilisation, were to be found frequently in 19th-century memoirs written about Indian railway journeys, where the formidable figure of the European stood in stark contrast to the meek silhouettes of Indian onlookers. See Chatterjee, *The Great Indian* Railways, pp. 81–83.

133. *Ibid.*, pp. 100–107.

134. Harris, 'The Smell of "Macbeth"', p. 485; Sukic, 'Odours and Aromas in *Love's Labour's Lost*', 2015.

135. Beaumont, *Nightwalking*.

136. Henri, *Critique of Everyday Life*, pp. 213–14.

137. Carlyle, *Collected Works*, p. 77.

138. Angela Vicario and Bayardo San Roman are characters in Gabriel Garcia Marquez's *Chronicle of a Death Foretold,* Trans. Gregory Rabassa (London: Jonathan Cape, 1982). Newlywed Angela is returned to her maternal home, after her husband Bayardo learns that she is not a virgin. Separated from her husband by twenty years, she writes frequent letters to him, while knitting a yarn, in the town of Riohacha. Bayardo returns after twenty years with all her letters, unopened.

139. Dickens, *Great Expectations*, p. 94.

140. Blumel, *George Orwell and the Radical Eccentrics*, pp. 67–102.

141. Nasta, 'Between Bloomsbury and Gandhi', p. 153.

142. Campion, 'Interview with Susheila Nasta', 2017.

143. Anand, *Conversations in Bloomsbury*, p. 49.

144. Desai, *Bye-bye Blackbird*, p. 71.

145. Mintz, *Sweetness and* Power, p. 39.

146. Bayly, 'Looking behind Domestic Tranquillity'.

147. Advertisement: 'Horniman's Pure Tea is the Best', in Bell, *The Chemistry of Foods*.

148. Qtd. in Fabian, *Karl Marx Prince of Darkness*, p. 444.

149. Johnston, 'The Chemistry of Common Life', p. 490.

150. Beecher, *How to Make Homes Happy*, p. 418.

151. Reade, *Tea and Tea Drinking*, pp. 79–104.

152. De Quincey, *Confessions*, p. 141.

153. Schmitt, 'De Quincey, Opium and Tea', p. 66.

154. Wilde, 'Ranjitsinhji Vibhaji, Maharaja Jam Sahib of Navanagar', 2011.

155. Bateman, *Cricket, Literature and Culture*, p. 135.

156. Fuller, *The Story of Noor Inayat Khan*, p. 68.

157. Beaumont, 'Brexit, Retrotopia and the Perils of Post-Colonial Delusions', pp. 379–90.

158. Personal correspondence (excerpt from Will Self's forthcoming book).

159. This is a rephrased version of lines from a sketch from the pilot of *A Bit of Fry & Laurie*. Hugh Laurie arrives at a library looking for *The West Indies: A Nation of Cricketers* by one Ted Cunterblast. On being offered a cut up version of the book, and later an amputated copy of the Wisden, both of which are meant to glorify English cricket, Laurie protests. Stephen Fry, who plays the librarian, goes on to narrate the virtues of English cricket and his own English identity.

160. Ballard, *The Unlimited Dream Company*, pp. 7–20.

161. Self, *Phone*, pp. 13–15.

162. The custom of hanging lovelocks seems to have started in Hungary, in the 1980s. Philipson, 'Hundreds of Couples Leave "Love Locks" Across London Ahead of Valentine's Day', *The Telegraph*, February 12, 2013.

163. Doyle, *The Sign of Four*, p. 44.

164. Chesterton, *Heretics*, p. 51.

165. Donne, 'Meditation', p. 575.

166. Keay, *The Honourable Company*, p. 13.

ACT I

Scene I: The Baptism

1. Neill, *Memoir of Rev. Patrick Copland*, pp. 12–13.

2. Dickens, *Our Mutual Friend*, p. 187.

3. Ackroyd, *London*, p. 96.

4. Churchill, *Speeches*, p. 179.

5. Qtd. in Collins and Lapierre, *Freedom at Midnight*, p. 14.

6. 'Sketches and Portraits from the History of the Mahomedan Dominion Over India', p. 91.

Scene II: Brewing a Colony in a Tea Cup

1. Evelyn, *Lives of Alfred the Great, Sir Thomas More, and John Evelyn*, p. 18.

2. Poole, Steven. 'What Does Boris Johnson Mean by "Teleological Construction"', in *The Guardian*, February 15, 2018,

3.   Pepys, *The Diary*, Vol. 1, pp. 254.

4.   Makepeace, 'A Most Fearefull and Dreadfull Fire', *British Library, Untold Lives Blog*, September 2, 2016

5.   Qtd. in Liu, *Tea Trade with China*, p. 142.

6.   Pepys, *The Diary*, Vol. 1, p. 254.

7.   Qtd. in Rappaport, *A Thirst for Empire*, p. 164.

8.   Mangham, 'Wilkie Collins', p. 385.

9.   Collins, *The Moonstone*, p. 105.

10. Cavert, *The Smoke of London*, p. 136.

11. Kelly, 'The 1992 Campaign', in *The New York Times*, October 31, 1992.

12. Mirza, *The Rise and Fall of the American Empire*, 171.

13. Geczy, *Fashion and Orientalism*, p. 28.

14. Beckert, *Empire of Cotton*, p. 48.

15. Qtd. in Ure, *The Cotton Manufacture of Great Britain*, p. 31.

16. Beckert, *Empire of Cotton*, p. 46.

17. Derrida, *Spectres of Marx*, p. 189.

18. Ackroyd, *London*, p. 96.

Scene III: An Indian Fish, Dead or Alive

1.   Neill, *A History of Christianity in India*, p. 375.

2.   Qtd. in O'Connor, *Chaplains of India*, pp. 41–42

3.   Shakespeare, *The Tempest*, p. 34.

4.   Ackroyd, *London*, p. 292.

5.   Habib, *Black Lives in the English Archives*, p. 183.

6.   'Guildhall Library Manuscripts Section: Black and Asian People Discovered in Records Held by the Manuscripts Section', in Institute of Historical Research, School of Advanced Study University of London.

7.   Visram, *Asians in Britain*, p. 13.

8.   Taylor, *Fielding's England*, p. 159.

9.   Qtd. in Ashton, *Social Life in the Reign of Queen Anne*, p. 81.

10. Visram, *Asians in Britain*, p. 9.

11. Woolf, *A Room of One's Own*, p. 71.

12. *Ibid.*, p. 73.

ACT II

Scene I: An Armenian in the City

1. 'The Dispatches of Field Marshal the Duke of Wellington', *The Quarterly Review*, Vol. 58, p. 92.
2. Prior, *Life and Character of the Right Hon. Edmund Burke*, pp. 517–18.
3. Chaudhury, *Trade, Politics and Society*, p. 129.
4. *Bengal, Past & Present*, Vol. 5, No. 1, p. 390.
5. Seth, *Armenians in India, from the Earliest Times to the Present Day*, p. 477.
6. Macknight, Thomas. *History of the Life and Times of Edmund Burke*, Vol. 1, p. 86
7. Malleson, *The Decisive Battles of India*, p. 68.
8. Walpole, *Letters*, p. 320.
9. Emin, *The Life and Adventures*, p. 26
10. *Ibid.*, pp. 34–37.
11. Qtd. in Murray, *Edmund Burke*, p. 64.
12. Montagu, *The Letters*, p. 51
13. Prior, *Memoir of the Life and Character of the Right Hon. Edmund Burke*, p. 519.
14. *Ibid.*

Scene II: The Orient Arrives

1. Fisher, *Counterflows to Colonialism*, p. 87.
2. Qtd. in Chatterjee, *The Black Hole of Empire*, p. 69.
3. Ihtishamuddin, *Travels*, p. 37–38.
4. *Ibid.*, p. 76.
5. Ihtishamuddin, *Travels*, p. 164.
6. *Ibid.*, p. 35.
7. Chatterjee, *The Black Hole of Empire*, p. 70.
8. Gleig, *Memoirs of the Life of Warren Hastings*, p. 375.
9. Lock, *Edmund Burke*, Vol. 2, p. 157.
10. Qtd. in Moon, *The British Conquest and Dominion of India*, p. 413.
11. Lock, *Edmund Burke*, Vol. 2, p. 34.
12. *History of the Proceedings and Debates of the House of Commons*, p. 485.

13. *Ibid.*
14. Gibbes, *Hartly House*, Vol. 2, p. 159.
15. Burke, *Correspondences*, p. 431.
16. George III, *The Correspondence of King George*, p. 261.
17. *Correspondence of the Right Honourable Edmund Burke*, Vol. 3, pp. 7–8.
18. Qtd. in *Gujarat State Gazetteers*, p. 73
19. Khan, *The Travels of Mirza Abu Taleb*, p. 18

Scene III: From an Indian Harem to a London Tavern

1. Qtd. in Willasey, 'Of Intelligence, an Assassination, East Indiamen and the Great Hurricane of 1808', 2014.
2. Khan, *The Travels of Mirza Abu Taleb*, p. 82.
3. *Ibid.*, p. 161.
4. *Ibid.*, p. 165.
5. *Ibid.*, p. 188.
6. *Ibid.*, p. 319.
7. *Ibid.*, p. 233.
8. *Ibid.*
9. *Ibid.*, p. 202.
10. *Ibid.*, p. 209.
11. *Ibid.*, p. 240.
12. *Ibid.*, p. 242.
13. *Ibid.*, p. 163.
14. *Ibid.*, p. 164.
15. *Ibid.*, p. 166.

Scene IV: Nurseries for Nabobs

1. Said, *Orientalism*, p. 212.
2. Qtd. in Fisher, *Counterflows to Colonialism*, pp. 119–20.
3. Qtd. in *Ibid.*, p. 127.
4. Qtd. in *Ibid.*, p. 128
5. Ali, *Observations on the Mussulmauns of India*, Vol. 1, 313.
6. Graham, *Journal of a Residence in India*, p. 13
7. 'Hertford College, General Examination' *The Asiatic Journal and Monthly Miscellany*, Vol. 5, p. 96.

Scene V: For the Sake of Mahomet

1. Wilde, *The Importance of Being Earnest*, p. 38.
2. Qtd. in Hazlitt, *Old Cookery Books and Ancient Cuisine*, p. 180.
3. Chatterjee, Arup K. 'How the Curry Came to London', in *Scroll*, June, 2017.
4. Macaulay, 'Minute', 1835.
5. Horne, *The Adventures of Naufragus*, p. 33.
6. Carey, *The Good Old Days of Honorable John Company*, p. 100.
7. Spear, *The Nabobs*, p. 36.
8. Henderson, *The Bengalee*, p. 408.
9. Collingham, *Curry*, p. 107.
10. *The British Critic, and Quarterly Theological Review*, Vol. 21, p. 24.
11. Henderson, *The Bengalee*, p. 408.
12. *The Nation and the Athenaeum*, Vol. 28, March, 1921, p. 920.
13. *The Spectator*, Vol. 108, February, 1912, p. 273.
14. 'Kitchen Melodies: Curry', p. 221
15. Soyer, *The Modern Housewife: Or, Ménagère*, p. 85.
16. Acton, *Modern Cookery in all its Branches*, p. 286.
17. Advertisement in *The Morning Post*, February 2, 1810.
18. Erredge, *The Ancient and Modern History of Brighton*, p. 235.
19. Mahomet, *Shampooing*, p. 77.
20. Sanghani, 'British Citizenship Test Is Just a "Bad Pub Quiz"', *The Telegraph*, June13, 2013.
21. 'And Mr Mohamed Too', *The Guardian*, April 9, 2002.
22. Mahomet, *The Travels of Deen Mahomet*, p. 101–102.
23. Roy, 'Origin of a Species: The First Indian to Publish a Book in English', *The Caravan*, December 1, 2015.
24. Collingham, *Curry*, p. 129.
25. Vivek Singh, qtd. in 'Curry House Founder Honored', *BBC*, September 29, 2005.
26. Mahomed, 'The Physiology and Clinical Use of the Sphygmograph', *Medical Times Gazette*, Vol. 1, No. 6, p. 63.
27. O'Rourke, 'Personal and Historical Perspectives: Frederick Akbar Mahomed', p. 212.
28. Cameron and Hicks, 'Frederick Akbar Mahomed and his role in the description of hypertension at Guy's Hospital', *Kidney International*, Vol. 49, p. 1500.
29. *Ibid.*, p. 1490.

ACT III

Scene I: Married to Empire

1. Ghosh, *Sex and the Family in Colonial India*, p. 163.
2. Qtd. in *Ibid.*, p. 167.
3. Dalrymple, *White Mughals*, p. 100.
4. 'A True Story', *The Indicator*, Vol. 1, pp. 319–20.
5. Dalrymple, *White Mughals*, p. 40.
6. Aveling, 'Autobiography of the Native Evangelist', *The Evangelical Magazine and Missionary Chronicle*, Vol. 33, p. 553.
7. Chatterton, *A History of the Church of England in India*, p. 91.
8. Sherwood, *The Lady of the Manor*, p. 257.
9. *The Brockport Republic*, Vol. 40, No. 22, February 27, 1896.
10. Mundy, *Pen and Pencil Sketches: Being the Journal of a Tour in India*, Vol. 1, pp. 369–72.
11. Scott, *Castle Dangerous*, 1832.
12. Qtd. in Fisher, *The Inordinately Strange Life of Dyce Sombre*, p. 268.
13. *The Calcutta Review*, Vol. 70, 1870, p. 459.

Scene II: Rag-tag of the Raj

1. Ackroyd, *London*, p. 208.
2. Qtd. in Visram, *Asians in Britain*, p. 11.
3. Visram, *Asians in Britain*, p. 44.
4. Roche, *Childhood in India*, p. 2.
5. Wilkins, *A Child's Eye View*, p. 11.
6. Fisher, 'Viewing the Early Twentieth-Century Institutional Interior Through the Pages of *Living London*', pp. 20–30.
7. *The Asiatic Journal and Monthly Register for British and Foreign India, China, and Australia*, Vol. 16, July-December, 1823, p. 67.
8. *Ibid.*, p. 57.
9. Fisher, *Counterflows to Colonialism*, p. 160.
10. *The Mariners' Church Gospel Temperance Soldiers' and Sailor's Magazine*, January 1843, p. 767.
11. *The Mariners' Church Gospel Temperance Soldiers' and Sailor's Magazine*, January 1845, p. 127.
12. *Ibid.*, p. 37.
13. *Westerly*, Vol. 29, 1984, p. 120.

14. Salter, *The Asiatic in England*, pp. 85–88.

15. Ackroyd, *London*, p. 666.

16. Visram, *Asians in Britain*, p. 68.

17. Erickson, *The Life of Queen Victoria*, p. 241.

18. *Ibid.*, p. 247.

19. Curzon, *Letters of a Vicereine*, p. 126.

Scene III: Scent of Steam

1. Sen, *Rajah Rammohun Roy*, p. 164.

2. Carpenter, *Rajah Rammohun Roy*, p. 115.

3. Qtd. in Zastoupil, *Rammohun Roy*, p. 119.

4. Zastoupil, *Rammohun Roy*, p. 127.

5. Bentham, *Collected Works*, Vol. 11, p. 7.

6. *Ibid.*, p. 66.

7. Letter from Lucy Aikin to William Ellery Channing, in Carpenter (ed.), *The Last Days in England*, p. 75.

8. Ray, 'Rammohun Roy and English Intellectuals', p. 184.

9. Singh, *Rammohun Roy*, 398.

10. Lamb, 'The Superannuated Man', p. 71.

11. Nowrojee and Meerwanjee, *Journal of a Residence of Two Years and a Half*, pp. 134–35.

Scene IV: The Baboos' Last Sigh

1. Kling, *Partner in Empire*, p. 21.

2. *Ibid.*

3. Dutta, *Calcutta*, p. 90.

4. Kripalani, *Dwarkanath Tagore*, p. 141.

5. Chatterjee, *The Great Indian Railways*, p. 84.

6. Qtd. in Kling, *Partner in Empire*, p. 169.

7. Qtd. in *Ibid.*, p. 170.

8. *Ibid.*, p. 171.

9. Qtd. in Mittra, *Memoir of Dwarkanath Tagore*, pp. 88–89.

10. Friedrich Engels, *The Condition of the Working Class in England*, p. 329.

11. Mittra, *Memoir of Dwarkanath Tagore*, p. 90.

12. *The Spectator*, Vol. 15, January, 1842, p. 750.

13. Bell, *British Folks & British India Fifty Years Ago*, p. 141.

14. *Ibid.*, p. 141–42.

15. Kling, *Partner in Empire*, p. 12.

16. Young, *The Second Maratha Campaign*, p. xvi.

17. Von Orlich, *Travels in India*, Vol. 2, p. 181.

18. *The Colonial Magazine and Commercial Maritime Journal*, p. 339.

19. Qtd. in Kling, *Partner in Empire*, p. 175.

20. Kling, *Partner in Empire*, p. 182.

21. Chatterjee, *The Great Indian Railways*, pp. 43–44.

22. Kripalani, *Dwarkanath Tagore*, p. 209.

23. Stocqueler, *The Memoirs of a Journalist*, p. 171.

24. Mozoomdar, *The Life and Teachings of Keshub Chunder Sen*, p. 221.

25. *Punch*, Vol. 57–60, p. 155.

26. Sen, *Diary, Sermons, Addresses & Epistles*, p. 239.

27. *Ibid.*, p. 175.

28. Mozoomdar, *The Life and Teachings of Keshub Chunder Sen*, p. 223.

29. Aravamudan, *Guru English*, p. 47.

30. Mozoomdar, *The Life and Teachings of Keshub Chunder Sen*, pp. 222–224.

31. Sen, *Diary, Sermons, Addresses & Epistles*, p. 28.

32. Mill, *Collected Works*, Vol. 6, p. 519.

33. Sen, *Diary, Sermons, Addresses & Epistles*, p. 38.

34. *Ibid.*, p. 398.

35. *Judy*, Vol. 11, p. 154.

36. Parekh, *Brahmarshi Keshub Chunder Sen*, p. 69.

37. Müller, *Biographical Essays*, pp. 49–166.

38. Qtd. in Visram, *Asians in Britain*, p. 115.

39. 'Letter from Charles Lamb to William Wordsworth', January 30, 1801, p. 763.

40. Ackroyd, *London*, p. 181.

41. Knight, (ed.), *London*, p. 37.

42. Sen, *Diary, Sermons, Addresses & Epistles*, p. 481.

ACT IV

Scene I: City of Counselors and Clients

1. Eliot, *The Waste Land and Other Poems*, p. 72.

2. Mody, *Pherozeshah Mehta*, p. 112

3. Ali, *The Spirit of Islam*, p. 11.
4. *Ibid.*, p. 192.
5. Baker, *The Last Englishmen*, p. 185.
6. Majumdar, *Family History*, p. 73.
7. Qtd. in Burton, *At the Heart of Empire*, p. 25.
8. Banerjea, *A Nation in Making*, pp. 12–14.
9. Qtd. in Lahiri, *Indians in Britain*, p. 155.
10. Qtd. in Mukherjee, *An Indian for All Seasons*, p. 8.
11. Qtd. in *Ibid.*, p. 155.
12. Mukharji, *A Visit to Europe*, p. 78–79.
13. *Ibid.*, p. 99–100
14. *Ibid.*, p. 100.
15. *Ibid.*, p. 105.
16. *Ibid.*, p. 132.
17. *The Spectator*, Vol. 63, 1889, p. 528.
18. Mukharji, *A Visit to Europe*, p. 90.

Scene II: Trains of Fact and Folklore

1. Sen, *Travels to Europe*, p. 82.
2. Qtd. in *ibid.*, p. 76.
3. Qtd. in *ibid.*, p. 81.
4. Roy, *Reminiscences: England and India*, p. 29.
5. Mukharji, *A Visit to Europe*, p. 34.
6. Shah, 'A Visit to the Tower of London', p. 209.
7. Roy, *Impressions of England*, p. 103.
8. Sen, *Travels to Europe*, p. 78–79.
9. Qtd. in *ibid.*, p. 84.
10. Tagore, *Selected Letters*, p. 90
11. Rhys, *Rabindranath Tagore*, p. 5.
12. Jack, 'Rabindranath Tagore was a Global Phenomenon', *The Guardian*, May 7, 2011.
13. Rabindranath. 'Letter to Sir William Rothenstein, November 26, 1932', p. 119.
14. Ghosh, '*Abol Tabol*: The Making of a Book', p. 245.
15. Malabari, *The Indian Eye*, p. 65.
16. *Ibid.*, p. 217–18.
17. Visram, *Asians in Britain*, p. 113.

Scene III: Raising the Bar

1.   Hobhouse, Mary, 'Progress of Female Education in India', *The Times*, April 13, 1888.
2.   Sorabji, *India Calling*, p. 52.
3.   Chambers, 'Indian Theatre in Britain', p. 157.
4.   *The March of India*, Vol. 13, 1961, p. 13.
5.   Naidu, *Speeches and Writings*, p. xiii.
6.   Sengupta, *Sarojini Naidu*, p. 89.
7.   Bubb, 'Tracing the Legacy of an Experimental Generation', p. 48.
8.   Naidu, *Speeches and Writings*, p. 105.
9.   *Ibid.*, p. 47–48.
10. Maher, 'Jinnah's Abode: No. 35, Russell Road', *The Express Tribune*, July 21, 2013.
11. 'Grey Wolf', in *India Today*, January 8, 2011.
12. Qtd. in Ahmed, *Jinnah, Pakistan and Islamic Identity*, p. 7.
13. Ahmad, *Quaid-i-Azam*, p. 159.
14. Qtd. in Bolitho, *Jinnah: Creator of Pakistan*, p. 19.
15. Qtd. in Moraes, *Jawaharlal Nehru*, p. 47.
16. Nehru, *The Essential Writings*, Vol. 2, pp. 593–94
17. Khan, *Words of Freedom*, p. 41.
18. Naidu, *Selected Poetry and Prose*, p. 144.
19. Qtd. in Dutt, *Romesh Chunder Dutt*, p. 62.
20. Qtd. in McCully, *The Origins of Indian Nationalism*, p. 301.
21. 'Britain's First Asian MP elected,' in *The Guardian*, July 26, 1892.
22. Banerjea, *A Nation in Making*, pp. 54.
23. Collins and Lapierre, *Freedom at Midnight*, p. 55.
24. Gandhi, *Collected Works*, Vol. 39, p. 42.
25. Gandhi, *Collected Works*, Vol. 10, p. 16–17.
26. Nanda, *Mahatma Gandhi*, p. 28.
27. Gandhi, *Collected Works*, Vol. 1, p. 93.
28. Gandhi, *Gandhi: The Man ...*, p. 31.
29. Gandhi, *Collected Works*, Vol. 39, p. 59.
30. Bubb, 'Three Iconic Indian Travellers in 1890s London,' p. 50.
31. Collingham, *Curry*, p. 178.
32. Gandhi, *Collected Works*, Vol. 1, p. 63.
33. Visram, *Asians in Britain*, p. 133.
34. 'Britain's First Asian MP elected,' in *The Guardian*, July 26, 1892.

35. *The First Indian Member of the Imperial Parliament*, p. 111.

36. Sheikh, *An Indian in The House*, p. 121.

37. Visram, *Asians in Britain*, p. 146.

38. *Ibid.*, p. 137.

39. Visram, *Ayahs, Lascars and Princes*, p. 96.

40. Qtd. in *ibid.*, p. 96–97.

41. Hinnels, *The Zoroastrian Diaspora*, p. 314.

Scene IV: A House of Uncommons

1. Visram, *Ayahs, Lascars and Princes*, p. 103.

2. Qtd. in Anand, *Sophia*, p. 229.

3. *Journal of Indian History*, Vol. 63, 1985, p. 98.

4. Gandhi, *Collected Works*, Vol. 9, p. 428.

5. *The Independent*, Vol. 63, 1909, pp. 58–59.

6. Iyer, *South Asian Affairs*, p. 62.

7. Datta, *Madan Lal Dhingra and the Revolutionary Movement*, p. 73.

8. *Ibid.*, p. 37.

9. Qtd. in *Ibid.*, p. 40.

10. Ward, *Maud Gonne*, p. 71.

11. *Britain and India*, Vol. 1, 1920, p. 96.

Scene V: A Theatre of Theatres

1. *The Indian Magazine and Review*, Vol. 43, No. 496, 1912, p. 99.

2. Chambers, Colin. 'Indian Theatre in Britain in the Early Twentieth Century,' p. 152.

3. Qtd. in *ibid.*, p. 153.

4. *Ibid.*, p. 156.

5. Qtd. in *ibid.*, p. 160.

6. Kehr, '*A Throw of Dice* and Summer Serials,' in *The New York Times*, July 15, 2008.

7. Bradshaw, 'Review: A Throw of Dice,' in *The Guardian*, August 24, 2007.

8. *Quaid-i-Azam Mohammad Ali Jinnah Papers*, pp. 566–69.

9. Chand, *History of the Freedom Movement in India*, p. 544.

10. *Quaid-i-Azam Mohammad Ali Jinnah Papers*, pp. 569.

11. Qtd. in Chakrabarty, *The Partition of Bengal and Assam*, p. 98.

12. Collins and Lapierre, *Freedom at Midnight*, p. 42.

13. Khan, *The Great Partition*, p. 115.
14. Kamran, 'Choudhary Rahmat Ali and his Political Imagination,' p. 87.
15. Aziz, *Rahmat Ali*, p. 352.
16. *Pakistan Movement: Historical Documents*, p. 115.
17. Aziz, *Rahmat Ali*, p. 85.
18. Qtd. in Ahmed, *Bengal Politics in Britain*, p. 37.
19. Qtd. in *ibid.*, p. 38.
20. Churchill, *The War Speeches*, p. 119.
21. Forward, 'Syed Ameer Ali: A Bridge Builder?', pp. 45–62.
22. Ansari, 'The Struggle to Create Muslim Space', 1910–1944, p. 86.
23. Qtd. in Visram, *Asians in Britain*, p. 199.
24. Lambert-Hurley, 'Atiya Fyzee in Edwardian London', p. 69.
25. Gandhi, *Understanding the Muslim Mind*, p. 51.
26. Qtd. in Gandhi, *Understanding the Muslim Mind*, p. 52.

ACT V

Scene I: Jewel in the Crown

1. Login, *Sir John Login and Duleep Singh*, p. 127.
2. Ranjan, Ramani, Agarwal, Chembolu and Dhiman, 'Kohinoor and its Travelogy: The Dialectic of Ownership and Reparations of an Artefact', p. 50.
3. *The Life of Swami Vivekananda*, p. 21.
4. Vivekananda, *The Complete Works*, Vol. 7, p. 499.
5. Vivekananda, *The Complete Works*, Vol. 2, p. 118. Also see, Wordsworth, 'Ode: Intimations of Immortality', li. 64, p. 24.
6. Vivekananda, *Letters*, p. 319.
7. Vivekananda, *The Complete Works*, Vol. 5, p. 190.
8. *The Life of Swami Vivekananda*, p. 60.
9. Vivekananda, *The Complete Works*, Vol. 2, p. 122.
10. Lawson, Alastair. 'Eton, the Raj and Modern India', in *BBC*, March 9, 2005.
11. Anand, *Sophia*, p. 30.
12. Kaye and Malleson, *History of the Indian Mutiny*, p. 34.
13. Bedi, 'India Finally Settles £1million Nizam Dispute', *The Telegraph*, April 12, 2008.
14. Balfour, *Famous Diamonds*, p. 144.

15. Zubrzycki, *The Mysterious Mr Jacob*, p. 2.
16. Bedi, 'India Finally Settles £1million Nizam Dispute'.
17. Collins, 'Preface', *The Moonstone*, p. 4.
18. Talairach-Vielmas, *Wilkie Collins, Medicine and the Gothic*, p. 77.
19. *The Spectator*, Vol. 44, June 1871, p. 442.
20. *Vanity Fair*, Vol. 23, January 1880, p. 61.
21. Collins, *The Moonstone*, p. 58.
22. Login, *Sir John Login & Duleep Singh*, p. 470.
23. Taylor, 'Revealed: The Woman Who Terrified the British Empire', *Independent*, May 25, 2009.
24. Qtd. in Visram, *Asians in Britain*, p. 174.
25. *Ibid.*
26. Singh, *Correspondence*, p. 375.
27. Roy, *Russo-Indian Relations in the Nineteenth Century*, p. 383.
28. Qtd. in Anand, *Sophia*, p. 289.
29. *Ibid.*
30. Anand, 'The Incredible Suffragette Princess Lost to History', *The Telegraph*, January 15, 2015.
31. Anand, 'Sophia, the Suffragette', *The Times of India*, January 11, 2015.
32. Anand, 'The Incredible Suffragette Princess Lost to History', *The Telegraph*, January 15, 2015.
33. Qtd. in Visram, *Asians in Britain*, p. 175.
34. Visram, *Asians in Britain*, p. 184.

Scene II: The Spirit and the Spectre

1. Mukherjee, 'Herabai Tata and Sophia Duleep Singh', p. 112.
2. Snaith, *Colonial Women Writers in London, 1890–1945*, p. 86.
3. Naidu, *Words of Freedom*, p. 75.
4. Naidu, *Speeches and Writings*, p. xxii.
5. Vernon, *Krishnamurti, the Invention of a Messiah*, p. 52.
6. Brendon, *The Decline and Fall of the British Empire*, p. 249.
7. Chopra, *A Joint Enterprise*, pp. xi–xii.
8. Qtd. in Lutyens, *J. Krishnamurti*, p. 54.
9. Lutyens, *J. Krishnamurti*, p. 663.
10. Squires, *Saklatvala*, p. 14.
11. Qtd. in Myers, 'Labour Against Empire', in *Jacobin*, February 19, 2018.
12. Saha, *Shapurji Saklatvala*, p. vii.

13.   Qtd. in Myers, 'Labour Against Empire', *Jacobin*, February 19, 2018.
14.   Wadsworth, *Comrade Sak*, p. 43.
15.   Qtd. in Marquand, *Ramsay MacDonald*, p. 488.
16.   Marx, *Political Writings*, p. 25
17.   Dutt, *Britain's Crisis of Empire*, Vol. 2, p. 131.
18.   Qtd. in Wadsworth, *Comrade Sak*, p. 97.
19.   Saha, *Shapurji Saklatvala*, p. 93.
20.   Qtd. in Wadsworth, *Comrade Sak*, p. 97.
21.   Kopf, *The Brahmo Samaj*, p. 111.
22.   Unwin, *The Story of Immigrants as Told in Obituaries from The Times*, p. 46.
23.   Myers, 'Labour Against Empire', *Jacobin*, February 19, 2018.
24.   *The Parliamentary Debates, House of Commons*, Vol. 180, 1925, p. 457.
25.   *The Labour Monthly*, Vol. 19, No. 1, January 1937, p. 52.
26.   Qtd. in Wadsworth, *Comrade Sak*, p. 49.
27.   Qtd. in Myers, 'Labour Against Empire', Jacobin, February 19, 2018.
28.   Qtd. in Saha, *Shapurji Saklatvala*, p. 76.
29.   Sheikh, *An Indian in The House*, p. 255.
30.   *The Communist International*, Vol. 13, 1936, p. 347.
31.   Qtd. in Saha, *Shapurji Saklatvala*, p. 101.

Scene III: The League of a Nation

1.   Menon, 'My Years in England', p. 17–18.
2.   'Mr Churchill on India', *Daily Telegraph*, February 24, 1931 (emphasis added).
3.   Churchill, Winston. *The Collected Essays*, Vol. 2, p. 226.
4.   Collins and Lapierre, *Freedom at Midnight*, p. 66.
5.   Potter, *The Nigel Barton Plays: Two Television Plays*, p. 106.
6.   Pillai, *The Courtesan, the Mahatma & the Italian Brahmin*, p. 271–73.
7.   Hall, '"Mephistopheles in a Saville Row Suit": V. K. Krishna Menon and the West', pp. 191-216.
8.   Pillai, *The Courtesan, the Mahatma & the Italian Brahmin*, p. 272-74.
9.   Khilnani, 'Nehru's Evil Genius', in *Outlook*, Vol. 47, No. 6-13, 2007.
10.   Nehru, *Jawaharlal. An Anthology*, p. 564.

11. Visram, *Asians in Britain*, p. 330.
12. Yeoman, 'Did Unity Mitford have Adolf Hitler's Love Child?', *The Times*, December 13, 2007.
13. Bose, *Life and Work*, p. 1954.
14. Toye, *The Springing Tiger*, p. 49.
15. *Ibid.*, p. 47.
16. Bose, *Words of Freedom*, p. 89.
17. *Report of the Delegation Sent to India by the India League, 1932*, p. xv.
18. Chakravarty, *V.K. Krishna Menon and the India League*, p. 285.
19. Qtd. in Faber, *Speaking for England*, p. 376.
20. *The Spectator*, Vol. 223, July 1969, p. 493.
21. Qtd. in Visram, *Asians in Britain*, p. 337.
22. Roosevelt, 'Letter to Winston Churchill, on April 11, 1942'.
23. Dilks, (ed.), *The Diaries of Sir Alexander Cadogan*, p. 582.

Scene IV: Between the Ink and the Deep Sea

1. Anand, *Conversations in Bloomsbury*, pp. 44.
2. *Ibid.*, pp. 62-63.
3. *Ibid.*, p. 63.
4. Chambers, *Britain Through Muslim Eyes: Literary Representations, 1780-1988*, p. 130.
5. Anand, 'On the Progressive Writers Movement', p. 1.
6. Ackroyd, *London*, p. 17.
7. Luthra, *Indian Broadcasting*, p. 94.
8. Visram, *Asians in Britain*, p. 261.
9. *Ibid.*, p. 267.

Scene V: If Empire be the Love of Food

1. Orwell, *The Complete Works*, Vol. 12, p. 183.
2. Collingham, *Curry*, p. 239.
3. Buettner, '"Going for an Indian": South Asian Restaurants and the Limits of Multiculturalism in Britain', p. 893.
4. Collingham, *Curry*, p. 2.
5. Monroe, *The Spicy Adventures of Curry*, p. 4.
6. 'Glasgow "invented" Tikka Masala', *BBC*, July 21, 2009.

7.   'Wanted, an Anglo–Indian Restaurant for London', in *Caterer*, June 15, 1891, p. 221.
8.   Malabari, *The Indian Eye*, p. 45.
9.   Qtd. in 'Shafi's Restaurant', *Making Britain*, The Open University.
10.   Collingham, *Curry*, p. 220.
11.   Monroe, *The Spicy Adventures of Curry*, p. 83.
12.   Collingham, *Curry*, p. 153.
13.   Highmore, *Ordinary Lives*, p. 158.
14.   Monroe, *The Spicy Adventures of Curry*, p. 83.
15.   Qtd. in Monroe, *Star of India*, p. 85.
16.   Qtd. in Assael, *The London Restaurant*, p. 168.
17.   Monroe, *The Spicy Adventures of Curry*, p. 87.
18.   Collingham, *Curry*, p. 218.
19.   Visram, *Asians in Britain*, p. 258.
20.   Collingham, *Curry*, p. 226
21.   Qtd. in Katy Gardner, '*Desh-Bidesh*', p. 361.
22.   Collingham, *Curry*, p. 225.
23.   Grigg, 'Myths About the Approach to Indian Independence', p. 204-205.
24.   Guha, *The Mahatma and the Netaji*, p. 127.
25.   Assael, 'Gastro-Cosmopolitanism and the Restaurant in Late Victorian and Edwardian London', pp. 681.
26.   Qtd. in Wasti, *My Reminiscences of Choudhary Rahmat Ali*, p. 118.
27.   Doyle, *A Study in Scarlet*, p. 2.
28.   Shakespeare, *The Tempest*, Act I, Sc. II, p. 19
29.   Kipling, *The Phantom Rickshaw, and Other Tales*, p. 66.
30.   Dickens, *A Tale of Two Cities*, p. 436.

References

Books, Essays in Collected Volumes and Old Periodicals

'A True Story'. 1822. *The Indicator*. London: Joseph Appleyard, (1) pp. 319-20.

ACKROYD, Peter. 2003. *London: The Biography*. London: Anchor Books.

ACTON, Eliza. 1845. *Modern Cookery in all its Branches: Reduced to a System of Easy Practice for Private Families*. London: Longman, Brown, Green & Longmans.

AGNANI, Sunil. 2017. 'The Reception of Edmund Burke's Imperial Ideas Relating to India, or Burke, the Brahmin and the Hot-House'. In *The Reception of Edmund Burke in Europe*, edited by Martin Fitzpatrick Peter Jones. London and New York: Bloomsbury, pp. 171–190.

AHMAD, Jamil-Ud-Din. 1966. *Quaid-i-Azam, as Seen by His Contemporaries*. Lahore: Publishers United.

AHMED, Akbar S. 1997. *Jinnah, Pakistan and Islamic Identity: The Search for Saladin*. London and New York: Routledge.

AHMED, Faruque. 2010. *Bengal Politics in Britain: Logic, Dynamics & Disharmony*. Morrisville: Lulu.

ALI, Meer Hasan. 1832. *Observations on the Mussulmauns of India: Descriptive of their Manners, Customs, Habits and Religious Opinions: Made During a Twelve Years' Residence in their Immediate Society*. London: Parbury, Allen & Co. (1).

ALI, Syed Ameer. 2010. *The Spirit of Islam: A History of the Evolution and Ideals of Islam*. New York: Cosimo.

ALLANA, Gulam (ed.). 1977. *Pakistan Movement: Historical Documents*. Lahore: Islamic Book Service.

Allen's Indian Mail, and Register of Intelligence for British and Foreign India, China, and All Parts of the East. London: W.H. Allen & Co. 1856 (14).

ANAND, Anita. 2015. *Sophia: Princess, Suffragette, Revolutionary*. London and New Delhi: Bloomsbury.

ANAND, Mulk Raj. 1979. 'On the Progressive Writers Movement'. In *Marxist Cultural Movement in India*, edited by S. Pradhan. Calcutta: National Book Agency, (1) pp. 1–23.

——. 1981. *Conversations in Bloomsbury*, edited by Saros Cowasjee. New Delhi: Arnold-Heinemann.

ANSARI, Humayun. 2013. '"A Mosque in London Worthy of the Tradition of Islam and Worthy of the Capital of the British Empire": The Struggle to Create Muslim Space, 1910–1944'. In *India in Britain: South Asian Networks and Connections, 1858-1950* edited by Susheila Nasta. Basingstoke: Palgrave Macmillan, pp. 80–95.

APPADURAI, Arjun. 1988. 'Commodities and the Politics of Value' in *The Social Life of Things: Commodities in Cultural Perspective*, edited by Appadurai. Cambridge: University of Cambridge Press, pp. 3–63.

APPELBAUM, David. 2009. *Jacques Derrida's Ghost: A Conjuration*. Albany: State University of New York Press.

ARAVAMUDAN, Srinivas. 2011. *Guru English: South Asian Religion in a Cosmopolitan Language*. Princeton: Princeton University Press.

ASHTON, John. 1882. *Social Life in the Reign of Queen Anne: Taken from Original Sources*. London: Chatto and Windus, (1).

ASSAEL, Brenda. 2018. *The London Restaurant, 1840–1914*. London: Oxford University Press.

AVELING, Thomas. 1845. 'Autobiography of the Native Evangelist'. In *The Evangelical Magazine and Missionary Chronicle*. London: Thomas Ward & Co., (33) pp. 553–54.

AYYAR, A.S.P. 1942. *An Indian in Western Europe*. Madras: C. Coomaraswamy Naidu & Sons.

AZIZ, Khursheed Kamal. 1987. *Rahmat Ali: A Biography*. Stuttgart: Steiner Verlag Wiesbaden.

BANCE, Peter. 2009. *Sovereign, Squire & Rebel: Maharajah Duleep Singh and the Heirs of a Lost Kingdom*. London: Coronet House Publishing.

BANDYOPADHYAY, Sekhar. 2004. *From Plassey to Partition: A History of Modern India*. Hyderabad: Orient Longman.

BANERJEA, Surendranath. 1925. *A Nation in Making: Being the Reminiscences of Fifty Years of Public Life*. London and New York: Oxford University Press.

BAKER, Deborah. 2018. *The Last Englishmen*. Gurgaon: Penguin Random House.

BALFOUR, Ian. 1987. *Famous Diamonds*. London: Collins.

BALLARD, J.G. 2008. *The Unlimited Dream Company*. London: Harper Perennial.

BARROWS, Adam. 2011. *The Cosmic Time of Empire: Modern Britain and World Literature*. Berkeley & London: University of California Press.

BARTLEY, Paula. 2016. *Queen Victoria*. New York: Routledge.

BATEMAN, Anthony. 2016. *Cricket, Literature and Culture: Symbolizing the Nation, Destabilizing Empire*. London and New York: Routledge.

BAYLE, Pierre. 1826. *An Historical and Critical Dictionary, Selected and Abridged*. London: Hunt & Clarke, (2).

BEAUMONT, Matthew. 2015. *Nightwalking: A Nocturnal History of London*. London and New York: Verso Books.

BEBBINGTON, Gillian. 1972. *London Street Names*. London: B.T. Batsford.

BECKERT, Sven. 2014. *Empire of Cotton: A Global History*. New York: Vintage.

BECKETT, Francis. 1995. *Enemy Within: The Rise and Fall of the British Communist Party*. London: John Murray.

BEECHER, H.W. 1881. *All Around the House, Or, How to Make Homes Happy*. New York: D. Appleton.

BELL, John Hyslop. 1891. *British Folks & British India Fifty Years Ago*. London: John Heywood.

BENTHAM, Jeremy. 1843. *Collected Works*. (ed.) John Bowring. Edinburgh: William Tait, (11).

BHABHA, Homi K. 1994. *The Location of Culture*. New York & London: Routledge.

BHADURI, Saugata. 2020. *Polycoloniality: European Transactions with Bengal from the 13th Century to the 19th Century*. New Delhi and London: Bloomsbury.

BHOWNAGGREE, Mancherjee Merwanjee. 1916. *The Verdict of India*. London and New York: Hodder & Stoughton.

BIRDWOOD, William Riddell. 1946. *In My Time: Recollections and Anecdotes*. London: Skeffington & Son.

BLUMEL, Kristin. 2004. *George Orwell and the Radical Eccentrics: Intermodernism in Literary London*. New York and Basingstoke: Palgrave Macmillan.

BOHLS, Elizabeth. 2013. *Romantic Literature and Postcolonial Studies*. Edinburgh: Edinburgh University Press.

BOLITHO, Hector. 1954. *Jinnah: Creator of Pakistan*. London: John Murray.

BOSE, Subhas Chandra. 2010. *Words of Freedom: Ideas of a Nation*. New Delhi: Penguin.

——. 1954. *A Nation's Homage: Life and Work of Netaji Subhas Chandra Bose*. (ed.) P.D. Saggi. Bombay: Overseas Publications.

BRENDON, Piers. 2008. *The Decline and Fall of the British Empire*. London: Vintage Books.

BRESSEY, Caroline. 2004. 'Four Women: Exploring Black Women's Writing in London (1880–1920)'. In *Critical Perspectives on Colonialism: Writing the Empire from Below*, edited by Fiona Paisley and Kirsty Reid. Abingdon: Routledge, pp. 179–98.

Britain and India. 1920. London: (1).

BUBB, Alexander. 2013. 'Tracing the Legacy of an Experimental Generation: Three Iconic Indian Travellers in 1890s London'. In *India in Britain: South Asian Networks and Connections, 1858–1950*, edited by Susheila Nasta. Basingstoke: Palgrave Macmillan, pp. 46–63.

BURKE, Edmund. 1855. *The Works of the Right Honourable Edmund Burke: Reports on Administration of Justice in India. Charge against Warren Hastings*. London: H.G. Bohn, (4).

——.1844. *Correspondence of the Right Honourable Edmund Burke: Between the Year 1744 and the Period of His Decease, in 1797*. Charles William, Earl Fitzwilliam and Richard Bourke (eds). London: F. & J. Rivington, (3).

——. 1970. *Correspondences*. Cambridge: Cambridge University Press, (9).

BURTON, Antoinette. 1998. *At the Heart of the Empire: Indians and the Colonial Encounter in Late-Victorian Britain*. Berkeley and Oxford: University of California Press.

——. 2003. *Dwelling in the Archive: Women Writing House, Home, and History in Late Colonial India*. New York: Oxford University Press.

CALLAGHAN, J. 1993. *Rajani Palme Dutt: A Study in British Stalinism*. London: Lawrence and Wishart.

CAMPION, Charles. 2003. *The Rough Guide to London Restaurants*. London: Penguin.

CARLYLE, Thomas. 1851. *The Life of John Sterling*. London: Chapman & Hall.

——1851. *Collected Works*. London: Chapman & Hall, (20).

CAREY, W.H. 1906. *The Good Old Days of Honorable John Company: Being Curious Reminiscences Illustrating Manners and Customs of the British in India During the Rule of the East India Company from 1600 to 1858*. London: R. Cambray.

CARPENTER, Lant. 1833. *A Review of the Labours, Opinions, and Character of Rajah Rammohun Roy*. London: R. Hunter.

CARPENTER, Mary (ed.). 1866. *The Last Days in England of the Rajah Rammohun Roy*. London: Trubner & Co.

CAVERT, William M. 2016. *The Smoke of London: Energy and Environment in the Early Modern City*. Cambridge: Cambridge University Press.

CHAJES, Julie. 2019. *Recycled Lives: A History of Reincarnation in Blavatsky's Theosophy*. New York: Oxford University Press.

CHAKRABARTY, Bidyut. 2004. *The Partition of Bengal and Assam, 1932–1947: Contour of Freedom*. London and New York: Routledge Curzon.

CHAKRABARTY, Dipesh. 2000. *Provincializing Europe: Postcolonial Thought and Historical Difference*. Princeton: Princeton University Press.

CHAKRAVARTY, Suhash. 1997. *V.K. Krishna Menon and the India League*. New Delhi: Har-Anand Publications, (1).

CHAMBERS, Claire. 2015. *Britain Through Muslim Eyes: Literary Representations, 1780–1988*. New York: Palgrave Macmillan, 2015.

CHAMBERS, Colin. 2013. "'A Flute of Praise": Indian Theatre in Britain in the Early Twentieth Century'. In *India in Britain: South Asian Networks and Connections, 1858–1950*, edited by Susheila Nasta. London: Palgrave Macmillan.

CHAND, Tara. 1961. *History of the Freedom Movement in India*. New Delhi: Publications Division, Ministry of Information and Broadcasting, Government of India, (4).

CHAUDHURY, Sushil. 2017. *Trade, Politics and Society: The Indian Milieu in Early Modern Era*. London and New York: Routledge. *Modern Era*. London and New York: Routledge.

CHATTERJEE, Arup K. 2018. *The Great Indian Railways: A Cultural Biography*. New Delhi and London: Bloomsbury.

CHATTERJEE, Partha. 2011. *Lineages of Political Society: Studies in Postcolonial Democracy*. New York: Columbia University Press.

———. 2012. *The Black Hole of Empire: History of a Global Practice of Power*. Princeton: Princeton University Press.

CHATTERTON, Eyre. 1924. *A History of the Church of England in India Since the Early Days of the East India Company*. London: Society for Promoting Christian Knowledge.

CHAUDHURI, Nirad C. 1968. *The Autobiography of an Unknown Indian*. Berkeley and Los Angeles: University of California Press.

CHEYETTE, Bryan. 2013. *Diasporas of the Mind: Jewish and Postcolonial Writing and the Nightmare of History*. New Haven and London: Yale University Press.

CHESTERTON, G.K. 1905. *Heretics*. New York: John Lane Company.

CHOPRA, Preeti. 2011. *A Joint Enterprise: Indian Elites and the Making of British Bombay*. London and Minneapolis: University of Minnesota Press.

CHOUDHURI, Mina. 2006. *Glimpses of the Justice System of Presidency Towns, 1687–1973*. New Delhi: Regency Publications.

CHURCHILL, Winston. 1951. *The War Speeches*. London: Cassell.

———. 1957. 'A History of English Speaking Peoples: Famous Men in a Century of Wars'. In *Life Magazine*. Chicago: Time Inc, 3(3), pp. 85–112.

———. 1976. *The Collected Essays*. Michael Wolff (ed.). London: Library of Imperial History, (2).

———. 2013. *Never Give In!: Winston Churchill's Speeches*. London and New York: Bloomsbury.

CLARKE, P.F. 2002. *The Cripps Version: The Life of Sir Stafford Cripps, 1889–1952*. London and New York: Allen Lane.

COLLINGHAM, Lizzie. 2006. *Curry: A Tale of Cooks and Conquerors*. London and Oxford: Oxford University Press.

COLLINS, Larry And Dominique Lapierre. 1975. *Freedom at Midnight*. London and New York: Simon and Schuster.

COLLINS, Wilkie. 1970. *The Moonstone*. New York: AMS Press.

Condition of India: Being the Report of the Delegation Sent to India by the India League in 1932. 1934. London: India League.

CONWAY, Suzanne. 2006. 'Ayah, Caregiver to Anglo-Indian Children, c. 1750–1947'. In *Children, Childhood and Youth in the British World*, edited by Simon Sleight, and Shirleene Robinson. Basingstoke: Palgrave Macmillan, pp. 52–55.

COWASJEE, Saros. 1977. *So Many Freedoms: A Study of the Major Fiction of Mulk Raj Anand.* Bombay: Oxford University Press.

CURZON, Mary. 1985. *Lady Curzon's India: Letters of a Vicereine.* London: Weidenfeld & Nicolson.

DAHIYA, Hema. 2013. *Shakespeare Studies in Colonial Bengal: The Early Phase.* Newcastle upon Tyne: Cambridge Scholars Publishing.

DALRYMPLE, William. 2004. *White Mughals: Love and Betrayal in Eighteenth-Century India.* New Delhi and New York: Penguin.

———. 2012. *Return of a King: The Battle for Afghanistan.* London: Bloomsbury.

———. with Anita Anand. 2017. *Koh-i-Noor: The History of the World's Most Infamous Diamond.* London and New Delhi: Bloomsbury.

DATTA, Vishwa Nath. 1973. *Madan Lal Dhingra and the Revolutionary Movement.* New Delhi: Vikas Publications.

DAVIES, Alfred Mervyn. 1939. *Clive of Plassey: A Biography.* London and New York: C. Scribner's Sons.

DAVIS, John R. 1999. *The Great Exhibition.* London: Sutton.

DAVIS, Mike. 2010. *Late Victorian Holocausts: El Nino Famines and the Making of the Third World.* London and New York: Verso.

DE QUINCEY, Thomas. 1826. *Confessions of an English Opium Eater.* New York: John Taylor.

DENNET, Daniel C. 2013. *Intuition Pumps and Other Tools for Thinking.* New York and London: W.W. Norton.

DERRIDA, Jacques. 1976. *Of Grammatology.* Gayatri Chakravorty Spivak (trans.). Baltimore: Johns Hopkins University Press.

———. 1995. *Archive Fever: A Freudian Impression*, in *Diacritics.* _____, 25(2), pp. 9-63.

———. 2007. *Psyche: Inventions of the Other.* California: Stanford University Press, (1).

———. 2012. *Specters of Marx: The State of the Debt, the Work of Mourning and the New International.* New York and London: Routledge.

DESAI, Anita. 1984. *Bye-bye Blackbird.* New Delhi: Orient Paperback.

DICKENS, Charles. 1864. *Great Expectations.* London: Chapman & Hall.

———. 1868. *A Tale of Two Cities.* London: Chapman & Hall.

——. 1891. *Our Mutual Friend*. London: Chapman and Hall Ltd., (2).

DILLINGHAM, W. 2008. *Being Kipling*. New York: Palgrave Macmillan.

DILKS, David (ed.). 1972. *The Diaries of Sir Alexander Cadogan, O.M., 1939–1945*. New York: G. P. Putnam's & Sons.

DONNE, John. 1838. 'Meditation'. In *Complete Works, with a Memoir of his Life*, edited by Henry Alford. London: John W. Parker, (3) pp. 574–75.

DOYLE, Arthur Conan. 1887. *A Study in Scarlet*. London: Ward Lock & Co.

——. 1890. *The Sign of Four*. London: Spencer Blackett.

DR BLACK. 1805. 'History of the Smallpox'. In *The European Magazine & London Review*. London: Philological Society of London & James Asperne, (47) pp. 186–91.

DUTT, Rabindra Chandra. 1968. *Romesh Chunder Dutt*. New Delhi: Publications Division, Ministry of Information and Broadcasting, Government of India.

DUTT, Rajani Palme. 1950. *Britain's Crisis of Empire*. London: Lawrence & Wishart, (2).

DUTTA, Krishna. 2003. *Calcutta: A Cultural and Literary History*. Oxford: Signal Books.

EADE, John. 1996. 'Nationalism, Community, and the Islamisation of Space in London'. In *Making Muslim Space in North America and Europe*, edited by Barbara Daly Metcalf. Berkeley and London: University of California Press, pp. 217–33.

ELIOT, Thomas Stearns. 2011. *The Waste Land and Other Poems*. Ontario and London: Broadview Press.

EMIN, Joseph. 1918. *The Life and Adventures*. Calcutta: Baptist Mission Press.

ENGELS, Friedrich. 1958. *The Condition of the Working Class in England*. London: Macmillan.

ERICKSON, Carolly. 1997. *Her Little Majesty: The Life of Queen Victoria*. New York: Simon & Schuster.

ERREDGE, J.A. 1867. *Brighthelmstone, Sussex: The Ancient and Modern History of Brighton*. Brighton: W.J. Smith.

EVANS, Elisabeth. 2008. *Threshold Modernism: New Public Women and the Literary Spaces of Imperial London*. Cambridge and New York: Cambridge University Press.

FATHAH, Nawaz Jung. 1890. *Extracts from the Diary of the Nawab Mehdi Hasan Khan Fathah Nawaj Jung*. London: Talbot Bros.

FABER, David. 2005. *Speaking for England: Leo, Julian and John Amery, the Tragedy of a Political Family*. London: Free Press.

FABIAN, George. 2011. *Karl Marx Prince of Darkness*. Bloomington: Xlibris.

Factory Miscellaneous Records, The Public Despatches, And The Bengal Inventories, No. 23.

FADERMAN, Lillian. 2013. *Scotch Verdict: The Real-Life Story That Inspired 'The Children's Hour'*. New York: Columbia University Press.

FERGUSON, Niall. 2018. *The Square and the Tower: Networks and Power, from the Freemasons to Facebook*. London and New York: Penguin.

FISHER, Fiona. 2016. 'Viewing the Early Twentieth-Century Institutional Interior Through the Pages of Living London'. In *Residential Institutions in Britain, 1725–1970: Inmates and Environments*, edited by Jane Hamlett, Lesley Hoskins, and Rebecca Preston. Abingdon: Routledge, pp. 17–34.

FISHER, Michael H. 2000. *The First Indian Author in English: Dean Mahomed (1759–1851) in India, Ireland, and England*. New York and Oxford: Oxford University Press.

———. 2006. *Counterflows to Colonialism: Indian Travellers and Settlers in Britain, 1600–1857*. New Delhi: Permanent Black.

———. 2006. 'Working Across the Seas: Indian Maritime Labourers in India, Britain, and in Between, 1600–1857'. In *Coolies, Capital and Colonialism: Studies in Indian Labour History*, edited by Rana P. Behal and Marcel van der Linden. Cambridge and New York: Cambridge University Press, pp. 21–46.

———. 2006. 'Bound for Britain: Changing Conditions of Servitude, 1600–1857'. In *Slavery and South Asian History*, edited by Indrani Chatterjee. and Richard M. Eaton. Bloomington: Indiana University Press, pp. 187–209.

———. 2010. *The Inordinately Strange Life of Dyce Sombre: Victorian Anglo-Indian MP and 'Chancery Lunatic'*. London: C. Hurst.

———. 2013. 'South Asians in Britain up to the Mid-Nineteenth Century'. In *Routledge Handbook of the South Asian Diaspora*, edited by Joya Chatterji. and David Washbrook. New York and Oxon: Routledge, pp. 123–35.

Fisher's Colonial Magazine. 1842. London: Fisher, Son & Co.

FORBES, Geraldine Hancock. 1996. *Women in Modern India*. Cambridge: Cambridge University Press, 2 (4).

FOSTER, William. 1925. *The English Factories in India (1665–1667)*. Oxford: Clarendon Press.

FOUCAULT, Michel. 2002. *The Order of Things: An Archaeology of Human Sciences*. New York & London: Routledge.

FROST, George H. 1882. *Engineering News and American Contract Journal*. New York: Engineering News Publishing Co., New York, (9).

FULLER, Jean Overton. 1952. *Madeleine: The Story of Noor Inayat Khan, George Cross, M.B.E., Croix de Guerre with Gold Star*. London: Gollancz.

GADAMER, Hans-Georg. 2004. *Truth and Method*. Joel Weinsheimer. and Donald G. Marsh (trans.). London and New York: Continuum.

GANDHI, M.K., 2000. *Collected Works*. New Delhi: Publications Division, Ministry of Information and Broadcasting, Government of India, (1).

——. 2000. *Collected Works*. New Delhi: Publications Division, Ministry of Information and Broadcasting, Government of India, (9).

——. 1963. *Collected Works*. New Delhi: Publications Division, Ministry of Information and Broadcasting, Government of India, (10).

——. 1963. *Collected Works*. New Delhi: Publications Division, Ministry of Information and Broadcasting, Government of India, (39).

GANDHI, Rajmohan. 1986. *Eight Lives: A Study of the Hindu-Muslim Encounter*. Albany: State University of New York Press.

——. 1986. *Understanding the Muslim Mind*. New Delhi: Penguin.

——. 2007. *Mohandas: True Story of a Man, His People*. London: Penguin.

——. 2008. *Gandhi: The Man, His People, and the Empire*. Berkeley: University of California.

GARDNER, Katy. 2001. '*Desh-Bidesh*: Sylheti Images of Home and Away'. In *Race and Ethnicity: Solidarities and Communities*, edited by Harry Goulbourne. London and New York: Routledge, pp. 361–78.

J.M. Campbell. 1877. *Gazetteer of the Bombay Presidency: Gujarat: Surat and Broach*. Bombay: Government Central Press, (2).

GECZY, Adam. 2013. *Fashion and Orientalism: Dress, Textiles and Culture from the 17th to the 21st Century*. London and New York: Bloomsbury.

GEORGE III. 1928. *The Correspondence of King George, from 1760 to December 1783*. John William Fortescue (ed.). London: Macmillan and Co.

GERMAN, Lindsey and John Rees. 2012. *A People's History of London*. London and New York: Verso.

GHOSH, Amitav. 1988. *The Shadow Lines*. New Delhi: Ravi Dayal.

GHOSH, Durba. 2006. *Sex and the Family in Colonial India: The Making of Empire*. Cambridge: Cambridge University Press.

GHOSH, Siddhartha. 2004. '*Abol Tabol*: The Making of a Book'. In *Print Areas: Book History in India*, edited by Swapan Chakravorty. and Abhijit Gupta. New Delhi: Permanent Black, pp. 242–56.

GIBBES, Phoebe. 1789. *Hartly House, Calcutta*. Dublin: William Jones.

GILHAM, Jamie. 2014. *Loyal Enemies: British Converts to Islam, 1850–1950*. New York and Oxford: Oxford University Press.

GLASSE, Hannah. 1774. *The Art of Cookery, Made Plain and Easy*. London: W. Strahan, J. and F. Rivington, J. Hinton.

GLEIG, G.R. 1841. *Memoirs of the Life of Warren Hastings*. London: Richard Bentley (1).

GOPAL, Priyamvada. 2005. *Literary Radicalism in India Gender, Nation and the Transition to Independence*. London and New York: Routledge.

GORE, Catherine Grace Frances. 1833. *The Sketch Book of Fashion*. London: R. Bentley (1).

GRAHAM, Maria. 1813. *Journal of a Residence in India*. London and Edinburgh: George Ramsay & Co.

GRIGG, John. 1995. 'Myths About the Approach to Indian Independence'. In *Adventures with Britannia: Personalities, Politics and Culture in Britain*, edited by Douglas K. Hyland, James Clifton and John Hutton. London: I.B. Tauris, pp. 203–220.

GUHA, Samar. 1986. *The Mahatma and the Netaji: Two Men of Destiny of India*. New Delhi: Sterling Publishers.

Gujarat State Gazetteers. 1961. Ahmedabad: Directorate of Government, Gujarat State.

HABIB, Imtiaz. 2008. *Black Lives in the English Archives, 1500–1677: Imprints of the Invisible*. London: Routledge.

HALL, Ian. 2015. '"Mephistopheles in a Saville Row Suit": V. K. Krishna Menon and the West'. In *Radicals and Reactionaries in*

Twentieth-Century International Thought, edited by Hall. New York: Palgrave Macmillan, pp. 191–216.

HASTINGS, The Marquess of. 1858. *The Private Journal*. Marchioness of Bute (ed.). London: Saunders & Otley, (2).

HAZLITT, William Carew. 1886. *Old Cookery Books and Ancient Cuisine*. London: Elliot Stock.

HENDERSON, Henry Barkley. 1829. *The Bengalee: Or, Sketches of Society and Manners in the East*. London: Smith, Elder & Co.

___. 1818. 'Hertford College, General Examination'. In *The Asiatic Journal and Monthly Miscellany*. London: W.H. Allen & Company, (5) pp. 95–96.

HIETARANTA, Pertti. 2017. 'Cognitive Economy and Mental Worlds: Accounting for Translation Mistakes and Other Communication Errors'. In *Empirical Modelling of Translation and Interpreting*, edited by Silvia Hansen-Schirra, Oliver Czulo and Sascha Hofmann. Berlin: Language Science Press, pp. 441–464.

HIGHMORE, Ben. 2011. *Ordinary Lives: Studies in the Everyday*. London and New York: Routledge.

HILL, S.C. 1985. *Bengal in 1756-1757: A Selection of Papers Dealing with the Affairs of the British in Bengal During the Reign of Siraj ud-Daula*. New Delhi: Manas Publications, (3).

HINNELLS, John R. 2005. *The Zoroastrian Diaspora: Religion and Migration*. Oxford: Oxford University Press.

——. 2008. 'Parsis in India and the Diaspora in the Twentieth Century and Beyond'. In *Parsis in India and the Diaspora*, edited by John R. Hinnells and Alan Williams. Abingdon and New York: Routledge, pp. 255–76.

HIRO, Dilip. 2005. *The Longest August: The Unflinching Rivalry Between India and Pakistan*. New York: Nation Books.

HOBHOUSE, Mary. 1888. 'Progress of female Education in India'. London: *The Times*.

HOBSBAWM, Eric. 1983. 'Inventing Traditions'. In *The Invention of Tradition*, edited by Eric Hobsbawm & Terence Ranger. Cambridge: Cambridge University Press, pp. 1–14.

HOPKIRK, Peter. 1996. *Quest for Kim: In Search of Kipling's Great Game*. London: John Murray.

HORNE, M J. 1827. *The Adventures of Naufragus*. London: Smith, Elder & Cornhill.

'Horniman's Pure Tea is the Best' (Advertisement). 1883. In James Bell, *The Chemistry of Foods*. London: Chapman & Hall.

HUTTON, J.H. and L.S. Vaidyanathan. 1932. *Census of India, 1931*. New Delhi: Manager of Publications, Government of India, 1(1).

IHTISHAMUDDIN, Mirza. 1827. *Travels of Mirza Itesa Modeen, in Great Britain and France*. James Edward Alexander (trans.). London: Parbury, Allen & Co.

IRVING, Washington. 1871. *Bracebridge Hall, or The Humorists: A Medley*. Philadelphia: J.P. Lippincott & Co.

IYER, Raghavan (ed.). 1960. *St Antony's Papers: South Asian Affairs*. London: Chatto & Windus, (1).

JACKSON, Peter. 2010. 'A Cultural Politics of Curry: The Transnational Spaces of Contemporary Commodity Culture'. In *Hybrid Cultures— Nervous States: Britain and Germany in a (Post)Colonial World*, edited by Ulrike Lindner, Maren Möhring, Mark Stein and Silke Stroh. New York and Amsterdam: Rodopi, pp. 167–88.

JELAVICH, Barbara. 1974. *St. Petersburg and Moscow: Tsarist and Soviet Foreign Policy, 1814–1974*. Bloomington: Indiana University Press.

JOHANYAK, Debra. 2010. '"Turning Turk," Early Modern English Orientalism, and Shakespeare's *Othello*'. In *The English Renaissance, Orientalism, and the Idea of Asia*, edited by Debra Johanyak and Walter S.H. Lim. New York: Palgrave Macmillan, pp. 77–96.

___. 1985. *Journal of Indian History*. Calcutta: Department of Modern Indian History, University of Calcutta, (63).

JOYCE, James. 1978. *Finnegans Wake*. New York and London: Garland Publishing, Book I, Chapters 6–7.

Judy. 1870. London: September, (11).

KAMRAN, Tahir. 2017. 'Choudhary Rahmat Ali and his Political Imagination'. In *Muslims Against the Muslim League*, edited by Ali Usman Qasmi and Megan Eaton Robb. Cambridge and New York: Cambridge University Press, pp. 82–108.

KAYE, John and George Bruce Malleson. 1897. *History of the Indian Mutiny of 1857–8*. London: Longmans & Green.

KEAY, Anna. 2012. *The Crown Jewels*. London: Thames & Hudson.

KEAY, John. 1991. *The Honourable Company*. London: Harper Collins.

KEAY, Julia. 2014. *Farzana: The Woman Who Saved an Empire*. London: I.B. Tauris.

KEITH, Michael. 2005. *After the Cosmopolitan?: Multicultural Cities and the Future of Racism*. London and New York: Routledge.

KHAIR, Tabish, Martin Leer, Justin D. Edwards and Hannah Ziadeh (eds). 2006. *Other Routes: 1500 Years of African and Asian Travel Writing*. Oxford: Signal Books.

KHAN, Abu Taleb. 1810. *The Travels of Mirza Abu Taleb Khan in Asia, Africa, and Europe: During the Years 1799 to 1803*. Charles Stewart (trans.). London: Longman, Hurst, Rees, and Orme.

KHAN, Abdul Ghaffar. 2010. *Words of Freedom: Ideas of a Nation*. New Delhi: Penguin.

KHAN, Muhammad Mojlum. 2013. *The Muslim Heritage of Bengal: The Lives, Thoughts and Achievements of Great Muslim Scholars, Writers and Reformers of Bangladesh and West Bengal*. Markfield: Kube Publishing.

KHAN, Yasmin. 2017. *The Great Partition: The Making of India and Pakistan*. New Haven and London: Yale University Press.

KINCAID, Dennis. 1938. *British Social Life in India 1608–1937*. London: Taylor & Francis.

KIPLING, Rudyard. 1890. *The Phantom Rickshaw, and Other Tales*. Allahabad and Lahore: A.H. Wheeler & Company.

'Kitchen Melodies: Curry' In *Punch*, Vol. 10. Punch Office, London: January-June, 1846, p. 221.

KLING, Blair B. 1976. *Partner in Empire: Dwarkanath Tagore and the Age of Enterprise in Eastern India*. Berkeley and London: University of California Press.

KLUGMANN, James. 1968. *History of the Communist Party of Great Britain: Vol. 1: Formation and Early Years, 1919–1924*. London: Lawrence and Wishart.

KNIGHT, Charles (ed.). 1841. *London*. London: Charles Knight, (9).

KOPF, David. 1959. *The Brahmo Samaj and the Shaping of the Modern Indian Mind*. Calcutta: Gupta Brothers.

KRIPALANI, Krishna. 1981. *Dwarkanath Tagore, a Forgotten Pioneer: A Life*. New Delhi: National Book Trust.

KUMAR, Anuradha. 2015. *Across the Seven Seas: Indian Travellers' Tales from the Past*. London and New Delhi: Hachette.

KUMAR, Amitava. 2002. *Bombay-London-New York*. New York and London: Routledge.

KUTTY, V. K. Madhavan. 1988. *V. K. Krishna Menon*. New Delhi: Publications Division, Ministry of Information and Broadcasting, Government of India.

LAMB, Charles. 1825. 'The Superannuated Man'. In *the London Magazine*. London: Hunt & Clarke, (2) pp. 67–73.

LAHIRI, Shompa. 2013. *Indians in Britain: Anglo–Indian Encounters, Race and Identity, 1880–1930*. Abingdon and New York: Routledge.

———. 2017. 'Patterns of Resistance: Indian Seamen in Imperial Britain'. In *Language, Labour and Migration*, edited by Anne J. Kershen. Abingdon: Routledge, pp. 169–172.

LAMBERT-HURLEY, Siobhan. 2013. 'Forging Global networks in the Imperial Era: Atiya Fyzee in Edwardian London'. In *India in Britain: South Asian Networks and Connections, 1858–1950*, edited by Susheila Nasta. Basingstoke: Palgrave Macmillan, pp. 64–79.

LEASOR, James. 1957. *The Plague and the Fire*. New Delhi: Affiliated East-West Press.

LEFEBVRE, Henri. 1991. *Critique of Everyday Life*. John Moore (trans.). London: Verso.

Charles Lamb. 2012. 'Letter from Charles Lamb to William Wordsworth'. January 30, 1801. in *Romanticism: An Anthology*, edited by Duncan Wu. Chichester: Wiley Blackwell, pp. 762–63.

LEPPERT, Richard. 1993. *The Sight of Sound: Music, Representation, and the History of the Body*. California, London: California University Press.

LIPSON, Ephraim. 1929. *The Economic History of England*. London: A & C Black, 1929.

LIU, Yong. 2007. *The Dutch East India Company's Tea Trade with China*. Leiden: Brill.

Lives of Alfred the Great, Sir Thomas More, and John Evelyn. 1845. London: James Burns.

LOCK, F. P. 2006. *Edmund Burke*. Oxford and New York: University of Oxford Press, (1, 2).

LOGIN, E. Dalhousie. 1915. *Recollections; Court Life and Camp life, 1820–1904*. London: Smith, Elder & Co.

LOGIN, Lena Campbell. 1890. *Sir John Login and Duleep Singh*. Lahore: University of Punjab, Department of Languages.

LOHMAN, Sarah. 2016. *Eight Flavors: The Untold Story of American Cuisine*. New York: Simon Schuster.

LONDON, Jack. 1904. *People of the Abyss*. New York and London: Macmillan.

LUTHRA, H.R. 1986. *Indian Broadcasting*. New Delhi: Publications Division, Ministry of Information and Broadcasting, Government of India.

LUTYENS, Mary. 1975. *Krishnamurti: The Years of Awakening*. New York: Farrar, Straus and Giroux.

———. 1980. *Edwin Lutyens*. London: John Murray.

——. 2005. *J. Krishnamurti: A Life*. London and New Delhi: Penguin.

MACKNIGHT, Thomas. 1858. *History of the Life and Times of Edmund Burke*. London: Chapman & Hall (1).

MAGILL, Frank N. (ed.). 1999. *The 17th and 18th Centuries: Dictionary of World Biography*. Oxon and New York: Routledge, (4).

MAHOMED, Frederick Akbar. 1872. 'The Physiology and Clinical Use of the Sphygmograph'. In *Medical Times Gazette*. J. & A. Churchill, New Burlington Street, London, (1).

MAHOMET, Sake Dean. 1794. *The Travels of Dean Mahomet, a Native of Patna in Bengal, Through Several Parts of India, While in the Service of the Honourable the East India Company*. Cork: J. Connor, (1).

——. 1838. *Shampooing: Or, Benefits Resulting from the Use of the Indian Medicated Vapour Bath*. Brighton: William Fleet.

MALABARI, Behramji. 1895. *The Indian Eye on English Life*. Bombay: Apollo Printing Works.

MALHOTRA, Ashok. 2012. *Making British Indian Fictions: 1772–1823*. New York: Palgrave Macmillan.

MALLESON, George Bruce. 1885. *The Decisive Battles of India, from 1746 to 1849 Inclusive*. London: W.H. Allen.

MANGHAM, Andrew. 2010. 'Wilkie Collins (1824–1889)'. In *A Companion to Crime Fiction*, edited by Charles J. Rzepka and Lee. Chichester: Wiley Blackwell, pp. 281–89.

MARQUAND, David. 1977. *Ramsay MacDonald*. London: Jonathan Cape.

MARX, Karl. 1974. *Political Writings: The First International and After*. David Fernbach (ed.). London and New York: Vintage Books.

MAJUMDAR, Janaki Agnes Penelope. 2003. *Family History*. Antoinette Burton (ed.). New Delhi: Oxford University Press.

MCCABE, Ina Baghdiantz. 1999. *The Shah's Silk for Europe's Silver: The Eurasian Trade of the Julfa Armenians in Safavid Iran and India (1530–1750)*. Atlanta: Scholars Press.

MCLUHAN, Marshall. 1962. *The Gutenberg Galaxy: The Making of Typographic Man*. Toronto: University of Toronto Press.

MONTAGU, Elizabeth. 1813. *The Letters*. London: Matthew Montagu, (3).

MOON, Penderel. 1989. *The British Conquest and Dominion of India*. London: Gerald Duckworth & Co.

MARSHALL, Peter. 1979. 'Masters and *Banians* of Eighteenth Century Calcutta'. In *The Age of Partnership. Europeans in Asia Before*

Dominion, edited by B.B. Kling and M.N. Pearson. Honolulu: University Press of Hawaii.

MATHEW, K.M. 1988. *History of the Portuguese Navigation in India, 1497–1600*. New Delhi: Mittal Publications.

MATHUR, Saloni. 2007. *India by Design: Colonial History and Cultural Display*. Berkeley: University of California Press.

MCLEOD, John. 2008. 'Mourning, Philanthropy, and M.M. Bhownaggree's Road to Parliament'. In *Parsis in India and the Diaspora*, edited by John R. Hinnells and Alan Williams. Abingdon and New York: Routledge, pp. 136–56.

MELVILLE, Lewis. 1996. *The Life of William Makepeace Thackeray*. Richard Pearson (ed.). Oxon and New York: Routledge.

MENON, Meena and Uzramma. 2017. *A Frayed History: The Journey of Cotton in India*. New Delhi: Oxford University Press.

MENTZ, Søren. 2005. *The English Gentleman Merchant at Work: Madras and the City of London 1660–1740*. Copenhagen: Museum Tusculanum Press.

METCALF, Barbara Daly (ed.). 1996. *Making Muslim Space in North America and Europe*. Berkeley, Los Angeles and London: University of California Press.

METCALF, Barbara D. and Thomas R. Metcalf. 2002. *A Concise History of India*. Cambridge: Cambridge University Press.

METCALFE, Richard. 1877. *Sanitas Sanitatum Et Omnia Sanitas*. London: Co-operative Printing Co.

MILL, John Stuart. 1963. *Collected Works*. Toronto: University of Toronto Press, (6).

MILLARD, Candice. 2016. *Hero of the Empire: The Boer War, a Daring Escape, and the Making of Winston Churchill*. London: Penguin.

MINTZ, Sidney W. 1986. *Sweetness and Power: The Place of Sugar in Modern History*. New York: Penguin.

'Minutes of Evidence Taken before the Select Committee on Indian Territories.' 1852-53. In *Reports from Committees, East India*, Sixth Report, Vol. 29 (London: House of Commons, 1852-53).

MIRZA, Rocky M. 2007. *The Rise and Fall of the American Empire: A Re-Interpretation of History, Economics and Philosophy: 1492–2006*. Victoria: Trafford Publishing.

MITTRA, Kissory Chand. 1870. *Memoir of Dwarkanath Tagore*. Calcutta: Thacker, Spink & Co.

MODY, Hormasji Peroshaw. 1967. *Pherozeshah Mehta*. New Delhi: Publications Division, Ministry of Information and Broadcasting, Government of India.

MONROE, Jo. 2005. *Star of India: The Spicy Adventures of Curry*. Chichester: Wiley.

MORAES, Frank. 1959. *Jawaharlal Nehru*. New Delhi: Jaico.

MOZOOMDAR, Protap Chunder. 1887. *The Life and Teachings of Keshub Chunder Sen*. Calcutta: J.W. Thomas Baptist Mission Press.

MUKHARJI, Trailokya Nath. 1889. *A Visit to Europe*. Calcutta: W. Newman & Co.

MUKHERJEE, Meenakshi. 2009. *An Indian for All Seasons: The Many Lives of R.C. Dutt*. New Delhi: Penguin.

MUKHERJEE, Rudrangshu. 2015. *Nehru and Bose: Parallel Lives*. London and New Delhi: Penguin.

MUKHERJEE, Sumita. 2012. 'Herabai Tata and Sophia Duleep Singh: Suffragette Resistances for India and Britain, 1910–1920'. In *South Asian Resistances in Britain, 1858–1947*, edited by Rehana Ahmed and Sumita Mukherjee. London and New York: Continuum, pp. 106–124.

MUNDY, Godfrey Charles. 1832. *Pen and Pencil Sketches: Being the Journal of a Tour in India*. London: John Murray, (1).

MURRAY, Robert Henry. 1931. *Edmund Burke: A Biography*. London and Oxford: Oxford University Press.

MÜLLER, Friedrich Max. 1884. *Biographical Essays*. London: Longmans, Green.

NAIDU, Sarojini. 1925. *Speeches and Writings*. Madras: G.A. Natesan & Company.

——. 1993. *Selected Poetry and Prose*. Makarand Paranjape (ed.). New Delhi: Harper Collins.

——. 1996. *Selected Letters 1890s to 1940s*. Makarand Paranjape (ed.). New Delhi: Kali for Women.

——. 2010. *Words of Freedom: Ideas of a Nation*. New Delhi: Penguin.

NANDA, B.R. 1958. *Mahatma Gandhi: A Biography*. London: George Allen and Unwin.

NANDY, Ashis. 1983. *The Intimate Enemy: Loss and Recovery of Self Under Colonialism*. New Delhi and London: Oxford University Press.

NARAVANE, M.S. 2006. *Battles of the Honourable East India Company: Making of the Raj*. New Delhi: APH Publishing Corporation.

NASTA, Susheila. 2008. 'Between Bloomsbury and Gandhi? The Background to the Publication and Reception of Mulk Raj Anand's *Untouchable*'. In *Books Without Borders*, edited by Robert Fraser and Mary Hammond. Vol. 2: Perspectives from South Asia. Basingstoke and New York: Palgrave Macmillan, pp. 151–69.

NEFF, J.U. 2005. *The Rise of the British Coal Industry*. London: Frank Cass & Co., (2).

NEILL, Edward Duffield. 1871. *Memoir of Rev. Patrick Copland: Rector Elect of the First Projected College in the United States: A Chapter of the English Colonisation of America*. New York: Charles Scribner & Co.

NEILL, Stephen. 1984. *A History of Christianity in India: The Beginnings to AD 1707*. Cambridge University Press.

NEHRU, Jawaharlal. *An Anthology*. 1980. New Delhi: Oxford University Press.

———. 2003. *The Essential Writings*. New Delhi: Oxford University Press, (2).

NIKHILANANDA, Swami. 1975. *Vivekananda: A Biography*. Calcutta: Advaita Ashrama.

NIETZSCHE, Friedrich. 1974. *The Gay Science*. Walter Kaufmann (trans.). New York: Vintage Random House.

NIERSTRASZ, Chris. 2015. *Rivalry for Trade in Tea and Textiles: The English and Dutch East India Companies (1700-1800)*. London: Palgrave Macmillan.

NOLAN, Edward Henry. 1859. *The Illustrated History of the British Empire in India and the East ... to the Suppression of the Sepoy Mutiny in 1859*. London: James S. Vertue, (1).

NOWROJEE, Jehangeer and Hirjeebhoy Meerwanjee. 1841. *Journal of a Residence of Two Years and a Half in Great Britain*. London: A.H. Allen & Co.

O'CONNOR, Daniel. 2012. *Chaplains of the East India Company, 1601–1858*. New York: Continuum.

OBORNE, Peter. 2014. *Wounded Tiger: A History of Cricket in Pakistan*. London and New York: Simon & Schuster.

ORWELL, George. 1998. *The Complete Works*. London: Secker & Warburg, (12).

PALSETIA, Jesse S. 2005. *The Parsis of India: Preservation of Identity in Bombay City*. Leiden: Leiden & Boston, Brill.

PANAYI, Panikos. 2008. *Spicing up Britain: The Multicultural History of British Food*. London: Reaktion.

PARANJAPE, Makarand R. 2012. *Making India: Colonialism, National Culture, and the Afterlife of Indian English Authority.* Berlin: Springer.

PAREKH, Manilal C. 1926. *Brahmarshi Keshub Chunder Sen.* Calcutta: Oriental Christ House.

PATEL, Dinyar Phiroze. 2015. 'The Grand Old Man: Dadabhai Naoroji and the Evolution of the Demand for Indian Self-Government'. Doctoral Dissertation. Cambridge, MA: Harvard University.

PEPYS, Samuel. 1926. *The Diary.* London: G. Bell, (1).

PERERA, Sonali. 2014. *No Country: Working-Class Writing in the Age of Globalisation.* New York: Columbia University Press.

PILLAI, Manu S. 2019. *The Courtesan, the Mahatma & the Italian Brahmin: Tales from Indian History.* Chennai: Westland.

POTTER, Dennis. 1968. *The Nigel Barton Plays: Two Television Plays.* London: Penguin.

PRICE, Leah. 2012. *How to Do Things with Books in Victorian Britain.* Princeton University Press.

PRIOR, James. 1826. *Memoir of the Life and Character of the Right Hon. Edmund Burke.* London: Baldwin, Cradock and Joy, (2).

Punch, Vols. 57-60. Punch Office, London: January-June, 1871.

RAPPAPORT, Erika. 2017. *A Thirst for Empire: How Tea Shaped the Modern World.* New Jersey: Princeton University Press.

RAJAMANNAR, Shefali. 2012. *Reading the Animal in the Literature of the British Raj.* New York: Palgrave Macmillan.

RAY, S.N. 2005. 'Rammohun Roy and English Intellectuals'. In *Raja Rammohun Roy: An Apostle of Indian Awakening,* edited by S.K. Sharma. New Delhi: Mittal Publications. pp. 177–189.

RAY, Utsa. 2015. *Culinary Culture in Colonial India: A Cosmopolitan Platter and the Middle Class.* Delhi: Cambridge University Press.

READE, Arthur. 1884. *Tea and Tea Drinking.* London: Sampson Low, Marston, Searle and Rivington.

REDDY, Sheela. 2017. *Mr and Mrs Jinnah: The Marriage that Shook India.* New Delhi: Random House.

REID, Stuart. 2017. *The Battle of Plassey 1757: The Victory That Won an Empire.* Barnsley: Frontline.

REID, Walter. 2016. *Keeping the Jewel in the Crown: The British Betrayal of India.* London and New Delhi: Random House.

Reports from Committees of the House of Commons. 1804. London: House of Commons, (5).

RESCHER, Nicholas. 2003. *Epistemology: An Introduction to the Theory of Knowledge.* Albany: State University of New York.

Reports from Committees of the House of Commons: Reprinted by Order of the House. 1806. London: House of Commons, (6).

RHYS, Ernst. 1914. *Rabindranath Tagore.* New York: Macmillan.

RITCHIE, John Gerald. 1920. *The Ritchies in India: Extracts from the Correspondence of William Ritchie, 1817–1862; and Personal Reminiscences of Gerald Ritchie.* London: J. Murray.

ROBERTS, Edwin A. 1997. *The Anglo–Marxists: A Study in Ideology and Culture.* London: Rowman & Littlefield.

ROCHE, George. 1994. *Childhood in India: Tales from Sholapur.* London and New York: The Radcliffe Press.

ROSSELLI, John. 1974. *Lord William Bentinck: The Making of a Liberal Imperialist, 1774–1839.* Berkeley and Los Angeles: University of California Press.

ROY, A.K. 1905. *Impressions of England.* Calcutta: New Arya Mission Press.

ROY, Amrit Lal. 1888. *Reminiscences: England and American Part 2, England and India.* Calcutta: Royal Publishing House.

ROY, Biren. 1982. *Calcutta, 1481–1981: Marshes to Metropolis.* Calcutta: National Council of Education.

———. 2000. *The Prelude to Empire: Plassey Revolution of 1757.* New Delhi: Manohar Publishers.

ROY, Purabi. 1999. *Russo–Indian Relations in the Nineteenth Century: A Selection of Documents: English Translation.* New Delhi: Asiatic Society.

ROY, Tirthankar. 2018. *A Business History of India: Enterprise and the Emergence of Capitalism from 1700.* New York and Cambridge: Cambridge University Press.

ROYLE, Nicholas. 1995. *After Derrida.* Manchester: Manchester University Press.

RUSHDIE, Salman. 1991. 'Imaginary Homelands'. In *Imaginary Homelands: Essays & Criticism* (1981–91). London: Granta, & Penguin, pp. 9–21.

SAHA, Panchanan. 1970. *Shapurji Saklatvala: A Short Biography.* New Delhi: People's Publishing House.

SAID, Edward. 1979. *Orientalism.* New York and London: Vintage.

SAKLATVALA, Sehri. 1991. *The Fifth Commandment: A Biography of Shapurji Saklatvala.* London: Miranda Press.

SALTER, Joseph. 1873. *The Asiatic in England: Sketches of Sixteen Years' Works Among Orientals*. London: Seeley, Jackson & Halliday.

SCHMITT, Cannon. 2002. 'Narrating National Addictions: De Quincey, Opium and Tea'. In *High Anxieties: Cultural Studies in Addiction*, edited by Janet Farrell Brodie and Marc Redfield. London: University of California Press, pp. 63–84.

SCOTT, Walter. 1833. *Castle Dangerous*. Edinburgh: Robert Cadell.

SEN, Amiya P. 2012. *Rammohun Roy: A Critical Biography*. London: Penguin.

SEN, Colleen Taylor. 2009. *Curry: A Global History*. London: Reaktion Books.

SEN, Keshub Chunder. 1938. *Keshub Chunder Sen in England: Diary, Sermons, Addresses & Epistles*. Calcutta: Navavidhan Publication Committee.

SEN, Simonti. 2005. *Travels to Europe: Self and Other in Bengali Travel Narratives, 1870–1910*. Hyderabad: Orient Longman.

SENGUPTA, Jayanta. 2009. *Nation on a Platter: The Culture and Politics of Food and Cuisine in Colonial Bengal*. Cambridge and New Delhi: Cambridge University Press.

SENGUPTA, Padmini Sathianadhan. 1966. *Sarojini Naidu: A Biography*. New Delhi: Asia Publishing House.

SELF, Will. 1998. 'Tough Tough Toys for Tough Tough Boys'. In *Tough Tough Toys for Tough Tough Boys*. London: Bloomsbury, pp. 109–154.

———. 2017. *Phone*. London and New York: Penguin.

SETH, Mesrovb Jacob. 1897. *History of the Armenians in India: From the Earliest Times to the Present Day*. London: Luzac & Co.

———. 1937. *Armenians in India, from the Earliest Times to the Present Day*. Calcutta: Jacob.

SHAH, Syed A.M. 1893. 'A Visit to the Tower of London'. In *The Indian Magazine*. National Indian Association, based in Maida Vale, London, 24(268) pp. 208–210.

SHAHANI, Dayaran Gidumal. 1888. *The Life and Life-work of Behramji M. Malabari: Being a Biographical Sketch, with Selections from his Writings and Speeches on Infant Marriage and Enforced Widowhood, and also His 'Rambles of a Pilgrim Reformer'*. Bombay: Educational Society Press.

SHAKESPEARE, William. 1733. *The Tempest*, in *Collected Works*. Mr Theobald (Collated, Annotated and Edited). London: Bettesworth, Hitch, Tonson, Wellington, et al, (1) pp. 1–76.

——. *A Midsummer Night's Dream*. In *Collected Works*. pp. 77–149.

SHEIKH, Mohamed. 2018. *An Indian in The House: The Lives and Times of the Four Trailblazers Who First Brought India to the British Parliament*. Cirencester: Mereo Books.

SHELLEY, Percy Bysshe. 1994. *Fragments of an Unfinished Drama*. London: Chadwyck-Healey.

SHERWANI, Latif Ahmed. 1987. *Pakistan in the Making: Documents and Readings*. Lahore: Quaid-i-Azam Academy.

SHERWOOD, Mary Martha. 1828. *The Lady of the Manor: Being a Series of Conversations on the Subject of Confirmation: Intended for the Use of the Middle and Higher Ranks of Young Females*. London: F. Houlston, (6).

SINCLAIR, Iain. 2007. *London: City of Disappearances*. London: Penguin.

SINGH, Duleep Maharajah. 1977. *Correspondence*. In *History of The Freedom Movement in The Punjab*, edited by Ganda Singh. Patiala: Punjabi University Press, (3).

SINGH, Iqbal. 1983. *Rammohun Roy: A Biographical Inquiry into the Making of Modern India*. New Delhi: Asia Publishing House, (2, 3).

ANON. 1843. 'Sketches and Portraits from the History of the Mahomedan Dominion Over India'. In *The Asiatic Journal and Monthly Miscellany*. London: W.H. Allen & Co., (40) pp. 91–101.

SMITH, Al. 1970. *Dictionary of City of London Street Names*. New York: Arco.

SNAITH, Anna. 2010. 'The Hogarth Press and the Networks of Anti-Colonialism'. In *Leonard and Virginia Woolf, The Hogarth Press and the Networks of Modernism*, edited by Helen Southworth. Edinburgh: Edinburgh University Press, pp. 103–127.

——. 2014. *Modernist Voyages: Colonial Women Writers in London, 1890–1945*. New York: Cambridge University Press.

SOMBRE, David Ochterlony. 1849. *Dyce Mr Dyce Sombre's Refutation of the Charge of Lunacy Brought Against Him in the Court of Chancery*. Paris.

SORABJI, Cornelia. 1934. *India Calling*. London: Nisbet & Co.

SOYER, Alexis. 1851. *The Modern Housewife: Or, Ménagère. Comprising Nearly One Thousand Receipts, for the Economic and Judicious Preparation of Every Meal of the Day, and Those for the Nursery and Sick Room*. London: D. Appleton.

SPEAR, Percival. 1998. *The Nabobs: A Study of the Social Life of the English in Eighteenth Century India*. New Delhi and London: Oxford University Press.

SQUIRES, Mike. 1990. *Saklatvala: A Political Biography*. London: Lawrence & Wishart.

STIMSON, Robert. 2008. 'Goodbye to India'. In John Elliott, Bernard Imhasly and Simon Denyer edited, *Foreign Correspondent: Fifty Years of Reporting South Asia*. New Delhi: Penguin.

STOCQUELER, Joachim Hayward. 1873. *The Memoirs of a Journalist*. London and Bombay: The Times of India.

SUBRAHMANYAM, Sanjay. 1990. 'Europeans and Asians in an Age of Contained Conflict'. In *The Political Economy of Commerce: Southern India 1500–1650*. Cambridge and New York: Cambridge University Press.

TALAIRACH-VIELMAS, Laurence. 2009. *Wilkie Collins, Medicine and the Gothic*. Cardiff and London: University of Wales Press.

TAGORE, Rabindranath. 1997. *Selected Letters*, edited by Krishna Dutta and Andrew Robinson. Cambridge: Cambridge University Press.

———. 2011. 'Letter to Sir William Rothenstein, November 26, 1932'. In *The Essential Tagore*, edited by Fakrul Alam and Radha Chakravarty. Cambridge and London: The Belknap Press of Harvard University Press, pp. 118–120.

TAYLOR, Duncan Burnett. 1967. *Fielding's England*. London: Dobson.

TAYLOR, Miles. 2018. *Empress: Queen Victoria and India*. New Haven and London: Yale University Press.

TENNYSON, Lord Alfred. 1879. *Poetical Works*. New York: Manhattan Printing and Publishing Co.

THACKERAY, William Makepeace. 1911. *The Collected Works: Ballads and Verses. Miscellaneous Contributions to Punch*. London: Macmillan.

THAROOR, Shashi. 2007. *Nehru: The Invention of India*. New Delhi: Penguin Viking.

The Asiatic Journal and Monthly Register for British and Foreign India, China and Australia, Vol. 16. London: Kingsbury, Parbury & Allen, 1823.

The British Critic, and Quarterly Theological Review, Vol. 21. London: C. & J. Rivington, 1824.

The Brockport Republic, Vol. 40, No. 22. New York: February 27, 1896. Available at: https://newspaperarchive.com/brockport-republic-feb-27-1896-p-1/ (Accessed on 21 October 2016).

The Calcutta Review, Vol. 24. Sanders, Cones & Co., 1855.

The Calcutta Review, Vol. 70. Calcutta: Thomas S. Smith, 1880.

The Colonial Magazine and Commercial Maritime Journal, Vol. 1. London: Fisher, Son & Co., August-December, 1842.

The Communist International, Vol. 13. London: Workers Library Publishers., 1936.

'The Dispatches of Field Marshal the Duke of Wellington', *The Quarterly Review*, Vol. 58. London: John Murray, 1837, pp. 82–107.

The Evangelical Magazine and Missionary Chronicle, Vol. 20. London: Ward & Co., January, 1842.

The First Indian Member of the Imperial Parliament, Being a Collection of the Main Incidents Relation to the Election of Mr. Dadabhai Naoroji to Parliament. Madras: Addison & Co., 1892.

The Independent, Vol. 63. New York: July-December, 1909.

The Indian Magazine and Review, Vol. 43, No. 496. London: April 1912.

The Indian Review, Vol. 21. Madras: G.A. Natesan, 1970.

The Labour Monthly, Vol. 19, No. 1. London: Labour Publishing Company, January, 1937.

The Life of Swami Vivekananda, Vol. 3. Calcutta: Advaita Ashrama, 1915.

The London Chronicle, Vol. 107. London: J. Wilkie, 1810.

The March of India, Vol. 13. New Delhi: Publications Division, Ministry of Information and Broadcasting, Government of India, 1961.

The Mariners' Church Gospel Temperance Soldiers' and Sailor's Magazine. London: Temperance British and Foreign Seaman, Soldiers' and Steamers' Friend Society & Bethel Flag Union, January, 1843.

The Morning Post. London: 2 February, 1810.

The Nation and the Athenaeum, Vol. 28. London: March, 1921.

The Parliamentary Debates, Official Report, House of Commons, Vol. 180. London: H.M. Stationery Office, 1925.

The Parliamentary Register: Or, History of the Proceedings and Debates of the House of Commons, First Session of the Fifteenth Parliament, Vol. 2. London: J. Debrett, 1793.

The Spectator: A Weekly Journal of News, Politics, Literature and Science, Vol. 15. London: Joseph Clayton, January, 1842.

The Spectator: A Weekly Review of Politics, Literature, Theology and Art, Vol. 44. London: John Campbell, June, 1871.

The Spectator: A Weekly Review of Politics, Literature, Theology and Art, Vol. 63. London: F.C. Westley, 1889.

The Spectator, Vol. 108. London: F.C. Westley, February, 1912.

The Spectator, Vol. 223. London: F.C. Westley, July, 1969.

TIMBS, John. 1860. *Anecdote Biography. William Pitt, Earl of Chatham, and Edmund Burke*. London: Richard Brentley.

TOYE, Hugh. 1959. *The Springing Tiger: A Study of a Revolutionary.* London: Cassell.

UNWIN, Peter (ed.). 2013. *Newcomers' Lives: The Story of Immigrants as Told in Obituaries from The Times.* London and New York: Bloomsbury.

URE, Andrew. 1836. *The Cotton Manufacture of Great Britain Systematically Investigated.* London: Charles Knight, (1).

Vanity Fair: A Weekly Show of Political, Social, & Literary Wares. 1880. Vol. 12. London: Ranken & Co., (12).

VERNON, Roland. 2001. *Star in the East: Krishnamurti, the Invention of a Messiah.* London and New York: Palgrave.

VIGASIN, Aleksei Alekseevich and Purabi Raya. 1999. *Russo–Indian Relations in the Nineteenth Century.* Calcutta: Asiatic Society.

VISRAM, Rozina. 2002. *Asians in Britain: 400 Years of History.* London: Pluto Press.

———. 2015. *Ayahs, Lascars and Princes: The Story of Indians in Britain 1700–1947.* London: Routledge.

VIVEKANANDA, Swami. 1989. *The Complete Works.* Calcutta: Advaita Ashrama, (2, 5, 6 and 7).

———. 1981. *Letters.* Calcutta: Advaita Ashrama.

VISHWANATHAN, Gauri. 2015. *Masks of Conquest: Literary Study and British Rule in India.* New York: Columbia University Press.

VISVANATHAN, Shiv. 1997. *A Carnival for Science: Essays on Science, Technology and Development.* Calcutta and Mumbai: Oxford University Press.

VON ORLICH, Leopold. 1845. *Travels in India: Including Sinde and the Punhab.* London: Longman, Brown, Green & Longmans, (2).

WADSWORTH, Marc. 1998. *Comrade Sak: A Political Biography.* London: Peepal Tree.

WARD, Margaret. 1990. *Maud Gonne: A Life.* Kitchener: Pandora.

WALPOLE, Horace. 1844. *Letters.* Philadelphia: Lea and Blanchard, (1).

WASTI, S. M. Jamil. 1982. *My Reminiscences of Choudhary Rahmat Ali.* Karachi: Royal Book Co.

WATES, Nick. 1976. *The Battle for Tolmers Square.* London: Routledge & Keegan.

WEAVER, Gordon. 2006. *Conan Doyle and the Parson's Son: The George Edalji Case.* Cambridge: Pegasus Elliot Mackenzie.

WEINREB, Ben, Christopher Hibbert, Julia Keay, and John Keay. 2008. *The London Encyclopaedia.* Photography by Matthew Weinreb. London: Macmillan.

WELSH, Alexander (ed.). 1968. *Thackeray: A Collection of Critical Essays*. London: Prentice-Hall.

WEMYSS, Georgie. 2009. *The Invisible Empire: White Discourse, Tolerance and Belonging*. Farnham: Ashgate.

WERTHEIMER, Egon. 1929. *Portrait of the Labour Party*. London: G. P. Putnam.

Westerly. 1984. Perth: University of Western Australia Press, (29).

WHITE, Daniel E. 2013. *From Little London to Little Bengal: Religion, Print, and Modernity in Early British India, 1793–1835*. Baltimore: Johns Hopkins University Press.

WHITE, Florence. 2000. *Good Things in England*. London: Persephone Books.

WHITE, Hayden. 1973. *Metahistory: The Historical Imagination in Nineteenth-Century Europe*. Baltimore and London: Johns Hopkins University Press.

WILDE, Oscar. 1899. *The Importance of Being Earnest*. London: Leonard Smithers & Co.

WILKINS, Joyce. 1992. *A Child's Eye View: 1904–1920*. Brighton: Book Guild.

WILLIAMS, Raymond. 1973. *The Country and the City*. New York: Oxford University Press.

WINSLOW. Forbes (ed.). 1850. *Journal of Psychological Medicine and Mental Pathology*. New Burlington Street, London, (3).

WOOD, Ernest. 1964. 'No Religion Higher than Truth'. In *The American Theosophist*. Theosophical Society in America, Wheaton 52(12) pp. 287–90.

WOLPERT, Stanley. 1984. *Jinnah of Pakistan*. New York: Oxford University Press.

WOOLF, Virginia. 1935. *A Room of One's Own*. London: Hogarth Press.

WORDSWORTH, William. 1884. *Ode: Intimations of Immortality from Recollections of Early Childhood*. Boston: Lothrop & Co.

——. 1850. 'Residence in London (Book 7)'. In *The Prelude, Or, Growth of a Poet's Mind: An Autobiographical Poem*. New York: D. Appleton & Co., pp. 169–204.

WRIGLEY, Edward Anthony and Roger Schofield. 1981. *The Population History of England, 1541–1871. A Reconstruction*. Cambridge, MA: Harvard University Press.

YOUNG, James. 1990. *The Second Maratha Campaign, 1804–1805: Diary of James Young*. D.D. Khanna (ed.). New Delhi: Allied Publishers.

ZAIDI, Z. H. (ed.). 1993. *Quaid-i-Azam Mohammad Ali Jinnah Papers*. Lahore: Quaid-i-Azam Papers Project, National Archives of Pakistan, (10).

ZASTOUPIL, Lynn. 2010. *Rammohun Roy and the Making of Victorian Britain*. New York: Palgrave.

ZUBRZYCKI, John. 2017. *The Mysterious Mr. Jacob: Diamond Merchant, Magician and Spy*. Melbourne: Transit Lounge Publishing.

ZUBRZYCKI, John. 2012. *The Mysterious Mr Jacob: Diamond Merchant, Magician and Spy*. New Delhi and London: Random House.

Articles and Essays in Journals

ALAVI, Hamza. 1989. 'Nationhood and the Nationalities in Pakistan'. *Economic and Political Weekly*, 24(27): 1527–34.

ALVI, Anjum. 2007. 'India and the Muslim Punjab: A Unified Approach to South Asian Kinship'. *The Journal of the Royal Anthropological Institute*, 13(3): 657–78.

ARNOLD, David. 2012. 'The Problem of Traffic: The Street-life of Modernity in late-colonial India'. *Modern Asian Studies*, 46(1): 119–41.

ASSAEL, Brenda. 2013. 'Gastro-Cosmopolitanism and the Restaurant in Late Victorian and Edwardian London'. *The Historical Journal*, 56(3): 681–706.

BADRUDDOJA, Roksana. 2006. 'White Spaces and Brown Traveling Bodies: A Project of Re-working Otherness'. *International Review of Modern Sociology*, 32(1): 1–34.

BALLARD, Roger. 1972. 'Family Organisation Among the Sikhs in Britain'. *New Community*, 2: 12–24.

BARTLETT, James. 2007. 'Dean Mahomet: Travel Writer, Curry Entrepreneur and Shampooer to the Kind'. *History Ireland*, 15(5): 8–9.

BASU, Anuradha. 1998. 'An Exploration of Entrepreneurial Activity among Asian Small Businesses in Britain'. *Small Business Economics*, 10(4): 313–26.

BEAUMONT, Paul. 2018. 'Brexit, Retrotopia and the Perils of Post-Colonial Delusions'. *Global Affairs*, 3(4–5): 379–390.

BEETHAM, Margaret. 2008. 'Good Taste and Sweet Ordering: Dining with Mrs Beeton'. *Victorian Literature and Culture*, 36(2): 391–406.

BHATTACHARYA, Bhashwati. 2005. 'Armenian European Relationship in India, 1500–1800: No Armenian Foundation for European Empire?'. *The Journal of the Economic and Social History of the Orient*, 48(2): 277–322.

BICKHAM, Troy. 2008. 'Eating the Empire: Intersections of Food, Cookery and Imperialism in Eighteenth-Century Britain'. *Past & Present*, 198: 71–109.

BOYCE, Charlotte. 2012. 'Representing the "Hungry Forties" in Image and Verse: The Politics of Hunger in Early-Victorian Illustrated Periodicals'. *Victorian Literature and Culture*, 40(2): 421–49.

BROWN, Judith. 1999. 'M. Gandhi: A Victorian Gentleman: An Essay in Imperial Encounter'. *The Journal of Imperial and Commonwealth History*, 27(2): 68–85.

BUCHAN, Alastair. 1968. 'Multicoloured Britain'. *International Journal*, 23(4): 520–530.

BUETTNER, Elizabeth. 2006. 'Cemeteries, Public Memory and Raj Nostalgia in Postcolonial Britain and India'. *History and Memory*, 18(1): 5–42.

——. 2008. '"Going for an Indian": South Asian Restaurants and the Limits of Multiculturalism in Britain'. *The Journal of Modern History*, 80(4): 865–901.

BURTON, Antoinette. 1998. 'From Child Bride to "Hindoo Lady": Rukhmabai and the Debate on Sexual Respectability in Imperial Britain'. *The American Historical Review*, 103(4): 1119–46.

CAMERON, J. Stewart and Jackie Hicks. 1996. 'Frederick Akbar Mahomed and his role in the description of hypertension at Guy's Hospital'. *Kidney International*, 49: 1488–1506.

CHANDRA, Sudhir. 1996. 'Rukhmabai: Debate over Woman's Right to Her Person' *Economic and Political Weekly*, 31(44): 2937–47.

CIECKO, Anne. 1999. 'Representing the Spaces of Diaspora in Contemporary British Films by Women Directors'. *Cinema Journal*, 38(3): 67–90.

CLAIBORNE, Louis F. 1973. 'Law and Race in Britain'. *The Annals of the American Academy of Political Science*. Blacks and the Law, 407: 167–178.

CREWE, Emma and Uma Kothari. 1998. 'Gujurati Migrants' Search for Modernity in Britain'. *Gender and Development*. [Migration and Mobility], 6(1): 13–20.

D'SOUZA, Eugene J. 2000. 'Nazi Propaganda in India'. *Social Scientist*, 28(5/6): 77–90.

DALY, Suzanne and Ross G. Forman. 2008. 'Introduction: Cooking Culture: Situating Food and Drink in the Nineteenth Century'. *Victorian Literature and Culture*, 36(2): 363–73.

DENT, Robert W. 1965. 'Shakespeare's Life and Times'. *Shakespeare Quarterly*, 16(3): 64–76.

DHONDY, Faroukh. 1986. 'An Emergent Ethnic Culture in Britain'. *India International Centre Quarterly*, 13(2): 207–215.

ENGBERG, Jens. 1966. 'Royalist Finances During the English Civil War, 1642–1646'. *The Scandinavian Economic History Review*, 14(2): 73–96.

FISHER, Michael H. 2007. 'Excluding and Including "Natives of India": Early-Nineteenth-Century British-Indian Race Relations in Britain'. *Comparative Studies of South Asia, Africa and the Middle East*, 27(2): 303–314.

FISHER, Michael H. and Mehdi Abedi. 1990. 'Bombay Talkies, the Word and the World: Salman Rushdie's *Satanic Verses*'. *Cultural Anthropology*, 5(2): 107–159.

FORWARD, Martin. 1995. 'Syed Ameer Ali: A Bridge Builder?'. *Islam and Christian–Muslim Relations*, 6(1): 45–62.

FRANK, Andre Gunder. 1990. 'On the Silk Road: An "Academic" Travelogue'. *Economic and Political Weekly*, 25(46): 2536–39.

FREEDMAN, Paul. 2011. 'American Restaurants and Cuisine in the Mid-Nineteenth Century'. *The New England Quarterly*, 84(1): 5–59.

FURBER, Holden. 1969. 'Asia and the West as Partners Before "Empire" and After'. *The Journal of Asian Studies*, 28(4): 711–121.

GANAPATHY-DORÉ, Geetha. 2009. 'Shakespeare in Rushdie'. *Atlantis*, 31(2): 9–22.

GARDNER, Katy. 1993. '*Desh-Bidesh*: Sylheti Images of Home and Away'. *Man*, New Series, 28(1): 1–15.

———. 2008. 'Keeping Connected Security, Place, and Social Capital in a "Londoni" Village in Sylhet'. *The Journal of the Royal Anthropological Institute*, 14(3): 477–95.

GHOSH, Partha S. 2012. 'To and Fro India, with Love'. *India International Centre Quarterly*, 39(2): 54–66.

GITHIRE, Njeri. 2010. 'The Empire Bites Back: Food Politics and the Making of a Nation in Andrea Levy's Works'. *Callaloo*, 33(3): 857–73.

GLEDIC, Bojana. 2012. 'The (Dis)Position of Immigrants in the 1960s London of Anita Desai's *Bye-Bye Blackbird*. *Rocky Mountain Review*, 66(Special Issue: Border Crossing): 58–72.

GOPAL, Priyamvada. 2013. 'Speaking with Difficulty: Feminism and Antiracism in Britain after 9/11'. *Feminist Studies*, 39(1): 98–118.

GREGORY, James and F.R. Hist. S. 2005. *British Vegetarianism and the Raj*. Plymouth University.

HARRIS, Jonathan Gil. 2007. 'The Smell of "Macbeth"'. *Shakespeare Quarterly*, 58(4): 465–486.

HAY, Stephen. 1989. 'The Making of a Late-Victorian Hindu: M.K. Gandhi in London, 1888–1891'. *Victorian Studies*, 33(1): 74–98.

HENDERSON, Heike. 2015. 'Kebab in London: Transnational Experiences and the Role of Food in Yadé Kara's "Café Cyprus"'. *Rocky Mountain Review*, 69(2): 182–199.

HENRY, N., C. McEwan and J. S. Pollard. 2002. 'Globalisation from Below: Birmingham: Postcolonial Workshop of the World?'. *Area*, 34(2): 117–27.

HIRO, Dilip. 1979. 'Indians in Britain'. *India International Centre Quarterly*, 6(3): 217–24.

HOLTZMAN, Jon D. 2006. 'Food and Memory'. *Annual Review of Anthropology*, 35: 361–78.

HOPKINS, A.G. 2008. 'Rethinking Decolonisation'. *Past & Present*, (200): 211–47.

HUSSAIN, Asaf. 2005. 'The Indian Diaspora in Britain: Political Interventionism and Diaspora Activism'. *Asian Affairs*, 32(3): 189–208.

HUSSAIN, Feryad. 2009. 'The Mental Health of Muslims in Britain: Relevant Therapeutic Concepts'. *International Journal of Mental Health*, 38(2): 21–36.

HUTTUNEN, Tuomas. 2004. 'Representation of London in *The Shadow Lines* by Amitav Ghosh'. *Literary London: Interdisciplinary Studies in the Representation of London*, 2(1), Available at: http://www.literarylondon.org/london-journal/march2004/huttunen.html. (Accessed on 20 February 2018).

International Human Genome Sequencing Consortium. 2004. 'Finishing the Euchromatic Sequence of the Human Genome'. *Nature: International Journal of Science*, 431: 931–45.

ISRAEL, Nigel B. 1992. '"The Most Unkindest Cut of All"—Recutting the Koh-i-Nur'. *Journal of Gemmology*, 23(3): 176.

JACOBS, Michael. 1985. 'Immigration Controls and Racism'. *Economic and Political Weekly*, 20(25/26): 1075–76.

JACKSON, Peter. 2002. 'Geographies of Diversity and Differences'. *Geography*, 87(4): 316–23.

JAZEEL, Tariq. 2012. 'Postcolonial Spaces and Identities'. *Geography*, 97(2): 60–67.

JOHNSTON, James. 1855. 'The Chemistry of Common Life'. *The Edinburgh Review*. London: Longman, Brown, Green & Longmans, 101: 480–500.

JUPP, James. 2010. 'Immigration and Race in the British General Election'. *AQ: Australian Quarterly*, 82(2): 32–37.

JUSSAWALLA, Feroza. 1988/1989. 'Chiffon Saris: The Plight of South Asian Immigrants in the New World'. *The Massachusetts Review*, 29(4): 583–95.

KARMAKAR, Chandrima. 2015. 'The Conundrum of "Home" in the Literature of the Indian Diaspora: An Interpretive Analysis'. *Sociological Bulletin*, 64(1): 77–90.

KENNEDY, Dennis. 1998. 'Shakespeare and Cultural Tourism'. *Theatre Journal*. Shakespeare and Theatrical Modernisms, 50(2): 175–88.

KENNEDY, Michael. 2010. '"Where's the Taj Mahal?": India Restaurants in Dublin Since 1908'. *History Ireland*. The Elephant and Partition: Ireland and India, 18(4): 50–52. KHAN, Hafeez-ur-Rahman. 1961. 'Pakistan's Relations with the Commonwealth: Political and Strategic Aspects'. *Pakistan Horizon*, 14(2): 128–38.

KHILNANI, Sunil. 2007. 'Nehru's Evil Genius'. *Outlook*, 47(6–13).

KLAUSEN, Jytte. 2005. 'Europe's Muslim Political Elite: Walking a Tightrope'. *World Policy Journal*, 22(3): 61–68.

LEWIS, Gordon K. 1971. 'An Introductory Note to the Study of Race Relations in Great Britain'. *Caribbean Studies*, 11(1): 5–29.

LOURENÇO, Inês and Rita Cachado. 2012. 'Hindu Transnational Families: Transformation and Continuity in Diaspora Families'. *Journal of Comparative Family Studies*. The Indian Family: A Revisit, 43(1): 53–70.

MACCREADY, Paul. 1999. 'An Ambivalent Luddite at a Technological Feast'. *Designfax*. Available at: http://www.designfax.net/archives/0899/899trl_2.asp. (Accessed on 20 September 2017).

MACEY, Ruth. 2012. '"Mangoes and Coconuts and Grandmothers": Food in Transatlantic South Asian Writing'. *South Asian Atlantic Literature, 1970–2010*. Edinburgh and London: Edinburgh University Press.

MARTINOT, Steve. 2007. 'Immigration and the Boundary of Whiteness'. *Race/Ethnicity: Multidisciplinary Global Contexts. Transnational Migration, Race and Citizenship*, 1(1): 17–36.

MAXEY, Ruth. 2012. 'Home and Nation in South Asian Atlantic Literature'. *South Asian Atlantic Literature, 1970–2010*. Edinburgh University Press.

MCGARR, Paul M. 2010. '"A Serious Menace to Security" British Intelligence, V. K. Krishna Menon and the Indian High Commission in London, 1947–52'. *The Journal of Imperial and Commonwealth History*, 38(4): 441–69.

MAY, Derwent. 2013. 'Letter from London' *The Hudson Review*, 66(2): 262–67.

MAY, Jon, Jane Wills, Kavita Datta, Joanna Herbert and Cathy McIlwaine. 2007. 'Keeping London Working: Global Cities, the British State and London's New Migrant Division of Labour'. *Transactions of the Institute of British Geographers*. New Series, 32(2): 151–67.

MENON, V.K. Krishna. 1974. 'My Years in England'. *Socialist India*. New Delhi: All India Congress Committee Office, December, 1974; republished from *The Sunday Times*, London, 1963, 10(2): 17–19.

MILLER, Henry. 1966. 'Race Relations and the Schools in Great Britain'. *Phylon*, 27(3): 247–267.

MURTY, M. Ram. 2011. 'The Meeting of Sri Ramakrishna and Swami Vivekananda'. *The Vedanta Kesari*, pp. 310–13, 349–51, 391–95.

NANDY, Ashis. Winter 2002–Spring 2003. 'Ethnic Cuisine: the Significant "Other"'. *India International Quarterly*. India: A national Culture?, 29(¾): 246–51.

NASSER, Noha. 2004. 'Southall's Kaleido-scape: A Study in the Challenging Morphology of a West London Suburb'. *Built Environment (1978–)*. The Cosmopolis: Emerging Multicultural Spaces in Europe and North America, 30(1): 76–103.

NASTA, Susheila. 2011. 'Sealing a Friendship: George Orwell and Mulk Raj Anand at the BBC (1941–43)'. *Wasafiri*, 26(4): 14–18.

O'ROURKE, Michael F. 1992. 'Personal and Historical Perspectives: Frederick Akbar Mahomed'. *Hypertension*, 19(2): 212–17.

OOMMEN, T.K. Winter 2002–Spring 2003. 'Demystifying the Nation and Nationalism'. *India International Quarterly*. India: A National Culture?, 29(¾): 259–74.

____. 2003. 'Pakistan and the World (Chronology: January-March 2003)'. *Pakistan Horizon*, Kashmir, 56(2): 149–201.

PANAYI, Panikos. 1991. 'Middlesbrough 1961: A British Race Riot of the 1960s?'. *Social History*, 16(2): 139–153.

PANT, Pushpesh. 2013. 'Food and the Making of the Nation'. *India International Quarterly*, 40(2): 1–34.

PORTMAN, Anne. 2014. 'Mother Nature has it Right: Local Food Advocacy and the Appeal to the "Natural"'. *Ethics and the Environment*, 19(1): 1–30.

PRASCH, Thomas. 2008. 'Eating the World: London in 1851'. *Victorian Literature and Culture*, 36(2): 587–602.

RAMJI, Hasmita. 2006. 'British Indians "Returning Home": An Exploration of Transnational Belongings'. *Sociology*, 40(4): 645–62.

RANJAN, Amit, Suhaas Ramani, Aanchal Agarwal, Akshita Chembolu, and Manika Dhiman. 2018. 'Kohinoor and Its Travelogy: The Dialectic of Ownership and Reparations of an Artefact'. *Coldnoon: International Journal of Travel Writing & Travelling Cultures*, 6(4): 49–72, Available at: https://coldnoon.com/journal/dandelion-february-2018/kohinoor-and-its-travelogy-the-dialectic-of-ownership-and-reparations-of-an-artefact/. (Accessed on 20 December 2018).

RAY, Sukumar. 1987. 'Selected Letters'. *South Asia Research*, 7(2):188–236.

RAY, Utsa. 2012. 'Eating "Modernity": Changing dietary practices in colonial Bengal'. *Modern Asian Studies*, 46(3): 703–730.

RODEN, Claudia. 2003. 'London's Mongrel English Cuisine'. *AA Files*, (49): 68–69.

ROGOV, Daniel. 2012. 'Rumblings from the World of Food'. *Gastronomica*, 12(2): 1–6.

ROY, Modhumita. 2010. 'Some Like It Hot: Class, Gender and Empire in the Making of Mulligatawny Soup'. *Economic and Political Weekly*, 45(32): 66–75.

RUTTEN, Mario and Pravin J. Patel. 2003. 'Caste-based Differences and Contested Family Relations: Social linkages between India and Britain'. *Etnofoor*. Kinship. 16(1): 75–96.

SANDHU, Sukhdev. 1999. 'London: Post-Colonial City: Conference at the AA, 12–13 May 1999'. *AA Files*, (38): 63–66.

SARTRE, Jean-Paul. 1970. 'Intentionality: A Fundamental Idea of Husserl's Phenomenology'. *Journal of the British Society for Phenomenology*, 1(2): 4–5.

SCHAFFER, Gavin. 2010. '"Till Death Us Do Part" and the BBC: Racial Politics and the British Working Classes 1965–75'. *Journal of Contemporary History*, 45(2): 454–77.

SCHAEFER, Richard T. 1976. 'Indians in Great Britain'. *International Review of Modern Sociology*, 6(2): 305–327.

SCOTT, Sam and Paul Brindley. 2012. 'New Geographies of Migrant Settlement in the UK'. *Geography*, 97(1): 29–38.

SEN, Sharmila. 2002. 'Foreign Accents: Notes upon My Return to the Diaspora'. *The Women's Review of Books*, 19(5): 8–9.

——. 2008. 'The Saracen's Head'. *Victorian Literature and Culture*, 36(2): 407–31.

SENGUPTA, Jayanta. 2010. 'Nation on a Platter: The Culture and Politics of Food and Cuisine in Colonial Bengal'. *Modern Asian Studies. The Politics of Work, Family and Community in India*. 44(1): 81–98.

SHAH, A.M. 2006. '*The Indian Sociologist*, 1905–14, 1920–22'. *Economic and Political Weekly*, 41(31): 3435–39.

SHAH, Saeeda. 2004. 'The Researcher/Interviewer in Intercultural Context: A social Intruder!'. *British Educational Research Journal*, 30(4): 549–575.

SHARMA, Shailja. 2001. 'Salman Rushdie: The Ambivalence of Migrancy'. *Twentieth Century Literature. Salman Rushdie.* 47(4): 596–618.

SHUKLA, Sandhya. 2001. 'Locations for South Asian Diasporas'. *Annual Review of Anthropology*, 30: 551–572.

SINCLAIR, Iain. 1993. 'Living in Restaurants'. *Mississippi Review. New British Fiction*, 21(3): 96–132.

SRINIVAS, Tulasi. 2006. '"As Mother Made It": The Cosmopolitan Indian Family, "Authentic" Food and the Construction of Cultural Utopia'. *International Journal of Sociology of the Family*. Globalisation and the Family, 32(2): 191–221.

TAYLOR, George. 2003. '"From the Slurry to the Curry": The Politics of Food Regulation and Reform in Ireland'. *Irish Studies in International Affairs*, 14: 149–64.

TENENBAUM, Harriet R. and Martin D. Ruck. 2012. '"British Adolescents and Young Adults" Understanding About the Religious and Nonreligious Rights of Asylum-Seeker Youth'. *Child Development*, 83(3): 1102–15.

VARLEY, H. L. 1953. 'Imperialism and Rudyard Kipling'. *Journal of the History of Ideas*, 14(1): 124–135.

VERMA, Jatinder. 1989. 'Transformations in Culture: The Asian in Britain'. *RSA Journal*, 137(5400): 767–78.

WALKER, Martin. 2006. 'Europe's Mosque Hysteria'. *The Wilson Quarterly (1976–)*, 30(2): 14–22.

'Wanted, an Anglo-Indian Restaurant for London'. *Caterer* (London: June 15, 1891) p. 221.

WATERS, Chris. 1997. '"Dark Strangers" in Our Midst: Discourses of Race and Nation in Britain, 1947–1963'. *Journal of British Studies*, 36(2): 207–238.

WEBER, Donald. 1997. '"No Secrets Were Safe from Me": Situating Hanif Kureishi'. *The Massachusetts Review*, 38(1): 119–35.

YEATS, George. 2012. 'Shakespeare's Victorian Legacy: Text as Monument and Emendation as Desecration in the Mid-Nineteenth Century'. *Victorian Literature and Culture*, 40(2): 469–86.

YEBRA, José M. 2011. 'The Moving Lines of Neo-Baroque in Will Self's "Dorian: An Imitation"'. *Atlantis*, 33(1): 17–31.

YENNING, Dan. 2011. 'Cultural Imperialism and Intercultural Encounter in Merchant Ivory's *Shakespeare Wallah*'. *Asian Theatre Journal*, 28(1): 149–67.

YOUNG, Paul. 2008. 'The Cooking Animal: Economic Man at the Great Exhibition'. *Victorian Literature and Culture*, 36(2): 569–86.

ZEIGLER, Garrett. 2007. 'East of the City: "Brick Lane" Capitalism, and the Global Metropolis'. *Race/Ethnicity: Multidisciplinary Global Contexts*. Transnational Migration, Race, and Citizenship, 1(1): 145–67.

ZLOTNICK, Susan. 1996. 'Domesticating Imperialism: Curry and Cookbooks in Victorian England'. *Frontiers: A Journal of Women Studies*. Gender, Nations and Nationalisms, 16(2/3): 51–68.

Newspaper Articles and Online Resources

'Ahmed Ali'. *Making Britain*. The Open University, Available at: http://www.open.ac.uk/researchprojects/makingbritain/content/ahmed-ali. (Accessed on 20 December 2018).

'Amiya Nath Bose'. *Making Britain*. The Open University, Available at: http://www.open.ac.uk/researchprojects/makingbritain/content/amiya-nath-bose. (Accessed on 20 December 2018).

'An Abandoned Ayah'. *Untold Lives*. British Library, Available at: http://blogs.bl.uk/untoldlives/2016/10/an-abandoned-ayah.html (Accessed on 20 December 2018).

Anand, Anita. 2015. 'Sophia, the Suffragette'. *The Times of India*, January 11, Available at: https://timesofindia.indiatimes.com/home/sunday-times/Sophia-the-suffragette/articleshow/45839386.cms. (Accessed on 20 December 2018).

———. 2015. 'The Incredible Suffragette Princess Lost to History ... Until Now'. *The Telegraph*, 15 January, Available at: https://www.telegraph.co.uk/women/womens-life/11345857/Incredible-suffragette-princess-was-lost-to-history...until-now.html. (Accessed on 20 December 2018).

———. 2018. '100 years on, the Forgotten Indian Princess Who Played a Key Role in the British Suffrage Movement'. *Scroll*, 8 February, Available at: https://scroll.in/article/867841/100-years-on-the-forgotten-indian-princess-who-played-a-key-role-in-the-british-suffrage-movement. (Accessed on 20 December 2018).

'And Mr. Mohamed Too'. *The Guardian*, 9 April, 2002, Available at: http://www.theguardian.com/world/2002/apr/09/religion.uk. Accessed on 2 January 2016.

'Atiya Fyzee'. *Making Britain*. The Open University, Available at: http://www.open.ac.uk/researchprojects/makingbritain/content/atiya-fyzee. (Accessed on 20 December 2018).

'Attia Hosain'. *Making Britain*. The Open University, Available at: http://www.open.ac.uk/researchprojects/makingbritain/content/attia-hosain. (Accessed on 20 December 2018).

BAYLY, Christopher. 'Looking Behind Domestic Tranquillity' in 'Early Victorian Tea Set'. *A History of the World in 100 Objects*, *BBC*, Available at: http://www.bbc.co.uk/ahistoryoftheworld/objects/FWYgWOCSSpKKuF3pctC6tA. (Accessed on 11 May 2018).

BATES, Stephen. 2004. 'Letter from Queen Victoria points to affair with Brown'. *The Guardian*, 16 December, Available at: https://www.theguardian.com/uk/2004/dec/16/monarchy.stephenbates. (Accessed on 14 December 2018).

BEDI, Rahul. 2008. 'India Finally Settles £1 million Nizam Dispute'. *The Telegraph*, 12 April, Available at: https://www.telegraph.co.uk/news/worldnews/1584818/India-finally-settles-1million-Nizam-dispute.html. (Accessed on 20 December 2018).

BHAGAT, Smriti, Moira Burke, et al. 2016. 'Three and a Half Degrees of Separation'. *Facebook Research*, 4 February, Available at: https://research.fb.com/three-and-a-half-degrees-of-separation/ (Accessed on 20 December 2018).

'Bibliophile Bookshop'. *Making Britain*. The Open University, Available at: http://www.open.ac.uk/researchprojects/makingbritain/content/bibliophile-bookshop. (Accessed on 20 December 2018).

BOULGER, George Simonds and Rebecca Mills. 'David Lester Richardson'. *The Oxford Dictionary of National Biography*, Available at: http://www.oxforddnb.com/view/10.1093/ref:odnb/9780198614128.001.0001/odnb-9780198614128-e-23550 (Accessed on 11 August 2018).

BOURKE, Joanna. 2018. 'Owner of Indian Restaurants Chain Masala Zone Makes Brexit Visa Plea'. *Evening Standard*, 9 January, Available at: https://www.standard.co.uk/business/owner-of-indian-restaurants-chain-masala-zone-makes-brexit-visa-plea-a3735396.html. (Accessed on 20 September 2018).

BRADSHAW, Peter. 2007. 'Review: *A Throw of Dice*'. *The Guardian*, 24 August, Available at: https://www.theguardian.com/film/2007/aug/24/drama.worldcinema1. (Accessed on 20 December 2018).

'Britain's Curry Houses Disappearing—50 Percent to Close Within 10 Years'. *The Telegraph*, February 23, 2017. Available at: http://www.telegraph.co.uk/news/2017/02/22/britains-curry-houses-feeling-heat-owners-arent-innovative-enough/. (Accessed on 25 September 2017).

'Britain's First Asian MP elected (From the Archive, 26 July 1892)'. *The Guardian*, July 26, 2013. Available at: https://www.theguardian.com/theguardian/2013/jul/26/election-naoroji-finsbury-1892. (Accessed on 20 December 2018).

CAMPION, Sonali. 'Interview with Susheila Nasta'. *South Asia at LSE, The London School of Economics and Political Science* (blog), Available at: https://blogs.lse.ac.uk/southasia/2017/02/02/before-independence-there-was-a-synergy-between-india-and-britain-that-came-from-a-shared-language-which-persists-today-susheila-nasta/. (Accessed on 20 September 2018).

CHATTERJEE, Arup K. 2017. 'How the Curry Came to London (and Why after the UK election, it May Never Taste the Same Again)'. *Scroll*, 8 June 8. Available at: https://scroll.in/magazine/839613/how-the-curry-came-to-london-and-why-after-the-uk-election-it-may-never-taste-the-same-again. (Accessed on 20 December 2018).

CHOPRA, Deepak. 2011. 'You Are Home to Millions of Microbes!'. *Huffington Post*, 24 June, Available at: https://www.huffingtonpost.com/deepak-chopra/weekly-health-tip-you-are_b_852800.html. (Accessed on 20 December 2018).

'Choudhary Rahmat Ali'. *Making Britain*. The Open University, Available at: http://www.open.ac.uk/researchprojects/makingbritain/content/choudhary-rahmat-ali. (Accessed on 20 December 2018).

'Clive, George (d.1779), of Wormbridge, Herefs'. *The History of Parliament*. Available at: https://www.historyofparliamentonline.org/volume/1754-1790/member/clive-george-1779 (Accessed on 20 December 2018).

Colorado Historic Newspaper Collection. 1899. 'A Chef from India: New York Women Go Wild Over Him'. *County Park Bulletin*, 17 November. Available at: https://www.coloradohistoricnewspapers.org/cgi-bin/colorado?a=d&d=PCB18991117.2.35&e=-------en-20--1--img-txIN%7ctxCO%7ctxTA--------0-- (Accessed on 20 December 2018).

'Curry House Founder Honored'. *BBC*, 29 September, 2005, Available at: http://news.bbc.co.uk/2/hi/uk_news/england/london/4290124.stm. (Accessed on 2 January 2016).

DEACON, Michael. 2016. 'Next Time, I'm Bringing Goggles and a Black & Decker'. *The Telegraph*, 13 October 13, Available at: https://www.telegraph.co.uk/food-and-drink/restaurants/michael-deacon-reviews-calcutta-street-london-next-time-im-bring/. (Accessed on 20 October 2018).

'Don't Tinker with Tikka or Mess with Masala'. *The Telegraph*, 24 March, 2004, Available at: https://www.telegraph.co.uk/news/uknews/1457612/Dont-tinker-with-tikka-or-mess-with-masala.html. (Accessed on 15 October 2017).

'G.V. Desani'. *Making Britain*. The Open University, Available at: http://www.open.ac.uk/researchprojects/makingbritain/content/g-v-desani. (Accessed on 20 December 2018).

GANDER, Paul. 2013. 'Ethnic Foods Shaping UK Market'. *Food Manufacture*, 12 August, Available at: https://www.foodmanufacture.co.uk/Article/2013/08/13/Ethnic-foods-how-authentic-are-they. (Accessed on 20 September 2018).

'Glasgow "invented" Tikka Masala'. *BBC*, 21 July, 2009, Available at: http://news.bbc.co.uk/2/hi/uk_news/scotland/glasgow_and_west/8161812.stm. (Accessed on 20 December 2018).

GRAY, John. 2019. 'British Populism and Brexit'. *A Point of View, BBC Sounds*, 19 July, Available at: https://www.bbc.co.uk/programmes/m0006v09. (Accessed on 07 September 2019).

'Grey Wolf'. *India Today*. January 8, 2011, Available at: https://
www.indiatoday.in/magazine/leisure/story/20110117-grey-
wolf-745476-2011-01-08. (Accessed on 20 December 2018).

GROSE, Thomas K. 2016. 'Indian Food Curries Less Favor in the
UK'. *US News*, 14 December, Available at: https://www.usnews.
com/news/best-countries/articles/2016-12-14/indian-food-
long-a-staple-in-british-cuisine-facing-decline. (Accessed on 25
September 2017).

'Guildhall Library Manuscripts Section: Black and Asian People
Discovered in Records Held by the Manuscripts Section'. *Institute of
Historical Research*, School of Advanced Study, University of London,
Available at: https://www.history.ac.uk/gh/baentries.htm (Accessed
on 20 February 2018).

HAMID, Shahela. 2005. 'A Study of Language Maintenance and Shift
in The Sylheti Community in Leeds'. Doctoral Dissertation. York:
University of York.

'Has Narendra Modi changed India?'. *The Briefing Room, BBC Sounds*,
May 23, 2019. Available at: https://www.bbc.co.uk/programmes/
m00057vj. (Accessed on 7 September 2019).

'India League'. *Making Britain*. The Open University, Available at:
http://www.open.ac.uk/researchprojects/makingbritain/content/
india-league. (Accessed on 20 December 2018).

'Indian Restaurants'. *Making Britain*. The Open University, Available at:
http://www.open.ac.uk/researchprojects/makingbritain/taxonomy/
term/31. (Accessed on 20 December 2018).

'Indira Devi'. *Making Britain*. The Open University, Available at:
http://www.open.ac.uk/researchprojects/makingbritain/content/
indira-devi. (Accessed on 20 December 2018).

'Iqbal Singh'. *Making Britain*. The Open University, Available at:
http://www.open.ac.uk/researchprojects/makingbritain/content/
iqbal-singh. (Accessed on 20 December 2018).

JACK, Ian. 2011. 'Rabindranath Tagore was a Global Phenomenon,
So Why is he Neglected?'. *The Guardian*, 7 May 7, Available at:
https://www.theguardian.com/commentisfree/2011/may/07/
rabindranath-tagore-why-was-he-neglected. (Accessed on 20
December 2018).

JACOB, Satish, 2000. 'Indian MPs demand Kohinoor's Return'.
BBC, 26 April 26, Available at: http://news.bbc.co.uk/2/hi/south_
asia/727231.stm. (Accessed on 20 December 2018).

JACOBSON, Howard. 2019. 'The Language of Leaving'. *A Point of View*, in *BBC Sounds*, 14 July Available at: https://www.bbc.co.uk/sounds/play/m0006n26. (Accessed on 20 August 2019).

JAHANGIR, Rumeana. 2009. 'How Britain Got the Hots for Curry'. *BBC*, 26 November 26, Available at: http://news.bbc.co.uk/2/hi/8370054.stm. (Accessed on 20 December 2018).

JOHNSON, Robert Wood. 2019. 'Don't Let Smears About US Farms Trap Britain into the EU's Museum of Agriculture'. *The Telegraph*, 1 March 1, Available at: https://www.telegraph.co.uk/news/2019/03/01/dont-let-smears-us-farms-trap-britain-eus-museum-agriculture/. (Accessed on 20 April 2019).

'Joseph Salter'. *Making Britain*. Open University, Available at: http://www.open.ac.uk/researchprojects/makingbritain/content/joseph-salter (Accessed on 20 December 2018).

KEBBLE, Mark. 2016. 'Veeraswamy: Adding Spice to London for 90 Years'. *The Resident*, 27 June 27, Available at: https://www.theresident.co.uk/food-drink-london/veeraswamy-adding-spice-london-90-years. (Accessed on 20 September 2018).

KEHR, Dave. 2008. 'New DVDs: *A Throw of Dice* and Summer Serials'. *The New York Times*, 15 July 15, Available at: https://www.nytimes.com/2008/07/15/movies/homevideo/15dvds.html?_r=1&oref=slogin. (Accessed on 20 December 2018).

KELLY, Michael. 1992. 'The 1992 Campaign: The Democrats—Clinton and Bush Compete to Be Champion of Change; Democrat Fights Perceptions of Bush Gain'. *The New York Times*, 31 October, Available at: https://www.nytimes.com/1992/10/31/us/1992-campaign-democrats-clinton-bush-compete-be-champion-change-democrat-fights.html. (Accessed on 20 December 2018).

KESVANI, Hussein. 2016. 'Curry in Crisis, Bollywood Bored of London: How India's Perceptions of Britain are Changing'. *New Statesman*, 18 November, Available at: https://www.newstatesman.com/politics/uk/2016/11/curry-crisis-bollywood-bored-london-how-india-s-perceptions-britain-are-changing. (Accessed on 25 September 2017).

'Khwaja Kamaluddin'. *Making Britain*. The Open University, Available at: http://www.open.ac.uk/researchprojects/makingbritain/content/khwaja-kamaluddin. (Accessed on 20 December 2018).

KRISHNAMURTI, Jiddu. 'Beyond Violence: London, Fourth Public Talk—30th May 1970—"The Religious Mind,"' in 'Teachings'.

Jiddu Krishnamurti (website), Available at: https://jkrishnamurti. org/content/part-iii-chapter-3-london-4th-public-talk-30th-may-1970-%E2%80%98-religious-mind%E2%80%99. (Accessed on 20 December 2018).

'Krishnarao Shelvankar'. *Making Britain.* The Open University, Available at: http://www.open.ac.uk/researchprojects/makingbritain/content/krishnarao-shelvankar. (Accessed on 20 December 2018).

KUMAR, Anuradha. 2015. 'How an Indian Took Shampooing to England'. *Scroll,* 9 November, Available at: http://scroll.in/article/768015/how-an-indian-took-shampooing-to-england. (Accessed on 2 January 2016).

LAWSON, Alastair. 2005. 'Eton, the Raj and Modern India'. *BBC,* 9 March, Available at: http://news.bbc.co.uk/2/hi/south_asia/4309213. stm. (Accessed on 20 December 2018).

MACAULAY, Thomas Babington. 'Minute by the Hon'ble T. B. Macaulay, dated February 2, 1835'. University of Columbia (website), Available at: http://www.columbia.edu/itc/mealac/pritchett/00generallinks/macaulay/txt_minute_education_1835. html. (Accessed on 20 December 2018).

MACGREGOR, Neil. 2012. 'London Becomes Rome'. *Shakespeare's Restless World,* BBC, 2 May, Available at: https://www.bbc.co.uk/sounds/play/b01h73pq. (Accessed on 20 September 2018).

———. 2012. 'From London to Marrakech'. *Shakespeare's Restless World,* BBC, 9 May, Available at: https://www.bbc.co.uk/sounds/play/b01gvrxk. (Accessed on 20 September 2018).

———.2019. 'India and How it Sees Britain'. *As the World Sees Britain,* BBC, 20 March, Available at: https://www.bbc.co.uk/sounds/play/w3csygxd. (Accessed on 20 October 2019).

'Mahatma Gandhi, Football Legend'. *FIFA,* 22 October, 2010, Available at: https://www.fifa.com/news/mahatma-gandhi-football-legend-1322010. (Accessed on 20 December 2018).

MAHER, Sanam. 2013. 'Jinnah's Abode: No. 35, Russell Road'. *The Express Tribune,* 21 July, Available at: https://tribune.com.pk/story/578135/jinnahs-abode-no-35-russell-road/. (Accessed on 20 December 2018).

MAJUMDAR, Bappa and Soumi Bhattacharya. 2004. '*Gitanjali*: Lost and Found'. *The Telegraph,* India, 4 April, Available at: https://www. telegraphindia.com/states/west-bengal/gitanjali-lost-and-found/cid/759193. (Accessed on 20 December 2018).

MAKEPEACE, Margaret. 2016. 'A Most Fearefull and Dreadfull Fire'. *Untold Lives*, British Library, 2 September, Available at: http://blogs.bl.uk/untoldlives/2016/09/a-most-fearefull-and-dreadfull-fire.html. (Accessed on 20 February 2018).

MALIK, Sonia. 2010. 'Jinnah as a Fashion Icon'. *The Express Tribune*, 14 November, Available at: https://tribune.com.pk/story/75202/jinnah-as-a-fashion-icon/. (Accessed on 20 December 2018).

Map of Early Modern London (website), Available at: https://mapoflondon.uvic.ca/index.htm. (Accessed on 15 July 2018).

MCCULLY, Bruce T. 1935. 'The Origins of Indian Nationalism According to Native Writers'. *The Journal of Modern History*, 7(3): 295–314.

Morrissy-Swan, Tomé. 2019. 'Deconstructed Cottage Pie and Indian Scotch Eggs: Meet the Man Taking Anglo-Indian Cuisine to the Next Level'. *The Telegraph*, 28 January, Available at: https://www.telegraph.co.uk/food-and-drink/features/deconstructed-cottage-pie-indian-scotch-eggs-meet-man-taking/. (Accessed on 20 October 2019).

'Mr. Churchill on India'. *Daily Telegraph*, February 24, 1931, Available at: https://www.britishnewspaperarchive.co.uk/search/results/1931-02-24?NewspaperTitle=Derby%2BDaily%2BTelegraph&IssueId=BL%2F0000327%2F19310224%2F&County=Derbyshire%2C%20England. (Accessed on 20 December 2018).

'Mulk Raj Anand'. *Making Britain*, The Open University, Available at: http://www.open.ac.uk/researchprojects/makingbritain/content/mulk-raj-anand. (Accessed on 20 December 2018).

'Mulk Raj Anand'. *Modernist Archives Publishing Project*, Available at: https://www.modernistarchives.com/person/mulk-raj-anand. (Accessed on 20 September 2019).

MYERS, Matt. 2018. 'Labour Against Empire'. *Jacobin*, 19 February, Available at: https://www.jacobinmag.com/2018/02/labour-party-shapurji-saklatvala-communist. (Accessed on 20 December 2019).

'Narayana Menon'. *Making Britain*, The Open University, Available at: http://www.open.ac.uk/researchprojects/makingbritain/content/narayana-menon. (Accessed on 20 December 2018).

NEHRU, Jawaharlal, 2016. 'We Want no Caesars: Nehru's Warning to Himself'. *The Caravan*, 14 November, Available at: https://caravanmagazine.in/vantage/want-no-caesars-nehrus-warning. (Accessed on 20 December 2018).

O'CARROLL, Lisa. 2019. 'Food Fight: Doubts Grow Over Post-Brexit Standards'. *The Guardian*, 6 March, Available at: https://www. theguardian.com/politics/2019/mar/06/food-fight-doubts-grow-over-post-brexit-standards. (Accessed on 20 April 2019).

O'Yeah, Zac. 2014. 'Back in Time: Mahatma Gandhi's Unpublished Guide to London'. *National Geographic Traveller, India*, 6 June, Available at: http://www.natgeotraveller.in/back-in-time-mahatma-gandhis-unpublished-guide-to-london/. (Accessed on 20 December 2018).

'Our History'. YMCA, Indian Student Hostel, London, Available at: http://www.indianymca.org/our-history/. (Accessed on 20 December 2018).

'P.N. Haksar'. *Making Britain*. The Open University, Available at: http://www.open.ac.uk/researchprojects/makingbritain/content/p-n-haksar. (Accessed on 20 December 2018).

PARACHA, Nadeem F. 2018. 'Smokers' Corner: Politics of Appeasement'. *Dawn*, 11 November, Available at: https://www.dawn.com/news/1444756. (Accessed on 20 December 2018).

PETTIT, Harry. 2017. 'Is this Britain's earliest curry? New recipe book recreates an 18th Century spicy chicken dish'. *Daily Mail*, 27 March, Available at: https://www.dailymail.co.uk/sciencetech/article-4353808/Is-Britain-s-earliest-curry.html (Accessed on 20 October 2018).

PHILIPSON, Alice. 2013. 'Hundreds of Couples Leave "Love Locks" Across London Ahead of Valentine's Day'. *The Telegraph*, 12 February, Available at: https://www.telegraph.co.uk/news/newstopics/howaboutthat/9864004/Hundreds-of-couples-leave-love-locks-across-London-ahead-of-Valentines-Day.html. (Accessed on 20 February 2018).

POOLE, Steven. 2018. 'What Does Boris Johnson Mean by "Teleological Construction"'. *The Guardian*, 15 February, Available at: https://www.theguardian.com/books/2018/feb/15/boris-johnson-teleological-construction-steven-poole. (Accessed on 20 December 2018).

POWELL, Enoch. 2007. '"Rivers of Blood" Speech'. *The Telegraph*, 6 November, Available at: https://www.telegraph.co.uk/comment/3643823/Enoch-Powells-Rivers-of-Blood-speech.html. (Accessed on 20 September 2018).

PRASANNARAJAN, S. 2005. 'M.A. Jinnah: A Secularist or a Sophisticated Communalist in Nationalist Garb?'. *India Today*,

27 June, Available at: https://www.indiatoday.in/magazine/cover-story/story/20050627-mohammad-ali-jinnah-a-secularist-or-a-sophisticated-communalist-787403-2005-06-27. (Accessed on 20 December 2018).

'Pulin Behari Seal'. *Making Britain*. The Open University, Available at: http://www.open.ac.uk/researchprojects/makingbritain/content/pulin-behari-seal. (Accessed on 20 December 2018).

QAMAR, Saadia. 2017. 'The Ever Lingering Fate of the Fyzee Rahamin Art Gallery'. *The Tribune*, 10 July, Available at: https://tribune.com.pk/story/1454059/ever-lingering-fate-fyzee-rahamin-art-gallery/. (Accessed on 20 December 2018).

RAYNER, Jay. 2003. 'Enduring Love'. *The Guardian*, 19 January, Available at: http://www.theguardian.com/lifeandstyle/2003/jan/19/foodanddrink.restaurants. (Accessed on 2 January 2016).

'Researchers Trim Count Of Human Genes To 20,000-25,000'. *Science Daily*, 21 October, 2004, Available at: https://www.sciencedaily.com/releases/2004/10/041021075155.htm. (Accessed on 20 December 2018).

ROBINSON, Amy Elizabeth. 2005. 'Tinker, Tailor, Vagrant, Sailor: Colonial Mobility and the British Imperial State, 1880–1914'. Doctoral Dissertation (Stanford University).

RODIONOVA, Zlata. 2016. 'Brexit-backing Curry Industry Says It Feels "Betrayed" by Theresa May's Immigration Clampdown'. *The Independent*, 4 November, Available at: http://www.independent.co.uk/news/business/news/brexit-latest-immigration-curry-industry-theresa-may-betrayal-a7398196.html. (Accessed on 25 September 2017).

ROOSEVELT, Franklin D. 'Letter to Winston Churchill, on April 11, 1942'. *Foreign Relations of the United States: Diplomatic Papers, 1942* (the British Commonwealth; the Far East) Vol. I, Office of the Historian, Department of States, United States of America, Available at: https://history.state.gov/historicaldocuments/frus1942v01/d530. (Accessed on 20 December 2018).

ROY, Nilanjana. 2015. 'Origin Of a Species: The First Indian to Publish a Book in English'. *The Caravan: A Journal of Politics and Culture*, 1 December, Available at: http://www.caravanmagazine.in/reviews-essays/origin-of-a-species-first-indian-publish-english-book. (Accessed on 2 January 2016).

RUDDICK, Peter. 'Under Fire: UK Ethnic Restaurants are "Losing Diners" to Supermarkets'. *Big Hospitality*, https://www.bighospitality.

co.uk/Article/2013/04/25/Under-fire-UK-ethnic-restaurants-are-losing-diners-to-supermarkets. (Accessed on 20 September 2018).

'Russia's Onward March; Progress in Asia and India Is Her Goal. Native Indians Who May Help Her—The Story of Duleep Singh's Going to Russia'. *The New York Times*, 9 October, 1887, Available at: https://www.nytimes.com/1887/10/09/archives/russias-onward-march-progress-in-asia-and-india-is-her-goal-native.html. (Accessed on 20 December 2018).

'Said Amir Shah'. *Making Britain*. The Open University, Available at: http://www.open.ac.uk/researchprojects/makingbritain/content/said-amir-shah. (Accessed on 20 December 2018).

'Sajjad Zaheer'. *Making Britain*. The Open University, Available at: http://www.open.ac.uk/researchprojects/makingbritain/content/sajjad-zaheer. (Accessed on 20 December 2018).

'Samuel Fyzee Rahamin'. *Making Britain*. The Open University, Available at: http://www.open.ac.uk/researchprojects/makingbritain/content/samuel-fyzee-rahamin. (Accessed on 20 December 2018).

SANGHANI, Radhika. 2016. 'British Citizenship Test is Just a "Bad Pub Quiz"'. *The Telegraph*, 13 June, Available at: http://www.telegraph.co.uk/news/uknews/immigration/10119281/British-citizenship-test-is-just-a-bad-pub-quiz.html. (Accessed on 2 January 2016).

'Sasadhar Sinha'. *Making Britain*. The Open University, Available at: http://www.open.ac.uk/researchprojects/makingbritain/content/sasadhar-sinha. (Accessed on 20 December 2018).

'Savitri Devi Chowdhary'. *Making Britain*. The Open University, Available at: http://www.open.ac.uk/researchprojects/makingbritain/content/savitri-devi-chowdhary. (Accessed on 20 December 2018).

SEN, Amrita. 2015. 'Early Women Travellers and the East India Company'. *Untold Lives*, British Library, 22 October, Available at: https://blogs.bl.uk/untoldlives/2015/10/early-women-travellers-and-the-east-india-company.html. (Accessed on 20 December 2018).

SENAPATHY, Kavin. 2016. 'Deepak Chopra Says Bacteria Listen To Our Thoughts'. *Forbes*, 27 January, Available at: https://www.forbes.com/sites/kavinsenapathy/2016/01/27/deepak-chopra-says-bacteria-listen-to-our-thoughts/#62addfbe6386. (Accessed on 20 September 2018).

'Shafi's Restaurant'. *Making Britain*. The Open University, Available at: http://www.open.ac.uk/researchprojects/makingbritain/content/shafis-restaurant. (Accessed on 20 December 2018).

'Shah Abdul Majid Qureshi'. *Making Britain*. The Open University, Available at: http://www.open.ac.uk/researchprojects/makingbritain/content/shah-abdul-majid-qureshi. (Accessed on 20 December 2018).

'Shah Jolal Restaurant'. *Making Britain*. The Open University, Available at: http://www.open.ac.uk/researchprojects/makingbritain/content/shah-jolal-restaurant. (Accessed on 20 December 2018).

SONIN, Adam. 2013. 'The Hampstead Years of Rabindranath Tagore: First Indian Writer to become Nobel Laureate'. *Ham & High*, 6 April, Available at: https://www.hamhigh.co.uk/news/heritage/heritage-the-hampstead-years-of-rabindranath-tagore-first-indian-writer-to-become-nobel-laureate-1-2003671. (Accessed on 20 December 2018).

SPECTOR, Ilya. 2017. 'Did Indian Aristocrats Live in the Russian Empire?'. *Russia Beyond*, 14 April, Available at: https://www.rbth.com/arts/history/2017/04/14/did-indian-aristocrats-live-in-the-russian-empire_742473. (Accessed on 20 December 2018).

'Sudhindra Nath Ghose'. *Making Britain*. The Open University, Available at: http://www.open.ac.uk/researchprojects/makingbritain/content/sudhindra-nath-ghose. (Accessed on 20 December 2018).

'Sukhsagar Datta'. *Making Britain*. The Open University, Available at: http://www.open.ac.uk/researchprojects/makingbritain/content/sukhsagar-datta. (Accessed on 20 December 2018).

SUKIC, Christine. 2015. '"I smell false Latin, dunghill for unguem": Odours and Aromas in *Love's Labour's Lost*'. *Actes des congrès de la Société française Shakespeare*, (32), Available at: https://journals.openedition.org/shakespeare/3289#ftn1. (Accessed on 20 August 2019).

'Sunity Devee'. *Making Britain*. The Open University, Available at: http://www.open.ac.uk/researchprojects/makingbritain/content/sunity-devee. (Accessed on 20 December 2018).

'Surat Alley'. *Making Britain*. The Open University, Available at: http://www.open.ac.uk/researchprojects/makingbritain/content/surat-alley. (Accessed on 20 December 2018).

TAYLOR, Jerome. 2009. 'Revealed: The Woman Who Terrified the British Empire'. *Independent*, 25 May 25, Available at: https://

www.independent.co.uk/news/people/news/revealed-the-woman-who-terrified-the-british-empire-1690412.html. (Accessed on 20 December 2018).

'The Perfect Storm: The United Kingdom, Brexit and Its History'. *The Briefing Room, BBC Sounds*, 5 September, 2019, Available at: https://www.bbc.co.uk/sounds/play/m00081xc. (Accessed on 7 September 2019).

'The Victoria'. *Famous Diamonds*, Available at: http://famousdiamonds.tripod.com/victoriadiamond.html. (Accessed on 20 December 2018).

'The War to End all Wars'. *BBC*, 10 November, 1998, Available at: http://news.bbc.co.uk/2/hi/special_report/1998/10/98/world_war_i/198172.stm. (Accessed on 10 May 2018).

TATKO, Victoria K. 1998. 'Speaking of the Raj: Kipling, Forster, and Scott on the English Language in British India'. Masters Thesis. 1742. Available at: http://thekeep.eiu.edu/theses/1742

'Venu Chitale'. *Making Britain*. The Open University, Available at: http://www.open.ac.uk/researchprojects/makingbritain/content/venu-chitale. (Accessed on 20 December 2018).

WILDE, Simon. 2011. 'Ranjitsinhji Vibhaji, Maharaja Jam Sahib of Navanagar (Ranjitsinhji or Ranji) (1872–1933)'. *Oxford Dictionary of National Biography*, Available at: https://www.oxforddnb.com/view/10.1093/ref:odnb/9780198614128.001.0001/odnb-9780198614128-e-35190. (Accessed on 20 September 2017).

WILLASEY, Tim. 2014. 'Of Intelligence, an Assassination, East Indiamen and the Great Hurricane of 1808'. *The Victorian Web*, Available at: http://www.victorianweb.org/history/empire/india/37.html. (Accessed on 20 December 2018).

'William Winstanley Pearson (1881–1923)'. Visva Bharati (website), Available at: http://www.visvabharati.ac.in/W-W-Pearson.html. (Accessed on 20 December 2018).

YEOMAN, Fran. 2007. 'Did Unity Mitford have Adolf Hitler's Love Child?'. *The Times*, 13 December, Available at: http://www.timesonline.co.uk/tol/news/uk/article3042944.ece. (Accessed on 20 December 2018).

'Z.A. Bokhari'. *Making Britain*. The Open University, Available at: http://www.open.ac.uk/researchprojects/makingbritain/content/z-bokhari. (Accessed on 20 December 2018).

Films and Media

ATTENBOROUGH, Richard (dir.). 1982. *Gandhi.* Perf. John Briley, Ben Kingsley, Candice Bergen, Edward Fox, John Gielgud and Trevor Howard. Goldcrest Films, International Film Investors, National Film Development Corporation of India, Indo–British Films, Columbia Pictures, United Kingdom and India.

CHOPRA, Aditya (dir.). 1995. *Dilwale Dulhania Le Jayenge.* Perf. Shahrukh Khan, Kajol Devgan, Amrish Puri, Farida Jalal, et al. Yash Raj Films, India.

DICK, Kirby and Amy Ziering Kofman (dirs.). 2002. *Derrida.* Perf. Jacques Derrida. Jane Doe Films and Zeitgeist Films. United States of America.

FELLOWES, Julian (created). 2010–15. *Downton Abbey.* Perf. Hugh Bonneville, Elizabeth McGovern, Maggie Smith, Jim Carter, Michelle Dockery, Laura Carmichael, Jessica Brown Findlay, Robert James-Collier, Dan Stevens, et al. ITV Studios, Carnival Films, WGBH-TV, United Kingdom.

FRY, Stephen and Hugh Laurie. 1989. *A Bit of Fry & Laurie.* Season 1. BBC1 and BBC2.

MICHELL, Roger (dir.). 1999. *Notting Hill.* Perfs. Julia Roberts, Hugh Grant, et al. PolyGram Filmed Entertainment, Working Title Films & Universal Pictures, United States of America and United Kingdom.

MORAHAN, Christopher, Jim O'Brien, Ken Taylor and Irene Shubik (created). 1984. *The Jewel in the Crown.* Perf. Paul Scott, Art Malik, Geraldine James, Saeed Jaffrey, Peggy Ashcroft, et al. Granada Television, ITV Studios, United Kingdom.

O'CONNOR, Andrew, Jesse Armstrong & Sam Bain (created). 2003–2015. *Peep Show.* Perf. David Mitchell, Robert Webb, et al. Objective Productions, All3Media, Channel 4, United Kingdom.

VISVANATHAN, Shiv. 2015. 'Ethics, Memory and Innovation' (Lecture). OP Jindal Global University, Available at: https://www.youtube.com/watch?v=JFS5fZM2e7A. (Accessed on 20 September 2018).

WOOD, Nick (dir.). 2012–2016. *Citizen Khan.* Perf. Adil Ray, Bhavna Limbachia, Maya Sondhi, et al. BBC1, United Kingdom.

Index

About the Author

Arup K. Chatterjee lives around New Delhi. He received his doctorate from the Center for English Studies, Jawaharlal Nehru University. He is the Founder Chief Editor of *Coldnoon: International Journal of Travel Writing & Travelling Cultures. He has authored The Purveyors of Destiny: A Cultural Biography of the Indian Railways and The Great Indian Railways.* He teaches at O.P. Jindal Global University.